To Set at Liberty

The Social World of Biblical Antiquity, Second Series, 11

JOHN HALL 'JACK' ELLIOTT

To Set at Liberty

Essays on Early Christianity and its Social World in Honor of John H. Elliott

edited by

Stephen K. Black

Sheffield Phoenix Press

2014

Published by Sheffield Phoenix Press
Department of Biblical Studies, University of Sheffield
45 Victoria Street, Sheffield S3 7QB

www.sheffieldphoenix.com

A CIP catalogue record for this book
is available from the British Library

Typeset by the HK Scriptorium
Printed by Lightning Source

Hardback 978-1-907534-92-8

Contents

Abbreviations

AB	Anchor Bible
ABD	*Anchor Bible Dictionary*
ANTC	Abingdon New Testament Commentaries
ABRL	Anchor Bible Reference Library
BDAG	W. Bauer, F.W. Danker, W.F. Arndt and F.W. Gingrich, *Greek-English Lexicon of the New Testament and Other Early Christian Literature* (Chicago: University of Chicago Press, 3rd edn, 2000)
BAR	*Biblical Archeological Review*
BibInt	*Biblical Interpretation*
BibSem	Biblical Seminar
BNTC	Black's New Testament Commentary
BTB	*Biblical Theology Bulletin*
BWANT	Beiträge zur Wissenschaft vom Alten und Neuen Testament
BZNW	Beihefte zur *ZNW*
CBQ	*Catholic Biblical Quarterly*
CBR	*Currents in Biblical Research*
CTM	*Currents in Theology and Mission*
EKKNT	Evangelisch-Katholischer Kommentar zum Neuen Testament
ETL	*Ephemerides theologicae lovanienses*
FOC	The Fathers of the Church
FRLANT	Forschungen zur Religion und Literatur des Alten und Neuen Testaments
HNT	Handbuch zum Neuen Testament
HTS	*Hervormde teologiese studies*
ICC	International Critical Commentary
JAAR	*Journal of the American Academy of Religion*
JBL	*Journal of Biblical Literature*
JETS	*Journal of the Evangelical Theological Society*
JSHJ	*Journal for the Study of the Historical Jesus*
JSJ	*Journal for the Study of Judaism*
JSJSup	*Journal for the Study of Judaism*, Supplement Series
JSNT	*Journal for the Study of the New Testament*
JSNTSup	*Journal for the Study of the New Testament*, Supplement Series
JSOT	*Journal for the Study of the Old Testament*
JSP	*Journal for the Study of the Pseudepigrapha*

LCL	Loeb Classical Library
LNTS	Library of New Testament Studies
LTJ	*Lutheran Theological Journal*
LXX	Septuagint
MM	J.H. Moulton and G.Milligan, *The Vocabulary of the Greek Testament.* London, 1930.
MT	Masoretic text
NIB	New Interpreter's Bible
NICNT	New International Commentary on the New Testament
NovT	*Novum Testamentum*
NovTSup	*Novum Testamentum*, Supplements
NTL	New Testament Library
NTS	*New Testament Studies*
PCNT	Paideia: Commentaries on the New Testament
PG	Patrologiae cursus completus: Series graeca, edited by J.-P. Migne (162 vols.; Paris: Lutetiae, 1857–1886)
PGM	*Papyri graecae magicae: Die griechischen Zauberpapyri* (ed. K. Preisendanz; 2 vols.; Stuttgart: Teubner, 2nd edn, 1973)
PMLA	*Papers of the Modern Language Association*
PRSt	*Perspectives in Religious Studies*
RB	*Revue biblique*
RES	*Revue des études sémitiques*
RQ	*Revue de Qumran*
SBEC	Studies in the Bible and Early Christianity
SBL	Society of Biblical Literature
SBLDS	SBL Dissertation Series
SBLMS	SBL Monograph Series
SBS	Stuttgarter Bibelstudien
SBT	Studies in Biblical Theology
SNTSMS	Society for New Testament Studies Monograph Series
SNTU	Studien zum Neuen Testament und seiner Umwelt
STDJ	Studies on the Texts of the Desert of Judah
StEv	*Studia evangelica*
TAPA	*Transactions of the American Philological Association*
TDNT	*Theological Dictionary of the New Testament* (ed. G. Kittel and G. Friedrich; trans. G.W. Bromiley; 10 vols.; Grand Rapids, Eerdmans, 1964–1976)
THNT	Theologischer Handkommentar zum Neuen Testament
TNTC	Tyndale New Testament Commentaries
VT	*Vetus Testamentum*
WBC	Word Biblical Commentary
WUNT	Wissenschaftliche Untersuchungen zum Neuen Testament
ZNW	*Zeitschrift für die neutestamentliche Wissenschaft*

List of Contributors

David E. Aune, Walter Professor of New Testament and Christian Origins, University of Notre Dame, Indiana, United States.

S. Scott Bartchy, Professor of Christian Origins and History of Religion Emeritus, University of California at Los Angeles, United States.

Alicia J. Batten, Associate Professor of Religious Studies and Theological Studies, Conrad Grebel University College/University of Waterloo, Ontario, Canada.

Stephen K. Black, Adjunct Professor of Classical Studies and Theology and Religious Studies, University of San Francisco, California, United States.

Zeba A. Crook, Associate Professor of Religion, Carleton University, Ottawa, Canada.

Richard E. DeMaris, Professor of New Testament, Valparaiso University, Indiana, United States.

Jonathan A. Draper, Professor of Religion, University of Kawazulu-Natal, South Africa.

Dennis C. Duling, Professor of Religious Studies and Theology Emeritus, Canisius College, New York, United States.

Philip F. Esler, Portland Chair in New Testament Studies, University of Gloucestershire, England.

Norman K. Gottwald, Professor of Biblical Studies Emeritus, New York Theological Seminary, United States.

David G. Horrell, Professor of New Testament Studies, University of Exeter, England.

Ralph W. Klein, Christ Seminary-Seminex Professor of Old Testament Studies Emeritus, Lutheran School of Theology at Chicago, Illinois, United States.

Stuart L. Love, Professor of Religion Emeritus, Pepperdine University, California, United States.

James P. Mackey, Thomas Chalmers Professor of Theology Emeritus, University of Edinburgh, Scotland.

Bruce J. Malina, Professor of New Testament and Early Christianity Emeritus, Creighton University, Nebraska, United States.

Halvor Moxnes, Professor of New Testament Emeritus, University of Oslo, Norway.

John J. Pilch, Lecturer, Odyssey Program, Johns Hopkins University, Maryland, United States.

Richard L. Rohrbaugh, Paul S. Wright Professor of Christian Studies Emeritus, Lewis & Clark College, Oregon, United States.

Herman C. Waetjen, Professor of New Testament Emeritus, San Francisco Theological Seminary, and the Graduate Theological Union, California, United States.

Robert L. Wilken, William R. Kenan Professor of the History of Christianity Emeritus, University of Virginia, United States.

Ritva H. Williams, Pastor, St Stephen's Lutheran Church (ELCA), Cedar Rapids, Iowa, United States.

Introduction

Stephen K. Black

Our honoree, John H. Elliott—Jack, as friends and colleagues know him—literally wrote the book on social-scientific criticism and its application to studying the origin and development of the early church. *What Is Social Scientific Criticism?* (Elliott 1993) is a landmark in exegetical methodology, the product of more than twenty-five years of bringing the social sciences into the exegetical task of biblical interpretation.[1] Jack argued not that social sciences should replace the traditional methods used in exegesis (text criticism, historical criticism, redaction criticism, rhetorical criticism, etc.), but that it should supplement them. Arguing that texts have a '*social dimension*' and give witness to '*social phenomen[a]*' (1993: 9), Jack outlined the ways in which social-scientific criticism can and should be employed in interpreting biblical documents. Jack had already demonstrated how the method works 'in action' with his celebrated *A Home for the Homeless* (1981), a study of the social situation of the community addressed by 1 Peter; he would again demonstrate it with his voluminous Anchor Bible commentary on the same letter (2000). Hardly limited to biblical Petrine literature, Jack's use of social-science methods has illuminated everything from the household in Luke's Gospel to persistent circum-Mediterranean fear of the 'evil eye' and its many references in the Bible and other ancient literature. Several authors in this volume testify to the influence of Jack's work on their own scholarship. Jack's vigor and productivity has influenced now two generations of scholars (and counting!).

A Personal Testimony from a Former Student

I first met 'Dr Elliott' in the late summer of 1992, when I enrolled as a graduate student in the Department of Theology and Religious Studies at the University of San Francisco. The faculty saw fit to assign Dr Elliott, the Prot-

1. See Norman Gottwald's contribution to this volume for the inspiration behind the use of social sciences in biblical interpretation.

estant professor of long-standing, as my advisor.[2] I soon became not only his student but his graduate research assistant. One of my first tasks as his assistant was to assemble the appendices for the recently completed manuscript of the aforementioned *What Is Social-Scientific Criticism?* I had not read the manuscript but was captivated by what is now Appendices 2 and 3. Descriptors such as '2.1.1.2. Status/rank/class (according to status of family and place of origin; gender; age; personal liberty or servitude [free/freed/slave]; wealth; ethnic origin; citizenship [local; Roman]; occupation; education)' (1993: 112) were both puzzling and provocative. Someone with a more limited secretarial interest in the material would have better served him. For while arranging these statements labeled under the rubrics of 'Data Inventory for Synchronic Social Analysis of Early Christian Groups', and 'Data Inventory for Diachronic Analysis of Social-Historical Phases and Trends', I was taking my time, studying them, and putting them together with what I heard Jack say in class. I was receiving a primer in social-scientific methodology, *and getting paid for it*! Concurrently, I was enrolled in Jack's seminar 'The Origins of Judaism and Christianity'. In a shameless attempt to impress my boss and professor, I wrote a paper subjecting Eusebius of Caesarea's account of the Council of Nicaea to the social-scientific analysis I had learned only from Jack's appendices, complete with parenthetical references to said. In what I later learned was characteristic of him, Jack was encouraging and liberal with his praise, and—gulp!– ruthless with his criticism. As his students and a few contributors to this volume can attest, Jack has a unique ability to be at one and the same time both gentle and encouraging as well as bluntly direct and honest, while all the time being supportive. Informing me of what I lacked in understanding, Jack then proceeded to present me with a bibliography of material I needed to read—*statim*!—to broaden and deepen my own understanding of social-scientific analysis and its application. Several of the authors represented in that bibliography are also represented in the present edited collection.[3] Only somewhat chagrined that I took more to post–New Testament literature, Jack insisted that social-scientific work was relevant to the fields of patristics and late antiquity. He was, of course, correct, something I hope my own contribution to this volume demonstrates.

The Purpose and Plan of This Book

In spite of Jack's immense influence in the fields of biblical scholarship and the social world of Mediterranean antiquity, there has not yet been a

2. Jack holds the distinction of being the non–Roman Catholic with the longest full-time appointment in a theology department in a Jesuit university in the United States.

3. Especially Bartchy, Gottwald, Malina, Pilch and Waetjen. Members of the Context Group may be amused to learn that among the names on those bibliographies was none other than the Roman economic historian Tenney Frank!

collection of essays written and published in his honor.[4] Such a volume is overdue. Indeed, the enthusiasm of the contributors to this endeavor, many of whom write touching tributes to Jack's personal and professional influence on their life and work, is a testament to this sentiment.

The title of this Festschrift, a phrase Jesus quoted from the prophet Isaiah (Lk. 4.18; Isa. 61.1), is suggestive of two interrelated aspects of Jack's vocation as scholar and minister of the gospel: his pioneering work in liberating the biblical texts from historically anachronistic readings so that the social life and culture of biblical antiquity can speak on its own terms; and his commitment to service in the church, especially its social justice mission. A quick perusal of Jack's abundant works (a list of which is printed at the end of this volume) reveals that his publications reflect both of these personal commitments. His larger scholarly works—especially on 1 Peter and social-scientific criticism—are well known. Less well known are his publications in church quarterlies and homiletical manuals. His recent work as president and founding board member of The Center and Library for the Bible and Social Justice is a testament to his ongoing involvement at the intersection of these commitments.[5]

The first contribution to this volume, Norman Gottwald's *encomium* to Jack, is a tribute to the Rev. Dr John H. Elliott's scholarly, ecclesiastical and political allegiances. It is also a fascinating glimpse into the origins of social-scientific methodology from one who shared with Jack and others the dynamic time and place of its origins.

David Aune's 'The Use of the Term "Magic" as a Socio-Religious Category in the Study of the Greco-Roman World and Early Christianity' argues that the use of the term 'magic' is an inappropriate modern designation used to describe a variety of ritual procedures common in Greco-Roman antiquity. Professor Aune demonstrates that our English term 'magic' carries more and different meanings than the ancient Greek μαγεία and thus provides no heuristic value in examining the religions of Greco-Roman antiquity, including early Christianity.

Scott Bartchy's '"Stickless" in Corinth: How Paul Sought to Recover his Authority' concerns Paul's response to questions about his apostolic identity in Corinth and argues that Paul sought to overcome divisions and disagreements within that community over his apostolic authority by abandoning traditional means for enforcing one's authority—the ῥάβδος (stick) (1 Cor. 4. 21), understood both literally and metaphorically—for one that invites

4. But see Stegemann, Malina and Theissen 2002. Their volume contains a dedication to Jack, who because of illness was unable to attend the 1999 conference on which this collection of essays was based. However, the essays contained therein were not originally conceived or written to honor Jack with his scholarship in mind.

5. See Elliott 2011, and Norman K. Gottwald's contribution to this volume.

imitation of a less hierarchical family and political model. Readers familiar with Bartchy's work on Paul will recognize that this is a model built on sibling relations. Only here, Bartchy tantalizes the reader with recent studies in neuroscience related to imitation.

Alicia Batten's 'The Characterization of the Rich in James 5' examines the role of Greco-Roman literary satire and argues that James used this literary form in his polemic against the rich. In particular, Batten illustrates how James's descriptions of the rich make use of the 'effeminate male' common in satire.

My own contribution, 'Ethnic Judeans and Christian Identity Formation in John Chrysostom's *Adversus Judaeos*', argues that the targets of John Chrysostom's homiletical invective in this series were *ethnic* Judeans (as opposed to 'Jews' practicing a 'religion' called 'Judaism'). Making use of social-scientific studies on ethnicity and studies of religion in the ancient Mediteranean and Near Eastern worlds, I argue that Chrysostom's invective was designed to give an alternative identity not only to ethnic Judeans in his congregation but also those of non-Judean descent.

Zeba Crook's 'Manufacturing Memory and Community: Luke 7.36-50 as a Test Case' argues that Luke's version of the story about the woman who anoints Jesus, which is radically different from that in the other Gospels, was 'manufactured' in part for the purpose of creating a specific Lukan communal identity, a chief marker of which was compassion for 'sinners'. Crook's contribution is also noteworthy for a particular 'memory' of the honoree.

Richard DeMaris's essay, 'The Gospel of Mark as a Therapeutic Ritual Script', reminds us that the Gospels were composed in an oral culture and postulates the notion that as Mark's Gospel was recited in ancient congregations it functioned as a ritual script with curative and therapeutic qualities whereby its participants appropriated the healing power of Jesus. But DeMaris also finds in this analysis a key to resolving the conundrum of Mark's Gospel: why does Mark portray Jesus as so powerful in the beginning, yet so powerless at the end? The Gospel coheres, argues DeMaris, around 'rites of affliction'.

Jonathan Draper's 'Disease, Table and Economy in Luke 16.19-31' explores the Parable of the Rich Man and Lazarus, focusing on the 'impure' body of Lazarus and why he was at the gate outside the rich man's property, while even dogs were allowed in to beg and fight for scraps. Drawing on Mary Douglas's analysis of the body as a 'social map' and anthropological studies on the 'geography of the dinner table' Draper shows how an early layer of the Jesus tradition (if not Jesus himself) sought to redraw the social boundaries of Israel, flipping the social hierarchy.

Dennis Duling's 'Following your Nose: Social-Historical and Social-Scientific Directions in New Testament Osmology' presents recent scholarship on smell and odor and calls for biblical exegetes to develop this 'scent-sitivity' in interpreting the New Testament. Duling's essay is marked not only by its humor but by his suggestions of what is possible when one 'follows the scent' in the New Testament.

In 'Beware the Messiah! *Psalms of Solomon* 17 and the Death of Jesus', Philip Esler uses a 'thought experiment' to postulate that the Jerusalem Temple priesthood was in possession of a copy of *Psalms of Solomon* 17, interpreted rumors of Jesus' words and deeds in light of it, and were consequently motivated to seek his death at the hands of the Romans.

In dialogue with Jack's pioneering work on 1 Peter, David Horrell's '"Honour Everyone . . ." (1 Peter 2.17): The Social Strategy of 1 Peter and its Significance for Early Christianity' argues that through 1 Peter's formula (fear God, honor the emperor), the author resists imperial power in a way that becomes standard for later Christian discourse on imperial power.

Ralph Klein's 'Resist the King! The Attitude toward the Emperor in Bel and the Dragon and in Daniel 1–6' demonstrates that these works are not only a criticism of idolatry but also a not-so-subtle criticism of imperial pretensions to rule.

In 'Spirit Agression in the Gospel according to Luke', Stuart Love examines the role of the Holy Spirit and its contrasting evil spirit of aggression in Luke's Gospel. Making use of anthropological models of spirit aggression, Love argues that Jesus' mission as Luke portrays it, while filled with God's Holy Spirit, is constantly challenged by the aggressive spirit of evil.

James Mackey's contribution, 'What Do the Twin Trials of Jesus Tell Us about Who and What He Was and Was Not?', argues that the real trial of Jesus was before Caiaphas rather than Pilate, and that the real charge was not sedition but blasphemy—a human being claiming equal status with God. More importantly, Mackey argues that the equality with God that the authorities accused Jesus of claiming (something Jesus explicitly denied) had nothing to do with the equality of substance found in later Trinitarian theology; rather, it was based on reports of Jesus' Torah violations that made it seem as if he were claiming 'equality of legislative power and status' with God.

Bruce Malina's 'Were There "Authors" in New Testament Times?' argues that the term 'author' is anachronistic when applied to ancient 'writers' (the preferred term). This is so not only because of modern notions of authorship that involve 'personal' insight and inspiration, as well as issues of copyright and intellectual property, but because the model of writing in antiquity more closely resembled either 'craftsmen' working with set forms, or 'modes of collaboration', the latter of which Malina finds evident in the Pauline corpus.

With terrorist attacks in Norway and the United States as its background, Halvor Moxnes's essay, 'Jesus beyond Nationalism—in Light of Terroism', revisits the study of the historical Jesus, questioning the implicit nationalism in historical Jesus scholarship and focusing our attention on Jesus' aims and the community of diversity he advocated under the banner of 'the kingdom of God'. In an important way, Moxnes's essay challenges the focus of identity based on ethnicity.

In 'Cross-Cultural Psychology and the Bible: A Model for Understanding Jesus' Psychological Development', John Pilch develops a cross-cultural psychological model to posit the development of ancient figures such as Jesus. Here Pilch offers an alternative to the Western Jungian notion of developmental stages, one more culturally appropriate to the Mediterranean world of biblical antiquity.

Richard Rohrbaugh's essay, 'The Social Function of Genealogies in the New Testament and its World', calls us to pay more careful attention to those places in biblical writings we tend to skip over as not very interesting (if not irrelevant)—namely the genealogies. In the ancient Mediterranean world genealogical references were 'attention grabbers' for the ancient reader. They encoded and communicated the patterns and protocols of ancient social interaction.

Herman Waetjen finds 'Intimation of the Year of Jubilee in the Parable of the Wicked Tenants'. Noting that in its earliest form the parable was addressed to the chief priests, scribes and elders of Israel, Waetjen argues that the parable functions as a mirror, showing the ruling elite that they have been evicted from God's vineyard and replaced by the poor they were guilty of oppressing with their land tenure policies.

Robert Wilken's '1 Peter 2.13-17 and Martyrdom', looks at the reception of this Petrine text regarding honoring everyone but fearing God in the context of the martyr communities of the second century. He argues that 1 Peter helped Christian martyrs draw the clear distinction between respecting imperial authorities and insisting on worship of God alone.

In 'The Interests of the Shrewd Steward and his Interpreters', Ritva Williams performs an 'ideology critique' on the common interpretation of the Parable of the Dishonest Manager in Lk. 16.1-8a. This interpretation typically recognizes the rich landholder as the good guy, while his steward is 'dishonest', and therefore the bad guy. Williams reveals that this interpretation does not reflect the interests of Jesus, Luke, Luke's community or, indeed, any early interpreters of the parable through the Reformation. Rather, these interests, all of which reflect a pre-industrial agrarian context, recognize the 'shrewdness' of the steward who manages to walk the fine line between providing relief to the victim of his master's greed and at the same time finding honor for the master.

We hope that the essays contained in this volume will give its honoree some things to think about, build upon, and perhaps even argue with.

References

Elliott, John H.

1981 *A Home for the Homeless: A Sociological Exegesis of 1 Peter, its Situation and Strategy* (Philadelphia, PA: Fortress Press, 2nd edn, 1990; Eugene, OR: Wipf & Stock, 3rd edn, 2005).

1993 *What Is Social Scientific Criticism?* (Guides to Biblical Scholarship; Minneapolis, MN: Fortress Press).

2000 *1 Peter: A New Translation with Introduction and Commentary* (AB, 37B; New York: Doubleday/Random House).

2011 'Refugees, Resident Aliens, and the Church as Counter-Culture', in *Liberating Biblical Study: Scholarship, Art and Action in Honor of the Center and Library for the Bible and Social Justice* (ed. Laurel Dykstra and Ched Meyers; Eugene, OR: Cascade Books): 197-212.

Stegemann, Wolfgang, Bruce J. Malina and Gerd Theissen (eds.)

2002 *The Social Setting of Jesus and the Gospels* (Minneapolis, MN: Fortress Press).

John H. Elliott: An Encomium

Norman K. Gottwald

John H. Elliott, better known to friends and colleagues as 'Jack', is solidly established in the scholarly world as a master interpreter of 1 Peter and an ardent advocate of social-scientific criticism in biblical studies. It is precisely by insisting on the social-critical method that Jack has been able to show that the 'resident aliens and strangers' addressed in 1 Peter are to be understood literally as Christ-believing social refugees forced to live on the margins of Greco-Roman society in Asia Minor. His detailed defense of that hypothesis in *A Home for the Homeless,* first published in 1981, has won him a primary position among Petrine scholars, even as his view of the book is contested among those who adhere to the conventional view that these folk are spiritual 'pilgrims and strangers', in the vein of the hymn, 'This world is not my home, I'm just passing through'.

Jack has gone on to provide us with the first systematic presentation of social-scientific criticism in a book whose title goes straight to the point, *What Is Social-Scientific Criticism?* (1993). While this work illustrates sociological methods and models with New Testament texts, it constitutes a manual that one can use to interrogate any biblical text, with the result that his directives for the method are entirely appropriate to Hebrew Bible exegesis. During the 1960s and 1970s social-critical methods were adopted by an increasing number of scholars in both Testaments. As usually happens when new paradigms and methods enter an established discipline, social-scientific criticism came under attack from scholars devoted to traditional textual and historical inquiry. The major objections raised by critics have been twofold. The first is the allegation that the agenda of interpreters using social-scientific methods is to replace the historical-critical method in its entirety or at least demote it into insignificance. The second objection is that modern sociological approaches, however well intentioned their use, are emphatically unsuited for studying ancient societies.

Jack tackled those objections with brio, and he did so in the most convincing manner possible, not by abstract argument, but by writing on 1 Peter as a test case. Employing the customary textual and historical-critical methods, he supplemented these time-honored tools with a penetrating social-critical analysis of the situation and strategy of the biblical text. As a result, he was able to show how the 'resident aliens and strangers' of 1 Peter were actually marginalized refugees struggling to survive in the hostile social environment of Asia Minor, and that the language of marginality in the book is not figurative but painfully literal. Viewed in this way, historical method was not rejected but rather was built upon and enriched by the sociological perspective, throwing light on the tenor of 1 Peter that otherwise seemed harsh and over-wrought. By the skillful employment of sociological studies of sectarian movements, Jack established that the judicious use of modern sociological theory and method is quite appropriate for New Testament studies. In the case of 1 Peter, as in many other biblical books, there are facets of the subject matter that only sociological studies have been able to elucidate. And in due time, drawing on his years of social-scientific study of New Testament texts, Jack prepared the ultimate 'how-to' manual on the principles and practices of the social-scientific mode of biblical interpretation. In a sense, this is an elevated 'Social-Scientific Criticism for Dummies'. In short, Jack's 'big' books on 1 Peter (he later wrote a major commentary on the epistle) and his 'little' book on the theory and practice of social-scientific criticism, went a very long way toward showing that the objections leveled at it are baseless.[1]

Jack comes to his studies with a solid training in the textual and historical tools of biblical studies, beginning with classical languages in high school and the full panoply of theological studies at Concordia College and Concordia Seminary, capped by postgraduate study in Germany. His subsequent teaching at Concordia Seminary was cut short by the fundamentalist climate in the Lutheran Church—Missouri Synod that, along with a visit to Selma, gave him a shocking immersion in ecclesial and secular politics that served him well when he moved to the Bay Area to join the faculty of the University of San Francisco, a Jesuit institution. Jack had begun teaching at the University of San Francisco when I first met him in the midst of the 1960s protest movements. He and I were among theological faculty members at Bay Area institutions of higher learning who supported the protests and participated in many of the demonstrations. Before long, several of us began reflecting on what the social conflicts we were living through had to do with our biblical scholarship. This led to organizing a study group, for which we intentionally chose the cumbersome name, Bay Area Seminar for the Study of Theology and Related Disciplines, because it yielded the handy acronym BASTARD! Provocative as the name was, it was not far removed from the disdain of some of our colleagues, and administrators in particular,

1. The big books on 1 Peter are Elliott 1981 [rev. 1990] and the Anchor Bible commentary (Elliott 2000); the little how-to book on social-scientific criticisms is Elliott 1993.

for indeed we were suspected of doubtful parentage in mixing biblical studies and social sciences in an unholy union.

The seminar prompted us to two lines of action. For one, in an attempt to be sociologically conversant, we set about immersing ourselves in sociological literature that we had never before read or had read only superficially. In our discussions, we started off by critiquing narrowly religious interpretations of the Maccabean war of liberation in an effort to understand the interests of all parties involved and the precipitating factors that led to war. We moved on to apply sociological method to other biblical texts and topics, in the Hebrew Bible, the prophets, the Deuteronomic reform, and the origins of Israel and, in the New Testament, the politics of Jesus, the parables, and the impact of Roman rule in Palestine. As he reports, the main body of Jack's *A Home for the Homeless* was taking shape with the stimulation of this company of scholar-activists, as well as subsequent work of Anne Wire, Herman Waetjen, Marvin Chaney and myself.[2] If you were interested in critical social study of the Bible, the Bay Area was definitely the place to be from the mid-sixties until the group disbanded with retirements and relocation of members to other academic posts in the early eighties.

It is emphatically noteworthy that in 1981, in *A Home for the Homeless,* Jack was still characterizing his method as 'sociological exegesis', but by 1993, with the publication of *What Is Social-Scientific Criticism?,* Jack was calling his method 'social-scientific criticism'. Therein lies a change much larger than it first appears, but what exactly is its significance? In 1981, sociological exegesis could be argued for in a period when many of us had not yet fixed on a common term for what we were practicing. Sociological exegesis was a reasonable term to use. After all, Jack and others of us were exegeting biblical books by what we took to be sociological methods (distinguishable from historical-critical methods). The discipline was sharply focused on adequate biblical exegesis. Two things happened in the 1970s and 1980s that altered the subdiscipline, one fairly technical and the other of deep and far-reaching significance. For one thing, practicing 'sociological' critics came to realize that sociology was only one of several social sciences that were being employed in biblical studies, others being, for example, anthropology, political science and economics. Thus, to speak of social-scientific criticism aligned us with the commonly accepted nomenclature within the broad field of the social sciences.

The more consequential reason for the change in nomenclature was a divergence of paths among scholars doing so-called sociological exegesis. As social-critical study was gathering steam in the 1960s and 1970s, it seemed adequate to include all of us in the same camp, particularly since

2. Gottwald 1979; Elliott 1981; Chaney 1983; Waetjen 1989; Wire 1990.

we faced strong opposition among biblical scholars to anything 'social' or 'sociological', across the board in Hebrew Bible and New Testament studies. What constituted the 'split' among us was a difference in understanding what 'sociological exegesis' entailed. One wing of social-critical scholars came to understand their work as social *description*, whereas numbers of us, Jack in the forefront, thought that the heart of our task was to develop social *theory* about the Israelite and early church formations once they were correctly described. An admittedly extreme example of the social description model was a study of Antioch with a view to throwing light on the first four centuries of Christian life in that city. It happens to be that we possess an immense amount of social and archaeological information about Antioch in that period. A huge amount of social description was collected, but the participants on the project were unable in the end to agree on a conceptual model to make sense of Christianity in that well-documented city during the centuries studied (Meeks and Wilken 1978). By contrast, although Jack collects a considerable body of data about the region of Asia Minor where the churches were located and to which the epistle was addressed, he refuses to stop with description. He proposes that a sectarian model goes a long way to understanding the vulnerable position of the churches of that region, and he elucidates the biblical text as seen through the prism of a conceptual model of sectarianism. In accord with the social-theoretical approach, Jack consistently asks what sort of social practice is indicated by the biblical text and by what concepts that practice may be best understood.

A feature of Jack's scholarship that has characterized his way of working is his commitment to serious conversation with other biblical interpreters. It is striking that he has played a major role in several academic working groups, beginning with BASTARD, and reaching beyond to the Society of Biblical Literature, the Catholic Biblical Association, and, most importantly, with the Context Group, composed internationally of social and cultural critics meeting twice yearly for more than twenty years, in pursuit of the meanings of biblical texts when viewed through the lenses of social and political theory. Even in retirement, his questing mind has found regular expression in the Pacific Coast Theological Society, which examines a whole range of theological topics and not simply biblical subjects. No aspect of Jack's work exhibits his blend of academic rigor, church commitment and social activism more vividly than his involvement over the years in the sanctuary movement, as his congregation, the University Lutheran Chapel in Berkeley, has offered asylum to war resisters and Central American political refugees. Jack views this ministry to the marginalized as comparable to, and inspired by, early Christian communities of 'resident aliens and strangers', such as the one he has discovered and shared with us in 1 Peter. Not being averse to social action that serves self-interest, Jack played a major leadership role in the protracted, ultimately successful, struggle to unionize the faculty of the University of San Francisco. Not to be overlooked was his teaching stint at the Pontifical Biblical Institute in Rome, where he served as the first and only Lutheran since the Reformation to be so honored.

Jack's most recent project is the Center and Library for the Bible and Social Justice, which began as a vision that he, Herman Waetjen and I shared to establish a research library and educational center connecting biblically informed activists and justice-oriented scholars in order to develop an empowering use of the Bible for achieving social justice today. It originated with each of us wondering what would become of our libraries at our passing. We observed that often we academics postpone decisions about the fate of our treasured books, sometimes leaving it to others to dispose of them. We did not want our collections to be sold off piecemeal or to fall into private hands. So we have donated our books relevant to the theme of the Bible and social justice to a research and educational center now located at the Stony Point Conference Center, thirty-five miles north of Manhattan. Others have begun to donate books; we have formed as a nonprofit organization, appointed a board of directors, and already have sponsored two seminars attended by pastors and social activists eager to explore biblical resources for the work they are doing (see www.clbsj.org). This is precisely the sort of imaginative undertaking to bring together 'academy, sanctuary and street' that has embodied Jack's life-long understanding of how scholarship should empower the church and equip social activists with biblical insights and tools. It is altogether fitting that Jack serves as the president of the newly launched Center and Library.

Finally, there is one consuming interest of Jack's that I am uncertain how to celebrate, but I think it has to be recognized because it has engaged so much of his attention in recent decades. I speak of his research on 'the evil eye', understood as a look or gaze believed to cause injury or misfortune, even death, to others. Jack has compiled a surprisingly large number of references to the evil eye cross-culturally in all the major societies of Mediterranean antiquity. In fact, the number of references is so vast that his work on this subject may require two volumes to do it justice. Because of the frequency of evil eye citations in both Testaments, I suspect it will be a revelation to biblical interpreters when the work is published. Meanwhile, he has shared some of his research in articles (Elliott 1988, 1990, 1991, 1992, 1994, 2005, 2007). It seems to me that this evil eye project illustrates two things about Jack. It shows how extensive and intensive his research characteristically is, and it shows his willingness to explore topics that others would call tangential to biblical studies but which in the end are likely to make an unforeseen contribution to biblical exegesis. But of course this virtual hobby of Jack's needs no justification or defense.

In conclusion, I find it difficult to exaggerate the work that Jack has accomplished as scholar, teacher and agent for social justice. His distinction is not alone in the work he has done, which is abundant in itself, but lies in the unusual trajectory of his life. In an after-dinner autobiographical presentation a few years ago at a meeting of the Pacific Coast Theological Society, Jack returned again and again to the paradoxes and ironies of his life, marked as it has been by inexplicable contradictions posing sharp incongruities between what he expected and what actually occurred. He tells of an early ambition to be a forensic chemist that gave way to a theological teaching career. Schooled as a very American boy from the Bronx, he found himself in Germany for a postgraduate degree and a plunge into another culture. Set for a career in teaching at Concordia, the flagship seminary of his denomination, the bulk of his teaching has been at a Roman Catholic university. Devoted to the rigors of historical criticism, Jack moved rapidly to the practice and advocacy of social-scientific theory. Taught that religion and politics don't mix, Jack was swept into the tumult of civil rights and anti-war fervor, and even turned to unionizing faculty. Is there a leitmotif running through the paradoxical and ironic twists and turns of his life and career? I believe there is, and Jack articulates it clearly in his opening autobiographical remarks when he says, 'In retrospect it appears that I regularly found myself living as a stranger or resident alien on someone else's turf, or being somewhat removed from the conventional center of things, and often peering over onto someone else's academic, or confessional, or cultural backyard' (Elliott 2009). What is surprising is the relative ease with which Jack has made these twists and turns so that he has been able to set up camp on each of the new 'turfs' as they become his playing field. Is it any wonder that Jack, the self-perceived stranger and resident alien, has been uniquely prepared to give voice to the strangers and resident aliens of 1 Peter?

References

Chaney, Marvin L.

1983 'Ancient Palestinian Peasant Movements', in *Palestine in Transition: The Emergence of Ancient Israel* (ed. D.N. Freedman and D.F. Graf; Sheffield: Almond Press): 39-90.

Elliott, John H.

1981 *A Home for the Homeless: A Sociological Exegesis of 1 Peter, its Situation and Strategy* (Philadelphia, PA: Fortress Press, 2nd edn, 1990; Eugene, OR: Wipf & Stock, 3rd edn, 2005).

1988 'The Fear of the Leer. The Evil Eye from the Bible to Li'l Abner', *Forum* 4.4: 42-71.

1990 'Paul, Galatians, and the Evil Eye', *CTM* 17: 262-73.

1991 'The Evil Eye in the First Testament: The Ecology and Culture of a Pervasive Belief', in *The Bible and the Politics of Exegesis: Essays in Honor of*

Norman K. Gottwald on his Sixty-Fifth Birthday (ed. David Jobling *et al.*; Cleveland, OH: Pilgrim Press): 147-59.

1992 'Matthew 20:1-15: A Parable of Invidious Comparison and Evil Eye Accusation', *BTB* 22: 52-65.

1993 *What Is Social Scientific Criticism?* (Guides to Biblical Scholarship; Minneapolis, MN: Fortress Press).

1994 'The Evil Eye and the Sermon on the Mount: Contours of a Pervasive Belief in Social Scientific Perspective', *BibInt* 2: 51-84.

2000 *1 Peter: A New Translation with Introduction and Commentary* (AB, 37B; New York: Doubleday/Random House).

2005 'Jesus, Mark, and the Evil Eye', *LTJ* (Victor Pfitzner FS) 39: 157-68.

2007 'Envy and the Evil Eye: More on Mark 7.22 and Mark's "Anatomy of Envy"', in *In Other Words: Essays on Social Science Methods and the New Testament in Honor of Jerome H. Neyrey* (ed. Anselm C. Hagedorn *et al.*; Sheffield: Sheffield Phoenix Press): 87-105.

2009 'Autobiographical Remarks', Pacific Coast Theological Society Meeting, April 18.

Gottwald, Norman K.

1979 *The Tribes of Yahweh: A Sociology of the Religion of Liberated Israel, 1250–1050 B.C.E.* (Maryknoll, NY: Orbis Books).

Meeks, Wayne A., and Robert L. Wilken

1978 *Jews and Christians in Antioch in the First Four Centuries of the Common Era* (Society of Biblical Literature Sources for Biblical Study, 13; Missoula, MT: Scholars Press).

Waetjen, Herman C.

1989 *A Reordering of Power: A Socio-political Reading of Mark's Gospel* (Minneapolis, MN: Fortress Press).

Wire, Antoinette C.

1990 *Corinthian Women Prophets: A Reconstruction through Paul's Rhetoric* (Minneapolis, MN: Fortress Press).

The Use of the Term 'Magic' as a Socio-Religious Category in the Study of the Greco-Roman World and Early Christianity

David E. Aune

Preface

In many respects, Jack Elliott is a model *Neutestamentler*: he is a rigorous, energetic and creative New Testament scholar who is a pioneer in the application of social-science methodology to the study of the biblical text (Dvorak 2007), particularly 1 Peter; he is an inspiring and demanding teacher who devoted thirty-four years to the Department of Theology and Religious Studies at the University of San Francisco; he is a person of faith with an ecumenical orientation as a Lutheran, teaching in a Roman Catholic educational institution; and he is one who has deep concerns with the relevance of the Bible to social justice issues. Jack's interests and mine intersect particularly in his expertise in his application of social-scientific methodology in the study of the pervasive belief in the 'evil eye', often regarded as a subcategory of ancient 'magic'. For years, he has collected references in primary and secondary sources to the cross-cultural phenomenon of the evil eye and has also contributed a series of articles on aspects of the subject over the years (Elliott 1988, 1990, 1991, 1994, 2004, 2011), with the ultimate goal of publishing a major monograph on the subject, a volume that I eagerly await. *Amico et socio* Jack Elliot: *ad multos annos, amice*!

The Problem

Those of us who are engaged in the study of various aspects of the ancient world face a common dilemma: the social, cultural and linguistic distance that separates us from the objects of our inquiry. While historical scholarship has tried to guard itself against the ever-present danger of understanding the ancient world in terms of the norms and values of modern Western civilization, attempts to be fully aware of our presuppositions are not always successful. On a rough analogy with the 'observer effect' in physics, which suggests that measurements of certain systems cannot be made without affecting the systems, it is difficult for scholars investigating ancient religions to avoid projecting alien presuppositions onto the objects of inquiry. The focus of this essay is the argument that 'magic' is a dysfunctional and misleading heuristic category for studying the religious practices and beliefs of antiquity, since the reification of the category 'magic' reshapes and rearranges the evidence to fit a modern agenda. While some concepts or categories are difficult to define, like 'religion'[1] and 'mystery cults', others such as 'magic' and 'gnosticism' are doubtful categories that deserve to be dismantled and discarded (Williams 1996).

As a younger scholar (rushing in where angels fear to tread),[2] I tried to define 'magic' in a lengthy essay that appeared in 1980.[3] Since 1979, I confess to having written more than a dozen articles on various aspects of ancient 'magic'.[4] Recently, after struggling with the problem and looking at it from various angles for nearly thirty years, I revisited the same issue with the awareness that I knew far less about the subject than I had earlier. In Aune 2008, I abandoned the two-part definition of 'magic' that I had earlier proposed, and I was also skeptical of the analytical utility of using the term 'magic' (which I regularly put in quotations marks to indicate its heuristic inadequacies) as a concept for categorizing ancient socio-religious phenomena, a skepticism that I shared with an intimidatingly small number of other scholars.[5] Many scholars of antiquity, though they rarely attempt to define magic, nevertheless obviously find the concept useful and even

1. Smith (1962) regards 'religion' as a modern Western invention that, when used of antiquity, only distorts what it seeks to illuminate.

2. Naturally, I'm suppressing the first part of this allusion to a phrase of Alexander Pope (1688–1744), 'For fools rush in where angels fear to tread' (Pope 1711), from his *An Essay on Criticism*.

3. Aune 1980: 1507-57 (reprinted in Aune 2006a: 368-420). The following definition appeared in Aune 1980: 1515 and Aune 2006a: 376: 'Throughout the remainder of this study, therefore, magic is defined as that form of religious deviance whereby individual or social goals are sought by means alternate to those normally sanctioned by the dominant religious institution.... Religious activities which fit this first and primary criterion must also fit a second criterion: goals sought within the context of religious deviance are magical when attained through the management of supernatural powers in such a way that the results are virtually guaranteed.'

4. In addition to two lengthy general articles (Aune 1980 and Aune 2008), I have also written a variety of other articles on ancient magic (in chronological order): (1) Aune 1979: 3.213-19; (2) contributing translator to Betz 1986, 1992; (3) Aune 1987; (4) Aune 1990; (5) Aune 1995a; (6) Aune 1995b; (7) Aune 1997; (8) Aune 2004; (9) Aune 2005; (10) Aune 2006b; (11) Aune 2012a; (12) Aune 2012b.

5. Throughout this essay, whenever I use what I regard as such doubtful categories as 'magic', 'magical' and 'magician', I have placed the term in quotation marks. However, when I am discussing the views of those who regard 'magic' and its cognates as legitimate categories I have refrained from putting those terms in quotation marks.

indispensable in categorizing certain constellations of religious phenomena in the ancient world. Like United States Supreme Court Justice Potter Stewart, who famously articulated his threshold test for obscenity in *Jacobellis v. Ohio* (1964), these scholars may not be able to define magic, but they know it when they see it.

Analytical Tools

There are two analytical approaches to our subject that hold some promise of aiding us in restraining our subjectivities: the emic/etic distinction and the differences between the orders or levels of discourse. In 1954, linguist Kenneth Pike proposed a linguistic theory that he understood corresponded to an analogous problem facing anthropologists in dealing with Third World cultures. Pike distinguished between two approaches to understanding other languages and cultures: (1) The 'emic' approach (based on the linguistic term 'phonemic') describes human behavior, belief and language in terms meaningful to cultural insiders, that is, what goes on inside their heads or aspects of social life that are real and important to them as cultural participants. (2) An 'etic' approach (based on the term 'phonetic'), on the other hand, describes human behavior, belief and language in terms meaningful to a cultural outsider, that is, aspects of social life that exist only outside of the minds of the cultural participants and which are thought to have cross-cultural validity (Harris 1976).[6] The best way to get inside people's heads, of course, is to interview them and ask them questions, either in their language or through an interpreter, about what they think and feel about various matters. However, biblical scholars are not anthropologists interviewing native informants, but historians interrogating ancient texts.

While the emic/etic distinction has proven useful in anthropology and ethnology, an insider's perspective into ancient religious practices and beliefs is difficult if not impossible to achieve (Frankfurter 1993: 88). I will therefore focus on what I consider a more useful analytical tool that is appropriate for scholars of antiquity who deal primarily with the interpretation of texts: the three levels or orders of discourse (Flood 2006; Gunnell 1998). First-order discourse consists primarily of what can be learned from ancient Greco-Roman literature, papyri and inscriptions about ancient religious traditions, institutions, practices and beliefs, including prayers,

6. The emic/etic distinction was first proposed by structural linguist Kenneth Pike (1954), who used linguistics as a model for emic analysis. Pike proposed viewing socio-cultural phenomena as a whole as an analogue of language (Harris 1976: 333). According to Pike (1967: 38), 'Two units are different etically when instrumental measurements show them to be so. Units are different emically only when they elicit different responses from people acting within the system.'

hymns, oracles, festivals, rituals and myths. An important segment of these ancient religious practices is a spectrum of ritual procedures that is widely, though not consistently, categorized as 'magic', a concept of modern third-order discourse (see below) that is typically thought to include most of the following types of religious or quasi-religious rituals: healing, exorcism, divination, curse tablets (*tabellae defixionum*), necromancy, incantations, the evil eye, uses of divine names, and amulets.

Second-order discourse consists of the gathering and arranging of first-order data through description, definition and classification and is concerned with what those who are involved in religious practices say about what they are doing and what they say about what others are doing. Thus, second-order discourse typically involves the formulation of a theology or ideology of religious beliefs and practices. Second-order discourse can also include negative evaluations of religious beliefs, practices and practitioners considered inappropriate, dangerous, socially deviant or illegal. The extensive negative critique of *magicae vanitates* ('the vain beliefs of magic') by Pliny the Elder (*Naturalis historia* 30.1-18) belongs to the realm of second-order discourse.

Third-order discourse, as applied to ancient religious beliefs and practices, includes data from first- and second-order discourse used by modern scholars and involves their analysis using modern methods and approaches developed within the academy, including anthropology, ethnology, sociology, social psychology, sociology of religions and history of religions. Third-order discourse is therefore based on an etic perspective, that is, the perspective of the outsider rather than the insider.

Frenschkowski on Magic in Antiquity

In this chapter, I will focus attention on the recent and comprehensive article on ancient magic by Marco Frenschkowski (2010) of the University of Leipzig in the *Reallexikon für Antike und Christentum*. While there are many other treatments of ancient magic that could be selected,[7] I have chosen Frenschkowski's article for several reasons: (1) it is a comprehensive and learned discussion of magic in the ancient world, (2) it is relatively long and detailed (c. 33,000 words), (3) the author makes extensive use of many primary and secondary sources, and (4) it is both recent and up-to-date. Since a summary of this richly detailed and complex article is not possible

7. Other possible candidates for criticism include the multi-authored article on 'Magie, Magier' in Cancik and Schneider 1999. This article, though much shorter than the one by Frenschkowski, divides the subject matter into five subcategories, written by five different scholars of antiquity: (1) alter Orient (Franz Wiggermann), (2) Judentum (Irina Wandrey), (3) Griechenland und Rom and (4) Christentum (Fritz Graf and Sarah Iles Johnson), and (5) Islam (Isabel Toral-Niehoff).

in this context and would hardly do it justice, my focus will be aspects of the article that shed light on the author's use of the concept *Magie*.

The Concept and Theories of Magic

Frenschkowski begins his article with an extensive section labeled *Begriff und Theorien*, that is, 'Concept and Theories' (cols. 858-76), alternating between using the singular forms of the synonyms *Begriff* and *Konzept* (both meaning 'concept'), making it clear that the he understands *Magie* as a conceptual umbrella that he, along with many others in the field, uses to categorize a particular configuration of religious phenomena in the ancient world. With thousands of articles and hundreds of books that deal with the term magic in their titles, the author has no difficulty in amassing a huge bibliography of secondary sources, which tend to use the term magic in the same overarching way.

Under the subheading *Begriffsgeschichte* ('history of the concept'), he observes that Iranian origin of the lexemes μάγος and μαγεία was widely known in antiquity and originally referred to Median priests and their ritual practices. He cites several passages in Herodotus in which the *Magier* (here magi) are described as sacrificial priests, interpreters of dreams and royal counselors. In the Greek language area, *Magier* oscillates between the pejorative meanings *Zauberer* ('sorcerer') and *Scharlatan* ('charlatan'), though for many writers, like Herodotus, the term retains positive connotations. Even for authors of the Roman period (e.g. Strabo, Plutarch, Pausanias), authentic information about *Magier* was readily available in eastern Anatolia, Mesopotamia and Iran (col. 862). 'Nevertheless', claims Frenschkowski (col. 863),[8]

> the connotations of the semantic field of *Magie* in the Roman period no longer presumed an Iranian cultural background, but was increasingly blanketed with the semantic field of *Zauber* and gradually became primarily a label for delegitimizing specific practices and also as an abbreviation for the fascination of particular rituals displaying power.

The author then turns to a discussion of aspects of the *Begriffsumfeld*, or 'conceptual field' of magic (cols. 863-64), which includes the noun γόης, originally referring to a type of shaman, but which soon came to refer to a sorcerer (*Zauberer*) and was used as a defamatory term in the Roman period, though it was superseded by μάγος by the Hellenistic period (col. 864).

8. 'Dennoch konnotiert das Wortfeld "M[agie]", in römischer Zeit mehrheitlich mich mehr einen iran[ischen] Kulturellen Hintergrund, sondern deckt sich zunehmend mit dem Wortfeld "Zauber" u[nd] wird damit zu einem zentralen Dislegitimierungslabel für spezifische Praktiken, aber auch zu einer Abbreviatur für das Faszinana bestimmter Rituale privater "Machtausübung"'.

At this point let me call attention to Frenschkowski's semantic sleight of hand: he has taken the category *Magie* from modern third-order discourse and identified it with the second-order Greek terms *μάγος* and *μαγεία*. For Frenschkowski (and many others) magic functions as a modern overarching term for a kaleidoscope of ancient religious phenomena arbitrarily grouped together under that category. Note that he refers to the semantic field of *Magie* and of *Zauber*, modern German words, when he should be exclusively concerned with the semantic field of *μάγος* and of *μαγεία*. Years ago, James Barr (1961: 107-60; 1962: 50-58) cautioned the academy about two types of linguistic error made by biblical theologians, 'the concept method' and 'etymologizing', both of which are in evidence here.[9] The concept method imposes a concept on a word, despite the fact that a single word, like the English word 'magic', can belong to several semantic domains,[10] with the effect of overwhelming its distinct semantic meanings (i.e. the word *μαγεία* did not mean all that the modern word *Magie* means),[11] while 'etymologizing' is confusing a word's history with its meaning (i.e. the fact that the Greek word *μαγεία* is typically translated magic or *Magie* in modern Greek lexicons, using these transliterated glosses with their third-order meaning to translate the Greek word as if that revealed the semantic meaning of the word in various contexts).

The first section of Frenschkowski's article concludes with two sections on theory, the first on 'Religious and Social-Scientific Theories [of Magic]' (cols. 871-73) and the second on 'The Task of a Contemporary Theory [of Magic]' (cols. 873-76). In the first section he briefly catalogs the views on magic of several important nineteenth- and twentieth-century scholars, most belonging to the usual list of suspects, including Frazer, Mauss, Hubert, Malinowski, etc. More recently, he notes, there have been repeated calls for dropping magic as a heuristic social-scientific category and replacing it with a less burdened concept, such as 'ritual acts to gain power', referring to the work of Kippenberg and Aune (col. 873). He then makes a remarkable statement (col. 873):[12]

9. More recently, see Louw 1982: 23-31.

10. A semantic field or domain is a group of words that share a set of meanings or whose meanings overlap (strictly speaking, there is no such thing as synonyms in the sense that no two lexical items ever have identical meanings). See Louw and Nida 1988 for a Greek–English dictionary arranged in semantic domains and subdomains.

11. For an example of this kind of category mistake, see Berding 2000. Among those who recognize the differences between the Greek word *μαγεία* and the modern word magic see Graf 1997: 26 and Dickie 2001: 25.

12. 'Der vorliegende Artikel orientiert sich daher sowohl am antiken Wortfeld als auch an metaprachlichen bzw. Kulturwissenschaftlichen M[agie]konzepten, ohne sich auf eine enge Definition festzulegen'.

> The present article is therefore oriented as much on the ancient semantic field as on the metalinguistic or social-scientific conceptions of magic without proposing a narrow definition.

The first part of this statement *appears* to deal with first- and second-order discourse by referring to the 'ancient semantic field [of magic]', while the second part clearly deals with third-order discourse by referring to modern social-scientific concepts of magic. However the phrase 'the ancient semantic field [of magic]' in reality constitutes third-order discourse, since Frenschkowski actually uses the concept of magic throughout this entire introductory section as a modern construct imposed on the ancient evidence to which he refers. A further noteworthy feature of this statement is that the author not only resists proposing a narrow definition of magic, he does not explicitly provide any explicit definition of magic at all. In actuality, however, he does provide an implicit definition, for the entire article functions as a definition of magic, since what he has done, as have many predecessors, is to bundle various discrete phenomena together under the one category, *Magie*, even though the constituent elements of his construction could better be discussed as discreet but connected aspects of the religions of antiquity.

He then argues (col. 873): [13]

> A contemporary theory of magic must distinguish more precisely between objective and metalinguistic considerations, hence between the investigation of ancient terms and concepts, on the one hand, and the final formation of a modern social-scientific nomenclature, on the other.

Here the author wants to distinguish between what I have designated first- or second-order discourse (i.e. objective considerations and ancient terms and concepts) and third order discourse (i.e. metalinguistic considerations and modern social-scientific nomenclature). This is what he says ought to be done, but he does not actually do it. For example, though he mentions the necessity of investigating ancient terms and concepts, this discussion is limited to a few Greek and Latin terms at the beginning of his sections on *Begriffsgeschichte*, 'history of the concept' (col. 858), and *Begriffsumfeld*, 'conceptual field' (col. 863), while he says virtually nothing about the terms used in other ethnolinguistic areas when discussing the ancient Near East (Egypt, Syria, Iran, Mesopotamia), the Old Testament and Judaism.[14]

13. 'Eine gegenwärtige Theorie der M[agie]. must daher auf jeden Fall präzise zwischen objekt- u. metasprachlichen Bestimmungen unterscheiden, also zwischen der Unstersuchung der antiken Begriffe u. Konzepte einerseits, u. der definierenden Ausbildung einer moderning kulturwissenschaftlichen Terminolog anderseits'.

14. One would suppose that this problem could be solved if each of the major ethnolinguistic areas of the ancient world were treated by specialists in those areas, such as the '*Magie, Magier*' articles in Cancik and Schneider 1999. However, even here it is

The author observes, correctly, that the problem of identifying cross-cultural constants in magic remains a debated issue, but one persistent feature of magic he insists on is the notion of alterity or difference in various ways (col. 874). In various places in the article he calls attention to types of socio-religious conflict in which members of dominant groups tended to use synonyms of magic and magician in a pejorative sense to stigmatize minorities with whom they were in opposition (col. 874), accusing them of improper, deviant or illegal beliefs and practices. The ancients had a vast arsenal of accusations to throw at their opponents (including cannibalism, infanticide and incest, to name a few of the more popular slanders), so that limiting their weapons to magic as the one overarching concept for this castigation is reductionistic. Such conflict was sometimes generated by the gender hierarchy of antiquity (cols. 880-82), partly reflected in the prominence of female witches over male magicians in parts of the ancient Near East. Gender antagonism in early Judaism is pithily expressed in *m. Abot* 2.7: 'Where there are many women, there are many witches'. The Acts of the Apostles and the apocryphal acts portray Paul and other Christian missionaries as in conflict with the world of pagan religious practices, occasionally using the terms μάγος and μαγεία, dramatized in the comic scene of the overpowering of the seven sons of Sceva, Jewish exorcists (Acts 19.13-16), and the voluntary burning of 'magical' books worth 50,000 silver coins by Christian converts in Ephesus (Acts 19.19). The opposition between 'magic' and miracle is an important theme in both the canonical Acts and the apocryphal acts (col. 922). The conception of pagan deities as demons (1 Cor. 10.20-21) becomes a standard Christian way of defaming all pagan religious practices (col. 924).

Magic in Greece and Rome

In discussing magic in Greece and Rome (cols. 876-99), Frenschkowski begins with a helpful discussion of sources, including the technical or professional writers who transmitted information about pharmacology, astrology, alchemy and magical spells sometimes accompanying descriptions of ancient ritual practices (col. 877). Other important sources include drawings and inscriptions found on amulets, curse tablets, magical bowls and magical gems.

One of the more important sources for our knowledge of ancient magic is the corpus of Greek and Coptic magical papyri (col. 877-78), complex ritual texts in which the rituals of public cults appear to have been recycled (col. 886). If we ask what is so 'magical' about the 'magical' papyri, the author

only in the section on '*Griechenland und Rom*' that the irresistible attraction of μαγεία and μάγος leads to a brief discussion of those Greek lexemes.

had earlier observed that there was a broad scholarly consensus that the corpus of texts from classical antiquity labeled as magical papyri are appropriately categorized (col. 876). But isn't the criterion of 'broad consensus' simply the Forty Million Frenchmen Can't Be Wrong[15] argument?

The author then turns to a discussion of the constitutive elements of magical rituals and some of their major features (cols. 882-91). Ritual in general exhibits a limited repertoire of features, lending itself to cross-cultural comparison. He discusses the basic features *Zaubersprüche*, magical spells (cols. 883-84), which are often lengthy litanies with syncretistic features using divine epithets and magical words as well as complicated ritual instructions (col. 883). While ascetic preparations for performing the rituals preserved in the magical papyri are identical with those of religious rites, there are some exceptions, such as ritual nudity, which is more common to magical than religious ritual (col. 888).

Certainly a central problem remains: how can magical rituals be distinguished from religious rituals? Since Frenschkowski has earlier assured the reader that 'not every symbolic ritual action is magical' (col. 874), the question naturally arises, how one can objectively distinguish magical from non-magical ritual without defining what one means by magic or magical ritual? Here some assembly is required, for the reader is forced to put together some of the distinctive features of magical ritual from the hints dropped by the author throughout his article. Part of the answer might be their distinctive content, the frequent use of so-called magical words, and the mention of the gods and goddesses of magic, particularly chthonic deities (e.g. Hekate, Persephone), and other deities found in magical contexts, such as Hermes, Agathodaimon, Seth-Typhon, Anubis and the Jewish Iao (cols. 889-90). Another part of the answer might be the practice of threatening the gods, which is clearly in opposition to typical religious forms of addressing the deities in prayer (col. 891). Another characteristic might be the pragmatism of magical ritual, which often focused attention on obtaining money, sex, success and revenge (col. 891). Yet another part of the answer might be the automatic or *ex opere operato* ('from the work done') character of magical ritual (col. 918).

In my view, it makes little sense to distinguish 'magical' ritual from religious ritual for several reasons. First, in the Greco-Roman world, the worship of the gods took place in public cults, domestic cults, mystery cults and private religious practices. Very little is known about the rituals and liturgies of domestic cults (not to mention the mystery cults) and even less is known about private religious practices, except for the ritual texts

15. 'Forty Million Frenchmen Can't Be Wrong' was actually the title of a 1927 hit song by Willie Raskin, Billy Rose and Fred Fischer comparing the free attitude of the Parisians of the 1920s with censorship and prohibition in the United States.

that many label 'magical rituals'. Second, the modern Western understanding of religion is largely conditioned by assumption of the paradigmatic character of forms of post-Enlightenment Catholicism, Orthodoxy, Protestantism and Judaism. Since many of the rituals preserved in the Greek and Coptic 'magical' papyri contain features that appear morally offensive, self-aggrandizing, self-centered and even malevolent, it is easy for us to categorize such beliefs and practices as antithetical to the values inculcated by modern Western forms of religious faith. Thus, the concept 'magic' seems to many to be an appropriate conceptual garbage can in which such practices can be conveniently quarantined. Third, on the other hand, if we are willing to understand the religious practices of antiquity in their integrity, with all of their differences from the world of norms and values which is an implicit part of our social knowledge, then the reasons for quarantining that which offends our sensibilities to the category of 'magic' will disappear.

Concluding Observations

In this essay, I have argued that the modern third-order category 'magic' provides no heuristic value for the investigation of the religions of antiquity. Quite the contrary, using that concept facilitates the projection of modern sensibilities onto the religious beliefs and practices of antiquity by separating those beliefs and practices that are palatable to modern tastes from those that are not. Though it is hard to unscramble scrambled eggs, we can make a start by rejecting the concept of 'magic' since it does more harm than good. How can we talk about 'magic' if we reject the term, aside from the likely fact that 'magic' in book titles aids sales? It is more important to focus on the individual components of the complex reality of ancient religion, including prayer, ritual, exorcism, curse tablets, divination and the like.

References

Aune, David E.

1979 'Magic, Magician', in *International Standard Bible Encyclopedia* (ed. G.W. Bromily; Grand Rapids, MI: Eerdmans, rev. edn): 3.213-19.

1980 'Magic in Early Christianity', in *Aufstieg und Niedergand der römischen Welt*, Part II, 23/2 (ed. H. Temporini and W. Haase; Berlin: Walter de Gruyter): 1507-57.

1987 'The Apocalypse of John and Graeco-Roman Revelatory Magic', *NTS* 33: 481-501.

1990 'Magical Papyri', in *Mercer Dictionary of the Bible* (ed. Watson E. Mills; Macon, GA: Mercer University Press): 540-41.

1995a 'Jesus (im Zauber)', *Reallexikon für Antike und Christentum* (Stuttgart: Anton Hiersemann): 17.821-37.

1995b 'Iao', *Reallexikon für Antike und Christentum* (Stuttgart: Anton Hiersemann): 17.1-12.

1997 'Amulets', in *The Oxford Encyclopedia of Archaeology in the Near East* (ed. Eric M. Meyers; 6 vols.; New York: Oxford University Press): 1.113-15.

2004 'Divination and Prophecy: Christianity', in *Religions of the Ancient World: A Guide* (ed. Sarah Iles Johnson; Cambridge, MA: Harvard University Press): 390-91.

2005 'Circle', in *The Encyclopedia of Religion* (ed. Lindsay Jones; Detroit, MI: Thomson Gale; Macmillan Reference USA, 2nd edn): 3.1790-95.

2006a 'Magic in Early Christianity', in *Apocalypticism, Prophecy, and Magic in Early Christianity: Collected Essays* (WUNT, 199; Tübingen: Mohr Siebeck): 368-420.

2006b 'Kreis', *Reallexikon für Antike und Christentum* (Stuttgart: Anton Hiersemann): 17.1053-70.

2008 ''Magic', in *Early Christianity and its Ancient Mediterranean Context: A Survey of Some Recent Scholarship,* in *Neues Testament und Magie: Verhältnisbestimmungen* (ed. Tobias Nicklas and Thomas J. Kraus), *Annali di storia dell'esegesi* 24.2: 229-94.

2012a 'Kan Jesus kaldes magiker?', *Bibliana* 13: 20-23.

2012b 'The Polyvalent Imagery of Rev 3:20 in the Light of Greco-Egyptian Divination Texts', in *Greco-Roman Culture and the New Testament: Studies Commemorating the Centennial of the Pontifical Biblical Institute* (ed. David E. Aune and Frederick E. Brenk; NovTSup, 153; Leiden: Brill): 167-83.

Barr, James

1961 *The Semantics of Biblical Language* (Oxford: Oxford University Press, 1961).

1962 *Biblical Words for Time* (SBT, 33; London: SCM Press).

Berding, Kenneth

2000 'Confusing Word and Concept in "Spiritual Gifts": Have We Forgotten James Barr's Exhortations?', *JETS* 45: 37-51.

Betz, Hans Dieter (ed.)

1986 *The Greek Magical Papyri in Translation including the Demotic Spells* (Chicago: University of Chicago Press).

1992 *The Greek Magical Papyri in Translation including the Demotic Spells* (Chicago: University of Chicago Press, 2nd edn).

Cancik, Hubert, and Helmuth Schneider (eds.)

1999 'Magie, Magier', *Der neue Pauly: Enzyklopädie der Antike* (Stuttgart: Verlag J.B. Metzler): 7.657-73.

Dickie, Matthew

2001 *Magic and Magicians in the Greco-Roman World* (London: Routledge).

Dvorak, James D.

2007 'John H. Elliott's Social-Scientific Criticism', *Trinity Journal* 28: 252-78.

Elliott, John H.

1988 'The Fear of the Leer: The Evil Eye from the Bible to Li'l Abner', *Forum* 4: 42-71.

1990 'Paul, Galatians and the Evil Eye', *CTM* 17: 262-73.

1991 'The Evil Eye in the First Testament: The Ecology and Culture of a Pervasive Belief', in *The Bible and the Politics of Exegesis: Essays in Honor of Norman Gottwald on his Sixty-Fifth Birthday* (ed. David Jobling, D.T. Sheppard and P.L. Day; Cleveland, OH: Pilgrim Press): 147-59.

1994 'The Evil Eye and the Sermon on the Mount: Contours of a Pervasive Belief in Social Scientific Perspective', *BibInt* 2: 51-84.

2004 'Jesus, Mark and the Evil Eye', *LTJ* 39: 157-68.

2011 'Social-Scientific Criticism: Perspective, Process and Payoff: Evil Eye Accusation at Galatia as Illustration of the Method', *Hervormde theologiese studies* 61: 114-23.

Flood, Gavin

2006 'Reflections on Tradition and Inquiry in the Study of Religions', *JAAR* 74: 54-57.

Frankfurter, David

1993 'Luke's μαγεία and Garrett's "Magic"', *Union Seminary Quarterly Review* 47: 81-89.

Frenschkowski, Marco

2010 'Magie', in *Reallexikon für Antike und Christentum* (ed. Georg Schöllgen *et al.*; Stuttgart: Anton Hiersemann): 23.857-957.

Graf, Fritz

1997 *Magic in the Ancient World* (Cambridge, MA: Harvard University Press).

Gunnel, John

1998 *The Orders of Discourse* (Lanham, MD: Rowman & Littlefield).

Harris, Marvin

1976 'History and Significance of the Emic/Etic Distinction', *Annual Review of Anthropology* 5: 329-50.

Louw, J.P.

1982 *Semantics of New Testament Greek* (Philadelphia, PA: Fortress Press; Chico: Scholars Press).

Louw, J.P., and Eugene A. Nida (eds.)

1988 *Greek–English Lexicon of the New Testament Based on Semantic Domains* (2 vols.; New York: United Bible Societies).

Pike, Kenneth

1954 *Language in Relation to a Unified Theory of the Structure of Human Behavior* (Glendale, CA: Summer Institute of Linguistics).

1967 *Language in Relation to a Unified Theory of the Structure of Human Behavior* (The Hague: Mouton, 2nd edn).

Pope, Alexander

1711 *An Essay on Criticism* (London: Printed for W. Lewis).

Smith, Wilfred Cantwell

1962 *The Meaning and End of Religion* (New York: Macmillan).

Williams, Michael Allen

1996 *Rethinking 'Gnosticism': An Argument for Dismantling a Dubious Category* (Princeton, NJ: Princeton University Press).

'Stickless' in Corinth: How Paul Sought to Recover his Authority

S. Scott Bartchy

> What would you prefer? Am I to come to you with a stick, or with love in a spirit of gentleness? (1 Cor. 4.21).[1]

Jack Elliott and I first met in 1976 at a session of the newly created section of the Society of Biblical Literature for exploring the use of the social sciences in interpreting the New Testament. When I learned then that he planned to be on sabbatical leave in Europe during the next academic year, I invited him to come to Tübingen, Germany, and serve as a senior research scholar in the then relatively new Institut zur Erforschung des Urchristentums there, of which I had become the director a few years earlier. He accepted, and, as he notes in the introduction to his path-breaking *A Home for the Homeless,* he wrote a substantial portion of that book in his office in that research center.

In addition to our beginning a long-term friendship that year, Jack benefitted me greatly in at least two ways. First, he challenged me to move forward from my established interest in the social history of the early Christ-followers (see Bartchy 1973) to a deep interest in the dominant cultural values and social codes in the early Roman Empire, that is, to thinking like a cross-cultural anthropologist. My embrace of this emphasis led to Jack encouraging me to join him and others in the creation of The International Context Group in 1990. Second, while in Tübingen, he invited me to join him in participating in a scholars' conference dealing with *materialistische Exegese,* held at a well-known retreat center in Germany, at which I met German scholars, many of whom knew my work and some of whom have become lifelong friends. As a result of all this and in gratitude, I am both honored and delighted by this opportunity to honor Jack Elliott by this modest inquiry into Paul's relationships with his converts.

1. Unless otherwise noted, all biblical quotations are cited in the words of the NRSV.

The Challenge of Social-Science Interpretation

A major benefit of social-science analysis of ancient documents is the challenge it presents to think concretely about the everyday relationships and cultural/behavioral assumptions of those who wrote, read and heard whatever words I see before me. As Bruce J. Malina has succinctly written, 'The purpose for using anthropological models in New Testament study is precisely to hear the meaning of the documents in terms of the social systems in which they were originally proclaimed' (2001: xi). In response to this challenge, I have sought to keep myself from imposing the values and behavioral standards of my own social system when exegeting all documents from other cultures and other times, including the letters of Paul. This may be most obvious in my various articles dealing with Paul of Tarsus (Bartchy 1999, 2003, 2005, 2009); in this essay I seek to push further into the social world that framed the relationships between Paul and his converts. In this inquiry, I will explore the extent to which Paul's converts in Corinth granted him greater authority over their lives than they gave to their parents, extended family, friends, patrons and any other influential persons. In particular, how strongly could Paul warn these Christ-followers that he would not be lenient with them and might even be 'severe in using the authority that the Lord had given' him (2 Cor. 13.10) before he risked losing them back into the arms of their respective skeptical families and friends? All exegetes known to me have largely ignored the continuing presence and possible weighty influence of these persons in the lives of Paul's converts and the challenge they presented to his authority.[2]

The Challenges to Paul's Authority

As Paul's uncontested letters abundantly reveal, both his converts and his opponents frequently questioned and even ignored his authority.[3] Schol-

2. For the relativizing of blood-family solidarity in the Jesus tradition see Barton 1994. Barton does comment briefly on the ways in which Paul's teaching also challenged traditional family ties (5-8), but he says nothing about the disapproving responses of the unconverted family members, except in the case of the *Acts of Paul and Thecla* (written about 185–195 CE). Karl Olav Sandnes provides a foundation for thinking about the responses of the unconverted in his article dealing with family solidarity (1997: 154-56).

3. These letters strongly indicate that those to whom Paul wrote were still at the 'storming' (rather than 'norming' or 'performing') stage of group development as described by Bruce J. Malina. That is, Paul's letters reveal a time in a group's life characterized by 'group members arguing with each other and heaping criticism on the leader'. Malina contrasts this period with the later 'norming' stage into which Paul sought to lead his converts, and Malina recommends reading Paul's letter to Romans from the viewpoint of this second stage. Yet Malina finds no examples among Paul's groups of any of

ars as well as most casual readers of these letters have observed that Paul was quite aware that many of his converts had ceased following him and were looking to others for leadership. Apparently, Paul's leadership style and his goals for transforming their behavior were bewildering, resulting in his converts granting greater authority to less challenging leaders. The most obvious cases of such pushback are reflected in his defense of his apostolic activity and authority in his letter to the Galatians and in 2 Corinthians 10–13. While this resistance may not be so obvious in 1 Corinthians, it is still clear from the tone of appeal that begins in 1 Cor. 1.10 that some (or many?) of the Corinthians are following other leaders such as Apollos and Cephas rather than Paul—even though Paul was the first to come all the way to them with 'the good news of Christ' (2 Cor. 10.14). To my knowledge, this observation has not yet resulted in asking sufficiently if it was something in Paul's style of leadership and manner of treating his converts that confused and disappointed them and made other, more conventionally acting leaders more attractive to them.

Seriously Overestimating Paul's Authority

The fact that Paul's letters gained such great authority over time that they were included in the Christian canon of Scripture has made it far too easy for both scholars and casual readers to overestimate and seriously exaggerate how much authority his converts continued to grant to the historical Paul following their initial positive responses to him. Indeed, arguably the major hindrance to understanding what Paul specifically intended to communicate to the various hearers of his letters is the context in which modern readers first 'meet' Paul—in the Bible. There can be no question that both male and female readers of the Bible have for many centuries used selected parts of the Pauline tradition to sanctify systems of domination in various cultures, including patriarchy, divinely appointed kingship and slavery. Largely as a consequence of such practices, historians and exegetes have focused their attention on Paul's own uses of power and claims of authority. Seemingly implicit in many scholars' analysis has been their assumption that Paul enjoyed the kind of extensive and profound authority among his converts that he came to have during later centuries.[4]

them having arrived at the 'performing' stage. Even the criteria for leadership presented in the Pastoral Letters 'still look like items desired and not yet realized' (2001: 208-10).

4. See, e.g., Elizabeth Castelli's widely cited presentation of Paul as a leader who sought to dominate his followers and used his call to imitate him to emphasize his privileged position in a 'natural', hierarchical social structure (1991: 89-117).

Paul the Pharisee Knew How to Use a Stick

Earlier in his life, when Paul was a Pharisee and initiated his persecution of Judean Christ-followers, he certainly must have had a 'stick', that is, some kind of effective and acknowledged threat, as he sought to influence fellow Judeans to remain in the way of life in which they had been raised.[5] That is, he was seeking to hinder them from embracing a new way of thinking and acting. Then he had a strong and long-standing tradition, a sense of family solidarity and a respected social framework on his side. But now, as a Christ-follower, Paul had precisely the opposite task: to introduce a new way of thinking and acting and to encourage his converts to abandon their 'comfort zones', whether Judeans or gentiles, including the approval and authority of their parents, the respect of their friends and even their views about Divine Power. Now they were to be radically resocialized into persons manifesting the gentle and patient 'fruit of the Spirit' (Gal. 5.22).[6]

But Did Paul as Christ's Apostle Still Have a 'Stick'?

Kathy Ehrensperger has published an excellent and extensive reframing of this debate in her *Paul and the Dynamics of Power* (2009), in which she points to the many ways that Paul did not seek to maintain ongoing relationships of control over his converts. Rather, she concludes, correctly in my judgment, that Paul 'exercised power-over the communities in a transformative way' (197). 'He only has authority in relation to them inasmuch as he is building them up (2 Cor. 10.8)' (198). Ehrensperger argues persuasively that Paul did not 'claim or aim at establishing a position of domination or control', noting the usually overlooked fact that he repeatedly left behind

5. While Paul does identify himself as one who 'violently persecuted the church of God and tried to destroy it' (Gal. 1.13; see also 1 Cor. 15.9; Phil. 3.6; and Paul's violent reputation noted in 1 Tim. 1.13), he does not indicate who or what institution authorized him to do so; and what he actually did 'violently' remains rather vague. Likewise, the author of the book of Acts notes simply that following the stoning of Stephen, Paul (Saul) began to destroy the church, putting both men and women in prison; there is no reference, however, to where this prison was or who authorized Paul to arrest these people (8.3). A few paragraphs later, the author of Acts states that Paul obtained letters from the high priest in Jerusalem to present to the synagogues in Damascus, authorizing him to take Christ-followers, both men and women, as prisoners back to Jerusalem (9.1-2; 22.5; 26.10-12). The historical problem here is that neither Paul himself nor any other ancient source verifies any authority the high priest had to demand such extradition.

6. Three of the canonical Gospels and the *Gospel of Thomas* note specifically that becoming a follower of Jesus could result in alienation from one's family of origin. See Mt. 10.34-37; Lk. 12.51-53; 14.26; Jn 9.13-23; *Gos. Thom.* 16, 101. See also Barton 1994.

the house churches he had founded. While later keeping in touch with many of them through letters and colleagues, he pushed on to the west (Rom. 15.14-29) and separated himself from his converts in the hope of their continuing empowerment by God's Spirit in Christ (199).

In an attempt to press further in the analysis of Paul's interactions with his converts, I seek here to imagine what Paul could actually do to discipline or punish his converts, a question that I have not found discussed in any of the commentaries or articles that I have read dealing with the Corinthian correspondence or any of Paul's other letters. What hold do we imagine that Paul had on his converts, such that his disapproval, however expressed, could make a serious difference in their lives? What price could he make any of his converts pay for not obeying him? What do we suppose Paul could have done, if indeed he had come to the Corinthian converts 'with a stick' or 'a rod', as the Greek term ῥάβδος is usually translated?[7] And when later he warns the Corinthians that he will 'not be lenient' when he comes to them for the third time (2 Cor. 13.1-4) and hopes that he will 'not have to be severe in using the authority' that the Lord has given him (13.10), what specific actions do contemporary readers think that he had in mind—personal rejection, shouting at them (would that have made any difference to those who challenged Paul's authority?), or calling for the Corinthian Christ-followers to shun a convert who rejects Paul's authority (as in 1 Cor. 5.1-5)? Paul did think that it was important to claim that he was not trying to shame them (1 Cor. 4.14). But after they had just heard Paul's strong words of rebuke in ch. 3, his assurance may have been faint comfort to those for whom Paul's judgment and approval already meant something.[8]

Could Punishment Encourage Transformation?

After imagining whatever means Paul might have used to punish his converts, it becomes important, I think, to reflect on the potential consequences of such possible actions. To what degree, if any, would such treatment of his converts contribute positively or negatively to Paul's goal of resocializing them, that is, leading them to 'live by the Spirit' and to be filled with the 'fruit of the Spirit', characteristics that he identifies as 'love, joy, peace, patience, kindness, generosity, faithfulness, gentleness, and self-control' (Gal. 5.16, 22)? By whatever means of punishment Paul thought to use,

7. See Daube (1966: 68) for a listing of the relevant LXX passages.

8. In her recent and helpful commentary on 1 Corinthians, Pheme Perkins reads this denial of an attempt to shame the Corinthians as Paul's stepping back and giving his hearers 'a glimpse of the writer puzzling over the words to put on the page', after recounting how much and how often he had been humiliated himself (2012: 80).

would he by his own example have been inadvertently hindering the transformation of his converts by the Spirit? If he came to them with a stick, even in view of the harshness and thrashings for which pedagogues could be known (see Bradley 1991: 55-56), would not such a negative example of interpersonal relationships have placed an unintended but significant barrier between his converts and his own goal of changing both their convictions and their behavior? Note carefully here that first-century pedagogues had authority over their charges because they had been given such power within the structure of the family who owned them or hired them. In that framework, many pedagogues continued to exert forceful influence over their charges even after they became adults.[9] In Paul's case, however, he had to operate without such a surrogate family structure being firmly recognized, making it all the easier for his converts to challenge his claim to be a leader worthy of their giving him ongoing authority over them.

In short, how did Paul's own behavior clarify and support his message, such that he could urge his converts to imitate him (see 1 Cor. 4.16; 11.1; 1 Thess. 1.6; see also Gal. 4.12)? On the other hand, might these Christ-followers have found imitating the behavior of those whom Paul criticizes as 'pseudo apostles' (2 Cor. 11.13) and ironically as 'super apostles' (2 Cor. 11.4-5; 13.11) more in tune with the way they had been raised, including imitating their parents, according to the dominant cultural values and social codes—and thus less demanding of serious personal and social transformation than Paul?

Paul's Own Example Critical to his Persuasiveness

Would not Paul's own behavior, especially his own way of treating others, including his converts, have been essential to demonstrate and clarify the meaning of his 'gospel' and to exemplify the truth of his rhetoric? Would not at first his manner of treating those traveling with him, such as Timothy and Titus (probably also, at least, Sosthenes and Silvanus) have been a critical factor in how his converts perceived and received him? And would not his exemplary manner of relating to his converts have been essential to his credibility in seriously redefining their understanding of Divine Power and their relationship to that new reality in their lives? In what follows, I propose some answers that I hope will persuade this book's honoree.

9. For example, even after Claudius, the later emperor, became an adult, the pedagogue his family had chosen for him accompanied him and disciplined him. According to Suetonius, Claudius complained in a petition that his pedagogue was a 'barbarian' who was inclined 'to discipline him as savagely as possible for any reason under the sun' (*Claudius* 2.2.).

Authority—How to Gain it, How to Use It, How to Keep It?

Very little of the scholarly analysis of Paul's assertions of his authority has paid sufficient attention to the fact that while authority may be claimed, it does not exist until it is granted by those who willingly give that power over them to an institution, a group, or a person. While power can coerce, authority results from gained assent. As Bengt Holmberg observes,

> in an authority relation there is something in the ruler's person or behavior that effects willing compliance on the part of the subordinate. He is constrained to submit to the other, not by an external means, but out of the conviction that it is right to do so (1980: 131).

It is a question of acknowledged legitimacy, and Paul's own behavior has frequently been undervalued as the critical factor in his gaining and maintaining such ongoing assent from his converts. While they had obviously granted him great authority when they first responded positively to Paul, his letters make clear that they had begun to have second thoughts about following his lead. Why?

Parents and Patrons Already Had Great Authority over Paul's Converts

Many, if not most, of the fathers, mothers, siblings, friends, patrons and perhaps employers of these Christ-followers must have repeatedly warned them to 'come to their senses' and return to blood-family solidarity and the practice of traditional and honorable cultural values and social codes. These good folks must have exerted pressure on Paul's converts to give up Paul's culturally suspect views and their new 'in-Christ' identity and to come back to the 'real world' in which they had been raised. It may well be that Paul was not the first or only wandering teacher (including various stripes of cynic philosophers) they had encountered who had challenged traditional Greco-Roman values and social codes. In any case, these folks knew that such teachers were bad for family solidarity and one's social health. Such unconvinced people among the Christ-followers' relatives and friends must have said that these Christ-followers' foolishness, and the potential social alienation that would befall them if they continued to listen to Paul, would certainly become evident in five or ten years, if not before.[10]

10. In my exegesis of 1 Cor. 7.20-21, I argue that when Paul exhorted his converts to 'stay in the calling (in Christ)', to affirm and confirm their new identity, he was urging his converts to stop thinking of themselves as they did earlier in their lives—and as outsiders probably still viewed them. He was exhorting them not to 'cave in' to those who were pressuring them to go back to their old way of socially defining themselves,

Paul had to be aware that, in light of the pushback against his authority, his strong assertion of that authority ('with a stick'?) might result in his losing his converts back to their earlier, socially approved existence in familial solidarity. That is, if Paul had indeed come to them in a spirit of punishment (a way of personal relating that both Paul and they knew well from how they all had been raised), he would have been working against his own desire to transform his converts. He would have given them, especially the males among them, implicit permission to go back to or to continue patterns of domination, retaliation and punishment—behavior that had been essential in their own, earlier relationships. Many of the men may have indeed welcomed such a tacit encouragement of their old honor-seeking and dominating ways of relating to one another as well as to those outside the group. They would have been 'off the hook' and potentially back in the good graces of family and friends. Paul had led them out of their comfort zone into a process of transformation of their lives by acting in ways that displayed the meaning of his strong words. If he had then unexpectedly acted 'with a stick', his behavior would have certainly dulled the cutting edge of those words.

Authority and Influence—without Domination

Had Paul actually come to the Corinthians 'with a stick', he would have made a seriously counterproductive move with regard to his true, long-range goal for his converts—for them to mature into Holy Spirit-filled earthen vessels. Frequently Paul sought to convince his converts that his authority was of a peculiar kind granted to him by the 'crucified Christ'. In that context, I see Paul negotiating, often out of profound frustration with their slow growth toward that maturity, to continue to have a non-dominating influence on those who did accept his 'cruciform' authority, while not further alienating those who were resisting his efforts to resocialize them into the image of Christ.

Paul must have known that the key to his success in this regard was his own Christ-like, Spirit-filled behavior. As one who had been raised according to the dominant values and social codes in ancient Mediterranean culture, Paul must also have known that he had undertaken a super-human task as he sought to lead the Corinthians into a less arrogant, less competitive, less envy-filled way of acting. As he wrote in 1 Cor. 4.12-13 (just before the 'stick' passage), 'When reviled, we bless, when persecuted, we endure, when slandered, we speak kindly'. Such counter-intuitive responses make clear that Paul himself as a Christ-follower had been undergoing a very

including those among Paul's opponents who sought to persuade his converts to define themselves ethnically (by circumcision, 7.18-19).

serious, Spirit-led resocialization process, in sharp contrast to the values by which his parents and other significant adults in his life had raised him.

When, then, in 1 Cor. 4.16 Paul urged his converts to imitate him (see also 1 Cor. 11.1), the behavior they were to emulate was his strikingly countercultural, non-authoritarian, non-retaliatory response to these many experiences of dishonor and humiliation in his life. As Paul's severe challenge to traditional values became increasingly clear to his converts, did they begin to have cold feet? As Paul clarified the implications of his gospel for their lives together, had Paul's agenda for transformation begun to lose its persuasive power?

In any case, Paul would have dramatically reinforced his critique of traditionally honorable behavior when he came to the Corinthians 'with love (ἀγάπῃ) in a spirit of gentleness' rather that 'with a stick'. If, on the other hand, he had come to them 'with a stick', he would have reinforced their own previous socialization, the very way of living that he was seeking to transform. Even a casual reading of 1 Corinthians displays many of Paul's converts in Corinth as ones who sought to live according to their own compromises between the values with which they had been raised and the 'new creation' values 'in Christ' (2 Cor. 5.17). For example, some of the (better-off) Corinthians were initiating lawsuits against other converts, and thereby displaying for all to see that they did not yet take one another seriously as 'brothers and sisters' (1 Cor. 6.1-8), Paul's favorite term for his converts (forty such uses in 1 Corinthians alone).

When Paul responded to this report by asking 'Why not rather be wronged? Why not rather be defrauded? ' (1 Cor. 6.7), it is easy to imagine that many of them thought, 'Paul, you can't be serious! You are no longer talking rationally.' They could have quickly thought of solid, traditional and honorable reasons for not being wronged. Further, their unconverted family members and friends would have reinforced their judgment that Paul was indeed a fool (see 2 Cor. 11.16), and totally unworthy of being given any authority. Yet, Paul certainly was very serious and could recount many times as a Christ-follower when he had been wronged and did not retaliate.

Why Then Even Mention Coming to Corinth with 'a Stick'?

Did Paul mention the possibility of his coming to the Corinthians 'with a stick' to stress in sharp contrast the alternative values that he had consistently lived by when he was among them? Was he assuming that some of them would really have preferred for him to act in 'the old-fashioned way' and thus ironically reminding them that he really did not have a stick anymore? Certainly the behavior of many of the Corinthians sorely vexed Paul and tempted him to try to take shortcuts, if he could, on the way to their transformation. Yet, Paul's continuing desire was to be accepted and honored as a trustworthy leader without first caving in to the temptation to seek to dominate them and to (re)gain his authority in their lives by conforming to their familiar 'old creation' patterns of behavior (see Bartchy 2005: 56-58).

The temptation for Paul to act in a dominating manner must have been greatly exacerbated by the arrival in Corinth of those whom Paul ironically labeled 'super apostles' (2 Cor. 11.5). Their troubling behavior must have exasperated him even more than that of his Corinthian converts. For, at least according to his view of the matter, these leaders had indeed arrived with a real stick—and been too well received. In Paul's eyes these super apostles were really 'pseudo apostles', not least because they took advantage of his converts and preyed upon them (probably financially), acting arrogantly and lording it over them, making slaves of the converts and even slapping their faces—literally or with some severe, calculated insult (2 Cor. 11.19-21) (see Harris 2005: 784-87). Such forms of leadership must have felt familiar to those who were raised with authoritarian values, values that in our culture we would probably regard as child abuse—psychological, if not also physical.

This kind of behavior certainly presented no challenge for the Corinthians to abandon their own inclination to dominate as many persons as they could (including one another) and to compete for honor at the expense of others.[11] While these opposing leaders may have preached some ideas with which Paul would not have disagreed (he does not seem to criticize their 'theology' as such), their own leadership style had resulted in giving a significantly different day-to-day behavioral meaning to words that sounded the same.

Paul's 'Stickless' Rhetorical Strategy

Without any question, in 1 Corinthians 4, Paul is employing every rhetorical means that he has as a Christ-follower in his attempt to overcome the spiritual arrogance of his converts in Corinth. In the following chapters, he then seeks to motivate them to practice a directly related, transformed behavior. The actual use of a 'stick', however, is strikingly (!) not one of those means. In 4.8-13, Paul has already ironically stressed his lack of power as traditionally measured: 'We are fools for Christ's sake, but you are wise in Christ. We are weak, but you are strong. You are held in honor but we in disrepute.' In distinct contrast to Castelli's claim that 'one is hard-pressed to produce a univocal, concrete expression of what exactly the Corinthians are being called to imitate' (1991: 109), Paul's stress in this passage on his refusal to

11. Fee concludes that the community as a whole was at fault because it had tolerated or even adopted the behavior patterns of the arrogant (1987: 190).

retaliate and use power for himself is unambiguously the behavioral context in which Paul urges his converts to imitate him. Then in 1 Cor. 11.1 Paul explicitly exhorts them to imitate him, as he imitates Christ in not seeking his 'own advantage but that of many'.

Did Paul Then Play the 'Father' Card?

While 'pulling out all the stops' in his tools of persuasion, Paul sought to emphasize his unique, seminal role in calling them to Christ. In 1 Cor. 4.15, he reminded his Corinthian converts that even though they might have 'ten thousand guardians (παιδαγωγούς) in Christ' they did 'not have many fathers (πατέρας)'. It has become conventional then in English translations to render the following sentence (also in v. 15) as 'Indeed, in Christ Jesus I became your *father* through the gospel' (my emphasis; so the NRSV, TNIV, NIV, and even the usually literal NASB). Yet, Paul did not actually use the term 'father' (πατήρ) in this sentence. Rather, what Paul wrote was 'in Christ Jesus through the gospel I begot you (ἐγέννησα)', with the term 'begot'—correctly translated in the KJV—emphasized by being the final word in the sentence.

Many scholars see here no particular intention by Paul to avoid using the term πατήρ for himself. See, for example, Gordon Fee, in his substantial commentary on 1 Corinthians, who justifies accepting the translation 'father' by contrasting it with the previous phrase, 'you do not have many fathers (πατέρας)' (1987: 185-86). T.J. Burke, who has written an excellent exposition of Paul's family metaphors, also takes for granted that the term 'father' is the appropriate rendering of ἐγέννησα and then builds his argument on wide-ranging evidence he gathers from the uses of πατήρ in Paul's cultural world (2003).

However, the fact that in his letter to Philemon (v. 10) Paul again avoided referring to himself as the πατήρ of Philemon's slave Onesimus (despite many English translations that use 'father' here) and again wrote ἐγέννησα instead, suggests that Paul sought in his discourse to invoke the image of the inseminating and nurturing parent without exploiting the dominance-loaded potential in the term πατήρ.[12] The tone of his next sentence reinforces this reading. That is, Paul appealed (παρακαλῶ) to his converts to imitate his self-effacing and serving behavior; he appealed to them rather than sternly ordering them, as a father in his cultural world would have been expected to do.[13]

12. I find it quite interesting that in the German translations known to me the term ἐγέννησα is always rendered *gezeugt*, except in the (Roman Catholic) *Einheitsübersetzung* where *euer Vater geworden* is the unsurprising rendering.

13. This may suggest that Paul was aware in some way of the tradition emphasized in Mt. 23.9 according to which Jesus exhorted his followers 'Call no man father on earth, for you have one Father—the one in heaven'.

Indeed, the engaging tone of Paul's discourse in many of his letters springs from his employing the language of appeal. Such is the case when Paul sought Philemon's cooperation in treating the slave Onesimus no longer as a slave but as 'a beloved brother'—as both Onesimus and Philemon had become to Paul himself (vv. 9-16). Further, it is noteworthy that in 1 Cor. 1.10, Rom. 15.30, and 1 Thess. 5.12 Paul makes his appeal to his 'brothers and sisters' rather than to his 'children' as such. To be sure, Paul occasionally referred to his converts as his 'offspring' (using τέκνον, not παῖς), as in 1 Thess. 2.11 and here in 1 Cor. 4.17 where he praises Timothy as his 'beloved and faithful' emissary, whom he sent to remind the Corinthians of Paul's 'ways in Christ Jesus'.[14] What Paul did not do is claim that 'because I am your father you must obey me!' In that sense, Paul never played his culture's well-known 'father card'.

However persuasive this line of reasoning proves to be, I suggest that it is time to think more about the tension between Paul's view of his converts as a 'family' (if often a dysfunctional one) who should now be practicing together the values of a well-functioning family and the obvious fact that 'family' was not yet the self- or group-perception of many of them. If, as seems clear from the Corinthian letters, the Christ-followers there had not yet embraced in any substantial way thinking of themselves together as a surrogate family, as true sisters and brothers, how effective would Paul's insisting on their obedience because he was their 'father' have been in inclining them to grant him more authority, even if he had done so?

What Then about Paul as a Maternal Figure?

Beverly Roberts Gaventa has made a splendid contribution to our enriched understanding of Paul's intended relationships with his converts by focusing our attention on the maternal imagery in his letters. She also calls attention to the way in which many English translations of Paul's letters obscure Paul's choice of 'begetting' language. Then she adds to the discussion her emphasis on the biological act in question as 'a single event in past time', as 'the initial stage of Christian preaching and conversion', rather than as a metaphor for ongoing care and concern for his converts (2007: 6).[15]

14. Pheme Perkins notes that in Paul's culture 'it was assumed that the philosopher provided his students with the living example of his teaching. But the effectiveness of imitation depends on living in the presence of the exemplary teacher, not reading the occasional letter' (2012: 80). So Paul sought to fill that gap by sending Timothy, one of his closest associates.

15. T.J. Burke appropriately seeks to correct Gaventa's strong emphasis on the punctiliar role of the father as begetter by calling attention to a Greco-Roman father's obliga-

It is maternal rather than paternal imagery that Paul used in 'contexts referring to the ongoing nature of the relationship between Paul and the congregations he founded' (6). After observing that Paul called on paternal imagery in only four passages (apart from his many references to God as father), Gaventa emphasizes that he used maternal imagery far more often, a fact that as she notes is virtually ignored in most discussions of Paul's letters (7). Characteristic of this maternal imagery is the reference to an extended period of time: the time of pregnancy, the time of physically nurturing an infant, the care provided by a nurse. For example, in 1 Thess. 2.7 Paul wrote, 'We were gentle (or like young children) among you, like a nurse tenderly caring for her own children'. In 1 Cor. 3.2 he describes himself as a nursing mother who gave them 'milk to drink, not solid food'.[16] And in Gal. 4.19-20 we read his words: 'My children (τέκνα) for whom I am again in the pain of childbirth until Christ is formed in you, I wish that I were present with you now and could change my tone, for I am perplexed about you'.[17]

Gaventa writes, 'When Paul presents himself as a mother, he voluntarily hands over the authority of a patriarch in favour of a role that will bring him shame, the shame of the female-identified male' (13-14). In a further compelling insight, Gaventa connects this astonishing nursing-mother metaphor to Paul's apostolic identification with the crucified Jesus (see 1 Cor. 1.18; 2.2-3), and both images profoundly challenge their culture's standard for a 'real man' (σκληρός ἀνήρ) (48-50). Every male was programmed to reestablish this 'tough guy' reputation in every encounter with other males. Yet, as Gaventa observes, in contrast to the neglect of recent generations of readers and scholars, earlier readers such as Origen, Methodius, Gregory of Nyssa and Anselm of Canterbury all found comfort in contemplating Paul's role as a nursing mother. Indeed, Anselm praised Paul as 'our greatest mother' (15).

Nevertheless, the Question of Possible Punishment Remains—But How?

A few sentences after Paul again in 2 Cor. 10.1 appealed (παρακαλῶ) to his converts, this time explicitly 'by the meekness and gentleness of Christ',

tion to exercise continuous concern for his children through education and by providing an example to imitate, especially for his sons (2003: 107).

16. Gaventa coins a new phrase, 'a metaphor squared', to describe what she identifies as a 'double switch' in this sentence. 'First, he metaphorizes (with apologies for the barbarism) the gospel as milk, then he "squares" that image by metaphorizing himself as the mother whose body supplies the milk' (2007: 5).

17. Gaventa comments at length on the complexities involved in interpreting these interrelated maternal metaphors (2007: 29-39).

at the end of a long Greek sentence that runs from vv. 3-6, he wrote the enigmatic words: 'We are ready to punish every disobedience when your obedience is complete' (10.6). First, what sense does it make to wait until their 'obedience is complete' (presumably, obedience to Christ), when any punishment would seem to be superfluous? Murray Harris sensibly asks: 'Why would Paul plan to punish the Corinthians for their disobedience only after their obedience had reached completion?' Would not remission of any planned punishment rather be called for? He then suggests that the disobedience is no longer that of Paul's converts, but of outsiders (2005: 685). But I ask, what authority and what means would Paul have had to punish outsiders? So this passage remains obscure and confusing to me.

But second, to come back to a major question in this essay, what could Paul actually do to punish anyone? For those outside the group of his converts, he obviously had no authority. For those inside the group who did not accept his authority, his situation was apparently not much better. Nevertheless, T.J. Burke refers to the 'vast power' at Paul's disposal and concludes his informative article on 1 Cor. 4.14-21 with this sentence: 'Paul's hope is that the Corinthians will amend their ways so that he can avoid using the rod which he as a loving parent has every right to exercise' (2003: 113). Yet, if many (most?) of the Corinthians were challenging his authority, not yet regarding one another as brothers and sisters—as family— and not yet recognizing him as their 'father', what 'right' had they given him to discipline them with a parental 'stick'?

Other commentators on 2 Corinthians seem to have been more interested in reflecting on the kinds of disobedience Paul had in mind than in reflecting on the actual options for punishment that Paul could inflict. At least Murray Harris notes that 'what form the punishment would take is not stated' (685). He comments that 'the mere expulsion of the intruders from the Corinthian congregation would scarcely amount to a penalty' and suggests that 'perhaps we should think of some formal "handing over" to Satan that would precipitate physical illness and suffering (cf. 1 Cor. 5.4-5)' (686). Since we have no evidence of Paul actually taking such punishing action on his own against his opponents, should we conclude that carrying out any effective discipline would have required the cooperation of the remaining obedient Corinthians?

In private correspondence, my Context Group colleague Dennis Duling has suggested that, as I reflect on Paul's conflicts with some of his converts, I might do well to think about the way internal conflict was treated in the congregational process detailed in Mt. 18.15-17. In his 1999 *BTB* article dealing with this fascinating passage, Duling cites the sober comments of Davies and Allison in their commentary on Matthew. 'Reproving one's brother is always a most delicate matter, and one must undertake the sad task in a spirit of love and humility' (1991: 751). While it is not difficult for me to imagine that this would have been the spirit in which Paul would have acted on his warnings, my problem is imagining that the group(s) of converts in Corinth had remained in sufficient solidarity with Paul to join him in carrying out disciplinary actions beyond the one he describes in 1 Corinthians 5. As Duling notes, 'Paul himself lamented that there was no "wise man" to handle internal affairs' among the Corinthians (see 1 Cor. 6.5) with 'direct expulsion of unrepentant sinners' as a consequence (1999: 18).

Thus I ask: Did Paul conclude that he had no other choice but to risk taking one step back in the transformation process of his converts in order for them again to take the hoped-for 'two steps' toward their own maturing in Christ? While the evidence makes this conclusion seem likely, I am still puzzling over what Paul could do to 'punish' his converts that would not either drive them away or undermine his own attempts to resocialize them by the transforming Spirit of God. Was not his long-range goal to see his converts manifesting the fruit of the Spirit that he stresses specifically in Galatians 5 and implies as Christ-filled behavior in virtually every paragraph in his letters?

Paul's Own Behavioral Example as a Decisive Factor

Before Paul came to them, his converts would have been urged explicitly and implicitly to imitate their parents and to shape their lives by imitating those good people who lived according to the dominant cultural values and social codes. So by urging his converts to imitate both him (as he imitated Christ—1 Cor. 11.1) and those who were already living according to his example (Phil. 3.17), Paul was certainly not introducing the concept or practice of imitation into their lives. Rather he was urging them to consider his own life and his way of treating both those traveling with him and them as an alternative and worthy model for changing their own behavior. In Brian Dodd's insightful monograph *Paul's Paradigmatic 'I': Personal Example as Literary Strategy* (1999), the author finally comes to the following firm conclusion: Paul's personal example was 'intrinsic to Paul's leadership and literary style'.[18] Dodd then notes what would seem to be a truism: 'all who follow expect those who lead to embody the values they represent and proclaim' (238). To this obvious observation I add that the pressure on such leaders, then as now, to 'embody the values they represent' increases

18. See also Bruce J. Malina's distinction between the role of a manager and the less formal role of a leader (1986: 107). Paul had no ascribed, traditional, blood lineage or legal position in the lives of his converts; he was not their recognized manager. By contrast, as Malina notes, leaders such as Paul are defined as those who have achieved their influence and authority by *what they have actually done for their followers* (my emphasis), initiating a relationship of some kind of generalized reciprocity.

directly ('geometrically', one could say) with the intensity of their challenging and undermining the currently dominant cultural values and the related social codes. Thus I ask, was Paul's urging his converts to imitate him different in any structural or psychological way from Jesus' urging people to 'follow him' in living out his own strong challenges to the dominant cultural values and social codes?

Imitation and Neuroscience

Recent research on mirror neurons suggests a potential way forward in examining the importance of Paul's call to imitation. This research provides a solid scientific basis for the absolutely critical role that imitation plays in the process by which human beings become human. While space prohibits a thorough investigation, I offer here a brief sketch.[19]

According to Marco Iacoboni, a path-breaking neuroscientist at UCLA, a convergence has been found between cognitive models of imitation derived from social psychology studies on mimicry and empathy and recent empirical findings from the neurosciences (2009).[20] These social-psychology studies have demonstrated that mimicry and imitation are pervasive and automatic; they facilitate mechanisms of mirroring at both single-cell and neural-system levels that support how we think and how we construct our social lives.

The Corinthians had certainly grown up imitating the adults around them whom they respected. Even when they too became adults, there was no question about whether their beliefs and behaviors would continue to be influenced by conscious or automatic imitation of others. Rather, the fundamental question was: Who were the Corinthians going to imitate—their parents, others in their extended family, their patrons, their friends, the 'super apostles', or Paul (as he imitated Christ)?

A Metaphorical, Rhetorical 'Stick'?

It has not been my intent or interest to portray Paul as an ideally mature example of the 'new creation' values that he sought to live by and to make effective in the lives of his converts. Yet he certainly regarded himself as an adequate model to begin imitating. Was he then sufficiently self-aware to realize that not everything he wrote would move his converts in a straight line toward the goal of their spiritual and social transformation? As he wrote to his doubting converts in Galatia, he was deeply perplexed by their behav-

19. For a fuller explanation, see my forthcoming *Call No Man Father*.

20. Iacoboni directs UCLA's Transcranial Magnetic Stimulation Lab at the Ahmanson-Lovelace Brain Mapping Center.

ior; and his frequently aggressive tone in that letter reveals his profound disappointment in their vulnerability to leaders who opposed him. Did Paul's perplexity and frustration amidst the challenges to his authority that he faced result in his resorting to traditional rhetorical threatening and exaggerating his power in his attempt to affect changes in the lives of those he sought to influence—ways of relating to others that he had in principle rejected?

Paul's profound exasperation with the relative success of the 'super apostles' among the Corinthians is certainly the context for exegeting his apparently paradoxical comments about being 'severe' (ἀπότομος) in using his Christ-given authority to build up rather than to tear down anyone (see Bartchy 2005:58-60). There must have been many days when Paul wished that he could accomplish his goals by using a 'stick', as he had earlier in his life as a persecutor of the Christ-followers. As a Christ-follower himself, however, he must have known that the actual use of that option would have been risky and potentially counterproductive behavior. No matter how weak his opponents perceived him to be, Paul knew that his strength was based on acting with agape-love 'in a spirit of gentleness'. Paul at his best, according to his own transformed values, was indeed 'stickless' in Corinth.

References

Bartchy, S. Scott

1973 *Mallon Chrēsai: First Century Slavery and the Interpretation of 1 Corinthians 7:21* (SBLDS, 11; Missoula, MT: University of Montana Press; repr. 1985, Atlanta, GA: Scholars Press; 2003, Eugene, OR: Wipf & Stock).

1999 'Undermining Ancient Patriarchy: The Apostle Paul's Vision of a Society of Siblings', *BTB* 29: 68-78.

2003 'Who Should Be Called Father? Paul of Tarsus between the Jesus Tradition and *Patria Potestas*', *BTB* 33: 135-47.

2005 '"When I'm Weak, I'm Strong": A Pauline Paradox in Cultural Context', in *Kontexte der Schrift,* Bd. II (Festschrift Wolfgang Stegemann; ed. Christian Strecker; Stuttgart: W. Kohlhammer): 49-60.

2009 'The Domestication of a Radical Jew: Paul of Tarsus', in *Maven in Blue Jeans* (Festschrift Zev Garber; ed. Steven L. Jacobs; West Lafayette, IN: Purdue University Press): 7-16.

Barton, Stephen C.

1994 *Discipleship and Family Ties in Mark and Matthew* (New York: Cambridge University Press).

Bradley, Keith R.

1991 *Discovering the Roman Family: Studies in Roman Social History* (New York: Oxford University Press).

Burke, Trevor J.

2003 'Paul's Role as "Father" to his Corinthian "Children" in Socio-Historical Context (1 Corinthians 4:14-21)', in *Paul and the Corinthians: Studies on a Community in Conflict. Essays in Honour of Margaret Thrall* (ed. T.J. Burke and J.K. Elliott; Leiden: Brill): 95-114.

Castelli, Elizabeth
1991 *Imitating Paul: A Discourse of Power* (Louisville, KY: Westminster John Knox).
Davies, W.D., and D.C. Allison
1991 *A Critical and Exegetical Commentary on the Gospel according to Saint Matthew.* Vol. 2 (ICC; Edinburgh: T. & T. Clark).
Daube, David
1966 'Paul a Hellenistic Schoolmaster?', in *Rationalism, Judaism and Universalism* (Festschrift Leon Roth; ed. Raphael Lowe; New York: Humanities Press).
Dodd, Brian
1999 *Paul's Paradigmatic 'I': Personal Example as Literary Strategy* (JSNTSup, 177; Sheffield: Sheffield Academic Press).
Duling, Dennis
1999 'Matthew 18:15-17: Conflict, Confrontation, and Conflict Resolution in a "Fictive Kin" Association', *BTB* 29: 4-22.
Ehrensberger, Kathy
2009 *Paul and the Dynamics of Power: Communication and Interaction in the Early Christ-Movement* (New York: T. & T. Clark).
Fee, Gordon D.
1987 *The First Epistle to the Corinthians* (NICNT; Grand Rapids, MI: Eerdmans).
Gaventa, Beverly Roberts
2007 *Our Mother Saint Paul* (Louisville, KY: Westminster John Knox).
Harris, Murray J.
2005 *The Second Epistle to the Corinthians: A Commentary on the Greek Text* (Grand Rapids, MI: Eerdmans).
Holmberg, Bengt
1980 *Paul and Power: The Structure of Authority in the Primitive Church as Reflected in the Pauline Epistles* (Philadelphia, PA: Fortress Press).
Iacoboni, Marco
2009 *Mirroring People: The Science of Empathy and How We Connect with Others* (New York: Farrar, Straus & Giroux).
Malina, Bruce J.
1986 *Christian Origins and Cultural Anthropology: Practical Models for Biblical Interpretation* (Atlanta. GA: John Knox).
2001 *The New Testament World: Insights from Cultural Anthropology* (Louisville, KY: Westminster John Knox, 3rd edn).
Perkins, Pheme
2012 *First Corinthians* (PCNT; Grand Rapids, MI: Baker Academic).
Sandnes, Karl Olav
1997 'Equality within Patriarchal Structures: Some New Testament Perspectives on the Christian Fellowship as a Brother- or Sisterhood and a Family', in *Constructing Early Christian Families* (ed. Halvor Moxnes; New York: Routledge): 150-65.

The Characterization of the Rich in James 5

Alicia J. Batten

Introduction

For approximately the past decade I have attended Context Group meetings, held in a variety of hospitable locations throughout North America and sometimes, internationally. It is primarily in such a 'context' that I have had the privilege of interacting with Jack Elliott. Jack's work and wisdom have aided me in a variety of ways. For instance, in addition to his *opera* on 1 Peter, Jack has assisted in the redemption of the letter of James from the status of New Testament 'junk mail' (Elliott 1993: 71); for he has joined others in arguing persuasively that James is a much more coherent document, both rhetorically and thematically, than previously discerned (Elliott 1993). Additionally, one of the pieces of advice that Jack has shared with members of the Context Group over the years is never to pass over older scholarship too quickly (some Contexters will remember the discussion about the importance of ancient historian Tenney Frank's work, for example). The fact that many nineteenth-century scholars were so steeped in classical literature and languages often means that their work is a goldmine of possible literary parallels and allusions that sometimes lies dormant, awaiting further exploration. The following discussion therefore attempts to pay tribute to Jack's *œuvre et sagesse* by continuing to focus on a piece of the 'junk mail', and by demonstrating how some of the material in J.B. Mayor's 1892 commentary on James has contributed to some of the conclusions reached.

Before turning to the specific arguments of the essay, it is worth recalling that James is indebted to a wide variety of sources and traditions for its creation. We find references to famous characters from Israelite lore, such as Abraham, Rahab, Job and Elijah, as well as examples from the Septuagint, as found in the use of Prov. 3.34 in Jas 4.6. In addition, although the letter never explicitly claims to be citing Jesus, James is aware of a form of a collection of Jesus' teachings. There is a wide range of views as to how many correspondences can be found between James and Jesus traditions (see Deppe 1989: 231-33), but the average is eighteen, which is striking for such a short letter, and close to every verse in James has been examined as possessing a potential connection to Jesus' teachings (Batten 2009: 73).

James is also appreciated as a literary text, employing unusual vocabulary, stylistic sophistication (Dibelius 1975: 34-38), and Graeco-Roman argumentative techniques. There is no consensus as to the overall rhetorical structure of the letter, but convincing arguments have been made that portions of the letter conform to rhetorical patterns, such as the elaboration of a theme exercise and portions of diatribe, evident in James 2 (Watson 2007). Recent work argues that the letter's author also uses *aemulatio*, an ancient type of paraphrase that creatively alters a prior, and known, tradition, such as a saying of Jesus, in order to suit the literary and social context of James's text. This practice not only impresses the audience by demonstrating how deftly the author has maneuvered and shaped a teaching to suit his own setting, it also counts on the authority of the original speaker to lend clout to the message (Kloppenborg 2007: 142).

Given this level of literary skill, it is not surprising to observe that James reflects an awareness and use of Hellenistic philosophical ideas. Various studies (Jackson-McCabe 2001; Kloppenborg 2010; O'Rourke Boyle 1985) cogently illustrate how Hellenistic principles, such as the idea of the unity of virtue or the Stoic notion of 'implanted reason' or the perception of endurance as a central force that both trains body and soul, surface in James. The letter may be deeply Judean, but comparable to the writings of Philo and others, it has arisen within a rich mix of literatures, ideas and practices. Any analysis of James must therefore take into account this myriad of traditions that have contributed to its conception and design; the text does not emerge from a unique culture or literature.

This essay explores James 5, especially the first six verses, and argues that the author draws upon reasonably standard types of imagery drawn particularly from Graeco-Roman satire and invective, in order to denounce the wealthy. James is not some type of Hellenistic Judean Juvenal, but his tone, at times, is comparable to that of the satirist. When one considers some of the descriptive details, it becomes apparent that the rich are 'effeminated'—a word used by Peter Brown (1988: 347) to translate Ambrose's *effeminat* (*De officiis ministrorum* 1.28.138)[1]—'gendered' as female, and dishonored as such. Although J.B. Mayor never came to this overall conclusion about the rich in James 5, some of the parallels that he draws between various words in Jas 5.1-6 and Greek literature elicit the idea that such is the case.

1. As Brown (1988: 347) writes, for Ambrose to 'surrender any boundary line was to court the ancient shame of the Roman male—it was to "become soft", to be "effeminated"'.

Poverty, Wealth and the Effeminate Male in Graeco-Roman Literature

Before turning to Mayor's as well as other parallels, it is important to remember that terms such as 'poor' and 'rich' are always relative, both in the present day and in antiquity. In classical Greek writings, greed and luxury are reviled and linked to barbarians, but the mendicant is not good. Rather, he is assumed to be low and of the mob, while the well-born person, provided he is generous, is associated with positive qualities (de Ste Croix 1981: 425-26). Some later philosophical writers, such as Philodemus, are as contemptuous of poverty (πτωχεία) as they are of greediness because it means that one will be preoccupied with survival just as one could be obsessed with acquisitiveness (Balch 2004: 184). Prosperity was not problematic provided that the wealth had been justly and honestly procured for such material security was considered necessary for a life of self-sufficiency (Finley 1973: 35-61). If one could not provide for one's own needs, or worse, if a person were destitute, he or she was vulnerable to physical harm and more likely to succumb to illness, disease and starvation (see Fagan 2011: 490).

Paupers and other marginal people were also socially and politically on the edge, excluded from much of civic life, including associations, gymnasia, and the baths (Morley 2006: 33-35). As such, the poor were subject to shame. Neville Morley alerts us to Juvenal's comment that 'of all the woes of luckless poverty none is harder to endure than this, that it exposes men to ridicule' (*Sat.* 3.153-54 [trans. Ramsey 1940: 43]). Such an example might be insulting to the truly destitute in Rome (Morley 2006: 35), for whom food and shelter were much higher priorities, but it does reveal an assessment of a dimension of poverty that was very real; material impoverishment meant living in a state of perpetual humiliation.

Throughout the Roman Empire, the poor and humiliated were everywhere—in the cities and especially the countryside. Given that the economy was pre-industrial, subsistence or near-subsistence level farmers, laborers, artisans, traders and others would comprise the largest single segment of the population of a big city such as Rome and its surrounding area (Friesen 2008: 20). Access to land, which was always in finite supply and the main source of security for loans (Osborne 2006: 5), was likely the most important factor as to whether a farm family survived or perished (Garnsey 1998: 213). There are ongoing debates among economic historians about the precise population percentage break-down among the different social levels within Roman society, but it is generally agreed that the wealthiest segment of the population was very small and extraordinarily rich (Jongman 2007: 600), with some affluent Romans owning hundreds of slaves to take care of their multiple residences and land holdings (Harris 2007: 527). The elites were well aware that land was an enduring asset, and they controlled the bulk of it, preferring to provide raw materials because it was a more profitable enterprise than investing in the creation of manufactured goods (Kehoe 2007: 569).

The age-old civic practice of *euergetism* among the Greeks supplied assistance to some, but there is no evidence that such acts of beneficence were perceived as 'poor relief' (Osborne 2006: 6). Nor was the provision of foodstuffs or other necessities by benefactors a lasting solution, as it was, by nature, *ad hoc* and dependent on the goodwill of wealthy individuals who expected honors in return for their largesse (Garnsey 1988: 82-82). Likewise, the Roman Empire did not develop any sort of 'system' that would assist those suffering from hunger or other side effects of poverty, but would place pressure on rich individuals to provide in moments of crisis such as a large food shortage, and the 'stark contrast between public poverty and private affluence persisted' (Garnsey 1988: 84). At certain moments the city of Rome did feed the poor, but such a practice was exceptional and owing to the fact that the poor had become a political force with which the rulers had to reckon (Finley 1973: 40; Osborne 2006: 14).

The political power of the impoverished in Rome also brought the contrasts between rich and poor into greater focus (Osborne 2006: 15). Despite the lack of interest in alleviating the concrete sufferings and privations of the indigent, it is in Roman literature that we observe authors self-identifying as poor in order to create a gulf between themselves and the super-rich, whom they sometimes criticize for particular behaviors and lifestyles. Thus, when Roman authors write of poverty, it is more as a contrast to wealth than a glorification of or even strong interest in poverty itself. Martial, for example, depicts himself as a poor poet, even though he was a landowner, educated and eventually received favours from a range of patrons. He was hardly poor, yet he claims to be poverty stricken in a variety of epigrams (*Ep.* 2.90; 5.13; 6.82). As Greg Woolf has argued, poets such as Martial had a range of reasons for adopting the *persona* of poverty, the most consistent being that such a *persona* was 'to achieve a distance from wealth, when [the] attack is directed against wealth, the wealthy or the abuse of riches' (Woolf 2006: 98). By taking on the identity of a needy person, the author creates a moral chasm between himself and the target of his criticism: the affluent and manipulative patron. Here, being poor *is not to be wealthy*, but it had very little to do with what the urban poor, reviled and forgotten, were actually experiencing.

It is also in Roman literature that we find the emergence of the figure of the virtuous labourer or noble person of simple means. Writers such as Juvenal speak of country lads, 'with hair cut close and uncurled'; sons of shepherds 'of open countenance and frank modesty, such as those ought to be who are clothed in glowing purple' (*Sat.* 11.150-55 [trans. Ramsey 1940: 231, 233]). Those who engage in hard physical work are deemed honourable. Dio Chrysostom writes an extended discourse contrasting poverty and wealth, reflecting on the lives of farmers, hunters and shepherds, among others. He states that poverty (πενία)

> is no hopeless impediment to a life and existence befitting free men who are willing to work with their hands, and leads them on to deeds and actions that are far better and more useful and more in accordance with nature than those to which riches are wont to attract most men (*Or*. 7.103 [trans. Cohoon 1932: 343]).

Similarly, Plutarch pays tribute to the Elder Cato, who is depicted as working in the fields alongside his slaves and sharing their simple fare at table (*Cato Major* 2–3). Plutarch describes Cato's 'bodily habit', which, because 'he was addicted from the very first to labour with his own hands . . . was very serviceable' (*Cat. Maj.* 1.3-6 [trans. Perrin 1948: 305]). Such characterizations of hard-working people were 'assimilated to the land owning class' (Morley 2006: 35), for we do not find texts expressing admiration for the impoverished beggar, or even worse, the slave—the ultimate poor person who clung to a meagre and usually brutal existence (Scheidel 2006: 58). Men such as the Elder Cato or Dio's noble country labourers become stock *exempla*, useful in shaping notions of masculinity and virtue to which Roman men should aspire (Woolf 2006: 89). Despite some appeals to poverty and the simple life in literary accounts, such references are intended more as rhetorical means of critiquing vices such as luxury and greed, or, as a means of shaping various virtues, including those associated with ideal masculinity, bravery and endurance, than they are of drumming up support for the poor, or of taking a sustained interest in the plight of the destitute.

Neediness, then, and the simple life of the hard-working labourer were useful tropes employed by some ancient writers to serve as contrasts when they engaged in criticism on topics such as greed, banqueting and sexual licentiousness. Affluence on its own did not invite abuse, but to indulge in wasteful, luxurious living and to fail to live up to the masculine ideal was another thing altogether. Just as it was not admirable to be a hungry beggar, it was wrong to be a rich glutton. The interrelated excesses of overeating, sexual impropriety and financial waste were featured in invective, including that of the Roman Latin writer Catullus, who ties gluttony to financial and sexual insatiableness (Richlin 1988: 361).[2] Linked to such vices was womanishness, and one means of denouncing an indulgent man in invective and satire was to accuse him of effeminacy, while women were condemned

2. In her study of food imagery in Catullus, Richlin suggests that 'the mention of food belongs to the erotic, whereas the description of it belongs to invective; or possibly, the idea of food on the table belongs to the erotic, whereas the mechanics of ingestion and excretion belong to invective' (1988: 355).

for promiscuity. Through such censure, not only did the writer intend to dishonour the recipient(s), he 'assert[ed] his power over him or her' (Richlin 1992: 140).

It is important to stress here that physiognomy was a preoccupation for Greeks and Romans from at least the classical period on. People were scrutinized for their dress, their gait, their body, and their facial expressions, as each of these personal traits was understood to be revealing of character and disposition. 'Masculine' and 'feminine' as categories were not solely linked to the biology of man and woman, but to specific behaviours. Thus, women could only become 'friends' with men, or at least gain more of a mutual relationship with them, if they became more male. Men, however, would not want to act in a manner that could appear to be more female, for if they did, they would lose honour (Moxnes 1997: 281).

Ancient handbooks relentlessly analyse male and female features and were useful for effeminate male detection (Gleason 1990). Women are typically portrayed as softer, feebler, and prone to fits of emotion, such as anger and loss of control. Writers would sometimes base these characteristics upon their observations of animals. In his *Physiognomics*, Pseudo-Aristotle says that that lion has the greatest male characteristics, for this animal has a vigorous walk, 'and his whole body is well-jointed and muscular, neither very hard nor very moist. . . . These then are his bodily characteristics; in character he is generous and liberal, magnanimous and with a will to win; he is gentle, just and affectionate towards his associates' (*Physiogn.* 809 b 15-35 [trans. Hett 1963: 113). In contrast, the author thinks that the panther reflects more female characteristics, including 'fleshy' (σαρκώδης) haunches and thighs, a small face, large mouth and small eyes, 'and its character is petty, thieving and generally speaking, deceitful' (810a 1-8). But these are only *some of the most outstanding* features of the male and female, for the treatise continues discussing the hind quarters, which if narrow and bony are strong, *and male*, but if fat and fleshy, are weak or soft (810a 35)[3] and therefore female, right down to the ankles, which again, if strong and well jointed, are brave in character, 'witness the male sex', while if they are 'fleshy and ill-jointed', are 'weak in character; witness the female sex' (810a 25-30). A first-century writer, Polemo of Laodicea, writes similarly, stating that the female has 'feeble ribs, larger, fleshier hips . . . knock knees, dainty finger tips and toes, the rest of the body moist and flabby, with soft limbs and slackened joints . . . etc. But the male is in every way opposite to this description, and it is possible to find masculine qualities also in women' (2. 1. 192-94F [trans. Gleason 1990: 392]). As Maud Gleason points out, the categories of male and female here 'are independent of anatomical sex'

3. Here he uses the word μαλακοί, which is consistently associated with the female.

(Gleason 1990: 392). Male and female qualities are polar opposites used to assess the character of the subject, particularly those subjects whose masculinity is suspect, or, as Gleason says, 'lukewarm' (Gleason 1990: 392).

One of the noted character deficiencies of these suspicious men was extravagant spending and a luxurious lifestyle. Effeminacy and reckless expenditure were regularly paired. Some Roman authors considered the introduction of rare goods, such as rich foods, jewels, unusual fabrics and even exotic animals, as sources of moral and financial decline, for it led to Roman covetousness for opulence (Pliny the Elder 33.149) and the draining of Roman coffers (Berg 2002: 56). Eastern leaders who traded such things are depicted by Quintus Curtius as effeminates, such as the kings of India, who bathe in perfume, comb their hair often and even hear formal requests from clients while they are with their hairdresser (*Historiae Alexandri magni* 8.22). Greeks, as well, identified non-Greeks, or barbarians, as 'girly' (see Dio, *Ad Alexandrinos* 32.3). To be a 'real man' was a public virtue for many Greeks; it meant to have 'leadership over oneself', and to reflect that self-control in every dimension of life (Moxnes 1997: 270-71), including one's financial affairs.

In addition to feasting and spending money, dancing and other forms of debauchery were considered to be 'unmasculine' activities. The effeminate banqueter was the target of rhetorical invective, usually satirical, due to his imbibing and carousing, including, often, sexually submissive behaviour. According to Anthony Corbeill, 'the stigma of convivial excess stems from anxiety over what constitutes—and what deconstitutes—Roman masculinity' (Corbeill 1996: 128-29). Such excess meant that one was not capable of self-management, and loss of self-control over bodily desires in the form of gluttony and wantonness was inextricably linked to fiscal profligacy. Thus verbs of eating, devouring, boiling and consuming, in both Greek and Latin, were associated with bankruptcy and wasting money, an association that often appears in comical invective (Corbeill 1996: 132). It may seem surprising that corpulence is only occasionally attacked, probably because the ancients assumed that wealthy men were well fed, and social value was placed upon wealth, as mentioned, and the self-sufficiency and political clout it provided (Corbeill 1996: 142-43).

In addition, because the effeminate male lacked self-control, he was politically weak, which made him all the more worrisome. For example, Cicero exhibits concern about two consuls, Hirtius and Pansa, who, he says, are 'full of lusting and lounging of the most effeminate nature. If they don't yield the helm, there's the greatest danger of everything being shipwrecked' (*Epistulae ad familiares* 16.27.1 = SB 352; trans. Corbeill 1996: 143). Corbeill thinks that such undermining of individuals is not simply meant to insult or create humour, but to expose such people as politically troublesome and risky for they undermined the sense of order, poise and prestige that was preserved by the ideal Roman male. In addition, he agrees with Catharine Edwards that the effeminate male was a violation of what some perceived to be the natural order; an order in which men and women had distinctive roles (Edwards 1993: 87). A womanish man was thus a political hazard, he was perceived to be intellectually feeble and lazy[4] and a 'failure within nature itself' (Corbeill 1996: 146).

Other specific areas that came under scrutiny were dress, adornment, walk, physical movements such as scratching the head with one finger, and voice. Cross-dressing and fastidiousness with regard to clothes or hair invite ridicule (see Corbeill 1996: 159-69). Dio laments the adornment of the rich, both men and women, and counsels that the poor should not be involved in trades that serve the immoderate lifestyles of wealthy people, such as the decoration of homes with precious stones, ivory or gold (*Orations* 7.117). The younger Seneca particularly complains about effeminate men wearing rings (*Naturales quaestiones* 7.31.2; cited in Corbeill 1996: 164 n). Certain movements, including being overly graceful, were suspicious (Richlin 1992: 92),[5] as was a high, shrill, or sing-song voice (see Dio Chrysostom *Or.* 33.52; Gleason 1990: 399). Although it was acceptable for men to weep in certain situations, public mourning was understood primarily as the task of women (Erker 2009: 135-36). Overly emotional expressions of grief and distress met disapproval by writers such as Cicero, however, for such behaviour did not embody appropriate self-discipline (Erker 2009: 137). Composure and self-control were essential to Roman conceptions of masculinity and needed to be manifested in dress, gait, movement and speech (see Dio Chrysostom, *Or.* 32.54; Moxnes 1997: 272). In deviating from what it meant to be an ideal male, the 'she-man' was undermining a whole set of values and power relations with which many ancients were deeply invested. He became a source of jokes and derision, and the accusation or even suggestion of effeminacy emerged as a significant form of undermining a person's character.

Effeminacy and James 5

Such contextual information is relevant to the description of the rich in the opening section of James 5. Luke Timothy Johnson has compellingly argued that Jas 5.1-6 is part of the larger unit of Jas 4.11–5.6, which focuses on the theme of arrogance (1995: 292). Arrogance includes speaking evil against and judging others (4.11-12), planning to do business and make

4. On the lazy intellects of 'soft' young men, see Seneca the Elder (*Controv.* 1, pr. 8-9).

5. Richlin (1992: 92) cites the example of a joke ascribed to Cicero about his son-in-law Piso. Apparently Cicero advised his daughter to learn to walk like her husband (see Macrobius, *Saturnalia* 2.3.16).

a profit (4.13), and, obviously, boasting in arrogance or false pretensions (ἀλαζονεία in 4.16). Hoarding treasures (5.1-3), exploiting labourers (5.4), living in luxury (5.5) and condemning and killing the righteous one (5.6), which is likely a recollection of a tradition known to Wis. 2.12 (LXX), are all consistent with the behaviour of an arrogant person.

In Jas 5.1-6 the author is likely drawing upon a variety of traditions (although no Septuagint text is directly cited),[6] as he elaborates on the behaviour of these arrogant rich. He is probably using some form of Q 6.24 and Q 12.33-34 (woes to the rich and the teachings about treasures), as has been observed elsewhere (see Kloppenborg 2007: 137-41). The focus here, however, is on *how* he describes the rich (οἱ πλούσιοι) and to what extent the portrait of them finds resonance with some of the ideas discussed earlier in this essay.

First, James uses the verbs κλαίω and ὀλολύζω, as he describes the rich weeping and howling from the miseries that are coming upon them. Ὀλολύζω appears nowhere else in the New Testament, but it is often used for violent grief in other literature, and the Septuagint employs it in several prophetic texts, including the wailing in anticipation of the day of the Lord (eg. Isa. 13.6 LXX), or the weeping and wailing of drunkards and wine drinkers (Joel 1.5 LXX). It is here that some of J.B. Mayor's observations are especially helpful, however. He indicates that in Homer and Herodotus, the verb delineates the 'joyful outcries of women in the worship of Athene' (Mayor 1892: 142),[7] recalling the practice of women ululating (from the Latin, *ululatus*). The author of James does not have 'joy' in mind here, but it is important to recall that Graeco-Roman writers, while accepting of men's tears, argue that even when it is in grief, such crying must not be exaggerated. Mourning rituals and gestures were 'gendered' in Greek and Roman contexts. As Corbeill has documented through the examination of a range of visual and literary evidence, 'women take on the role of grieving loss in the domestic sphere while male behavior demonstrates public recognition of the deceased's passing' (2004: 73). While women wailed and tore at their hair, the men might 'greet the dead with a salute' (Corbeill 2004: 73). Moreover, women, who were expected to weep and wail in certain circumstances, could be criticized for being overly emotional if they clawed at their hair, or mutilated themselves, as it was counter to the ideal of the quiet restrained life of the citizen (Erker 2009: 143, 157). The Romans even developed legislation that limited women's excessive displays of grief at funerals because such occasions were becoming sites of competition among elites in order

6. Todd Penner points out that this denunciation has a prophetic style. The calls for the rich to cry out and weep recall Lam. 1.2 and Isa. 14.31; 15.2-3 and create an atmosphere of a 'prophetic funeral dirge and mourning cry' (Penner 1996: 175).

7. See Homer, *Il.* 6.297; Herodotus, *Hist.* 4.189.

to advertise self-importance (see Cicero, *De legibus* 2.59). Not only were families vying for the most lavish funeral, but the most anguished one, with women lacerating their cheeks and breasts, lamenting loudly and chanting dirges (Corbeill 2004: 75). Plutarch will depict men crying (κλαίω), but 'it is often a generous pity for others, never a self-centered grief or anxiety for self' (Lateiner 2009: 128). The rich in James are crying for themselves, and they are wailing. Ὀλολύζω refers to a loud wailing, not a quietly sorrowful tearfulness. My interpretation is that the author is subtly, or perhaps not so subtly, signaling that these rich are howling like distraught women, out of control, as they lament their encroaching misery.

Next, the letter refers to the destruction of the 'wealth' (πλοῦτος) of the rich. It identifies the rotting of what are probably food stores (σήπω, 'to make rotten'), moth-eaten garments (ἱμάτια), and rusted gold and silver. John Kloppenborg points out how if James is drawing upon Q 12.33-34 in this passage, the author has introduced new images, such as clothing, and what are probably ornaments, thus making the sayings more comprehensible to an urban audience (2007: 139-40). I concur, and want to suggest that the specific references to dress and ornaments further underscore the possibility that the rich are characterized as somewhat 'female' given their specific investments. It is noteworthy that the rust from the gold and silver will 'eat' (φάγεται) the flesh of these wealthy, indicating that these metals are being worn *on the body*. Is James imagining affluent people sporting rings, as he does when he refers to a man with gold rings and fine clothing (Jas 2.2), that will now eat away at their fingers (Jas 5.3)? Does James have in mind a person similar to Chariton's effeminate man, who wears perfume, dons cosmetics and sports multiple rings (*De Chaerea et Challirhoe* 1.4.9)?[8] One could imagine that in James, the image intended is that of numerous rings that have become too tight, causing them to cut into or 'eat' at the pudgy digits of the rich. And given some of the Graeco-Roman nervousness about men wearing rings, is the author again attempting to convey the image of the rich as 'womanish'?

When the letter refers to the 'flesh' of the rich it uses the plural of σάρξ (σάρκας). Mayor states that the plural refers to the 'fleshy parts' of the body, as attested to by classical and later writers (as well as in the LXX), while σάρξ

8. James's depiction of the rich here also finds parallels to Lucian's discussion of a 'millionaire' who comes to Athens, and struts about, earning ridicule from onlookers. Lucian says of the man's other 'vulgarities [that] they turned into jest in the same way—the number of his rings, the over-niceness of his hair, the extravagance of his life' (*Nigrinus* 13 [trans. Harmon 1927: 113, 115]). Likewise, Lucian claims that the philosopher Nigrinus states, 'are not the rich ridiculous? They display their purple gowns and show their rings and betray an unbounded lack of taste' (*Nigrinus* 21 [trans. Harmon 1927: 121]).

refers to the entire body (Mayor 1892: 144-45). In the New Testament, the plural appears only here and several times in the book of Revelation, where it shows up consistently in the context of the 'eating' of the flesh, whether it is that of the harlot (Rev. 17.16), who will be eaten by the beast, or of kings, captains, horses and men, free and slave, great and small, whose flesh will be part of the supper of God, and gorged on by the birds (19.18, 21). In the Septuagint, *σάρκας* also emerges in the context of eating. It is used in reference to the flesh (or fleshy parts) of Israelite sons and daughters (Lev. 26.29), of Jezebel (2 Kgs 9.36), or in Jdt. 16.17, when the Lord will seek vengeance by sending fire and worms into the fleshiness of the nations that rise up. The fact that *σάρκας* refers to that which is ingested indicates that is it the fatty parts—edible morsels—that are what these authors have in mind, not the body as a whole. The texts refer to the fleshy parts of both males and females and support the notion that the author of James is depicting the rich as 'soft', or flabby, especially in light of the other details in the letter thus far considered. If these rich are 'fleshy', then they resemble females, recalling the physiognomic handbooks surveyed earlier.

Verse 5 declares plainly that these rich have lived in extravagance. James 5.5 employs the unusual ἐτρυφήσατε, which appears elsewhere in the New Testament only as a noun in 2 Pet. 2.13 in the context of describing the false teachers who revel, possibly in love feasts, making it clear that these people have lived luxuriously. Some classical Greek authors use this word regularly as an adjective to describe effeminates: those who live softly or who are fastidious and dainty (Liddell and Scott 1968: 1831). The present participle τὸ τρυφῶν means 'effeminacy' in Aristophanes' *Vespae* (1455). Perhaps this is an even more blatant identification of these rich as womanly, and we have tended to overlook the connotation because this is the only place in which it figures as a verb in the New Testament. Furthermore, the text underscores the self-indulgence of the well heeled by claiming that they have lived on the earth ἐσπαταλήσατε,[9] another interesting term that connotes living softly, and in some contexts, the adjective can describe ornaments or food delicacies (Liddell and Scott 1968: 1625). Forms of this word are sometimes associated with women (see LXX Ezek. 16.49; 1 Tim 5.6) but also with a foolish reveler (Sir. 21.15) and those who are compared to swine (*Barn.* 10.3).

9. Mayor (1892: 147) points out that the *Shepherd of Hermas* (Herm. *Sim.* 61.6.1-2) also associates these two words when he refers to τὰ πρόβατα ταῦτα ὡσεὶ τρυθῶντα ἦν καὶ λίαν σπαταλῶντα who are taken care of by a young shepherd who turns out to be an angel of luxury and deceit (6.2). Notably, Hermas (*Sim.* 61.2.3) also refers here to the notion of the 'double-minded' or 'double-souled' (δίψυχος) person, who repeatedly appears in James (1.8; 4.8).

The author refers to further feeding when he says that the wealthy have 'fed' or 'fattened' (as this form of τρέφω is often translated) their hearts. There is no other instance of this phrase in ancient literature of which we are aware (Mayor 1892: 148). Homer (*Od.* 9.246) uses a form of τρέφω to refer to milk turning into cheese (Mayor 1892: 148), which reflects the 'fattening' or 'thickening' idea that is also connoted here. Its use in James reinforces the debauchery of the rich consistent with Graeco-Roman characterizations of effeminate men.

The denunciation of the rich is further emphasized through the charges against them for their mistreatment of labourers and the righteous. The notion that effeminate, indulgent and wealthy men were exploitative of others in order to further their own gain is not unusual, as it further associates them with women's behaviour. Preferring private advantage over the welfare of others was perceived as a feminine trait. As Edwards points out, '[i]n neglecting the public good for the pursuit of his own private desires [a man] became like a woman, in Roman eyes' (1993: 85). Greedy merchants, those who seek to 'trade and get gain' (Jas 4.13), were especially vulnerable to satirical attacks, such as the trader Catullus, who in Juvenal's twelfth satire throws the results of his conspicuous consumption and greed overboard in order to save his life during a storm at sea. Catullus tosses to sea some purple garments, 'such as would have benefited a soft Maecenas' (*Sat.* 12.39 [Ramsay, 1940: 239]), and he is compared to a eunuch beaver that loses a testicle.[10]

It is especially interesting that James should speak of the exploitation of labourers by the rich and the fact that it is the cries of the harvesters that have reached the ears of the Lord of hosts. The author may be deliberately contrasting the sloth, softness and greed of the rich with the toiling farm worker, who models, in some ways, the physically strong and noble country labourer, and who, as we have seen, was admired by some ancient moralists. It is precisely these ones who call upon the Lord of hosts, who hears them. James then strikes a final blow against the affluent by declaring how they have condemned and killed the righteous one (τὸν δίκαιον), which is probably a reference to the Israelite tradition of the poor and righteous person who is executed by the self-indulgent wealthy (LXX Wis. 2.10, 12; 1 *En.* 96.7-8).

In Jas 5.7-11, the author provides further contrast to the practices of the rich. He refers to the farmer (v. 7) who is patient or long-tempered (μακρόθυμος) (v. 8) (see Mayor 1892: 149), the suffering prophets (v. 10)

10. As Warren S. Smith explains, 'the goods of Catullus, the loss of which turns him into a eunuch beaver, serve merely as a reminder of the corruption from which the narrator, busy with sacrifices, seems so remote: effeminacy, luxury, conspicuous consumption, and bribery' (1989: 293).

as well as the figure of Job (v. 11), who embodies the Roman male virtue of 'steadfastness' or 'endurance' (ὑπομονή) (v. 11). All are clearly contrasted to the soft, indulgent rich, and like the harvesters, are comparable to the noble labourers found in Graeco-Roman literature, such as the Elder Cato, or Dio's hunters and shepherds. In James 5, they are admirable *exempla* whom the writer hopes his audience will imitate. They uphold masculine virtue, as opposed to effeminate weakness. They are anything but the soft, wealthy people who exploit their workers and do not manifest endurance. The author of James likely thought that the rich are incapable of even lifting a pitchfork!

The Audience

Does James imagine that some in his audience would identify with these rich, whom he has sought to discredit so thoroughly? Recent work on the letter argues that it was likely sent to a somewhat educated, metropolitan community, given the letter's literary and rhetorical sophistication, its interests in psychagogy, and adaptation of Jesus traditions to a more urban milieu (Kloppenborg 2010: 71). The audience may well have consisted of a mixture of people of varying social levels. Perhaps some members identified quite readily with the 'poor' in James, while others may have recognized some of their own practices, aspirations and attitudes to which the letter writer objects, including some of the activities associated with wealthy people in Jas 4.11–5.6. Most were likely somewhere in between these two poles, and the writer warns them to avoid the behaviours of the rich and to care for the poor among them.

If the author of this text has been influenced, perhaps indirectly, by elements of Graeco-Roman invective and satirical writing, it is worth thinking about its function and audience in comparison to satirical letters. As James is considered by many to be a literary letter (Francis 1970; Tsuji 1997; Niebuhr 1998), we are only witnessing one side of a fictional dialogue. The audience members are therefore comparable to eavesdroppers, some of whom, because the letter is 'oblique and indirect' as many satirical letters were (Braund 1999: 58), saw themselves reflected variously by different characters and groups in the text, despite the fact that they are clearly exhorted to care for the poor. In reference to James 2, for example, Wesley Wachob has argued that James understood his readers to be 'God's chosen poor' (Wachob 2000: 167). However, like Martial, these people may not have been materially impoverished, and the author's identification of them as 'the poor' could have served as a means of distancing some members, at least, from the conduct of the rich, and promoting a more communitarian social ethic in which the addressees provided for the needs of those who were materially less well off. In Jas 4.11–5.11, the author denounces the wealthy in very uncomplimentary terms, repudiating them as effeminates, and presents the patient farmer and Job, who endure, as exemplars. It is possible that James was presuming that there were such rich people in his audience (see Kloppenborg 2007: 138-39), although there is no evidence that he has specific individuals in mind. James 4.11–5.11 is calling for those who could identify with such behaviours to change, and using one of the most uncomplimentary characterizations, that of effeminacy, to do so. Satirical letters generally leave the audience 'free to identify with the situation of any of the characters, as it wishes' (Braund 1999: 58). Therefore, some of James's readers likely saw themselves reflected in aspects of Jas 4.11–5.6, and the letter writer has effectively exposed how their behaviour is dishonourable and subject to eschatological judgment.

Conclusion

The letter of James is a deeply Judean text, indebted as it is to Israelite traditions. But it is also a letter crafted in the context of the Graeco-Roman world. As has been documented, aspects of its form, rhetoric and conceptual patterns find clear parallels in Graeco-Roman materials. Given the tremendous importance of the masculine ideal found in Greek and Roman writings, and the scrutiny applied to those men who did not adequately embody that ideal, there is no reason to think that such concerns would not have left their mark on letters such as James. It will be worthwhile to continue this line of exploration in James: to systematically analyse the rest of the letter for imagery and themes that tap into portrayals of masculine and feminine in order to determine how these powerful and important cultural and social values play out elsewhere throughout the letter. These values endured (Gleason 1990: 203), and accusations of effeminacy were widespread. Subsequent Christian writers, such as Clement of Alexandria (*Paedagogus* 3.11.74), upheld this manly ideal, and it continued on, furnishing the basis for characterizing early Christian martyrs as strong men versus their effeminate non-Christian persecutors (Kuefler 2009: 247).

References

Aristotle (Pseudo)

1963 *Physiognomics* (trans. W.S. Hett; LCL; London: Heinemann; Cambridge, MA: Harvard University Press).

Atkins, Margaret, and Robin Osborne (eds.)

2006 *Poverty in the Roman World* (Cambridge: Cambridge University Press).

Balch, David L.

2004 'Philodemus, "On Wealth" and "On Household Management": Naturally Wealthy Epicureans against Poor Cynics', in *Philodemus and the New Testament World* (ed. John T. Fitzgerald, Dirk Obbink and Glenn S. Holland; NovTSup, 111; Leiden: Brill): 177-96.

Batten, Alicia J.
2009 *What Are They Saying about the Letter of James?* (Mahwah, NJ: Paulist Press).
Berg, R.
2002 'Wearing Wealth: *mundus muliebris* and *ornatus* as Status Markers for Women in Imperial Rome', in *Women, Wealth and Power in the Roman Empire* (ed. P. Setälä, R. Berg, R. Hälikkaä, M. Keltanen, J. Pölönen and V. Vuolanto; Acta Instituti Romani Finlandiae, 25; Rome: Institutum Romanum): 15-73.
Boyle, Marjorie O'Rourke
1985 'The Stoic Paradox of James 2.10', *NTS* 31: 611-17.
Braund, Susanna Morton
1999 *The Roman Satirists and their Masks* (London: Bristol Classical Press, repr).
Brown, Peter
1988 *The Body and Society: Men, Women and Sexual Renunciation in Early Christianity* (Lectures on the History of Religions, 13; New York: Columbia University Press).
Corbeill, Anthony
1996 *Controlling Laughter. Political Humor in the Late Roman Republic* (Princeton, NJ: Princeton University Press).
2004 *Nature Embodied: Gesture in Ancient Rome* (Princeton, NJ: Princeton University Press).
Deppe, Dean B.
1989 *The Sayings of Jesus in the Epistle of James* (PhD diss., Vrije Universiteit, Amsterdam).
Dibelius, Martin
1975 *James: A Commentary on the Epistle of James* (rev. Heinrich Greeven; trans. Michael A. Williams; Hermeneia; Philadelphia, PA: Fortress Press).
Dio Chrysostom
1932 *Discourses I-XI* (trans. J.W. Cohoon; LCL; London: Heinemann).
Edwards, Catharine
1993 *The Politics of Immorality in Ancient Rome* (Cambridge: Cambridge University Press).
Elliott, John H.
1993 'The Epistle of James in Rhetorical Social Scientific Perspective. Holiness–Wholeness and Patterns of Replication', *BTB* 23: 71-81.
Erker, Darja Šterbenc
2009 'Women's Tears in Ancient Roman Ritual', in Fögen 2009: 135-60.
Fagan, Garrett G.
2011 'Violence in Roman Social Relations', in *The Oxford Handbook of Social Relations in the Roman World* (ed. Michael Peachin; New York: Oxford University Press): 467-95.
Finley, Moses I.
1973 *The Ancient Economy* (Berkeley, CA: University of California Press).
Fögen, Thorsten (ed.)
2009 *Tears in the Graeco-Roman World* (Berlin: Walter de Gruyter).
Francis, Fred O.
1970 'The Form and Function of the Opening and Closing Paragraphs of James and John', *ZNW* 61: 110-26.

Friesen, Steven J.

2008 'Injustice or God's Will? Early Christian Explanations of Poverty', in *Wealth and Poverty in Early Church and Society* (ed. Susan Holman; Holy Cross Studies in Theology and History; Grand Rapids, MI: Baker Orthodox Press): 17-36.

Garnsey, Peter

1988 *Famine and Food Supply in the Graeco-Roman World: Responses to Risk and Crisis* (Cambridge: Cambridge University Press).

1998 *Cities, Peasants and Food in Classical Antiquity: Essays in Social and Economic History* (Cambridge: Cambridge University Press).

Gleason, Maud

1990 'The Semiotics of Gender: Physiognomy and Self-Fashioning in the Second Century C.E'., in *Before Sexuality: The Construction of Erotic Experience in the Ancient Greek World* (ed. David M. Halperin, John J. Winkler and Froma I. Zeitlin; Princeton, NJ: Princeton University Press): 389-415.

Harris, William V.

2007 'The Late Republic', in Scheidel, Morris and Saller 2007: 511-39.

Jackson-McCabe, Matt A.

2001 *Logos and Law in the Letter of James: The Law of Nature, the Law of Moses and the Law of Freedom* (NovTSup, 100; Leiden: Brill).

Johnson, Luke Timothy

1995 *The Letter of James* (AB, 37A; New York: Doubleday).

Jongman, Willem M.

2007 'The Early Roman Empire: Consumption', in Scheidel, Morris and Saller 2007: 592-618.

Juvenal

1940 *Satires* (trans. G.G. Ramsay; LCL; London: Heinemann; Cambridge, MA: Harvard University Press).

Kehoe, Dennis

2007 'The Early Roman Empire: Production', in Scheidel, Morris and Saller 2007: 543-69.

Kloppenborg, John S.

2007 'The Emulation of Jesus Traditions in James', in Webb and Kloppenborg 2007: 121-50.

2010 'James 1:2-15 and Hellenistic Psychagogy', *NovT* 52: 37-71.

Kuefler, Mathew

2009 'Soldiers of Christ: Christian Masculinity and Militarism in Late Antiquity', in *Men and Masculinities in Christianity and Judaism* (ed. Björn Kronderfer; London: SCM Press): 237-58.

Lateiner, Donald

2009 'Tears and Crying in Hellenic Historiography: Dacryology from Herodotus to Polybius', in Fögen 2009: 105-34.

Liddell, Henry George, and Robert Scott

1968 *A Greek–English Lexicon* (Oxford: Clarendon Press, rev. edn).

Lucian

1927 *Nigrinus* (trans. A.M. Harmon; LCL; London: Heinemann).

Mayor, J.B.

1892 *The Epistle of St. James* (London: Macmillan).

Morley, Neville

2006 'The Poor in the City of Rome', in Atkins and Osborne 2006: 21-39.

Moxnes, Halvor

1997 'Conventional Values in the Hellenistic World: Masculinity', in *Conventional Values of the Hellenistic Greeks* (ed. Per Bilde, Troels Engberg-Pedersen, Lise Hannestad and Jan Zahle; Studies in Hellenistic Civilization, 8; Aarhus: Aarhus University Press): 263-84.

Niebuhr, Karl-Wilhelm

1998 'Der Jakobusbrief im Licht frühjüdischer Diasporabriefe', *NTS* 44: 420-43.

Osborne, Robin

2006 'Introduction: Roman Poverty in Context', in Atkins and Osborne 2006: 1-20.

Penner, Todd C.

1996 *The Epistle of James and Eschatology. Re-reading an Ancient Christian Letter* (JSNTSup, 121; Sheffield: Sheffield Academic Press).

Plutarch

1948 *Marcus Cato* (trans. Bernadotte Perrin; LCL; London: Heinemann; Cambridge, MA: Harvard University Press).

Richlin, Amy

1988 'Systems of Food Imagery in Catullus', *The Classical World* 81: 355-63.

1992 *The Garden of Priapus: Sexuality and Aggression in Roman Humor* (New York: Oxford University Press, rev. edn).

Scheidel, Walter

2006 'Stratification, Deprivation and Wuality of Life', in Atkins and Osborne 2006: 40-59.

Scheidel, Walter, Ian Morris and Richard Saller (eds.)

2007 *The Cambridge Economic History of the Greco-Roman World* (Cambridge: Cambridge University Press).

Smith, Warren S.

1989 'Greed and Sacrifice in Juvenal's Twelfth Satire', *TAPA* 119: 287- 98.

Ste Croix, G.E.M. de

1981 *The Class Struggle in the Ancient Greek World from the Archaic Age to the Greek Conquests* (Ithaca, NY: Cornell University Press).

Tsuji, Manabu

1997 *Glaube zwischen Vollkommenheit und Verweltlichung: Eine Untersuchung zur literarischen Gestalt und zur inhaltlichen Kohärenz des Jakobusbriefes* (WUNT, 2/93; Tübingen: J.C.B Mohr Siebeck).

Wachob, Wesley Hiram

2000 *The Voice of Jesus in the Social Rhetoric of James* (SNTSMS, 106; Cambridge: Cambridge University Press).

Watson, Duane F.

2007 'A Reassessment of the Rhetoric of the Epistle of James and its Implications for Christian Origins', in Webb and Kloppenborg 2007: 99-120.

Webb, Robert L., and John S. Kloppenborg (eds.)

2007 *Reading James with New Eyes. Methodological Reassessments of the Letter of James* (LNTS, 342; London: T. & T. Clark).

Woolf, Greg

2006 'Writing Poverty in Rome', in Atkins and Osborne 2006: 83-99.

Ethnic Judeans and Christian Identity Formation in John Chrysostom's *Adversus Judaeos**

Stephen K. Black

In my days as a student of Jack Elliott at the University of San Francisco he taught a course with Dr Rabbi David Davis, founding director of USF's Swig Program in Judaic Studies, called 'Jesus the Jew'.[1] The extremely popular course was not only a landmark in contemporary Jewish–Christian relations, the rigor of the course gave the lie to the naïve and uninformed notion that Jesus was somehow distinct from his ethnic and religious context. Several years after his retirement, however, Jack declared that were he to teach that course today, he would sacrifice the alliteration in the course title for a more historically and culturally accurate one, 'Jesus the Israelite' (Elliott 2007: 151). In the late 1990s, Jack was among several scholars reflecting on the problems associated with translating the New Testament term Ἰουδαῖος as 'Jew'.[2] For Jack this culminated in his 2007 article, 'Jesus the Israelite Was neither a "Jew", nor a "Christian": On Correcting Misleading Nomenclature'.[3] Drawing on the distinction between emic and etic references, Jack argued that Jesus and his followers saw themselves as 'Isra-

* I would like to thank the Saint Ignatius Institute at the University of San Francisco, especially its director (at the time), Sean Michaelson, S.J., and its assistant director, Barbara St Marie, for the leave and funding to spend the summer of 2012 as Research Fellow at the Centre for Medieval and Renaissance Studies (CMRS) at the University of Oxford, where the majority of the research and writing for this chapter took place. I would also like to thank CMRS and its senior dean, Dr Nicholas Crowe, and its principal, Dr Mark Philpott, for providing a collegial environment and gracious hospitality. Finally, I would like to thank Philip Esler and Wendy Mayer for reading and commenting on an earlier draft of this chapter.

1. The course was taught every year from 1980 through 1997, after which Rabbi Davis left for other ventures.

2. See, e.g., Pilch 1997.

3. Jack's 2007 article as it now appears is a revised version of two papers he delivered to professional associations: the 1997 meeting of the International Context Group in Prague, and the 2004 meeting of the Catholic Biblical Association in Halifax, Nova Scotia.

elites', 'Galileans', and 'Nazoreans' (emic references) and that they were so called by their fellow Israelites. Ἰουδαῖος was an outsider (Greek and therefore etic) term, sometimes used by insiders (Israelites) when communicating with outsiders as an accommodation. Jack argued that we ought to respect insider (emic) usage to avoid anachronistic and misleading nomenclature. Hence, Jesus was not a Jew but an Israelite. Further, because our understanding of Jews and Judaism (as well as Christians and Christianity) reflects fourth- rather than first-century usage, we ought to translate the appearance of Ἰουδαῖος as 'Judean' rather than 'Jew' in order to reflect first-century outsider (etic) meanings, which, from a Greek-speaking perspective, referred to the people who inhabited the land of Ἰουδαία, Judea. While there remains opposition to such a characterization,[4] in recent years many scholars—Jews and Christians alike—have argued similarly.[5] However, few scholars agree on when it becomes appropriate to refer to 'Jews' rather than 'Judeans'. I would like to honor my mentor and friend Jack Elliott by demonstrating that in at least one late-fourth-century case—the homiletical series of John Chrysostom known as *Adversus Judaeos*[6]—we should yet read Ἰουδαῖος as Judean rather than Jew.

In the autumn of 386, the year he was ordained to the presbyterate, John Chrysostom delivered a homily objecting that some members of his congregation were attending the synagogue for the festivals of Rosh Hashanah, Yom Kippur and Sukkoth. The following autumn he made a more concerted effort to stop them, preaching an additional six homilies on the subject.[7] During the course of the series he stressed that it is not possible *both* to participate in the Ἰουδαϊσμός of the synagogue *and* also participate in the mysteries of the Eucharist in the church. One had to choose. I argue that in these homilies we can and ought to read and understand John Chrysostom's use of Ἰουδαῖοι as well as Ἰουδαϊκοί and ἰουδαΐζοντες as references to *ethnic* Judeans, and Ἰουδαϊσμός as a reference to the ways, customs and manners of these Judeans.[8] We should understand their presence at the synagogue in

4. See, e.g., Levine 2006: 159-66, and Schwartz 2007.

5. See, e.g., Boyarin 1999 and 2003 (Jew); Malina 2000; Esler 2003, 2007, and 2009 (Christians).

6. The titles of John Chrysostom's homilies are not necessarily contemporaneous with Chrysostom himself; they are likely later scribal descriptions. See Mayer 2005: 315-21. I will be arguing on the basis of John Chrysostom's use of the various forms of Ἰουδαῖος within the homilies themselves.

7. For the order and dating of these homilies I follow Pradels, Brändle and Heimgartner 2002. Their dating accords better with the evidence than does that of Harkins 1979: l-lix. *Adversus Judaeos* 3 is not part of the original series but is nevertheless relevant.

8. In *Adversus Judaeos* Chrysostom used Ἰουδαῖος in its various syntactical forms 135 times, Ἰουδαϊκός 18 times, ἰουδαΐζων only 3 times (1.4 [849.56], 6.7 [916.10], 8.5

fourth-century Antioch as a normal expression of their ethnic attachment to rituals rooted in the ancient homeland of Israel/Judea. Furthermore, the ἰουδαΐζοντες of Chrysostom's homiletical series refer specifically to ethnic Judeans who were additionally believers in Jesus as the Messiah—or as he refers to them, 'those who are happily our members, those who appear to be among our troops, but are among those who attend the whole assembly' at synagogue during festivals.[9] This practice he sought to proscribe. Social-scientific studies on ethnicity as well as what we know of ancient Mediterranean and Near Eastern religions in general, and the role of the synagogue in the diaspora in particular, suggest that what Chrysostom was criticizing was not 'the religion of Judaism' as such, but Judean ethnic identity itself, which of course included distinctive religious practices. The specific language John Chrysostom used to discredit the synagogue and its adherents was kinship based, suggesting that he had in mind something similar to what we might call 'ethnicity'.[10] His kinship language sought not only to discredit the ethnic identity of Judeans but also to form a new identity he construed as distinctively Christian.

In what follows I will review modern social-scientific studies on ethnicity in order to identify and define what it means to say that the targets of John Chrysostom's invective were *ethnic* Judeans. Focusing on two specific 'ethnic indicators' I will then demonstrate the close association between ethnic groups, their religious practices and their 'land'.[11] The close association between these factors was common in the ancient Mediterranean

[934.56]), and Ἰουδαϊσμός six times (1.4 [849.13], 1.8 [856.31], 2.1 [857.58], 2.2 [859.4], 4.4 [876.23], 6.7 [914.47]). He spoke of the land of Ἰουδαία only twice: (1.6 [851.50]: ἄνδρας ἐκ τῆς Ἰουδαίας [men from Judea]; 2.122va [Pradels, Brändle and Heimgartner 2001: 34], specifying the land in which it was permissible to offer sacrifices). He never used the adverb ἰουδαϊκῶς in this series. John refered to Ἰσραήλ or Ἰσραηλίτης only 11 times and only while quoting or paraphrasing scripture. All references to the text of *Adversus Judaeos* are taken from PG 48, except where noted. The bracketed references refer to the columns and line numbers of that volume.

9. See *Adv. Jud.* 4.3 (875.2-6): Μᾶλλον δὲ πρὶν ἢ πρὸς Ἰουδαίους ἀποτείνασθαι, τοῖς ἡμετέροις ἡδέως διαλεξόμεθα μέλεσι, τοῖς δοκοῦσι μὲν μεθ' ἡμῶν τετάχθαι, θεραπεύουσι δὲ τὰ ἐκείνων, καὶ τὸν ἀγῶνα ἅπαντα ὑπὲρ αὐτῶν ἀνῃρημένοις (translations of all Greek texts are my own unless otherwise noted). Scholarship since the nineteenth century has historically interpreted such practices as evidence of 'Jewish Christianity' (see the review by Taylor 1990). Aside from the problem of classifying such groups (see Jackson-McCabe 2007), the terminology, however construed, tends to confuse 'religion' for 'ethnicity'. Ἰουδαῖος and Ἰουδαϊκός are ethnic terms, while Χριστιανός is not.

10. Most scholars agree that whatever else is entailed in 'ethnicity', kinship ties, even when fictive, are at its root. Note the comment of Hutchinson and Smith 1996: 3: 'Though the term "ethnicity" is recent, the sense of kinship, group solidarity, and common culture to which it refers is as old as the historical record'.

11. By 'land' I mean the geopolitical unit common to the group.

and Near Eastern worlds. I will follow this presentation with an analysis of how this association between ethnicity, religious practice, and land worked among exiles and other dispersed peoples. We will then be in a position to appreciate the specific language John Chrysostom used to discredit Judean ethnic identity and construct Christian identity using terms associated with kinship and ethnicity.

The Study of Ethnicity in the Social Sciences

The study of ethnicity as such is a relatively recent endeavor. The English word *ethnicity* is even more recent.[12] The coined term is based on the Greek word ἔθνος (*ethnos*), which originally meant any collective group.[13] In early Christian literature prior to the fourth century ἔθνη most frequently referred to Greeks, or other non-Judeans and non-Christians (see Bowersock 1990: 10-11). Its adjectival form ἐθνικός, commonly translated as *foreign* or *pagan*, is the basis of the English word *ethnic*, and into the twentieth century was typically and pejoratively rendered in English as *heathen*. On the one hand such renderings do capture the ancient Greek sense of 'others' as opposed to 'us'; on the other, such renderings are not helpful in social-scientific studies.

Importantly, *ethnicity* is distinct from *race*. The latter is still a popular term used to classify peoples (especially in the United States), but has been discredited by biological and social scientists as unscientific. Geneticists no longer use the term; the fact that hereditary physical traits do not follow clear 'racial' boundaries has rendered the term useless as a scientifically descriptive category. Similarly, social scientists have found no connection between hereditary characteristics in race and social and cultural variation (Eriksen 2010: 4-6). The term also suffers from its connection with the Nazis and other proponents of 'racist' ideology, who regarded race in an essentialist and primordial way. According to this understanding, groups of people classifiable by 'race' have certain distinctive physical and mental characteristics (frequently perceived as 'limitations') existing according to nature, specifically, in the blood. This is unsupported by any credible biological or social scientist. Instead, social scientists speak

12. The word was coined in 1942 by sociologists W. Lloyd Warner and Paul Lunt (Warner and Lunt 1942: 73).

13. Homer used the term to refer to flocks of birds and swarms of flies (*Il.* 2.459, 469), although it is worth noting that in both instances Homer employed a simile referring to the gathering armies preparing for battle. He also uses ἔθνος to mean a group of warriors (*Il.* 2.91; 3.32; 7.115; 11.724) and, collectively, the dead (*Od.* 10.526). Herodotus used it to refer to populations of people (1.6; 1.57; 1.203; 4.5; 4.17; 4.99; 4.108; 4.171-72; 4.183; 4.197; 7.161; 8.73).

of *ethnicity*. Unlike race, ethnicity is understood as a social and cultural construction.[14]

The sociological study of groups as ethnic owes its origins, like so much else in sociology, to Max Weber. In his 1922 posthumously published *Wirtschaft und Gesellschaft* (*Economy and Society*), Weber identified the inherently subjective nature of ethnic group classification: '"ethnic groups" [are] those human groups that entertain a *subjective belief* in their common descent because of similarities of physical type or of customs or both, or because of memories of colonization and migration' (1968: 389 [emphasis added]). For Weber, 'it does not matter whether or not an objective blood relationship exists' (1968: 389). This removed race as the primary determining factor in ethnic group formation. What was determinative for ethnicity was the body politic: 'it is primarily the political community, no matter how artificially organized, that inspires *the belief in* common ethnicity', a belief which persists 'even after the disintegration of the political community' (1968: 389 [emphasis added]). Further, Weber argued that ethnic ties are particularly strong among immigrants. Whenever 'emigration from a mother community remains for some reason alive, there undoubtedly exists a very specific and often extremely powerful sense of ethnic identity, which is determined by several factors: shared political memories or, even more importantly in early times, persistent ties with the old cult' (1968: 390). As we will see, this insight is particularly relevant for examining the ways in which Judeans in fourth-century Antioch were still tied to the ancient cultic practices of Israel.

Norwegian anthropologist Fredrik Barth has similarly argued for the subjective nature of ethnicity. However, he was less focused on political community and more on social organization. Barth argued that studies of ethnic groups ought to focus on the self-ascription of a group and the use of that ascription by others. In response to a tendency to regard cultural features as primordial principles in determining ethnicity, Barth argued that the common culture of ethnic groups is an implication of ethnic group organization rather than a primary definitional characteristic (1969: 11); indeed, ethnic groups continuously negotiate the social boundaries that define the group (1969: 15) and itself determines the significant cultural indicators. Thus, cultural indicators are the result of ethnic group formation, not the other way around. Important for Barth are the ways in which groups maintain social boundaries identified as ethnic. These boundaries are fluid and can

14. I am aware of the arguments of some scholars who persist in the use of the term 'race' on the grounds that this term too should be understood as a social and cultural construct. See, e.g., Buell 2005 and (with much less sophistication and nuance) Isaac 2004. See n. 61 below for why I think this is unhelpful and problematic.

shift over time and space as ethnic groups migrate or otherwise encounter other ethnic groups and their cultures.

Although theoretically foundational, neither Weber's nor Barth's studies are particularly helpful at indicating what specific markers or indicators identify a group as ethnic. More recent attempts at developing such indicators crystallized in the work of sociologist Anthony D. Smith of the London School of Economics. In his study *The Ethnic Origins of Nations* (1986), Smith argued that while the concept of nations and nationalism is modern, it is rooted in premodern notions of ethnicity that reach back into antiquity. The modern nation-state, then, reflects the durability of ethnic communities (1986: 16-17). In describing the 'foundations of ethnic community' Smith developed six 'chief features' that distinguish ethnic identity apart from other forms of collective identity (1986: 22-30). The first of these is a *collective name* for the ethnic group. Second, ethnic groups have *a common myth of origin and descent*. Third is a sense of *a shared history*. The fourth indicator of ethnic groups is *a distinctive shared culture* that includes language, religion, customs, institutions, laws, dress and the like. I will focus on this particular ethnic indicator in the analysis that follows. I will also focus on Smith's fifth indicator: an *association with a specific territory* or homeland the ethnic group considers its own. Importantly, Smith notes that the group need not physically occupy the land; 'what matters is that it has a symbolic geographical center, a sacred habitat' (1986: 28).[15] The sixth and final indicator of ethnic groups is that they share *a sense of solidarity* and identity.[16]

Two of Smith's ethnic indicators—a distinctive shared culture (indicator four), and an association with a specific territory (indicator five)—are particularly useful for identifying ethnic Judeans in the late antique diaspora. The distinctive shared culture necessarily focuses on, but is not limited to, 'religion', and brings into sharp relief the way 'religion was done' (Beckman 2005) in the ancient Mediterranean and Near Eastern worlds at large. An association with a specific territory also focuses us on the importance of place in ancient religion; it enables us to see how place was managed by diaspora peoples.

15. Anthony Smith makes the important point that ethnic groups 'do not cease to be *ethnie* when they are dispersed' (1986: 28).

16. What the work of Weber, Barth and Smith demonstrate is the *socially constructed* nature of ethnic identity. This has proven helpful in recent studies of ancient Greek ethnicity (Malkin 2001) and ethnicity in Hellenistic Egypt (Bilde 1992). Anthony Smith's indicators of ethnic identity have been influential in several studies of antiquity (Hall 1997, 2002; Esler 1998, 2003, 2007, 2009).

Ethnicity and Religion in the Ancient Mediterranean and Near East

Smith's study emphasizes one very critical aspect of ethnic groups that modern discussions of religion do not: the importance of distinctive religious practices as a key characteristic feature of ethnic groups. Contemporary assumptions about what constitutes religion, particularly the religions of Judaism and Christianity, tend to blur our vision when looking at ancient societies. Modern notions of religion are largely influenced by post-Enlightenment suppositions about belief, doctrine and morality that, although supported by a 'religious community', are by and large individually based (see Frankfurter 2003: 131).[17] The implications of this understanding are that religion is an element of human life that is discreet, separate from one's sense of kinship, ethnicity, and, as the famous national constitutions of the eighteenth century indicate, one's nation-state. Such notions of religion would have been unrecognizable in the ancient and late ancient Mediterranean world.[18]

Religion in antiquity was primarily about ritual actions performed in particular places as expression of one's kinship, ethnicity and citizenship in a particular body politic. In Mediterranean and Near Eastern antiquity ritual practices (religion) honoring gods permeated every unit of social organization and location. For example, readers of Greek mythology are quite familiar with the deity Zeus and several of his epithets ('father of gods and men', 'storm god', 'deep thundering', etc.). Much less familiar are Zeus Ktesios (of the household property), Zeus Herkeios (of the household boundary), Zeus Phratrios (of the neighborhood fraternity), Zeus Agoraios (of the marketplace), Zeus Boulaios (of the town council), and Zeus Polieos (of the city), to name only a few. All of these manifestations of Zeus are tied to specific social units, locales and ritual practices. The father of a Greek household would perform (daily) rituals at his home to honor Zeus Ktesios and Zeus Herkeios, the latter at an altar in the household courtyard.

17. Note also the recent article by Blowers 2011, where he challenges the very notion of 'community' in early Christianity as based on anachronistic notions projected on to Paul and other early 'Christians'.

18. See the classic and seminal study by Wilfred Cantwell Smith (1962) who traces the historical evolution of our notion of religion, and regards it as a *modern Western* invention that distorts our attempts to understand religion in antiquity. Some scholars have recently suggested that religion became a discreet area of human life under the influence of fourth-century Christianity. For a provocative discussion of the discourses that produced this see Boyarin 2004: 202-25. I do not deny that shifts were taking place in the fourth century, producing discourses about 'religion'. John Chrysostom's *Adversus Judaeos* was in fact part of that discourse. But none of these discourses produced what we now think of as 'religion'. Chrysostom's discourse presupposed the notion that religion was embedded in ancient conceptions of one's ethnicity.

He would also participate in the rituals associated with his neighborhood *phratres* (brotherhood) in honor of Zeus Phratrios. Originating in associations of kin who recognized a common ancestor, *phratres* were particularly important (see Bruit Zaidman and Schmitt Patel 1992: 86, and Hendrick 2010: 293). In Athens, it was through the various *phratres* that young men were enrolled as citizens, significantly, only after their kinship legitimacy had been established by means of rituals and sacrifices to Zeus Phratrios.[19] Additionally, a father would be a part of ritual celebrations in his *deme* (local district), *genos* (kinsmen [probably fictive]), and *phulē* (tribe) (Bruit Zaidman and Schmitt Patel 1992: 81-89). If he were a merchant, he would honor Zeus Agoraios; if he were on the town council (*boulē*), Zeus Boulaios. And if Zeus were a patron deity of his city, he would participate in the rituals at a multiday festival in honor of Zeus Polieos. Similar manifestations of Zeus would be honored in other cities and locales.[20] All of these deities were Zeus, but none of them were simply Zeus, the deity portrayed by Homer, Hesiod and other mythographers.[21] These 'Zeus examples' could be multiplied for practically every deity in the Greek pantheon in every Greek city. The specific locations of cultic centers were critically important as they indicated not only where the deity was honored, but also the specific context in which protection and favor from that deity was sought, be it the Greek *oikos*, the Greek *polis*, or whatever social unit in between. What this means, practically speaking, is that ethnicity in ancient Greece was an extended version of kinship that started with the household and ended with the *politeia* common to these kinship groups.[22] That is to say that the way religion was practiced in ancient Greece was in the specific locales of various kinship and ethnic groups (Athenians, Spartans, Corinthians, etc.). This has been called '*polis* religion' (see Sourvinou-Inwood 1988 [2000b],

19. These rituals were part of a three-day festival known as the *Apatouria*, literally, 'of the same father' (Mikalson 2010: 140-42; Bruit Zaidman and Schmitt Patel 1992: 65-66).

20. On the Greek gods, their functions, and their relationship to specific locales, see Bremmer 1994: 13 and Mikalson 2010: 32-36.

21. Note Herodotus's comment at 2.53 that Hesiod and Homer created for literary purposes the famous genealogies and characteristic features of the Olympian deities; prior to this such familial relationships between the deities, Herodotus claims, were unknown.

22. This was Aristotle's notion of state building (*Politica* 1252a-53a). See the important study of Nagle 2006. Note also our honoree's comments: 'The *oikos* thereby provided the model, the terminology and the ideological framework for the organization of the state as a whole, its smaller parts, its various types of subjects, and its administrative officials. . . . [T]he political connotations of *oikos* were known and even basic to the sociopolitical forms of life in the Mediterranean world as a whole' (Elliott 1990: 172-73).

1990 [2000a]),[23] even though it also encompassed one's home, neighborhood, village and tribe (Bruit Zaidman and Schmitt Patel 1992: 80-101).[24] As Jonathan Hall has demonstrated, these kinship and ethnic groups were supported as such by (constructed) ethnographies and genealogies, traces of which survive in Greek mythology (1997: 67-110). One finds like connections between ethnicity, *politeia* and religion throughout the ancient Mediterranean and Near Eastern worlds, even in ancient Israel.[25] Simply put, in Mediterranean and Near Eastern antiquity religious ritual played a key role in identifying an ethnic group. Such demonstration of the group to itself through ritual activity is one very key way in which a group recognizes and projects itself as ethnic (Hendrick 2010: 290). Practice and place were at the heart of ancient religious expression, and are notions at the heart of John Chrysostom's condemnation of Judeans in Antioch.

Association with an Ancestral Land among the Diaspora

In the first century CE the apostle Paul could specifically identify himself to others as a member of the ancient Israelite tribe of Benjamin (Phil. 3.5).[26] Paul was a native of Tarsus (Acts 21.39; 22.2), a city on the Mediterranean coast in the Roman province of Cilicia (current southeast Turkey). In spite of the fact that he spoke Greek and was apparently a citizen not only of the city of Tarsus but also of Rome (Acts 16.37-38; 22.25-29), Paul identified himself ethnically as a son of Israel, descended from the ancient tribe of Benjamin.[27] This brings into focus Smith's fifth indicator of ethnicity—namely, connection to an ancestral land even among diaspora peoples.

23. Sourvinou-Inwood's studies 'Further Aspects of Polis Religion' and 'What Is Polis Religion?' were originally published in 1988 and 1990 respectively. Both articles have been reissued in the 2000 work cited.

24. Note Kindt 2012, who objects to the narrow focus on *polis* religion. While hers is a helpful caution, her analysis does not undermine the connection between ethnicity and religious practice in the *polis*.

25. The literature on the subject is abundant. On Rome and its empire see Savage 1971, Wiseman 1995, Beard, North and Price 1998, Scheid 2003, Rives 2007 and Rüpke 2007; on ancient Mesopotamia see Van de Mieroop 1997, Beckman 2005, Limet 2005 and Snell 2011; on ancient Egypt see Černy 1979, Frankfurter 1998 and Assmann 2001; on ancient Israel, see the seminal study by Gottwald 1979.

26. See Duling 2003, who notes that Paul does *not* mention his immediate kin, genealogy, or city of origin (236-37).

27. See also 2 Cor. 11.22 where Paul responds to his Judean critics: 'Are they Hebrews (Ἑβραῖοί)? So am I. Are they Israelites (Ἰσραηλῖταί)? So am I. Are they descendants of Abraham (σπέρμα Ἀβραάμ)? So am I.' All three of these rhetorical questions use *emic* references to ethnicity.

Sources testify to the presence of Judeans residing in the city of Antioch from its foundation as a city c. 300 BCE (Josephus *Ant.* 12.119; *Apion* 2.39).[28] While initially these were likely retired mercenary soldiers who had served in Alexander's army, by the second century BCE Judeans were an identifiable community with their own *politeia* (Josephus *Wars* 7.43-44).[29] This means that the community living in Antioch called Ἰουδαῖοι by their fellow Greek-speaking Antiochenes was an immigrant community, one of several such communities in the cities of the Mediterranean world, and referred to in the scholarly literature as the diaspora. According to Anthony Smith, ethnic groups maintain a connection with a specific territory they call their own (1986: 28). This is also true of those members of the ethnic group who do not reside in that territory (see Hutchison and Smith 1996: 7), including the Judean diaspora of fourth-century CE Antioch. That this community was still identifiable as Ἰουδαῖοι—Judeans—in the fourth century, nearly seven centuries after their first members arrived in the city, is testament to the strength of their ethnic ties.

As the work of Frederik Barth shows, one of the ways that notions of ethnicity can shift over time and space is how ethnic groups negotiate their social boundaries under the influence of contact with other ethnicities. The ancient sources also attest to varying degrees of what is typically called 'cultural assimilation' to Antiochene (Greek) culture on the part of Judeans. Two pieces of evidence, both from the late first century CE, express the possible extremes. The first of these is the story of the Maccabean martyrs contained in *4 Maccabees,* likely written in 90–100 CE (Klauck 1989: 668-69). The story, set in second-century BCE Jerusalem during the reign of the Seleucid king Antiochus IV Epiphanes, narrates the martyrdom of the Judean priest, Eleazar, as well as seven brothers, at the hands of the Hellenistic king and his officials. Although the location is disputed, internal evidence as well as the existence of a known shrine dedicated to the 'Maccabean martyrs' in Antioch suggests that the martyrdom took place in Antioch (Schatkin 1974: 99-103).[30] On the surface, the story exhibits the ethnic conflicts between

28. See Kraeling 1932: 131, and Downey 1961: 79-80, the latter of whom notes that at its founding Antioch also included indigenous Syrians as well as Greeks and Macedonians.

29. By *politeia* I mean not 'citizenship' (a possible translation of the Greek word) in the *polis* of Antioch, but rather the right granted Judeans to live according to their own customs (*nomoi*), including religious practices (see Applebaum 1974: 436, 452). See also Kraeling 1932: 145-46 and, especially, Zetterholm 2003: 31-37, who judiciously reviews Josephus's references and various studies on them.

30. Meeks and Wilken (1978: 3) think that 'it seems more likely that the martyrdoms actually took place in Jerusalem', although they offer no refutation of the evidence set forth by Schatkin 1974. There remains debate about this subject, however. For a survey of the literature on the controversy see Mayer and Allen 2012: 90-94.

Judeans and Greeks in the second century BCE that are well known to scholars. However, the story reflects similar ethnic tensions in the first century CE (see Zetterholm 2003: 80-1). The second piece of evidence is from Josephus, written at approximately the same time as *4 Maccabees*. He tells of a certain Judean, Antiochus, who was the son of the *gerousiarch* in Antioch.[31] During the Judean War with Rome (66–70 CE) Antiochus entered the theater of Antioch and denounced his father and fellow Judeans, accusing some of plotting to burn the city, naming names as he did so. He then adopted Greek ways, including sacrificing to Greek gods (*War* 7.46-50). Obviously Antiochus stands at the other extreme, an example of someone who, though ethnically Judean, renounced this ethnic identity to adopt the ethnic identity (Greek) of the majority community in Antioch. These two examples represent the extreme options. However extreme, neither of these examples should surprise us, as they are two possible reactions to the adopted culture of immigrant peoples.

Magnus Zetterholm has studied these two stories in the context of 'cultural and religious differentiation' within immigrant communities. Noting studies of Hungarian immigrants to Sweden and Muslim immigrants to western Europe, Zetterholm posits three possible responses of an ethnic group to the 'host community' (in our case Antioch): (1) a *rejection* of one's native culture, including its religion, in favor of assimilation to the host culture; (2) an *intensification* of commitment to one's ethnic group, including its religion, as a way of preserving identity; (3) the formation of '*new manifestations*' of the ethnic group which adopts aspects of the host culture, while preserving, if altering, the customs of the original ethnic group (2003: 53-111). The third response is more typical among immigrant communities, and Zetterholm finds evidence of this in what he (and the majority of scholarship on the subject) calls 'Hellenistic Jews'.[32] While such hellenization might entail any number of features in a cultural hybridity, Zetterholm notes that the most identifiable of these is the adoption of the host language (Greek) and the host educational system (*paideia*) for elites. There also develops a degree of 'structural assimilation', that is, where members of the immigrant group develop primary social relationships with members of the host society, joining them in social cliques, clubs and other socio-political institutions.

31. A *gerousiarch* was the head of the council of Judeans in Antioch that adjudicated internal matters of the immigrant community of Judeans, and the body that negotiated with Hellenistic and Roman officials.

32. Zetterholm also sees as an example of this third type of 'new manifestation' what he calls 'Messianist Jews', who, although 'Jewish', recognized Jesus as the messiah (2003: 88-91).

Structural assimilation can lead to complete assimilation, as it seemed to have with Antiochus, but it need not. Zetterholm sees 'Hellenistic Jews' also involved in structural assimilation (see 2003: 55-90), while still maintaining their Judean ethnic identity. Under this category we might reasonably see the father of the aforementioned Antiochus. Evidence suggests that the *gerousiarchs* of Antioch had close ties with other local elites and good working relationships with Roman provincial governors. In the case of Antiochus's father, about whom we know almost nothing, we might also note the name he gave his son—the namesake of the Seleucid monarch after whom the very city was named!

There is clear evidence of this kind of structural assimilation in fourth-century Antioch as well. In 364 CE representatives of the Judean community in Antioch appealed to Libanius, the city's teacher of rhetoric, to intercede on their behalf with Priscianus, the Roman provincial governor of Palestine, over a matter concerning the appointment 'of a certain wicked old man' (πονηροῦ τινος γέροντος) to the Judean assembly (*gerousin*). According to Libanius, they were concerned that 'the chief of their officials' (τὸν τῶν ἀρχόντων τῶν παρ' αὐτοῖς ἄρχοντα), had already secured the appointment through Priscianus (Libanius, *Ep.* 1251). While there is controversy over the specific offices, as well as specific persons referred to by Libanius,[33] it is clear that members of the Judean community, if not their assembly, were close enough to civic elites (Libanius), if not imperial officials (Priscianus), to ask for assistance in their internal affairs.

While this all shows that Judeans existed as an immigrant community in Antioch, and how some Judeans responded to that host community, it does not necessarily show how they maintained a relationship with their homeland, Israel/Judea. This is especially problematic given that the cultic center (Temple) in Jerusalem was destroyed by the Roman armies in 70 CE and that Judeans were not allowed to reside in Judea in the aftermath of the Bar Kokhba revolt (132–135 CE). While it is easy to see how people who no longer live in the land can still exist as a distinct ethnic group with ties to their homeland, it is more difficult to see how this is the case when the homeland no longer exists as a homeland. For this and other reasons, much of the scholarship on this period insists that it is here that we should speak of 'Judaism' and 'being Jewish' as a distinctively *religious* phenomenon (see Segal 1986; Cohen 1999; Dunn 1991). Two interrelated considerations mitigate this interpretation, however.

First, social scientists point out that the attachment to homeland is 'symbolic' more than it is actual. As Anthony Smith reminds us, 'the association with' the homeland 'may be just a potent memory'. Physical possession of

33. For the opposing views compare Meeks and Wilken (1978: 7) against A.F. Norman (1992: 260-61 n. b).

the land is not important; what matters is 'a *symbolic* geographical center, a sacred habitat . . . to which it may *symbolically* return' (1986: 28; [emphasis added]). There is evidence of this emphasis in the diaspora. The symbolic nature of Judean attachment to its homeland was a highly rhetorical self-understanding, thanks in part to the unique history of Israel. This included not only its exodus from an alien land, but also, and more importantly, its experience of exile.

The immigrants of the diaspora were able to survive (even thrive) because they had 'expanded and adapted' exilic biblical theology (Kraabel 1987 [1992: 27]). The incursions of foreign powers into Israel—Assyria in 722 BCE and Neo-Babylonia in 597 and again in 587 BCE—had a profound impact on Israel's self-understanding. Here represented a shift from 'nation', ideologically supported by the cultic center of the Temple (as was the case throughout the Mediterranean and Near Eastern worlds), to that of a minority community gathered in synagogue (not the building, which was not yet in existence, but the gathered community). Many never returned from exile, choosing to remain in Babylonia or immigrating to other locations, especially after Alexander the Great's conquests. While many immigrants throughout the Greco-Roman world during the Hellenistic and early Roman imperial times lost touch with the cult of their kinship and homeland,[34] diaspora Judeans were able to maintain the cultic roots of their ethnic identity by means of the synagogue. 'Of all immigrant groups of the Roman Empire, only the Jews were prepared theologically and sociologically for Diaspora existence' (Kraabel 1987 [1992: 29]).[35] What it meant to be Israelite/Judean among the immigrants of the diaspora, especially following

34. According to the traditional narrative, the old civic cults were replaced 'politically' by Hellenistic ruler cults and 'spiritually' by the development of mystery cults as well as the philosophical emphases of Epicureanism, Stoicism and 'Middle' Platonism. See the standard portraits in Gehrke 1990: 185-92; Grant 1953: xi-xxxviii; Martin 1987; Peters: 1970: 446-79; Walbank 1992: 209-26; Koester 1995, 156-96; and more recently Tripolitis 2002. While these trends were significant, they are frequently overstated, as the loss of the old civic cults would have affected mostly immigrants. See Jonathan Z. Smith (1971) on 'native cults' in immigrant (diaspora) communities. See Mikalson (1998) on the persistence of the old cults in Athens during the Hellenistic era. It is also worth noting that ruler cults were *adaptations* that involved the ruler associating himself with an Olympian deity (the Seleucids, Apollo; the Ptolemies, Dionysus; the Macedonians, Heracles), rather than wholesale changes.

35. This also appears to be true for those who, as adults, adopt a Judean ethnic identity: 'when non-Jews adopted Judaism as proselytes they underwent such a thorough resocialization as to acquire in effect a new "ethnicity" in kinship and custom' (Barclay 1996: 408). See Barclay's larger discussion of this important issue in 1996: 402-13. Barclay's study presumes an understanding of 'Jew' and 'Judaism' as 'religious' indicators, the anachronism of which is ironically indicated by his observation, just quoted, that one can aquire multiple ethnic identities. On acquiring multiple ethnic identities see Esler

the banishment of Judeans from Palestine, was not so much focused on the geography of Judea as such, but rather its symbolic importance. This is not to say that diaspora Judeans were oblivious to the destruction of the Temple in 70 CE and the banishment of Judeans from Judea in 135 CE; evidence suggests these events were quite traumatic (Goodman 1992). It is only to say that 'homeland' meant more than the actual physical territory of Judea. As Kraabel trenchantly puts it: 'The common tie was, of course, the Homeland, not necessarily the Palestine of their own times, but the biblical Israel elevated to mythical status' (Kraabel 1987 [1992: 27]).

The second consideration mitigating the interpretation that following 135 CE we should speak of Judaism as a distinctively religious phenomenon is the role and function of the synagogue itself in diaspora communities.[36] For immigrants, what enabled them to 'return home' was cultic and ritual expression. As Max Weber noted, whenever 'emigration from a mother community remains for some reason alive, there undoubtedly exists a very specific and often extremely powerful sense of ethnic identity, which is determined by several factors: shared political memories or, even more importantly in early times, persistent ties with the old cult' (1968: 390). While other immigrants also lacked priesthood and temple of their homeland, thereby unable to offer cultic sacrifices, diaspora Judeans were unique in that they 'retained essential cultic practices—food laws, circumcision, Sabbath observance' (Kraabel 1987 [1992: 26]), as well as the seasonal festivals associated with ancient Israel, including the very ones John Chrysostom criticizes—Rosh Hashanah, Yom Kippur, Sukkoth and Passover. The synagogue as a public institution at once served to integrate diaspora Judeans in their host culture via its architecture (Kraabel 1987 [1992: 26]), yet also preserved the distinctive ethnic identities of its participants through its various communal activities and rituals.

Recent studies have demonstrated that the synagogue in the Second Temple period functioned as an extension of the Temple and homeland (Kraabel 1981 [1992: 265]; Binder 1999; Levine 2000). As Binder has shown, synagogues in Palestine as well as the diaspora 'served as subsidiary sacred precincts that extended spatially the sacrality of the Temple shrine and allowed Jews everywhere participation within the central cult' (1999: 32). The one major function of the Temple that was not a part of synagogue rituals was cultic animal sacrifice. In the synagogues themselves, cultic sacrifice was replaced by an emphasis on Torah reading and study, prayer, and monetary giving for animal sacrifice in Jerusalem (Binder 1999: 391). Following the destruction of the Temple in 70 CE, while the rabbis were busy reinterpret-

2003: 49-50. In Barclay's later work on Josephus, however, he examines 'the construction of ethnicity' and routinely translates Josephus's use of Ἰουδαῖος as 'Judean' (2007).

36. Here I mean the building as a place for gathering.

ing the significance of cultic rituals in light of the destruction of its ritual place (Neusner 1988: 41-65), synagogue leaders and Judeans in the diaspora continued as they had, minus the monetary donation for sacrifice in the Jerusalem Temple.[37]

Apart from the specific rituals associated with synagogues, certain architectural features of synagogues also suggest that they functioned as a means of 'returning home' to the land of Israel. All known synagogues, both in Palestine and in the diaspora, varied from the typical civic orientation archetype of Greco-Roman temples on an east–west axis and were instead oriented toward Jerusalem no matter the direction. This is true even of synagogues constructed *after* 70 CE.[38] Moreover, the Torah shrine on all known synagogues was on the wall nearest Jerusalem.[39] Reading from the scrolls contained in the shrine reminded the people who they were and where they came from.[40] At least one diaspora synagogue took this a step further. In the third-century synagogue at Dura Europos, just above the Torah shrine, were frescoes depicting the Temple mount and Temple façade (Levine 2000: 235-36), structures that by this time, of course, no longer existed. For diaspora Judeans the synagogue was the homeland and its Temple.[41] All of these features suggest that for diaspora Judeans to go to synagogue was to go 'home' again. For Judeans of the diaspora 'symbolic' attachment to the ancestral land was created and maintained through the rituals and the architectural structure of the synagogue.

These two considerations suggest that 'Judaism' post-135 CE was not a strictly 'religious' phenomenon. Judean ethnicity, exemplified by its ritual activity including those that maintained a (symbolic) relationship to the land of Judea, remained critically important in the diaspora. Thus, to suggest that the targets of John Chrysostom's invective were ethnic Judeans means very concretely that this sector of his congregation were descended from immigrants whose roots went back to ancient Israel/Judea. They maintained their

37. While evidence indicates *some* interaction between rabbis and synagogues in these years (see Levine 2000: 440-70), rabbis were not yet the synagogue leaders. Rather there were a variety of lay functionaries, including the *archon*, *gerousiarch*, *geron* and *archisynogogos*. For a discussion of these and other synagogue officials, see Binder 1999: 343-71.

38. See Levine 2000: 182, who says that synagogues were oriented toward Jerusalem, 'owing to their strongly felt religious and ethnic identification with Jerusalem'.

39. Some of these shrines were quite elaborate structures. Particularly impressive were the Torah shrines (*aediculae*) at Sardis and Ostia. See images in Levine 2000: 246, 257.

40. See Wilken's important discussion on the numinous quality of the scrolls (1983: 80-83).

41. Similarly, Kraabel 1987 (1992: 30) notes: 'The Diaspora was not Exile; in some sense it became a Holy Land, too'.

ties to their geographic homeland by means of centuries-old cultic rituals adopted from the homeland, including the Temple and its various institutions and rituals, adapted to suit the needs and restrictions of a diaspora community by means of the synagogue (see Gruen 2002: 105-32).[42] Many of them likely attended synagogue on the Sabbath, something that would have occasioned no conflict with their Eucharistic celebration in church a day later.[43] However, Judean festivals, which operated on a lunar calendar, might indeed occasion conflict. That they would have absented themselves from the weekly Eucharist to celebrate the festivals of the homeland might have given some pause, but it is easy to see how an annual festival tied to the ancient practices of the homeland would take precedence over a weekly celebration. John Chrysostom sought to change their thinking and practices by encouraging them to cut their ties to their Judean ethnic identity and to claim 'Christian' identity. In doing so, he was not only instructing these ἰουδαΐζοντες (judaizers), but also encouraging the non-Judeans of his congregation to understand their own identity in strictly Christian terms.

Adversus Judaeos *in Light of Ethnicity and Religion in the Ancient Mediterranean and Near East*

When read in light of social-scientific studies of ethnicity, as well as the role and function of cultic activity throughout the ancient world and the Judean diaspora in particular, it becomes possible to read John Chrysostom's *Adversus Judaeos* as an attack on Judean ethnic identity, inclusive of, but not limited to, 'religious' practice. If we understand the targets of his invective to be ethnic Judeans (rather than religious Jews) the language he employed becomes more comprehensible; for his attack presumes an understanding of a people (*ethnos*) and their cultic rituals noted above. This is evident by the vocabulary he used, specifically terms associated with household, descent group, kinship, tribe and family, which run throughout this homiletical series.[44] The use of these kinship terms, all associated with a distinctive *ethnos*, suggests that he had in mind something akin to our modern notion of ethnicity. These all have cultic implications but are not limited to religion.

42. The possibility that some ἰουδαΐζοντες (judaizers) were not originally Judean, but aquired this ethnic identity, does not affect the argument. See n. 35 above.

43. See Wilken 1983: 76: 'In their minds, there was no contradiction between going to the synagogue on Saturday to hear the reading of the Law and coming to church on Sunday to participate in the Eucharist'.

44. In *Adversus Judaeos* οἶκος (household) and οἶκος related terms occur over 150 times (οἰκεῖος [one's own property inclusive of people] 39 of these); γένος (descent group) 33 times; συγγένεια (kinship) 12 times; φυλή (tribe) 24 times, almost always in reference to the tribes of Israel. Familial terms: πατήρ 60 times; μήτηρ 14 times; ἀδελφός 67 times.

While Chrysostom sought to discredit Judean ethnicity and its ritual practices, this was not his end goal. Ultimately the purpose was to form an alternative identity—Christian—using kinship terms. Discrediting Judean ethnicity enabled him to construct a Christian identity that demonstrated the favor of Israel's God and applied it, using the same kinship language, to those who accepted and followed God's son and Christ, Jesus.

Discrediting Judean Ethnic Identity

In order to discredit Judean ethnicity, John Chrysostom employed a familiar rhetorical *topos*, the Greek rhetorical invective (*psogos*). No one has done more to place John Chrysostom's rhetoric in these homilies in its proper perspective than Robert Wilken. In his classic study, *John Chrysostom and the Jews*, Wilken demonstrated the need to read these homilies in the context of the basic rhetorical use of the *psogos*, invective against opponents, taught in the schools of rhetoric (1983: 112-16). Among the devices of slander encouraged in such schools was to highlight the opponent's bad upbringing or humble ancestry (sheep farmer, tradesman, criminal, etc.—anything to highlight non-elite background). This was typically peppered with accusations of gluttony, drunkenness, effeminate behavior (all features of *Adversus Judaeos*),[45] excessive laughter or gesticulation, criminal activity and the like. The truth of the accusations was another, rather irrelevant, matter.

One strategy of such invective was to slander the opponent's ancestry and heritage. Such slander was a direct attack on the honor of one's kinship and ethnicity. John Chrysostom employed precisely this component as the basic strategy in the invective against the Judeans; only here the attack was not against an individual, as was customary, but an entire people (*ethnos*). Here Chrysostom claimed that Judeans brought shame on their kinship line. 'Although called into adoption as sons', he says, 'they have fallen to kinship with dogs' (1.2 [845.39-41]). The language is quite strong and appealed to Mediterranean cultural norms regarding honor and shame, about which his listeners would have been keenly sensitive.

The honor status of a family was everything in ancient Mediterranean culture.[46] It was the social currency of the time, and losing it could be devastating to a kinship group. The honor of a kinship group, however, was

45. See, e.g., *Adv. Jud.* 1.2 where the obstinacy of the Judeans in refusing to accept Christ stems from gluttony and drunkenness (ἀδηφαγίας καὶ μέθης [846.25]), and where the Judeans at synagogue festivals are a gathering chorus of effeminates (χοροὺς μαλακῶν συναγαγόντες [846.66]) and a refuse heap of prostitutes (πεπορνευμένων γυναικῶν συρφετὸν [846.66–847.1]). See also Drake 2013: 78-98.

46. See Pitt-Rivers 1965, Gilmore 1987, Malina 2001: 27-57.

relatively stable; kinship groups who had honor had what social and cultural anthropologists call 'ascribed honor'. Apart from finding itself on the wrong side of a shift in political power, very few things could bring ruin to such kinship groups (see Malina 2001: 40-43). One of these things was criminal activity—especially murder and its consequent bloodguilt (μιαιφονία).

Bloodguilt most commonly stemmed from the killing of one's kin, an action that brought incredible shame and devastation to a family. Kin killing was a particularly heinous form of murder in the ancient Mediterranean world, and caused unbelievable suffering that destroyed the fabric of the ancient family. In collectivist societies kin-killing was seen as a form of self-killing.[47] It also brought the stain of pollution (μίασμα), the only remedy for which was exile and purification (Parker 1983). Examples of this abound in ancient literature. The subject was particularly poignant in the hands of Greek tragic playwrights. The stories of Orestes, Oedipus, Heracles, and the descendants of Cadmus are famous for the way in which they illustrate the shame and exile of those guilty of kin killing.[48] The Bible also provides evidence of the devastation and pollution caused by kin killing. In Genesis, the human race is itself threatened by Cain's murder of his brother Abel. When Yahweh ordered his exile (Gen. 4.12), Cain expressed the fear that his polluted status would lead to his own demise abroad:

> My punishment is greater than I can bear! Today you have driven me away from the soil, and I shall be hidden from your face. I shall be a fugitive and a wanderer of the earth and anyone who meets me may kill me (Gen. 4.13, NRSV).[49]

Chrysostom shared this cultural perspective on bloodguilt and judged the status of Judeans accordingly.[50] They were guilty of murdering their own

47. On collectivist societies versus individualist societies see Malina 2010. On kin-killing being a form of self-killing in the ancient world see Parker 1983: 123. Parker shows how Greek words for self-killing (αὐτοφόνος, αὐτοφόντης, αὐτοσφαγής, αὐτοκτόνος) are used by Greek tragedians to refer to kin killing (1983: 351).

48. For Greek tragedies see Aeschylus, *Choephoroe* and *Eumenides*; Sophocles, *Oedipus tyrannus* and *Oedipus coloneus*; Euripides, *Hercules furens* and *Bacchae*.

49. This is but one of several examples. See also 2 Samuel 13–18; 2 Kgs 21.6; 23.26-27. John Chrysostom refers to Cain's murder (φόνος) of Abel at *Adv. Jud.* 8.2 [930.1-25]). He claims God declared to Cain: αὐτὸ τὸ πρᾶγμα κηρύττει τὸν μιαιφόνον, 'the very act proclaims your bloodguilt' (930.23-4).

50. John Chrysostom would have been well aware not only of the biblical examples but also the examples from classical Greek literature from his own encyclical and rhetorical education, not to mention their performance at the theater in Antioch. See Coleman-Norton 1932. There are numerous references to tragic plays in Chrysostom's homilies. For these references, as well as Chrysostom's use of the theater and its perceived wickedness as a rhetorical device, see Leyerle 2001 (esp. 13-74).

children and prophets. Chrysostom articulated the issue in the explicit terms of kinship and bloodguilt:

> What kind of tragedy, which direction of lawlessness, is not concealed by their bloodguilt (μιαιφονίαις)? They offered their sons and daughters as sacrifices to demons. They failed to perceive the order of nature, forgot the pangs of birth, trampled under foot the rearing of children (παιδοτροφίαν κατεπάτησαν), and overturned from their foundations the laws of kinship (τῆς συγγενείας τοὺς νόμους) (1.6 [852.59-65]).

While killing the 'sons and daughters of Israel', most especially the prophets, was reprehensible, the killing of Jesus—'the son of your Lord'[51]—was particularly shameful.

> Since you killed the Christ, since you stretched out your hands, and since you spilled his honored blood, you have no righteousness, no forgiveness, and no defense. In days past, those reckless deeds were against God's servants Moses, Isaiah and Jeremiah. Even if your impiety was then evident, the extreme recklessness crowning your evil was yet to come. But now you have made all these past crimes seem trivial. You have reserved for yourself a transgression beyond all others because of your madness against Christ. . . . It is clear that you surpassed all your child-murders (παιδοκτονίας) and transgressions when you dared the far greater crime of killing Christ (6.2 [907.4-13, 17-19]).

Because John Chrysostom, like his fellow Nicene Christians, understood Jesus to be the incarnate son of God, adoption into God's 'family' now depended on acceptance of him.[52] His murder brought irreversible shame to the Judean people as a whole. As is fitting for those who have committed bloodguilt, they have been duly exiled for their crime (5.1 [884.21-4]).

Israel had interpreted its own exile of 586 BCE as punishment for its crimes, especially the crime of shedding blood. Examples from the biblical prophets abound.[53] The Deuteronomistic Historian even gave as a specific reason for the Babylonian exile the bloodguilt of the seventh-century BCE Judean king, Manasseh (2 Kgs 21.6, 16; 24.3-4).[54] His blood crimes were regarded as so heinous that not even the good reign of Josiah (2 Kgs 23.25)

51. 1.7 (854.14): Τοῦ Δεσπότου σου τὸν Υἱὸν ἀνεῖλον.

52. The relationship of the homiletical series *Adversus Judaeos* to the series against the Anomoeans (*De incomprehensibili Dei natura homilae*), which John interrupted to preach *Adversus Judaeos* 1, is worthy of further investigation in this connection.

53. A non-comprehensive list includes Isa. 5.7, 13; 26.20-21; 59.3; Jer. 2.34; 7.6 [repeated at 22.3]; 19.4; 22.17; 26.15; Lam. 4.13-15; Ezek. 7.23; 9.9; 12.1-6; 16.22, 36, 38; 18.10-13; 22.2-4, 6, 9, 11-16, 23-31; 23.36, 39, 45; 35.6; Mic. 3.10; 7.2; Nah. 3.1.

54. 2 Kgs 21.6 ('He made his son pass through fire' [NRSV]) is widely regarded to be a reference to Manasseh sacrificing his son. King Ahaz is said to have done the same (2 Kgs 16.3).

could reverse the stain of pollution brought on by Manasseh (2 Kgs 23.26-27). The exile itself was interpreted as purification for past sins.[55]

In spite of the fact that they had endured exile before, Chrysostom argued this one was permanent. This was indicated both by the prophecy of Christ and the length of time the exile had lasted. Christ's prediction was that, once destroyed, the Temple and Jerusalem were forever off-limits (*Adv. Jud.* 5.1 [884.2-17]). While their forefathers knew they would return to their land, Judeans now had 'no such hope of recovering their former citizenship (πολιτείαν)' (*Adv. Jud.* 4.4 [877.54-6]). Chrysostom thought history proved this. If it had been only a few years, or even decades, there might have been hope. But 'three centuries and more have passed since the capture of your land, and there has been no trace, not even a shadow has appeared, of the change you are expecting' (5.3 [888.59-62]).[56]

Because their exile was permanent, Chrysostom believed the Judeans were in a permanent state of pollution, no longer possessing the ritual means to purify themselves of their crimes. Here he relied on ancient cultic notions that religious ritual was a matter of time and place. Denying the legitimacy of diaspora existence, Chrysostom claimed that permanent exile prohibits the activity that would allow protection from God because God's law specifically prohibits the necessary ritual activity outside Jerusalem. Their Israelite ancestors exiled by Babylon following the destruction of the first Temple knew this well enough, and 'never sacrificed, nor sang hymns in an alien land' (*Adv. Jud.* 4.4 [877.48-9]). Without the Temple in Jerusalem, Chrysostom regarded the Judean festivals as null and void: 'In the matter of the Judean festivals, the Law exhorts observance not only of the time, but also of the place' (*Adv. Jud.* 4.4 [876.47-9]). And of the two, place is the most important (*Adv. Jud.* 4.4 [876.56–877.46]). Judeans of the synagogue might be able to keep the proper time, but not the more critical matter of place.[57]

It should not be lost on us that Chrysostom was declaring invalid the festival that purified Israel of its (annual) transgressions, including its bloodguilt—Yom Kippur, the Day of Atonement. This festival called for fasting, sacrifices and the ritual of the 'scapegoat', who bore deserved exile for

55. Again, purification of those exiled for bloodguilt is a theme common in ancient literature. See Aeschylus *Eumenides* and Euripides *Hercules furens*. For biblical references, see Isa. 4.3-4; Jer. 33.8; Ezek. 16.9; 22.15; 24.3-13; 36.25, 33.

56. Chrysostom was being disingenuous here. Only twenty-five years prior, in 362, the emperor Julian issued orders that the temple in Jerusalem be rebuilt, re-establishing the sacrificial cult there; the project was a failure, however. See Ammianus Marcellinus, *Res gestae* 23.1.2-3.

57. For a discussion of Chrysostom's distinctive emphasis on place in these homilies see Shepardson 2007. See also her recent book on place in Antioch (2014).

crimes of pollution (Lev. 16.6-10; see Smith 1987).[58] These rituals required priests, animal sacrifices and the Temple in Jerusalem, which Judeans no longer possessed. In *Adversus Judaeos* 6, preached on Yom Kippur in the year 387, Chrysostom mocked their lack of priests.

> Where is your high priest? Where is his robe, speaking platform, and sacred implements? Do not tell me about these patriarchs, who are shysters and merchant traders, filled with all transgressions. Tell me, what kind of priest is one who is not anointed according to that ancient custom, nor any other ritual? What kind of a priest does not sacrifice, nor has an altar, nor renders service? If you wish I will speak about the laws of the priesthood, how the ancient customs came into being in order that you might learn that those now called patriarchs are not priests at all. Rather, they act like priests and prepare for their role, but they cannot answer the call because in their response they are far removed from the truth (*Adv. Jud.* 6.5 [911.13-27]).

For Chrysostom, without the necessary priesthood and the cultic apparatus of the Jerusalem Temple, there was no atonement with God for Judeans. Simply put, the Ἰουδαῖοι were a shameful and disinherited ethnicity, and the Ἰουδαϊσμός of the synagogue was illegal because it was out of place.

For the ἰουδαΐζοντες, hanging on to a disinherited ethnic identity while claiming to be a follower of Christ was not only a contradiction, it called into question the purification of baptism and brought the stain of pollution (μιαρός, μίασμα) by association with those guilty of kin killing. 'Tell me, how can you bear to gather with men so possessed of unclean spirits, reared in such slaughter and murder? Do you not shudder?' (1.6 [852.51-4]). A few lines later, he continued:

> If a man killed your son, tell me, could you bear to look at him, or accept his greeting? Would you not flee from him as from an evil demon, as from the devil himself? They killed the son of your Lord, and you recklessly go into the same place with them? The one who was killed honored you by making you his own brother and co-heir; but you dishonor him by honoring those murderers and crucifiers (φονέας καὶ σταυρώσαντας), and by worshiping with them at their festivals (*Adv. Jud.* 1.7 [854.10-19]).[59]

58. The notion of a 'scapegoat' who bears the 'sins of the people' has received much attention in scholarly circles, most notably from Girard 1977. Jonathan Z. Smith 1987 argues persuasively, however, that the goat of Leviticus 16 carries off not sin but pollution. See also Janovitz 2011.

59. The problem of sharing a roof with someone guilty of kin killing is also well illustrated in ancient literature. See, e.g., Homer, *Il.* 24.479-505; Sophocles, *Oed. col.* 220-57; Euripides, *Andr.* 655-59; Gen. 4.12-13; 2 Sam. 4.24-33.

If ethnic Ἰουδαῖοι wanted to restore their honor, Chrysostom argued, they needed to abandon their ethnicity and adopt a new identity, one that acquired honor by means of God's son.

Christian Identity

John Chrysostom made use of kinship terms to identify what it means to be Christian. This was hardly a new strategy. Chrysostom inherited a tradition dating back to Jesus, where familial language helped describe the relationships within the early Jesus movement.[60] This language continued under Paul and later 'apostolic fathers', language particularly provocative given the household (*oikos*) context of the early church. These kinship identifiers were used frequently to contrast with Judean and Greek ethnicity in order to establish an alternative identity (Gal. 3.28-29).[61] Chrysostom drew on this tradition as a strategy to encourage the ἰουδαΐζοντες of his congregation to abandon their Judean ethnicity, but also to persuade his non-Judean members to redefine theirs.[62]

> They were the branches of the holy root, but they were broken off. We had no share in the root, but we bore the fruit of reverence. They knew the prophets from the beginning, but they crucified the one about whom the prophets foretold. We did not hear the divine pronouncements, but we did worship the one about whom they prophesied (1.2 [845.31-7]).

The 'they' (ἐκεῖνοι) of the passage refers to Ἰουδαῖοι (ethnic Judeans). The 'we' (ἡμεῖς) refers to 'gentiles' (i.e. those ethnically Greek who [previously] worshiped Greek deities).[63] This is supported both by the context and the

60. The scholarly literature is abundant. See, e.g., Moxnes 2003 (esp. 59-64).

61. This has been called 'ethnic reasoning' (Buell 2005). Unfortunately, this clever term is couched in a study that continues to use 'race' in spite of the call of social scientists to abandon this term. Buell rightly claims that both race and ethnicity are 'modern' categories; however, this is the only thing they have in common. See the above discussion on these terms (pp. 65-67) as classifications. In addition I would note that the two terms do not have the same heuristic value. The Greek noun γένος refers not to a 'race' but to a sociological 'descent group', even if fictively constructed. To translate and understand this term as 'race', understood however fictively, ignores the simple fact that 'race', with its modern abusive connotations of skin color and other distinctive physical and mental characteristics, carries far more negative baggage than does 'ethnicity'.

62. Isabella Sandwell has raised the important point that nearly all of Chrysostom's writings and homilies were attempts to construct Christian identity (2007: 11-20).

63. Chrysostom's congregation was likely made up primarily of ethnic Greeks, along with Syrians and Judeans. Jonathan Hall has argued that Greek ethnicity as such did not persist past the classical era and that 'Greek' was 'conceived more in cultural terms' by the fourth century BCE (Hall 1997: xiii). But as Philip Esler has pointed out, Hall lapses into 'primordialism' here, neglecting that there were people living through-

allusion to Paul.[64] It also fits the logic of Chrysostom's argument. A few lines later he adds:

> They who were called into adoption as sons, fell to kinship with dogs. We who were dogs, prevailed through the grace of God, put away our former irrationality, and were raised to the honor of sons (1.2 [845.39-43]).

This kinship reversal made it possible for other ethnicities to become part of God's 'kinship line' via his son, Jesus. But it also called for 'putting away' (ἀποτίθημι) indicators of Greek ethnicity, including the worship of Greek gods.

Chrysostom's end game was not simply to discredit Judean ethnicity. Indeed it was to discredit all ethnicity in favor of constructing a Christian identity using traditional terms associated with kinship and ethnicity. True, the overwhelming majority of his remarks were focused on discrediting Judean ethnicity. But the not-so-subtle message to his non-Judean audience members was that they needed to understand their own kinship relations differently. In his most pointed remarks to non-Judeans, Chrysostom spoke:

> Just as we call them [i.e. ἰουδαΐζοντες] out for transgressing the law, so also many of you for allowing their transgression; not only those who run off [to the synagogue] but also those of you who have the power to prevent them from running off but are not willing to stop them. Do not say to me: 'What do I have in common with him? He is a stranger (ἀλλότριος) and I do not know him'. If he is a believer and participates with you in the mysteries and comes into the same church, he is more properly of your household than all your brothers and kinsmen (καὶ ἀδελφῶν καὶ συγγενῶν καὶ ἐπιτηδείων καὶ πάντων ἐστὶν οἰκειότερος) (4.7 [882.4-12]).

The word ἀλλότριος, translated as 'stranger', connotes not so much someone personally unrecognizable, but rather a foreigner whose ways and customs are unknown, and who might be, potentially, an enemy (Liddell and Scott 1968: 70-71). For Chrysostom, an ethnic Judean who professes Christ and who also attends synagogue festivals might be in error, but he is certainly not a stranger, foreigner or enemy. He or she is 'kin', and non-Judeans should do everything in their power to recover their 'brother' or 'sister'.[65]

out the Mediterranean world who called themselves Greeks, spoke Greek, were educated in Greek literature and rhetoric, worshiped Greek gods, attended Greek *gymnasia* and theaters, and were engaged in ethnic conflict with non-Greeks in their various cities. 'The self-ascriptive and boundary-maintaining nature of ethnicity demands . . . that we regard such people as indeed possessing Greek ethnicity, whatever other ethnic identities they might claim' (2003: 57).

64. See *Adv. Jud.* 1.2 (845.46-47) and Rom. 11.17. Not only does Chrysostom follow Paul's 'root and branches' metaphor, he also follows him in the use of the term ἔθνη.

65. Chrysostom suggests at 2.3 (860-61) that women especially were frequenting the synagogue for festivals.

In a particularly poignant analogy, Chrysostom acknowledged that with the Judean festivals near an end, non-Judeans needed to be on the lookout to help their Judean brothers and sisters who have 'fallen in battle'.

> Let us not put aside forethought for our brothers, and neither let us fail to be caring even though it is not as timely as before. Notice what soldiers do whenever they return from a battle victorious. Returning from the route, they do not immediately run back to their tents, but first go back to the place of battle and lift up those in their ranks who have fallen, and bury those who have died. But if they should see among the dead bodies those still breathing, they give those not mortally stricken as much aid as possible, then lifting them up, they carry them back into camp. Then they pull out the arrow, summon the physicians, wash away the blood, apply medicine, and rendering all care, they bring them back to health (8.1 [928.25-40]).

The image is rich given that one fights on the same side in battles not with strangers or enemies, but with one's friends, if not kinsmen.[66]

This kinship construction of ethnically diverse peoples is designed so that Chrysostom's listeners see their identity in a new way. They have a 'common mother' (the church) and a common father (God).[67] They share brother and sisterhood through Christ, who has enabled their adoption into this 'family' (1.2 [845.39-43]; 1.7 [854.16-17]). Judean ethnicity must be abandoned because of its unique bloodguilt with respect to Jesus. But so also must non-Judean ethnicity (be it Greek, Syrian or whatever) be abandoned in favor of a Christian identity. Prior to acceptance of Jesus as God's son, non-Judeans were 'dogs' (1.2 [845.39-43]).[68] What mattered now was not one's birth ethnicity, but an identity acquired through adoption into God's family via God's very own son. For Christ 'has made you his own brother and co-heir (ἀδελφόν σε ποιῆσαι καὶ συγκληρονόμον αὐτοῦ)' (1.7 [854.16-17]). All who claimed the mantle of Christ, be they ethnic Judeans or Greeks, can and should transcend these shamed and dishonored ethnicities to adopt a more honored identity where brothers and sisters of a common mother (the church) and father (God) are established as God's children and heirs to God's inheritance.

66. Chrysostom's concern for 'recovery' of Judean 'brothers' runs throughout *Adv. Jud.* See, e.g., 1.8 (856.5-29); 4.7 (881.12-36); 8.2 (929.3-20).

67. Addressing his non-Judean listeners about their lost Judean 'brothers', Chrysostom says 'Our common mother has not lost a cloak, but our brother' (Ἡ μήτηρ ἡμῶν ἡ κοινὴ οὐ ἱμάτιον, ἀλλ' ἀδελφὸν ἀπώλεσεν) (1.8 [856.29-31]).

68. I have argued elsewhere (Black 2005) that Chrysostom railed against much of what passed for Greek cultural identity in late antiquity, especially Greek *paideia*. See especially Black 2005: 19-94. I now see this in terms of a larger program of Chrysostom's to establish a distinctive Christian identity, apart from birth or other aquired ethnicities.

References

Applebaum, S.

1974 'The Legal Status of the Jewish Communities in the Diaspora', in *The Jewish People in the First Century: Historical, Geographical, Political History, Social, Cultural and Religious Life and Institutions* (ed. S. Safrai, M. Stern, D. Flusser *et al.;* Assen: van Gorcum): 420-63.

Assmann, Jan

2001 *The Search for God in Ancient Egypt* (trans. David Lorton; Ithaca, NY: Cornell University Press).

Barclay, John M.G.

1996 *Jews in the Mediterranean Diaspora: From Alexander to Trajan (323 BCE–117 CE)* (Edinburgh: T. & T. Clark).

2007 *Flavius Josephus: Against Apion* (ed. Steve Mason; Flavius Josephus Translation and Commentary, 3; Leiden: Brill).

Barth, Fredrik (ed.)

1969 *Ethnic Group Boundaries: The Social Organization of Culture Difference* (Boston: Little, Brown).

Beard, Mary, John North and Simon Price

1998 *Religions of Rome* (2 vols.; Cambridge: Cambridge University Press).

Becker, Adam H., and Annette Yoshiko Reed (eds.)

2003 *The Ways That Never Parted: Jews and Christians in Late Antiquity and the Early Middle Ages* (Tübingen: Mohr Siebeck).

Beckman, Gary

2005 'How Religion Was Done', in *A Companion to the Ancient Near East* (ed. Daniel C. Snell; Oxford: Blackwell): 343-53.

Bilde, Per (ed.)

1992 *Ethnicity in Hellenistic Egypt* (Aarhus: Aarhus University Press).

Binder, Donald D.

1999 *Into the Temple Courts: The Place of the Synagogues in the Second Temple Period* (SBLDS, 169; Atlanta, GA: Society of Biblical Literature).

Black, Stephen K.

2005 Paideia, *Power and Episcopacy: John Chrysostom and the Formation of the Late Antique Bishop* (PhD diss., Graduate Theological Union, Berkeley, CA).

Blowers, Stanley

2011 'The Concept of "Community" and the History of Early Christianity', *Method and Theory in the Study of Religion* 23: 238-56.

Bowersock, Glen W.

1990 *Hellenism in Late Antiquity* (Ann Arbor, MI: University of Michigan Press).

Boyarin, Daniel

1999 *Dying for God: Martyrdom and the Making of Christianity and Judaism* (Stanford, CA: Stanford University Press).

2003 'Semantic Differences; or "Judaism"/"Christianity"', in Becker and Reed 2003: 65-85.

2004 *Boarder Lines: The Partition of Judaeo-Christianity* (Philadelphia, PA: University of Pennsylvania Press).

Bremmer, Jan N.

1994 *Greek Religion* (Oxford: Oxford University Press).

Bruit Zaidman, Louise, and Pauline Schmitt Patel

1992 *Religion in the Ancient Greek City* (trans. Paul Cartledge; Cambridge: Cambridge University Press).

Buell, Denise Kiber

2005 *Why This New Race: Ethnic Reasoning in Early Christianity* (New York: Columbia University Press).

Černy, Jaroslav

1979 *Ancient Egyptian Religion* (Westport, CT: Greenwood Press).

Cohen, Shaye

1999 *The Beginnings of Jewishness: Boundaries, Varieties, Uncertainties* (Berkeley, CA: University of California Press).

Coleman-Norton, P.R.

1932 'St Chrysostom's Use of the Greek Poets', *Classical Philology* 27: 213-21.

Downey, Glanville

1961 *A History of Antioch in Syria: From Seleucus to the Arab Conquest* (Princeton, NJ: Princeton University Press).

Drake, Susanna

2013 *Slandering the Jew: Sexuality and Difference in Early Christian Texts* (Divinations: Rereading Late Ancient Religion; Philadelphia, PA: University of Pennsylvania Press).

Duling, Dennis

2003 '"Whatever gain I had . . .": Ethnicity and Paul's Self-Identification in Phil 3.5-6', in *Fabrics of Discourse: Essays in Honor of Vernon K. Robbins* (ed. D.B Gowler, G. Bloomquist and D.F. Watson; Harrisburg, PA: Trinity Press International): 222-41.

Dunn, James D.G.

1991 *The Parting of the Ways: Between Christianity and Judaism and their Significance for the Character of Christianity* (London: SCM Press).

Elliott, John H.

1990 *A Home for the Homeless: A Social-Scientific Criticism of I Peter, its Situation and Strategy* (Philadelphia, PA: Augsburg Fortress, repr. of 1981 edn with new introduction).

2007 'Jesus the Israelite Was neither a "Jew", nor a "Christian": On Correcting Misleading Nomenclature', *JSHJ* 5.2: 119-54.

Eriksen, Thomas Hylland

2010 *Ethnicity and Nationalism: Anthropological Perspectives* (London: Pluto Press, 3rd edn).

Esler, Philip

1998 *Galatians* (London: Routledge).

2003 *Conflict and Identity in Romans: The Social Setting of Paul's Letter* (Minneapolis, MN: Fortress Press).

2007 'From *Ioudaioi* to Children of God: The Development of a *Non-Ethnic* Group *Identity* in the Gospel of John', in *In Other Words: Essays on Social Science Methods and the New Testament in Honor of Jerome H. Neyrey* (ed. Anselm C. Hagedorn, Zeba A. Crook and Eric Stewart; Sheffield: Sheffield Phoenix Press): 106-37.

2009 'Judean Ethnic Identity in Josephus' *Against Apion*', in *A Wandering Galilean: Essays in Honour of Seán Freyne* (ed. Zuleika Rodgers *et al.*; Leiden: Brill): 73-91.

Frankfurter, David

1998 *Religion in Roman Egypt: Assimilation and Resistance* (Princeton, NJ: Princeton University Press).

2003 'Beyond "Jewish Christianity": Continuing Religious Sub-cultures of the Second and Third Centuries and their Documents', in Becker and Reed 2003: 131-44.

Gehrke, Hans Joachim

1990 *Geschichte das Hellenismus* (Munich: Oldenbourg).

Gottwald, Norman K.

1979 *The Tribes of Yahweh: A Sociology of the Religion of Liberated Israel, 1250–1050* B.C.E. (Maryknoll, NY: Orbis Books).

Gilmore, David (ed.)

1987 *Honor and Shame and the Unity of the Mediterranean* (Washington, D.C.: American Anthropological Association).

Girard, René

1977 *Violence and the Sacred* (trans. P. Gregory; Baltimore, MD: Johns Hopkins University Press).

Goodman, Martin

1992 'Diaspora Reactions to the Destruction of the Temple', in *Jews and Christians: The Parting of the Ways A.D. 70–135* (ed. James Dunn; Tübingen: Mohr Siebeck): 27-38.

Grant, Federick (ed.)

1953 *Hellenistic Religions: The Age of Syncretism* (New York: Liberal Arts).

Gruen, Erich

2002 *Diaspora: Jews amidst Greeks and Romans* (Cambridge, MA: Harvard University Press).

Hall, Jonathan M.

1997 *Ethnic Identity in Greek Antiquity* (Cambridge: Cambridge University Press).

2002 *Hellenicity: Between Ethnicity and Culture* (Chicago: University of Chicago Press).

Harkins, Paul (trans.)

1979 *Saint John Chrysostom: Discourses against Judaizing Christians* (FOC, 68; Washington, DC: Catholic University of America Press).

Hendrick, Charles W., Jr

2010 'Religion and Society in Classical Greece', in *A Companion to Greek Religion* (ed. Daniel Ogden; Oxford: Wiley-Blackwell): 283-96.

Hutchinson, John, and Anthony D. Smith (eds.)

1996 *Ethnicity* (Oxford: Oxford University Press).

Isaac, Benjamin

2004 *The Invention of Racism in Classical Antiquity* (Princeton, NJ: Princeton University Press).

Jackson-McCabe, Matt (ed.)

2007 *Jewish Christianity Reconsidered: Rethinking Ancient Groups and Texts* (Minneapolis, MN: Fortress Press).

Janovitz, Naomi

2011 'Inventing the Scapegoat: Theories of Sacrifice and Ritual', *Journal of Ritual Studies* 25: 15-24.

Kindt, Julia

2012 *Rethinking Greek Religion* (Cambridge: Cambridge University Press).

Klauck, Hans-Josef

1989 *4. Makkabäerbuch* (ed. Hermann Lichtenberger; Jüdische Schriften aus hellenistisch-römischer Zeit 3/6; Gütersloh: Gütersloher Verlagshaus).

Koester, Helmut

1995 *Introduction to the New Testament*, vol. 1: *History, Culture, and Religion of the Hellenistic Age* (New York: de Gruyter, 2nd edn).

Kraabel, A. Thomas

1981 'Social Systems of Six Diaspora Synagogues', in *Ancient Synagogues: The State of Research* (ed. Joseph Gutmann; Chico, CA: Scholars Press): 103-21 (reprinted in Overman and MacLennan 1992: 257-67).

1982 'The Roman Diaspora: Six Questionable Assumptions', *Journal of Jewish Studies* 33: 445-64 (reprinted in Overman and MacLennan 1992: 1-20).

1987 'Unity and Diversity among Diaspora Synagogues', in *The Synagogue in Late Antiquity* (ed. Lee I. Levine; Philadelphia, PA: ASOR): 49-60 (reprinted in Overman and MacLennan 1992: 21-33).

Kraeling, Carl H.

1932 'The Jewish Community at Antioch', *JBL* 51.2: 130-60.

Levine, Amy-Jill

2006 *The Misunderstood Jew: The Church and the Scandal of the Jewish Jesus* (San Francisco, CA: Harper).

Levine, Lee I.

2000 *The Ancient Synagogue: The First Thousand Years* (New Haven, CT: Yale University Press).

Leyerle, Blake

2001 *Theatrical Shows and Ascetic Lives: John Chrysostom's Attack on Spiritual Marriage* (Berkeley, CA: University of California Press).

Liddell, Henry George, and Robert Scott

1968 *A Greek–English Lexicon* (Oxford: Clarendon Press, rev. edn).

Limet, Henri

2005 'Ethnicity', in *A Companion to the Ancient Near East* (ed. Daniel C. Snell; Oxford: Blackwell).

Malina, Bruce

2000 'Three Theses for a More Adequate Reading of the New Testament', in *Practical Theology: Perspectives from the Plains* (ed. Michael Lawler and Gail S. Risch; Omaha, NE: Creighton University Press): 33-60.

2001 *The New Testament World: Insights from Cultural Anthropology* (Louisville, KY: Westminster John Knox Press; 3rd edn).

2010 'Collectivism in Mediterranean Culture', in *Understanding the Social World of the New Testament* (ed. Dietmar Neufeld and Richard E. DeMaris; London: Routledge).

Malkin, Irad (ed.)

2001 *Ancient Perceptions of Greek Ethnicity* (Cambridge, MA: Harvard University Press).

Martin, Luther H.

1987 *Hellenistic Religions: An Introduction* (Oxford: Oxford University Press).

Mayer, Wendy

2005 *The Homilies of St John Chrysostom: Provenance, Reshaping the Foundations* (Orientalia christiana analecta, 273; Rome: Pontificium Institutum Orientalium Studiorum).

Mayer, Wendy, and Pauline Allen

2012 *The Churches of Syrian Antioch (300–638 CE)* (Late Antique History and Religion, 5; Leuven: Peeters).

Meeks, Wayne A., and Robert L. Wilken

1978 *Jews and Christians in Antioch in the First Four Centuries of the Common Era* (SBL Sources for Biblical Study, 13; Missoula, MT: Scholars Press).

Mikalson, Jon D.

1998 *Religion in Hellenistic Athens* (Berkeley, CA: University of California Press)

2010 *Ancient Greek Religion* (Oxford: Wiley-Blackwell, 2nd edn)

Moxnes, Halvor

2003 *Putting Jesus in his Place: A Radical Vision of Household and Kingdom* (Louisville, KY: Westminster John Knox Press).

Nagle, D. Brendon

2006 *The Household as the Foundation of Aristotle's* Polis (Cambridge: Cambridge University Press).

Neusner, Jacob

1988 *From Testament to Torah: An Introduction to Judaism in its Formative Age* (Englewood Cliffs, NJ: Prentice-Hall).

Norman, A.F. (ed. and trans.)

1992 *Libanius Autobiography and Letters,* vol. 2 (LCL; Cambridge, MA: Harvard University Press).

Overman, J. Andrew, and Robert S. MacLennan

1992 *Diaspora Jews and Judaism: Essays in Honor of, and in Dialogue with, A. Thomas Kraabel* (South Florida Studies in the History of Judaism, 41; Atlanta, GA: Scholars Press).

Parker, Robert

1983 *Miasma: Pollution and Purification in Early Greek Religion* (Oxford: Clarendon Press).

Pitt-Rivers, Julian

1965 'Honour and Social Status', in *Honour and Shame: The Values of Mediterranean Society* (ed. J.G. Peristiany; London: Weidenfeld & Nicolson): 19-77.

Peters, F.E.

1970 *The Harvest of Hellenism: A History of the Near East from Alexander the Great to the Triumph of Christianity* (New York: Touchstone).

Pilch, John

1997 'Are There Jews and Christians in the Bible?' *HTS* 53: 119-25.

Pradels, Wendy, Rudolf Brändle and Martin Heimgartner

2001 'Das bisher vermisste Textstück in Johannes Chrysostomus, *Adversus Iudaeos*, Oratio 2', *Zeitschrift für antikes Christentum* 5.1: 23-49.

2002 'The Sequence and Dating of the Series of John Chrysostom's Eight Discourses *Adversus Iudaeos*', *Zeitschrift für antikes Christentum* 6: 90-116.

Rives, James B.
2007 *Religion in the Roman Empire* (Oxford: Blackwell).
Rüpke, Jörg
2007 *Religion of the Romans* (trans. Richard Gordon; Cambridge: Polity Press).
Sandwell, Isabella
2007 *Religious Identity in Late Antiquity: Greeks, Jews, and Christians in Antioch* (Cambridge: Cambridge University Press).
Savage, David W. (ed.)
1971 *The Imprint of Roman Institutions* (New York: Holt, Rinehardt & Winston).
Schatkin, Margaret
1974 'The Maccabean Martyrs', *Vigiliae christianae* 28: 97-113.
Scheid, John
2003 *An Introduction to Roman Religion* (trans. Janet Lloyd; Bloomington, IN: Indiana University Press).
Schwartz, Daniel R.
2007 '"Judean" or "Jew"? How Should We Translate *Ioudaios* in Josephus', in *Jewish Identity in the Greco-Roman World* (ed. J. Frey, D. Schwartz and D. Gripentrog; Leiden: Brill): 3-27.
Segal, Alan F.
1986 *Rebecca's Children: Judaism and Christianity in the Roman World* (Cambridge, MA: Harvard University Press).
Shepardson, Christine
2007 'Controlling Contested Places: John Chrysostom's *Adversus Iudaeos* Homilies and the Spatial Politics of Religious Controversy', *Journal of Early Christian Studies* 15.4: 483-516.
2014 *Controlling Contested Places: Late Antique Antioch and the Spatial Politics of Religious Controversy* (Berkeley, CA: University of California Press).
Smith, Anthony D.
1986 *The Ethnic Origins of Nations* (Oxford: Basil Blackwell).
Smith, Jonathan Z.
1971 'Native Cults in the Hellenistic Period', *History of Religions* 11: 236-49.
1987 'The Domestication of Sacrifice', in *Violent Origins: Walter Burkert, René Girard, and Jonathan Z. Smith on Ritual Killing and Cultural Formation* (ed. R.G. Hamerton-Kelly; Stanford, CA: Stanford University Press): 191-235.
1990 *Drudgery Divine: On the Comparison of Early Christianities and the Religions of Late Antiquity* (Chicago: University of Chicago Press).
Smith, Wilfred Cantwell
1962 *The Meaning and End of Religion* (Minneapolis, MN: Fortress Press; repr., 1991).
Snell, Daniel C.
2011 *Religions of the Ancient Near East* (Cambridge: Cambridge University Press).
Sourvinou-Inwood, Christiane
2000a 'What Is *Polis* Religion?', in *Oxford Readings in Greek Religion* (ed. Richard Buxton; Oxford: Oxford University Press): 13-37.
2000b 'Further Aspects of *Polis* Religion?', in *Oxford Readings in Greek Religion* (ed. Richard Buxton; Oxford: Oxford University Press): 38-55.

Taylor, Joan E.
1990 'The Phenomenon of Early Jewish Christianity: Reality or Scholarly Invention?', *Vigiliae christianae* 44: 313-34.
Tripolitis, Antonía
2002 *Religions of the Hellenistic-Roman Age* (Grand Rapids, MI: Eerdmans).
Van de Mieroop, Marc
1997 *The Ancient Mesopotamian City* (Oxford: Clarendon Press).
Walbank, F.W.
1992 *The Hellenistic World* (Cambridge, MA: Harvard University Press; rev. edn).
Warner, W. Lloyd, and Paul S. Lunt
1942 *The Status System of a Modern Community* (Yankee City Series, 2; New Haven, CT: Yale University Press).
Weber, Max
1968 *Economy and Society* (trans. G. Roth and C. Wittich; 2 vols.; Berkeley, CA: University of California Press).
Wilken, Robert L.
1983 *John Chrysostom and the Jews* (Transformation of the Classical Heritage, 3; Berkeley, CA: University of California Press).
Wiseman, Timothy P.
1995 'The God of the Lupercal', *Journal of Roman Studies* 85: 1-22.
Zetterholm, Magnus
2003 *The Formation of Christianity in Antioch: A Social-Scientific Approach to the Separation between Judaism and Christianity* (London: Routledge).

Manufacturing Memory and Community: Luke 7.36-50 as a Test Case

Zeba A. Crook

> Storytelling about the past is thus not merely something communities do; it is, in important ways, what they are (Olick 2006: 6).

When I first saw John H. Elliott, as he was known to me then, he was sitting behind a huge cello. His hands moved fluidly in competing directions: the one moved laterally, drawing the bow slowly across the strings, the other vertically, eliciting precise notes with a duration that spoke of sorrow. I needed to know how it all worked, how he knew where to place his thick fingers on a board without frets, but I was new, and he was John H. Elliott. So I sat and listened. Perhaps it was because he was done, or because he noticed my attention, but he called me over, introduced himself as Jack, and talked to me about how he was playing. What followed was an illustration of why I could never be a cello player, and why I would always feel welcome by Jack in the Context Group.

Jack Elliott epitomizes *communitas* in every sense of the word. He is a fierce defender and tireless supporter of the work of the academic community he helped to found, namely the Context Group, and he has devoted a good deal of his intellectual energies to gaining a better understanding of the communities that early Christians founded. In his widely read and critically received 1981 book, *A Home for the Homeless*, Elliott argued that 1 Peter's use of the term πάροικος is best understood not as serving a metaphorical function, referring to and giving hope to Christians who felt alien in this world, and promising them a better life in the world to come. Rather, Elliott argued that the term referred to the concrete social, political and geographical experiences of homelessness that members brought with them into the community: these people were without social status—artisans, freedmen, slaves, rural dwellers, and so on—and they came together in the Jesus movement. First Peter was written therefore to exhort them toward solidarity with one another, as members of a new, enduring household, a home for those without a home.

In this paper, I would like to explore how memory theory, a relatively recent addition to the study of Christian origins, can supplement Elliott's interest in community and identity formation, and to recommend Luke's story of the woman who anointed Jesus' feet (Lk. 7.36-50) as a scribal location where community formation and memory intersect.

Memory in New Testament Studies

Two characteristics have emerged from much of the work being done by those who use memory theory to study earliest Christianity. The first is a primary focus on the historical Jesus, and how material about Jesus might have come to its present form in the canonical Gospels (Allison 2010; Le Donne 2011; Dunn 2003a, 2008; Keener 2009). This interest in memory is largely concerned with how eyewitnesses remember, and then how they transmit their memories to others down a chain. The second and related characteristic is an assumption about the primary reliability of human memory (Le Donne 2011; Dunn 2003b; Keener 2009; McIver 2011). In this regard, orality is frequently thought to be the closest cousin to memory: ancient people remembered well because oral cultures were accustomed to remembering and transmitting orally and with accuracy (Bailey 1991; Gerhardsson 1961). This trajectory within memory theory in New Testament studies argues that the period between the teaching mission of Jesus and the writing of the Gospels was marked by oral transmission of Jesus' teaching that was mostly reliable. The common claim is that the 'gist' (McIver 2011: 58) or the 'impression' (Dunn 2007: 187) or impact (Dunn 2008: 90) of Jesus' teachings was always retained. A desire to remain faithful to the actual teachings of Jesus, coupled with a nod toward the human limitations of memory, results, according to Dunn, in a stable core around which subtle and largely irrelevant details might change, which Dunn calls 'variation within the same' (Dunn 2003b: 212) or 'same yet different' (Dunn 2011: 38). This is a move wholly supported by McIver (2011) and Le Donne (2011).

One of the strongest contributions of memory and orality theory to the study of the historical Jesus is the observation that the quest for the *ipsissima verba* of Jesus is wholly misguided, since it requires us to imagine that sayings of Jesus would have functioned inertly, taking on layers of secondary tradition, but not in any way influencing how that tradition came to overlay the sayings (Kirk 2005: 29). Jan Assmann puts it best when he complains about the passivity implied in the notion of 'tradition':

> Rome is not just a vast open-air museum in which the past is preserved and exhibited, but an inextricable tangle of old and new, of obstructed and buried material, of detritus that has been reused or rejected. In this way tensions arise, rejections, antagonisms, between what has been censored and uncensored, the canonical and the apocryphal, the orthodox and the

> heretical, the central and the marginal, all of which makes for cultural dynamism. . . . This is why the concept of tradition, as usually understood, is completely inadequate as a description of this phenomenon. 'Tradition' refers to the business of handing down and receiving, as well as the continued existence of what has been received (Assmann 2006: 25).

Dunn has complained that the default model for explaining or imagining the transmission of pre-Gospel Jesus material is textual, and not, more reasonably, oral (Dunn 2003a). Dunn may well be correct about this, but it is not at all clear that we have access to what lies behind (or beneath) the *literary* Gospels. One ought not to assume that one can get to the period of oral transmission by reading literary or scribal productions.

Not all approaches to memory theory seek to reconstruct the past (Williams 2011). In fact, some particularly fruitful approaches to memory are less interested in challenging or defending the historical accuracy of memory and are instead more interested in the twofold question of how collective, social, or cultural memory *happens*, and how it *functions* in the world (Schwartz 2005).[1] Alan Kirk puts it bluntly: Memory theory does not lend itself to 'drawing naive correspondences between "memory" and "history"' (Kirk 2010: 820). In this regard, it is always worth returning to Jeffrey Olick's mantra that 'memory is a process and not a thing, a faculty rather than a place. Collective memory is something—or rather many things we *do*, not something—or many things—we *have*' (2006: 13 [emphasis original]). Collective memory is not something people possess, nor is it something people access, like a database. It is rather an activity in which people participate, sometimes unconsciously, and one that is susceptible to numerous simultaneous and complex processes, including 'collective representations (publicly available symbols, meanings, narratives and rituals), deep cultural structures (generative systems of rules or patterns for producing representations), social frameworks (groups and patterns of interaction), and culturally and socially framed individual memories' (Olick 2006: 12).

Collective, social, or cultural memory refers to the memories people have of events they were not present for (Burke 1989: 98). They are therefore memories that are given to people, not memories they experience firsthand. Thus, collective memory first and foremost refers to how the past functions,

1. The terms collective, social and cultural memory are difficult to define, and far from technical terms with a single meaning or referent. Anthony Le Donne defines them thus: social memory refers to 'the ways that group ideologies inform individual memories'; collective memory refers to the way memories are 'shared and passed down by groups'; cultural memory 'broadens the scope of Collective Memory' (Le Donne 2007: 165). He also rightly warns that the various terms are used so interchangeably that the nuance of each term varies from author to author. In this paper, I use the term 'collective memory' as Le Donne defines it, but especially to distinguish it from individual memory.

how it is presented and represented in someone's present. The past is put to work in many ways: representations of the past can explain the past, they can shape personal and communal identity, establish or maintain community boundaries, and prescribe people's behaviour by presenting an ideal model from the past. And of course, there can be many competing spheres of communal identity: a broader community might support a particular cultural memory, but that memory might be contested by smaller communities within it. Like culture then, collective memory can be challenged, or simply constructed differently, by competing communities. Since the needs of the present dictate how the past is used and represented, since needs of the present dictate which parts of the past are acknowledged and which are not, and since every group's present needs are different, there naturally will be many versions of the past. This is, of course, precisely what we see in the writings of early Christianity, both canonical and extracanonical.

There is therefore an inextricable relationship between collective memory and the collective. People receive their collective memories from those around them. These memories are commonly about the community: where it came from, who comprises the community, what its people are like, how they differ from other communities, where they are going, and so on. Jan Assmann observes that social memory (which he is contrasting with the mythical past of cultural memory) 'is a matter of communication', and 'a function of our social life'; no less, it 'enables us to live in groups and communities, and living in groups and communities enables us to build a memory' (Assmann 2008: 109).[2] Elsewhere, he points out that 'The past is the decisive resource for consciousness of national identity. Whoever wishes to belong must share the group memory' (Assmann 2006: 87). Of course, this need not be limited to 'national identity'; his observations pertain to the identity of any collection of people, no matter how large or small, how socially or politically central or peripheral. The past can create a sense of unity in a group. That is, insofar as the group participates in the construction of its own past, everyone in the group shares a vested interest in that past (Assmann 2006: 94).

It is the heart of cultural, collective, or social memory that the past works in the service of the present. But collective memory has a future aspect as well, a point often missed or underemphasized by scholars. Kelber gives a modest nod in its direction, when he writes that 'Cultural memory . . . recognizes both a regressive gesture toward the past, seeking to retrieve as much of the past as seems appropriate, and a gesture to the present (and future), preserving what is deemed to be useful in the present' (Kelber 2005:

2. On the relationship between memory and community, see also Olick 1999, 344: 'Genuine communities are communities of memory that constantly tell and retell their constitutive memories'. A similar sentiment can be found in Fentress and Wickham (1992: 25).

226). Social memory seems to be oriented mostly toward the interplay between past and present, not present and future. Of course, when one is focused on *remembering*, that makes sense, but if one is focused on the full expanse of collective memory it makes less sense. For instance, collective memory can be future oriented when its primary concern is to create new memories. These are 'memories' that in fact do not have a past, material that only becomes social memory in the future once it is accepted as 'memory'. Focusing on the fact that memories can be manufactured, and exploring why they might be manufactured, shifts the focus of social memory from solely past–present to present–future (evidenced in Lieu 2004: 62-97).

Focusing on how memory functions within groups rather than on questions of accuracy and reliability, however fruitful that focus is, does not render the question of historical accuracy wholly moot. It may well be the case that when it comes to collective memory, the fact that the collective holds the memory matters much more than whether the memory is accurate or not. But it is also a fact that representations of the past change. This is called memory distortion. We may not be able to distinguish which version of a memory of the past is *the* correct one, and so in that regard the distinction is moot. But we can often tell that one memory is more original than another, that one memory is secondary. We do not need to know which if either version is original in order to recognize that one of them derives and departs from the other, and is therefore *further* from the original.

Writing about Egyptian anti-Judaism, Assmann avers that the 'notion "distorted memory" seems to presuppose that there something like "undistorted memory"' (1995: 366). Of course, there is not: all memory is distorted memory (Le Donne 2007: 167). But Assmann's discussion, quite properly, does not end there. At the same time that he accepts and embraces the fact that all memory is reconstructed and reinvented, he insists that 'some memories are *more distorted* than others and some traditions *more invented* than others' (1995: 366 [emphasis added]). Peter Burke offers some illustrations that show how the memory of a culture's recent heroes can be distorted when it succumbs to the pressures of collective memory, one of which is the attachment of myths to certain figures (Burke 1989: 104).

Burke refers to this process as mythogenesis, the process of myths attaching themselves to certain individuals, often completely independent of anything that individual did.[3] He writes that 'the central element in the explanation of this mythogenesis is the perception (conscious or unconscious) of a "fit" in some respect or respects between a particular individual and a current stereotype of a hero or villain—ruler, saint, bandit, witch, or whatever' (Burke 1989: 104). Figures can be transformed in the process, as

3. 'Myth' here is used by Burke not to refer to something 'inaccurate' in the story, but to refer to features that give a story a new and often symbolic meaning.

he shows: 'the cold and colourless William III into the popular Protestant idol "King Billy" can hardly be explained in terms of his own personality. Bandits turn into Robin Hoods, robbing the rich to give to the poor. Rulers travel their kingdom in disguise to learn about the condition of their subjects (Burke 1989: 104). In other words, people's memories of a revered figure from the past are not only fit into schemata, but these schemata can radically alter the memory of the character of that figure.

There might be a tendency to view memory distortion as essentially negative, because it removes us ever further from historically reliable information. This is true to a certain extent, but it does, as suggested above, miss the point of collective memory, which is not historical accuracy but present utility (Lieu 2004: 62). Distortions to memory can also be 'positive', in that they have 'a democratizing outcome or else because they bring about a necessary readjustment of values or value systems that are out of synch—anomalous—in a particular time and place' (Kammen 1995: 329-30). And, in the context of a discussion of a manufactured memory in a Gospel writing, it is important to point out that this can happen over a very short period of time: 'memories can readily, with scant embarrassment or challenge, be quietly repressed within a generation and replaced by alternate explanations' (Kammen 1995: 333). This has been abundantly illustrated also in the works of Hobsbawm and Ranger (1983) and Loftus (1993). Arjun Appadurai pleads that the past is not 'a limitless and plastic symbolic resource, infinitely susceptible to the whims of contemporary interest and the distortions of contemporary ideology' (1981: 201), but it is more complicated than this. Past actuality *can* serve as a constraint on the use of the past, but it does not always. Put differently, the past has no inherent qualities that *necessitate* a constraint on its use in the present. Sometimes there is little relation between the past and the use of the past.

The Uniqueness of Luke's Story

The episode of a woman anointing Jesus is one of those rare stories that appears in all four canonical Gospels—Mt. 26.6-13, Mk 14.3-9, Lk. 7.36-50, and Jn 12.1-8. The degree of verbatim parallels between the versions found in Matthew and Mark make it clear that Matthew has relied on Mark directly (Corley 2003: 67). That is, in terms of cultural memory, Matthew does not have access to a memory independent of Mark; the memory has come to him mediated through Mark. The question as it pertains to Luke is much more complicated. The versions found in Luke and Mark are startlingly different from each other. Indeed the degree of difference is noteworthy. It is, of course, not uncommon for Luke to edit Mark, and thus end up with a different version of a story. What is noteworthy here is the extent and the nature of the differences.

4

Details in common	Details in disagreement
The event happened in someone's house	The house is in Bethany in Mark, in the Galilee in Luke
	The event occurs two days before Jesus is executed in Mark, but during the period of Jesus' initial ministry in the Galilee in Luke
The house owner's name was Simon	Simon is a leper in Mark, a wealthy Pharisee in Luke
The setting is a public meal	
A woman is the central figure	The woman is characterless in Mark; she is a 'sinner' in Luke
An anointing happens	Mark has Jesus' head anointed; in Luke it is his feet
The ointment was transported in an alabaster container	The ointment is named as 'nard' in Mark; it is not named in Luke[4]
	The woman in Luke has wept on Jesus' feet and wiped both her tears and the ointment away with her hair
There is an objection to the actions of the woman	In Mark, it is unnamed people at the dinner who object; in Luke it is the host, Simon
There is a reason for the objection	In Mark, the objection is to the wastefulness of the expensive ointment; in Luke the objection is to the sinfulness of the woman who touches Jesus, a purity issue
There is a justification of the woman's actions	In Mark, Jesus justifies the waste on the grounds that the poor will always be around, and can always be helped; in Luke, Jesus justifies the act at great length, only to say that the woman has more to be grateful for, being the greater sinner
The anointing has a purpose	In Mark, the woman's act anticipates the treatment of his dead body; in Luke it is her sin offering
There is a concluding statement by Jesus	In Mark, Jesus' conclusion is that the woman's act will be remembered forever; in Luke it is that the woman's sins have been forgiven

4. Hearon implies that Luke contains the word nard (2005: 104). In fact, the term *nardos* is not found anywhere in the Gospel of Luke.

This table illustrates that there are very few details on which Mark and Luke agree without qualification: they share the outline of the story (event, objection, justification, concluding proclamation), and they share that the event happened at a meal. On every other detail, either they share it but share it with significant differences (e.g. whether the Simon in question was a leper or a Pharisee), or they wholly disagree (e.g. on the timing of the event, the use of the woman's hair). Also, what appears in this table is that the two stories share little more in common than the barest narrative skeleton.[5]

This invites the question: what is the source of Luke's story? For Holly Hearon, the shared nature of the story suggests that it represents a broadly held memory in the early church (Hearon 2005: 100-101).[6] Hearon smartly avoids attempting to discern which of the four versions is the more historical; rather, she focuses on how each version functions as social memory for Mark, Luke and John (she subsumes Matthew's intent under Mark's, since the two versions are very similar). But in so doing, she also cautions that Luke is likely not directly reliant on Mark for this story. Rather, he, like John probably, inherited his version of the story from circulating and competing social memories. Coakley reduces the number of strands of social memory from three (Mark, Luke and John) to two, describing Luke as '*distantly related* to both John and Mark' (Coakley 1988: 241[emphasis added]). It is understandable why one interested in memory theory (which does not include Coakley, since his work preceded the introduction of memory theory into biblical studies) would find such an explanation attractive, but it is not the only way memory theory can be used to explain Luke's unique story.

My objection to the suggestion that Luke's story derives from a strand of social memory independent of Mark is fourfold. First, if the versions of this story found in Mark and Luke represent two independent streams of memory, this really does not speak well of the reliability of human memory. In fact, to think of these two stories as originating from some historical event results in something of a comedy of errors, given how different the two versions end up being. Hearon at one point observes that the extant versions reveal 'a limited number of ways in which the story of "the woman

5. It might explain why in most synopses, including my own (Crook 2011), the Matthean and Markan versions are so often placed together and the Lukan version shown separately. Such an arrangement of pericopae implies that Luke is not reliant on Mark for this story. In the writing of this article, however, I have come to regret the decision to separate these pericopae in my synopsis. The literary parallels, while not extensive, are best explained as competing memories of a single event.

6. For brief summaries of scholarship concerning the sources for this story, see Corley 2003: 62-64, and Fitzmyer 1981: 684-87.

who anointed Jesus" can be told' (Hearon 2005: 107), but really the vastness of the difference between Mark and Luke shows us that that limit is not much of a limit at all.

Second, the suggestion that Luke's story is so different because that is how he inherited it returns us to the days of the form critics: an ironic critique, given the unrestrained disdain directed at form criticism among those who favour memory and orality (Bauckham 2006; Dunn 2003a; Kelber 2005: 231, 2006: 17; Kirk 2005: 1, 2010: 810). The form critics treated the Gospel writers like mere inheritors of tradition, giving them little more input into the creation of their Gospels than the arrangement of material. Redaction criticism replaced form criticism precisely on account of the limitations of the form-critical model: it does not cohere with the evidence of the Gospels, which reveal considerable creative input on the part of the Gospel writers, both at the level of story and arrangement and at the level of words said by and about Jesus. That we must reckon with the Gospel writers as authors in their own right is part of the reason redaction criticism became so popular. In fact, the *assumption* that Luke must have inherited this story fails adequately to come to terms with 'Luke's capacity for literary creativity' (Pesonen 2000: 95 n. 7).[7]

Third, there is some evidence of Lukan dependence on Mark, measured in the traditional way, namely by verbatim agreement. The agreements may not be extensive, but they are significant. We can observe that though the stories are quite different, they are different at the level of detail. Though these different details really do result in a different story, the fact remains that the two stories share the very same structure. Further, as a general rule, we know Luke relies literarily on Mark and Q, and though he also has much unique material, where a story structure is shared like this, there seems insufficient reason to assume Luke here is relying on anything other than Mark. This might appear to Dunn to be falling back on literary default settings, but the fact is, we only have Mark and Luke before us. They are literary products, and thus we ought to be at ease attending to their literary interdependence.

There are also verbatim agreements, however, which are difficult to ascribe merely to cultural memory. For instance, Mark and Luke share the detail that the ointment was carried in an alabaster container. Such specificity seems pointless in Mark. The syntax reveals that it was the ointment that was expensive (μύρου νάρδου πιστικῆς), and not the alabaster container. And when the people in Mark object, it is not over the fact that the alabaster

7. In this regard, Fitzmyer appears unwilling to consider the possibility of thoroughgoing Lukan creativity in this story. He will allow that the parable in the narrative is Lukan, but insists that the remainder of the story derives from L (1981: 684), which reflects the fact that the story survived in multiple oral forms (1981: 686).

container was smashed (συντρίβω) but that the ointment was used wastefully. Thus, the alabaster container does not figure at all in the narrative. Therefore, that Luke takes over that description is suggestive of direct borrowing. Moreover, that the word κατάκειμαι is used in both versions immediately before the woman enters the scene (Mk 14.3//Lk. 7.37) suggests direct literary dependence, especially given that Luke prefers the term κατακλίνω, which he just used, and which on two other occasions he adds to Markan material (Lk. 9.14, 15). After this, the two narratives depart so significantly that we should not expect any verbatim agreement.

Fourth, in addition to signs of direct dependence on Mark, there is also plenty of evidence of Lukan style in this pericope. Delobel points to seventeen instances of unique or strong Lukan vocabulary and phrases (Delobel 1966: 421-44) and eight words that are *hapax* in a number of ways (Pesonen 2000: 89).[8] This suggests that what has been changed in Luke's telling has been changed in Luke's voice. One could object that this signifies nothing more than that Luke inherited a story from oral tradition but told it in his own words, but that is assuming facts not in evidence. The evidence before us is literary, and it shows Luke relying on Mark for a story, and personally and radically redacting it.

I am, like many others (Corley 2003: 68-69; Goulder 1989: 397-406; Pesonen 2000: 99-101; Smith 2003: 224), inclined to take the position that Luke inherited this story from Mark, but then changed it to suit his own particular needs.[9] That the past is changed to suit new needs is the heart of redaction criticism and memory theory both. We can see in Luke's radical retelling of the story that he has not simply retooled a social memory: he has actually manufactured a new memory. He manufactures a memory of a story that involves a sinning woman anointing Jesus' feet (and not his head), that takes place in the Galilee (and not in Bethany), in the home of a Pharisee (and not in the home of a leper) early in Jesus' career (and not in the last days of his life), in which Simon (and not someone else) balks at the contact between Jesus and the sinful woman (and not at the waste), to which Jesus responds with a parable (and not with a rebuke against mistreating her

8. *Hapax legomena* are sometimes thought, by necessity, to indicate derivation from a source, but such a position is anything but certain when applied to a writer with Luke's vocabulary (Pesonen 2000: 89-90).

9. Unlike Corley, however, I leave without comment whether the core of the story itself can be traced back to a historical event in the life of Jesus, largely because the question of ultimate historicity, or lack thereof, has no bearing on understanding and commenting on how Luke has altered the Markan version, and to what purpose. And unlike Kilgallen, I leave unaddressed whether what Luke added (his focus is mostly the parable) was simply in order to make explicit something that was already implicit in a pre-Lukan version of the narrative (Kilgallen 2005: 532). For Kilgallen, the focus of the story is Christology: Jesus has the authority to forgive sin.

and an allusion to his immanent death), and which concludes with the issue of whether Jesus has the authority to forgive sins (and not with the remembrance of the woman's actions). The evidence available to us suggests that Luke inherited the structure of this story from Mark, and rejected all but a few of the details, thus radically changing the story. The purpose of his doing so is the issue we shall consider next.

Luke Constructs a Community

Commenting on the changes Luke has made to Mark, Kathleen Corley claims that it is implied in Mark that the woman is a sinner of a sexual nature, likely a prostitute, evidenced simply in her presence at the dinner.[10] But this is not the most obvious reading of the narrative available to us. If this were Mark's intent, it becomes difficult to explain why he would leave it unaddressed as he has. One would expect someone in the narrative to object to the presence of a stranger at a meal hosting such a special guest. Perhaps Mark's readers would have all agreed that the woman must be 'a female of questionable reputation' (Malina and Rohrbaugh 2003: 128-29). Or perhaps Mark's silence on the woman's identity or character is suggestive. Could Mark have meant to say nothing more about her than that she was a woman who crashed a party to adore Jesus? Doing so allows Mark to keep the narrative focus on the action of preparing Jesus for burial. By contrast, Luke's explicit comment about the woman's character, that she is a sinner from the city, must be attributed to Lukan redaction, and must be equally suggestive of Luke's narrative intent.[11] In addition, the changes Luke makes to Mark also reflect the fact that Luke is not interested in transmitting a story about Jesus' impending death and resurrection (Corley 2003: 68). Rather, Luke's interest is Jesus' kingdom and the community devoted to it. In this regard, Luke's depiction of the woman as a sinner is key.

Holly Hearon's analysis of this story is excellent. She shows that the meaning of Luke's story resides in its characters and not in the location of the story. This is signaled, in the first instance, by Luke's replacement of Mark's precise location (Bethany) with a vague location (the Galilee). It is signaled also by Luke's focus on the status of two of the main characters in the story: the identity of the host (a Pharisee) is mentioned twice in the first verse, and the woman is explicitly referred to as a sinner from the city. The

10. At the end of the article, however, it becomes clear that Corley thinks this applies to Mark's literary intent only, and does not apply to the historical woman herself (2003: 72).

11. That Luke intended, however, to convey the idea that the woman was a former slave who had achieved manumission through prostitution, as Corley (2003: 70) suggests, is more than the evidence can bear.

absence of names for both of these characters serves to keep the reader's attention on the status of each (Hearon 2005: 113; Pesonen 2000: 95).

Two other features of the story further suggest that the focus of the story is the status of the main actors. First, the objection of the Pharisee is not directed at the woman's action, but at her character.[12] Second, when Jesus defends the woman, though he focuses in part on her actions (and on Simon's inaction), it is really on her character as proxy-host (and Simon's failure of character) that is Jesus' focus: she is generous, selfless, adoring, and welcoming, and it was not even her obligation to be (Kilgallen 2005: 530). Hearon concludes that the character of the woman models for readers, who in Luke's estimation are also sinners, how to respond to Jesus (2005: 114). It functions therefore in Luke's construction of a community of followers.

This is a community whose focus is on saving sinners, not the already righteous.[13] Pesonen situates this story in Luke's 'theme of repentance and grace illustrated in encounters of Jesus and sinful people' (Pesonen 2000: 92). She writes that the 'sinner motif is so beautifully developed and so far from casual in the Gospel that it is hardly conceivable without the conscious, creative, and theologically thorough work of the redactor' (Pesonen 2000: 94). David Neale makes the point that sinners in Luke's Gospel are not historical figures (though they may once have been) but rather represent Lukan 'archetypes' to illustrate his theology of repentance (Neale 1991). As archetypes then, they would truly derive from Luke's deliberate construction of a community.

There are other features of Luke's vision of his community visible in this pericope. The first is that this story functions as part of Luke's greater narrative and theological interest in women.[14] Clearly, Luke's construction of his community makes room for women. According to Jane Via, 'women are viewed in this gospel as vehicles of revelation and voices of theological insight' (Via 1987: 50). They have a prominent role then in Luke's view of Jesus' kingdom of God. This is surely part of Luke's construction of a community identity.

Another feature of Luke's vision of his community is the context of a meal. Meal scenes are a unique feature of Luke: he has them far more often

12. I think Kilgallen (2005: 529) reads against the grain of the narrative when he argues that Luke's focus is on the actions of the woman and Simon, not on their status and character.

13. This is affirmed in this story, but also previously at Lk. 5.32 (Stagg 1997: 222).

14. Of Luke's forty-two stories featuring women, twenty-three are unique to him, a larger number of unique stories than can be found in any of the other Gospels.

than Matthew or Mark.[15] According to Halvor Moxnes, '[i]n Luke's Gospel, a meal functions as an effective metaphor for the banquet in the kingdom of God. . . . Jesus' meals have the function not of creating distinctions, but of bridging them and including people' (1988: 87-88). Moxnes goes on to say that the focus of the meal scenes is on 'who is invited to participate and for what purpose a host has gathered people together for a meal' (1988: 88). The debate (between Jesus and Simon the Pharisee) is about who is pleasing to God, and thus who belongs most in the community (Ford 1984: 71; Tiede 1982: 160). In the case of our story then, it would appear that the host has held a celebratory banquet for an honored guest (Jesus), likely with other honored guests there to meet or hear Jesus. But in the narrative, Jesus upends that guest list by insisting that a woman with a poor reputation has been better to Jesus than even the host. The focus is indeed on who will be invited to participate in his kingdom.

Luke's creativity, especially as it pertains to his construction of community, is evident in this entire section (Marshall 1978: 276). The theme of the entirety of Luke 7 is that the kingdom is designed for those without access to power, namely sinners and outsiders. The stories in this section all reflect this theme: Jesus helps a gentile (7.1-10), a widow (7.11-17), and a sinful woman (7.36-50). The story about John the Baptist's disciples interrogating Jesus even fits in here: Luke reports Q's statement of Jesus that 'Blessed is anyone who takes no offense at me' (Lk. 7.23): could this relate to our story in which the Pharisee takes offense at Jesus letting himself be touched by a sinner? What follows is Jesus' address to the crowds, in which he accepts the charge of focusing his attention on sinners (7.34), a line he also takes over from Q. Then, as if to make that very point, Luke inserts Mark's story of the woman who anoints Jesus, though heavily altered and turned into a sinful woman. Ellis is surely correct to claim that 'Nowhere in Luke is the art of a descriptive writer more evident' (Ellis 1966: 123). Indeed, Luke has manufactured a new memory in which Jesus forgives the sins of those who love him deeply (Kilgallen 2005: 533).

Memory and Community Identity

John Gillis has shown that the 'core meaning of any individual or group identity, namely a sense of sameness over time and space, is sustained by remembering, and what is remembered is defined by the assumed identity' (Gillis 1994: 3). There can be no identity without memory, nor even boundaries: 'remembering as well as forgetting—that is, the construction of

15. Luke 5.29-32; 7.36-50; 10.38-42; 15.1-2, 6, 9, 22-25; 16.19-25; 19.6-10; 22.14-22; 24.30-31; 24.41-43 (Moxnes 1988: 87).

the narrative of identity—are both acts of power and means of maintaining power; if they include, they of necessity will also exclude' (Lieu 2004: 65). Lieu offers a rich collection of examples of how Judean and Christian identities are shaped by the construction and use of the past, and Gruen reminds us to remain attentive to 'the manipulation of myths, the reshaping of traditions, the elaboration of legends, fictions, and inventions, the recasting of ostensibly alien cultural legacies with the aim of defining or reinforcing a distinctive cultural character' (Gruen 1993: 3).

Now, Gruen writes about the manufacturing of collective memories concerning the founding of Rome and Roman origins, and also of memories of the intimate relationship between Judeans and Greeks, especially of Alexander the Great's worshiping at the Judean Temple. These belong to the mythic past, to use Assmann's categorization, and as such, their origin is lost to us. But some collective memories, and, in particular, some manufactured memories, can be traced to a point of genesis. Such is the benefit of having multiple Gospels. Luke's redaction of Mark's story of a woman in Bethany anointing Jesus' head in preparation for burial, thorough-going enough to generate a whole new story, allows us to identify precisely the point of origin of the Christian memory of a sinning woman anointing his feet in the Galilee. Luke does this because he has something to say about the community of followers he is part of constructing. Lieu's remark about the Gospels in general applies no less to Luke individually: 'The Gospels represent distinctive "rememberings" of the Jesus story that maintain a reciprocal dialectic between the telling of the past and the needs of the present; in this way they have been seen as each constituting the "charter myth" of the foundation of the group"' (Lieu 2004: 87, citing Wills 1997: 179). The present needs of Luke, I have argued, have to do with the identity construction of the community for whom he writes. The editing of this story suggests that the story fits within a broader concern that Luke appears to have for compassion (van Staden 1991).

Luke cannot be unique in the way he has used some memories and manufactured others to aid in the construction of his community's identity. Consider Matthew's largely fictional and entirely symbolic genealogy, or his fulfillment formulas, also sometimes bearing little resemblance to the past it claims to represent. Or consider Mark's motif of secrecy in his memories of Jesus. Kelber is surely correct to conclude that 'gospel composition is unthinkable without the notion of cultural memory, which serves ultimately not the preservation of remembrances per se but the preservation of the group, its social identity and self-image' (1997: xxiii). Luke is doing exactly what we would expect him to do: he is not retaining memory of the past, as if drawing it from a storehouse, but is instead creating a new past 'that speaks to the needs of the present' (Kelber 2002: 57) and that will have a lasting impact on the future.

It is what we all do. The story I opened with, about Jack at the cello, did not happen. It is my own manufactured memory.[16] Sometimes memories can be manufactured accidentally; that is, the one relating the memory believes that the event being related really happened, or that it happened in the way it is being related. The teller might be unaware that she is confusing events, or players, or timing. In some instances, especially when relating memories of events one was not present for, one might not realize that the entire story one has inherited is manufactured. But memories can also be deliberately manufactured in order to make a point, to say something about the present or to perform some future task. That is the heart of social memory theory: the idea that the past is used to *do* something in the present. And sometimes, that 'past' can be a wholly manufactured past, even a mythical past. Luke did that with his creative and thorough rewriting of the story of the woman who anointed Jesus' feet, and I have done it with my story of Jack Elliott at the cello. With it I mean to express my gratitude to Jack for helping to build and sustain a community of scholars among whom I have come to feel at home.

References

Allison, Dale C.
2010 *Constructing Jesus: Memory, Imagination, and History* (Grand Rapids, MI: Baker Academic).

Appadurai, Arjun
1981 'The Past as a Scarce Resource', *Man* NS 16: 201-19.

Assmann, Jan
1995 'Ancient Egyptian Antijudaism: A Case of Distorted Memory', in *Memory Distortion: How Minds, Brains, and Societies Reconstruct the Past* (ed. D.L. Schacter; Cambridge, MA: Harvard University Press): 365-76.
2006 *Religion and Cultural Memory* (Stanford, CA: Stanford University Press).
2008 'Communicative and Cultural Memory', in *Cultural Memory Studies: An International and Interdisciplinary Handbook* (ed. Astrid Erll and Ansgar Nuenning; Berlin: de Gruyter): 109-18.

16. This, on the other hand, is unlikely to become a collective memory since I have confessed to having created it. But one never knows: it is widely known that George Washington did not in fact confess to having chopped down his father's cherry tree as a child, and yet this is still part of American collective memory (Nelson 2008: 40). This is an important lesson in the creation of collective memory: memories (manufactured or otherwise) become collective when they enter the collective memory stream, and there they often take on a life of their own. There is a collective memory held among a great many Germans still that German came very close to being the official language of the United States. The memory persists despite explicit denials from both the German and American governments (see http://usa.usembassy.de/germanamericans-language.htm, accessed July 16, 2014).

Bailey, Kenneth E.
1991 'Informal Controlled Oral Tradition and the Synoptic Gospels', *Asia Journal of Theology* 5: 34-54.
Bauckham, Richard
2006 *Jesus and the Eye Witnesses* (Grand Rapids, MI: Eerdmans).
Burke, Peter
1989 'History as Social Memory', in *Memory: History, Culture and the Mind* (ed. Thomas Butler; Oxford: Basil Blackwell): 97-113.
Coakley, J.F.
1988 'The Anointing at Bethany and the Priority of John', *JBL* 107: 241-56.
Corley, K.E.
2003 'The Anointing of Jesus in the Synoptic Tradition: An Argument for Authenticity', *JSHJ* 1: 61-72.
Crook, Z.A.
2011 *Parallel Gospels: A Synopsis of Early Christian Writing* (Oxford: Oxford University Press).
Delobel, J.
1966 'L'onction par la pécheresse', *ETL* 42: 415-75.
Le Donne, Anthony
2007 'Theological Memory Distortion in the Jesus Tradition', in *Memory and Remembrance in the Bible and Antiquity* (ed. Loren T. Stuckenbruck, Stephen C. Barton and Benjamin G. Wold; Tübingen: Mohr Siebeck): 163-77.
2011 *Historical Jesus: What Can We Know and How Can We Know It?* (Grand Rapids, MI: Eerdmans).
Dunn, James D.G.
2003a 'Altering the Default Setting: Re-envisaging the Early Transmission of the Jesus Tradition', *NTS* 49:139-75.
2003b *Christianity in the Making,* vol. 1: *Jesus Remembered* (Grand Rapids, MI: Eerdmans).
2007 'Social Memory and the Oral Jesus Tradition', in *Memory in the Bible and Antiquity* (ed. Loren T. Stuckenbruck, Stephen C. Barton and Benjamin G. Wold; Tübingen: Mohr Siebeck): 179-94.
2008 'Eyewitnesses and the Oral Jesus Tradition', *JSHJ* 6: 85-105.
2011 *Jesus, Paul, and the Gospels* (Grand Rapids, MI: Eerdmans).
Elliott, John H.
1981 *A Home for the Homeless: A Social-Scientific Criticism of I Peter, its Situation and Strategy* (Philadelphia, PA: Augsburg Fortress, repr. 1990 with new introduction).
Ellis, E. Earle
1966 *Gospel of Luke* (London: Nelson).
Fentress, J., and C. Wickham
1992 *Social Memory* (Oxford: Blackwell).
Fitzmyer, Joseph A.
1981 *The Gospel according to Luke* (Garden City, NY: Doubleday).
Ford, J. Massyngbaerde
1984 *My Enemy Is my Guest: Jesus and Violence in Luke* (Maryknoll, NY: Orbis Books).

Gerhardsson, Birger
1961 *Memory and Manuscript: Oral Tradition and Written Transmission in Rabbinic Judaism and Early Christianity* (Lund: Gleerup).

Gillis, John R.
1994 'Memory and Identity: The History of a Relationship', in *Commemorations: The Politics of National Identity* (ed. John R. Gillis; Princeton, NJ: Princeton University Press): 3-24.

Goulder, M.D.
1989 *Luke: A New Paradigm* (Sheffield: JSOT Press).

Gruen, Erich S.
1993 'Cultural Fictions and Cultural Identity', *TAPA* 123: 1-14.

Hearon, Holly
2005 'The Story of "The Woman Who Anointed Jesus" as Social Memory: A Methodological Proposal for the Study of Tradition as Memory', in *Memory, Tradition, and Text: Uses of the Past in Early Christianity* (ed. Alan Kirk and Tom Thatcher; Leiden: Brill): 99-118.

Hobsbawm, Eric, and Terence Ranger
1983 *The Invention of Tradition* (Cambridge: Cambridge University Press).

Kammen, Michael
1995 'Some Patterns and Meanings of Memory Distortion in American History', in *Memory Distortion: How Minds, Brains, and Societies Reconstruct the Past* (ed. D.L. Schacter; Cambridge, MA: Harvard University Press): 329-45.

Keener, Craig S.
2009 *The Historical Jesus of the Gospels* (Grand Rapids, MI: Eerdmans).

Kelber, Werner H.
1997 *The Oral and the Written Gospel: The Hermeneutics of Speaking and Writing in the Synoptic Tradition, Mark, Paul, and Q* (Bloomington, IN: Indiana University Press).
2002 'The Case of the Gospels: Memory's Desire and the Limits of Historical Criticism', *Oral Tradition* 17: 55–86.
2005 'The Works of Memory: Christian Origins as MnemoHistory—A Response', in *Memory, Tradition, and Text: Uses of the Past in Early Christianity* (ed. Alan Kirk and Tom Thatcher; Leiden: Brill): 221-48.
2006 'The Generative Force of Memory: Early Christian Traditions as Processes of Remembering', *BTB* 36: 15-22.

Kilgallen, John J.
2005 'What Does It Mean to Say That There Are Additions in Luke 7.36-50?', *Biblica* 86: 529-35.

Kirk, Alan
2005 'Social and Cultural Memory', in *Memory, Tradition, and Text: Uses of the Past in Early Christianity* (ed. Alan Kirk and Tom Thatcher; Leiden: Brill): 1-24.
2010 'Memory Theory and Jesus Research', in *Handbook for the Study of the Historical Jesus*, vol. 1: *How to Study the Historical Jesus* (ed. Tom Holmén and Stanley E. Porter; Leiden: Brill): 809-42.

Lieu, Judith M.
2004 *Christian Identity in the Jewish and Graeco-Roman World* (New York: Oxford University Press).

Loftus, Elizabeth F.
1993 'The Reality of Repressed Memories', *American Psychologist* 48: 518-37.
Malina, Bruce J., and Richard L. Rohrbaugh
2003 *Social-Science Commentary on the Synoptic Gospels* (Minneapolis, MN: Fortress Press).
Marshall, I. Howard
1978 *The Gospel of Luke* (Grand Rapids, MI: Eerdmans).
McIver, Robert K.
2011 *Memory, Jesus, and the Synoptic Gospels* (Atlanta, GA: Society of Biblical Literature).
Moxnes, Halvor
1988 *The Economy of the Kingdom: Social Conflict and Economic Relations in Luke's Gospel* (Philadelphia, PA: Fortress Press).
Neale, David A.
1991 *None but the Sinners: Religious Categories in the Gospel of Luke* (Sheffield: Sheffield Academic Press).
Nelson, Dana D.
2008 *Bad for Democracy: How the Presidency Undermines the Power of the People* (Minneapolis, MN: University of Minnesota Press).
Olick, Jeffrey K.
1999 'Collective Memory: The Two Cultures', *Sociological Theory* 17: 333-48.
2006 'Products, Processes, and Practices: A Non-Reificatory Approach to Collective Memory', *BTB* 36: 5-14.
Pesonen, Anni
2000 'The Weeping Sinner: A Short Story by Luke?' *Neotestamentica* 34: 87-102.
Schwartz, Barry
2005 'Christian Origins: Historical Truth and Social Memory', in *Memory, Tradition, and Text: Uses of the Past in Early Christianity* (ed. Alan Kirk and Tom Thatcher; Leiden: Brill): 43-56.
Smith, Dennis E.
2003 *From Symposium to Eucharist: The Banquet in the Early Christian World* (Minneapolis, MN: Fortress Press).
Staden, Piet van
1991 *Compassion—the Essence of Life: A Social-Scientific Study of the Religious Symbolic Universe Reflected in the Ideology/Theology of Luke* (Pretoria: University of Pretoria).
Stagg, Frank
1997 'Luke's Theological Use of Parables', *Review & Expositor* 94: 215-29.
Tiede, D.L.
1982 'Religious Propaganda and the Gospel Literature of the Early Christian Mission', in *Aufstieg und Niedergang der römischen Welt* (ed. Hildegard Temporini and Wolfgang Haase): 1705-29.
Via, E.J.
1987 'Women in the Gospel of Luke', in *Women in the World's Religions, Past and Present* (ed. Ursula King; New York: Paragon House): 38-55.
Williams, Ritva
2011 'BTB Readers' Guide: Social Memory', *BTB* 41: 189-200.
Wills, L.M.
1997 *The Quest of the Historical Gospel: Mark, John and the Origins of the Gospel Genre* (New York: Routledge).

The Gospel of Mark as a Therapeutic Ritual Script

Richard E. DeMaris

Far be it from me to suggest that our honoree has a split personality, but I would say that there are two distinct sides to Jack Elliott. There is the blustery, aggressive, in-your-face Jack who confronts interpretations he regards as inadequate or misguided, and attacks them with gusto. That Jack I nicknamed 'Jack Hammer' at a meeting some years ago. He confirmed the aptness of the nickname the very next day, when, in reference to a particularly weak piece of scholarship, he said that we needed to pulverize it. This is the Jack you hope to avoid triggering. When this Jack does explode, you hope the shrapnel misses you.

Yet there is another side to Jack, one that is not pugnacious and critical but creative and generative—even nurturing. Jack has generated a host of creative scholarship, but he has also encouraged creativity in others by mapping out where he thinks biblical studies should be going. This visionary side of Jack has inspired my scholarship, and my contribution to this volume owes a debt to an agenda-setting text he wrote twenty years ago, *What Is Social-Scientific Criticism?* (1993). The book drew my attention to ritual as a subject of study (1993: 133, 115) and to ritual studies as an interpretive approach or model that belonged to the larger program of social-scientific criticism (1993: 126). So although my attention has turned in recent years from Corinth and Paul to the Gospel of Mark, my approach has remained the same. What I offer in this chapter is an interpretation of Mark that is sensitive to ritual and informed by ritual theory.

Semeia vol. 67, which appeared almost twenty years ago and bears the title *Transformations, Passages, and Processes: Ritual Approaches to Biblical Texts*, may be the best point of departure for considering the Gospel of Mark as ritual (McVann 1994b). In it, Mark McVann's interpretation of Mark, 'Reading Mark Ritually: Honor–Shame and the Ritual of Baptism', and Carol J. Schersten LaHurd's response, 'Exactly What's Ritual about the Experience of Reading/Hearing Mark's Gospel?', identify and explore several important issues relevant to this chapter (McVann 1994a; LaHurd 1994). A brief consideration of McVann and LaHurd will set the table for the ritual interpretation of Mark articulated below.

Key points in each article are worth noting. McVann's ritual reading of Mark depended on Benoît Standaert's and Augustine Stock's rhetorical analyses, which found a concentric and chiastic structure (A-B-A′) in the Gospel, emphasizing its beginning or prologue (Mk 1.1-13), center (8.27–10.52, especially 8.27–9.1), and end or epilogue (16.1-8) (Standaert 1978: 427; 1997: 24-29; Stock 1989). According to Standaert, this rhetorical organization, and the dramatic nature of the narrative, belonged in a festive and commemorative setting; consequently, he hypothesized that Mark was read during the Paschal evening (Easter vigil) when the events of Christ's passion were recalled. Since this was the preferred time for baptism in the early church, Standaert ventured to call Mark an initiation text. In addition to a Paschal *haggadah*, therefore, Mark would have served as a baptismal liturgy. McVann supports and extends this interpretation, elaborating on the ritual aspect of Mark by introducing Victor Turner's work on rites of passage and the transformative aspect of ritual (Turner 1969; 1974). Turner distinguished ritual, which he considered transformative, from ceremonies, which he regarded as confirmatory (Turner 1967: 95).[1] To support the connection between Mark and baptismal practice posited by Standaert, McVann asserts the ubiquity of baptism in Mark: 'Mark's narrative is thus thoroughly imbued with baptismal imagery and themes, and baptismal imagery abounds at the three most important points in the Gospel's narrative structure, namely, the beginning, middle, and the end' (McVann 1994a: 186). Also in those key passages, McVann claims that they narrate what is essentially a rite of status transformation: Jesus' baptism in ch. 1 marked his transformation into God's adopted son and prophetic agent; Jesus initiated his followers into the way of true discipleship—the way of the cross—at the Gospel's midpoint (8.27-9.1); and the empty tomb narrative in ch. 16 signals a dramatic change in Jesus' status from death to life, from humiliation and shame to exaltation and honor. Thus the text, replete with baptismal imagery and filled with rites of passage, shows every indication of having been used in conjunction with the initiate's entry into the church via baptism, the Christian rite of passage par excellence.

LaHurd's positive and negative criticisms of McVann are equally instructive. On the positive side, she applauds McVann for introducing Turner's work on ritual process and transformation, because doing so helps make sense of the Marcan narrative as a whole—that Jesus undergoes a profound status transformation in the course of the story. Moreover, LaHurd concurs with McVann's claim that in several key episodes within the larger story, Jesus undergoes what is properly understood as a rite of passage. The three stages comprising a typical rite of passage are most evident in the opening

1. I assume that a ritual can be transformative or confirmatory, or sometimes both.

chapter, where Jesus departs from Nazareth and is baptized (separation), spends time in the wilderness (liminality), then returns to society to spread the good news (aggregation). Thus, she concludes, 'McVann has effectively demonstrated that Turner's stages can help illuminate dynamics within Mark's story of Jesus' (LaHurd 1994: 206).

LaHurd's approval of McVann's ritual analysis is not unqualified, however. For she finds Jesus' identity and status in the Gospel not only transformed but also, at many points, confirmed. To the extent that Mark focuses on revealing who Jesus is, she argues, that portion or aspect of it is confirmatory rather than transformative, which stands in tension with how McVann characterizes the Gospel. My own survey of the rites reported in Mark lends support to LaHurd's position. Of the approximately 158 rituals reported in Mark 1–11, 110 are largely transformative and 48 are mostly confirmatory. So while transformative ritual action dominates Mark, a closer look reveals that the Gospel is a mixture of transformative and confirmatory rituals.

More critically, LaHurd finds that McVann weakens his ritual analysis of Mark by placing too much emphasis on baptism, or, to put it more sharply, by finding baptism in too many places. As noted above, McVann finds baptismal imagery throughout the Gospel, but he does so by following Standaert and Stock in reading Mark through a Pauline lens. For it is only by introducing Paul's understanding of baptism as dying and rising with Christ (Rom. 6.1-11) that one can find a baptismal allusion in the cross and resurrection language at Mark's midpoint, and in the crucifixion and empty tomb narrative at the end. Even if the young man who flees naked at Jesus' arrest and reappears clothed in white at the tomb[2] alludes to the ritual of baptism—Standaert, Stock and McVann follow this interpretation—baptism is not a major theme in the closing chapters of Mark. McVann has limited and thus weakened his ritual analysis of Mark, LaHurd would say, by making baptism the primary or sole vehicle for ritual transformation.

The question of how present (or absent) baptism is in the text of Mark has implications for what McVann (and Standaert and Stock) claims about the purpose and *Sitz im Leben* of Mark. LaHurd poses several important questions in this regard toward the end of her critique. McVann argued that the emphasis on ritual transformation and ubiquity of baptism in the Gospel were evidence for setting and use: they mirrored the reality faced by initiates at Easter vigil and marked it as a baptismal liturgy. LaHurd accepts the logic of McVann's reasoning, but is unconvinced by his conclusion, because she finds less baptism and (ritual) transformation than he claims. Thus she asks, 'is there sufficient textual evidence that the ritual status transformation

2. Mark 14.51-52 and 16.5 use the same term for young man, νεανίσκος, which appears nowhere else in Mark. This line of interpretation is well laid out in Scroggs and Groff 1973.

of readers/hearers is a major concern of the Markan text?' (LaHurd 1994: 206). Hers is a rhetorical question whose answer is clearly 'no'.

The value of LaHurd's critique, beyond its effective criticism of McVann's interpretation of Mark, lies in the clarity it brings to the issue of ritual analysis in general. For it differentiates the application of a model or theory of ritual to a text in order to interpret it from determining whether a text arose from ritual activity and had a ritual function. LaHurd herself does not always keep the two tasks separated, and they are related issues. Still, she makes the distinction clear enough: while she appreciates McVann's application of Turner to the Gospel of Mark because it illuminates dynamics in it, she questions whether those who composed and/or preserved the Gospel of Mark intended it to be used or actually used it in a baptismal setting. LaHurd's critique of McVann broaches the important subject of *how* one determines whether a text arose in a ritual setting and had a ritual function or purpose.

With this distinction in mind—ritual theory as interpretive tool versus the possible ritual origins and function of a text—we now move to the ritual interpretation of Mark offered in this chapter. It has two steps. The first is what might be called an etic approach in which I use a ritual model heuristically to help us, outsiders to first-century Mediterranean society, make sense of the Gospel of Mark. The second is an exploration at an emic level into the origins and function of Mark in the first century. In this case the question is, did first-century Christ followers compose Mark in a ritual setting and use it for ritual purposes?

Theoretically there are dozens of ritual models or theories that could be applied to a text, but the number of models or theories that actually sheds light on a given text and advances the interpretation of it would be relatively small. LaHurd saw utility in McVann bringing a Turnerian perspective to bear on Mark, but I would question whether McVann's interpretation of Mark has improved our understanding of that Gospel. What interpretive impasse or problem is solved? It is already clear without resort to ritual theory that Jesus' baptism and passion signal major transitions in the narrative. Does it shed any further light on Mark to analyze those episodes as rites of passage? Even the causal reader notices profound change in Jesus' status in the course of the Gospel. Does considering it as a rite of transformation lead to greater understanding? I would want to hear a fuller presentation from McVann before I am convinced that it does.

This is not to say that Turner cannot be fruitfully applied to New Testament texts. A case in point is Christian Strecker's application of Turner's work on ritual to the apostle Paul, his letters, and his theology (Strecker 1999). My praise for *Die liminale Theologie des Paulus: Zugänge zur paulinischen Theologie aus kulturanthropologischer Perspecktive* is unrestrained:

> The great strength and appeal of this book lie in the fresh and satisfying solutions it proposes to some perennial problems in Pauline scholarship. For instance, Strecker suggests an inviting alternative to the dispute over whether Paul's 'Damascus experience' was a conversion or a call. Reading that event as an initiation allows Strecker to take the radical transformation that Paul underwent seriously while at the same time avoiding the problematic implications of characterizing it as a conversion (from Judaism to Christianity) (DeMaris 2001: 79).

What makes Strecker's analysis praiseworthy is not the use of Turner per se but the results of the application. Strecker's ritual analysis promises a solution to a long-standing problem in Pauline studies. Accordingly, a ritual reading of Mark might best be introduced as the solution to an interpretive problem.

What follows is an interpretation of Mark at the etic level, and we begin with a problem. The various theological, historical and literary approaches to Mark that hold sway over New Testament studies have not convincingly accounted for why the second evangelist presented the story's protagonist, Jesus, as he did. The problem is this: the difference between the way Jesus is portrayed in the first half of the Gospel is strikingly different from that of the second half. In chs. 1 to 10, Jesus appears as an overwhelmingly powerful figure, able to conquer the demonic by exorcising evil spirits right and left and to overcome sickness by bringing healing to those who approach him. In contrast, from ch. 11 to the end of Mark, Jesus seems powerless to resist concerted efforts to humiliate him and bring about his death (Collins 1992: 40-41). On its face, then, the Gospel of Mark makes little sense, for it seems to convey a contradictory or at least inconsistent message about who Jesus is.

The many attempts to reconcile the two Marcan portraits of Jesus have not met with success, because what these interpretations offer is not reconciliation of the two but the capitulation of one portrait to another. While Martin Kälher's provocative claim that the Gospels are passion narratives with extended introductions is dismissed as overstatement (Kähler 1896: 80 n. 1), studies of Mark invariably place primary emphasis on the passion narrative and make the preceding narrative subservient to it. In some studies, such as Theodore Weeden's *Mark: Traditions in Conflict*, the portrayal of Jesus as miracle worker represents an inadequate Christology that is corrected by the theology of suffering embodied in the passion narrative (Weeden 1971). In other studies, the cross or Jesus' death becomes the interpretive key to the whole Gospel, so that the powerful Jesus disappears. Such emphasis is nowhere more emphatically put than in the conclusion of *What Are They Saying about Mark?*, where Frank Matera writes,

> Anyone who has read through this book has become aware that the cross and death of Jesus play the central role in Mark's theology. It is to the

> credit of Markan scholarship that it has resolutely struggled with Wrede's messianic secret, a theological problem which has shown them that the cross stands at the center of Mark's theology. It is to the credit of Markan scholarship that it has struggled with the titles Son of God and Son of Man and discovered that neither can be understood apart from the cross. It is to the credit of Markan scholarship that it has doggedly pursued Mark's view of the disciples and discovered that in this Gospel discipleship cannot be grasped apart from the cross (Matera 1987: 95).

Still other studies assert that Mark's portrayal of Jesus is paradoxical, but this amounts to another way of stating (but not solving) the problem.

Yet no reader of Mark can miss the abundance and salience of healings and exorcisms in the first half of the Gospel, so much so that they outweigh Jesus' teachings in terms of amount and prominence. As Adele Yarbro Collins notes,

> The first eight chapters of Mark contain fifteen miracle stories. In addition to these specific accounts, five Markan summaries or editorial remarks mention Jesus' many healings or exorcisms or both. Furthermore, in the narrative about the appointment of the twelve, it is said that they were to be sent out to preach and to cast out demons (3:14-15). Immediately following is an elaborated pronouncement story whose core is a controversy over the source of Jesus' power to cast out demons (3:19b-35). Later the sending out of the twelve to preach and cast out demons is narrated (6:7-11) and their success in exorcising and healing is summarized (6:12-13). At least one-half of the narrative material in these first eight chapters is devoted to miracles (Collins 1992: 58-59).

Given the prominence of healings and exorcisms in Mark, interpretations that downplay them or subordinate them to another event in, or aspect of, Jesus' life fail to do justice to Mark. The powerful Jesus is not simply a foil for the powerless Jesus. How then can these two portraits be understood as compatible and even congruent?

A ritual approach to Mark provides a way of reconciling the two portraits. Scholars have introduced Catherine Bell's typology of ritual action to the study of Qumran literature (and community ritual) and the Old Testament Apocrypha and Pseudepigrapha (Kugler 2002; Arnold 2006; Davila 2004a), and the typology may be particularly useful for understanding Mark because of how Bell classifies and groups rituals. Her categories are sixfold, which she says strike a balance between completeness and simplicity (Bell 1997: 94). James Davila offers this useful summary of them:

1. *Rites of Passage* are, most basically, rites of birth, coming of age, marriage, and death. They may include rites of initiation.
2. *Calendrical Rites* are ritual observances of seasonal changes or commemorations of important historical events.

3. *Rites of Exchange and Communion* include various kinds of offerings to a deity, sacrifices (involving destruction of the offering and perhaps some type of communal consumption), prayer, incantation, divination, consultation of oracles, incubation, and fertility rites. These rites operate on a continuum between quid-pro-quo exchanges for benefits (material gains, atonement, spiritual advances, etc.) and nearly disinterested communion and devotion to the divine.
4. *Rites of Affliction* have the purpose of mitigating the influence of negative forces/states such as demonic spirits, sins, and impurity. They include rituals of healing, exorcism, purification, along with self-afflicting and purificatory preparation for encounters with the divine (such as voluntary trance and possession, and vision quest), as well as oaths and curses intended to mobilize negative forces against oath breakers or enemies, and executions of malefactors to purify the community.
5. *Feasting, Fasting, and Festivals* are cultural performances expressing commitment to the religion, society, community, etc. These include lamentations, processions, games and contests, pilgrimages, and carnivals and rituals of reversal.
6. *Political Rites* display and promote the power of political institutions, using symbolic representation to make these institutions seem natural or part of the order of things. They include royal rites, enthronement rituals, legal ceremonies, ceremonies of warfare, and ritual dramas with a political end (Davila 2004b; cf. Bell 1997: 93-137).

From the angle Bell provides, we see that much of what transpires in Mark 1–10 falls under category no. 4, rites of affliction (which some scholars refer to as cult of affliction or possession cult [Skultans 2005: 1.56-69]). Not just the obvious material, such as the numerous healings and exorcisms, belongs here. The baptism and temptation sequence, because it involves the spirit possession of Jesus, and the transfiguration, because it entails ecstatic experience, fit under the category. We are also alerted by Bell's category to how tightly healing and exorcism are tied to issues of pollution and purification, which is reflected at numerous points in the Marcan narrative: exorcism involves the removal of unclean spirits (1.23, 26, 27; 3.11; 5.2, 8, 13; 6.7; 7.25); the woman who touches Jesus' garment is both healed and purified (5.25-34). The discourse about defilement in ch. 7 also fits under the rubric of rites of affliction, for it concerns purity, which is achieved and maintained by rites of affliction.[3]

3. Bell's ritual taxonomy, particularly the rubric of affliction, needs to be clearly distinguished from what Susan Garrett calls cultural models of affliction (Garrett 1995). Bell's use of the category falls toward the etic end of the scale, Garrett's toward the emic.

The key events of Jesus' final days in Jerusalem, beginning with the triumphal entry in Mark 11 and ending with his crucifixion in ch. 15, can also be understood as rites of affliction. The particular rite that Jesus underwent in those chapters is what I have labeled a curative exit rite, which came to expression in various forms in the ancient Mediterranean world: *pharmakos*, *devotio*, scapegoat (DeMaris 2008: 91-111). In the face of a crisis brought on by pollution, unholiness, illness, plague, military defeat, or other impairment or threat, a community would resort to a curative exit rite in order to restore wholeness and thereby preserve itself. The rite included both status elevation rites, by which a community member was designated, and status degradation rites, such as spitting, mocking, cursing, deriding, beating and stoning, by which the community transferred its ills, impurities, and iniquities to the designee for disposal. The designee's forced exit from the community (and, sometimes, death) completed the rite.

The closing chapters of Mark bear the telltale marks of a curative exit rite: a designee undergoes status transformation and ejection (DeMaris 2008: 94, 108). The Jesus who was declared king as he enters Jerusalem (11.1-11), who as authoritative prophet challenged the Temple complex and predicted its downfall (11.15-19; 13.1-37), who gained such respect from the populace that his opponents could not publicly check him (11.18; 12.12) and were even won over by him (12.32)—these events bring about Jesus' elevation in status—is the same Jesus who days later underwent status degradation rites. Those rites occupy much of the passion narrative: (1) Jesus' betrayal, arrest and desertion (14.43-50); (2) a sham trial before the ruling Jerusalemite elite at which Jesus is spat on, blindfolded and beaten (14.53-65); (3) a sham trial before Pilate that results in Barabbas, a murderer and insurrectionist, being acclaimed worthier than Jesus (15.1-15); (4) a mock investiture of Jesus as king during which he is struck and spat on (15.16-20); and (5) Jesus' crucifixion, a very demeaning form of execution, at which he is publicly derided by all parties present, even those crucified with him (15.25-32). This final humiliation takes place outside Jerusalem, where the soldiers have taken him. By giving the story of Jesus' final days the shape of a curative exit rite, the Gospel writer is able to find something profoundly important and positive in a series of events that were otherwise tragic.

It is useful to repeat here what I wrote earlier about the overall interpretation of Mark that results from reading the closing chapters of Mark as a curative exit rite:

> What does the gospel of Mark look like read through a ritual lens? The story of Jesus in Galilee, which leads up to the passion narrative, tells us much about Jesus but also describes a world that is terribly out of order. Illness and demon possession are prevalent, indicating that the land is no longer healthy. Likewise, the land has become unholy. The system of purification, with the Jerusalem Temple at its center, has failed, as evidenced

> by Jesus' devastating critique of the system (chap. 7) and the Temple (chap. 11). If the opening and middle chapters of Mark describe a world infected by unwholeness and unholiness, then the closing chapters present the ritual solution to the crisis: the designation of someone, via rites of elevation and degradation, who will bear the land's illness away (DeMaris 2008: 108).

Through the wider lens of Bell's rites of affliction, we see a related but slightly different picture. From that vantage point, we see Jesus acting on individuals to eliminate pollution, remove impairment and restore human wholeness in the opening chapters of Mark. As the story progresses, such activity expands to a societal and even cosmic level, for the passion narrative involves all Jerusalem and even a larger whole: at Jesus' death darkness is over the whole earth; the curtain of the Temple is torn in two. What unites the beginning and the end of Mark is common ritual action—action that is rectifying, healing, redressive, restorative, purifying, curative. The Gospel as a whole coheres around rites of affliction.

Finding unity in the Gospel of Mark by introducing Bell's ritual taxonomy enables the modern reader to make sense of Mark. It may also provide leads for determining Mark's origin and function, but it does not settle the matter. After all, an ancient narrative filled with reports about food, diet and eating would not necessarily have originated in the context of dining. Nor would it necessarily have been used in conjunction with dining ritual. Determining that Mark coheres around rites of affliction is important and maybe even necessary evidence for claiming that Mark developed in a ritual setting or served as a ritual text, but is not sufficient evidence.

What more do we need to make a case for Mark's ritual origins and function? This is the second step in the interpretation offered in this chapter. It is more speculative than the first, in part because the church of the second, third and fourth centuries and later referred to Mark infrequently, so we are in the dark as to how it was used (Moloney 2002: 1; Schildgen 1999: 37). Also, the application of speech-act theory, orality studies and performance theory to the New Testament encourages us to understand Mark in new ways, so that we need to picture the Gospel functioning more like a script than a text in the church, which was largely illiterate (Gilfillan Upton 2006; Horsley, Draper and Foley 2006; Shiner 2003). In other words, Mark was composed to be read aloud, and dramatically so, and most ancient believers encountered Mark aurally; so it is appropriate to consider the performance of Mark and the effect it may have had on the listeners. While this approach is congenial with understanding Mark as ritual in general, it underscores the necessary speculation entailed in imagining what a performance of Mark was like and what it accomplished specifically. The nonverbal communication of the reciter/presenter/performer comes into play, which is virtually impossible to reconstruct, along with the likelihood that reciters modified Mark according to audience and situation.

This second step in the ritual interpretation of Mark raises doubts about a broad consensus among New Testament scholars that Mark had its roots in the proclamation about Jesus Christ and that the Gospel writer's aim was to present the story of Jesus and engender belief in him. Interpreters describe Mark's purpose variously—kerygmatic (O'Grady 1979: 157), didactic (Boring 2006: 21-22), catechetical (Collins 1992: 90), exhortatory (Best 1983: 51), apologetic, polemical (Weeden 1971: 162-68), explanatory—but the essential function is invariably the same: to inform and to persuade. This is not a surprising consensus, since this is how texts typically function in literate cultures; but it is anachronistic, since the ancient church and ancient Mediterranean society as a whole was an oral culture, and texts function differently in such a setting. If not to communicate and convince, therefore, how did Mark function?

Scholarship in an allied field, classics, may provide assistance in answering this question. Richard Seaford's study of ancient Attic tragedy argues that performance of it enhanced social cohesion. Seaford maintains that the intense emotion the ancient Greeks associated with attending a tragedy is best understood collectively. It was not an emotional release or personal catharsis—this is an individualist, hence anachronistic, reading—but the shared feeling of solidarity experienced by the audience as it responded to the tragedy it witnessed. The common response would have been group lamentation (Seaford 1994: 86-92, 139-43; 2000: 32, 43). Seaford finds not only a social effect but a political one as well: the tragedies would have increased democratic cohesion among the Athenians (Seaford 2000: 34-37). Tragic presentation of powerful individuals' crimes and their disastrous consequences gave expression to the Athenians' deeply conflicting attitudes toward contemporary oligarchs and tyrants of the past who could unify the state but also threaten it and its democratic elements. One would not want to push the analogy too far, given their profoundly different social locations and genres, but perhaps Mark, like Greek tragedy, had a socially ameliorative and unifying effect on the circle of hearers.

Magical practices among ancient Christians, though documentation of them is relatively late, may also give insight into how Mark functioned ritually. Of particular interest is the phenomenon of *historiolae*, as it suggests that narrative texts were thought to embody a certain power that could be invoked for palliative, curative, or protective ends (Frankfurter 1995). *Historiolae* (little stories) are

> short narrations inserted into written or spoken spells, usually evocative of longer tales that are well known. For example, a Coptic Christian spell first sketches a story of how Jesus and the angel Michael relieved a doe's

> labor pains; implicit is the presumption that the patient for whom the spell is recited will similarly be relieved (Johnston 2004: 145).

These short narratives typically came from the Gospels and were sometimes paired with imperatival or performative language that directed the beneficial power, as in this amulet text:

> Holy, holy, holy, lord . . . and he who has healed again, who has raised Lazarus from the dead even now on the fourth day, who has healed Peter's mother-in-law, who has also accomplished many unmentioned healings in addition to those they report in the sacred gospels: Heal her who wears this divine amulet of the disease afflicting her . . . (Meyer and Smith 1994: 38, no. 13 [=*PGM* 2.227]).

Sometimes the narrative excerpt stood alone. The healing spell below introduces the narrative passage in such a way as to suggest its application, but is not explicit or directive. Whoever pronounced the spell may have supplied additional language relevant to the situation:

> Curative Gospel according to Matthew. And Jesus went about all of Galilee, teaching and preaching the gospel of the kingdom, and healing every disease {and every disease} and every infirmity among the people. And his fame spread into all of Syria, and they brought him those who were ill, and Jesus healed them (Meyer and Smith 1994: 33, no. 7 [=Oxyrhynchus 1077 and *PGM* 2.211]).

Given the heavy concentration of healing and exorcism stories in Mark—heavier than any other Gospel, canonical or noncanonical—it is probable that Mark emerged and developed in a circle of reciters keen on highlighting Jesus' curative powers. Was the aim of composition simply to inform hearers about the miraculous deeds of Jesus? To answer 'yes' would ignore the influence a written text had in oral culture, the powerful effect the spoken word had on an audience, and the use of Gospel narratives in healing rituals. Certainly we should not be surprised if a text thick with healings and exorcisms were pressed into use in the early Christian health care system, given the very limited availability of health care in the ancient Mediterranean world (Avalos 1999). Later additions to Mark lend credibility to the claim that curative and protective ritual practices were central to the Marcan tradition. The so-called Longer Ending of Mark refers to exorcism, protection from snake bite and poison, and healing in a mere eleven verses (16.9-20).

Further attention to the content of Mark, along with its likely date of composition, suggests an additional use for Mark, a use related to those described above. The appearance of Mark coincided with the disappearance of the Jerusalem Temple, the center and monumental embodiment of the Judean purity system. The destruction of the Temple necessitated a dramatic reformulation of that system because a primary mechanism for pollution removal—sacrifice at the Temple—was gone (Hanson and Oakman 2008: 135). That reformulation was anticipated by the Gospel of Mark, in which Jesus attacks the existing understanding of purity and defilement in ch. 7, assails the Temple functionaries in ch. 11, and predicts the Temple's destruction in ch. 13. The miraculous tearing of the Temple veil at Jesus' death marks the climax of the reformulation, for the intertwining of the two events signals Jesus' displacement of the Temple. The death of Jesus marks the completion of the *pharmakos* rite, which Jesus underwent to restore wholeness and holiness to the people. What the Temple-centered purity system had once done, Jesus now did. Access to, and participation in, the *pharmakos* rite could be realized every time the story was retold or reenacted. For hearers of Mark, then, it could function as a rite of purification.

This second step in the ritual interpretation of Mark, which has attempted to establish the origins and function of the Gospel, concludes that Mark arose not for purposes of communication and persuasion. Rather, its primary function was therapeutic: socially unifying and ameliorative, palliative and curative, restorative and purificatory. The aim was not to spread the good news but to derive community benefits from the story and the events it recalled.

References

Arnold, Russell C.D.

2006 *The Social Role of Liturgy in the Religion of the Qumran Community* (STDJ, 60; Leiden: Brill).

Avalos, Hector

1999 *Health Care and the Rise of Christianity* (Peabody, MA: Hendrickson Publishers).

Bell, Catherine

1997 *Ritual: Perspectives and Dimensions* (Oxford: Oxford University Press).

Best, Ernest

1983 *Mark: The Gospel as Story* (Edinburgh: T. & T. Clark).

Boring, M. Eugene

2006 *Mark: A Commentary* (NTL; Louisville, KY: Westminster John Knox).

Collins, Adela Yarbro

1992 *The Beginning of the Gospel: Probings of Mark in Context* (Minneapolis, MN: Fortress Press).

Davila, James R.

2004a 'Ritual in the Pseudepigrapha', in *Anthropology and Biblical Studies: Avenues of Approach* (ed. Louise J. Lawrence and Mario I. Aguilar; Leiden: Deo Publishing): 158-83.

2004b 'Ritual in the Old Testament Apocrypha' (paper presented at the Symposium on Anthropology and the Old Testament, Glasgow, August 27).

DeMaris, Richard E.

2001 Review of *Die liminale Theologie des Paulus: Zugänge zur paulinischen Theologie aus kulturanthropologischer Perspecktive*, by Christian Strecker, in *BTB* 31: 79.

2008 *The New Testament in its Ritual World* (London: Routledge).

Elliott, John H.

1993 *What Is Social-Scientific Criticism?* (Guides to Biblical Scholarship, New Testament Series; Minneapolis, MN: Fortress Press).

Frankfurter, David

1995 'Narrating Power: The Theory and Practice of the Magical *Historiola* in Ritual Spells', in *Ancient Magic and Ritual Power* (ed. Marvin Meyer and Paul Mirecki; Religions in the Graeco-Roman World, 129; Leiden: E.J. Brill): 457-76.

Garrett, Susan R.

1995 'Paul's Thorn and Cultural Models of Affliction', in *The Social World of the First Christians: Essays in Honor of Wayne A. Meeks* (ed. L.M. White and O.L. Yarbrough; Minneapolis, MN: Fortress Press): 82-99.

Gilfillan Upton, Bridget

2006 *Hearing Mark's Endings: Listening to Ancient Popular Texts through Speech Act Theory* (Biblical Interpretation Series, 79; Leiden: Brill).

Hanson, K.C., and Douglas E. Oakman

2008 *Palestine in the Time of Jesus: Social Structures and Social Conflicts* (Minneapolis, MN: Fortress Press, 2nd edn).

Horsley, Richard A., Jonathan A. Draper and John Miles Foley (eds.)

2006 *Performing the Gospel: Orality, Memory, and Mark* (Minneapolis, MN: Fortress Press).

Johnston, Sarah Iles

2004 'Magic', in *Religions of the Ancient World: A Guide* (ed. Sarah Iles Johnston; Harvard University Press Reference Library; Cambridge, MA: Harvard University Press): 139-52.

Kähler, Martin

1896 *Der sogenannte historische Jesus und der geschichtliche, biblische Christus* (Leipzig: Deichert, 2nd edn).

Kugler, Rob

2002 'Making All Experience Religious: The Hegemony of Ritual at Qumran', *JSJ* 33.2: 131-52.

LaHurd, Carol J. Schersten

1994 'Exactly What's Ritual about the Experience of Reading/Hearing Mark's Gospel?', in McVann 1994b: 199-208.

Matera, Frank J.

1987 *What Are They Saying about Mark?* (New York: Paulist Press, 1987).

McVann, Mark

1994a 'Reading Mark Ritually: Honor–Shame and the Ritual of Baptism', in McVann 1994b: 179-98.

McVann, Mark (ed.)

1994b *Transformations, Passages, and Processes: Ritual Approaches to Biblical Texts* (Semeia, 67; Atlanta, GA: Scholars Press).

Meyer, Marvin, and Richard Smith (eds.)

1994 *Ancient Christian Magic: Coptic Texts of Ritual Power* (San Francisco, CA: HarperSanFrancisco).

Moloney, Francis J.

2002 *The Gospel of Mark: A Commentary* (Peabody, MA: Hendrickson Publishers).

O'Grady, John F.

1979 'The Origins of the Gospels: Mark', *BTB* 9: 154-64.

Schildgen, Brenda Deen

1999 *Power and Prejudice: The Reception of the Gospel of Mark* (Detroit, MI: Wayne State University Press).

Scroggs, Robin, and Kent I. Groff

1973 'Baptism in Mark: Dying and Rising with Christ', *JBL* 92: 531-48.

Seaford, Richard

1994 *Reciprocity and Ritual: Homer and Tragedy in the Developing City-State* (Oxford: Clarendon Press).

2000 'The Social Function of Attic Tragedy: A Response to Jasper Griffin', *Classical Quarterly* 50: 30-44.

Shiner, Whitney

2003 *Proclaiming the Gospel: First-Century Performance of Mark* (Harrisburg, PA: Trinity Press International).

Skultans, Vieda

2005 'Affliction: An Overview', *Encyclopedia of Religion* (15 vols.; Detroit, MI: Thomson Gale/Macmillan Reference, 2nd edn): 1.56-69.

Standaert, Benoît

1978 *L'évangile selon Marc: Composition et genre littéraire* (Nijmegen: Stichting Studentenpers).

1997 *L'évangile selon Marc: Commentaire* (Lire la Bible, 61; Paris: Les Éditions du Cerf, 2nd edn).

Stock, Augustine

1989 *The Method and Message of Mark* (Wilmington, DE: Michael Glazier).

Strecker, Christian

1999 *Die liminale Theologie des Paulus: Zugänge zur paulinischen Theologie aus kulturanthropologischer Perspecktive* (FRLANT, 185; Göttingen: Vanderhoeck & Ruprecht).

Turner, Victor W.

1967 *The Forest of Symbols: Aspects of Ndembu Ritual* (Ithaca, NY: Cornell University Press).

1969 *The Ritual Process: Structure and Anti-Structure* (Chicago: Aldine).

1974 *Dramas, Fields, and Metaphors: Symbolic Action in Human Society* (Symbol, Myth, and Ritual; Ithaca, NY: Cornell University Press).

Weeden, Theodore J.

1971 *Mark: Traditions in Conflict* (Philadelphia, PA: Fortress Press).

Disease, Table and Economy in Luke 16.19-31

Jonathan A. Draper

Introduction

This paper arises out of a concern to explore the implications of the Jesus tradition and its attitude toward disease and healing in the face of the crisis of HIV/AIDS in South Africa. I am delighted to offer it in honour of John H. Elliott, whose ground-breaking book *A Home for the Homeless: A Sociological Exegesis of 1 Peter, its Situation and Strategy* (1981) offered me and many others a refreshingly new model for the application of social-scientific theory to ancient texts which has substantially influenced my own study. Attention to the social sciences has enabled New Testament scholars to revisit old interpretations with fresh perspectives that often speak more clearly to modern crises. It may seem somewhat odd to apply social-scientific theory on disease and healing to the well-known story of Dives/Rich Man and Lazarus. At first glance it does not seem to be very apposite. It is not a healing story in which Jesus shows his power over disease or demons. In fact, it is a parable widely used in sermons on riches and poverty rather than on disease. However, the connection is not as arbitrary as it at first seems. After all, Lazarus is suffering from a skin disease and its social consequences, a disease that labels him a social deviant, marginalizes him and from which he dies in the end—yet it is not the end. Is it simply a story about the need to give to the poor, or could it be read as a story about the social and economic location and consequences of disease, offering insights into Jesus' (or at least Luke's) own approach to the social aspects of disease? How does Lazarus's disease relate to his exclusion from the rich man's table? Ernest van Eck, in his helpful study of the parable using patron–client theory comments, 'The reason why Lazarus ended up at the gate of the rich man can only be speculated upon' (2009: 353). Read from the perspective of the relationship between the body and society, however, van Eck's analysis can be taken further, as I will demonstrate in what follows.

Previous Research on the Parable of the Rich Man and Lazarus

Most of the research into this parable has focused either on its implications for ethical economic behaviour or on its sources. The first major study on the parable in 1918 was a source-critical study by H. Gressmann, *Vom reichen Mann und armen Lazarus: Eine literargeschichtliche Studie*. He argued for an Egyptian source for the parable, citing the story of Setme and his son Si-Osiris, who pass a funeral and observe the burial of a rich man and a beggar. Si-Osiris, who is a god in disguise, then shows his father that the rich man is being punished in the underworld for his wicked deeds, while the beggar is being rewarded for his good deeds. We have then, in common with Jesus' parable, the combination of the theme of wealth and poverty, and a picture of the fate of the two men in the next world. However, unlike the Egyptian parallel, Jesus' parable says nothing about the relative moral behaviour of the two men. Gressman also examines various Judean[1] parallels to this story and argues that Jesus knew and used a version of the story from popular Judean culture. The Judean parallels, like the Egyptian one, stress the moral consequences in the next life of good or bad deeds, though balancing those consequences with rewards received in this life for good and bad behaviour. The parallels in (late) rabbinic texts are provided by both Bultmann (1968: 197) and Jeremias (1971: 182-87) as providing the background to Jesus' use of the story. Ronald Hock (1987), on the other hand, rightly stresses the parallels in Graeco-Roman literature, particularly Lucian's dialogues *Gallus* and *Cataplus*, though without adding significantly to the interpretation of the parable itself.

A problem with these source-critical interpretations of the parable is that they do not account for the refusal of the request by the rich man to be allowed to return and warn his living brothers about the consequences of their uncaring behaviour, which is the main point of the story in the parallels. Bultmann (1968: 197) suggests a later 'polemical change' which disrupts Jesus' simple parable. Jeremias (1971: 186), on the other hand, finds here bedrock teaching of Jesus through comparison with other Synoptic

1. The use of the term 'Jewish' in studies of first century CE literature is problematic, since it often assumes an anachronistic unity based on later Rabbinic writings where there was in fact diversity (see Elliott 2007). 'Judean' was an outsider label used in the Graeco-Roman world for the Israelite people, whereas the insider term they used to refer to themselves seems to have been 'all Israel' (Tomson 1986; 2000). Here I will use 'Judean' to refer to the southern temple state and its region, including the inhabitants of Jerusalem, its elite and its envoys. I will use 'Israelite' to refer to 'all Israel' in an inclusive sense, where the inhabitants of Galilee and the diaspora of Israel are also in mind.

tradition, so that Lazarus 'is only a secondary figure' since 'Jesus does not want to comment on a social problem, nor does he intend to give teaching about the after-life, but he relates the parable to warn men who resemble the brothers of the rich man of the impending danger'. Both interpretations weaken the force of the parable in my opinion. While agreeing that the background of the story may lie in Egyptian and Israelite common popular tradition, an excellent study by Richard Bauckham (1991) points out that the central point of Jesus' parable is quite different: it is the stark contrast in economic and social living conditions—luxury versus beggary—that determines the fate of the two men, since nothing is said at all about the moral behaviour of either of them. It is simply a story of eschatological reversal and says little about 'human destiny after death'. Bauckham points out that the request for a return of the departed to warn the living is refused in the story, unlike other similar ancient Near Eastern stories, and that the story offers no explanation about how the living would know about the events it describes. This, he argues, is paradoxically the point of the story:

> The story in effect deprives itself of any claim to offer an apocalyptic glimpse of the secrets of the world beyond the grave. It cannot claim eyewitness authority as a literal description of the fate of the dead. It has only the status of parable. It is part of a story told to make a point. The point is no more than the law and the prophets say—and that no more than the law and the prophets say is required. . . . By refusing an apocalyptic revelation from the world of the dead, the parable throws the emphasis back onto the situation with which it began (Bauckham 1991: 245-46).

Hence the story is really a warning to the rich about their uncaring behaviour, since the story clearly has an economic reference and draws on the tradition of reversal often found in trickster tales and carnival, which according to James C. Scott (1990: 135-82) is characteristic of oppressed peasant societies. Recent social-scientific readings of the parable have rightly emphasized the way in which its message relates to the 'moral economy of the peasant' (Sahlins 1972; Scott 1976), in which the economy is not separated from the moral order but embedded in it (see Moxnes 1988: 75-98, esp. 89-90). Ernest van Eck's interesting study of the parable turns appropriately to the model of patron–client relationships in the ancient world against the background of the exploitation of the peasantry which reduced them to the kind of penury represented by Lazarus, producing an unbridgeable gap between patrons and clients. However, ironically, van Eck's interpretation would leave the patron–client system intact if only it is practiced generously: 'This is the result of patrons not being patrons. Real patrons are children of Abraham and they look after the poor' (2009: 9).

Why Is Lazarus outside the Gate?

My own interpretation of this parable focuses on why Lazarus is outside the gate. This interpretation is informed by Mary Douglas's work on the body as a social map (developed in Douglas 1966, 1982 and 1999). Douglas argues that 'dirt' is a fundamental boundary marker for society: it relates to what is included and what is excluded in any social sphere. Additionally, she argues that social boundaries and the relative problems and experiences a society has with those boundaries (internal and external) will be marked out physically or in terms of dirt taboos of the body. Attitudes to boundaries will manifest in terms of form, external boundaries, internal boundaries and internal structure. A society that is under extreme pressure on its outward boundaries will manifest strong taboos vis-à-vis the boundaries of the physical body, particularly the orifices, mouth, anus, sexual organs and so on. Israel, as a society under constant threat of invasion, shows a particular obsession with the bodily boundaries, particularly food and sex (and to a lesser extent with excrement). Strong internal social contradictions and ambiguities will manifest themselves in an obsessive concern with purity laws, washing and unenforceable taboos that depend on self-monitoring (e.g. *zab*, body flux of blood or semen). Douglas develops this theme with regard to Israel in her two key works. In *Purity and Danger* (1966: 41-57) she argues that the dietary rules in Leviticus 11 represent the organizing principles of symbolic system of the Israelite social universe in which the prohibition of pork carries no special emphasis but is only prohibited as one of a series of 'anomalies' within this symbolic system of relations. In response to criticism of her hypothesis, she argues in *Natural Symbols* (1982: 38-41) that the special abhorrence of pork that characterizes later Jewish culture was the result of repeated military invasion by outside powers and the attempt by Antiochus Epiphanes to force the sacrifice of pigs and the eating of pork on the Jewish people as a part of his attempted integration of his empire around Greek religion. Practices such as the resolute avoidance of pork in ancient Israel, like Friday fasting among expatriate Irish Catholic labourers in London, 'gain significance as symbols of allegiance simply by their lack of meaning for other cultures' (1982: 40). The purity of the body is shorthand for observation of the whole law, and the preservation of its boundaries is shorthand for resistance to military and cultural invasion. In an article entitled 'Deciphering a Meal' (1971), Douglas focuses attention on the way the dinner table in particular serves as a marker of social boundaries in all societies, internal and external; anthropologists call this the 'geography of the dinner table'.

Philip Esler highlights the importance of this theory for the study of Luke–Acts (1987: 71-109). Esler points to the predominance of table imagery in the book of Acts and questions where 'a legitimation of table fellowship between Jews and gentiles forms a vital arch in the symbolic universe which Luke creates for his community' (1987: 109). This makes a *prima facie* case for examining attitudes to table as boundary markers not only in Acts but in the Gospel of Luke as well.

With regard to our parable, Douglas's theory raises the question, 'Why, after all, is Lazarus lying outside the gate, when all and sundry—including dogs—are inside the gate observing (and participating, in as far as they can, even if not reclining at table) the rich man's opulent meals?' This is a significant question when the geography of the Mediterranean dinner table is taken into consideration. Being observed by social inferiors in such public acts of benefaction is a central aspect of a host's status in an honour–shame society, essential for acquired honour as opposed to ascribed honour (see Moxnes 1996; Malina 2001: 32-33). Exchange of banquets established *koinonia,* or friendship, between social equals and required reciprocity but also proclaimed and cemented the inferior position of the social unequals. The lavish gift of food (e.g. grain), public benefactions as well as access to power and services for social inferiors, established a relationship of dependency between patron and client (Moxnes 1991; Elliott 1996). There were, of course, differences between Israelite peoples and other Mediterranean societies with regard to meal practice; but recent studies have shown a remarkable convergence of practice in Mediterranean societies, including Israelite society, when it comes to rituals of dining, practices that differed significantly from our own preconceptions with regard to meals. In a study by Dennis Smith, *From Symposium to Eucharist: The Banquet in the Early Christian World* (2003), he argues that there was a clear 'social code' governing the operation of banquets in the ancient world. Smith (2003: 260-63), like Bauckham, sees in the Parable of the Rich Man and Lazarus the theme of eschatological reversal, in which the same tropes of the meal are found in the opulence of the Rich Man during his earthly life and Lazarus's dining with Abraham in the afterlife.

Meals in the Mediterranean world served to mark out and ritualize social boundaries by participation or non-participation. As we have noted, they built and consolidated social relations—particularly between equals, but also between patrons and clients—and created webs of mutual obligation. The seating of a person at the table was especially significant in marking out status and hierarchy. This was achieved by a remarkable degree of public display. In other words, the whole point of such geographical marking was the extent to which everyone could observe it. Those who were not included in the seating arrangements were not thereby excluded from the theatre of performance. Women, for instance, who were not by and large allowed to sit at table, with the exception of courtesans for the pleasure of male guests, and, perhaps, elite women who might even be patrons of a feast (see Smith 2003: 42-44; Osiek and MacDonald 2005). It seems that the situation was more fluid in the first century CE than it had been in earlier Graeco-Roman society (Corley 2010: 5-20). Nevertheless, women were present at meals to cook and serve, and their usual exclusion from the seating arrangements marked out for all their subordination to men. Servants hovered around, and uninvited guests, singers, prostitutes, beggars and dogs were also present or might wander in. Ramsay MacMullen (1981: 34-42) has described graphically the way in which beggars, the homeless, prostitutes and just about anyone might hover around temple feasts and public banquets in particular. However, this would likely be true at any formal meal. Such potential openness is one of five central characteristics of the ancient Mediterranean meal identified by Smith (2003: 23-25; cf. Klinghardt 1996: 84-97). Hal Taussig, drawing on Klinghardt, has observed also (2009: 26, 68, 82-84) that there was an upsurge in the intrusion of uninvited guests and unruly behaviour by such gate-crashers during the Hellenistic period. He argues, somewhat unconvincingly in my opinion, that this was related to the ritual creation of *communitas* during a period of rapid social change in 'the polyglot Hellenistic society' (2009: 82-85). Mary Douglas's theory would certainly indicate a relationship between such behaviour and a weakening of social boundaries as well as social structure (grid and group). There does not seem to be the same evidence of disorder in Israelite meals, but there is evidence of relatively open access to banquets.

If we read the Jesus tradition around meals with close attention, then we see that such public participation by social marginals was normal. So, for instance, a woman could walk in off the streets hearing that Jesus is eating in a particular house and wash his feet (Mk 14.3; Mt. 26.7-10; John 12). Luke 7.36-50 notes that a prostitute can come off the street and do the same. However, such conduct could bring shame on the woman or the man or both. A peasant with a low social status but a reputation as a prophet, such as Jesus, might be invited to a banquet for his entertainment value, but his low status would be marked by deliberate withholding of the courtesies due to equals: his feet are not washed, he is not greeted with a kiss and his head is not anointed with oil as, we are to understand, was the case with the other guests who were Simon's social equals (Lk. 7.36-50):

> Then turning toward the woman, he said to Simon, 'Do you see this woman? I entered your house; you gave me no water for my feet, but she has bathed my feet with her tears and dried them with her hair. You gave me no kiss, but from the time I came in she has not stopped kissing my feet. You did not anoint my head with oil, but she has anointed my feet with ointment (Lk. 7.44-46, NRSV).

We are not told whether Jesus was reclining at table, or whether he ate with the other guests. Taussig (2009: 82-85) indicates that some sages might come simply to get a hearing, and, while some elite performers might be among the reclining guests, probably the majority were not. The fact that his feet were not washed indicates that Jesus was brought in as a famous prophet only to entertain the guests at the *symposion*, so that he would have had to stand or sit on the floor awaiting his time to perform.

We also hear in the tradition that dogs had open access to the table. In the story of the healing of the Syrophoenician woman's daughter in Mk 7.24-30 (// in Mt. 15.21-28 but omitted by Luke), which is significant for its information on the table, the boundaries of Israel and the right of non-Israelites to share in the healing of Jesus, we read,

> Now the woman was a Gentile, of Syrophoenician origin. She begged him to cast the demon out of her daughter. He said to her, 'Let the children be fed first, for it is not fair to take the children's food and throw it to the dogs'. But she answered him, 'Sir, even the dogs under the table eat the children's crumbs' (Mk 7.26-28, NRSV).

Beggars would doubtless have vied with the dogs for food, hovering around the edge of the table, their marginal position re-enforced by their undignified scramble and tussle with dogs.

This whole picture of the table in antiquity reminds me very vividly of what I have observed at feasts and public meals in the Zulu community. Special guests will be invited and given special seats indicating their relative importance, but the whole community turns up anyway, invited or not, once they hear a feast is imminent. Even enemies will come, since failure to attend might indicate a social grudge or witchcraft. Beggars in rags and dogs (taking care to avoid being kicked) are hovering around the edges. No one is turned away. Indeed, the presence of the poor reinforces the status of the rich and the important. Who is conducted to the top table, where they sit, what food they are offered and in what order, maps out their status. Who is served the liver, the tongue and the prime haunch? Who gets to cut the meat and pass it out? Who is the first to receive? Who is served beer or fine drink and who is served watered-down orange juice. Women in traditional settings do not sit at the same table as men, for instance. Elite women will sit at a separate table; others will be preparing and serving food. The person who throws the feast will indicate how this is to be done and who is to be honoured.

So why is Lazarus sitting outside at the gate, longing for scraps, while beggars, dogs and others of low status can be present at the margins of the table? What marks him out as different is his disease. He is covered in sores. A beggar without sores might hover around the table with the dogs, but a beggar *with* sores that are clearly suppurating could not. He has damaged skin and a broken body, and that brings the clear threat of impurity to the whole community. His body maps out the social fears and endangered boundaries of the first-century Judean social universe. Hence he is shut outside, where the dogs lick his filthy open sores but, ironically, could subsequently go inside and fight for scraps at the feast.

The Geography of the Table in Luke 14.1–16.31

The link between this parable and geography of the table is not accidental in Luke. The parable is woven into the structure of this section of Luke, where 13.25–17.10 is chiastically structured to challenge the traditional geography of the table in Mediterranean society. What I have termed a Prelude and Postlude are perhaps only peripherally attached to the sequence, but I have included them since they indicate Luke's overall pattern of table and economy. The structure is (loosely) as follows, with the theme of table and meal emphasized in italics:

[A. Prelude: First and last 13.25-30 (to someone on the way)
Dining with Jesus now, dining with Abraham, Isaac and Jacob in the kingdom later
Refusing Jesus now, excluded from the feast in the kingdom later]
- B. Dining with a pharisaic ruler 14.1-24 [to lawyers and Pharisees]
  Healing of man with dropsy standing in front of the table
  Controversy about healing on the Sabbath: Saying of the son/ox in the pit
  Parable of place of honour at table—go low first
  Invite those who can't pay you back—poor, lame, blind
  Parable of the Wedding Feast
  - C. Counting the cost 14.25-35 [to crowds]
    Hate father and mother, life: carry cross
    Parable: Building a tower
    Parable: Going to war
    Parable: Salt losing its flavour
    - D. Accusation: This man receives sinners and eats with them 15.1-32 [to Pharisees and scribes]
      Parable of Lost Sheep: *rejoice/feast with me*
      Parable of Lost Coin: *rejoice/feast with me*
      Parable of Prodigal Son: rejoice/feast with me
      - spending inheritance wastefully and sinfully
      - eating pods with swine
      - eating calf with father
      - refusal to share meal with unclean/ sinner by brother
  - C′. God and mammon 16.1-13 [to disciples]
    Parable of Dishonest Steward: Friends can build community not just break it

Faithfulness/ unfaithfulness in little or much: Money little beside true riches
Two masters: God and mammon incompatible masters
B′. Counteraccusation: Pharisees are lovers of money and their behaviour an abomination in God's eyes 16.14-31 [to Pharisees]
Entering the kingdom violently
Divorce is adultery
Parable: Rich Man and Lazarus
- exclusion of the poor and diseased man from table
- exclusion of rich man from Abraham's [table]

[A′. Postlude: Parable of Servant and Master at Table 17.7-10)
(to disciples)
Lower status people should not expect thanks for serving at table since it is simply their duty]

The theme of table and meal (emphasized by italics), with the concomitant reference to insider/outsider and to social status tied up with wealth which is encoded in the table, weaves in and out of the narrative of 14.1–16.31, with what I have termed a Prelude and a Postlude that prepare for and continue the theme, connecting the passage with the wider narrative.[2] The central unit in the ring composition addresses the accusation of the Pharisees, 'This man receives sinners and eats with them' (15.2). His direct address to the scribes and Pharisees in B, D, B′ alternates with his address to the crowds/ disciples in [A], C, C′, [A′]. Jesus' own position throughout the section is insistence that the usual dinner table status is reversed in the kingdom he proclaims: go to the bottom of the table first and do not hanker after the top position; invite those who cannot pay you back and who are not your equals; feast with those who have been lost and are found; assume the position of a servant and not the position of the master at table. This is a radical critique of the Mediterranean meal and its role in re-enforcing status, wealth and domination. The Parable of the Rich Man and Lazarus serves as a climax to the series of teachings, addressing and dismissing the Pharisees' charge that he receives sinners and eats with them by denying in effect that

2. There have been many attempts to explain the structure and coherence of the 'Journey' narrative in Luke's central section (9.51–19.46). Many have seen an intricate chiastic structure here (see the bibliography provided by Frank J. Matera 1993: 61-2 n. 11; note especially C.H. Talbert 1974: 51-56). However, it would be too great a task to extend the patterns observed here with the gospel as a whole. While sceptical of such elaborate chiasms for Luke as a whole, Matera (1993) uses the concrete markers of place and time changes, together with the addressees of Jesus' discourses, to structure the Journey narrative. I also view these signals as key structural markers in a smaller chiastic structure.

the sick man outside the gate is a sinner, while warning them that they are the ones in danger of judgment because of their failure to care for the needy.

The Moral Economy of the Kingdom

Luke is certainly aware of the relationship between table, health and the economy (if we can use this anachronistic term). The sections C′ and B′ in particular connect the theme of the table with the question of mammon and love of money (φιλαργυρία). As Moxnes (1988: 139-53) has pointed out, a key feature of a patron was the appearance of not loving money (ἀφιλάργυρος). In theory, giving to others on the part of a patron was disinterested, but the benefaction usually involved obvious material benefits to the patron. Precisely because benefactions brought such benefits, a patron might make them in secret to ward off envy of other patrons (Malina 2001: 125; Pilch 1992: 164; Watson 2010: 24-35). The central section D contains the key accusation that Jesus receives sinners and eats with them (15.2), signaling a loss of honour, since he would be eating not with equals but with social inferiors. A rebuttal of this accusation determines the arrangement of the material that follows.

Three parables that follow provide examples of something/somebody lost and then found amid great rejoicing: a lost sheep (15.3-7), a lost coin (15.8-10) and a lost son (15.11-32). Feasting is mentioned only in the third, the Parable of the Prodigal Son, but summoning friends to rejoice with one would almost certainly imply feasting. The purpose of the feast is not here to promote the honour of the person who throws the feast but to express joy at finding and affirming life: 'But we had to celebrate and rejoice, because this brother of yours was dead and has come to life; he was lost and has been found' (15.32). The fourth parable, that of the Dishonest Manager (16.1-13), has often caused consternation, since it seems to approve dishonest financial behaviour. However, we should note that the steward is only accused or slandered with the charge of wasting his master's money: there is no evidence that he had done so, only his master's word. The Greek word διαβάλλω can indeed mean 'to charge with' in a juristic sense, but usually seems to mean 'to malign' or to accuse out of suspicion and resentment, envy or calumny (Liddell and Scott 1968: 389-90; Fitzmyer 1985: 1099 acknowledges this but simply dismisses this possibility). A trial would not normally be the outcome of such a master's accusation, but dismissal or worse still (16.2). If the behaviour of the steward once he hears of the master's plans is anything to go by, he may well have been in trouble for failing to screw the maximum profit out of the unfortunate indebted peasant farmers to whom the master had lent money to be repaid with interest. Usury was contrary to the Torah (Exod. 22.24; Lev. 25.36-37; Deut. 23.20-21) but was practiced by the master nevertheless (cf. 'Q' in Lk. 19.23 = Mt. 25.27).

The steward's response is to go even further in mitigation of their plight, by writing off the interest on the debt, contrary to his master's instructions but in conformity with Torah. His master could not reverse his steward's action without exposing his own breach of the usury laws. Hence, his master's grudging comment on his acumen (16.8). By relieving the debt of the tenants, the steward obtains their gratitude and the assurance of receiving hospitality at their table later. The master is shamed, and the steward receives honour, a reversal of the patron–client status hierarchy that is approved by Jesus: 'And I tell you, make friends for yourselves by means of dishonest wealth so that when it is gone, they may welcome you into the eternal homes' (16.9). It is a 'trickster' story that proclaims that God is on the side of the poor and not of the wealthy who exploit them: 'You cannot serve God and wealth' (16.13).

The parables call forth ridicule from the Pharisees, who are 'lovers of money' (φιλάργυροι) and whose goal is honour before others (ὑμεῖς ἐστε οἱ δικαιοῦντες ἑαυτοὺς ἐνώπιον τῶν ἀνθρώπων). However, God who knows the hearts sees such behaviour as an abomination (16.14-15). Interestingly, the conclusion of the Parable of Lazarus which provides a reaffirmation of the sufficiency of the Law and the prophets, is prefigured by the reference to 'law and the prophets' (16.16, with a somewhat opaque reference to violence against the kingdom) which follows the Parable of the Dishonest Manager and introduces 'Q' material about the kingdom (Lk. 16.16//Mt. 11.12, 13; 4.23; Lk. 16.17//Mt. 5.17, 18; Lk. 16.18//Mt. 5.31, 32; 19.19) concerning the immutability of Torah. Torah stands for justice and the relief of the suffering of the poor and the oppressed, which is the good news of the kingdom (Lk. 4.16-21). Jesus' reversal of the honour–shame culture of the elite is directly related to his 'moral economy of the kingdom' and plays itself out around the table. It situates the Parable of the Rich Man and Lazarus within a critique of the whole patron–client network that characterized and defined the Roman Empire and its (conquered) client states, but with a particularly Judean character.

Disease, Impurity and Exclusion from Table

The story of Lazarus, then, could be read as a parable about disease, impurity and exclusion from table, even though no act of healing by Jesus is envisaged. I offer this preliminary and imprecise structuring of the story:

A. There was a rich man
    who was dressed in purple and fine linen
        and who feasted sumptuously every day.
    B. And at his gate lay a poor man named Lazarus
        covered with sores

who longed to satisfy his hunger with what fell from the rich man's table
even the dogs would come and lick his sores.
B′. The poor man died
and was carried away by the angels
to be with Abraham.
A′. The rich man also died
and was buried.
In Hades, where he was being tormented
he looked up
and saw Abraham far away with Lazarus by his side.
C1. He called out,
'Father Abraham have mercy on me
and send Lazarus to dip the tip of his finger in water
and cool my tongue
for I am in agony in these flames'.
C2. But Abraham said
c1. 'Child, remember that during your lifetime you received your good things
and Lazarus in like manner evil things
c2. but now he is comforted here
and you are in agony.
c3. Besides all this, between you and us a great chasm has been fixed
so that those who might want to pass from here to you cannot do so
and no one can cross from there to us'.
D1. He said
'Then, father, I beg you to send him to my father's house
for I have five brothers
that he may warn them
so that they will not also come into this place of torment'.
D2. Abraham replied
'They have Moses and the prophets
they should listen to them'.
E1. He said
'No, father Abraham; but if someone goes to them from the dead
they will repent'.
E2. He said to him
'If they do not listen to Moses and the prophets
neither will they be convinced
even if someone rises from the dead'.

The parable does, as has often been noted, fall into two natural sections. In the first section, there is a chiastic arrangement: A–B, the opposed situations in life of the rich man and then Lazarus; B′–A′ the opposed situations in death of Lazarus and then the rich man. Finally there is a series of three exchanges between the rich man and Abraham (C1-2, D1-2, E1-2), in which the request for a return from the dead to warn the living is posed and rejected. It is possible C, D, E represents a later elaboration of the simple story of reversal found in A–B–B′–A′, which could stand by itself.

The significant opposition in the first section of the story, however, is not so much characterized by a reversal of wealth as by a reversal of the inside and outside status conveyed by disease and impurity. On earth Lazarus lies outside the gate, excluded from house and from meal: his broken penetrated body licked by unclean dogs provides confirmation of his impurity. The rich man excludes the possibility of touching Lazarus by shutting him out in the street. Nothing is said about any relation of sickness to sin on the part of Lazarus or about judgment. Instead, Lazarus's situation is depicted simply: his disease has resulted in poverty and exclusion from table and extreme hunger as a result. The picture of the animal realm intruding into the human body, transgressing its boundaries, licking the open sores, emphasizes the situation of his broken, unclean body. No cure is possible for the disease. The man dies. The rich man's situation is described equally simply: his wealth enables him to express and maintain his bodily and social insider status by providing daily feasts, where inclusion or exclusion at the table signals social boundaries. Exclusion of unclean Lazarus allows him to maintain his ritual and social purity.

In the second section, the situation is reversed. Whereas he was excluded on earth from normal social relations in Israel because of his broken body and impurity, Lazarus is now reclining in Abraham's bosom at a feast in heaven, in the typical position of honoured guest at table, as a sign of his full inclusion in Israel. The situation suggests the eschatological feast of Lk. 13.25-30. The heavy emphasis on touch and embrace points to the embodied nature of the contrast. The rich man, by way of contrast, is now excluded from (eschatological) Israel, since Abraham is 'far away'. His exclusion is marked out in an embodied position of separation and distance accompanied by heat and thirst.

The final three sections represent an attempt at plea bargaining on the part of the rich man, but they also refer in an ironic way to the reversal of the role of diseased and impure Lazarus. The rich man wishes Lazarus to dip his finger in water and cool his tongue. In other words, he opens himself to the penetration of his formerly pure body by Lazarus's formerly impure fingers. Whereas before the dogs licked Lazarus's sores, here the rich man seeks to lick Lazarus's finger. Water was regarded by the rabbis and by the Qumran community as particularly liable to pollution and the conveyance of impurity (hence while community members may eat the ritually pure food of the community after one year, they are not allowed to share the ritually pure drink until after two years probation), so the point is particularly apposite. Abraham's reply to his request both emphasizes the reversal of roles and the separation between the rich man and Israel in the afterlife: a great chasm is set between them. No further contact is possible! His postmortem impurity is extended indefinitely.

This leads to the request to send Lazarus back to life to warn the brothers of the rich man. This is a common motif in ancient stories. However, here it is refused, the opposite of the usual story. The reason may lie in the nature of the episode: if, as commonly thought, Israelite culture did not make a dualistic distinction between body and soul (see, e.g., Brown 1978), and Lazarus comes back to life, he will, presumably be back in a broken, impure, diseased and excluded body.[3] The rich man's brothers would not receive him in such a body any more than he had, nor would Lazarus gain admission to speak to them within the gate. Does the rich man imagine him returning in bodily form but healed now from his disease and impurity? If not, how could the return possibly serve its purpose? Only a change in social and cultural attitudes toward the broken bodies of the diseased and impure would enable people to hear any warning from those who had died of those diseases. The implied reference to Jesus' resurrection—'they would not believe even if someone were to rise from the dead' (16.31)—reinforces the bodily aspect of the resurrection and the continuance of the marks of Jesus' crucifixion because of the emphasis on the bodily nature of Jesus' resurrection in Luke's account: 'Look at my hands and feet. It is I myself. Touch me and see; no ghost has flesh and bones as you can see that I have. . . . Have you anything here to eat?' (24.39-41).

The second point made by the story is that Israel already has sufficient warning in Moses and the prophets and does not need anything further. The protection of (human) life takes precedence over the purity laws, as in Mk 7.1-23 and the 'Q' saying in Lk. 13.15 and 14.5 (//Mt. 12.11-12). The purpose of the parable is not to give the hearer a way out (God will give you a second chance); neither is the purpose to theologize about life after death or postmortem judgment of sins. The point of the parable is that we are responsible *now* for our attitudes and behaviour. As in the Deuteronomic and prophetic tradition of the Hebrew Bible, God is the protector of the widow, the

3. This is not the place for a discussion of this complicated question, but Paul goes to great lengths to try and escape the question of how a fleshly resurrected body would be received by his concept of a 'spiritual body' in 1 Cor. 15. The 'great chasm' fixed between the dead and the living reflects this problem, which would not have arisen in Graeco-Roman culture.

orphan, the stranger and the poor (e.g. Deut. 14.29; 16.11, 14; 26.12-13; Isa. 10.2; Ezekiel 34; Amos 3.6; 4.1; 8.4-6), and God holds us accountable for our behaviour toward them. Among the poor, Luke's narrative includes the excluded, outcast, diseased and stigmatized, like Lazarus in the parable. Healing begins and ends with the removal of social stigma. There are purity rules in the law of Moses, but the fundamental laws are 'Love God and love your neighbour as yourself' (cf. Mk 12.29-31//Mt. 22.36-39//Lk. 10.27). In Mk 7.13 Jesus rebukes the scribes, 'So with your human rules you make of no account the laws of God'. This is the point with which the parable concludes.

Setting aside the purity laws in the face of human need is a characteristic of Jesus' teaching and healing action in the Synoptic tradition. So he touches the leper, takes the hand of Peter's mother-in-law and the dead girl, and sends the healed person home to her/his village. He eats with Levi the tax collector and other publicans and sinners. He restores them to community. This is the significance of table within the renewed eschatological Israel that Jesus seeks to embody among his followers. Social and physical healing are integrally linked.

Body Boundaries and Israel's Boundaries

As we noted in our brief exposition of Mary Douglas's theory of the body as social map, meal and table are crucial social markers of belonging and status, of social inclusion and exclusion. Pollution codes operate in dialectic with moral codes, especially in areas that are impossible to police publicly. Persistent transgression of pollution codes results in a person being labeled a deviant and marginalized, so that ideally the codes reinforce social cohesion and social boundaries, especially in times when a community is faced with invasion and cultural erosion. However, Mary Douglas notes that this dialectic can go wrong in two directions. First, '[e]asy purification enables people to defy with impunity the hard realities of their social system' (1966: 137). In other words, people can hide gross violations of their social obligations to help the poor in Israel (the widows, orphans and strangers) behind fulfilling the ritual purity codes. Second, pollution fears in times of system breakdown 'provide independent grounds for breaking the moral code which at one time they worked to support' (1966: 138). In other words, the purity rules designed to reinforce social cohesion and the solidarity of all Israel in the face of threats from outside become the very means to exclude the majority of the population from what the powerful define as 'all Israel'. The poor are labeled as impure transgressors of the code and therefore defined as the *'am ha-arets* who are now outside the boundaries of Israel.

So in the face of Roman imperial political and cultural intrusion, 'all Israel' comes increasingly to be restricted to members of a particular purity group within Israel, such as the *haburoth* of the Pharisees or the *yaḥad* of the Essenes, even though the purpose of the rules was 'to protect the political and cultural unity' of Israel (Douglas 1966: 124). This created grave internal contradiction in the internal lines of the community and therefore, in terms of Douglas's model, exaggerated avoidance of the sources of pollution in those things that enter and/or affect the body: food, drink, sex, bleeding bodies and broken skin. These things have economic implications, since commerce is essentially a matter of exchange with the concomitant threat of pollution. Hence, economic obligation, marriage and charity become confined to one's own purity group, and the sharing of resources outside it, even with one's own family, is forbidden as *korban* (e.g. Mk 7.11; Draper 2009). The food of the *haburah* is seen as equivalent to the pure food of the priests on temple service and so cannot be shared with those who are impure, even if they are starving. The great reversal represented by the story of the Rich Man and Lazarus has economic implications, but the more fundamental reversal is the dining of the unclean and marginalized Lazarus with the patriarch Abraham, founder of Israel, and the exclusion from Abraham's table of the ritually pure and social insider, the rich man of the story. Jesus 'dines with tax collectors and sinners', and those who dine with Jesus now dine with Abraham later. Those who refuse to dine with Jesus, instead feasting with their elite social equals now, will be refused access to Abraham's table later (Lk. 13.22-30).

Abraham is mentioned fifteen times in Luke, of which eleven are unique to his Gospel. Otherwise, the name occurs only once in Mark and parallels (Mk 12.26//Mt. 22.32//Lk. 20.37), three times in Q (Lk. 3.8 [twice]//Mt. 3.9 [twice]; Lk. 13.28//Mt. 8.11) and three times in the genealogy of Matthew. In the special Lukan material, Abraham is the heir of God's merciful and unfailing promises, which will result in the reversal of present disaster, deprivation, poverty and exclusion. In Mary's song (1.46-55) God's promise to Abraham means scattering the proud, bringing down the powerful and uplifting the lowly, filling the hungry and sending the rich away empty; in Zechariah's song (1.68-79) the promise to Abraham means rescue from enemies and restoration to the service of God; for the woman crippled for eighteen years (13.10-17), the promise means being set free from bondage (on the Sabbath day) and reassurance that she too is a daughter of Abraham; for Lazarus (16.19-31) the promise to Abraham means reversal of disease, hunger and exclusion by reclining in Abraham's bosom at the eschatological banquet from which the uncaring rich are excluded; for Zacchaeus (19.1-10), the promise to Abraham means restoration to community from exclusion because of his despised (impure) profession and his dishonesty and reassurance that he too is a son of Abraham.

Luke or Jesus?

We cannot, of course, step lightly from Luke's narrative to Jesus' act and word, still less Jesus' intentionality. The story of the Rich Man and Lazarus is structured carefully and deliberately into Luke's narrative. The twin foci on table and healing in relation to the poor are both proven concerns of Luke. So too is an understanding of boundaries and marginalization (cf. Draper 1996). So too is the emphasis on Abraham. However, it is entirely possible that this story derives from an earlier layer of the Jesus tradition. As the analyses of various source and form critics have shown, the story belongs to an oral tradition with widespread attestation in Hebrew, which may well be related to or derive from a narrative from Egypt. The parallels from Graeco-Roman literature are less convincing, though not insignificant. This indicates but does not require a Palestinian origin, so that Luke may fairly be assumed to be using earlier tradition available to him. It could be that Luke has emphasized the role played by wealth and table in the story as wrong in and of itself, which is absent in the forms of the story prior to Luke. This, again, would match his general redactional emphasis (set out programmatically in Lk. 4.18-19). However, while the final form and location in the narrative belong to Luke's redaction, we could argue that the underlying parable goes back behind it and may faithfully represent Jesus' attitude to the question of disease, stigma and healing in the context of the social crisis of 'all Israel' in Palestine under Roman rule. There may be some truth in Joachim Jeremias's insistence that parables are passed on more faithfully than other forms of the early Jesus tradition (Jeremias 1971: 29-30).

Conclusion

This parable represents a forcible challenge to our attitudes to the many in our communities in South Africa who are living with HIV/AIDS. Many of us are afraid to eat and drink with them. When they cannot hide their condition any longer, they are often ostracized. They may die in social exclusion and under a heavy condemnation, which is all the more devastating when it is unspoken, though it is expressed often enough. People living with HIV/AIDS may be condemned from the pulpit as having brought it on themselves through promiscuity. Even wives who contract AIDS from unfaithful husbands are regarded as guilty and may even be blamed for causing the death of their husbands. The situation of people living with AIDS in South Africa is like that of Lazarus. Despite the national catastrophe that has unfolded among us in the form of HIV/AIDS, people living with HIV/AIDS still sit at the gate waiting for scraps to fall from our national budget, although that situation is beginning to change. For us today, Jesus' story of reversal of the positions of the rich man and Lazarus would see the people living with HIV/AIDS welcomed into the arms of father Abraham, while we who are 'pure' and have not suffered stigma and pain would face exclusion in the afterlife! We cannot even plead ignorance, any more than the rich man in the story: 'If they do not listen to Moses and the prophets, neither will they be convinced if someone should rise from the dead' (Lk. 16.27-31). We have not only Moses and the prophets but also the parable of the Jesus tradition.

The purpose of the story is to shock its hearers into changing their attitudes and behaviour. Disease does not make a person unclean; social injustice and failure to care for those in need make one unclean. HIV/AIDS is a sickness, not a punishment from God. On the contrary, those living with the disease should be counted, like Lazarus, especially beloved by God. Our society is challenged not to leave them lying outside the gate begging for scraps of our bounty but allocate the resources needed to halt the spread of HIV/AIDS and care adequately for those living with HIV/AIDS.

References

Bauckham, R.
1991 'The Rich Man and Lazarus: The Parable and the Parallels', *NTS* 37: 225-46.

Brown, C.
1978 'Soul', *The New International Dictionary of New Testament Theology*, vol. 3 (ed. C. Brown; Exeter: Paternoster): 676-89.

Bultmann, R.
1968 *The History of the Synoptic Tradition* (trans. John Marsh; Oxford: Blackwell; repr. 1972).

Corley, Kathleen E.
2010 *Maranatha: Women's Funerary Rituals and Christian Origins* (Minneapolis, MN: Fortress Press).

Douglas, M.
1966 *Purity and Danger: An Analysis of the Concepts of Pollution and Taboo* (London: Routledge).
1971 'Deciphering a Meal', in *Myth Symbol and Culture* (ed. C. Geertz; New York: W.W. Norton): 61-81.
1982 *Natural Symbols* (New York: Pantheon; rev. edn with new Introduction).
1999 *Leviticus as Literature* (Oxford: Oxford University Press).

Draper, J.A.
1996 '"Was there no-one left to give glory to God except this foreigner?' Breaking the Boundaries in Luke 17:11-19', in *Archbishop Tutu: Prophetic Witness in South Africa* (ed. L.D. Hulley, L. Kretzschmar and L.L. Pato; Cape Town: Human & Rousseau): 222-29.
2009 'What Goes In and What Comes Out: Reading Mark 7 and Zulu Culture in the Context of Communal Healing', in *Broken Bodies and Healing*

Communities: The Challenge of HIV and AIDS in the South African Context (ed. Neville Richardson; Pietermaritzburg: Cluster Publications): 61-82.

Eck, E. van
2009 'When Patrons Are Not Patrons: A Social-Scientific Reading of the Rich Man and Lazarus (Lk 16:19-26)', *HTS* 65.1: 346-56.

Elliott, John H.
1981 *A Home for the Homeless: A Sociological Exegesis of 1 Peter, its Situation and Strategy* (Philadelphia, PA: Fortress Press).
1996 'Patronage and Clientage', in *The Social Sciences and New Testament Interpretation* (ed. Richard Rohrbaugh; Peabody, MA: Hendrickson Publishers): 144-56.
2007 'Jesus the Israelite Was neither a "Jew" nor a "Christian": On Correcting Misleading Nomenclature', *JSHJ* 5.2: 119-54.

Esler, Philip E.
1987 *Community and Gospel in Luke–Acts: The Social and Political Motivations of Lukan Theology* (Cambridge: Cambridge University Press).

Fitzmyer, Joseph A.
1985 *The Gospel according to Luke X–XXIV* (AB, 28a; Garden City, NY: Doubleday).

Gressmann, H.
1918 *Vom reichen Mann und armen Lazarus: Eine literargeschichtliche Studie* (Berlin: Verlag der königlich Akademie der Wissenschaft).

Hock, R.F.
1987 'Lazarus and Micyllus: Greco-Roman Backgrounds to Luke 16:19-31', *JBL* 106: 448-55.

Jeremias, Joachim
1971 *New Testament Theology*, vol. 1 (London: SCM).

Klinghardt, Matthias
1996 *Gemeinschaftsmahl und Mahlgemeinschaft: Soziologie und Liturgie frühchristlicher Mahlfeiern* (Tübingen: Francke Verlag).

Liddell, Henry George, and Robert Scott
1968 *A Greek–English Lexicon* (Oxford: Clarendon Press).

MacMullen, Ramsey
1981 *Paganism in the Roman Empire* (New Haven, CT: Yale University Press).

Malina, Bruce J.
2001 *The New Testament World: Insights from Cultural Anthropology* (Louisville, KY: Westminster John Knox, 3rd edn).

Matera, Frank J.
1993 'Jesus' Journey to Jerusalem (Luke 9.51–19.46): A Conflict with Israel', *JSNT* 51: 57-77.

Moxnes, Halvor
1988 *The Economy of the Kingdom: Social Conflict and Economic Relations in Luke's Gospel* (Philadelphia, PA: Fortress Press).
1991 'Patron–Client Relations and the New Community in Luke–Acts', in *The Social World of Luke–Acts: Models for Interpretation* (ed. Jerome H. Neyrey; Peabody, MA: Hendrickson Publishers): 241-68.
1996 'Honour and Shame', in *The Social Sciences and New Testament Interpretation* (ed. Richard Rohrbaugh; Peabody, MA: Hendrickson Publishers): 19-40.

Osiek, C., and M. Y. MacDonald
2005 *A Woman's Place: House Churches in Earliest Christianity* (Minneapolis, MN: Fortress Press).
Pilch, John J.
1992 'Secrecy in the Mediterranean World: An Anthropological Perspective', *BTB* 24: 151-57.
Sahlins, M.
1972 *Stone Age Economics* (Chicago: Aldine).
Scott, James C.
1976 *The Moral Economy of the Peasant* (New Haven, CT: Yale University Press).
1990 *Domination and the Arts of Resistance* (New Haven, CT: Yale University Press).
Smith, D.
2003 *From Symposium to Eucharist: The Banquet in the Early Christian World* (Minneapolis, MN: Fortress Press).
Talbert, Charles H.
1974 *Literary Patterns, Theological Themes and the Genre of Luke–Acts* (Missoula, MT: Scholars Press).
Taussig, Hal
2009 *In the Beginning Was the Meal: Social Experimentation and Early Christian Identity* (Minneapolis, MN: Fortress Press).
Tomson, Peter J.
1986 'The Names Israel and Jew in Ancient Judaism and in the New Testament', *Bijdragen, tijdschrift voor filosofie en theologie* 47: 120-40, 266-89.
2000 '"Jews" in the Gospel of John as Compared with the Palestinian Talmud, the Synoptics and Some New Testament Apocrypha', in *Anti-Judaism and the Fourth Gospel: Papers of the Leuven Colloquium, 2000* (ed. R. Bieringer, D. Pollefeyt and F. Vandecasteele-Vanneuville; Leiden: van Gorcum): 301-40.
Watson, D.F.
2010 *Honor among Christians: The Cultural Key to the Messianic Secret* (Minneapolis, MN: Fortress Press).

Following your Nose: Social-Historical and Social-Scientific Directions in New Testament Osmology

Dennis C. Duling

> Odor is many things: a boundary-marker, a status symbol, a distance-maintainer, an impression management technique, a schoolboy's joke or protest, and a danger-signal—but it is above all a statement of who one is. Odors define the individual and the group, as do sight, sound, and the other senses; and smell, like them, mediates social interaction (Synnott 1993: 438).

It is my great honor to have known 'Jack' Elliott as a colleague and scholar for more than thirty years, and as a personal friend almost as long. Both he and Linde have been houseguests of my spouse, Gretchen, and me. Jack and I have discussed and socialized at society meetings, especially the Context Group, which he for many years planned, chaired and entertained with his wonderful wit. Jack's dedication to theory and method (1986; 1993), and to exegetical detail (2000), marks his research. He is a marvelous teacher, an inspiring lecturer, and ever ready to help scholars and students with his encyclopedic knowledge, extensive bibliographies and encouragement.

For many years Jack has gathered data and written about the evil eye (1988, 1990, 1991, 1992, 1994, 2005, 2007, 2011). So it seems appropriate to write about another human sense organ, the nose. In Western culture the nose has never had the status of the eye, good or evil; 'seers' see with in-sight, but 'smellers' just smell (the transitive/intransitive ambiguity says much). Yet, I hope that the closeness of the nose to the eye on the face and the historical honor the former pays to the latter are symbolic for my relationship to, and affection for, Jack.

Introduction

Noseaphobia and osmophobia have been dominant throughout most of Western culture. In the English language the nose is abused with epithets—'schnoz', 'snout', 'snoot', 'honker', 'hooter'—and most nose expressions are uncomplimentary: 'brown-nose', 'nose up to', 'lead around by the nose', 'pay through the nose', 'look down one's nose', 'turn up one's nose', 'thumb one's nose' and just plain 'nosy'. Pinocchio's growing proboscis is a cultural symbol of dishonesty. The noses of Cyrano de Bergerac, C.D. Bales, and Jimmy Durante (the 'Schnozzola') will bring forth smiles. Patrick Süskind's novel *Perfume: Story of a Murderer*, also an award-winning film, critiques the Enlightenment by linking a serial killer of beautiful and fragrant virgins with putrid Paris and perfumery (Donahue 1992). TV ads in our Lysol and Listerine culture show us how to protect ourselves from 'offensive', 'strong' or 'tough' odors.

The nose usually 'takes it on the nose'. Sight and hearing, the 'distant' senses, are labeled the 'primary' senses; smell, taste and touch, the 'proximity' senses, are labeled the 'secondary' senses. Popular attitudes about the nose and odor, scratch-and-sniff books for children, smell museums and puerile olfactory humor in the media have led to the widespread opinion that, as olfactory historian Mark Jenner puts it, '[s]mells fit uneasily into the world of serious scholarship' (2011: 336).

Yet, the academic smellscape is changing. Serious scientific research on smell today ranges from flatulence (Ig Nobel Prize 2004; Suarez *et al.* 1997) to pheromones (Wilson 1992; Stern and McClintock 1998). The Concordia University Sensoria Research Team (CONSERT) at the University of Montreal led the way and set a high standard. There is an Institute of Olfactory Research at Warwick University, a Taste and Smell Research Foundation in Chicago, a Centre for the Study of the Senses (CenSes) hosted by the Institute of Philosophy, School of Advanced Study, University of London. There is an extensive on-line 'Research Directory' and bibliographies on 'sensuous scholarship' that track smell research in the humanities and the social sciences. One can also find a 'Smell Report' by the Social Issues Research Center (SIRC). Digital Scent Technologists experiment with scents for theater, film, computer printers and 'Smell-o-Vision'. The Nobel Prize for Physiology or Medicine has been awarded to Richard Axel and Linda Buck, who demonstrated that the human brain can distinguish over ten thousand smells (Axel and Buck 2004).

Olfactory research related to the Bible and the early Christ movements, as one might suspect, has been somewhat limited, but that is also changing. Excellent studies of ancient spices, perfumes and the spice trade related to the Bible already existed (e.g. Van Beek 1960; Miller 1969; Nielsen 1986; cf. Matthew 1992), and they are now joined by impressive historical and social-scientific studies related to the Bible. Béatrice Caseau's Princeton dissertation, Εὐωδία*: The Use and Meaning of Fragrances in the Ancient World and their Christianization (100–900* AD*)* (1994), tracks smell in Greco-Roman antiquity and the emergent churches. Susan Ashbrook Harvey's *Scenting Salvation: Ancient Christianity and the Olfactory Imagination* (2006) explores smell, particularly incense, in the early churches.

Deborah Green's *The Aroma of Righteousness: Scent and Seduction in Rabbinic Life and Literature* (2011) includes whiffs from the Hebrew Bible and Roman culture. These important works do not focus on the New Testament as such, but Harold Attridge's excellent article on the 'aroma of Christ' in 2 Cor. 2.14-17 (2003) is an example of what is possible.

In this chapter, I sketch smell research in Western history, sociology and anthropology; note some olfactory classification systems and a possible research paradigm; summarize the sensorium of the Mediterranean world; develop some emphases in the Hebrew Bible; and comment briefly on a few New Testament passages. My operating hypothesis is that the earliest Christ believers participated in the rich olfactory environment of the Mediterranean world much more than the influential odoriphobic Greek philosophers who preceded them or the odoriphobic Christian theologians who followed them.

Tracking Sensorial History and Sensorial Social Science

Western intellectuals during the eighteenth and nineteenth centuries usually subscribed to the theory that 'savages' in small-scale, non-literate societies were closer to the animals in their sensorial evolution than to 'more advanced' Euro-Americans. For example, the pioneer of physical anthropology, Paul Broca (1824–1880), influenced by Charles Darwin, argued that the 'ascent of man' (no pun intended) from the apes was accompanied by a diminished sense of smell and an enhanced sense of sight (Furlow 1996: 39). Sigmund Freud (1856–1939) associated the rise of rational civilization with the suppression of animalistic and human female sense of smell (Mavor 2006: 282). Meanwhile, materialist scientists and philosophers (both empiricists and rationalists) focused almost exclusively on smell as a physical response to the external environment and virtually ignored cultural constructions.

These views have diminished or disappeared. Cross-cultural sensorial research on smell was undertaken in the Torres Islands by Alfred Cort Haddon in 1898 (Haddon 1935), but the credit for highlighting cultural constructions of sense impressions goes to sociologist Georg Simmel, who in 1908 proposed a 'sociology of the senses' as a new field of research (1908b: 646-60 [1992]; see 1908a [1997]: 110-11) and emphasized that the act of humans smelling other humans, whether it leads to revulsion or attraction, is integral to social interaction (Simmel 1908b [1992]: 736). Yet Simmel continued to believe that the ability of modern Westerners to sense others had declined with the march of civilization (1908a [1997]: 118-19). Two generations later, *Annales* social historian Lucien Febvre analyzed statements about odors mentioned in past literary sources, compared them to his own perceived olfactory sensitivity and concluded that the decline of the sense of smell in the West took place from the sixteenth to the eighteenth century (1982 [orig. French 1942]).

The theory of a decline in the Western olfactory sense has a related social constructionist variant: the decline in the *cultural importance* of smell. Constance Classen of the Concordia University Sensoria Research Team (CONSERT) writes, 'If one contrasts the cultural role of smell in the pre-modern West with its present role, that an olfactory decline in fact occurred appears an inescapable conclusion' (1993: 36). She locates this sort of decline in the eighteenth and nineteenth centuries when scientists and philosophers 'decided that while sight was the pre-eminent sense of reason and civilization, smell was the sense of madness and savagery' (1994a: 3-4; cf. 1993, ch. 1). Classen's key illustration for this (implied evolutionary) judgment is that rose gardens, once cultivated for their fragrance, are now cultivated for their visual beauty. Other CONSERT members agree (Classen, Howes and Synnott 1994). So does Mark Smith, who goes so far as to say, 'histories of the sense promise to rescue us from an Enlightenment conceit with visuality that is not only pernicious in its silent effect on historical writing but also responsible for a sometimes misleading, partial, and distorted "view" of the past' (2003: 167).

Influential cultural historian Alain Corbin also believes that an 'olfactory revolution' took place in the eighteenth century, but he offers a different explanation: olfactory 'scents-itivity' was *heightened*, but in a particular way (1986 [French 1982]; Mennell 1987). After examining histories of science, medicine, hygiene, public health, literature, architecture and urban planning, Corbin concludes that the revolution took place among the powered and perfumed aristocratic classes, especially in putrid Paris. The 'aroma *Angst*' of these upper social classes shifted the olfactory code from organic, natural-world smells to the odors of the lower classes. 'Repugnance of smell now focused on the poor man's hovel and latrines, the peasant's dung, the greasy and fetid sweat impregnating the worker's skin, rather than on the oppressive vapor of the putrid crowd in general' (1986: 230). Organizational theorist Martin Corbett offers a pungent, symbolic illustration: eighteenth-century Paris excrement collectors responded to their social stigmatization by mooning aristocrats, taunting them with scatological expletives and pelting them with poop (2006: 225-26). Corbett reinforces the point with observations about eighteenth-century scientific and technical developments in disinfection, fumigation and ventilation (2006: 224-26), and Mark Jenner stresses the effect of aroma *Angst* about city planning (2011: 338, n. 23). Aristocratic scents-itivities were then passed on to the middle classes (Howes 1991a: 144-46). It should be added that some scholars reject olfactory evolution. They argue that such theories create an unwarranted divide between nature and culture and ignore earlier periods of sense-itized aromaphilia and aromaphobia (e.g. Jenner 2000: 138; 2011: 338-42; Smith 2007; Low 2009: 8).

The CONSERT scholars have made significant advances. David Howes concluded that a 'sensual revolution' is taking place. He proposed a new sub-field of anthropological research called 'anthropology of the senses' (1991b). A generation earlier, sociologists Gale Peter Largey and David Rodney Watson offered an innovative analysis on how olfactory stereotypes create *we/they* social boundaries of attraction/avoidance, social hierarchies and cultural judgments about moral status (1972). Constance Classen expanded this approach by analyzing how olfactory stereotypes—she calls them the 'odor of the other'—create *we/they* social boundaries and social hierarchies based on class, ethnicity, race, urban/rural differences, national origins and gender (1992; 1993; 2005). Anthony Synnotte, who anticipates a 'sociology of smell' (1991a), concentrates on the sensory codes of the modern West (1993; cf. Classen, Howes and Synnott 1994). There are other contributors outside the CONSERT circle. Susan Rasmussen researches West African olfactory codes (1999). Kelvin E.Y. Low criticizes Western olfactory scholars for ignoring non-Western *urban* environments and analyzing the sensorium with an overly simplified bipolarism—'the good smelling good, the bad smelling bad' (2009: 19-27). Low makes theoretical progress by including 'everyday life experience' phenomenology, social interactionist theory and ethnomethodology. He also generates non-Western, urban sensorial data by interviewing Singaporians' experiences of smelling the lower classes, men and women in relation to the four officially recognized ethnic categories in Singapore, that is, 'Chinese', 'Malay', 'Indian' and 'Others'.

In summary, despite Western cultural tendencies to odoriphobia and earlier academic avoidance, there has emerged a body of serious, cross-disciplinary social historical and social-scientific olfactory research. There are now sensorial academic fields, including sensorial history, sensorial sociology, sensorial psychology, sensorial anthropology, sensorial ethnology and sensorial archaeology. The breadth of this new academic interest is illustrated by the essays in David Howes's *Empire of the Senses: The Sensual Culture Reader* (2005) and Jim Drobnick's *The Smell Culture Reader* (2006).

The Senses, Olfactory Classification Systems, and a Research Paradigm

Physical scientists have differing opinions about the number of human senses. 'The big five'—seeing, hearing, touching, tasting and smelling—are common, but some scholars argue for more senses (e.g. temperature [thermoception], balance [equilbrioception], time [chronoception], pain [nociception] and so forth). It is usually held that the senses interact. Thus, some researchers think that all the senses in a society should be examined and classified in order to determine 'sense ratios' and deduce the society's sensory hierarchy (Howes 1991b: 168; 1991c [CONSERT]; Howes, Synnott and Classen 2007 [CONSERT]). This 'whole society' approach can be briefly illustrated with traditional anthropological studies of three small-scale 'scents societies'.

The Kapsiki of the north Cameroon in West Central Africa have fourteen olfactory lexemes. These include smells of various animals, urine, animal feces, human feces, milk, millet beer, edible food, roast food, spoiled food, fresh meat, old grain, rotting corpses and any fleeting smell. Kapsiki men (not women) say that white people, like toads, smell 'milky-scented' (Almagor 1987: 108; Van Beek 1992: 43).

The Andaman Islanders in the Bay of Bengal order their whole society by smell. They have a 'calendar of scents' that describes the seasons in terms of odoriferous flowers and plants. Each smell season has its own 'aroma-force' (power) that can be internalized by eating fruits from that season. They even distinguish regions and villages by their smell (Classen, Howes and Synnott 1994: 95-98; Rasmussen 1999).

Finally, the Daasanach of southwestern Ethiopia order their two dry and two wet, rainy seasons by a succession of odors and categorize all outsiders by their smell. The majority pastoralists claim superiority over the minority fishermen: cattle smell is 'good'; fish smell is 'bad'. To distinguish themselves, the pastoralists 'often wash their hands in cattle urine; men smear manure on their bodies to advertise the fertility of their herds' (Classen 1992: 139). They believe that foul-smelling fish and fishermen threaten the whole social order (Almagor 1987: 110-17; Classen 1992: 138-40, 142; 1993: 83-85).

Because this 'whole society' approach is more difficult to examine in large-scale societies, other analysts prefer to focus on individual cases or a single sense (Drobnick 2006: 1-9; Low 2009: 15), which with regard to smell is called an 'olfactocentric strategy'. Constance Classen believes that both designs are possible and necessary (1997: 410). It is also important to distinguish between the everyday 'practical' sensorium and cultural beliefs and symbols, to be aware that sensory orders change over time, to understand that different subgroups can have different olfactory hierarchies and to realize that outside researchers can have sensorial biases (Howes and Classen 1991: 257-58).

As noted, Largey and Watson moved social-scientific study forward by proposing four olfactory classifications for analyzing interpersonal and intergroup sensory relations (1972). They are:

1. odor/group stereotypes (religious, racial, ethnic, national; class; urban/rural; age)

2. odor-based moral statuses (fragrant smells = moral purity [e.g. virginity, suitability for marriage]; foul smells = moral laxity [sinners, prostitutes, sorcerers, witches, heretics; the 'fart taboo'])
3. 'odor avoidance' (the skunk symbol) and 'odor attraction' (the rose symbol)
4. 'management of the olfactory environment' (odorizing, deodorizing, washing, gargling, incensing, fumigating).

The CONSERT researchers build on these four by

a. classifying people, animals and plants by their natural odor
b. classifying people, animals and plants by symbolic odors attributed to them (cf. Largey and Watson 1972: 1)
c. classifying groups within a society by natural and symbolic odors (cf. Largey and Watson 1972: 1)
d. classifying space related to environmental odors of different territories and places;
e. classifying the cosmos by odor
f. establishing a value system based on olfactory symbolism (e.g. 'good' and 'bad' odors; cf. Largey and Watson 1972: 2) (Classen, Howes and Synnott 1994).

Howes and Classen also develop sensorial research paradigms (1991) that here I revise and present in an 'olfactocentric' form. This involves an investigation of

1. olfactory language or olfactory linguistic code (words, metaphors, quantity)
2. olfactory artifacts and aesthetics
3. nose decoration and description (illustrative of a culture's sensory order)
4. children's views of noses, their sensory sensibilities and their education about smell
5. alternatives to dominant olfactory code (men/women; sensory handicaps)
6. the place of olfaction in sensory communication
7. the olfactory environment, natural or constructed, including space and bodies
8. the emphasis on olfactory elements, sequence, olfactory specialists in ritual
9. the importance of olfaction in mythology (the sensual ability and environment of gods, goddesses, heroes, etc.)
10. olfaction in cosmology (calendars, myths, spirit world, this world and the next).

Finally, Howes and Classen distinguish between doing field research and library research (1991: 259-60) and, for the latter, propose selecting a piece of literature and proceeding as follows: (1) compiling a list of its references to senses or sensory phenomena; (2) categorizing the data into intra-model sets, such as found in the sensorial classifications and the research paradigm above; (3) analyzing the relations between these modalities in relation to cultural experience; and (4) establishing the hierarchy of the senses.

It should be remembered, as Low has pointed out (2009), that bipolarism exists. Scholars often refer to 'scents societies' versus 'non-scents societies' (Classen 1992: 133) and other, similar bipolar categories (Almagor 1987: 107; Howes 1991b; see Caseau 1994: iv). 'Scents societies' are said to have more extensive olfactory classification systems, more extensive olfactory vocabularies, less concern to suppress odors and more interest in the views of others and their own olfactory environments. Theoretically, this anthropological approach is a type of constructionism. It implies linguistic and cultural relativity (Ayabe-Kanamura *et al.* 1998).

A Sniff of the Ancient Mediterranean Sensorium

Study of small-scale scents societies 'scents-itize' researchers. A whole culture approach to a complex, urbanized, commercialized advanced agrarian society is not feasible or even possible here. However, sniffing out representative ideas from the Mediterranean sensorium will suggest that although Mediterranean society was not a 'scents society' with extensive olfactory vocabularies and concepts, it was very sensitive to unpleasant smells. Thus, people, especially aristocrats, indulged themselves with all sorts of fragrances. Béatrice Caseau keyed this sensorium to the core values of honor and shame: olfactory pleasure was honorable; olfactory displeasure was dishonorable (Caseau 1994: 117-93).

The unpleasant, malodorous smells of the ancient Mediterranean environment are best illustrated by the typical Mediterranean city. Sociologist Rodney Stark offers a compact description:

> Given limited water and means of sanitation [open sewer ditches, chamber pots, pit latrines], and the incredible density of humans and animals, most people in Greco-Roman cities must have lived in filth beyond our imagining. Tenement cubicles were smoky, dark, often damp, and always dirty. The smell of sweat, urine, feces, and decay permeated everything. Outside, on the street, it was little better—mud, open sewers, manure, and crowds. In fact, human corpses—adult as well as infant—were sometimes just pushed into the street and abandoned. . . . And even if the wealthiest households could provide ample space and cleanliness, they could not prevent many aspects of the filth and decay surrounding them from penetrating their homes. Given that the stench of these cities must have been overpowering for many miles—especially in warmer weather—even

> the richest Romans must have suffered. No wonder they were so fond of incense. Moreover, Greco-Roman cities must have been smothered in flies, mosquitoes, and other insects that flourish where there is much stagnant water and exposed filth. And, like bad odors, insects are very democratic (Stark 1991: 194).

Archaeologists cannot verify this description directly, but multidisciplinary case studies of organic matter in various stages of decay can, as archaeologist Lásló Bartosiewicz argues (2003), and ancient literature has numerous references that support it. Two odoriferous examples will make the point: human waste and human disease.

Disposing of human waste was a perpetual problem in the cities of antiquity. In ancient Rome, for example, the urban poor lived in the upper storeys of tiny high-rise slum tenement buildings with no running water or toilets (Wallace-Hadrill 2003). They had several options to relieve themselves (Scobie 1986; Taylor 2005). They could trudge down many flights of stairs to the streets, which at night were dangerous, to urinate or defecate in alleys or behind bushes and statues, or urinate in terracotta urine jars that shop owners provided for urgent needs in front of their shops, or visit a public latrine, hopefully not too far away (Taylor 2005: 55-59). Or, what is much easier, they could throw their waste from chamber pots out a window to the street below where it might land on some unsuspecting passerby, which is indicated by laws forbidding this practice (*Digest* 43.10.1.5; Juvenal, *Sat.* 3.269-77; Scobie 1986: 416).

A second example comes from the malodors of human disease. The ancient medical tradition attributed to Hippocrates contains many graphic descriptions of 'acrid' or 'bilious' disease symptoms related to urine, stool, intestinal discharges, vomit, phlegm and flatus (*Epidemiae* 3). Where there was the odor of disease, the stench of death was often not far behind (Classen 1994b: 42-44; Hope and Marshall 2000).

Given ubiquitous everyday life experiences of foul smells in Mediterranean cities, it is not surprising that Mediterranean urban elites responded with osmologies of fragrance expressed in myths about the divine and practices of the human. People honored their deities by portraying them in aromatic environments and filling their temples with flowers and incense (Classen, Howes and Synnott 1994: 45-48). The Greeks, for example, said that their deities fed on and smelled like immortal-giving ambrosia and that their gods and goddesses spread their pleasurable scent everywhere they went (Caseau 1994: 218-21). A *Homeric Hymn* to Aphrodite indicates that the goddess, madly in love with Anchises, went 'to Cyprus, to Paphos, [where] she disappeared into her fragrant temple . . . and there the Graces bathed her and rubbed her with olive oil, divine oil, as blooms upon the eternal gods—ambrosial bridal oil that she had ready perfumed' (*Hymn Hom.* 5 [*ad Ven.*] 58-63 [West 2003: 165]).

Across the Mediterranean Sea in aroma-loving and perfume-producing Egypt, it was believed that Nefertem, who emerged at creation as an infant out of the opening of a giant odiferous lotus blossom, the symbol of rebirth, was the god of perfume (Wilkinson 2003: 133; cf. Manniche 1999). One could also smell Isis, who had a garlanded crown, perfumed feet and breath like the fragrant spices of Arabia (Apuleius, *Metamorphoses* 11.3-4). Among the Romans, Flora, the goddess nymph of spring and the flowers, exhaled spring roses (Ovid, *Fasti* 5.2), and Venus, the goddess of love and sensuality, was venerated, bathed and garlanded with sweetly scented myrtle. Her devotees offered her incense, myrtle, mint and sheaves of rushes in clustered roses (Ovid, *Fasti* 4.23).

From the human side, olfactory pleasure and honor required pleasant smells in human environments. Béatrice Caseau writes, 'the omnipresence of fragrances can be observed from one end of the Mediterranean to the other end, and from the earliest Antiquity to Medieval times, though we can admit that there existed a peak in the consumption of incense, spices and perfumes during the early Roman Empire' (Caseau 1994: 1). Osmo-manipulation was common at public baths, gymnasia, banquets, weddings, funerals and major spectacles such as games and imperial victory processions. Incense spiced up the opening of the Olympics, trailed triumphal entrances, enhanced crossroad shrines, fumigated public buildings, anointed the statues of gods and emperors and dominated the liturgies of the *lares*. There was a tremendous demand for imported fragrances: roses from Cyrene, perfumes from Capua and spices from the Orient, especially Arabia (Miller 1969).

There were also influential writers on smell. 'The Father of Botany', Theophrastus of Eresus on the Island of Lesbos (c. 371–287 BCE), wrote *Concerning Odors*, the first such treatise known. He covered such topics as spices and plants, oils for perfumes, good and bad odors, perfumes and their ingredients, their lack of distinctive names, the relation of smell to decaying matter, the animals' superior sense of smell, ointments for healing, and the irony that good-smelling plants spoil food and bad-smelling spices enhance food, except for wine (ΠΕΡΙ ΟΣΜΩΝ or *De odoribus* [Theophrastus *Historia plantarum* 324-89]; Harvey 2006: 32-33)! Similar descriptions are found in Dioscorides (c. 40–90 CE), whose illustrated five-volume *Concerning Medical Matters* (c. 64 CE) informed medical practice for some fifteen hundred years (Gunther 1933; Osbaldeston and Wood 2000; Beck 2005). Among the Romans, Pliny the Elder's *Natural History* (c. 77–79 CE) recorded the olfactory capabilities of animals (*Nat.* 11) and the scents of plants (*Nat.* 12), and in the process he mentions over sixty aromatics and the ingredients of perfumes (*Nat.* 13). He believed that the Persians were the first to use unguents, that the Greeks learned about them from a chest that Alexander the Great took from the defeated Persian King Darius III, and that his countrymen came to the view that '[t]he pleasure of perfume . . . [is] . . . among the most elegant and also most honorable enjoyments in life' (*Nat.* 13.1 [Rackham 1955: 99]; cf. Classen, Howes and Synnott 1994: 13); yet, he himself believed that perfumes 'lose their scent at once, and die in the very hour when they are used. Their highest recommendation is that when a woman passes by her scent may attract the attention even of persons occupied in something else—and their cost is more than 400 denarii per pound!' (*Nat.* 13.4 [Rackham 1955: 111]). Thus, although they give pleasure, they are in the last analysis decadent and disgraceful, a costly indulgence that even found its way into Roman military camps (cf. Harvey 2006: 33-36).

A Few Smell Samples from the Hebrew Bible

The Hebrew Bible offers especially interesting perspectives on the Mediterranean aromascape (Green 2011, ch. 3). Despite the warnings that no one can see God's face and live (Exod. 33.20; cf. 3.6), the Bible contains anthropomorphic statements that God has a nose (*'aph*) that 'burns hot' in anger (Exod. 32.1; Deut. 29.28), emits smoke (Ps. 18.8) and is 'long' when he is 'long-suffering' or merciful (Exod. 34.6). In contrast to perpetually anosmic idols (Deut. 4.28; Ps. 115.6), then, Yahweh has the sense of smell and his anger can be soothed by the 'pleasing odor' of sacrificial offerings (e.g. Gen. 8.21; Exod. 29.18, 25, 41; Lev. 1.9; 26.31). In short, Yahweh's nose is a conduit of 'regular interaction and communication' (Green 2011: 72, 76).

Olfactory pleasure typical of Mediterranean elites everywhere was also common among Judean elites. Prophets, priests and kings were anointed with precious, fragrant oils, and kings were designated *m^{e}shîach*, 'anointed one'. Processions to temples were perfumed, and temples were filled with peculiar fragrances. When the Queen of Sheba (Arabia!) visited Solomon, she had 'a very great retinue, with camels bearing spices' (1 Kgs 10.1 = 2 Chron. 9.1, NRSV). In the Wisdom literature, Wisdom spreads her wonderful fragrance like chosen myrrh (Sir. 24.20). Before going to seduce Holofernes, Judith anointed herself with precious aromatic oils (Jdt. 10.3).

Smells of the body, whether naturally secreted or humanly created, pervade 'almost every line and scene in the [Song of] Songs—often explicitly, but sometimes suggestively' (Green 2011: 84). A woman's secretions are better than spices (Song 1.3); she 'gives forth' enticing fragrances, 'opening to the man' (Green 2011: 85-89). The aroma of her clothing 'is like the scent of Leb[v]anon' (a word-play on Hebrew *levonah*, 'frankincense') (4.11). Her body is a sweet smelling garden (4.9-16; Green 2011: 87-94; Alter 2012), fragrant with aromatic, exotic spices and oils. She invites her lover to blow on her garden, to 'enter' (sexually penetrate) it (cf. Gen. 16.2). Her 'channel' is an orchard of pomegranates, a sexually symbolic fruit (Song

4.13). Sexually explicit seductive fragrances are also found in Proverbs. The adulterous wife entices her lover to have sexual relations while her husband is away on a long trip. She says,

> I have perfumed my bed with myrrh, aloes, and cinnamon.
> Come, let us take our fill of love until morning . . . (Prov. 7.17-19, NRSV).

Yet, the formula for making incense given to Moses in the priestly writings (Exod. 30.34-38) contains a clear warning not to confuse the sacred and the profane: 'Whoever makes any like it to use as perfume shall be cut off from the people' (Exod. 30.38, NRSV).

Odoriphobia among Ancient Philosophers and Early Christian Theologians

One might think that the ancient philosophers and theologians would have shared the fondness for fragrances typical of Mediterranean elites. The Greek philosopher Aristippus (c. 435–350 BCE) did, for he ranked bodily pleasures over mental pleasures (Diogenes Laërtius 2.8), but the most influential philosophers distrusted the senses (Synnott 1991b: 62-63). Plato's views are mixed. On the one hand, he contrasted reason and sense perception (*Theaetetus* 184b-187a [esp. 186d]), and in his famous 'Allegory of the Cave' he demonstrated his belief that human sense perception is deceptive (*Respublica* 7.514a-517c). On the other hand, in his *Timaeus* he judged that sight is the greatest good among the senses because by making possible the observation of the days, seasons and years, it produces mathematics, the notion of time, research into the universe and philosophy (*Tim.* 47a-b). He was also affirmative about sound and hearing because, 'bestowed upon us' by the gods they produce music that has harmony and 'motions akin to the revolutions of the Soul within us' (*Tim.* 47c-d [Bury 1942: 109]; cf. Jütte 2005: 34-36). Smell, however, did not get Plato's equal admiration, although he offered an analysis of it. He observed that smells are perceived when the state of matter undergoes change, that is, when it is 'moistened or putrefied or melted or vaporized', for example, when air changes to water (mist) or water changes to air (smoke), suggesting that smells are 'thinner than water and thicker than air'. The result is that smells are a 'half-formed class', therefore not well distinguishable by names, but simply 'pleasant' or 'painful' (*Tim.* 66d-67a [Bury 1942: 171]). Finally, smells, unlike many substances, can be pleasurable without any antecedent of pain (*Resp.* 9.584b). An example is perfume, one of the greatest of pleasures (*Tim.* 65a).

Aristotle's osmology was even more influential in Western culture, although he was not always clear (Johansen 1996). He keyed on the five bodily senses and reflected on them (*De anima* 2.5.416b33–12.424b19), especially in terms of his theory of perception or change, that is, their potentiality and actuality, actuality always defining what is potentiality (*De an.* 2.5.417a6-418a7). Thus, the sense faculty is potentially (e.g. potentially hot) what the sense object really is (e.g. actually hot). However, in the case of smell, it is not easy to determine the sense faculty because it is not easy to determine the sense object (*De an.* 2.9.421a9-421b2; cf. *De sensu et sensibilibus* 4.440b32). He ranked seeing and hearing ('mediated' or 'distant' senses) at the top of his sense hierarchy because they make the greatest contributions to humanity (beauty and music), while taste and touch ('contact' or 'tactical' senses) are at the bottom because they can be abused (gluttony and lust). Although smell is similar to taste discrimination and derives vague names from more identifiable and precise flavors—sweet taste, sweet smell (*De an.* 2.9.421a26-b2)—it is dry in comparison to taste, and mediated in contrast to taste. Ultimately, smell is in between the distant and contact senses, and distinctive. It cannot be abused like taste and touch, but it is imperfectly mediated (in both air and water), indirectly perceived, illusive and ambiguous. Aristotle also noted that compared to the animals humans have a poor and inaccurate sense of smell (*De an.* 2.9.421a8-13).

Susan Ashbrook Harvey comments that the paradoxical tension between olfactory pleasure in Mediterranean culture and olfactory disdain among most ancient philosophers ultimately meant the 'relegation of smell to relative insignificance, albeit recognizing the usefulness of smells for certain practical points of knowledge'. She adds that 'Christian thinkers would present a similar paradox, informed by their particular contexts of discussion' (2006: 105). Constance Classen calls the patristic perspective 'the scent of sanctity and the stench of sin' (1992; 1993; 1994b: 1). The 'scent of sanctity' refers to the idea that God, angels, saints, ascetics and martyrs were thought to have a fragrant aroma. The 'scents of sin' refers to attitudes about perfumes and cosmetics, which had worldly and erotic connotations, as well as the odors of decay, disease and death, all associated with the devil and demons. Initially, incense was also included because it symbolized immoral pagan houses and temples, and the fact that Roman sacrificial shrines were used to test whether Christ believers were loyal to Rome. Ascetic-minded Origen was representative. He concluded that the good man should not offer incense, but rather a sweet-smelling prayer that ascends from a pure conscience (Origen, *Contra Celsum* 17). In relation to the scent of sanctity, Harvey surmises that in the real world the spaces and bodies of eremitic, anchorite ascetics surely offended their cenobite brothers and sisters; yet, they were said to have had a divinely smelling aroma—especially in death. Eventually, however, aromatic oils and incense made a comeback, the former in healing and prebaptismal anointing, the latter in the celebration of the Eucharist. These aromas were too deeply rooted in the culture and the Bible to be abandoned forever (Caseau 1994: 3; Brattston 2007).

While medieval cities fared no better than ancient ones—they were often worse—and the need for fragrances continued, medieval theologians continued the mainly negative judgment of the key philosophers and patristic theologians (Classen, Howes and Synnott 1994: 51-66). There are many examples. Plagues were believed to be caused by the fetid smells of disease and death. Medieval sermons, commentaries and penitentials related the sense of smell to two of the seven deadly sins, gluttony and lust. Although the olfactory sense fared somewhat better during the Renaissance, most theologians considered smell to be a 'lower' animal nature, subject to the pestilential breath of evil spirits. The nose became a phallic symbol in bawdy Germanic literature and art (Stewart 1995), but in ecclesiastical art it was virtually ignored (Nordenfalk 1985). Odoriphobia during the Enlightenment and more recent times has already received sufficient attention.

A New Testament 'Olfactionary' and an Impressionistic Sensorial Hierarchy

The New Testament is a late selection of twenty-seven miscellaneous books, thus in terms of literary research not a single piece of literature; neither does it represent the 'whole culture' of the Mediterranean. Thus, analysis must be modest.

An initial exploration turns up twenty-nine olfactory terms that can represent a minimal New Testament olfactory lexicon, or an 'olfactionary'. In the space here I can do no more than list them in translation: 'alabaster', 'aloes', 'altar' or 'censer', 'aroma' or 'fragrance', 'bowl' used in offerings, 'cinnamon', 'dill', 'frankincense', 'I anoint', 'I make an incense offering', 'I smell' or 'emit an odor' (pleasant or unpleasant), 'incense', 'incense burning', 'mint', 'myrrh', 'nose', 'oil' or 'olive oil', 'ointment' or 'perfume', 'pleasant odor' or 'ointment', 'rue', 'sacrifice' or '(burned) offering', 'scented', 'scented wood', 'sense of smell', 'smoke', 'spice', 'spices', and '(spike)nard'. This olfactionary suggests the general acceptance of the smells of everyday life and liturgy.

It is very instructive to look also at verb statistics for the 'big five' senses. As previously noted, while the New Testament is neither a single piece of literature nor a representation of the whole culture, these statistics will give at least a hint of a 'sense ratio' and an impression of what a New Testament sensory hierarchy might look like.

1. I see	ὁράω	449
	θεωρέω	58
2. I hear	ἀκούω	430
3. I touch	ἅπτω	39
4. I taste	γεύομαι	15
5. I smell	ὄζω	1

The two 'distant' senses at the top of this list express the importance of wise in-sight and hearing the Word of God in the canon of a predominantly oral culture. While the extreme imbalance is striking, I suggest that a brief survey of the New Testament shows that the relative paucity of terms and this impressionistic olfactory hierarchy are not the final olfactory breath.

Following the Scent of a Few New Testament Passages

The New Testament contains several anti-Temple statements (Mk 13.1-4// Mt. 24.1-3//Lk. 21.5-7; Acts 7.48; Jn 4.16-26; Hebrews). However, incense itself is not condemned or spiritualized, and, moreover, any implied negative judgment seems to be counterbalanced by other considerations. It is true that aromatic spices, wine and oil are listed in Revelation as part of a costly cargo that will no longer be bought when Rome is destroyed (Rev. 18.11-13), but, similar to the comment of Pliny, the focus is on the high cost, not the aromas. Be that as it may, there are further avenues of olfactory exploration.

1. Was Jesus a Putrid Peripatetic Who Become the Aromatic 'Anointed'?

As noted previously, Susan Ashbrook Harvey suggests that the real-world spaces and bodies of eremitic, anchorite ascetics would have probably offended their cenobite brothers and sisters, but they were nonetheless believed to be sweet-smelling holy men, especially in their deaths. Early Gospel traditions record that the wandering Jesus had no money, no food-bag, no change of clothes, no sandles on his feet and no place to lay his head (Mt. 10.9-10 = Lk. 10.3-4 [Q]; Lk. 9.58). No matter what the body odor of this homeless vagabond was, he was apotheized as the divinely appointed 'anointed' king and a son of God (Mt. 1.1-17; Rom. 1.3-4; Acts 2.36). Is there any parallel with the later ascetics?

Anthony Synnott thinks that although Jesus' lifestyle was ascetic and austere, 'with fasting, watches, prayer, poverty, chastity, and obedience', Jesus seemed to have had a mostly positive attitude toward the senses (1991b: 64). His healing methods included touch (Mk 5.23; 6.5), and his communal meals with his disciples and others (1 Cor. 11.17-34; Mk 2.13-17; 14.22-25//Mt. 26.26-29//Lk. 22.15-20) earned him the reputation among his opponents of being a glutton and a drunkard (Mt. 11.7-19 = Lk. 7.24-35 [Q]). Several stories indicate a mainly positive view of Jesus' aromatic environment. His disciples were said to complain about the cost of an alabaster jar of pure nard that an unknown woman used to anoint Jesus' head (Mk 14.3), but Jesus defended and memorialized her. Jesus reputedly honored a woman of the city who anointed his feet with myrrh (Lk. 7.37-38). Mary of Bethany was said to anoint Jesus' feet with costly ointment of pure nard, and without further comment the text reports that 'the house was filled with the fragrance of the ointment' (Jn 12.3).

Two of the three honorable gifts from the Magi for the infant Jesus (Mt. 2.11), frankincense and myrrh, were commonly linked (Song 3.6; Rev. 18.13). Frankincense was used primarily in incense, but also in perfume and medicine (Song 3.6; Van Beek 1992: 83). Myrrh was also used in incense, but more in cosmetics, perfumes, ointments, medicine and embalming (Van Beek 1960: 83-84; cf. Mk 15.23). The third gift, gold, a royal metal perhaps suggested by the royal and messianic associations of Isa. 60.6, does not fit the aromatic series. Possibly the original gift was incense. This interpretation is proposed by scholars because the Hebrew for 'gold', *zāhāb*, might have originally been South Arabic *ḏahab*, which could mean either 'gold' or 'incense' (Ryckmans 1951; Brown 1993: 176; Harvey 2006: 33). Were the fitting gifts for the Messianic child all aromatics, that is, *incense,* frankincense and myrrh?

2. Two Odoriferous Simons: The Tanner and the Fisherman

In the ancient world, dung-collectors collected feces and urine for tanners; often, they were the same persons. The district of the tanners was situated on the edge of, or outside, a city because of its offensive smell. Joachim Jeremias assembled rabbinic passages showing that tanning was a 'despised' trade (Jeremias 1969: 308, 310). The following comment is no doubt a bit of wry rabbinic humor: 'the world cannot exist without a perfumer and without a tanner—happy is he whose craft is that of a perfumer!' The rabbis quickly added, 'woe to him who is a tanner by trade!' (*Qid.* 82b; *Pes.* 65a; *B. Bat.* 16b). Although the tanner was probably accustomed to his malodorous environment, the tanner's wife had the unusual right to claim divorce and reclaim her dowry. According to *Mishnah Ketubot*, the wife could said, 'I thought that I could endure it, but now I cannot endure it!' (*Ket.* 77a).

The environment of fishermen was also odoriferous. Fish smell was prominent in fishing villages and seaports. Romans of all social strata loved the fish sauce delicacy *garum*, also used for medicine (Curtis 1991; Hanson 1997: 106-107). Processing *garum*, recipes for which can be found in Athenaeus (*Deipnosophistae* 3.116a-121d), involved open barrels of decaying fish parts rotting in the sun for weeks; indeed, *garum* producers, like tanners, seem to have been located at the edge of towns; some towns even outlawed its production. Seneca said, 'Do you not think that the so-called "Sauce from the Provinces", the costly extract of poisonous fish, burns up the stomach with its salted putrefaction?' (Seneca, *Ep.* 95 [Gummere 1925: 75]). Fishing was big business in Galilee, and *garum* was a major export (Josephus, *Wars* 3.516-20; Pliny, *Nat.* 31.95; Freyne 1995: 35; Hanson 1997: 106-107).

Simon son of Jonah, a Galilean fisherman, was named for his father (Mt. 16.17; Jn 21.17). In contrast, Simon the Tanner was named for his 'despised trade' (Acts 10.6). No doubt, both were adjusted to their odoriferous environments. However, given Daasanach prejudices about the smell of fishermen, one wonders what Simon the Tanner thought about the smell of Simon the fishermen, and likewise, what Simon the fisherman thought about the smell of Simon the Tanner. Perhaps it was fortunate that Simon the Tanner's house, where Simon the fisherman was a guest, was located by the windblown sea (Acts 10.6, 32).

3. Did Euodia Have a Euōdia?

The name of one of Paul's co-workers at Philippi was Euodia (Phil. 4.2; Dahl 1995), a name well attested in Greek and Latin inscriptions (Bauer [BDAG] 2000 [CIL 6]). Literally, εὐοδία (*euodia*) means 'a good journey', thus 'success'. She could be named, then, 'Success' (had she been a slave? Horsley 1979: 178-79 [95]). There is no textual evidence in Philippians that εὐοδία was ever confused with εὐωδία, which means 'aroma', and James Hope Moulton was skeptical about omicron/omega itacism or orthographic errors in Paul's writings; yet, he admitted that such itacism was widespread in Egypt, and he gives examples from Asia Minor (Moulton 1920: 73, 75). The 'pleasing aroma' of sacrifices that God loves to smell is translated in the Septuagint ὀσμὴ εὐωδίας (many LXX references), and Paul uses this exact same expression as a metaphor for the Philippians' gift to him (Phil. 4.18) in the very same literary context where he mentions Euodia. Carolyn Osiek speculates that Paul might have had in mind a Euodia/*euōdia* play on words (2000: 123). Did Euodia suggest *euōdia*? One can speculate further: was Euodia fragrantly perfumed? If she was, the result was the 'sweet smell' of 'Success'!

4. The Bi-aroma of Christ: 2 Corinthians 2.14-16a

In 2 Cor. 2.14 the thanksgiving that opens a possible letter fragment (2.14–6.13 + 7.2-4) weaves together two images: (a) a 'triumphal procession' (NRSV) led by God in Christ in which Paul, God's herald, and the other apostles spread knowledge of God as a 'fragrance' (τὴν ὀσμὴν) everywhere (cf. 4.5; 5.20–6.2; 6.11-13; 7.2-4), and (b) the apostles described as Christ's 'aroma' (εὐωδία) for God, a 'smell' (ὀσμή) that drifts from death to death among non-believers and life to life among believers. This mixed imagery is difficult to interpret. Rudolf Bultmann offered three possible options (Bultmann 1985: 65): (1) God and Christ are deities that, like the gods (e.g. Isis), emit pleasant fragrances; (2) Wisdom spreads like God's divine fragrance, as in Ben Sira (24.15; 39.13; 50.15); and (3) Torah wisdom works like a fragrant drug (*Ta'anith* 7a).

Another complication in this passage is that the verb θριαμβεύω, 'I lead in a triumphal procession', normally refers to a triumphal *military* procession, in which case the olfactory images might have referred to perfumes sometimes used to fumigate the stench of prisoners executed along the processional route (Schmidt 1995; see Suetonius, *Nero* 25.2; Song 3.6). However, since military imagery has difficulties in this context, Harold Attridge offers an alternative explanation, namely, θριαμβεύω refers to a *religious* procession (2003). Previously, Paul Brooks Duff had suggested the explanation 'epiphanic processions' during which deities such as Dionysus or Isis were believed to become manifest to the processional devotees (1991). Attridge, citing Apuleius's *Metamorphoses* 11.19, proposes that white-robed women devotees, garlanded with flowers, would have sprinkled the sacred processional way with 'blossoms from their bosoms' and 'various perfumes, a delightful balm shaken out in drops' (2003: 81-82).

If so, Paul uses odiferous religious processions as an analogy for describing both the spreading of the fragrant knowledge of God and the apostles as the smell of Christ, sweet-smelling to the believer, foul-smelling to the disbeliever.

Conclusion: The 'Essence'

The smells of the first century have been right under our noses all along, but we have been mostly 'a-osmatic', that is, more interested in *seeing* the Truth and *hearing* the Word. I have omitted much. In the New Testament there were other smells of place: poverty at Jerusalem, food at Antioch, Corinth, or Rome. There were the aromas of time and place: meat, fresh-baked bread and rich wine. There were figs, grapes, olives. There were flora and fauna. There was the death-stench of Lazarus, where the single instance of the verb 'I smell' occurs, and there were the burial spices of the women and Nicodemus (Mk 16.1//Lk. 24.1; Jn 19.39). There were swine, dogs and horses in the streets. There was the sweat on the brow of the peasant and the slave. And there were Greeks and Romans, who must have had an odor to the Easterners, and Easterners who must have had an odor to the Greeks and Romans.

It may (or may not) be that our sense of smell has declined since the sixteenth, seventeenth, and especially eighteenth centuries. Be that as it may, Western society tends toward osmophobia and counters unpleasant odors with an array of fragrances, deodorants and sprays. Scholars have often avoided the topic, but recently a new interest has appeared, and there is an increasing amount of serious olfactory scholarship. Some say that an 'olfactory revolution' is taking place. Perhaps the seductions of love and sex in the media of an open, postmodern society have helped to drive it. In any case, smells and 'the odor of the other' have become a matter for social-historical and social-scientific analysis. Social boundaries, social stratification and social-identity issues related to the cross-cultural study of olfaction are growing.

I suggest that research on olfaction beckons social-historical and social-scientific New Testament critics to get a better sense of the senses and the sensorium in the New Testament. Again, discoveries are right under our noses. While this chapter has barely sniffed the olfactory air of the New Testament and its environment, the few examples I have mentioned point to the potential for greater scents-itivity in exegesis. It is important to take a whiff, pick up the scent and follow your nose.

References

Almagor, Uri
1987 'The Cycle and Stagnation of Smells: Pastoralists–Fishermen Relationships in an East African Society', *RES* 14: 106-21.

Alter, Robert
2012 'Entering the Aromatic Garden of Love' http://jhom.com/topics/spices/levonah.html (last accessed February 27, 2013).

Attridge, Harold W.
2003 'Making Scents of Paul: The Background and Sense of 2 Cor. 2.14-17', in *Early Christianity and Classical Culture* (ed. John T. Fitzgerald, Thomas H. Olbricht and L. Michael White; Leiden: Brill): 71-88.

Axel, Richard, and Linda B. Buck
2004 'The Nobel Prize in Physiology or Medicine'. Press release. http://nobelprize.org/nobel_prizes/medicine/laureates/2004/press.html.

Ayabe-Kanamura, S., I. Schicker, M. Laska, R. Hudson, H. Distel, T. Kobayakawa and S. Saito
1998 'Differences in Perception of Everyday Odors: A Japanese–German Cross-cultural Study', *Chemical Senses* 23: 31-38.

Bartosiewicz, Lásló
2003 'There's Something Rotten in the State: Bad Smells in Antiquity', *European Journal of Archaeology* 6.2: 175-95.

Bauer, Walter, William F. Arndt, F. Wilber Gingrich and Frederick W. Danker [BDAG]
2000 *A Greek–English Lexicon of the New Testament and Other Early Christian Literature* (Chicago: University of Chicago Press, 3rd edn).

Beck, Lily Y. (trans.)
2005 *De materia medica by Pedanius Dioscorides* (Hildesheim: Olms-Weidmann). See Gunther 1934 and Osbaldeston and Wood 2000.

Brattston, David W.T.
2007 'Incense in Ante-Nicene Christianity'. http://www.churchsociety.org/churchman/documents/Cman_117_3_Brattston.pdf.

Brown, Raymond E.
1993 *The Birth of the Messiah* (New York, NY: Doubleday).

Bultmann, Rudolf
1985 *The Second Letter to the Corinthians* (trans. Roy A. Harrisville. Minneapolis, MN: Augsburg Press).

Bury, R.G. (trans.)
1942 *Plato,* vol. 7 (LCL; Cambridge, MA: Harvard University Press).
Caseau, Béatrice
1994 *Εὐωδία: The Use and Meaning of Fragrances in the Ancient World and their Christianization (100–900 AD)* (PhD diss., Princeton University, Princeton, NJ).
Classen, Constance
1992 'The Odor of the Other: Olfactory Symbolism and Cultural Categories', *Ethos* 20.2: 133-66. Revised in Classen, Howes and Synnott (eds.) 1994: 15-35.
1993 *Worlds of Sense: Exploring the Sense in History and across Cultures* (London: Routledge).
1994a 'Introduction. The Meaning and Power of Smell', in Classen, Howes and Synnott (eds.) 1994: 1-10.
1994b 'The Aromas of Antiquity', in Classen, Howes and Synnott (eds.) 1994: 13-50.
1997 'Foundations for an Anthropology of the Senses', *International Social Science Journal* 49/153: 401-12. On line: http://www.scribd.com/doc/48996829/Foundations-for-an-Anthropology-of-the-Senses.
2005 'The Witch's Senses: Sensory Ideologies and Transgressive Femininities from the Renaissance to Modernity', in Howes (ed.) 2005: 70-84.
Classen, Constance, David Howes and Anthony Synnott (eds.)
1994 *Aroma: The Cultural History of Smell* (London: Routledge).
Corbett, J. Martin
2006 'Scents of Identity: Organisation Studies and the Cultural Conundrum of the Nose', *Culture and Organization* 12.3: 221-32.
Corbin, Alain
1986 *The Foul and the Fragrant: Odor and the French Social Imagination* (trans. Miriam L. Kochan, Roy Porter and Christopher Prendergast; Cambridge, MA: Harvard University Press [French 1982]).
Curtis, Robert I.
1991 *Garum and Salsamenta: Production and Commerce in Materia Medica* (Studies in Ancient Medicine; Leiden: E.J. Brill).
Dahl, Nils Alstrup
1995 'Euodia and Syntyche and Paul's Letter to the Philippians', in *Social World of the First Christians*: *Essays in Honor Wayne Meeks* (ed. L. Michael White and O. Larry Yarbrough; Minneapolis, MN: Augsburg Fortress): 3-15.
Digital Scent Technology
http://www.digiscents.com/blog/index.php (last accessed February 27, 2013).
Donahue, Neil H.
1992 'Scents and Insensibility: Patrick Süskind's New Historical Critique of "Die neue Sensibilität", in *Das Parfum* (1985)', *Modern Language Studies* 22.3: 36-37.
Drobnick, Jim (ed.)
2006 *The Smell Culture Reader* (Oxford: Berg).
Duff, Paul Brooks
1991 'Metaphor, Motif, and Meaning: The Rhetorical Strategy behind the Image "Led in Triumph" in 2 Cor. 2.14', *CBQ* 53: 79-92.

Duling, Dennis C.
2007 'Making Sense of Scents: Ancient Mediterranean and Biblical Osmologies from a Social-Scientific Perspective, with a focus on the New Testament'. Presentation at Society of Biblical Literature Annual Meeting, San Diego, CA, November 18, 2007.

Elliott, John H.
1986 'Social-Scientific Criticism of the New Testament and its Social World: More on Method and Models', in *Social-Scientific Criticism of the New Testament and its Social World* (ed. John H. Elliott; Semeia, 35; Decatur, GA: Scholars Press).
1988 'The Fear of the Leer: The Evil Eye from the Bible to Li'l Abner', *Forum* 4: 42-71.
1990 'Paul, Galatians and the Evil Eye', *CTM* 17: 262-73.
1991 'The Evil Eye in the First Testament: The Ecology and Culture of a Pervasive Belief', in *The Bible and the Politics of Exegesis: Essays in Honor of Norman Gottwald on his Sixty-Fifth Birthday* (ed. David Jobling, D.T. Sheppard and P.L. Day; Cleveland, OH: Pilgrim Press), 147-59.
1992 'Matthew 20:1-15: A Parable of Invidious Comparison and Evil Eye Accusation', *BTB* 22: 52-65.
1993 *What Is Social-Scientific Criticism?* (Guides to Biblical Scholarship; Minneapolis, MN: Fortress Press).
1994 'The Evil Eye and the Sermon on the Mount: Contours of a Pervasive Belief in Social Scientific Perspective', *BibInt* 2: 51-84.
2000 *1 Peter: A New Translation with Introduction and Commentary* (AB, 37B; New York: Doubleday).
2005 'Jesus, Mark and the Evil Eye', *LTJ* 39: 157-68.
2007 'Envy and the Evil Eye: More on Mark 7.22 and Mark's "Anatomy of Envy"', in *In Other Words: Essays on Social Science Methods and the New Testament in Honor of Jerome H. Neyrey* (ed. Anselm Hagedorn, Zeba A. Crook and Eric Stewart; Sheffield: Sheffield Phoenix Press): 87-105.
2011 'Social-Scientific Criticism: Perspective, Process and Payoff: Evil Eye Accusation at Galatia as Illustration of the Method', *HTS* 61:114-23.

Febvre, Lucien
1982 'Smells, Tastes, and Sounds', in *The Problem of Unbelief in the Sixteenth Century: The Religion of Rabelais* (trans. Beatrice Gottlieb; Cambridge: Cambridge University Press, repr. [original French 1942]).

Freyne, Sean
1995 'Herodian Economics in Galilee', in *Modelling Early Christianity: Social-Scientific Studies of the New Testament in its Context* (ed. Philip F. Esler; London: Routledge): 23-46.

Furlow, F. Bryant
1996 'The Smell of Love', *Psychology Today* 29/2: 38-45.

Green, Deborah A.
2011 *The Aroma of Righteousness: Scent and Seduction in Rabbinic Life and Literature* (University Park, PA: Pennsylvania State University Press).

Gummere, Richard M. (trans.)
1925 *Lucius Annaeus Seneca: Moral Epistles*, vol. 3 (LCL; Cambridge, MA: Harvard University Press).

Gunther, R.T. (ed.)
1933 *The Greek Herbal of Dioscorides* (trans. John Goodyer, 1655; Oxford: Oxford University Press). See Osbaldeston and Wood 2000 and Beck 2005.

Haddon, Alfred Cort
1935 *Reports of the Torres Strait Expedition* (6 vols.; London: Cambridge University Press).

Hanson, K.C.
1997 'The Galilean Fishing Economy and the Jesus Tradition', *BTB* 27: 99-111. http://www.kchanson.com/ARTICLES/fishing.html (Section 7).

Harvey, Susan Ashbrook
2006 *Scenting Salvation: Ancient Christianity and the Olfactory Imagination* (Berkeley, CA: University of California Press).

Hope, Valerie M., and Eireann Marshall
2000 *Death and Disease in the Ancient City* (London: Routledge).

Horsley, G.H.R.
1979 *New Documents Illustrating Early Christianity,* vol. 4 (Sydney: Macquarie University).

Howes, David
1991a 'Olfaction and Transition', in Howes (ed.) 1991: 128-46.
1991b 'Sensorial Anthropology', in Howes (ed.) 1991: 167-91.
1991c 'The Varieties of Sensory Experience: A Comparative Study of the Influence of Culture on the Relation or Balance between the Senses', in *Senses*. The Concordia Sensoria Research Team (CONSERT). Concordia University, Montreal, Canada. http://www.david-howes.com/senses/Consert-Variety.htm (last accessed December 27, 2012).

Howes, David (ed.)
1991 *The Varieties of Sensory Experience: A Sourcebook in the Anthropology of the Senses* (Toronto, ON: University of Toronto Press).
2005 *Empire of the Senses: The Sensual Cultural Reader* (Oxford: Berg).

Howes, David, Anthony Synnott and Constance Classen
2007 'Anthropology of Odor (1990–1994)', in *Senses.* The Concordia University Sensoria Research Team. http://alcor.concordia.ca/~senses/Consert-Odor.htm (last accessed December 21, 2012).

Howes, David, and Constance Classen
1991 'Conclusion: Sounding Sensory Profiles', in Howes 1991a: 257-315 (without Epilogue and Bibliography) as 'Doing Sensory Anthropology', *Sensory Studies.* http://www.sensorystudies.org/sensorial-investigations//doing-sensory-anthropology/ (last assessed December 23, 2012).

'Ig Nobel Prize Awarded for Fish Flatulence Research' (at Harvard University).
2004 http://www.fishupdate.com/news/fullstory.php/aid/2035/Ig_Nobel_Prize_awarded_for_fish_fart_research.html

Jenner, Mark S.R.
2000 'Civilisation and Deodorisation? Smell in Early Modern English Culture', in *Civil Histories: Essays Presented to Sir Keith Thomas* (ed. Peter Burke, Brian Harrison and Paul Slack; Oxford: Oxford University Press).
2011 'Follow your Nose? Smell, Smelling, and their Histories', *American Historical Review* 116.2: 335-51.

Jeremias, Joachim

1969 *Jerusalem in the Time of Jesus* (trans. F.H. and C.H. Cave; Philadelphia, PA: Fortress Press).

Johansen, Thomas K.

1996 'Aristotle on the Sense of Smell', *Phronesis: A Journal for Ancient Philosophy* 41.1: 1-19.

Jütte, Robert

2005 *A History of the Senses: From Antiquity to Cyberspace* (Cambridge: Polity Press).

Largey, Gale Peter, and David Rodney Watson

1972 'The Sociology of Odors', *American Journal of Sociology* 77.6: 1021-34.

Low, Kelvin E.Y.

2009 *Scent and Scent-Abilitites: Smell and Everyday Life Experiences* (Newcastle upon Tyne: Cambridge Scholars Publishing).

Mavor, Carol

2006 'Odor di femina. Though You May Not See Her, You Can Certainly Smell Her', in Drobnick 2006.

Manniche, Lise

1999 *Sacred Luxuries: Fragrance, Aromatherapy and Cosmetics in Ancient Egypt* (photographs by Werner Forman; Ithaca, NY: Cornell University Press).

Matthew, Victor H.

1992 'Perfumes and Spices', *ABD* 5: 226-28.

Mennell, Stephen

1987 'Review of Alain Corbin, *The Foul and the Fragrant: Odor and the French Social Imagination*', *American Journal of Sociology* 93.3: 727-29.

Miller, James Innes

1969 *The Spice Trade of the Roman Empire, 29 B.C. to A.D. 641* (New York: Oxford University Press).

Moulton, James Hope, and Wilbert Francis Howard

1920 *A Grammar of New Testament Greek. Vol. 2: Accidence and Word Formation* (Edinburgh: T. & T. Clark).

Nielsen, Kjeld P.

1986 *Incense in Ancient Israel* (Leiden: E.J. Brill).

'Nobel Prize in Physiology or Medicine'. Press release

2004 http://nobelprize.org/nobel_prizes/medicine/laureates/2004/press.html (last accessed December 22, 2012). See Axel and Buck.

Nordenfalk, Carl

1985 'The Five Senses in Late Medieval and Renaissance Art', *Journal of the Warburg and Courtauld Institutes* 48: 1-22.

Osbaldeston, Tess Anne, and R.P.A. Wood (eds.)

2000 *Dioscorides. De materia medica. Being An Herbal with Many Other Medicinal Materials* (trans. John Goodyer, 1655; Johannesburg: Ibidis Press cc. On-line pdf.). See Gunther 1933 and Beck 2005.

Osiek, Carolyn

2000 *Philippians. Philemon* (ANTC; Nashville, TN: Abingdon Press).

Rackham, Harris (trans.)

1955 *Pliny's Natural History,* vol. 4 (LCL; Cambridge, MA: Harvard University Press).

Rasmussen, Susan
1999 'Making Better "Scents" in Anthropology: Aroma in Tuareg Sociocultural Systems', *Anthropological Quarterly* 72.2: 55-74.
Ryckmans, Gonzague
1951 'De l'or, de l'encens, et de la myrrhe', *RB* 58: 372-76.
Schmidt, T.E.
1995 'Mark 15:16-32: The Crucifixion Narrative and the Roman Triumphal Procession', *NTS* 41: 1-18.
Scobie, Alex
1986 'Slums, Sanitation, and Mortality in the Roman World', *Klio* 68.2: 399-433.
Sense of Smell Institute Bibliography
2013 http://www.senseofsmell.org/resources/bookshelf_detail.php?value=Culture.
Simmel, Georg
1908a 'Sociology of the Senses', in *Simmel on Culture: Selected Writings* (ed. David Frisby and Mike Featherstorne; London: Sage, 1997): 109-19.
1908b *Sociologie: Untersuchungen über die Formen der Vergesellschaftung* (Berlin: Duncker & Humblot, repr. 1992).
Smith, Mark M.
2003 'Making Sense of Social History', *Journal of Social History* 37.1: 165-86.
2007 'Producing Sense, Consuming Sense, Making Sense: Perils and Prospects for Sensory History', *Journal of Social History* 40/4: 841-58.
Stark, Rodney
1991 'Antioch as the Social Situation for Matthew's Gospel', in *Social History of the Matthean Community: Cross-Disciplinary Approaches* (ed. David L. Balch; Minneapolis, MN: Fortress Press): 189-210.
Stern, K., and Martha K. McClintock
1998 'Regulation of Ovulation by Human Pheromones', *Nature* 392: 177-79.
Stewart, Alison
1995 'Large Noses and Changing Meanings in Sixteenth-Century German Prints', *Faculty Publications and Creative Activity, Department of Art and Art History.* Paper 7.[AQ any more info available?]
Suarez, F., J. Furne, J. Springfield and M. Levitt
1997 'Insights into Human Colonic Physiology Obtained from the Study of Flatus Composition', *American Journal of Physiology* 272: 1028-33.
Süsskind, Patrick
1986 *Perfume: The Story of a Murderer* (New York: A.A. Knopf).
Synnott, Anthony
1991a 'A Sociology of Smell', *Canadian Review of Sociology and Anthropology* 28.4: 437-59.
1991b 'Puzzling Over the Senses: From Plato to Marx', in Howes (ed.) 1991a: 61-76. www.udel.edu/History/.../611.../Synnott_Puzzling_over_senses.pdf.
1993 *The Body Social: Symbolism, Self and Society* (London: Routledge).
Taylor, Craig
2005 'The Disposal of Human Waste: A Comparison between Ancient Rome and Medieval London', *Past Imperfect* 11: 53-72. On-line by subscription (July 15, 2014).

Van Beek, G.W.
1960 'Frankincense and Myrrh', *BAR* 2: 99-126.
Van Beek, Walter E.A.
1992 'The Dirty Smith: Smell as a Social Frontier among the Kapsiki/Higi of North Cameroon and North-Eastern Nigeria', *Africa* 62: 38-58.
Wallace-Hadrill, Andrew
2003 'Domus and Insulae in Rome: Families and Housefuls', in *Early Christian Families in Context. An Interdisciplinary Dialogue* (ed. David L. Balch and Carolyn Osiek; Grand Rapids, MI: W.B. Eerdmans): 3-18.
Wilkinson, Richard
2003 *The Complete Gods and Goddesses of Ancient Egypt* (London: Thames & Hudson).
Wilson, H. Clyde
1992 'A Critical Review of Menstrual Synchrony Research', *Psychoneuroendocrinology* 17.6: 565-91.
West, Martin L. (trans.)
2003 *Homeric Hymns, Apocrypha, Lives of Homer* (LCL; Cambridge, MA: Harvard University Press).

Beware the Messiah! *Psalms of Solomon* 17 and the Death of Jesus

Philip F. Esler

Introduction

Most of us can point to events that were pivotal in our lives. One such event for me was meeting Jack Elliott at the International SBL Conference in Copenhagen in 1989 when I was still working full-time as a barrister in Sydney, Australia. I had read his *A Home for the Homeless* when doing my doctorate in Oxford seven years earlier, and here I was meeting the man himself. As well as talking about the Apocalypse, he suggested I join a group of mainly U.S. biblical critics interested in the social sciences who had been meeting annually. This led me to fly to Portland, Oregon, in March 1990 for what became the first meeting of the Context Group. So taken was I with the way the Group worked, both intellectually and personally, that I soon began giving thought to exchanging my legal career for a full-time academic post, leading to a move to the University of St Andrews, Scotland, in 1992. From 1989 Jack Elliott has helped me with my own work and has been a close friend, with his wife, Linde, showing me numerous kindnesses and extending me hospitality in their home near San Francisco, and elsewhere along the way. So it is a great honor for me to be able to contribute to this volume. He was indeed present when the first version of this essay was presented at a Context Group meeting several years ago.

This essay aims to make a fresh contribution to our historical understanding of why Jesus was killed. Using a thought experiment, I will explore aspects of the social context of Galilee and Judea in the 30s of the first century CE in order to highlight certain historical factors relevant to any attempt to explain Jesus' death and propose one possible (I do not submit probable) explanation for it. 'Thought experiments are devices of the imagination used to investigate the nature of things'.[1] My thought experiment, which Jack Elliott described as an 'emic scenario' in commenting on the first version of

1. 'Thought Experiments', *Stanford Encyclopedia of Philosophy* (http://plato.stanford.edu/entries/thought-experiment/).

this essay, will take the form of (a) assuming that the priestly authorities in Jerusalem possessed a copy of *Psalm of Solomon* 17 ('the most sustained messianic passage of the Second Temple period' [Chester 2007: 340]), and of (b) considering how they would have responded upon receiving intelligence of the words and actions of Jesus in Galilee and Judea. I will suggest that they would have formed the view either that he was the Messiah foretold in that text or that there was a real likelihood of a significant number of Judeans coming to believe he was that figure and, having reached that view, encouraged the Romans to crucify him.

The Psalms of Solomon and their Original Context

There are eighteen psalms in this collection, and most scholars believe they were written in Hebrew and later translated into Greek and Syriac.[2] It has been suggested that they represent the work of more than one author, and this view draws support from the collaborative nature of literary composition in the largely oral social context of the first century BCE (see Botha 2012: 113-31). They were composed around the mid first century BCE, from about 70 to 45 BCE,[3] as shown by their references to the turbulent events that ensued when the Hasmonean queen Alexandra (the widow of Alexander Jannaeus) died in 67 BCE and war immediately broke out between her sons Hyrcanus II and Aristobulus II. This conflict led to Pompey's arrival in Palestine, his entry into Jerusalem in 63 BCE, his capture of the Temple and the transportation of Judean prisoners to Rome to appear in his triumph.[4]

These events, referred to in several of the psalms,[5] provide a date *a quo,* and, given the richness of the allusions to these events, the date of composition was probably fairly soon after 63 BCE. One of the psalms refers unmistakably to the death of Pompey on the coast of Egypt in 48 BCE (2.26-27), described in poignant detail by Plutarch (*Pompey* 77-80). *Psalm of Solomon* 17 can actually be dated more exactly (and earlier) than this, since although it refers to the capture of the Temple and alludes to the dispatch of Aristobulus and his relatives to Rome to grace Pompey's triumph in 61 (17.12), it makes no mention of his escaping from Rome and raising a revolt in Palestine in 57 BCE (Josephus, *Ant.* 14.6). Furthermore, there

2. See Wright 2007 for a critical edition of the Greek text and an English translation (which is radically different from that in Wright 1985).

3. For discussion of various possibilities within this period, see Viteau 1911: 38-45; O'Dell 1961–62: 241; de Jonge 1985: 161; and Wright 1985: 641.

4. See Schürer 1973: 229-42. The Roman triumph functioned as a ritual of status elevation for the *triumphator* and of status degradation for the vanquished (see Esler 1995a: 241-45).

5. For example, *Pss. Sol.* 2.1, 2 and 6; 8.15-21; and 17.5-14.

seems to be a reference to *Pss. Sol.* 11.2-5 in *Bar.* 5.5-8 (Wright 1985: 647-48), a text that is usually dated to the end of the first century CE, and this provides a useful *terminus ad quem*. Yet there is no other allusion to these psalms extant from the first century, and the next evidence for them comes in the mention of 'Eighteen Psalms of Solomon' in the list at the beginning of Codex Alexandrinus, to be dated to the fifth century CE (Wright 1985: 639). Although the relevant leaves of the Codex are missing, that these psalms should be mentioned in Codex Alexandrinus at all, something that cannot be said of any of the other works collected by Charlesworth (1983 and 1985), testifies to their importance in certain early Christian (and possibly Judean) circles.

Two considerations suggest that the author or authors of the psalms and their audience were likely to have been Judeans in the mainstream of Judean life and not, for example, those who had separated off into particularist in-groups. First, *Pss. Sol.* 10.6-7 states that 'the devout shall give thanks in the assembly of the people (ἐκκλησίᾳ λαοῦ)' and 'the synagogues (συναγωγαὶ) of Israel will glorify the Lord's name'.[6] The author thus aligns his audience with people who will attend the 'assembly of the people', which is probably a reference to the *Hever ha-Yehudim*, the Council of the Judeans, convened by the Hasmonean leader in his role of high priest,[7] and the synagogues in Jerusalem. Those synagogues were the most likely venue for the earliest public performances of the *Psalms of Solomon*, where their promulgation represented a specific example of the way texts were published in an oral context like this (see Botha 2012). Second, contrary to those who have argued for Pharisaic or Essene aspects to these psalms,[8] there is nothing in them that speaks to particularist interests in Israel. What we find is an expression of understandings based on the Mosaic law and Judean scripture with which a majority of Judeans would have identified (Embry 2002: 121).

The Psalms of Solomon in the First Century CE *and the Jerusalem Priesthood*

The likely exposure of such Judeans, Jerusalemites especially, to the oral performance of these psalms and the existence of manuscript or manuscripts containing them throughout the first century CE mean that we must consider the role of memory in their continuing impact. Anthony Le Donne has recently sought to apply social memory theory to understanding the

6. English translation Wright 1985: 661.

7. The expression *kohen gadol wa-hever ha-Yehudim*, 'High Priest and Council of the Judeans', is common on Hasmonean coins (see Schürer 1973: 603-605).

8. For a refutation of the theory that Pharisees produced these psalms, see O'Dell 1961–62. Also see the literature cited in Wright 2007: 8-9.

historical Jesus but in a way that has wider application (Le Donne 2009). He has proposed that memories are preserved in groups over time but also 'refracted' as they are shaped by new influences. Thus we have a system of mnemonic continuity and adaptation, a hermeneutical spiral moving forward in time. A particular manifestation of this process, highlighted by Le Donne, is that of typology, which is 'a means of interpreting the roles of relatively new characters (in the narratives of story and history) by the great characters of metanarratives' (2009: 56). He describes metanarratives, in turn, as stories that are 'so culturally significant and so well known that they become standards of significance, by which all similar stories are measured and interpreted' (2009: 56). Within a relevant group, a memory (for example, of a great figure from the past) can be refreshed and adapted to new circumstances and situations so that it serves a new role or produces a new impact in the present (Le Donne 2009: 70-77).[9]

There is no doubt that the contemporaries of Jesus used figures from Israelite tradition typologically to interpret certain of their contemporaries. Thus the Gospels refer to the possibility that figures with major roles in Judean tradition are about to appear or have appeared in Israel, often in the guise of living persons active in that setting. Such figures include the Messiah (χριστός),[10] 'he who is to come',[11] John the Baptist,[12] and Elijah.[13] Two considerations suggest that expectations like this probably reflect historical reality in first-century CE Galilee and Judea. First, these Gospel instances represent details of the sort that it is difficult to see people simply inventing: they satisfy a criterion of historicity that Mark Goodacre has designated 'accidental information' (2012: 168). Second, there is evidence both within and outside of the New Testament that a number of people did actually appear in the first century claiming to be such figures or having that status ascribed to them. Some of these have been called 'sign prophets' (see Barnett 1981 and Gray 1993). For example, in about 45–46 CE Theudas appeared (as a latter-day Joshua) and invited a large group of people to join him at the Jordan where he promised to part the water (cf. Joshua 3) and provide them an easy passage (Josephus, *Ant.* 20.97). There was also an Egyptian prophet (mentioned both in Josephus and Acts)[14] who gathered a

9. Although beyond the scope of this essay, it is worth noting here that social identity theory provides another way of understanding the role of great individuals from the past in the present as prototypes or exemplars of group identity (see Smith and Zarate 1990: 244-46).

10. Mt. 2.4; Lk. 3.15; Mk 8.29 and cf. Mt. 16.16 and Lk. 9.20; Mk 12.35 and cf. Mt. 22.42; Mk 14.61 and cf. Mt. 26.63 and Lk. 22.67.

11. Mt. 11.3 and Lk. 7.19.

12. Mk 8.27-28 and cf. Mt. 16.13-14 and Lk. 9.18-19.

13. Mk 8.27-28 and parallels and Mk 9.11 and cf. Mt. 17.10.

14. Josephus, *War* 2.259-63, and *Ant.* 20.169-71; Acts 21.38.

large band in the period 52–58 CE, promising (again in the guise of Joshua) that the walls of Jerusalem would fall at this command. The Egyptian also had kingly pretensions: after overpowering the Roman garrison he would reign over the people (τοῦ δήμου τυραννεῖν).[15] There were other, unnamed figures who promised to liberate and exhibit signs redolent of Moses and Joshua (Barnett 1981: 682-83, 684-86). Having reviewed the data, Barnett reasonably concludes that the style of operation of the sign prophets was 'modelled upon the great figures of Israel's Exodus–Conquest, Moses and Joshua' (Barnett 1981: 689).

It is worth noting what happened to the two most prominent sign prophets. Theudas and his followers were attacked by Roman troops; many were killed, and he was captured and had his head cut off (Josephus, *Ant.* 20.98). The Romans attacked the crowd gathered by the Egyptian, but he escaped (Josephus, *War* 2.259-63; *Ant.* 20.169-71). Nor should we forget the example of Herod in Matthew 2. Faced with the possibility that 'the King of the Judeans' (Mt. 2.2) had recently been born in Bethlehem, he ruthlessly sought to rid himself of this threat to his power by killing all male children under two in Bethlehem and the surrounding hills. No doubt the story is fictional, but Matthew must have regarded it as a socially realistic description of how the ruler in Jerusalem would react to someone who might take his place.

On the basis that first-century CE Judeans were primed to expect the reappearance of great figures from the past, we may now introduce the *Psalms of Solomon*, especially *Pss. Sol.* 17, and begin our thought experiment of assuming that the Jerusalem priesthood was familiar with it and was interpreting Jesus typologically in relation to its Davidic and messianic protagonist.

There were several ways in which the priests in Jerusalem could have been aware of the figure predicted in *Pss. Sol.* 17. The first and most likely route is that they possessed or had access to a copy of *Pss. Sol.* 17; Jerusalem was the likeliest place to find it: as David Goodblatt has noted, 'Jerusalem was the religious and intellectual capital of the country, so we would expect it to be a center of book production, possession, and collection' (2006: 44). Second, perhaps the various psalms in the *Psalms of Solomon* were still being read to Jerusalem synagogue congregations in the 30s of the first century. Third, a priest or priests in the 30s could have been told about them by a parent who had heard them being read as far back as 60 BCE.

Given the power, sometimes enacted, of Judean collective memory crystallizing typologically in first-century CE persons, it is probable that the priests, including the high priest, would have interpreted developments in

15. Josephus, *War* 2.262.

Judea and Galilee contemporaneous with them in light of the *Pss. Sol.* 17 figure. From 18 to 36 CE the high priest was Caiaphas. He was appointed by the Roman procurator Valerius Gratus and removed by Vitellius (Josephus, *Ant.* 18.4.2; 18.4.3), Pilate's replacement. Since Caiaphas was high priest throughout the procuratorship of Pilate (26 to 36 CE) and Pilate did not replace him, it is probable that good working relations existed between the two men. In view of the coincidence of interest between political authorities and a dominant religion, they are likely to have cooperated against common threats (such as the sign prophets mentioned above). It is also highly probable that they were receiving reports of what Jesus was saying and doing in Galilee and Judea. There is evidence for such a Jerusalem-based interest in Jesus in Mk 3.22. Most probably the Jerusalem authorities, like other political powers in the region (see Dvornik 1974), engaged in espionage in relation to any persons they thought threatened the status quo. How would they have assessed what they were hearing about Jesus in relation to the messianic figure in *Pss. Sol.* 17 and what would they have done?

Correspondences between the Historical Jesus and Psalm of Solomon 17

Comparing what the historical Jesus likely said and did with the message of *Pss. Sol.* 17 reveals several correspondences that quite possibly would have caught the attention of the high priest and other authorities, causing them to act against Jesus. These correspondences are:

1. Teaching on the kingdom of God
2. Notions of the Davidic king and Messiah
3. Attitude toward the Temple and priesthood
4. Beliefs about the reconstituted tribes of Israel and land distribution
5. Teaching on the 'children of God'
6. Beliefs about the *sinlessness* of the king/Messiah and the *repentance* of the people
7. Notions about power in the Holy Spirit

I will deal with each of these in turn, outlining these ideas as they appear in *Pss. Sol.* 17 and examining how the Jerusalem priesthood likely would have understood them and how they might have aligned their interpretation with intelligence about Jesus' actions and words.

1. The Kingdom of God

A major area of correspondence between *Pss. Sol.* 17 and Jesus is that of God's kingship. *Psalm of Solomon* 17 begins and ends (vv. 1 and 46) with assertions of God's eternal kingship couched in almost identical terms. The text leaves no doubt that any other claims to kingship divorced from this reality are spurious. There is wide agreement among New Testament critics that Jesus preached the kingdom of God whatever else he did, as can be seen in a just a sample of scholarship on the subject.[16] Allison lists fifty-eight separate sayings about the kingdom in the Synoptic Gospels (2010: 164-68). While the kingdom of God no doubt served a polyvalent function in Jesus' teaching, two meanings for which there is considerable New Testament evidence are (a) God's dynamic activity as a ruler, his kingship (similar to *Pss. Sol.* 17.1 and 46); and (b) the result of that activity, his realm, including a spatial sense.[17] Allison suggests that probable instances of the first meaning include Lk.1.33; 11.20//Mt. 12.28; Lk. 13.20//Mt. 13.31; and Lk. 17.20-21, while noting that it is often hard to distinguish whether the expression means reign or rule (Allison 2010: 202).

One of the more plausible suggestions in relation to the meaning 'reign' for 'kingdom', made by Bruce Chilton on the basis of research into the Targums (especially of Isaiah), is that Jesus was referring to the intervention of God in strength on behalf of his people and was emphasizing not the abstract nature of the kingdom but the dynamic, personal presence of God, his saving, usually future activity (Chilton 1979; 1994). Such a message is extremely close to that in *Pss. Sol.* 17.3:

> We hope in God our saviour,
> because the strength of our God is forever merciful,
> and the kingdom of our God is forever over the foreigners (ἔθνη)
> in judgment.[18]

Judean priests who heard that Jesus was preaching the imminent intervention of God in history may not necessarily have regarded that as a bad thing, even if it did involve judgment against foreigners, but their Roman masters would have been extremely unhappy. How could the Israelite God's arrival in strength to judge them be anything other than most unwelcome, since it would be quite antithetic to their rule in Jerusalem? And how could the teaching of that forthcoming event by Jesus not be, in some sense at least, seditious? Yet this would have been only the beginning of their concerns, for *Pss. Sol.* 17 speaks of a human king as well as a divine one.

2. A (Davidic) King and Messiah

At *Pss. Sol.* 17.21 the author introduces the Davidic king, in a section that extends to v. 43. First comes a prayer that the Lord will 'raise up for them

16. See Perrin 1963, 1976: 54-63; Riches 1982: 87-111; Chilton 1979, 1984; 1994; Allison 2010: 164-204 (citing a rich array of secondary literature).

17. See Allison 2010: 168-99, with an insistence on the importance of the latter meaning in the Synoptic Gospels.

18. Translations of *Pss. Sol.* 17 are my own.

their king, the son of David' to be 'king over your child Israel' (v. 21). The psalmist has strong views on how he wants God to have this figure behave. He prays that God will give him the strength:

> to destroy unrighteous rulers,
> to purify Jerusalem of the foreigners who are trampling her to destruction,
> with wisdom and righteousness to drive out the sinners from their inheritance,
> to smash the arrogance of the sinner like a potter's jars,
> with an iron rod to shatter (συντρῖψαι) all their existence,
> to destroy the unlawful foreigners
> with the word of his mouth,
> so that at his threat the foreigners will flee from this presence,
> and to condemn sinners by the word in their heart (vv. 22-25).

The expression 'word of his mouth' is probably an allusion to the description in Isa. 11.1-5 (LXX) of the rod who will spring from the root of Jesse who, *inter alia*, 'will smite (πατάξει) the earth with the word of his mouth' (v. 4), for which the MT reads 'rod of his mouth'. It should be noted, however, that συντρίβω (inf. συντρῖψαι), which means 'break in pieces', is a much stronger verb than πατάσσω (fut. πατάξει).

He will be a righteous king, χριστὸς κυρίου, the Lord's Messiah (v. 32).[19] The Lord himself is his king. He will have mercy on foreigners who fear him. He will strike the earth with the word of his mouth forever. He will bless the Lord's people with wisdom and happiness. He himself will be free from sin and drive out sinners by the power of his word (vv. 34-36). He will not grow weak, because God has made him powerful in the Holy Spirit and wise in understanding with strength and righteousness (v. 37).

How would the priesthood, especially Caiaphas the high priest, and Pontius Pilate, the Roman procurator in the 30s, have responded if they had thought Jesus was this figure or that a significant proportion of the population were coming to think that he was? What would they have considered was in store for them and what would they have done about it? We should note at the outset that *Pss. Sol.* 17.21-43 identifies two groups who will be affected by the actions of the Davidic king: (a) (unrighteous) rulers (vv. 22, 36) and sinners (vv, 23, 24, 25, 36), who are almost certainly Israelites (*inter alia*, because they will be driven from their inheritance; v. 23), and (b) foreigners (vv. 22, 24, 25, 28, 29, 30), who, *inter alia*, are trampling Jerusalem to destruction (v. 22).

In the 30s of the first century CE Caiaphas would surely have interpreted himself and his family, and perhaps other priests, as the unrighteous rulers

19. For a discussion of the messianic nature of the figure in this psalm, see Davenport 1980.

and sinners targeted in this text for destruction (v. 22), expulsion (v. 23), the shattering of their existence with an iron rod (v. 23) and condemnation (v. 25), while noting with concern the reference to the purification of Jerusalem with holiness (v. 30), which must apply to the Temple above all. Pilate would have regarded himself and the Roman garrison based in the Fortress Antonia, which was constructed on the northwest corner of the Temple Mount, as the 'foreigners' mentioned in the text. They were the foreigners of whom Jerusalem would be purified (v. 22), who would be destroyed (ὀλεθρεῦσαι) by a word of his mouth (v. 24), who would flee from his presence (v. 25), who would not be permitted to reside among them (v. 28) and who would be enslaved under his yoke (v. 30).

There is a recent discussion as to how warlike this Davidic king and Messiah is. Atkinson has argued that *Pss. Sol.* 17 describes a violent and militant Davidic messiah who will lead Israel in war against foreigners oppressing Israel (Atkinson 2004: 129-79). Le Donne, on the other hand, has sought to play down the warlike dimensions, suggesting that the figure in *Pss. Sol.* 2.9 has been run through the mnemonic lens of Isa. 11.4 so that 'the coming king is portrayed as a person of wisdom and peaceful domination' (Le Donne 2009: 125). Certainly the author carefully excludes his reliance on an army:

> For he will not hope in horse or rider or bow,
> nor will he multiply for himself gold and silver for war,
> nor concentrate hopes in a multitude for a day of war (v. 33).

Nevertheless, Le Donne's presentation of him neglects the violent imagery of v. 24, where he uses an iron rod to shatter the existence of sinners and the word of his mouth to destroy foreigners. The text imagines his word operating as a devastating sonic weapon. Not only does the Davidic king use an iron rod and his word for violent purposes, his wisdom and righteousness have the power 'to drive out sinners from their inheritance' (v. 23). There is no justification for Le Donne to suggest that 'the figure relies on divine intervention' (Le Donne 2009: 129). Well might Caiaphas and Pilate fear *him*.

Many scholars believe that the *titulus* hung on Jesus' cross, which included the words 'the King of the Judeans' (Mt. 27.37; Mk 15.26; Lk. 23.38; Jn 19.19), was authentic (see Bammel 1984: 363; and Schneider 1984: 403); as such, it provided an explanation from the Romans to onlookers as to why he was crucified.[20] John Collins has noted that 'Jesus was crucified as "King of the Jews", and this suggests that he was viewed as a messianic pretender and that the kingdom he proclaimed was understood,

20. See Horsley (1994b: 413-14), who argues against seeing in the words of the *titulus* the exact nature of the charge that had been made against him.

at least by some of his followers, as a messianic kingdom' (Collins 1998: 259).[21] While this is highly probable, for the purposes of this essay a more precise point can be made: either Pilate considered Jesus as a king of the Judeans or considered it likely that his followers so regarded him. So we have a Jesus who both proclaims God's kingdom and is himself regarded as a king. This is very close indeed to the (Davidic) king in *Pss. Sol.* 17. On the assumption that Pilate had been alerted by Caiaphas to this similarity, the role envisaged in that text for this king would have provided them both with ample reason to want Jesus killed.

While we are secure in the view that the Romans connected Jesus with a claim to kingship, what led them to that view and, perhaps, to align him with the figure in *Pss. Sol.* 17 is far less certain. Although there are some Gospel references to Jesus being a king or having the trappings of kingship (e.g. Mk 10.35-40; Mt. 2.2; 4.1-11; and Lk. 19.11-27), it is difficult to relate any of these to the historical Jesus. It is, however, possible that what is called the triumphal entry of Jesus into Jerusalem, if historical, played a part in this view. In Mk 11.1-11 Jesus enters Jerusalem on a donkey, in manifest fulfillment of the saying in Zech. 9.9: 'Your king comes to you . . . humble and riding on a donkey', while the crowd cries out, 'Blessed is the coming kingdom of our ancestor David'. Nevertheless, the Gospel accounts do connect this event with a claim to kingship, although more strongly in Mark (11.1-11; kingdom of David), Luke (19.28-44; the king who comes in the name of the Lord) and John (12.12-19: king of Israel) than in Matthew (21.1-11; son of David). There are some grounds for optimism in regarding a modest arrival by Jesus into Jerusalem on a donkey in fulfillment of Zech. 9.9 as rooted in memory and as historical (see Le Donne 2009: 191-200).

Does the use of *Pss. Sol.* 17 by Caiaphas and Pilate also explain the odd fact that there is no trace in the Gospels or elsewhere of any of Jesus' disciples having been crucified with him? This is rather unexpected in light of the way that at other times in the first century CE, as noted above, the Romans attacked both sign prophets and their followers. *Psalm of Solomon* 17.33 explicitly states that this king will not rely on soldiers, gather resources for war, or foment hopes for a day of war. Did the Judean high priest and the Roman procurator consider that Jesus was a king who would not lead a band of warriors and that there was therefore no need to execute any of his followers, even though he himself had to be killed?

Lastly on this point, one of the most significant aspects of the messiah in *Pss. Sol.* 17 is his *Davidic* ancestry, an idea long established in Israelite tradition (see Pomykala 1995). Now although the Synoptic tradition came to assert the Davidic ancestry of Jesus very strongly, the question arises as

21. For a recent discussion arguing that Jesus was executed as 'King of the Jews', see Allison 2010: 233-40.

to whether the historical Jesus himself made this claim or the claim was made of him. Paul attributes Davidic descent to Jesus in Rom. 1.3 (possibly citing a pre-Pauline creed). In Mark's Gospel Jesus is addressed as 'son of David' by the blind Bartimaeus (10.47, 48). This may be pre-Marcan since it comes across as an incidental detail in the narrative, and Davidic descent is something Mark does not develop elsewhere, although the idea of Davidic descent is raised in connection with the entry of Jesus into Jerusalem (Mk 11.10). Perhaps the most intriguing piece of evidence in relation to this question comes in Mk 12.35-37, where Jesus raises the claim of the scribes that the messiah must be a son of David in such a way as to cast some doubt over whether the claim is correct. If this originates in the career of the historical Jesus, might not the context for it have been a notion abroad that Jesus was claiming to be of Davidic descent, a notion that he was seeking to rebut (perhaps because he believed he had a messianic role but knew he was not descended from David)?[22] Others may have been making the claim for him, and this alone would have been enough to cause apprehension among the Jerusalem leadership, while he himself sought to discount the idea.

3. Attitude toward the Temple and Priesthood

Psalms of Solomon 17.5 states that 'They took away with violence (μετὰ βίας ἀφείλαντο)'. As far as the first century BCE was concerned, this was a reference to the Hasmonean leadership, which embraced kingly and priestly roles in the one person. A very graphic condemnation of people who can only be the Temple priesthood occurs in *Pss. Sol.* 8, where they are alleged to have stolen from the sanctuary, walked on the place of sacrifice while unclean and defiled the sacrifices (vv. 11-13). In *Pss. Sol.* 2, moreover, the author attributes the Romans' profanation of the place of sacrifice (τὸ θυσιαστήριον) (v. 2) to the fact that 'the sons of Jerusalem defiled the sanctuary of the Lord (τὰ ἅγια κυρίου); they were profaning the offerings of God with lawless acts' (v. 3). These actions were either being committed by the priests or, at least, permitted by them.

Misappropriation by priests had a history in Israel that stretched back to the period of the judges. In the practice described in 1 Sam. 2.12-17, the sons of Eli take sacrificial meat provided by Israelites, 'by force' (κραταιῶς) if necessary (1 Sam. 2.16; LXX). The role of the Temple within the economic and political system of Palestine in the first century BCE was based on the broad dynamics that had been a feature of life in the Near East for as long as temples had existed there. Once a culture had achieved what sociologists Lenski and Lenski describe as the advanced agrarian stage, when the use

22. That Jesus had a messianic sense of himself is supported by the probable historicity of his claim 'I will destroy this temple and in three days build another'. See Theissen 1992.

of a plough meant peasants produced more than they needed for subsistence, a dominant elite arose that used military force to take control of the surplus (see Lenski and Lenski 1982). The social and political structures, at a general level, that arose in response to these surpluses were extremely significant. A tiny ruling elite (2 to 5 percent of the population), living in cities and assisted by various types of retainers, exercised power over large numbers of peasants and extracted a significant proportion of their surplus production. All this allowed the elite to maintain a comfortable, even luxurious, life in the city and the religious cult or cults that were located there.

In the first century CE the Temple continued to be economically dependent on other Judeans, of whom the peasantry comprised the largest proportion, both with respect to tithes and the Temple tax (which was compulsory, not voluntary),[23] and the priests continued to use their position to enrich themselves. The broad economic and political position of the Temple as the institution whereby the Jerusalem urban elite, especially the priesthood, maintained and legitimated their exactions from the rest of the population continued in much the same way in the first century CE. This now occurred, however, in collaboration with the Romans, whose *imperium* ensured the political stability necessary for the process to operate with minimal interruption. This dimension should not be forgotten as forming the context in which a text such as *Pss. Sol.* 17 would have been received.[24]

The main evidence for this malpractice is as follows:[25]

(a) Chapter 7 of the *Testament of Moses* (dated just prior to 30 CE) describes priestly corruption. Although the text is fragmentary, the priests are referred to as 'godless and destructive', as 'deceitful', 'false in every way imaginable', as people who 'consume the goods of the poor, saying their acts are according to justice'. They commit criminal deeds all day long, so as to enjoy feasting and to behave like princes (see Priest 1983: 930). Archaeological evidence has illuminated the luxurious lifestyle of the Jerusalem priesthood in the first century (Mazar 1975: 84-86; Avigad 1983: 129-30).

(b) In a Talmud passage (*b. Pesaḥ.* 57a) there is a reference to high priestly families violently taking from the peasants: 'Woe is me because of

23. Bauckham 1988.

24. In a careful and detailed response to the original form of this essay delivered at a meeting of the Context Group many years ago, Wolfgang Stegemann disagreed with my highlighting oppression of the peasantry by the priests. While I have greatly profited from this critique in reworking this essay, I regard the mention of the violent misappropriation reported in v. 5, in the context of the external data cited in the next paragraph, as the key evidence for my view.

25. See Bauckham 1988 and Evans 1989; 1995b (who has unfortunately overlooked Bauckham 1988).

the house of Boethus, . . . Hanan etc. . . . for they are high priests, and their sons are treasurers, and their sons-in-law are temple overseers, and their servants beat the people with clubs' (quoted in Horsley 1994a: 75). Richard Bauckham has shown that this passage represents an authentic tradition from before the fall of Jerusalem, when four main high priestly families kept a firm control on the affairs of the Temple (Bauckham 1988: 79-80).

(c) During the 50s and 60s high priests sent servants to the threshing-floors to take tithes by force from ordinary priests, some of whom starved as a result (Josephus, *Ant.* 20.181, 206-207).

(d) 4Q251 has evidence of priestly corruption: 'They will rob their neighbours and oppress one another'.

(e) There are three passages in the Isaiah Targum where criticism is directed at the first-century CE priesthood. Two of these (Isa. 5.1-7 and 28.1-13) refer to oppression by the priests (Evans 1995b: 328-30).

(f) In the Targum of Jer. 7.9 the religious leaders are specifically called 'thieves' and on other occasions they are called 'robbers of money', and there are pejorative references to 'the scribe and priest' (Evans 1995b: 330-33), no doubt because the scribes were the agents of the priests in their larceny.

(g) During the Judean revolt the Temple archives containing the debt records were burnt (Josephus, *War* 2.17.6). Not all the creditors would have been priests, but some must have been; and the fact that the debt records were kept in safe custody in the Temple must have solidified the impression that the priesthood was implicated in the oppression of the peasantry.

So how does what Jesus said and did in relation to the Temple relate to the material in *Pss. Sol.* 17 and other *Psalms of Solomon* in light of the historical context just set out? Two aspects of the Jesus traditions might very well have caused the Jerusalem elite and their Roman protectors to be concerned about a possible relationship between Jesus and the Davidic king and messiah in *Pss. Sol.* 17 in this area:

(a) the incident in the Temple (Mt. 21.12-17; Mk 11.15-18; Lk. 19.45-48; Jn 2.13-22), and
(b) the prophecy of Jesus that he would destroy the Temple and in three days rebuild it (Mk 14.58).

I will deal with these in turn.

Most commentators accept the historicity of the incident in the Temple, even though discussion rages as to the significance of Jesus' actions.[26] E.P. Sanders has proposed that Jesus' action was not a protest against dishonesty or improper religious polity but a prophetic demonstration symbolizing the imminent destruction of the Temple that was interpreted by Mark and the

26. For a neglected article on this historicity of the incident (a reference I owe to K.C. Hanson), see Eppstein 1964.

others as a cleansing to tone down its militancy. He argues that the 'eschatological' prophet was to destroy the Temple before building a new one, and this was a symbol of the destruction. For Sanders, what Jesus did had nothing to do with 'corruption', and there is no evidence of corruption in the first-century Temple (1985: 61-71). Sanders has rightly been criticized for the implausibility of this interpretation of Jesus' action in the Temple as a symbol of both destruction of the existing Temple and *replacement with a new one*, when in the light of other Judean traditions we would expect more emphasis on the new than the old (Bauckham 1988: 79-81). A more fundamental criticism, however, is that Sanders fails to factor into his discussion the economic and political significance of the Temple as parasitic on the Judean population in the manner set out above.

It is noteworthy that the Synoptic Gospels stress the relation of the incident to dishonest practice (Mk 11.15-18; Mt. 21.12-17; Lk. 19.45-48),[27] using the 'robbers' den' quotation from Jer. 7.11. This forges a powerful point of connection between *Pss. Sol.* 17 and Jesus. The description of the Temple as a 'robbers' den' may well be historical and align Jesus precisely with the outlook of the sources just cited which saw in the Temple priesthood people who took far more than their just dues, and also with the statement about violent misappropriation in *Pss. Sol.* 17.5. It is possible to analyse the four elements of Mark's account of what Jesus did in the Temple along these lines: He drove out those who were buying and selling because of the high prices being charged; he overturned the tables of the money-changers (controlled by the priesthood and holding stocks of Tyrian half-shekels necessary to pay the Temple tax) because they were charging an exorbitant commission on their exchange; he upset the seats of those selling doves because the Temple priests (who had a monopoly on their sale) were demanding an excessive price from the poor who bought them for sacrifice; and he prevented any vessel (σκεῦος) from being carried through the Temple because such an item held the flour, oil and wine sold for sacrifice which was sold at an excessively high price (see Bauckham 1988: 75-77).

It is also likely that Jesus did indeed utter the prophecy about destroying and rebuilding the Temple, as Gerd Theissen (1992) has shown. Although it is impossible to determine whether Jesus made the prophecy in conjunction with the incident, as suggested by Jn 2.13-22 (but not the Synoptics), this remains an intriguing possibility. The fact that Jeremiah 7, which the Synoptic Gospels have Jesus quote for its 'robbers' den' reference in v. 11 (Mt. 21.13; Mk 11.17; Lk. 19.46), goes on to warn of the destruction of the Temple (vv. 12-15) shows how naturally Jesus could have raised this theme in connection with what he did in the Temple with respect to the 'robbers'.

27. John 2.13-22 has Jesus attack it for commercial activity, rather than dishonesty.

Psalms of Solomon 17.30 states of the Davidic king that he is going to 'honour the Lord in a prominent place on the earth, and he will purify Jerusalem with holiness'. Does this indicate that he will build a new temple? If so, we have direct link between Jesus' prophecy and *Pss. Sol.* 17.

It is therefore possible that Jesus' demonstration in the Temple and his prophecy about its destruction and rebuilding played a large role in his death, perhaps because he appeared to Judean priests and Roman legate as just too similar to a messiah whose appearance spelt doom for all of them.

4. Reconstituted Tribes of Israel and Land Distribution

The tribes of Israel appear in *Pss. Sol.* 17.26 in the context of the coming judgment by the messiah and, more importantly, in v. 28, where it states, 'He will distribute them on the land according to their tribes, the resident alien and the foreigner will no longer reside among them'. There are two important dimensions to this distribution. As to the first dimension, there may appear to be a reference to the return of those Israelites to Israel who had been scattered among other peoples, which is a common feature of Israelite tradition concerning the end-time (cf. Isa. 49.22; 60.4; 66.20; *Bar.* 5.5-9). Indeed this tradition is the subject of *Pss. Sol.* 11 and appears in *Pss. Sol.* 17.31. Yet none of these passages mentions that the returning Israelites will be settled on the land according to their tribes; rather, they have in view a return to Jerusalem only. Michael Fuller wrongly suggests that in *Pss. Sol.* 17 'the locus of the re-gathered ones will be the exalted Temple' (2006: 169). While *Pss. Sol.* 17.31 refers to Israelites who will return from abroad, *Pss. Sol.* 17.28 means that they will be redistributed on the land. What we have in *Pss. Sol.* 17, in fact, is the idea that the Davidic king will repeat the process that first occurred after the Israelites crossed the Jordan under Joshua, arrived in Canaan, and were then allocated various parts of the country as their own (Josh. 13.1–14.5). Re-establishing the tribes on the land is of a piece with the projected role of the assembly of the tribes (συναγωγῇ φυλῶν) in *Pss. Sol.* 17.44, which is similar to the assembly of Israelites mentioned frequently in Joshua. We have seen above how sign prophets acting in the guise of Joshua fell foul of the Romans later in the first century CE; a text that raised the spectre that someone acting like Joshua would also have caused the Jerusalem authorities grave anxiety in the 30s.

The second dimension is less securely featured in the text but cannot be ignored. We must bear in mind that the displacement of peasantry from their land, due to debt especially, was a continuing problem in the Near East. The land tended to fall into the hands of wealthier peasants or even the local aristocracy, in the latter case resulting in the latifundialization for which there is evidence in Galilee during the first century CE (Freyne 1995: 33-35). In this context, the action by the messiah in distributing the tribes on the land would have been seen as a decisive action on behalf of displaced peasantry and a grave threat to those who benefited from their displacement, including wealthier priestly families and the Temple authorities who were presumably receiving a tithe from the farms and olive groves in question.

Related to the first dimension is the likelihood that Jesus gathered twelve special disciples about him, in a manner that could easily have been interpreted as revealing an intention to appoint them to rule over the twelve tribes. A good case can be made for the historicity of the incident when James and John ask that they be allowed to sit on his right and his left in his glory (Mk 10.35-45), which causes annoyance to the other disciples, since it is difficult to imagine this tradition being invented at any time (Sanders 1985: 146-47). Here the context seems to be one in which the king will dine with his chosen twelve gathered about him, one to lead each tribe; and this seems to be related to the Q saying that these disciples shall sit upon thrones judging the twelve tribes of Israel (Mt. 19.28; Lk. 22.30), which Luke connects with the messianic banquet.

As to the second dimension, Jesus would have alarmed the Jerusalem priesthood in this connection if they had heard anything suggesting that he was taking the part of the peasant or had an interest in the position of the tribes. Douglas Oakman has indeed argued that the 'Our Father' should be interpreted as a peasants' prayer, which responded to their economic and political exploitation, especially the indebtedness which led to hunger and the way the court system favoured the wealthy (Oakman 1986: 152-56; 1999). William Herzog (1994) has also interpreted the parables of Jesus as addressed to the non-elite in their circumstances of economic difficulty and oppression. If Herzog's interpretation is correct, reports of parables carrying this type of message that reached Jerusalem would have caused the authorities there considerable alarm.

5. The Children of God

Psalms of Solomon 17.27c states of those whom the messiah will favour: 'For he will know them, that they are all sons of their God'. It should be noted, however, that God is never directly referred to or addressed as 'Father' in the psalm. Nevertheless, the sonship-of-God theme in the psalm connects with some evidence that the historical Jesus developed a self-understanding of his followers as fictive kin under the fatherhood of God. The main sign of this is the 'Our Father' (Mt. 6.9-13; Lk. 11.2-4), the historicity of which I accept, at least in its shorter Lucan form. As noted in the previous section, it is possible that the Lord's Prayer itself was a peasants' prayer, referring to matters pertaining to dispossession, such as debt and the legal procedures for debt recovery. We should also bear in mind the strand in the tradition that speaks of the followers of Jesus leaving their relatives (Mt. 10.34-38; Lk. 12.51-53 and 14.26-27), in relation to which Jerome Neyrey (1995) has argued that the experience of the followers of Jesus, alienated from their own families, underlies the Q version of the Beatitudes. This type of experience may well have stimulated Jesus to stress the fictive kinship that his followers shared, possibly as far as his fostering a sense among them that they were 'sons of God', at least to the extent that they prayed to God as father, even if they did not designate themselves in exactly those terms.

6. Sinlessness of the King and Repentance of the People

In *Pss. Sol.* 17 the sin of the author's ingroup is blamed for the usurpation of power by the Hasmoneans (v. 5). Sin is also repeatedly attributed to those condemned in the text (vv. 5, 8, 20, 23 and 25). It is no surprise, therefore, that the problem of sin will be addressed by the Davidic king and messiah. He will judge the tribes and will not tolerate unrighteousness among them, so that any wicked person will not live among them (v. 27). Moreover, the messiah himself will be sinless and will drive out sinners (v. 36). The text thus indicates that being free from sin and unrighteousness will be necessary for Judeans who live in the time of the messianic king, even if repentance itself is not mentioned in *Pss. Sol.* 17.

While sinlessness may be something that was not predicated of either Jesus or his followers in the period up to his death,[28] the need for repentance is prominent in the Synoptic tradition precisely in relation to the nearness of the kingdom of God:

> The time is fulfilled and the kingdom of God is at hand.
> Repent and believe in the gospel (Mk 1.15).

While it is doubtful whether the historical Jesus used the expression 'believe in the gospel', since it looks like a post-Easter formulation, many commentators would grant that a call to repentance was a part of his message (Perrin 1976: 90-102; Riches 1982: 87-112). The Jerusalem priesthood might well have interpreted a call for repentance by someone like Jesus as a necessary preparatory step for the attainment of the state of sinlessness that is lauded in *Pss. Sol.* 17, especially if linked to the kingdom of God that appears in vv. 1, 3 and 46.

We need to be careful, however, about exactly what kind of repentance this was and to recognize that Jesus may have been employing widely known Judean traditions in so doing (Sanders 1985: 106-13). Nevertheless, our hypothesized priests in Jerusalem, comparing what they were hearing about Jesus with the picture of the messiah in the psalm, would probably have seen in this aspect of Jesus' preaching one more link to that threatening figure.

28. The idea of Jesus as sinless certainly developed later, as is evident in 2 Cor. 5.21; Heb. 4.15 and 7.26; 1 Pet. 3.22 and 1 Jn 3.5, for example.

7. Powerful in the Holy Spirit
The Davidic king in *Pss. Sol.* 17 is described as being 'powerful in the Holy Spirit' (v. 37). This is an allusion to Isa. 11.2-5, also alluded to elsewhere in *Pss. Sol.* 17, which speaks of a branch of the root of Jesse on whom will rest the Spirit of the Lord and who, in wisdom and righteousness, will vindicate the poor and humble of the earth and slay their oppressors with his powerful word. There is a direct connection made in this Isaian passage between the Spirit of God and the rectification of prevailing patterns of social and economic injustice. And in Isaiah the 'humble' must include the peasants. The passage from Isaiah, in its original form and in its appropriation in *Pss. Sol.* 17, represented disturbing news for the elites who controlled Palestine. The psalm declares, after all, that the Davidic messiah will drive out rulers (ἄρχοντας, v. 36).

This material becomes relevant to the historical Jesus, given the role the Spirit probably had or been perceived to have had in his ministry. Certainly we can discount some information in the Gospel traditions on this subject (especially in Luke) as a product of later reflection, a retrojection of post-Easter charismatic experience and insight onto the earlier period. But can we discount all of it? A reasonable case can be made for some historicity attaching to the account of Jesus having been accused by scribes who came down from Jerusalem of casting out demons by Satan (Mk 3.22-30). His answer is that, in fact, it is by the Holy Spirit that he casts out demons and, moreover, that blasphemy against the Holy Spirit is a sin that will not be forgiven. This dispute makes good sense in a context where the Jerusalem authorities are becoming concerned that people are claiming that Jesus' ability to exorcise demons rests on his being filled with the Holy Spirit, since this evokes precisely the spectre of the dangerous messiah in *Pss. Sol.* 17.35-37.

Conclusion

This comparison of some of what we know about the life and death of Jesus with what was predicted of the Davidic king and messiah in *Pss. Sol.* 17 reveals, accordingly, significant areas of overlap. We will never discover if the Jerusalem priests were ticking off features of the messiah in their text of *Pss. Sol.* 17 against what they were gradually learning about Jesus, culminating in his dramatic actions and teaching in the Temple. Nevertheless, this remains an intriguing possibility. I have shown that there were enough correspondences for them and the Romans to want Jesus killed and that much evidence suggests this is what the rulers in Jerusalem would have done to such a figure. Moreover, in carrying out this exercise we have been able firmly to situate Jesus within prophetic and messianic traditions in Israel that aligned those sent by God with the poor and humble of the land, the long-suffering peasantry whose maltreatment by Temple priesthoods stretched back centuries. Conducting such a thought experiment on *Pss. Sol.* 17 thus allows a fresh examination of what led to Jesus' death.

References

Allison, Dale C.
2010 *Constructing Jesus: Memory, Imagination, History* (London: SPCK).

Atkinson, Kenneth
2004 *I Cried to the Lord: A Study of the Psalms of Solomon's: Historical Background and Social Setting* (JSJSup, 84; Leiden: Brill).

Avigad, Nahman
1983 *Discovering Jerusalem* (Nashville, TN: Thomas Nelson).

Bammel, Ernst
1984 'The *Titulus*', in *Jesus and the Politics of his Day* (ed. Ernst Bammel; Cambridge: Cambridge University Press): 353-64.

Barnett, P.W.
1981 'The Jewish Sign Prophets—A.D. 40–70: Their Intentions and Origin', *NTS* 27: 679-97.

Bauckham, Richard
1988 'Jesus' Demonstration in the Temple', in *Law and Religion: Essays on the Place of the Law in Israel and Early Christianity* (ed. Barnabas Lindars; Cambridge: James Clarke): 72-89.

Botha, Pieter J.J.
2012 *Orality and Literacy in Early Christianity* (Biblical Performance Criticism, 5; Eugene, OR: Cascade Books).

Charlesworth, James H. (ed.)
1983 *The Old Testament Pseudepigrapha: Apocalyptic Literature and Testaments,* vol. 1 (London: Dartman, Longman & Todd).
1985 *The Old Testament Pseudepigrapha: Apocalyptic Literature and Testaments,* vol. 2 (London: Dartman, Longman & Todd).

Chester, Andrew
2007 *Messiah and Exaltation*: *Jewish Messianic and Visionary Traditions and New Testament Christology* (WUNT, 207; Tübingen: Mohr Siebeck).

Chilton, Bruce
1979 *God in Strength: Jesus' Announcement of the Kingdom* (SNTU B, 1; Freistadt: Plöchl; repr. 1987 as BibSem, 8; Sheffield: JSOT Press).
1994 'The Kingdom of God in Recent Discussion', in Chilton and Evans 1994: 255-80.

Chilton, Bruce (ed.)
1984 *The Kingdom of God in the Teaching of Jesus* (Issues in Religion and Theology, 5; Philadelphia, PA: Fortress Press).

Chilton, Bruce, and Craig A. Evans (eds.)
1994 *Studying the Historical Jesus: Evaluations of the State of Current Research* (Leiden: E.J. Brill).

Collins, John
1998 *The Apocalyptic Imagination: An Introduction to Jewish Apocalyptic Literature* (Grand Rapids, MI: Eerdmans, 2nd edn).

Collins, John J., and G.W.E. Nickelsburg (eds.)
1980 *Ideal Figures in Ancient Judaism: Profiles and Paradigms* (SBL Septuagint and Cognate Studies, 12; Chico, CA: Scholars Press).
Davenport, Gene L.
1980 'The "Anointed of the Lord" in Psalms of Solomon 17', in Collins and Nickelsburg 1980: 67-92.
Dvornik, Francis
1974 *Origins of Intelligence Services: The Ancient Near East, Persia, Greece, Rome, Byzantium, the Arab Muslim Empires, the Mongol Empire, China, Muscovy* (New Brunswick, NJ: Rutgers University Press).
Embry, Brad
2002 'The Psalms of Solomon and the New Testament: Intertextuality and the Need for a Re-Evaluation', *JSP* 13: 99-136.
Eppstein, Victor
1964 'The Historicity of the Gospel Account of the Cleansing of the Temple', *ZNW* 55: 42-58.
Esler, Philip F.
1995a 'God's Honour and Rome's Triumph: Responses to the Fall of Jerusalem in 70 CE in Three Jewish Apocalypses', in Esler 1995b: 239-58.
Esler, Philip F. (ed.)
1995b *Modelling Early Christianity: Social-Scientific Studies of the New Testament in its Context* (London: Routledge).
Evans, Craig A.
1989 'Jesus' Action in the Temple and Evidence of Corruption in the First-Century Temple', in *Society of Biblical Literature 1989 Seminar Papers* (ed. David J. Lull; Atlanta, GA; Scholars Press): 522-39.
1995a *Jesus and his Contemporaries: Comparative Studies* (Leiden: E.J. Brill).
1995b 'Jesus' Action in the Temple and Evidence of Corruption in the First-Century Temple', in Evans 1995a: 319-44.
Freyne, Sean
1995 'Herodian Economics in Galilee: Searching for a Suitable Model', in Esler 1995b: 23-46.
Fuller, Michael E.
2006 *The Restoration of Israel: Israel's Re-gathering and the Fate of the Nations in Early Jewish Literature and Luke–Acts* (BZNW, 158: Berlin: de Gruyter).
Goodacre, Mark
2012 'Criticizing the Criterion of Multiple Attestation: The Historical Jesus and the Question of Sources', in *Jesus, Criteria, and the Demise of Authenticity* (ed. Chris Keith and Anthony Le Donne; London: T. & T. Clark): 152-69.
Goodblatt, David
2006 *Elements of Jewish Nationalism* (Cambridge: Cambridge University Press).
Gray, Rebecca
1993 *Prophetic Figures in Late Second Temple Jewish Palestine: The Evidence from Josephus* (Oxford: Oxford University Press).
Herzog, William R., II
1994 *Parables as Subversive Speech* (Louisville, KY: Westminster/John Knox Press).
Horsley, Richard A.
1994a *Sociology and the Jesus Movement* (New York: Continuum, 2nd edn).

1994b 'The Death of Jesus', in Chilton and Evans 1994: 395-422.

Jonge, M. de

1985 'The Psalms of Solomon', in *Outside the Old Testament* (ed. M. de Jonge; Cambridge Commentaries on the Writings of the Jewish and Christian World, 4; Cambridge: Cambridge University Press): 159-77.

Le Donne, Anthony

2009 *The Historiographical Jesus: Memory, Typology, and the Son of David* (Waco, TX: Baylor University Press).

Lenski, Gerhard, and Jean Lenski

1982 *Human Societies: An Introduction to Macrosociology* (New York: McGraw Hill, 4th edn).

Mazar, B.

1975 *The Mountain of the Lord: Excavating in Jerusalem* (Garden City, NY: Doubleday).

Neyrey, Jerome H.

1995 'Loss of Wealth, Loss of Family and Loss of Honour: The Cultural Context of the Original Makarisms in Q', in Esler 1995b: 139-58.

Oakman, Douglas

1986 *Jesus and the Economic Questions of his Day* (SBEC, 8; Lewiston, NY: Mellen).

1999 'The Lord's Prayer in Social Perspective', in *Authenticating the Words of Jesus* (ed. Bruce Chilton and Craig A. Evans; Leiden: Brill): 137-86.

O'Dell, J.

1961–62 'The Religious Background of the Psalms of Solomon (Re-evaluated in the Light of the Qumran texts)', *RQ* 3: 131-64.

Perrin, Norman

1963 *The Kingdom of God in the Preaching of Jesus* (Philadelphia, PA: Westminster Press).

1976 *Rediscovering the Teaching of Jesus* (New York: Harper & Row).

Pomykala, Kenneth E.

1995 *The Davidic Dynasty Tradition in Early Judaism: Its History and Significance for Messianism* (SBL Early Judaism and its Literature, 7; Atlanta, GA: Scholars Press).

Priest, J.

1983 'Testament of Moses: A New Translation and Introduction', in Charlesworth 1983: 919-34.

Riches, John

1982 *Jesus and the Transformation of Judaism* (New York: Seabury Press).

Sanders, E.P.

1985 *Jesus and Judaism* (London: SCM Press).

Schneider, G.

1984 'The Political Charge', in *Jesus and the Politics of his Day* (ed. Ernst Bammel; Cambridge: Cambridge University Press): 403-14.

Schürer, Emil

1973 *The History of the Jewish People in the Age of Jesus Christ (175 B.C.–A.D. 135),* vol. 1 (rev. and ed. Geza Vermes, Fergus Millar and Martin Goodman; Edinburgh: T. & T. Clark).

Smith, Eliot R., and Michael A. Zarate
1990 'Exemplar and Prototype Use in Social Categorization', *Social Cognition* 8 (1990): 243-62.

Theissen, Gerd
1992 'Jesus' Temple Prophecy: Prophecy in the Tension between Town and Country', in *Social Reality and the Early Christians: Theology, Ethics and the World of the New Testament* (ed. Gerd Theissen; Edinburgh: T. & T. Clark): 94-114.

Viteau, J.
1911 *Les Psaumes de Salomon: Introduction, texte grec et traduction* (Paris: Letouzey et Ané).

Wright, Robert B.
1985 'Psalms of Solomon: A New Translation and Introduction', in Charlesworth 1985: 639-70.
2007 *The Psalms of Solomon: A Critical Edition of the Greek Text* (London: T. & T. Clark).

‘Honour Everyone . . .’ (1 Peter 2.17): The Social Strategy of 1 Peter and its Significance for Early Christianity*

David G. Horrell

John H. Elliott has done more than any other scholar to rehabilitate 1 Peter, which he once (now famously) referred to as ‘an exegetical step-child’ (Elliott 1976). The title of his 1976 review of research on 1 Peter, focused on the then recently published third edition of Francis Beare’s commentary (Beare 1970 [1947]), has been very frequently cited, capturing as it does a programmatic goal for studies of 1 Peter, a goal he has led the way in fulfilling. From his doctoral dissertation, published as a monograph in 1966, to the crowning achievement of his magisterial Anchor Bible commentary, published in 2000, and in subsequent publications too, Jack has shown how much this short letter yields for the understanding of early Christianity. He is, to use another of his memorable neologisms, a ‘primopetrophile’ par excellence (see Elliott 2000: xiii). His monograph *A Home for the Homeless* (Elliott 1981/1990) not only opened up new perspectives on 1 Peter but also pioneered social-scientific analysis of a NT text, analysing both the social situation of the addressees and the social strategy of the letter.[1] The ensuing debate with David Balch, whose monograph *Let Wives Be Submissive* was published in the same year (Balch 1981), has remained one of the most influential and significant debates about 1 Peter and its social strategy (published in Talbert 1986).[2] As someone who has also spent a fair bit of time engaged with this particular letter, and who has benefited from Jack’s

* This essay was first drafted during a short period of research as a Visiting Fellow at the Catholic University of Leuven. I would like to thank the university, and in particular my host, Reimund Bieringer, for the award of the fellowship. I am also very grateful to Stuart Macwilliam, Wei-Hsien Wan and Travis B. Williams for very helpful comments on my draft.

1. For a summary of Elliott 1981 as a landmark in the social-scientific interpretation of 1 Peter, see Horrell 2014.

2. For example, in a review of research on 1 Peter, Mark Dubis comments that ‘[o]ne of the principal debates related to the study of 1 Peter has been that between Elliott and Balch’ (Dubis 2006: 212). For a more extended review of the debate, and subsequent reactions to it, see Bechtler 1998: 10-22, 112-18; Horrell 2007b: 111-17 (revised and extended in Horrell 2013: ch. 7).

input and encouragement—through responses to papers at conferences, sending copies of publications, commenting on draft essays and so on—I am especially grateful for this opportunity to join in honouring Jack's scholarly achievements. As someone committed to writing a major commentary on 1 Peter, I confess to feeling daunted at the prospect of 'following in his steps' in this regard when Jack has provided such a thorough and comprehensive work that encapsulates the fruits of a lifetime of engagement with 1 Peter (Elliott 2000).

My aim in this essay is to build (not uncritically) on Elliott's work on the social strategy of 1 Peter through a study focused on 1 Pet. 2.17. For Elliott, 1 Peter represents 'a response to those problems with which conversionist sects in general must struggle' (Elliott 1981: 102). Thus, the letter constitutes an attempt to sustain and promote the solidarity of the group, to maintain its distinctiveness and sense of estrangement in relation to the world (Elliott 1981: 106-48). My argument with regard to 1 Pet. 2.17 will be that, in just eleven Greek words, the author neatly encapsulates the essentials of his view concerning the Christian community's character, conduct and relationship to the world, expressing a stance that would prove to be both innovative and influential in establishing the contours of Christian existence in community and in society. As such, he promotes the solidarity and internal cohesion of the Christian movement, but also encourages a positive stance toward the world, albeit one carefully nuanced and limited in light of the specific pressures of imperial demands and possible persecution. Developing this argument requires a close analysis of the context and structure of the verse, and then an investigation of each of its components.

The Context and Structure of 1 Peter 2.17

The first main section of 1 Peter describes the glorious salvation to which God has called his elect and holy people. The second major section of the letter, which begins at 2.11, focuses on 'the consequences for the behavior of Christians in the structures of society' (Goppelt 1993: 151), specifically 'the need for honorable, upright behaviour and doing what is right in the face of hostility, abuse, and undeserved suffering' (Elliott 2000: 81). The opening two verses, 2.11-12, marked with the introductory ἀγαπητοί (cf. 4.12) and serving as a kind of headline to what follows, express both dimensions of the Christians' ambivalent relationship to the world. As Leonhard Goppelt remarks, 'these two verses provide fundamental direction—first negatively and then positively—for the behavior of Christians in society' (Goppelt 1993: 155). Their distinction and distance are first expressed in an emphatic repetition of their estranged identity (ὡς παροίκους καὶ παρεπιδήμους), an identity that implies and requires separation from 'fleshly desires' (σαρκικῶν ἐπιθυμιῶν) such as characterized both their former lives and still characterize the lives of those among whom they live (4.2-4). But immediately another leitmotif of the letter is also stressed: the need to 'do good', that is, to live in such a way that those who currently criticize and condemn the Christians may be 'won over' (2.12-15; 2.20; 3.6; 3.11-17; 4.19).

In 2.13-17 we find a section of instruction concerning responsibility toward those in authority, with notable parallels to Rom. 13.1-7, before a section dealing with duties within the context of various relationships within the household (2.18–3.7).[3] The extended section of instruction is connected by repeated use of the verb ὑποτάσσω (ὑποτάγητε [v. 13], ὑποτασσόμενοι [v. 18], ὑποτασσόμεναι [3.1, 5]). The section that runs from 2.13 to 2.17 comes to a close with a series of concise imperatival instructions, 'stated asyndetically' (Elliott 2000: 497). The words πᾶς and βασιλεύς form something of an *inclusio* with v. 13,[4] and a connection with the immediately preceding verse is apparent in the sense that it is precisely as free people who are God's slaves that they are to conduct themselves in the manner now specified (cf. Michaels 1988: 130). Verse 17 itself consists of four phrases, each of which consists of an imperative and an object:

17a πάντας τιμήσατε,
17b τὴν ἀδελφότητα ἀγαπᾶτε,
17c τὸν θεὸν φοβεῖσθε,
17d τὸν βασιλέα τιμᾶτε.

The most immediate question is how to make sense of the relationship between the four imperatives. The two main proposals are either that the verse is structured chiastically, given the opening and closing use of τιμάω;[5] or that the first imperative functions as a general headline, which is applied more specifically in the following instructions, given the author's choice to begin the series with an aorist (τιμήσατε) and to follow this with three present imperatives (ἀγαπᾶτε, φοβεῖσθε, τιμᾶτε).[6] The first proposal is favoured by Elliott (2000: 497), who further notes how this draws a distinction between external relations (A, A′, 17a, d) and internal relations (B, B′, 17b, c). This analysis stresses in particular the double use of τιμάω, while the second proposal stresses the distinction in tenses.

3. Brox (1989 [1979]: 116), for example, sees 2.13-17 as part of a wider section of traditional materials on the subject of 'Unterordnungs-Ethik' adopted by the author, though not part of the household code as such. Balch (1981: 118, 129), sees the 'household duty code' as extending from 2.11 to 3.12.

4. So Elliott 2000: 485, 497. Cf. also Michaels 1988: 132.

5. Notably Bammel 1964-65; also Kelly 1969: 112; Brox 1989 [1979]: 122-23; Légasse 1988: 384; Achtemeier 1996: 187. Windisch (1930 [1911]: 64) already identifies it as a 'vierzeilige Sentenz', divided into two 'Doppelzeiler'.

6. See esp. Snyder 1991; also Martin 1992: 204. Such a view is reflected in NIV and NEB; contrast RSV, NRSV, ESV *et al.*

The main weakness of the first proposal is its failure to give an adequate explanation for the change from aorist to present.[7] It is true that the aorist is the dominant tense for imperatives in the letter,[8] but this leaves the switch to the present needing explanation. One should assume that the change of tense bears some significance, unless no sense can be made of it.[9]

The objections raised against the second view, which largely focus on questions about whether the latter three instructions can plausibly be seen as specific instantiations of the first, are either insubstantial or, I want to argue, can be answered adequately.[10] There are points for and against both proposals, but on balance I think the second seems preferable, especially in view of recent perspectives on the aspectual function of the Greek tenses.[11] And, as I hope to show, there is no reason why loving the community of Christians, reverencing God and honouring the emperor cannot all be seen as appropriate expressions of the broad and general expectation that the Christians will act in ways that are honourable.[12]

7. Bammel (1964-65: 279-80) simply illustrates the fact that commentators have not agreed on the significance of the change in tenses without offering a cogent explanation for it. The fact that the aorist 'gives the entire series an unambiguous imperative quality (by themselves the present imperatives could be read as indicatives . . .)' (Michaels 1988: 130) does not explain the shift to the present tense, given the author's general preference for the aorist imperative.

8. Michaels 1988: 130. Aorist imperatives are found at 1.13, 15, 17, 22; 2.2; 4.1, 7; 5.2, 5, 6, 8, 9, 12, 14; present imperatives at 3.3; 4.12, 13, 15, 16 [*bis*], 19 (the last four of which are third-person imperatives) and conceivably at 2.11 (if we read ἀπέχεσθε).

9. Kelly 1969: 112, considers that 'too much has been made of the change of tenses' and that this is probably one example of 'inexplicable tense variations in imperatives in the NT', citing Rom 6.13 and 2 Tim. 4.5. Neither of these instances is strictly comparable, though, especially the former (in the latter it depends on whether νῆφε is in any sense a summary command for those that follow). Cf. also Légasse 1988: 384 with n. 5. On the difficulties, see Feldmeier 2005: 110 n. 362.

10. See esp. Snyder 1991: 213-15. Kelly 1969: 112, for example, finds it 'incredible' that fearing God could be included under the general rubric of honouring all. Grudem 1988: 122 lists a number of objections. Elliott 2000: 498, likewise thinks it unlikely that the first clause can be a summary statement, 'since 17b and c involve other, different actions concerning the brotherhood and God that are not illustrations of showing honor to all'.

11. Also notable as a point in favour of this interpretation is the (rather later) rendering of Theophylact, *Expositio in Epist. 1. Pet.* 363 (in Migne PG 125, col. 1216): πάντας τιμήσατε, τὴν ἀδελφότητα μὲν ἀγαπῶντες, τὸν δὲ θεὸν φοβούμενοι, τὸν βασιλέα τιμῶντες (also cited in Martin 1992: 204 n. 236). A little later in the same column of Migne's PG, Theophylact also cites the verse exactly as it appears in our text, indicating that he knew it in this form, but understood it in the sense suggested by his paraphrase.

12. To the objection that this leaves out any specific indication as to how the Christians are to relate to their non-Christian neighbours in general—a point made by Grudem 1988: 122—it may be noted that the context particularly concerns the kind of behaviour

In relation to the particular issue of the change from aorist (for the first imperative) to present (for the remaining three), recent studies of the Greek verbal system have stressed the importance of aspect in understanding the choice of tenses. The aorist is generally used to express a perfective, external, or summary perspective, while the present gives an imperfective, internal, or progressive (open-ended, ongoing) view.[13] With regard specifically to imperatives, Daniel B. Wallace suggests that in general 'the aorist puts forth *a summary command*', and Stanley Porter sees 1 Pet. 2.17 as an instance 'where the aorist imperative serves as a summary-term for the following specifying or particularizing present imperatives'.[14] This suggests a plausible grammatical explanation for the choice of tenses, on the assumption that the first imperative functions as a summary headline. It remains to be shown, however, whether the grammatical perspective can plausibly be supported exegetically.

Honour Everyone (v. 17a)

The opening command, πάντας τιμήσατε, highlights the importance of honour as a central cultural value for the author and his contemporaries. Bruce Malina must be credited with bringing the importance of honour and shame as Mediterranean cultural values to the attention of NT scholars, while Elliott has shown how prominent are such values in the formulation of the Gospel in 1 Peter (Malina 1981: 25-50; 2001: 27-57; Elliott 1995). While I have sometimes felt some skepticism about a tendency to assume that honour and shame must be the controlling values even in texts where the vocabulary is not present,[15] and while Elliott perhaps extends the semantic

required for a 'good' Christian life ἐν τοῖς ἔθνεσιν (v. 12): the instructions that begin in v. 13 'are ways in which the Christians are to carry out the command in verse 12, the good deeds which they are to do and which the non-believers will see' (Snyder 1991: 213).

13. Cf. Porter 1994: 21, drawing on his broader study (Porter 1989); Wallace 1996: 501.

14. Wallace 1996: 485 (italics original); Porter 1994: 54, cf. 227; also Porter 1989: 360. Cf. also BDF §337.2. Hort 1898: 146, sees the aorist as 'the most forcible tense for the exhortation'; Michaels 1988: 130, sees it as 'programmatic'; Achtemeier 1996: 187-88, sees the choice of aorist as due to the influence of the aorist in v. 13, but offers a weak explanation for the choice of the present tenses. A different assessment of the general distinction between aorist and present imperatives is given by Campbell 2008: 79-100, who argues that the aorist generally conveys a specific instruction, while the present is general. However, he does not discuss 1 Pet. 2.17, though he notes that the author of 1 Peter 'bucks existing trends' (87) by preferring the aorist imperative in general, and using it for 'general instruction' (87).

15. See, for example, Horrell 2000: 90-93, in criticism of Esler 1995; Esler 1998: 127-40. Philip Esler responds to the criticism in the same issue of *JSNT* (Esler 2000).

range of these values rather far in his analysis of 1 Peter (cf. Elliott 1995: 174-75), there can be little doubt that they are prominent in 1 Peter's lexical and cultural perspective. Steadfast faith will result in τιμή (1.7; cf. 2.7), not shame (2.6; cf. 4.16). In specific relationships, husbands should show τιμή to their wives (3.7).

This last example might already suggest the possibility that πάντας τιμήσατε could serve as a summary headline to denote the kind of behaviour deemed appropriate for Christians in all their various relationships. The plausibility of this construal would also seem to be enhanced by the notable parallel Elliott cites in Plutarch, where the 'knowledge of what is honourable (τὸ καλόν) and what is shameful (τὸ αἰσχρόν)', which philosophy can enable one to attain, entails a wide range of modes of appropriate relationship:

> to reverence the gods (θεοὺς μὲν σέβεσθαι), to honour one's parents (γονέας δὲ τιμᾶν), to respect one's elders, to be obedient to the laws, to yield to those in authority (ἄρχουσιν ὑπείκειν), to love one's friends (φίλους ἀγαπᾶν), to be chaste with women, to be affectionate with children, and not to be overbearing with slaves (*Mor.* 7DE [*De lib. ed.*], Eng. trans. Babbitt 1949: 35; cf. Elliott 2000: 498).

In the Hebrew Bible too there is sufficient indication that an appropriately worshipful and reverent relationship to God might be described as 'honouring' God (e.g. 1 Sam. 2.30; 15.30; Dan. 11.38-39). In the NT there are also plenty of instances where an appropriate relationship toward God is described in terms of offering 'honour' (Jn 5.23; Rom. 1.21; 2.23; 1 Cor. 6.20; 1 Tim. 1.17; 6.16; Rev. 4.11; 5.13; also *Did.* 4.1).[16] It does not, then, seem difficult to conceive that 'honour everyone' might include the duty to honour God, a duty that would be specifically enacted through the offering of reverence or worship (*pace* Kelly 1969: 112, quoted in n. 10 above).

More generally, offering appropriate honour to others—whether divine or human—is depicted as the proper pattern of conduct, not least in LXX texts (e.g. Wis. 14.15 [for gods]; 14.17 [for a king]; Sir. 3.3, 5, 8 [for one's father]). Honour is also used in the NT to denote a basic value that should pervade human conduct, including in the household and in marriage (e.g. Mk 10.19 [quoting Exod. 20.12; Deut. 5.16]; 1 Thess. 4.4; 1 Tim. 6.1; Heb. 13.4; cf. also Gen. 30.20). Particularly pertinent to the question of whether 'honour everyone' could also serve as a suitable headline for the specific injunction to show love to other Christians is Rom. 12.10, where the two ideas are juxtaposed: τῇ φιλαδελφίᾳ εἰς ἀλλήλους φιλόστοργοι, τῇ

16. The most common word in NT doxologies is of course δόξα, which Elliott (1995: 174) includes within the semantic field of honour. In the LXX both δοξάζω and τιμάω are used for the Hebrew *kabed*.

τιμῇ ἀλλήλους προηγούμενοι. It seems perfectly plausible, then, to regard the exhortation to 'love the family of believers' (NRSV) as the specific form that the overall instruction to 'honour everyone' might well take, when related to the Christian community's internal relationships (*pace* Elliott 2000: 498, quoted in n. 10 above). The exhortation to 'honour everyone' can be well understood as a kind of summary command, encapsulating the Christian's responsibility in all the main spheres of relationship. This summary exhortation also suggests that the social strategy of 1 Peter is not to be construed entirely in terms of developing community cohesion and stressing distinctiveness and separation from the world, but rather encapsulates a positive pattern of relating to both outsiders and insiders.[17]

Love the Brotherhood (v. 17b)

The first specific injunction is τὴν ἀδελφότητα ἀγαπᾶτε. As is generally the case in the NT, with the (important) exceptions of Mt. 5.44//Lk. 6.27; Lk. 6.35; and 1 Thess. 3.12, the instruction to show love in human relationships is focused internally on the Christian community. This is certainly the focus in 1 Peter (1.22; 3.8; 4.8; 5.14; see esp. Thorsteinsson 2010: 105-16). Also common in early Christian literature, especially in Paul's letters, is the designation of fellow Christians as ἀδελφοί.[18] In 1 Peter this label is used only once, in relation to an individual (5.12); the conviction that the community members constitute a group of siblings is expressed using the substantive ἀδελφότης (also in 5.9) and by denoting the kind of love they should share for one another as φιλαδελφία (1.22; cf. 3.8). As Runar Thorsteinsson remarks, 'on the whole, ἀγάπη in 1 Peter is primarily presented as the underlying moral principle for the Christian brotherhood' (Thorsteinsson 2010: 116). With this brief injunction, the author therefore expresses *in nuce* what Elliott has identified as key elements of his social strategy: to reinforce the 'internal cohesion' and 'distinctive collective identity' of the Christian communities, encouraging bonds of love and commitment among the members (Elliott 1981: 270; cf. 107, 140, *et passim*).

17. The former aspects of 1 Peter's social strategy are stressed, though not exclusively, by Elliott (1981; 1986), notably in debate with Balch (1981; 1986), who argued that the letter (and specifically its domestic code) represented an apologetic strategy of assimilation to society (see n. 2 above). According to Elliott, 'the letter affirms the distinctive communal identity and seeks to strengthen the solidarity of the Christian brotherhood so that it might resist external pressure urging cultural conformity and thereby make effective witness to the distinctive features of its communal life, its allegiance and its hope of salvation' (Elliott 1986: 78).

18. See further Horrell 2001; Aasgaard 2004. On the use of such sibling language in non-Jewish or Christian associations, see Harland 2009: 63-81.

However, the specific word he chooses to denote the community is notable, even if it is difficult to render into English in a concise but non-gender-specific way.[19] As Elliott (2000: 499) notes, the author here uses 'a unique *collective* term for the entire *community of brothers and sisters*, consonant with his employment of collective terms elsewhere in the letter'. The use of -οτης to form abstract substantive nouns from 'adjectives and substantives of the second declension' is common in later Greek (BDF §110.1). But ἀδελφότης is indeed uncommon, especially prior to 1 Peter, and its occurrence here may constitute the first time it is used in the concrete sense to denote a community of ἀδελφοί—'the brotherhood', or 'the siblinghood'—as distinct from the abstract sense of 'familial affection', or 'brotherly bonds' (as in 1 Macc. 12.10, 17; *4 Macc.* 9.23; 10.3, 15; 13.19, 27; Dio Chrysostom, 38.15 [ἡ ἀδελφότης . . . ἐστὶν ἀδελφῶν ὁμόνοια]; Vettius Valens, *Anthology* 1.1.17, 38; Hermas *Mand.* 8.10).[20] For example, the word occurs only very rarely in inscriptions from Asia Minor, and when it does in the period prior to 1 Peter's composition, it is used in the abstract sense: 'the Peoples . . . who have taken oaths over newly-burnt offerings and made blood-offerings for their natural alliance, eternal concord, and brotherhood with each other (ὑπὲρ τῆς πρὸς ἀλλήλους φ[ύσει] συμμαχίας καὶ ὁμονοίας [αἰ]ωνίου καὶ ἀδελφότητος)'.[21]

In subsequent Christian literature, however, the term becomes common as a designation for the Christian community. As F.J.A. Hort noted long ago: '[t]he word does not earlier [than 1 Peter] occur in this [concrete] sense (indeed it is rare even in the abstract sense), but was speedily taken up into Christian literature, Latin as well as Greek' (Hort 1898: 146). For example,

19. I shall use the word 'brotherhood' as the most lexically similar single word, as does Elliott 2000: 499-500, though the gender-specific implications of this term are unfortunate and inappropriate to the Greek term. The English word 'siblinghood' could perhaps be deployed for this purpose, though it is hardly established in common parlance.

20. LSJ, 21, lists only 1 Pet. 2.17 and 5.9 for the substantive 'the brotherhood'. Some of the instances in *4 Maccabees* (10.3, 15) could be seen as acquiring a more substantive sense, but phrases such as οὐκ ἀρνήσομαι τὴν εὐγενῆ ἀδελφότητα (10.15) are best understood in the sense of 'our noble family ties' (so NRSV). In any case, the date of 4 Maccabees may well be around, or slightly later than, the date of 1 Peter; for a date of 90–100 CE, see Barclay 1996: 449; Klauck 1989: 668-69.

21. *Aphrodisias* 179 (= *IAph* 2007 8.210), c. second century BCE (Greek and Eng. translation from http://insaph.kcl.ac.uk/iaph2007/iAph080210.html). For the same inscription see also *IK Kibyra* 2. A search of the Packard Humanities inscriptions database for Asia Minor (at http://epigraphy.packhum.org/inscriptions) yielded only this example from the first century CE and earlier. Other (Christian) examples date from the third century (cited at n. 23 below) and the sixth–seventh century (*Monumenta Asiae Minoris antiqua* 4.37[1]).

in Polycarp's letter to the Philippians (*Phil.* 10.1), almost certainly influenced by 1 Peter (cf. Eusebius, *Hist. eccl.* 4.14.9)[22] the addressees are urged to be 'lovers of the brotherhood' (*fraternitatis amatores*, this section of his letter being extant only in Latin), roughly equivalent to the Greek οἱ τὴν ἀδελφότητα ἀγαπῶντες (cf. Theophylact, cited in n. 11 above). In *1 Clement* the addressees are praised for their efforts ὑπὲρ πάσης τῆς ἀδελφότητος (*1 Clem.* 2.4). Other instances occur in patristic literature, where the word is used to denote the Christian community in general, the local congregation (as in *Hist. eccl.* 6.45.1), or a religious or monastic community, or as a form of address to members of councils, groups of bishops or clergy (see Lampe, *PGL*, 31). Likewise, a late third-century Christian inscription, although somewhat incomplete, from a cemetery in Phrygia, wishes 'peace to all the brotherhood' (εἰρήνῃ πάσῃ τῇ ἀδελ̣[φότητ̣]ι).[23] So, while the author of 1 Peter is by no means unique in describing the Christians' duty to love one another as siblings, he does encapsulate this duty in a highly concise form, and initiates a substantive use of ἀδελφότης that would henceforth become common Christian vocabulary.

Fear God, Honour the Emperor (v. 17c-d)

I treat the last two phrases of the verse in a section together, since their significance, I shall argue, emerges particularly from their juxtaposition. The first phrase indicates how the addresses are to honour God: τὸν θεὸν φοβεῖσθε. The meaning of φοβέομαι in this context (as with the Latin *timeo*, which we shall encounter below) is well captured by J.P. Louw and E.A. Nida: 'to have profound reverence and respect for deity, with the implication of awe bordering on fear—"to reverence, to worship"' (Louw and Nida 1988: §53.58).[24] The 'fear of the Lord' is well established in the Hebrew Bible and LXX as a fundamental and central requirement for the people of God (e.g. Deut. 6.2; 10.12; Ps. 34.9; Prov. 1.7; Sir. 1.11-14). The NT and early Christian literature repeat the same conviction (e.g. Acts 9.31; 2 Cor. 5.11; Rev. 15.4; *1 Clem.* 3.4; 23.1; Polycarp *Phil.* 2.1; 4.2; 6.2-3; *Did.* 4.9-10). Again, the author of 1 Peter expresses this duty concisely, though not in any specifically striking or innovative way.

The second phrase, τὸν βασιλέα τιμᾶτε, repeats the verb used in the opening summary instruction, indicating, significantly, that the attitude to be displayed toward the emperor is (only) that which is to be shown, in

22. For the connections between 1 Peter and Polycarp, *Phil.*, including some 'virtually certain citations', see Elliott 2000: 143.

23. In Ramsay 1897: 720 §655. Cf. §654, a similar cemetery stone, which has the functionally equivalent phrase, εἰρήνῃ πᾶσι τοῖς ἀδελφοῖς.

24. Cf. also BDAG, 1061 §2; MM, 673 (5399 §2); *TDNT* 9.189-219.

appropriate ways, to all people.[25] A similar point is made in v. 13, where the emperor is (only) a 'human creature', ἀνθρώπινη κτίσις, like everyone else.[26] On the other hand, the juxtaposition of God and emperor indicates that these belong together in terms of considering what kind of attitude should be displayed toward figures who are in some sense preeminent. Taken together with the previous phrase, the author here gives a carefully worded and nuanced indication of the Christians' responsibilities toward God and the emperor: less enigmatic than Mk 12.17 and par., and more equivocal in urging loyalty and submission than Paul (Rom. 13.1-7). Commentators have long noted the influence of Prov. 24.21:[27] φοβοῦ τὸν θεόν . . . καὶ βασιλέα.[28] Yet, given this parallel, the author's use of two different verbs to distinguish responsibility toward God and emperor is significant and (one must assume) deliberate (cf. Sir. 7.31, distinguishing God and priest in a similar way).[29] While honour can also be appropriately directed toward God (or the gods), the author denotes φόβος as the specifically required attitude, avoiding this in the case of the emperor.

The importance and influence of the distinction drawn here by the author of 1 Peter may be shown by setting out some of the later Christian texts that reflect a similar distinction, or use the same vocabulary, mostly (and significantly) in martyrologies and apologetic works, from the second-century onward. For example, in his interrogation before execution, Polycarp refuses to 'swear by the genius of Caesar (τὴν καίσαρος τύχην)', at the same time expressing what he sees as his Christian duty to render honour (τιμή) to rulers (*Mart. Pol.* 10.1-2; cf. 8.2; 9.2). The specific phrasing found in 1 Peter is very closely echoed in the *Acts of the Scillitan Martyrs* (180 CE).[30] Urged by the proconsul to 'swear by the Genius of our lord the emperor' (*iura per genium domini nostri imperatoris*) the (soon to be) martyrs reply: 'We have none other whom we worship[31] but our Lord God who is in heaven. . . . Honour to Caesar as Caesar, but worship only to God' (*Nos non habemus*

25. Cf. Elliott 2000: 501.

26. Here, as Elliott (2000: 489) notes, the author adopts an expression in which 'imperial power is subtly but decisively demystified, desacralized, and relativized'.

27. E.g., Hort 1898: 146; Windisch 1930 [1911]: 64.

28. Theophilus of Antioch interestingly renders the phrase Τίμα . . . θεὸν καὶ βασιλέα, in a context where, heavily influenced by 1 Pet. 2.17 (see below), he insists that the emperor should be honoured, not worshipped, since God alone should be worshipped (*Ad Autol.* 1.11 [Grant 1970: 14-17]).

29. Φοβοῦ τὸν κύριον καὶ δόξασον ἱερέα. Noted also by Windisch 1930 [1911]: 64.

30. It is striking (and unfortunate) that this text is not included among the citations of 1 Pet. 2.17 listed in *Biblical patristica* 1: 528. Also cited in Elliott 2000: 501; Feldmeier 2005: 110 n. 364, and earlier, as part of the *testimonia veterum* for 1 Peter, by Bigg 1901: 11.

31. On the meaning of *timeo* here, see at n. 24 above.

alium quem timeamus nisi domnum Deum nostrum qui est in caelis.... Honorem Caesari quasi Caesari; timorem autem Deo [*Act. Scil.* 8-9]).

Another martyrology, recounting a trial that took place around 180–185 CE, similarly draws on the language of 1 Pet. 2.17 in articulating reasons for a refusal to 'swear by the Genius of our lord the emperor' (ὄμοσον τὴν τύχην τοῦ κυρίου ἡμῶν) (*Mart. Apollonius* 3 [Musurillo 1972: 91]). 'Would you want me to swear', Apollonius replies, 'that we pay honour to the emperor (βασιλέα τιμῶμεν) and pray for his authority? If so, then I would gladly swear, calling upon the one, true God. . . For he [Christ] taught us . . . to obey any law passed by the emperor and to respect him, but to worship God alone' (βασιλέα τιμᾶν, θεὸν σέβειν μόνον. *Mart. Apol.* 6, 37 [Musurillo 1972: 93, 101]).

In an apologetic work dating from shortly after 180 CE, Theophilus of Antioch sets out strongly and fully his reasons for the Christians' refusal to worship the emperor, again drawing clearly on the language of 1 Pet. 2.17:[32]

> I will pay honour to the emperor (τιμήσω τὸν βασιλέα) not by worshipping him (οὐ προσκυνῶν αὐτῷ) but by praying for him. I worship the God (θεῷ . . . προσκυνῶ) who is the real and true God.... You will say to me, 'Why do you not worship the emperor?' Because he was made not to be worshipped (προσκυνεῖσθαι) but to be honoured with legitimate honour (τιμᾶσθαι τῇ νομίμῳ τιμῇ). Similarly, worship (προσκυνεῖσθαι) must be given to God alone.... Honour the emperor (τὸν δὲ βασιλέα τίμα) by wishing him well, by obeying him, by praying for him . . . (Theophilus, *Ad Autolycus* 1.11 [Grant 1970: 14-15]).

Tatian likewise describes himself willing to obey and respect the ruler, up to a point: 'for a human being is to be honoured in a way fitting for a human being, only God is to be feared' (τὸν μὲν γὰρ ἄνθρωπον ἀνθρωπίνως τιμητέον, φοβητέον δὲ μόνον τὸν θεὸν [*Oratio ad Graecos* 4]).[33]

Tertullian declares, 'a Christian is an enemy of no one' (*Christianus nullius est hostis*), particularly not of the emperor (*nedum imperatoris*): as one appointed by God, the Christian 'must love, reverence, honour, and wish him well (*diligat et reuereatur et honoret et saluum uelit*), together with the whole Roman Empire' (*Ad Scapulam* 2.6). Here Tertullian goes somewhat further than 1 Peter in the devotion he seems prepared to offer to the emperor, but the immediately following comments make clear that the parameters of the distinction between what is rightly offered to the emperor, as a human being, on the one hand, and to God, on the other, remain clear:

> In this way, then, do we honor the emperor (*colimus . . . imperatorem*), as is both lawful for us and expedient for him, as a man next to God: who has received whatever he is from God; who is inferior to God.... This is why

32. Again it is unfortunate that this text is not listed in *Biblia patristica* 1.528.
33. This text is also noted by Elliott 2000: 501.

> we also offer sacrifice for the welfare of the emperor, but to God, who is our God and his—and in the way God commanded us, with pure prayer (*Ad Scap.* 2.7-8 [Arbesmann *et al.* 1950: 153]).

Elsewhere he explicitly cites 'Peter' for the teaching that 'the king indeed must be honoured (*regem quidem honorandum*)' but 'only . . . when he is far from assuming divine honours (*a diuinis honoribus longe est*)' (*Scorpiace* 14.3 [Thelwall 1885: 648]). Another indirect reference to 1 Pet. 2.17 may be made a little later in Arnobius's *Adversus nationes*, in the context of a discussion about honouring the gods, where the writer states that Christians 'have been taught by the higher commands to honor even human beings, of whatever rank and whatever fortune they may be' (7.15 [McCracken 1949: 494]).

While these are instances where the more or less direct influence of 1 Pet. 2.17 may be seen, the stance encapsulated in τὸν θεὸν φοβεῖσθε, τὸν βασιλέα τιμᾶτε characterizes the position expressed in a wider range of material. Tertullian spends a significant amount of his *Apology* (*Apol.* 29–36) insisting that, while Christians refuse 'to offer sacrifice for the well-being of the emperor' (*Apol.* 28.2; cf. 10.1), they show respect and loyalty toward him, praying for his welfare (*Apol.* 30.1; 33.1, etc.). Indeed, from early times, Christians followed Jews[34] in this respect (1 Tim. 2.1-3; *1 Clem.* 60.4–61.2; cf. also Polycarp, *Phil.* 12.3; Theophilus, *Ad Autol.* 1.11; Origen, *Contra Celsum* 7.64-66; 8.64; *Acts Cyprian* 1.2).[35] Tertullian echoes 1 Peter in his

34. Elliott (2007) is among those who have argued that the terms 'Jew', 'Jewish', etc., are anachronistic and inappropriate for the ancient context, and propose 'Judean' instead, reflecting the view that geographical territory or homeland was the decisive factor in the labelling of ethnic identities. I have not researched the topic sufficiently to argue a case either way with conviction, but remain at present not entirely convinced by the call to abandon entirely the use of 'Jew', 'Jewish' (and 'Christian', similarly) for the early period. Reasons for hesitation include the following: (1) anachronism is certainly a risk when using such labels, but this risk applies to all sorts of terms, which inevitably change their associations through time. Changing the terms is not the only way to alert readers to the historical and cultural 'gap'; (2) various factors may contribute to the construction of ancient ethnicities, and the territorial facet should perhaps not always be regarded as determinative (cf. Sechrest 2009: 54-109; Johnson Hodge 2007: 52-54); (3) there are significant risks in abandoning the term 'Jew', since such a move may appear to break any religio-ethnic connection between contemporary Jews and the people described in our ancient texts and effectively to 'de-Judaize' the NT (see Levine 2006: 159-66).

35. On Jewish practice of praying for rulers (and offering sacrifices, not to the emperor himself, but to their God for the emperor's welfare), see (on prayers) Ezra 6.10; *Abot* 3.2; and (on sacrifices) 1 Macc. 7.33; Philo, *Leg. Gai.* 279-80; Josephus, *Apion* 2.76-78; cf. Elliott 2000: 500. Tertullian's remarks cited above (*Ad Scapulam* 2.8) combine both notions: the sacrifice offered on behalf of the emperor is precisely the sacrifice of prayer.

remarks: 'Of course, I will call the emperor Lord, but only in the customary meaning of the word, if I am not forced to call him Lord in place of God. So far as he is concerned, I am a free man [cf. 1 Pet. 2.16]. For, I have one Lord, the omnipotent and eternal God . . .' (*Apol.* 34.1 [Arbesmann *et al.* 1950: 90]).[36] Also a broader stance, congruent with the teaching of 1 Peter, is the insistence that Christians are good people, who live in ways that are good and honourable, except insofar as this refusal to reverence any but their one true God is deemed a crime (e.g. *Diognetus* 2.6-10; 5.1–6.4; Justin, *1 Apol.* 4–7; Tertullian, *Apol.* 1–3).

Two Arguments on the Significance of 1 Peter 2.17

The texts cited above date, of course, from some time after the likely period of 1 Peter's composition, so we need to reflect on what their significance is for the interpretation of our text. I propose two arguments.

The first argument is not indisputable, and may not convince all (including Jack Elliott, I suspect), namely, that the careful formulation in 1 Pet. 2.17 reflects a context in which this distinction is both pertinent and necessary, namely, one similar to that known to us from Pliny's letter, written not many years after the time of 1 Peter, in which Christians—accused and slandered by their hostile contemporaries—might face the demand to worship the emperor or the gods of Rome (Pliny *Ep.* 10.96). Many scholars, including Elliott, see 1 Pet. 2.17 as evidence against the idea that the letter reflects any 'official' or imperial persecution, or expresses any critical stance toward Rome. Stephen Bechtler, for example, puts it clearly:

> the one passage in the letter in which the emperor is explicitly mentioned—2.13-17—tells against imperial persecution. Here the letter enjoins fear of God and honor of the emperor in a single breath and commands subjection to the emperor as ὑπερέχων. Nor does 1 Peter elsewhere exhibit the kind of hostility to, or at least wariness of, Rome to be expected in a document dealing with imperial persecution.[37]

Elliott has been influential in arguing that the suffering experienced by the addressees of 1 Peter is a matter of informal hostility and slander and not of imperial persecution, and argues forcefully that the parallels with the situation depicted by Pliny are few, and of no relevance for the interpretation of 1 Peter (e.g., Elliott 2000: 792-93).[38] This has become something

36. Cf. also Minucius Felix, *Octavius* 29.4-5.

37. Bechtler 1998: 50; cf. Elliott 2000: 502: 'this passage [2.13-17] offers strong incidental support for the conclusion that Rome played no discernible role in the hostility and sufferings encountered by the addressees'; Michaels 1988: lxiii.

38. My counterarguments for seeing parallels with Pliny are set out in Horrell 2007a: 370-76; 2013: 183-97.

of a consensus in recent studies of 1 Peter, especially in English.[39] Yet the evidence from Christian sources in the second century and beyond suggests that 2.13-17, and v. 17 in particular, fits rather well into a setting where a measured but conscious resistance to imperial demands is required, including the specific context of trials.

When Leonhard Goppelt says that the issue of 'divine homage paid to the emperor', which Goppelt sees arising especially in the time of Domitian, 'lies quite clearly outside the purview of 1 Peter' (1993: 45) it seems he has not sufficiently seen the significance of the distinction drawn in 2.17 (and in 2.13-14). And when Marta Sordi, citing the same phrase from the *Acts of the Scillitan Martyrs* quoted above, claims that it was these late-second-century martyrs who 'were the first to formulate reasons why their refusal [of the imperial cult] had to be made' (Sordi 1994: 177), it seems she has likewise failed to appreciate the precise formulation of the same stance in 1 Peter, where the essential theological reasoning is concisely conveyed: only (the one) God is to be worshipped, so the emperor may (only) be honoured. The fact that 1 Peter's phrasing here 'may have been inspired by Prov 24.21' (Elliott 2000: 500), as we have noted above, only increases the likelihood of his facing some such situation: Why, given the scriptural teaching φοβοῦ τὸν θεόν . . . καὶ βασιλέα, would the author introduce the careful distinction he does, if he were not aware of the need to draw a line in the sand marking the limits of Christian obedience to Rome? Without confrontation with the *imperium* as part of its context, the precise wording of 1 Pet. 2.17 lacks a *Sitz im Leben*.

My second argument is (I think) less controversial and can be stated more briefly: 1 Peter here sets out in a remarkably clear, concise and influential way the stance—one I have elsewhere called 'polite resistance' (Horrell 2007b; 2013: ch. 7)—that would, in the following centuries, essentially define the church's position vis-à-vis Rome. Whatever the situation faced by the author and recipients of 1 Peter, the phrase τὸν θεὸν φοβεῖσθε, τὸν βασιλέα τιμᾶτε conveys in a few words what many later martyrs and apologists would essentially find themselves needing to say.[40] Indeed, the allusions to 1 Pet. 2.17 surveyed above demonstrate the importance and widespread

39. Cf. the comments in the overviews of research by Dubis 2006: 203; Webb 2004: 383. For a discussion of scholarship on this topic, and of recent challenges to the consensus, see Williams 2012a; and the more detailed treatment of suffering in 1 Peter in Williams 2012b.

40. Brox 1989 [1979]: 123, sees neither any critical significance in the verbal distinction drawn here nor any critical stance toward the emperor expressed in vv. 13-14. By contrast, Spörri (1925: 94) rightly notes how in 2.17 1 Peter breaks the ultimate authority of the state, if only 'delicately' (*zart*): 'Damit ist die Allmacht der staatlichen Gewalt durchbrochen, ihr Autorität nicht als die höchste und letzte anerkannt, auf dem Standpunkt des römischen Imperiums eine Ungesetzlichkeit revolutionärster Tendenz.

influence of the careful distinction set out in our text. More broadly, the letter's instruction that Christians should be people who demonstrably do what is good, and keep themselves innocent of any wrongdoing (2.12, 15, 20; 3.6, 10-11, 13, 16-17; 4.19), while at the same time retaining an exclusive allegiance to God and to Christ, establishes the contours for much subsequent Christian teaching and apologetic.

Conclusion

In just eleven Greek words, with typical literary and theological skill, the author of 1 Peter sets out the essential contours of Christian existence in the world. In these four imperatives, the social strategy of the letter is summarized. The distinctiveness and internal solidarity of the community are stressed and reinforced in the injunction to love the members of the community, the 'brotherhood', and in the imperative to worship (only) the one God, whom the author declares as 'the God and Father of our Lord Jesus Christ' (1.3). In his substantive use of the term ἀδελφότης the author makes an innovative move in developing Christian vocabulary that would be frequently taken up thereafter. At the same time, the headline imperative indicates that this is not a stance of sectarian withdrawal, nor one in which outsiders are to be treated with contempt or hostility. It is not only internal solidarity and distinctiveness from society that the author is concerned to stress. On the contrary, all people are to be honoured. In the specific instruction to honour the emperor, both dimensions of the community's existence in the world, and specifically in the empire, are carefully delineated: as decent citizens, Christians will offer the emperor honour, and will accept the judicial authority with which he and his emissaries reward good behaviour and punish wrongdoing (2.13-14). Yet as members of a brotherhood whose ultimate allegiance is to the one true God, to whom alone reverent fear is due, they will only honour the emperor, and will not worship him—even if such a stance is punished as evil rather than recognized as good. As later martyr-accounts show, that stance was indeed regarded as sufficiently rebellious and intransigent to warrant the death penalty, when circumstances combined to bring Christians to trial. These later accounts, along with apologetic writings, also indicate how influential was the concise distinction between 'honouring' the emperor and 'fearing' God, set out for the first time in our text. First Peter 2.17 is, then, a remarkably concise and precise formulation, which encapsulates *in nuce* both the social strategy of the letter and the parameters within which much mainstream Christian social teaching would fall. Here, as in other respects—such as its use of the

Freilich ist diese Möglichkeit des Ungehorsams gegen die Obrigkeit im 1. Ptbf nur zart, aber doch unverkennbar angedeutet.'

terms γένος (2.9) and χριστιανός (4.16)[41]—the author of 1 Peter makes innovative moves that would prove influential for the construction of Christian identity and the delineation of Christian existence in an often hostile world. On the basis of this verse alone we find plenty to affirm Elliott's judgment that 1 Peter is 'one of the most socially significant writings of the early church' (Elliott 1990: xxxii).

References

Aasgaard, Reidar
2004 *'My Beloved Brothers and Sisters!' Christian Siblingship in Paul* (JSNTSup, 265; London: T. & T. Clark).
Achtemeier, Paul J.
1996 *1 Peter* (Hermeneia; Philadelphia, PA: Fortress Press).
Arbesmann, Rudolph, Emily Joseph Daly and Edwin A. Quain (trans.)
1950 *Tertullian, Apologetical Works, and Minucius Felix, Octavius* (FOC, 10; Washington, DC: Catholic University of America Press).
Babbitt, Frank Cole
1949 *Plutarch's Moralia,* vol. 1: 1A–86A (LCL; London: Heinemann; Cambridge, MA: Harvard University Press).
Balch, David L.
1981 *Let Wives Be Submissive: The Domestic Code in 1 Peter* (SBLMS, 26; Atlanta, GA: Scholars Press).
1986 'Hellenization/Acculturation in 1 Peter', in *Perspectives on First Peter* (ed. Charles H. Talbert; Macon, GA: Mercer University Press), 79-101.
Bammel, Ernst
1964-65 'The Commands in I Peter II.17', *NTS* 11: 279-81.
Barclay, John M.G.
1996 *Jews in the Mediterranean Diaspora from Alexander to Trajan (323* BCE*–117* CE*)* (Edinburgh: T. & T. Clark).
Beare, Francis W.
1970 [1947] *The First Epistle of Peter* (Oxford: Blackwell, 3rd edn).
Bechtler, Steven R.
1998 *Following in his Steps: Suffering, Community, and Christology in 1 Peter* (SBLDS, 162; Atlanta, GA: Scholars).
Bigg, Charles
1901 *A Critical and Exegetical Commentary on the Epistles of St. Peter and St. Jude* (ICC; Edinburgh: T. & T. Clark).
Brox, Norbert
1989 [1979] *Der erste Petrusbrief* (EKKNT, 21; Zurich: Benziger; Neukirchen-Vluyn: Neukirchener Verlag, 3rd edn).
Campbell, Constantine R.
2008 *Verbal Aspect and Non-Indicative Verbs: Further Soundings in the Greek New Testament* (Studies in Biblical Greek, 15; New York: Peter Lang).

41. On which see, respectively, Horrell 2012 and 2007a.

Dubis, Mark

2006 'Research on 1 Peter: A Survey of Scholarly Literature since 1985', *CBR* 4: 199-239.

Elliott, John H.

1966 *The Elect and the Holy: An Exegetical Examination of 1 Peter 2:4-10 and the Phrase βασίλειον ἱεράτευμα* (NovTSup, 12; Leiden: Brill).

1976 'The Rehabilitation of an Exegetical Step-Child: 1 Peter in Recent Research', *JBL* 95: 243-54, repr. in Talbert 1986: 3-16.

1981 *A Home for the Homeless: A Sociological Exegesis of 1 Peter, its Situation and Strategy* (Philadelphia, PA: Fortress Press); repr. with new 'Introduction' as *A Home for the Homeless: A Social-Scientific Criticism of 1 Peter, its Situation and Strategy* (Minneapolis, MN: Fortress Press, 1990).

1986 '1 Peter, its Situation and Strategy: A Discussion with David Balch', in Talbert 1986: 61-78.

1995 'Disgraced yet Graced: The Gospel according to 1 Peter in the Key of Honor and Shame', *BTB* 25: 166-78.

2000 *1 Peter: A New Translation with Introduction and Commentary* (AB, 37B; New York: Doubleday).

2007 'Jesus the Israelite Was neither a "Jew", nor a "Christian": On Correcting Misleading Nomenclature', *JSHJ* 5.2: 119-54.

Esler, Philip F.

1995 'Making and Breaking an Agreement Mediterranean Style: A New Reading of Galatians 2:1-14', *BibInt* 3: 285-314.

1998 *Galatians* (New Testament Readings; London: Routledge).

2000 'Models in New Testament Interpretation: A Reply to David Horrell', *JSNT* 22.78: 107-13.

Feldmeier, Reinhard

2005 *Der erste Brief des Petrus* (THNT, 15/1; Leipzig: Evangelische Verlags-anstalt).

Goppelt, Leonhard

1993 *A Commentary on I Peter* (Grand Rapids, MI: Eerdmans).

Grant, Robert M.

1970 *Theophilus of Antioch, Ad Autolycum* (Oxford Early Christian Texts; Oxford: Clarendon).

Grudem, Wayne A.

1988 *1 Peter* (TNTC; Leicester: Inter-Varsity Press).

Harland, Philip A.

2009 *Dynamics of Identity in the World of the Early Christians: Associations, Judeans, and Cultural Minorities* (London: T. & T. Clark).

Horrell, David G.

2000 'Models and Methods in Social-Scientific Interpretation: A Response to Philip Esler', *JSNT* 22.78: 83-105.

2001 'From ἀδελφοί to οἶκος θεοῦ: Social Transformation in Pauline Christianity', *JBL* 120: 293-311.

2007a 'The Label Χριστιανός: 1 Pet 4:16 and the Formation of Christian Identity', *JBL* 126: 361-81.

2007b 'Between Conformity and Resistance: Beyond the Balch–Elliott Debate towards a Postcolonial Reading of 1 Peter', in *Reading 1 Peter with New Eyes: Methodological Reassessments of the Letter of First Peter* (ed. Robert

L. Webb and Betsy Bauman-Martin; LNTS, 364; London: T. & T. Clark): 111-43.

2012 '"Race", "Nation", "People": Ethnic Identity-Construction in 1 Peter 2.9', *NTS* 58: 123-43.

2013 *'Becoming Christian': Essays on 1 Peter and the Making of Christian Identity* (LNTS; London: T. & T. Clark).

2014 'Ethnicity, Empire, and Early Christian Identity: Social-Scientific Perspectives on 1 Peter', in *Reading 1–2 Peter and Jude A Resource for Students* (ed. Eric Mason and Troy Martin; Atlanta, GA: SBL): 135-49.

Hort, F.J.A.

1898 *The First Epistle of St. Peter I.1–II.17: The Greek Text with Introductory Lecture, Commentary, and Additional Notes* (London: Macmillan, repr. Eugene, OR: Wipf & Stock, 2005).

Johnson Hodge, Caroline

2007 *If Sons, then Heirs: A Study of Kinship and Ethnicity in the Letters of Paul* (New York: Oxford University Press).

Kelly, J.N.D.

1969 *A Commentary on the Epistles of Peter and Jude* (BNTC; London: A. & C. Black).

Klauck, Hans-Josef

1989 *4. Makkabäerbuch* (ed. Hermann Lichtenberger; Jüdische Schriften aus hellenistisch-römischer Zeit, 3/6; Gütersloh: Gütersloher Verlagshaus).

Légasse, Simon

1988 'La soumission aux autorités d'après 1 Pierre 2.13-17: version spécifique d'une parénèse traditionelle', *NTS* 34: 378-96.

Levine, Amy-Jill

2006 *The Misunderstood Jew: The Church and the Scandal of the Jewish Jesus* (New York: HarperCollins).

Louw, J.P., and E.A. Nida

1988 *Greek–English Lexicon of the New Testament Based on Semantic Domains* (New York: United Bible Societies, 2nd edn). Cited from the electronic edition in BibleWorks 6.

Malina, Bruce J.

1981 *The New Testament World: Insights from Cultural Anthropology* (Atlanta, GA: John Knox; London: SCM, 1st edn).

2001 *The New Testament World: Insights from Cultural Anthropology, Third Edition, Revised and Expanded* (Louisville, KY: Westminster John Knox).

Martin, Troy W.

1992 *Metaphor and Composition in 1 Peter* (SBLDS, 131; Atlanta, GA: Scholars Press).

McCracken, George E. (trans.)

1949 *Arnobius of Sicca: The Case against the Pagans*, vol. 2, Books 4–7 (Ancient Christian Writers, 8; Westminster, MD; Newman Press).

Michaels, J. Ramsey

1988 *1 Peter* (WBC, 49; Waco, TX: Word Books).

Musurillo, Herbert

1972 *The Acts of the Christian Martyrs: Introductions, Texts and Translations* (Oxford: Clarendon Press).

Porter, Stanley E.

1989 *Verbal Aspect in the Greek of the New Testament, with Reference to Tense and Mood* (Studies in Biblical Greek, 1; New York: Peter Lang).

1994 *Idioms of the Greek New Testament* (Sheffield: Sheffield Academic Press, 2nd edn).

Ramsay, William M.

1897 *The Cities and Bishoprics of Phrygia,* vol. 1, part 2 (Oxford: Clarendon Press).

Sechrest, Love L.

2009 *A Former Jew: Paul and the Dialectics of Race* (LNTS, 410; London: T. & T. Clark).

Snyder, Scot

1991 '1 Peter 2:17: A Reconsideration', *Filologia neotestamentaria* 4: 211-16.

Sordi, Marta

1994 *The Christians and the Roman Empire* (London: Routledge).

Spörri, Theophil

1925 *Der Gemeindegedanke im ersten Petrusbrief: Ein Beitrag zur Struktur des urchristlichen Kirchenbegriffs* (Neutestamentliche Forschungen, 2.2; Gütersloh: Bertelsmann).

Talbert, Charles H. (ed.)

1986 *Perspectives on First Peter* (Macon, GA: Mercer University Press).

Thelwall, S. (trans.)

1855 *Ante-Nicene Fathers, Vol. 3: Latin Christianity: Its Founder, Tertullian* (ed. Philip Schaff; Ante-Nicene Fathers; 10 vols.; Edinburgh: T. & T. Clark; repr. Grand Rapids, MI: Eerdmans).

Thorsteinsson, Runar M.

2010 *Roman Christianity and Roman Stoicism: A Comparative Study of Ancient Morality* (Oxford: Oxford University Press).

Wallace, Daniel B.

1996 *Greek Grammar beyond the Basics: An Exegetical Syntax of the New Testament* (Grand Rapids, MI: Zondervan).

Webb, Robert L.

2004 'The Petrine Epistles: Recent Developments and Trends', in *The Face of New Testament Studies: A Survey of Recent Research* (ed. Scot McKnight and Grant R. Osborne; Grand Rapids, MI: Baker): 373-90.

Williams, Travis B.

2012a 'Suffering from a Critical Oversight: The Persecutions of 1 Peter within Modern Scholarship', *CBR* 10: 271-88.

2012b *Persecution in 1 Peter: Differentiating and Contextualizing Early Christian Suffering* (NovTSup, 145; Leiden: Brill).

Windisch, Hans

1930 [1911] *Die katholischen Briefe* (HNT, 15; Tübingen: Mohr Siebeck, 2nd edn).

Resist the King! The Attitude toward the Emperor in Bel and the Dragon and Daniel 1–6

Ralph W. Klein

My friendship with Jack Elliott goes back more than fifty years, when he was in his last year and I was in my first at Concordia Seminary. We both later taught at Concordia, though not at the same time. A number of mutual friends and frequent conversations at the annual meetings of the Society of Biblical Literature and the Catholic Biblical Association nourished our friendship.

In his magisterial commentary on 1 Peter (Elliott 2000: 401, 494), Jack reflects on the epistle's attitude toward the emperor: 'Be subordinate to every human creature because of the Lord, whether to the emperor as supreme, or to governors as sent by him to punish those who do what is wrong or to praise those who do what is right. . . . Honor everyone; love the brotherhood; revere God; honor the emperor' (1 Pet. 2.13-14, 17). Jack notes that the Petrine author's view of civil government stands midpoint between the thoroughly positive position of Paul and the entirely negative view of the author of Revelation, who depicts civil authorities as agents of Satan. In the view of 1 Peter's author, subordination is obligatory not because the emperor is divine or a minister of God but because he, like all creatures, deserves respect from subordinates. Christians can show such respect when it does not impinge on the reverence that is due to God alone. It is a pleasure to contribute to this *Festschrift* an essay that deals with a far different attitude to a king or emperor than that in 1 Peter: that of the apocryphal work known as Bel and the Dragon.

Preserved in two Greek versions (Old Greek and Theodotion), Bel and the Dragon was probably written originally in a Semitic language, and may have been composed in Jerusalem in the first quarter of the second century BCE (Collins 1993: 418). According to the Old Greek version, Daniel was a priest. In both translations he is designated as a 'companion' to the king. The real name of the author of the book of Daniel and Bel and the Dragon is unknown but the legendary character who is featured in the Danielic literature is possibly based on Ezek. 14.14, where Noah, Daniel and Job are paragons of righteousness, or on Ezek. 28.3, where the prophet says of the king of Tyre, 'You are indeed wiser than Daniel'.[1]

The Depiction of the King in Bel and the Dragon

A major theme of Bel and the Dragon is its polemic against idolatry, and specifically against the god Bel (vv. 1-22) and a divine dragon[2] (vv. 23-27), both of whom are exposed as frauds by Daniel and come to ignominious ends. While any discussion of Bel and the Dragon must deal with the issue of idolatry, our major attention will be on another major theme: the naïveté of the king, his inability to stand up to those who oppose him, the fickleness of his decisions and his easy resort to excessive violence toward any who disagree with him. In Theodotion the king is identified in v. 1 as Cyrus, but that name is not repeated in the rest of the narrative, and in the Old Greek the king is anonymous throughout. The author of Bel and the Dragon provides a caricature of this imperial ruler and subtly urges resistance to such a foreign king that is similar in many ways to the attitude toward the king in Daniel 1–6. The two themes have much in common. The polemic against idolatry does not arise from the fear that the faithful might succumb to the worship of 'other gods',[3] but as part of the anti-empire message throughout the book. Just as the king is exposed as a brutal and vacillating weakling, so the gods of the empire have as shaky a claim on authority and power as the empire itself does.

The King in the Story of Bel

The king in Bel and the Dragon revered the voracious Bel and went every day to worship him (v. 4). According to Theodotion, the Babylonians provided twelve bushels of choice flour, forty sheep and six measures of wine to the god Bel on a daily basis.[4] The king sharply criticized Daniel for remaining true to his God, and the king was convinced that Bel was alive[5] since this idol ate and drank much every day. In Theodotion Daniel laughed

1. All biblical and apocryphal translations are from the NRSV.

2. In this article I use the traditional name 'dragon' whereas Collins (1993: 406, 414) suggests a translation 'serpent', and Moore (1977: 141) a translation 'large snake'.

3. Moore 1977: 127 says that the primary purpose of this book was to ridicule paganism.

4. In the Old Greek the Babylonians provided twelve bushels of choice flour, but only four sheep. Excessive meat eating was frowned on in antiquity. The liquid contribution of the priests in the Old Greek was six measures of oil instead of wine, but in vv. 15 and 21 wine is mentioned.

5. See the references to the living God in Dan. 6.20, 26.

at the gullible king, causing him to lose his temper.[6] Daniel insisted that Bel was only clay inside and bronze outside and did not really eat or drink anything. The king immediately proposed a contest to determine whether Bel was alive, and the losing side in the contest—the seventy priests of Bel or Daniel—would face execution. If the priests of Bel could not show who was eating the provision they would die, but if they proved that Bel was in fact eating the provisions, Daniel would die (vv. 3-9).

The seventy priests of Bel provided food and wine for Bel, but had left the premises of the temple when Daniel, alone in the presence of the king, scattered ashes throughout the whole temple. Leaving the temple, Daniel and the king shut the door and sealed it with the king's seal. When Daniel and the king arrived at Bel's temple the next day, the king asked whether the seals had been broken, and Daniel assured him that they were intact. The king, however, saw that the food was gone and jumped to a false conclusion. The king shouted in triumph and declared: 'You are great, O Bel, and in you there is no deceit at all!' (vv. 10-18).

Daniel laughed at the king for the second time (v. 19) and kept the king back from barging into the temple. At Daniel's urging the king looked at the footprints revealed by the scattered ashes and conceded that these were the footprints of men, women and children who had entered the temple of Bel surreptitiously through secret doors during the night and devoured all the things that had been offered to Bel.[7] The king lost his temper again and executed the priests of Bel and their families.[8] The king who had asked Daniel the day before why he did not worship Bel, and had reaffirmed that Bel was great when he had entered the temple, now turned over his god Bel to Daniel, who destroyed both the idol and its temple. Bel was proved to be false because he could not eat, whereas the priests and their families were executed because they had eaten inappropriately (vv. 19-22).

The King in the Story of the Dragon

The Babylonians had a second deity they revered, which was a great dragon. The king thought he had indeed bested Daniel this time since this

6. In the *Apocalypse of Abraham,* Abraham's father, Terah, laughed at the idol Barisat who had caught fire while supposedly tending a cooking fire: 'I laughed (and) said to myself, "Barisat, truly you know how to light a fire and cook food!" And it came to pass while saying this in my laughter, I saw (that) he burned up slowly from the fire and became ashes' (*Apoc. Abr.* 5.10-11).

7. So Theodotion. In the Old Greek they had merely taken the food home.

8. So Theodotion. In the Old Greek the king brought the priests out of the temple and handed them over to Daniel. He also gave Bel's provisions to Daniel and destroyed Bel himself.

god was clearly alive and therefore should be worshiped by Daniel. Daniel confessed steadfastly that he was an adherent of 'the Lord my God, for he is the living God'. He asked permission of the king to kill this god, without using standard military weapons. Amazingly, the king naïvely gave Daniel permission to kill the great dragon (vv. 23-26)!

Daniel boiled together several ingredients—pitch, fat and hair—none of them toxic in themselves, and fed them to the dragon, which promptly exploded. Three observations can be made. First, Daniel also will eat a boiled meal in the lions' den but will survive. Second, the dragon can be compared to the priests of Bel since neither the dragon nor the priests recognized that what they ate could lead to their death. Finally, both Bel and the dragon are proven to be powerless through food.[9] The dragon is different from Bel because he can eat, but it is exactly that ability that kills him since the dragon is unable to determine whether the food offered to him is lethal (v. 27).

The Babylonians put pressure on the king and charged: 'The king has become a Jew; he has destroyed Bel, and killed the dragon, and slaughtered the priests' (v. 28). Only the fourth charge—slaughtering the priests—can be directly laid at the king's door. Collins notes that by the end of the book the king has become a monotheist (v. 41), but even then it is not clear that he has become a Jew (Collins 1993: 415).[10] The king himself had not destroyed Bel (at least according to Theodotion) nor killed the dragon even though Daniel had. In any case, the Babylonians threatened the king and his household with death unless he would hand over Daniel. The supposedly mighty king gave in to this pressure and handed Daniel over to the Babylonians (vv. 28-30).

The Babylonians promptly threw Daniel into the lions' den where he stayed for six days. To seal Daniel's fate his would-be executioners did not give the lions their usual daily fare of two human bodies and two sheep[11] so that they would be ravenously hungry and sure to gobble up Daniel.[12] The cruelty of the king is again demonstrated in his contributing two humans

9. For a thorough discussion of the role that the ability or inability to eat plays in Bel and the Dragon, see Bergmann 2004: 262-83.

10. In 2 Macc. 9.17 the dying Antiochus made a vow to the Lord, who no longer had mercy on him, that he would become a Jew and would visit every inhabited place to proclaim the power of God. Earlier he had not allowed Jews to profess themselves to be Jews (2 Macc. 6.6). My use of the word Jew/Jews in this context is dictated by NRSV. I am well aware that Jack Elliott and other scholars consider this term anachronistic before the second century CE.

11. The two sheep are not mentioned in the Old Greek.

12. The Old Greek adds that death by the lions would deprive Daniel of a proper burial.

daily to the lions' diet. Daniel stayed in this lions' den for six days without harm (vv. 31-32).

Of course the lions were not the only ones who were hungry in their den. So was Daniel. An angel transported the prophet Habakkuk by the crown of his head from Judea to Babylon. Habakkuk took along with him a stew that he had intended to feed to some reapers. Habakkuk urged Daniel to eat the food that God had sent to him. Daniel ate, and God returned Habakkuk back to Judea. Since the prophet Habakkuk prepared Daniel's food, he consumed food that had been prepared according to the laws of *kashrut* and had not been in contact with idol worshipers (Bergmann 2004: 275; vv. 33-39).[13]

On the seventh day, the king came to the lions' den to mourn for Daniel. This contrasts with Daniel 6 where the sleepless Darius, who had fasted, hurried to the lions' den on the very first day because he was worried about the well-being of Daniel. Readers of Bel and the Dragon are bound to ask: 'Where has the king been for the last week?' When the fickle king saw that Daniel sat there alive, he shouted out, 'You are great, O Lord, the God of Daniel, and there is no other besides you' (v. 41). Only twenty-three verses earlier the king had shouted, 'You are great, O Bel, and in you there is no deceit at all!' The king pulled Daniel out of the lions' den and threw into the den those who had attempted to destroy Daniel. He watched as the lions gobbled them up. Only twelve verses earlier the king had caved before the Babylonians' demands and given them the right to destroy Daniel. The lions showed remarkable restraint for a week in not eating Daniel, but returned to their ravenous practices when the king's enemies were thrown into their den (vv. 40-42).

The king was loyal to the 'gods' Bel and the great dragon until Daniel exposed them both as frauds. The demise of these idols hints at the precarious hold that the king has on power. At first the king had badly misread the results of Daniel's attempt to prove that Bel was not a god. And the king was willing to double-cross Daniel by throwing him to the lions to save his own life. His punishments of the priests of Bel and their families and the Babylonians who had accused him of being a Jew were brutal. When Daniel was miraculously spared in the lions' den, the king acknowledged Daniel's God and denied that there were any other gods. Can the reader doubt that this king would double-cross Daniel again if he faced political pressure or threats of violence? Would not the reader suspect that the king would renege on his allegiance to Daniel's God at the first opportunity? The story of Bel and the dragon is devastating in its depiction of the king. The anonymity of the king, except for v. 1, allows him to represent a variety of royal figures whom the postexilic community would have experienced.

13. Compare the controversy over Persian food and drink in Dan. 1.5, 8-16.

The Picture of the Imperial King in Daniel 1–6

The first six chapters of Daniel have often been thought to provide examples of what it means to live faithfully in an alien culture, but they are better understood in my judgment as satirical attacks on the imperial system in general and the king as the embodiment of that imperial arrogance in particular. Satire often uses exaggeration, incongruity, reversal and parody. This strong resistance to the king is mixed with some accommodation to the realities of empire, which distinguishes these chapters from Daniel 7–12.[14] The imperial kings in Daniel 1–6 resort easily to violence, repent after manifestations of God's power and even confess the superiority of Israel's God, but soon fall back into their disregard for the religious claims of those whom they rule or force them into religiously compromised situations.

Daniel 1

In Daniel 1, we learn that Nebuchadnezzar's conquest of Jerusalem was done by the permission of the God of Israel: 'The Lord let King Jehoiakim of Judah fall into his [Nebuchadnezzar's] power, as well as some of the vessels of the house of God' (v. 2). Hence Nebuchadnezzar's military achievements were not solely his own. When Daniel and his three friends Hananiah, Mishael and Azariah were selected for training as Babylonian bureaucrats, Daniel refused to accept the daily portion of food and wine offered by the king, not so much because it violated the laws of *kashrut*, but apparently because Daniel did not want to accept food offered by the empire. Daniel was resisting hybridity, knowing that you are what you eat.[15] His request worried Ashpenaz, the chief of the king's eunuchs,[16] who feared that any deterioration in Daniel's physical condition would lead to violent punishment by the king. That is how ancient emperors were expected to rule. Ashpenaz's willingness to negotiate with Daniel, however, undercuts some of the power of the king. After living on this special diet for ten days, Daniel and his friends were better and fatter than the Babylonian control group. When the king gave Daniel and his friends their final examination after three years of education, no one was comparable to Daniel, Hananiah,

14. Drawing on the literary methodology of Mikhail Bakhtin, David M. Valeta (Valeta 2005 and 2008) understands the tales in Daniel as Menippean Satires, and reads the depiction of the king in Daniel 1–6 in a similar way to my own understanding.

15. This thought was suggested to me by Carolyn Leeb. She pointed out that hybridity can be syncretic (assimilative) or resistant (parody).

16. See Dan. 1.3, 7, 8, 9, 10, 11, 18. The NRSV and other English versions identify Ashpenaz as 'palace master' or something similar. The importance of understanding the term 'eunuch' literally will be discussed by Carolyn Leeb and me in our commentary on Daniel in the Wisdom Commentary Series, forthcoming.

Mishael and Azariah, and they were stationed in the king's court. They were ten times better than their competitors. In v. 19 the narrator ignores the Babylonian names the king's eunuch had given the four men (v. 6) and calls them by their Israelite names. The emperor and his officials had tried to deprive Daniel and his friends of their Israelite identity.

Daniel 2

In Daniel 2, Nebuchadnezzar lost sleep because of a dream he had. The power of Nebuchadnezzar was thus unmasked by insomnia (see also 6.18) and an involuntary dream.[17] He made an outrageous demand in v. 2 that his magicians, enchanters and sorcerers not only interpret the dream, but tell him also what he had dreamed. His expert assistants greeted him with this wish: 'O king, live forever',[18] even though by the end of the chapter we learn that not only will Nebuchadnezzar not live forever, but in fact the Babylonian Empire will be succeeded by three subsequent empires, each one of lesser value than its predecessor—gold, silver, bronze, iron.[19] Nebuchadnezzar underscored his absurd demand by threatening his assistants with being torn limb from limb and having their houses ruined. The king accused his assistants of stalling for time (v. 8), even though later he proved to be inconsistent when he granted Daniel's own request for additional time (v. 16). The assistants cut the king down to size when they insisted that no king has ever made such a request—even kings who were however great and powerful (v. 10). It seems that Nebuchadnezzar's assistants did not place him at such a powerful level, and they insisted that no humans could ever fulfill such a request to tell a king what he had dreamed.

The king again showed uncontrollable rage and commanded that all his wise men be executed (v. 12). The king who had promoted the four men at the end of ch. 1 now gave them the thankless job of executing the king's

17. 'In Daniel, however, it is not the dreams of the slaves but the interpretation of the dreams of the vanquisher by the vanquished that reveals these reveries as messages from God, and thus indicative of a greater power than earthly empires' (Valeta 2005: 322).

18. See also Dan. 3.9; 5.10; 6.21.

19. Scholars have long debated why the text of Daniel changes from Hebrew to Aramaic at 2.4b and does not revert to Hebrew until 8.1. Portier-Young has made the interesting proposal that the stories of Daniel 1–6 show resistance and accommodation and that the writers who joined the tales of Daniel 1–6 to the visions of Daniel 7–12 'made intentional use of two languages, Hebrew and Aramaic, to move their audience from a posture of partial accommodation and collaboration to one of total rejection of Seleucid hegemony and domination' (Portier-Young 2011: 227 and Portier-Young 2010). That is, the switch from the language of the empire (Aramaic) to Hebrew, the age-old language of Israel, marks this definitive transition.

Babylonian assistants. In Daniel's prayer for help he mentioned that God deposes kings and sets up kings. Their power is only a gift that can also be taken away. Daniel exposed the violent traits of Nebuchadnezzar by ordering the executioner Arioch not to carry out the king's threat to destroy the wise men of Babylon (v. 26). When Daniel addressed Nebuchadnezzar as 'king of kings' (v. 37), the title is more than a little ironic. After all, it is Daniel's God who has given Nebuchadnezzar all the power and responsibilities he claims. While Daniel assures the king that he is the head of gold in his dream, his kingdom is only one of four successive empires, and he clearly will not live forever. At the end of these kingdoms that will be destroyed by a divinely made stone—one not made by human hands—will come the kingdom of God that will never be destroyed (v. 44).

All pretensions of power by Nebuchadnezzar collapse when he falls on his face and worships Daniel, even commanding that a grain offering and incense be offered to him. The biblical text does not bother to countermand this order since every reader of Daniel will know that no human, not even Daniel, is to be worshiped. Nebuchadnezzar confessed Daniel's God as God of gods and Lord of kings and a revealer of mysteries (v. 47), all of which seems incongruous. The king promoted Daniel and gave him many great gifts and made him ruler over the whole province of Babylon just after Daniel had announced that Nebuchadnezzar's kingdom was only one of four and that that these kingdoms are doomed and will be replaced by a kingdom set up by God that shall never be destroyed. The king is seemingly so smitten by Daniel that at Daniel's request he also promoted Shadrach, Meshach and Abednego. Daniel, the vindicated interpreter, remained at the king's court where he had been since Dan. 1.19. The king's favorable attitude toward the four men will soon prove to be a mirage.

Daniel 3

Resistance to the king continues to be shown in Daniel 3, where the king is still Nebuchadnezzar but the resisters are Shadrach, Meshach and Abednego. Daniel does not appear in this chapter, and Shadrach, Meshach and Abednego do not appear after this chapter. Nebuchadnezzar erected a statue of ridiculous proportions, sixty cubits high by six cubits wide, or, in our measurements, ninety feet high and nine feet wide. How would such a statue withstand a windstorm? The king sent out invitations to the satraps, prefects, governors, counselors, treasurers, justices, magistrates and all the officials of the provinces to come to the dedication of this statue. All of these major and minor officials assembled in Dura and were instructed that when they would hear the sound of the horn, pipe, lyre, trigon, harp, drum and the entire musical ensemble, they were to fall down and worship the golden statue that the king had set up (v. 5). Whoever failed in this obligation would be thrown into a furnace of blazing fire (v. 6).

As the music sounded from all the musical instruments (v. 7; cf. vv. 10, 15), all the peoples, nations and languages fell down in unison and worshiped the golden statue that Nebuchadnezzar had set up. There is parody in the repeated listing of musical instruments at whose sound everyone is to worship the king's statue (see Avalos 1991: 580-88). The sycophantic Chaldeans then played their expected part, expressed a wish that the king would live forever (v. 9) and reported to the king that Shadrach, Meshach and Abednego paid no heed to the king, did not serve his gods and did not worship the golden statue that the king had set up. One suspects that their first accusation—that Shadrach, Meshach and Abednego paid no heed to the king—was the most egregious in the king's eyes. One also sees here a critique of the petty infighting among the imperial bureaucrats.

Nebuchadnezzar, as we would expect, again loses his temper (v. 13), and calls Shadrach, Meshach and Abednego on the carpet. The king gave them a choice: when they would hear all the musical instruments again, they could either fall down and worship the statue or be thrown into the fiery furnace. The king mocked their faith in advance: 'Who is the god that will deliver you out of my hands?' Here he echoes the arrogant taunt of the Rabshakeh of Sennacherib (Isa. 36.19-20; 37.11-12; 2 Kgs 18.33-35; 19.12-13).

The three resisters answered defiantly. They felt no need to make a defense before Nebuchadnezzar. They would be happy if God would deliver them, but even if he could not, they would not serve Nebuchadnezzar's gods or worship the golden statue he had set up. As Portier-Young observes, '[The three young men] trust in God, defy the king's edict, refuse to worship any God but Yahweh, proclaim their faith out loud and in public, and surrender their bodies to death, not to apostasy' (Portier-Young 2011: 261). These men give their lives regardless of any reward they might expect. '[This story] instills in the persecuted the conviction that acting for their own sake, for God's, and for one another's all aim toward the one end of covenant fidelity. Self-sacrifice does not negate this goal but allows them to attain it' (Portier-Young 2011: 260).

Again, Nebuchadnezzar had problems with anger management. He was so angry in fact that his face was distorted. At his orders the furnace was heated seven times more than was customary. Acting as if throwing people into a fiery furnace was a natural pattern of events, the king in his fury turned up the thermostat. Because the king's command was urgent and the furnace overheated, the flames killed the men who lifted the three resisters into the furnace.

When the king saw four figures instead of three in the furnace, and the three resisters walking around unbound, he addressed Shadrach, Meshach and Abednego in v. 26 as 'servants of the Most High God'. The golden statue that everyone was to worship or risk death goes unmentioned, and the king blessed the God of Shadrach, Meschach and Abednego, who had sent an angel to deliver his servants who trusted in him. The king now decreed that any people nation or language (v. 29; cf. v. 7) that utters blasphemy against the God of Shadrach, Meshach and Abednego would be torn limb from limb and their houses would be ruined. The king is 'equal opportunity' on threats. On the other hand, the king promoted Shadrach, Meshach and Abednego, whom shortly before he had thrown into the fiery furnace. While his effort to destroy Shadrach, Meshach and Abednego misfired (no pun intended), his threat to punish brutally any who did not worship their God says much about the character of emperors.

Daniel 4[20]

Although this chapter is largely a first-person report by Nebuchadnezzar[21] in vv. 1-18 and vv. 34-37, with Daniel referring to the king in the third person in vv. 19-33, criticism and mockery of the king can be detected throughout the chapter. Nebuchadnezzar begins with a letter addressed to all peoples, nations and languages that tells of God's benefactions to him. Nebuchadnezzar had had another dream that frightened and terrified him. When his professional interpreters could not explain his dream, Daniel, whom the king addressed by his Babylonian name, Belteshazzar, showed up uninvited.[22] He flattered Daniel/Belteshazzar by saying that he was endowed with a spirit of the holy gods and that no mystery was too difficult for him. The meaning of the dream he told Daniel is clear enough without any need for interpretation even though the magicians, enchanters, Chaldeans and diviners could not figure it out and the king himself needed all the help he could get (v. 7). A gigantic tree that provided food for all and a home for birds and other animals was chopped down by orders of a watcher who had come from heaven. Clearly the tree represents the king. His provision of food and shelter does not come from his magnanimity but as a consequence of taking people from their homelands. The king would now live with the animals and exchange his human mind for the mind of an animal. This condition, initiated by the watchers and holy ones, would last for seven years. Its purpose: that all may know that the Most High is sovereign over the kingdom

20. I follow the English verse numbers. Dan. 4.1 is 3.31 in Aramaic, and v. 4 in English is v. 1 in Aramaic.

21. I agree with the proposal that this story may once have featured Nabonidus instead of Nebuchadnezzar, but it is the latter king who is unequivocally present in the final form of the text.

22. The king had apparently forgotten about Daniel's skill and fidelity after the dramatic events of Daniel 1–2.

of mortals and would give the kingdom to whomever he chooses. This is quite a comedown for the great king of Babylon. The narrator expresses no anxiety about how the nations will feed and house themselves in the king's absence.

The king admitted that Daniel was endowed with a spirit of the holy gods, which was a good thing, since all the wise men of Nebuchadnezzar's kingdom could not interpret the dream (v. 18). But the king's confession is both transitory and shallow. Daniel hesitated to describe the meaning of this dream. His thoughts terrified him—it was not healthy to give bad news to the volatile king—but the king encouraged him to go on. Who could criticize Daniel for what he said in v. 19: 'My lord, may the dream be for those who hate you, and its interpretation for your enemies!' After identifying the king with the tree, Daniel talked about the king being great and strong, with his greatness and sovereignty reaching the ends of the earth. But the fate of the king, who would live with the wild animals, has a clear purpose: that the king learn that the Most High, the God of Israel, has sovereignty over human rule and gives such rule to whomever he chooses. The king would regain his kingdom only when he acknowledged that God/Heaven is sovereign. Daniel urged the king to atone for his sins with righteousness and for his iniquities with mercy to the oppressed, that is, to the ones he himself as king has oppressed. Daniel thus gives the king a last minute out: if he would reverse his sinful imperial policies, he could escape divine punishment.

A whole year later Nebuchadnezzar has not gotten the point, but paraded instead on the roof of the palace and said, 'Is this not magnificent Babylon, which I built by my mighty power and for my glorious majesty?' He is a self-made monarch, and the whole purpose of his state building projects is to garner glory for himself. A heavenly voice instantaneously[23] told Nebuchadnezzar that he had lost the kingdom. Nebuchadnezzar was driven from human society, ate grass like an ox, had his body washed with the dew of heaven, saw his hair grow as long as eagles' feathers and his nails become like birds' claws. The king eats like an animal, is homeless despite all his building projects, his appearance is unkempt, and his hands become grotesque. David Valeta believes that the 'madness' of Nebuchadnezzar may allude to Antiochus IV and his reputation for madness and erratic behavior (Valeta 2005: 31). In his praise for God after his recovery, Nebuchadnezzar acknowledged God's sovereignty and his freedom to do whatever he chooses. In other words, Nebuchadnezzar regained his kingdom when he admitted he himself had none. Nebuchadnezzar extolled the king of heaven and confessed: his works are truth; his ways are justice; and God is able to bring low those in walk in pride—like emperors, for example.

23. The king's words were still in his mouth.

Daniel 5

The transition to this chapter is abrupt since Belshazzar has become king with no word about Nebuchadnezzar's death. The new king presided over a banquet with heavy drinking. In a drunken condition the king ordered his servants to bring in the vessels Nebuchadnezzar had taken from the temple in Jerusalem. Then the king, his lords, his wives and concubines—clearly the listing of his sexual partners is not complimentary—toasted the gods of gold and silver, bronze, iron, wood and stone as they drank from the stolen temple vessels.

In the midst of this blasphemous toast a hand began to write on the wall, terrifying the king half to death: 'Then the king's face turned pale, and his thoughts terrified him. His limbs gave way,[24] and his knees knocked together' (Dan. 5.6). The king called for the usual professional interpreters, promising them royal clothing, jewelry and high rank in the kingdom. They failed to interpret, of course, which only caused the king more anxiety: 'King Belshazzar became greatly terrified and his face turned pale, and his lords were perplexed'. The bureaucrats know perfectly well what the king does to servants who fail to do impossible tasks. At this point the queen mother appeared and said, 'O king, live forever!' She recommended Daniel, who was like a person endowed with the spirit of the holy gods, and who had shown godlike wisdom during the reign of Belshazzar's 'father', Nebuchadnezzar.[25] 'He will give the interpretation'. Belshazzar explained the circumstances to Daniel and offered him the same rewards/bribes that had been offered to the professional interpreters. Daniel refused the gifts but gave Belshazzar his interpretation of the handwriting on the wall anyway. Daniel rehearsed the events of ch. 4, but was much more explicit in the criticism of Nebuchadnezzar: his heart was lifted up and his spirit was hardened so that he acted proudly. Daniel scolded Belshazzar for not humbling his heart even though he had known all this about his father. Belshazzar himself is accused of exalting himself against the Lord of heaven. He had praised the gods of silver, gold, bronze, iron, wood and stone, but the God in whose power was his very breath and to whom belong all his ways, he had not honored.

24. This expression is unclear. Literally translated it refers to the untying of knots, an idiom also used of Daniel's solving of problems in vv. 12 and 16. Al Wolters suggests this interpretation of all three passages: 'My proposal is that v. 5 refers to the king's panic-stricken loss of sphincter control, and that vv. 12 and 16 are a mocking and ironic allusion to this ignominious incontinence on the king's part' (Wolters 1991: 118).

25. Belshazzar was actually the son of Nabonidus, and he never advanced beyond the rank of regent. This is usually identified as one of the many historical errors in Daniel, and so it is. A modern reader, therefore, knows that Belshazzar's claims to the throne were even more vapid than the author of Daniel did.

The meaning of the Aramaic inscription itself is enigmatic, but Daniel interpreted it to mean that Belshazzar had been weighed and found wanting and that his kingdom would be given to the Medes and Persians. Despite Daniel's earlier refusal of the king's gifts, Belshazzar gave Daniel the three gifts anyway. That night Belshazzar was killed,[26] despite the queen mother's wish earlier in the day that he live forever. Belshazzar was succeeded by (the fictitious) Darius the Mede (see Collins 1993: 30-32).

Daniel 6

Darius appointed Daniel to a new position as one of three presidents to whom the satraps reported, and soon Daniel emerged as the leading president. The other presidents and satraps were jealous of Daniel, but they could find no grounds for complaint against him. They conspired against Daniel to catch him in connection with the law of his God. After the usual wish for a long life, they proposed to Darius that for the next thirty days no one should pray to anyone but the king, and failure to comply would lead to being thrown into the lions' den. The gullible king is persuaded to issue this brutal edict according to the law of the Medes and Persians, which cannot be revoked.[27] This provision will limit the king's options later.

Daniel knew that this document had been signed (v. 10), but he continued to pray three times a day before an open window, toward Jerusalem. Presumably these prayers were offered out loud, and so his accusers knew that he was praying to someone other than Darius. Daniel sins boldly against the emperor. The conspirators reported this violation to Darius and reminded the king of his previous edict that could not be changed. Legalistic obedience is more important than saving Daniel's life. The king himself reiterated that such a law of the Medes and Persians could not be revoked. Only when this provision was reiterated did they report Daniel's prayers, which were a classic case of civil disobedience. Darius made every effort to save Daniel until sunset, but he then caved in to their demands, much as the king did in Bel and the Dragon when his subjects accused him of becoming a Jew. In his moral weakness the king said to Daniel, 'May your God, whom you faithfully serve, deliver you!' Thus, even as he initiates a death sentence, the king acknowledges that Daniel is innocent. His hope that God would deliver Daniel contradicts his own decree that in this month no one should pray to any god but the king. The entrance to the den was covered and sealed with the king's seal and the signet of his lords.

26. We are not told by whom the king was killed. By Darius and/or by his forces? The narrator did not know and perhaps did not care.

27. This supposed characteristic of Persian laws is not attested in ancient documents.

The worried king went home, fasted and could not sleep. No 'diversions' (NRSV 'food') were brought to him, perhaps referring to his usual habit of frolicking with concubines or dancing girls (Collins 1993: 258 n. 48). At daybreak the king rushed to the lions' den and called anxiously: 'O Daniel, servant of the living God, has your God whom you faithfully serve been able to deliver you from the lions?' How ironic that Daniel, who was exposed to mortal danger because of his civil disobedience is credited with faithful service to the God to whom he had been praying. After wishing that the king might live forever,[28] Daniel reported that God had sent an angel and shut the lions' mouths. Daniel affirmed that he had been found blameless before God and had done no wrong to the king. The king was very glad about the fate of Daniel, but ordered that the conspirators, their wives and children be thrown into the lions' den. One can perhaps understand his pique toward Daniel's accusers, but his most brutal self is revealed when he also executes their wives and children. Before these folks hit the bottom of the den, they were overpowered by the lions, who broke in pieces all their bones. It was no accident that the lions had no appetite for Daniel.

Darius now made another decree directly opposite to his earlier decree that supposedly could not be revoked, but now is changed. He ordered that people should tremble and fear before the God of Daniel, who is living and who endures forever. God's kingdom will never be destroyed. This God had saved Daniel from the power of the lions. Daniel maintained his faithfulness even when that would expose him to capital punishment. But this chapter also portrays the king as easily fooled by his staff, and as a ruler who fails to act for the safety of Daniel even when he knew that Daniel was in the right. Darius affirmed that Daniel has served his God faithfully. When the king's foolish decree and justice collided, Darius opted for his foolish decree. His verdict on the conspirators was just but brutal: he also executed their wives and children.

Conclusion

I believe that previous commentators have underplayed the sharp critique of imperial powers that appears throughout the seven chapters of Bel and the Dragon and Daniel 1–6. Bergmann speaks of the positive attitude of Bel and the Dragon's author toward foreign rulers and uses this argument to date the apocryphal work before the time of Antiochus Epiphanes (Bergmann 2004: 265; cf. Collins 1993: 418, who also speaks about the sympathetic portrayal of the king in this chapter). On the contrary, the author of Daniel 6 portrays a king as brutal as Antiochus and who clearly knows better than to try to

28. This is the only time in Daniel that this expression is spoken by an Israelite.

execute Daniel. The tales in Daniel 1–6 are as critical of the empire as the visions in chs. 7–12. Who is more evil, the little horn who speaks arrogant things in Daniel 7 or the whole series of kings who observe the good character of Daniel and his friends time after time, but yield to every kind of political pressure or naïvely accept bureaucratic calumny against them? Perhaps the tales of Daniel 1–6 are older than the visions of Daniel 7–12,[29] but the usual reason for affirming that has been called into question since their main burden does not seem to be instruction on how to live faithfully in a foreign context, but rather an exposé of the pretentions of imperial power.

References

Avalos, Hector I.

1991 'The Comedic Functions of the Enumerations of Officials and Instruments in Daniel 3', *CBQ* 53: 580-88.

Bergmann, Claudia

2004 'The Ability/Inability to Eat: Determining Life and Death in *Bel et Draco*', *JSJ* 35: 262-83.

Collins, John J.

1993 *Daniel* (Hermeneia; Minneapolis, MN: Fortress Press).

Elliott, John H.

2000 *1 Peter* (AB, 37B; New York: Doubleday).

Moore, Carey A.

1977 *Daniel, Esther, and Jeremiah: The Additions* (AB, 44; Garden City, NY: Doubleday).

Portier-Young, Anathea E.

2010 'Languages of Identity and Obligation: Daniel as Bilingual Book', *VT* 60: 98-115.

2011 *Apocalypse against Empire: Theologies of Resistance in Early Judaism* (Grand Rapids, MI: Eerdmans).

Valeta, David M.

2005 'Court of Jester Tales? Resistance and Social Reality in Daniel 1–6', *PRSt* 32: 309-24.

2008 *Lions and Ovens and Visions: A Satirical Reading of Daniel 1–6* (Hebrew Bible Monographs, 12; Sheffield: Sheffield Phoenix Press).

Wolters, Al

1991 'Untying the King's Knots: Physiology and Wordplay in Daniel 5', *JBL* 110: 117-22.

29. Collins 1993: 418, argues that the identification of Daniel as a priest in Bel and the Dragon, in contradiction to Daniel 1, suggests a date before Daniel MT had become authoritative.

Spirit Aggression in the Gospel according to Luke

Stuart L. Love

For twenty-eight years I have counted John H. Elliott my mentor and friend. I remember vividly his encouragement and constructive criticism of my work at annual meetings of the Context Group in the United States, annual meetings of the Society of Biblical Literature, and international meetings of the Context Group in Spain, Germany, the Czech Republic and Russia. Rarely have I known a person with such deep human qualities, sensitivities to social problems, devotion to the church and to the work of New Testament scholarship for the sake of the church. At a personal level Jack would ask, 'Stu, how is your book on Matthew coming?' And when I finished it, and he read it, making suggestions, he immediately asked, 'Stu, what do you want to do next? Are you interested in something in Luke–Acts as you did in Matthew?' That's Jack Elliott. He supported me. He helped me. He encouraged me to do my best scholarship.

For all of our times together, and for the splendid lectures you gave at Pepperdine University enjoyed by all, but especially our students, and for the gracious friendship you and Linde have given to D'Esta and me, I want to say 'thank you'.

Introduction

> *'The Spirit of the Lord is upon me, . . . to let the oppressed go free, . . .'* (Lk. 4.18).

The purpose of this paper is to explore through the use of a social-scientific model of 'spirit aggression' representative examples in the Gospel of Luke of both the powerful, forceful work of the Holy Spirit in doing good, and the powerful, aggressive, oppressive 'spirit of evil' identified at its mythological source with the devil/Satan. On face value these appear to be two different trajectories within the writing, but I will demonstrate their essential confrontational interplay as a way of highlighting significant motifs of Luke's theological message. These lines of inquiry, which I am identifying as 'spirit aggression', are particularly evident in the healing activity of Jesus—'For if it is by the finger of God that I cast out demons, then the kingdom of God has come upon you' (Lk. 11.20).[1]

The Third Gospel gives significant weight to the work of the Spirit. For example, F.W. Horn, summarizing the significance of the Spirit in Luke–Acts, states, 'Luke is surely the theologian of the spirit, not only in terms of statistics (*pneuma* 106 times; *pneuma theou,* 75 times; *pneuma hagion,* 54 times) but also in terms of his reflection on primitive Christian testimony and ideas concerning the spirit from the perspective of a concept of salvation history' (1992: 277). Salvation history (see Baer 1926: 108), that is, Luke's understanding of the biblical account beginning with Abraham, then moving through the Davidic line to Christ and finally to the church's origin and mission (Holladay 2005: 175-76), highlights God's great acts of salvific deliverance in three periods: Israel (16.16; 3.18-20), Jesus (the climactic center), and the church (see Acts 7; 13.16-25). Accordingly, the Gospel of Luke works with this theme in two of the three periods—Israel (ending with the imprisonment of John in Lk. 3.20) and Jesus. The period of Israel is largely a time of promise as set forth, for example, in the birth stories of Luke 1–2. From the moment of Jesus' baptism, the Third Gospel marks the Spirit's concentrated and magnified intervention on the son of Mary.

Overview: An Active, Forceful Vocabulary for Good

Often a vigorous, dynamic vocabulary—as in, especially, Luke's use of verbs—advances the narrative as it depicts the aggressive power and involvement of the Spirit of God in the lives of individuals and of the believing community. The following limited litany demonstrates this truth: persons such as John, Elizabeth, Zechariah and Jesus are *filled* (ἐπλήσθη) with the Spirit (Lk. 1.15, 41, 67; 4.1). The Holy Spirit *comes upon (*ἐπελεύσεται) Mary as the power of the Most High *overshadows* her (ἐπισκιάσει σοι) (Lk. 1.35). The Spirit *rests* on Simeon (ἦν ἐπ'αυτόν) (Lk. 2.25) and *descends* on Jesus (περιστερὰν ἐπ'αυτόν) at his baptism (Lk. 3.22). *Full* (πλήρης) of the Spirit and *led* (ἤγετο) by the Spirit (Lk. 4.1), Jesus returns to Galilee 'filled with the *power* (δυνάμει) of the Spirit' (4.14) after which God *anoints* (ἔχρισέν) him with the Spirit to carry out his task of bringing good news to the poor (4.18; cf. Acts 10.38). Jesus' 'relationship to the Spirit' (Bovon 2002: 151), accordingly, is found as early as the angel's annunciation to Mary (1.35) and the descent of the Spirit at his baptism (3.22).[2]

1. Unless otherwise noted, all translations of text are the author's.

2. Angels, a significant topic in Luke, will not be treated in this paper due to space restraints.

Overview: An Active, Powerful Vocabulary for Evil

However, the converse is also true. If we can speak of the 'breath' or 'wind' of the Spirit of God empowering Jesus to do good, we can also identify the 'breath' or 'wind' of an aggressive, powerful spirit of evil identified at its mythological source with the devil/Satan (Bovon 2002: 141-42; see also Bovon 2006: 225-73).[3] This is not to say that Luke has a developed demonology, but as Bovon notes (2002: 141), 'he still has a few thoughts on the topic'. Humans 'are afflicted by the devil and suffer from him' (Bovon 2002: 141; cf. Garrett 1989: 37-60),[4] and such evil influence has its own vocabulary. In one passage (4.33), Luke combines *spirit, unclean,* and *demon (πνεῦμα δαιμονίου ἀκαθάρτου)*.[5] Green (1997: 222) believes that the 'additional adjectives are needed . . . to negate any possible confusion between the spirits at work in the narrative'. Green states further (1997: 222) that by 'attacking this one unclean spirit, the Spirit-empowered Jesus has initiated a ministry of "release" constituting an onslaught against all the forces of evil'. Scholarship has established (Twelftree 1985, 1993; Garrett 1989: 39-40) that in Luke the coming millennial age identifies the termination of the rule of Satan. The connection of the use of 'spirit' in this vein and associating it inextricably with Satan is inescapable in the story of the healing of the crippled woman (13.11, 16).

Once more, active verbs advance the narrative and depict the violent forceful power of evil in human life. People are *oppressed* (καταδυναστευομένους) by the devil (Acts 10.38). In their subjugation, they may have 'the spirit of an unclean demon' (4.33) or, as in the case of the women who follow Jesus, they first had been 'healed of evil spirits and infirmities' (8.2; τεθεραπευμέναι ἀπὸ πνευμάτων πονηρῶν καὶ ἀσθενειῶν). Warning his disciples, Jesus tells Peter, 'Satan has demanded (ἐξῃτήσατο) to sift all of you like wheat, . . .' (22.31).

Luke uses strong verbs to describe the demon-possessed. People are *thrown down* (ῥῖψαν) (4.35). Often, Legion is *seized* (συνηρπάκει) by an unclean spirit (8.29). In the case of an afflicted boy (9.37-43), a spirit, his father testifies, suddenly seizes (λαμβάνει) him. In the throes of the attack

3. Luke–Acts employs 'the devil/slanderer' (διάβολος) seven times (Lk. 4.2, 3, 6, 13; 8.12; Acts 10.38; 13.10) and 'Satan' (σατάν) seven times (Lk. 10.18; 11.18; 13.16; 22.3, 31; Acts 5.3; 26.18).

4. See Lk. 13.16; Acts 10.38; 26.18.

5. For the phrase 'unclean spirit' (ἀκαθάρτον πνεῦμα) see Lk. 4.33, 36; 6.18; 8.29; 9.42; 11.24; Acts 5.16; 8.7; 10.14, 28; 11.8; for 'demon' (δαιμόνιον/δαίμων) see Lk. 4.33, 35, 41; 7.33; 8.2, 27, 29, 30, 33, 35, 38; 9.1; 9.42, 49; 10.17; 11.14, 15, 18, 19, 20; 13.32; (17.18); for 'evil spirit' (πονηρὸν πνεῦμα) see Lk. 7.21; 8.2; Acts 19.12, 13, 15, 16; for 'spirit of divination' (πνεῦμα πύθωνα) see Acts 16.16; for other uses of 'spirit' (πνεῦμα) with malevolent intent or effects see Lk. 9.39; 11.26; 13.11.

the boy shrieks, convulses, foams at the mouth, after which the spirit *mauls* (συντρῖβον) him (9.39).

The effect of Jesus' healings situates his ministry within a struggle between two dominions: that of Satan and that of God. In the Beelzebul controversy, Jesus casts out demons 'by the finger of God' (11.20). The 'stronger person', Jesus asserts, *attacks, overpowers, takes away* (ἐπέρχομαι, νικάω, αἴρω) the strong man's armor, and *divides* (διαδίδωμι) his plunder (11.22). When the seventy return to Jesus they report that the demons *submit* (ὑποτάσσεται) to them (10.17). Jesus then, in a prophetic vision, recognizes that his own mission, shared with his followers, spells the decisive defeat of all the forces of evil—'I watched Satan fall from heaven like a bolt of lightning' (10.18). Bovon (2002: 142) summarizes this thought, 'Luke is aware of the power of supernatural forces that imprison humanity, but he knows far more about the power that can set the captives free'.[6]

A Social-Scientific Model of Spirit Aggression

To cast interpretive light on our topic I will create and then apply a social-scientific model of 'spirit aggression' to representative passages in Luke. The model will have two interrelated components: First, I will utilize certain etic insights from the work of Fritz Kramer (1987) pertaining to spirit possession among African tribes in the postcolonial European period that seem to parallel Luke's treatment of the Spirit. Second, I will set forth a taxonomic system of sickness and healing along the lines of witchcraft, sorcery and spirit aggression in societies like ancient Rome.

Spirit Possession among Sub-Saharan African Tribes

Based on Kramer's research, I will emphasize four points. First, there is an apparent similarity of terms common to the African tribal context and the biblical witness that includes Luke–Acts. The words translated from Hebrew or Greek as *spirit*, denoting 'wind', 'breath', or 'air', appropriately mean the same thing among African tribal groups—*spirit* denotes 'wind, breath or waft of air' (Kramer 1987: 67). Kramer states, 'The animation of spirit seems logical where that which can move independently is considered to be endowed with spirit, but it also reflects the fact that the spirit of a phenomenon is seen to be that which touches or moves a person' (1987: 67). Accordingly, one can find a parallel use of verbs. Both in the biblical accounts and in the tribal cultures verbs like *filled, possessed* and *led* characterize persons and groups that are spirit influenced. Kramer (1987: 64) affirms, 'the basic words in African languages which we translate as "spirit" denote first and foremost the spirit of something'.

6. See Acts 5.19; 12.7-10; 16.25-30.

Second, there is a certain dualism in the biblical and African examples. Among the African tribes one can be moved or possessed by the spirit (Benz 1972: 141), being *moved* indicating 'an encounter with the divine in its beatific, healing, regenerative form', and *possession* as 'being overwhelmed in the sense of being taken over by a demonic, infernal or evil spirit which makes itself evident in a person's personality in a harmful or destructive way'. Kramer (1987: 60) states, 'the difference between being moved and being possessed depends on which power is recognized as the agent. It is not difficult to find African equivalents of the "divine" and "demonic" powers named here. . . . [D]ualism was also at home in the African world pictures, even if it resisted reduction to the dualism of good and evil, God and Devil'. It should be noted that the data of Luke sets forth a dualism of good and evil, but does not embrace Iranian dualistic influences (Samain 1938: 451). Rather, emphases in Luke stress an arena of 'two empires' that 'are in opposition, one governed by God and angels, the other by Satan and demons' (Samain 1938: 451).

Third, in the formulation of an anthropological theory among African tribes, Kramer (1987: 57), citing Evans-Pritchard (1956: 106-10), asserts that 'spirits' and 'divinities' are 'refractions of social reality'. Evans-Pritchard's view stands over and against an older anthropology that spoke of 'manism' and 'animism'. Accordingly, care must be taken not to identify contemporary psychology and cosmology with that of spirit possession among African tribal cultures, and I suggest the same is true for the data of Luke. Instead of seeking understanding by means of modern rationalism or psychoanalytic interpretations, Kramer (1987: 58) believes that we need to follow the example of Lienhardt (1961: 151-52), who attempts to '"translate" the cosmology of the Dinka into modern language, and to make the divinities they believe in comprehensible as characteristic expression of their experience of the world'. To accomplish this, Lienhardt (1961: 151) uses a Latin word, *passiones,* which means 'the opposite of actions in relation to the human self'. Kramer (1987: 58) sums up particular implications of Lienhardt's view:

> But only with the aid of this counter notion can we convey properly the concept of the powers, the spirits and deities peculiar to the Dinka. The powers are 'the images of human *passiones* seen as the active sources of those *passiones*'. By putting it this way, the anthropologist is saying that we are guilty of simplification and overlooking a decisive meaning in the original if we translate what for the Dinka are 'images of *passiones*' as 'passions' or 'drives', and equate them with the id.

For example, following Kramer (1987: 58), when 'we say that someone has caught an illness, the Dinka say that someone has been seized by an illness'. As we will see, this insight is applicable to examples of healing in Luke. Kramer (1987: 59) sums up Lienhardt's (1961: 151-52) thought:

> This means that we should not conceive of the powers as entities, as bodies or substances with extension and location in space, nor of the human self as an independent whole; the powers act as self-determining subjects in the world and in the person. When these subjects dissociate in a person's self, when one power ousts another inside, the person embodies this power whose effects then fuse with the *passiones*.

Therefore, Kramer (1987: 61) believes it 'is wrong in the African examples to think of the devil as an abstract power of evil. The powers of the cosmos, both animals and landscapes, recur in the person possessed, so that we can truly speak of *passiones* as an experienced reality.'

Fourth, symptoms of spirit possession appear to be similar in both cultures. Kramer (1987: 61; see also Benz 1972: 125) describes the common indicators in the African examples: 'a sudden transformation to bestial behavior, deep sleep, raging, uncustomary, barbarian sounds and bestial cries, appalling grimaces and great agitation, such that the person concerned is unable to remain in one place and goes in search of solitude, etc.'. Perhaps the classic example (Hollenbach 1981: 567-88) of similar behavior interpreted politically is the account of the Gerasene demoniac called Legion (Lk. 8.26-39).

Spirit Aggression and Illness

A number of stories involve Jesus as an Israelite healer, a social reality that raises the question as to how illness is experienced and treated in advanced agrarian societies analogous to the Roman Empire. Hahn (1995: 24) writes, 'Anthropological observers in a variety of non-Western settings have noted that, in addition to roughly equivalent generic matters, sickness is connected to two broader phenomena: cosmological or religious forces, and social relationships and interpersonal conflicts'. In medical anthropology (Pilch 1986: 102), 'illness' denotes a social-cultural perspective in which 'many others besides the stricken individual are involved'. Both patients and healers are 'embedded in a cultural system', and it is the 'whole system that heals' (Pilch 1986: 102). Attitudes and actions are embedded in the total fabric of life (Blum and Blum 1965: 20). The Blums (1965: 20) add, 'Health beliefs and practices must be viewed within the context in which they occur, since focusing on them in isolation distorts or detracts from their meaning and function'. Jesus as an Israelite healer should not be viewed in isolation, but in association with the cultural *system* (Pilch 1985: 143; 2000). Systems theory (Hahn 1995: 2; Blum and Blum 1965: ch. 2; Allbaugh 1953), accordingly, considers social relations and cultural expectations of societies in understanding sickness and healing. Sickness and healing belong to the organized patterns of thinking, judging and behaving shared by members of a society. This arrangement is different from the biomedical approach largely operative in advanced industrial societies like the United States and northern Europe, in which the focus too often is on a narrow hierarchy of molecules, cells, organs and human bodies (Hahn 1995: 97). Persons in advanced industrial settings do not readily see Jesus' healing activity as essential to his task in a social-political sense.

In societies like ancient Rome, sickness and healing may be classified along the lines of witchcraft, sorcery and spirit aggression (Murdock 1980: 73; Foster 1976: 773-82). 'Without exception', Murdock states (1980: 82; see Pilch 1991: 200-209; 1992: 253-6), 'every society in the sample which depends primarily on animal husbandry for its economic livelihood regards spirit aggression as either the predominant or an important secondary cause of illness'. Spirit aggression assumes (Pilch 1986: 102, 104) that sickness is a misfortune due to the effect of cosmic forces on human lives. Sun and moon belong to the array of cosmic forces. The sun's power gives warmth and life; it also causes headaches. Seeds, women and the moon wax and wane together, and ill people may be moonstruck (Blum and Blum 1965: 31-32).[7]

Further, I maintain that the religious and political implications of scenes such as the Beelzebul controversy (11.14-23) hinge on whether Jesus casts out demons by the prince of demons (11.15) or by the 'finger of God' (11.19). Luke's language is unequivocal, forceful, uncompromising and violent (11.20-23). Jesus' ministry of healing is situated within the struggle between two dominions—Satan and God—in which Luke presents Jesus as a Spirit-led servant–prophet who struggles with the religious and political powers of Jerusalem.

Finally, a word concerning magic and magical practices is in order. Magical practices flourish in pre-industrial settings (Sjoberg 1960: 275; Blum and Blum 1965: 21, 31-35) among all social groups, but especially among lower-class urbanites and villagers. Sjoberg states (1960: 277-78), 'Restorative magic has prevailed in feudal orders from the most ancient ones in the Near East to those in the Greek and Roman periods, in Central and Eastern Asia, in medieval Europe and pre-Columbian America, down to those that survive today'. Since evil spirits upset the order of life, causing illness or other social or physical disasters, magical practices ward off evil and correct imbalances in the spiritual order. Magical rituals presume 'the sympathy of word, deed, and concept: peasants believe that by naming their wish, what they wish shall be, with the proviso that the energies of the supernaturals will be enlisted toward this end' (Blum and Blum 1965: 31-32). Whether Jesus is a Hellenistic magician is a question that has sparked provocative discussion among scholars (Hull 1974; Smith 1978; Kee 1986;

7. The demon-possessed son in Matthew 17 is literally *moonstruck* (σεληνιάζεται) (17.15), that is, he is under the moon's cosmic influence or power. Often the Greek is translated to indicate that the boy is an *epileptic*.

Garrett 1989; Twelftree 1993; Meier 1994). Our purpose is not to decide whether Jesus was a magician or 'charismatic healer' (Theissen and Merz 1998: 305-308), but to consider how afflicted persons might perceive and respond to Jesus. Therefore, the employment of the term 'magic' is used in a non-pejorative sense 'as the art of influencing the superhuman sphere of the spirits, demons, angels and gods' (Theissen and Merz 1998: 305 n. 22). Having set forth the model we now turn to its application.

Applying the Model

In organizing our representative data we will follow Luke's view of salvation history in the Third Gospel (set forth above): Israel and Jesus.

Israel

Drawing from the work of Kramer in our model, four points of comparison can be demonstrated. First, like the African example, there is the common usage of *spirit* terminology in Luke (1.15, 35, 41, 67; 2.25-27). Second, those 'moved' by the Spirit, John (1.15), Elizabeth (1.41), Zechariah (1.67) and Simeon (2.25-27) are *filled* with the Spirit, that is they have 'an encounter with the divine' in a powerful 'beatific' fashion (Kramer 1987: 60). They are 'moved' but not 'possessed' (Kramer 1987: 60). Bovon indicates (2002: 36 n. 56) that in 'the NT one finds πίμπλημι ("to fill") almost exclusively in Luke'. Luke 'indicates with this word the presence of the Holy Spirit' (Benoit 1956-57: 169-94; see 1.15, 41, 67; 2.25, 26; 3.16). Consequently, the Spirit has 'residence in the Baptist', even before his birth (1.15; see 1.76). John, like Samson (Judg. 13.4) and Samuel (1 Sam. 1.11), also children of divine promise, is required to abstain from *strong drink* so that only the Holy Spirit fills him. His mighty prophetic mission is to lead the people back to their God and in so doing restore their relationship with him. John functions as the forerunner of the messiah (Mal. 4.5-6) and his task is rendered *with the spirit and power of Elijah* (ἐν πνεύματι καὶ δυνάμει Ἠλίου, 1.17). John's message makes clear that God's coming kingdom will be *wrath* for those unprepared for its judgment (3.7). Setting their lives in order requires the crowds to share food and clothing with those in need (3.11; cf. Acts 2.44-47; 4.32-35). His message to tax collectors (who collaborated with foreign powers) and soldiers (who carried out the political will of foreign powers) corresponds with a social reputation of cheating and extortion. Ultimately, John's preaching is placed within the prospects of Isaiah's proclamation of Israel's restoration (3.4-6; see Isaiah 40).

In the case of Elizabeth (1.41), when Mary greets her kin the child in Elizabeth's womb leaps. As Fitzmyer (1981: 357-58) puts it, 'Elizabeth, filled with the holy Spirit, concludes that Mary is to give birth to "the Lord"'. Here, the force of the term *filled* (ἐπλήσθη) is best qualified by the verb used as a prophetic sign to Elizabeth, 'the babe *leaped* (ἐσκίρτησεν) in her womb', that is, the unborn child behaves like the clumsy jumping and love of motion in young animals (Bovon 2002: 58 n. 36). Bovon (2002: 59) compares Elizabeth's spirit-filled prophetic cry to the leaping of the child. A significant social refraction is underway by means of the lives of these two women. Mary, too, has experienced how divine power in the 'Holy Spirit' replaces masculine begetting (1.35).

In the final case of Zechariah (1.67), the father of John, 'filled with the Spirit' (ἐπλήσθη πνεύματος ἁγίου), utters a prophetic prayer of God-given wisdom amid the setting of his family's community (Dubois 1977: 100). The prayer answers the fundamental question, 'What then will this child become?' (1.66). Accordingly, God's historical deliverance for Israel begins anew. The prayer interweaves two stories, John and Jesus, into one tapestry depicting God's salvific purpose. In John and Jesus, God comes to set things right—to look favorably on his people, to redeem them, to raise up a savior who saves his people from their enemies, from all who hate them. John's task as prophet of the Most High is to go before the Lord to prepare his way, to provide knowledge of salvation 'by the forgiveness of their sins' (1.77). As a result, those who sit in darkness and in the shadow of death will have light to guide their feet into the way of peace. Zechariah's prayer, prompted by the Spirit's filling, accentuates the faithfulness of God in the coming deliverance and restoration of God's people.

Third, even though there are no explicit indicators of a dualism of God and Satan or of being demonically 'possessed' in the aforementioned data, there is an apparent proleptic adumbration of what is to come in the struggle between God and Satan identified especially in the hymn of Mary (1.46-55) and Zechariah's prayer (1.68-79). For example, in Mary's hymn, the Lord, as a merciful and powerful savior (1.47), has 'lowered the powerful' and 'raised up the lowly' (1.52). He has 'filled the hungry with good things' and 'sent the rich away empty' (1.53). The prayer of Zechariah petitions the 'Lord God of Israel' (1.68) to save his people from their enemies and all those who hate them (1.71, 74). Bovon states, 'When Luke analyzes the tragedy of human captivity, the devil is usually the true enemy . . .' (2002: 73; see Lk. 13.16; Acts 10.38).

Finally, I make a few observations concerning Evans-Pritchard's notion that 'spirits' are 'refractions of social reality' (Kramer 1987: 57), that is, they mark a change of direction, a bending, or alteration of the course of social reality. I will limit my observations to John the Baptist, but similar analyses could be made of Zechariah, Elizabeth, Mary and Simeon. As noted above, before his birth, John is 'filled' with the Holy Spirit (1.15, 41). His name, given before his birth (1.13), marks a departure from traditional familial practices (1.60-63). The child is reared not in his parent's village but in the desert, where he becomes 'strong in spirit' (1.80). All of these identity markers point the reader to a significant refraction of social expectations that manifest themselves and are connected inseparably to his preaching of repentance to Israel—a message that is set within the reign of Tiberius, the authority structures of the empire, the local rulers and the power brokers of the Temple (3.1-2).

Jesus

The application of our model now centers on the period of Jesus in which two spheres are considered: (1) the baptism (3.21-22), temptation (4.1-13) and outset of Jesus ministry in Nazareth (4.14-30); and (2) four representative examples of Jesus' work of healing and/or exorcism—the man with an unclean spirit (4.31-37), Simon's mother-in-law (4.38-39), the man with a withered hand (6.6-11), and the crippled woman (13.10-17).

The Baptism of Jesus. At his baptism (3.21-22) the Holy Spirit *descends* (καταβῆναι) upon Jesus in *bodily form* (σωματικῷ) *as a dove* (ὡς περιστερὰν), which is followed by the voice from heaven, 'You are my Son, the Beloved, with you I am well pleased' (3.22, NRSV). In keeping with our model, what transpires seems to follow Kramer's insight (1987: 141) of one 'being moved by the spirit'—that is, Jesus experiences a 'beatific' overwhelming. Two considerations are worthy of mention. First, out of Israel's past, Luke apparently draws upon the beginning of the first of the so-called Servant Songs (Isa. 42.1) as well as Ps. 2.7. If so, Jesus is anointed by the Spirit of the Lord as God's son to 'bring forth justice to the nations'. Second, the scene is so pivotal that it begins a sequence of events related to his temptation (4.1) and the beginning of his entire messianic task (4.14, 18-19; cf. Acts 10.37-38).

Culpepper (1995: 91), commenting on the Spirit descending upon Jesus as a dove 'in bodily form', believes Luke employs language that 'emphasizes both tangibility and inexpressibility'. Moreover, in a period previously viewed as dormant vis-à-vis the working of the Spirit in Israel, Luke apparently sees in the entire birth narrative a renewal of the activity of God's Spirit. Luke 'proclaims that God's Spirit has become active again at the end of time' (Culpepper 1995: 91). Jesus, at the inauguration of his mission, 'receives the affirmation and the gift of divine power' (Bovon 2002: 129). Accordingly, what takes place is consistent with a cosmology that is a 'characteristic expression' of his world (Lienhardt 1961: 151-52; see also Evans-Pritchard 1956: 106-10).

The Temptation of Jesus. With the temptation account we openly confront for the first time the dualism typical of 'spirit' in Luke's Gospel: on the one hand, the powerful, benevolent work of the Holy Spirit in Jesus; on the other, the powerful, aggressive, oppressive 'spirit of evil' identified at its mythological source with the devil/Satan in Luke–Acts. This follows our model not only in terms of an encounter with the divine and the presence of the demonic (Benz 1972: 141) but also because the scene poses a test of Jesus. Will he depend on God's provision for his needs (4.3-4)? Will he worship the devil (4.7; προσκυνήσῃς ἐνώπιον ἐμοῦ) in order to have the glory and authority of the kingdoms of the earth? Will he test God by casting himself down from the pinnacle of the temple wall to be saved by angels (see Ps. 91.11-12)? These are christological tests of the messiah (Luz 1989: 185), which means, using the language of Bovon (2002: 140), the 'theme is Christology, not merely ethics'. However, Green observes (1997: 196),

> the tests faced here encapsulate all the tests Jesus would meet during the course of his ministry. And tests would certainly continue—not merely where demonic forces or Satan himself is mentioned (e.g., 4:33-36; 22:3), but throughout his ministry as he encounters forces hostile to God's purpose. As we have learned, behind all such opposition stands the devil, so that Jesus can characterize his whole ministry with the language of testing (22:28).

Green adds (1997: 196 n. 44; see also Green 1989: 652-53; Busse 1978), this 'is most obviously true in the case of Jesus' healing activity, for in almost every account the source of the ailment is traced back to Satan—cf., e.g., 13.10-17; Acts 20.38'.

For example, the issue of 'bread' (subsistence) is implicit to the precarious situation facing the widow at Nain (7.11-17; see 1 Kgs 17.17-24; 2 Kgs 4.32-37; Lk. 4.25-26). By resuscitating her son not only is the woman's domestic survival ameliorated if not secured, the action also refutes any notion that her son's death was due to divine punishment. Or, in the feeding account of the five thousand (9.10-17), Bovon (2002: 359) observes, 'Christologically, Jesus appears as a prophet like Elijah and as the last prophet like Moses'. When Jesus blesses the food, 'he transfers his power to the bread and the fish; as in the healings (5.17; 6.19; 8.46), a δύναμις (*power*) goes forth from him and makes the miracle possible' (Bovon 2002: 357). This can be contrasted to the devil's temptation that Jesus exercise power to satiate his own hunger. Jesus stands in the biblical tradition of 1 Kgs 17.8-16 and the story of Elisha in 2 Kgs 4.42-44 in which the prophet 'nourishes the hungry people even better than the prophets did. Thus the Israelite belief is realized: "We will receive food to eat, and there will be some left over"' (Bovon, 2002: 358). Herbert (1964: 65-72; noted by Bovon, 2002: 358 n. 46) compares the feeding miracle to Jesus' refusal to transform the stone into bread (4.1-4) and contrasts the two episodes with each other.

Let us take an additional step. It is possible from a social-scientific perspective to view the three temptations as corresponding to three of the four major social domains that characterize advanced agrarian societies: economics, politics and religion. The only missing domain is kinship (family), and I believe that is so for a reason. These four spheres are embedded socially to the extent that one sphere's definition, structures and authority may be dictated by another sphere (Hanson 1994: 183-94). However, politics and kinship are so different that one may speak of political religion and domestic religion but not simply of religion. Or one may speak of political economy and domestic economy, but not simply of economy. Religious leaders such as Caiaphas, members of the Jerusalem Sanhedrin, and the Pharisees are political personages, and the Jerusalem Temple is a political edifice where sacrifices are made for the public good (Love 2009: 97). Obviously, the second temptation, the kingdoms of the world, illustrates the political domain. It is less apparent but not impossible to see political religion at the core of the Temple test in Jerusalem. Certainly Luke expresses a bitter irony that it is impossible for a prophet to be killed outside of Jerusalem (13.33, 34). The city and its Temple do not recognize the things that make for peace! These things are hidden from their eyes (19.41-42; see 23.27-31; 21.23-24).

Let us describe a bit more the political domain (Love 1997: 98-102). The Temple and palace constitute the commercial center and hub of wealth for the state. From these locations, rulers find legitimization and the ideological means for controlling the population. The economic structure of the political domain is fundamentally a redistributive network. This means that taxes and rents are levied on rural producers (kinship domain) and redistributed in the cities, estates and temple. Instead of feeding extra mouths in villages, the surplus ends up being used for other purposes by 'the ruling groups' (Rohrbaugh 1991: 156). When Jesus cleanses the Jerusalem Temple, he challenges its redistributive network (19.45-46). The involvement of the Israelite Temple priesthood explains why Herod and the Roman prefects appoint the Jerusalem high priests during the period of Jesus (Hanson and Oakman 2008: 137).

The opposite pole, the kinship domain, entails the household and family. Elliott (1991: 229) demonstrates in Luke–Acts that the household plays 'no part in Palestine's power structure except as the supplier of its economic resources and the object of its devouring policies'. Quite opposite to the Temple, the household is a social organization of reciprocity, not redistribution.

Let us now return to the temptation scene. Luke closes his account by reminding his audience that the devil departed from Jesus 'until an opportune time' (4.13). As previously noted, the reference is not limited to the time of his passion when Satan *enters/possesses* Judas (Εἰσῆλθεν δὲ σατανᾶς εἰς Ἰούδαν) (22.3), or when Jesus tells Peter that Satan 'has *demanded to sift all of you like wheat'* (ἐξῃτήσατο ὑμᾶς τοῦ σινιάσαι ὡς τὸν σῖτον) (22.31), or in the agony experienced on the Mount of Olives (22.39-46), or the arrest scene of Jesus (22.47-53), which ends with Jesus telling his opponents, '[b]ut this is your hour, and the power of darkness!' (22.53). Rather, Jesus' testing rivets on how he—as the Son of God—will carry out his mission regarding human issues of need, in the face of the entrenched powers emanating from the Temple, court, and synagogue. Confronted by the domains of social power radiating out from Jerusalem, his mission requires that his commitment and resolve to accomplish his task faithfully to God inevitably lead him to Jerusalem where he suffers and dies.

The Outset of Jesus' Ministry in Nazareth. Following our model of spirit possession we recognize, again, the use of common terminology, including not only the language of spirit but 'spirit' as an animation or as an endowment that also 'reflects the fact that the spirit of a phenomenon is seen to be that which touches or moves a person' (Kramer 1987: 67). Verbs like 'filled' and 'led' or an adjective like 'full' characterize the relationship of the Spirit to Jesus in Luke ch. 4. Jesus is 'full of the Holy Spirit, 'led by the Spirit', 'filled in the power of the Spirit', or, as stated a bit differently in the quotation from Isaiah 61, 'the Spirit of the Lord is upon me' (4.1, 14, 18). Bovon (2002: 151) states, 'These repetitions are anything but literary clumsiness. Luke is trying to say that, in Jesus, God's power and justice have become active and perceptible again in the world and in history'. One should keep in mind that a similar lexicon is used of John (1.15), Elizabeth (1.41), Mary (1.35), Zechariah (1.67) and Simeon (2.25). Bovon (2002: 151) summarizes the matter theologically, 'the Spirit of prophecy and the Spirit of fulfillment are one in Luke. In this way, he illustrates that the turning point in time has come'. Culpepper (1995: 103) believes that 'References to the Holy Spirit form a leitmotif linking John's preaching (3.16), the baptism of Jesus (3.22), the temptations (4.1), and the beginning of his ministry in Galilee (4.14)'.

The inaugural sermon and its hostile response provide a programmatic answer to the question, what kind of mission will Jesus pursue? Guided by the Spirit and in opposition to the devil's testing, Jesus' primary mission is 'to proclaim good news to the poor' (4.18). The poor are confronted continuously with subsistence issues (1.52-53; 6.20; 7.22; 14.13, 21; 16.20, 22; 18.22; 21.3); but the poor also are identified in the social world of Luke by a number of other 'disadvantaged conditions' such as 'education, gender, family heritage, religious purity, vocation, economics, and so on' (Green 1997: 211).[8] Luke uses a key verb, *to release* (ἀφίημι), twice: 'release to the captives' and 'release to those oppressed' (4.18).[9] Culpepper (1995: 106) states, 'Jesus released persons from various forms of bondage and oppression: economic (the poor), physical (the lame, the crippled), political (the

8. This can be seen in 4.16-30 through the examples of non-Israelites—the widow of Zarephath and the leprous Syrian Naaman.

9. Release means 'forgiveness' and by extension human wholeness—freedom from the devil's power (see 13.10-17; Acts 10.38).

condemned), and demonic. Forgiveness of sins, therefore, can also be seen as a form of release from bondage to iniquity (Acts 8.22-23)'. Having set forth Luke's use of the Spirit in relation to Jesus, we now examine four representative examples of his healing activity using both components of our model but especially healing observations related to agrarian societies like ancient Rome.

Four Examples of Jesus' Healing Activity. Our first two examples—the exorcism of a man with an unclean spirit in the Capernaum synagogue, a public, Sabbath-day setting (political, religious domain) (4.31-37) and the 'exorcism' of a fever from Simon's mother-in-law at Simon's house, a private, domestic location (kinship domain) (4.38-39)—advance Jesus' mission of 'release to the oppressed' (4.16-30). Our model of spirit aggression casts light on both accounts; that is, the stories illustrate how sickness and/or demon possession are connected to two broader phenomena: cosmological or religious forces and social relationships. In the case of the man, unabashedly if not redundantly, Luke identifies him as possessing 'the spirit of an unclean demon' (4.33). And yet, he is present at a religious communal gathering of Israelites on the Sabbath. When the demon cries out, 'Let us alone! What have you to do with us . . . have you come to destroy us?' (4.34), the reference to *us* most probably comprises the community of demons (Twelftree 1985: 95-106; 1993: 217-24; Garrett 1989: 39-40) and marks the power of Jesus against all the host of evil (4.1-13; 3.16; 11.14-23; 13.16). The social environs of Simon's house accents the extremity of the illness and the meticulousness of the act of healing in a social environment marked by thanksgiving and hospitality. In both settings Jesus rebukes the malady in a way that reminds us of Kramer's insight (1987: 58) that among the Dinka instead of saying that someone has 'caught an illness' tribal peoples will say that someone has been 'seized by an illness'. Jesus *rebukes him* (ἐπετίμησεν αὐτῷ) and commands the unclean spirit, '[b]e silent, and come out of him!' (4.35, NRSV). In the case of Simon's mother-in-law (Lk. 4.38-39), Jesus places himself 'above her'—that is, he bends down over her and verbally *rebukes the fever* (ἐπετίμησεν τῷ πυρετῷ), a redactional emphasis missing from Mark (1.31) and Matthew (8.15). The NRSV then translates, 'and it *left her*' (ἀφῆκεν αὐτήν). The fever entered her and the fever left her. The fever behaves like a 'demon'. Recognizing this reality, Pilch (1992: 253-56) entitles his article, 'A Spirit Named "Fever"'. Culpepper (1995: 111) states, 'The fever is seen as the cause of her illness, not a symptom of an infection'. This is helpful to modern readers, as Luke is not thinking rationalistically about illness in terms of modern medicine. Sickness for his social world is a misfortune due to the effect of cosmic forces on human lives. The woman suffers from spirit aggression. Jesus liberates her of spiritual oppression.

Apparently, in this instance there is no political/religious clash between Jesus and the synagogue authorities. However, that changes in chs. 6 and 13. The first case involves a man with a withered right hand (6.6-11//Mk 3.1-6//Mt. 12.9-14). As Jesus teaches, the scribes and Pharisees watch him to see if he would heal on the Sabbath, 'so that they might find an accusation against him' (6.7).[10] We now have a Sabbath controversy within the institutional setting of a synagogue. Concerning the man's condition, Culpepper (1995: 134) observes, '[o]nly Luke adds that it was the man's right hand, the hand normally used for work, gesturing and greeting. Since one performed chores of bodily hygiene with one's left hand, that hand was not to be presented in public. The man had lost the use of his good hand, presumably forcing him to use his left hand in public, thereby adding shame to his physical disability'. The reference to work raises a probable economic factor. The misfortune of the man's deformed condition has familial consequences in restricting his contribution to his household's survival. Healed, his family's productivity is assuredly ameliorated (kinship economics). Jesus invites the man to get up and join him before the entire assembly (6.8). The authorities' reaction to Jesus' riveting and deliberate demonstration carries forward the synagogue reaction at Nazareth (4.16-30). The authorities, are *filled with fury/hot anger* (ἐπλήσθησαν ἀνοίας) and discuss with one another what they might do to Jesus' (6.11).[11] Ironically, while Jesus is *filled* with the power of the Spirit, the political/religious authorities are *filled* with fury, not the liberating purposes of God.

The case of ch. 13 involves a crippled woman, the final example of a Sabbath controversy in a synagogue setting (13.10-17) and one that emphasizes the socially perceived link between illness and an evil spirit (13.11).[12] Drawing upon our healing model, the woman's condition should not be interpreted from a biomedical perspective (Wilkinson 1990: 70). Green (1997: 521) indicates that some describe her as having a 'protracted *spondylitis ankylopoietica*' or some form of '*hysteria*'. He rightly argues that Luke is not 'really interested in a biomedical diagnosis'. He attributes her condition,

10. This is the first synagogue clash after Jesus' inaugural sermon at Nazareth, but it is not the first conflict between Jesus and the political/religious authorities. See 5.17-26 where Pharisees and teachers of the law come from 'every village of Galilee and Judea and from Jerusalem' (a redactional feature of Luke's account) and charge Jesus with blasphemy.

11. Mark, as we might expect, is even harsher in his assessment. The Pharisees plot with the Herodians how they might 'destroy him' (3.6). Matthew omits the Herodians but agrees with Mark that the Pharisees wanted 'to destroy him' (12.14).

12. To interpret *spirit* as a 'weak spirit' (πνεῦμα ἀσθενείας) instead of 'spirit of infirmity' (NRSV) indicates not that the spirit is weak but that its 'aggression' *causes* weakness. In other words, the *illness* needs to square with Luke's subsequent statement that Satan had bound the woman for eighteen years (13.16).

instead, to a 'spirit'. What is needed, Green declares (1989: 521 n. 12), is an ethnomedical perspective: 'this woman's illness has a physiological expression but is rooted in a cosmological disorder'. I agree with this viewpoint. Green rightly observes (1997: 521; Hahn 1995: 27-28) that 'most of Luke's accounts of "illness" could more accurately be termed "disorder accounts"'.

The leader of the synagogue addresses the congregation by recalling the words of Deut. 5.13.[13] His goal is to maintain the reading and faithful teaching of the Law—that is, how one interprets the Sabbath law is critical to fostering Israelite identity. Certainly, the woman's misfortune has lasted 'eighteen years' and does not justify an infringement of Sabbath legislation. However, Jesus argues from a lesser issue of care for the needs of animals, a point granted by the teachers of the law (14.5), to the greater issue of care for an oppressed woman. If it is right to care for domestic animals on the Sabbath, it is right to relieve human distress. Identifying her as a 'daughter of Abraham' indicates that she, like Zacchaeus (19.9), is one of God's chosen people (Gen. 12.2-3). Her liberation from Satan's bondage is most appropriate at this time. Her affliction conflicts with God's purpose of salvation in his covenant with Abraham and the central reason for Jesus' ministry (4.18). Every aspect of the incident points to a communal setting. Honor and shame are at stake. The woman has lived a life of shame for eighteen years. Healed, she has honor among the congregants and her family, and she can be now, more than ever, a productive member of her family. Her opponents who claimed ascribed, institutional honor are shamed (13.17).

Conclusion

Space restraints prevent us from examining other examples in Luke or, for that matter, from opening up a wealth of evidence in the book of Acts, where the disciples of Jesus take up his role of rejected prophet. From the prophet Joel (3.1-5) Peter interprets the outpouring of the Spirit as the beginning of the last days—that is, the period of the church that is marked by prophecy and cosmic signs. Now, God's Spirit is poured out on 'all flesh', referring to all human beings, not just Israelites, sons and daughters and slaves: both men and women who prophesy, see visions and dream dreams (Acts 2.16-21).

It is sufficient to say that based on the evidence of our model and the Third Gospel, Jesus' mission is clearly set within a struggle between two opposing dominions: that of Satan and that of God. Jesus' mission is essentially situated within that struggle. Ultimately, God's Spirit-led servant–prophet is challenged by the religious and political powers of Jerusalem.

13. See also Exod. 20.9-10.

The heart of these hostilities is anticipated and adumbrated in the temptation account where—for the first time—the dualistic powerful, benevolent work of the Spirit in Jesus is resisted by the powerful, aggressive, oppressive 'spirit of evil' identified at its mythological source with the devil/Satan. As the writing unfolds, the stories of sickness and/or demon possession are connected by two broader phenomena: cosmological or religious forces and social relationships. I do not claim that the above insights are unknown to scholars of Luke–Acts, but have demonstrated that the use of a social-scientific model of spirit aggression casts additional light on the writing and better focuses our perceptions as to how Luke's audience would have heard the reading of the Third Gospel and how we can be a more empathetic audience.

References

Allbaugh, Leland G.

1953 *Crete: A Case Study of an Underdeveloped Area* (Princeton, NJ: Princeton University Press).

Baer, H. von

1926 *Der heilige Geist in den Lukasschriften* (BWANT, 3/3; Stuttgart: W. Kohlhammer).

Benoit, Pierre

1957 'L'enfance de Jean-Baptiste selon Luc 1', *NTS* 3: 169-94.

Benz, Ernst

1972 'Ergriffenheit und Bessenheit als Grundformen religiöser Erfahrung,' in *Ergriffenheit und Bessenheit* (ed. J. Zutt; Berne: Francke Verlag).

Blum, Richard, and Eva Blum

1965 *Health and Healing in Rural Greece: A Study of Three Communities* (Stanford, CA: Stanford University Press).

Bovon, François

2002 *Luke 1: A Commentary on the Gospel of Luke 1:1–9:50* (Minneapolis, MN: Fortress Press).

2006 *Luke the Theologian: Fifty-five Years of Research (1950–2005)* (Waco, TX: Baylor University Press, 2nd rev. edn).

Busse, Ulrich

1978 *Das Nazareth-Manifest Jesu: Eine Einführung in das lukanische Jesusbild nach Lk 4.16-30* (SBS, 91; Stuttgart: Katholisches Bibelwerk).

Culpepper, Alan R.

1995 *The Gospel of Luke: Introduction, Commentary, and Reflections* (NIB, 9; Nashville, TN: Abingdon Press).

Dubois, Jean-Daniel

1977 *De Jean-Baptiste à Jésus: Essai sur la conception lucanienne de l'esprit à patir des premiers de l'évangil* (Diss., Strasbourg).

Elliott, John H.

1991 'Temple versus Household in Luke–Acts: A Contrast in Social Institutions', in Neyrey 1991: 211-40.

Evans-Pritchard, E.E.
1956 *Nuer Religion* (Oxford: Oxford University Press).
Fitzmyer, Joseph A.
1981 *The Gospel according to Luke, I–IX* (AB; Garden City, NY: Doubleday).
Foster, George M.
1976 'Disease Etiologies in Non-Western Medical Systems', *American Anthropologist* 78: 773-82.
Garrett, Susan B.
1989 *The Demise of the Devil: Magic and the Demonic in Luke's Writings* (Minneapolis, MN: Fortress Press).
Green, Joel B.
1989 'Jesus and a Daughter of Abraham (Luke 13:10-17): Test Case for a Lukan Perspective on the Miracles of Jesus', *CBQ* 51: 643-54.
1997 *The Gospel of Luke* (New International Commentary on the New Testament; Grand Rapids, MI: Eerdmans).
Hahn, Robert A.
1995 *Sickness and Healing: An Anthropological Perspective* (New Haven, CT: Yale University Press).
Hanson, K.C.
1994 'BTB Readers' Guide: Kinship', *BTB* 24: 183-94.
Hanson, K.C., and Doug Oakman
2008 *Palestine in the Time of Jesus: Social Structures and Social Conflicts* (Minneapolis, MN: Fortress Press, 2nd edn).
Herbert, Arthur G.
1964 'History in the Feeding of the Five Thousand', *StEv* 2: 65-72.
Holladay, Carl R.
2005 *A Critical Introduction to the New Testament* (Nashville, TN: Abingdon Press).
Hollenbach, Paul W.
1981 'Jesus, Demoniacs, and Public Authorities: A Socio-Historical Study', *JAAR* 49: 567-88.
Horn, F.W.
1992 'Holy Spirit', in *ABD* (ed. David Noel Freedman; New York: Doubleday): 3.260-80.
Hull, John M.
1974 *Hellenistic Magic and the Synoptic Tradition* (SBT, 2/28, Naperville, IL: Allenson).
Kee, Howard Clark
1986 *Medicine, Miracle, and Magic in New Testament Times* (SNTSMS, 55; Cambridge: Cambridge University Press).
Kramer, Fritz
1987 *The Red Fez: Art and Spirit Possession in Africa* (London: Verso).
Lienhardt, Godfrey
1961 *Divinity and Experience: The Religion of the Dinka* (Oxford: Oxford University Press).
Love, Stuart L.
2009 *Jesus and Marginal Women: The Gospel of Matthew in Social-Scientific Perspective* (Matrix; Eugene, OR: Cascade Books).

Luz, Ulrich
1989 *Matthew 1–7: A Continental Commentary* (Minneapolis, MN: Fortress Press).
Meier, John P.
1994 *A Marginal Jew: Rethinking the Historical Jesus: Mentor, Message, and Miracles,* vol. 2 (ABRL; New York: Doubleday).
Murdock, George Peter
1980 *Theories of Illness: A World Survey* (Pittsburgh, PA: University of Pittsburgh Press).
Neyrey, Jerome (ed.)
1991 *The Social World of Luke–Acts: Models for Interpretation* (Peabody, MA: Hendrickson Publishers).
Pilch, John J.
1985 'Healing in Mark: A Social Science Analysis', *BTB* 15: 142-50.
1986 'The Health Care System in Matthew: A Social Science Analysis', *BTB* 16: 102-106.
1991 'Sickness and Healing in Luke–Acts', in Neyrey 1991: 181-209.
1992 'A Spirit Named "Fever"', *PACE* 21: 253-56.
2000 *Healing in the New Testament: Insights from Mediterranean and Medical Anthropology* (Minneapolis, MN: Fortress Press).
Rohrbaugh, Richard L.
1991 'The Pre-Industrial City in Luke–Acts: Urban Social Relations', in Neyrey 1991: 125-50.
Samain, P.
1938 'L'accusation de magie contre le Christ dans les évangiles', *ETL* 15: 440-62.
Sjoberg, Gideon
1960 *The Preindustrial City: Past and Present* (New York: Free Press).
Smith, Morton
1978 *Jesus the Magician* (San Francisco, CA: Harper & Row).
Theissen, Gerd, and Annette Merz
1998 *The Historical Jesus: A Comprehensive Guide* (Minneapolis, MN: Fortress Press).
Twelftree, Graham H.
1985 *Christ Triumphant: Exorcism Then and Now* (London: Hodder & Stoughton).
1993 *Jesus the Exorcist: A Contribution to the Study of the Historical Jesus* (Peabody, MA: Hendrickson Publishers).
Wilkinson, John
1990 *Health and Healing: Studies in New Testament Principles and Practices* (Edinburgh: Handsel).

What Do the Twin Trials of Jesus Tell Us about Who and What He Was and Was Not

James P. Mackey

My association with Jack Elliott began when I came from my native Ireland to the University of San Francisco in 1969, when he crafted my very best introduction to the United States by writing a most favourable review in the *Catholic Biblical Quarterly* of a book I had just published in Dublin and Chicago, entitled *The Problems of Religious Faith* (Chicago: Franciscan Herald Press, 1972). I found that Jack's exegetical work proved to be, both formally and informally, the most inspiring influence on my theologizing of any of my colleagues at USF. I hope that Jack may see in the following piece sufficient merit to reflect the worth of his influence on me when he was a most helpful and cooperative colleague.

In the doctrinal traditions of the main Christian churches Jesus has come down to us as prophet, priest and king. In addition, from the third century with the adoption of ancient Greek philosophical theology as the main tool for the culture-friendly expansion of the Christian faith, Jesus became a divine person equal to the one he prayed to as his Father and ours.

In my book *Jesus of Nazareth: The Life, the Faith and the Future of the Prophet* (Dublin: Columba Press, 2008), I used the biblical material on the twin trials of Jesus, among other bodies of material, in order to argue that neither was Jesus himself a priest of the cultic sacrificial kind nor did he ever ordain any such priests. In consequence, Calvary had nothing whatever to do with a cultic blood sacrifice (a human sacrifice in this case), required by divine justice as the price to be paid for the remission of the sins of the race. Thus, such cultic priesthoods and bloody sacrifices—even if now offered in an unbloody form, as my Roman Catholic Church claims—should have no place at all in the religion of those who would follow in the faith of Jesus. Further, I would argue that Jesus in his own estimation was no king, not even a pretender to the throne of David; indeed, such a pretence would be anathema to him, if only in view of the fact that Jesus regularly took the received and general image of the earthly monarch to be itself the very antithesis of what leadership in his prophetic movement should look like and manage to be. What about prophet then? In my forthcoming book, *The*

Prophet Jesus of Nazareth, I argue that this was the title that Jesus accepted and bore; not any old prophet, but rather the prophet of the time of fulfilment, the prophet like Moses that Moses himself had promised God would send, and whose prophecy would see fulfilment at last (Deut. 18.15-19).

All of which leaves just one other operation to be performed: a clinical operation on the traditional belief that Jesus was, and knew himself to be, very God. For traditional exegesis of the trial before the high priest has from time immemorial insisted that when the latter tore his garments at the blasphemy perpetrated by Jesus in answering in the affirmative his judge's question as to whether he was indeed the son of the living God, that meant that Jesus was claiming to be a divine person equal to the Father—if ever a blasphemy had to be punished by death, this was the one (Mk 14.61-64// Mt. 26.63-66).

But let us start at the beginning. Mark's 'gospel of Jesus Christ, the son of God', introduces us to Jesus with his arrival to join the redoubtable prophet John the Baptist on the banks of the river Jordan. This was to be the beginning of a working fellowship between these two prophets that had Jesus at one point sharing his baptismal duties with John, possibly believing John to be the prophet that Moses had promised for the time of fulfilment (Jn 4.2-24). That Jesus stayed with John for some time, and even rose in the ranks until he was co-baptizer with John, is more than hinted at in two scripture passages: first, when the evangelist John informs us that the Baptist's estimate of Jesus caused two of the former's disciples to follow the latter (Jn 1.35-37); second, when he records the fact that Jesus and John were baptizing at different places, and that 'Jesus was making and baptizing more disciples than John' (Jn 3.22-24; 4.1).[1] Indeed there is implicit confirmation of this in a story of Paul at Ephesus. It is telling that a group of these early disciples of John-and-Jesus could be found in the diaspora; for when Paul first thought of them as 'some disciples' (of Jesus alone, he would have assumed), he soon discovered that it was 'John's baptism' they had undergone, presumably under the hand of Jesus, and so Paul had them baptized again with the life-giving Spirit rather than the symbolic cleansing water (Acts 19.1-4). Then at some time roughly coincident with John's imprisonment and accidental execution, Jesus outgrew the *ethos* of John's prophetic movement, and made eucharist, not baptism, the definitive ritual of the true reign of God that both of these prophets had announced in virtually identical terms and with equal eschatological urgency: Matthew has John demand, 'repent, for the kingdom of heaven is at hand' (Mt. 3.2), while Mark has Jesus declare, 'The time is fulfilled, and the kingdom of God is at hand; repent and believe in the gospel' (Mk 1.14; see also Lk. 17.20-21).

1. All scripture citations are taken from the Revised Standard Version.

Now put yourself in the shoes of the officially designated guardians of Torah, the Temple authorities in Jerusalem: the priests with their attendant scribes, especially 'the scribes of the Pharisees', who were doubly zealous for the Law to its very letter. Imagine yourself in their place, and the mixed feelings you might well entertain in the case of particular prophets, or indeed about that somewhat motley class of prophets in general. Temple or court authorities might well have few worries about prophets officially appointed by themselves; for they could well depend on their appointees' well-developed sense of self-preservation were they to contemplate any pronouncement in the name of God that could threaten the authority or well-being of the appointing authorities. But these chaps who arrived self-propelled and rather wild from the wilderness, believing that they had sojourned with their Lord there as Israel did of old when she received perfect Torah for her dowry, and who, like Jesus on occasion, were happy to flee back to that desert again when priest or king might order their minions to come calling. That is a very different matter indeed; so that, from the very moment that one of these men from the wilderness appeared on the borders of civilization, shouting the odds about betrayal of Yahweh's rule and the consequences that would descend on all alike from the highest to the lowest, from priest to peasant and king to commoner, it should cause none of us, then or now, any surprise if the official guardians of Torah and the examining magistrates should send post-haste some of their minions, like mobile units of examining magistracy, who could confront these apparently self-appointed fellows, in order to report their findings to the ruling examining magistrates in Jerusalem.

So it is that from the beginnings of our Gospels we are told about the examining magistrates from Jerusalem arriving at public occasions on which our two prophets are active; however, upon examination they find two very different prophets, who meet a similar demise, but for very different reasons. John died for publicly condemning Herod for a clear and public breach of Torah in marrying against the law (Mk 6.17//Mt. 14.3). In Jesus' case, however, it was for his own clear, constant and conspicuous breaches of Torah that the examining magistrates reported him to Jerusalem, and that the highest magistracy, the Sanhedrin, eventually sentenced him to death.

From the beginning of the Gospels we are instructed of this contrast in style, symbolism and substance as we note and itemize the visitations of our two prophets by the travelling magistrates. John's Gospel ends its famous prologue with a contrast between law given by Moses and grace coming through Jesus (Jn 1.17). The heuristic power of this simple contrast is likely to dawn only slowly, and only upon the most attentive of readers. For John goes on immediately to note that 'the Jews sent priests and Levites from Jerusalem to ask (the Baptist), "who are you?"' (Jn 1.19). In answer John says he is not the Messiah, nor is he Elijah who was believed to precede *the* prophet of the end-time; and he certainly is not himself *the* prophet. Such passages may be dismissed as an expected piece of propaganda written into the Gospels by committed Jesus-followers; but even if it is just that, it nevertheless contains its grain of truth. For the Baptist himself seemed to recognize, when languishing without hope in Herod's prison, that he no longer believed that he could be *the* prophet; and so he sent emissaries to ask Jesus, 'are *you* he who is to come?' The answer arrives, according to Matthew, with more than a hint of grace: 'Go and tell John what you hear and see: the blind receive their sight and the lame walk, lepers are cleansed and the deaf hear, and the dead are raised up, and the poor have good news preached to them' (Mt. 11.4-5//Lk.7.22). *The* prophet may have more to do with God's grace healing and enriching all and promising eternal *shalom* than with any exclusive zealotry for Torah to the letter, including the punishments laid down for breaches of Torah and administered by God and man, a point that Jesus will continuously drive home as he heals on the Sabbath when healing is forbidden by the Law (Mk 3.1-6//Mt. 12.9-14//Lk. 6.6-11). In any case, the examining emissaries from Jerusalem never do find anything on which the Baptist, as he became known, could be condemned. They found only a fellow zealot for Torah who would die for defending it against even the mightiest in the land.

The experience of Jesus with the examining magistrates could not have been more different, when 'after John was arrested (he) came into Galilee, preaching the gospel of God, and saying: "The time is fulfilled, and the kingdom of God is at hand; repent and believe in the gospel"' (Mk 1.14). The ominous note is sounded already in Mark's first two chapters when Jesus 'entered the synagogue' and taught (in Capernaum, where he seems to have set up house for a time), and 'they were astonished at his teaching, for he taught them as one who had authority, and not as the scribes' (Mk 1.22). Ominous? Indeed yes. The scribes felt themselves bound to the very letter of Torah, tasked only with searching minutely for its specific and delivered meaning as the only authoritative teaching that they could then hand down. But this fellow? He simply behaved as if he had some innate authority to interpret Torah, an authority that could well take all beyond what any particular passage from the five books of Moses delivered. Such authority would take him well beyond the letter of the law to what could be called its fulfilment, at least in his very favourable view of his own teaching.

Here already the missionary scribes from Jerusalem had enough evidence to bring a charge against Jesus. But worse was to come, and in Mark's narrative, it came quickly. For Mark next tells the story of the healing of a paralytic, helped by four adventurous friends who jumped the queue by getting in through the roof of the house. Jesus admires the faith they showed in this escapade, and he immediately tells the paralytic, 'your sins are forgiven' (Mk 2.3-4). 'Now some of the scribes were sitting there', as they would be almost everywhere that Jesus made public appearances from now on, and they immediately cried 'blasphemy' (Mk 2.6-7). Why? Well, Torah contained lists of punishments for breaches, decreed by God through Moses; and there was a widespread belief that the very ills to which humankind was heir must be divine punishments for sins committed, even in a previous generation. So this Jesus is making himself equal to God in apparently teaching that the God of the Mosaic Torah is not their true God, but that the honour goes to a God of relentless grace who decrees no specified punishment for any sin but has forgiven all even before or as the sins are committed. Whoever can decide who is God and who is not must be the equal of any god.

The scribes stayed around apparently on this occasion at the house of Jesus in Capernaum long enough to witness a dinner party to which Jesus had invited guests, many of whom were known to be sinners (for tax collectors in the common prejudice now as then were pictured as choice sinners). Conscious, no doubt, of the symbolism of the meal as a proud ancient symbol of the age of fulfilment, the examining magistrates interpret this as a declaration by Jesus to the effect that the sinners as such will be seated at the banquet of the kingdom of God in eternal shalom on equal footing with the just (Mk 2.15-17). This kind of view is verified by Jesus according to Matthew's Sermon from the Mount (the handing down of the renewed and fulfilled Torah), when he preaches that the sun and the rain, joint sources of all life, its supports, healings and enhancements, are the gifts or graces of God to all, here and hereafter, whether the recipients be just or unjust, good or evil; so that we all should be sons and daughters of the heavenly *paterfamilias*, by never returning evil for evil, but only grace and goodness to all, a rule and kingdom of relentless grace (Mt. 5.43-48). Now any scribe, witless or wise, could easily see that in treating saint and sinner alike in thanking God (eucharist) for the grace of life, with all of life's supports and enhancements as a gift given equally to all, a perpetual gift therefore that was not to be appropriated by each for self, but first to be broken open and poured out by each to all, indiscriminately to good or bad alike, Jesus was urging us to behave likewise, as true sons and daughters of the Father of all, never to do anything but good to others—a very complete revision in terms of a rule of unconditional grace; a revision now passed off as fulfilment of an unfulfilled rule of punitive Torah.

Correspondingly, the sacrament of initiation that Jesus instituted, one that he substituted for John's baptism, was eucharist—though some of his followers (perhaps some of those who had been baptized by Jesus while he still worked with John) later re-introduced baptism, as John the evangelist notes (Jn 4.2)—and eucharist then remained a permanent feature of the whole prophetic movement that Jesus inaugurated. Eucharist is the signature sacrament that Jesus 'instituted', the only one he instituted and celebrated throughout his public ministry, and that he commanded his followers to continue after his death (1 Cor. 11.23-25). As things turned out, eucharist was as much a threat to the strict letter of Torah as John's baptism, which was meant to symbolize and effect the distinctive support and wholehearted celebration of Torah to the letter. Thus, Jesus was eventually executed for systematic and unapologetic breaches of the Mosaic Torah that he shamelessly—in his accusers' view—tried to justify in various ways, and even tried to pass off as the very fulfilment of the Law that Moses directly received, face to face with God, and handed down the mountain to God's chosen people.

Moreover, eucharist is no sacrament instituted by Jesus in the last hours of his life. Quite to the contrary, eucharist occurs so frequently in the Gospels as to leave no doubt about the fact that it is the distinctive sacrament of the prophetic movement led by Jesus, and that he personally instituted no other. For example, the story in all four Gospels of the feeding of the five thousand (Mt. 14.13-21; Mk 6.32.44; Lk. 9.10-17; Jn 6.1-5) and the similar story in Matthew and Mark of the feeding of the four thousand (Mt. 15.32-39; Mk 8.1-10) are paradigmatic eucharistic stories, as revealed by the formula used of taking food and drink, symbolic of all life, blessing or thanking (eucharist) God for it as God's gift (*gratia*, grace) equally to all, and in consequence breaking and pouring it out to all before being oneself likewise served by others. The most explicit eucharistic story on the point that God's grace is for all, just and unjust equally and alike, is the first eucharistic story in Mark that takes place at Jesus' own table (Mk 2.15-17); and of course, the eucharistic stories continue to appear in the account of the Jesus movement after the death of Jesus, as he had specifically ordered that they should (1 Cor. 11.24). The rule of law, surely now, is being replaced by the law of grace, as the examining magistrates see quite clearly, and no doubt report quite regularly to the priests in Jerusalem.

When in Mark's Gospel the examination of Jesus is taken over by the Pharisees (Mk 2. 16), they specifically focus on activities of Jesus that break Sabbath law, ranging from plucking ears of corn when hungry (Mk 2.23-24// Mt. 12.1-2//Lk. 6.1-2) to the much more general complaint of healing on the Sabbath (Mk 3.1-6//Mt. 12.9-14//Lk. 6.6-11). These incidents in Mark's and other Gospels draw various defensive responses from Jesus, responses that range from citing case law in his favour to the pronouncement of a radical principle of justification: 'The sabbath was made for man, not man for the sabbath' (Mk 2.27). Now that must range with the most radical humanistic kinds of principle ever to adorn human morality and jurisprudence; for if it means anything at all, it must mean that God, according to the opening chapters of the book of Genesis, initiated the creation itself for the good of all creatures—'and God saw that it was good, very good'—and not for his own glory, but so that the Sabbath rest, peace, shalom is symbol of the fulfilment time of all creation. We are back again with a rule of relentless grace rather than a rule of coercive law, and the scandalizing of scribes, priests and Pharisees is once again guaranteed (Mk 3.20-28). Along these lines the examining magistrates, with varied personnel but a standard focus on the Mosaic Torah and its predictable accusations of guilt for breaches thereof, signal ever more insistently the guilty verdict for a capital crime that the Sanhedrin will eventually hand down in its trial of Jesus.

The immediate family of Jesus, his mother, brothers and sisters, are the first to see this clearly. Having been singled out on the occasion of the first visit of Jesus to teach in the synagogue in his own country, merely to have their humble status serve as a reason to question the origin of Jesus' own apparent wisdom and power, the family do rally to the view that their most unenviably famous member was 'beside himself', and that the examining magistrates would sooner or later take him to the highest court in the land, the Sanhedrin, to face capital punishment for his offences against Torah, Moses and God. So the family members turn up at a public session of his to try to get him away, as his friends had done already, only to hear that his response to their request to talk to him was met with the caustic remarks: 'Here (you say) are my mother and my brothers! Whoever does the will of God is my brother, and sister, and mother' (Mk 3.32). A bit sanctimonious, you would have to say; for his mother in particular, we can be sure, was only trying to save her beloved son from what any half-wit could see was an already impending trial and execution. He could easily have gone out, brought her into his house and offered to the poor woman a few words of explanation of what was afoot, and do this without first requiring her credentials as a regular doer of the will of God, credentials of which he should have been already aware in any case (Mk 6.1-6; Lk. 4.16-30).

It would be worth any Gospel reader's while to pause at this point in order to make some general notes on what part 'the crowd' he taught on these very public occasions played in the promotion or demotion of his prophetic mission. Here, in the case of his appearance at his home synagogue, in Luke's version of the story, this particular crowd tried to kill him. Why? Apparently because he responded to this crowd's dismissal of his implied claims to be an appointed wise teacher on the grounds that he came from an uneducated family, and left them with the jibe that God often chose in the past to reroute prophets like him away from those who thought themselves the chosen ones. This retort so incensed his congregation that they crowded round and tried to kill him there and then; but he escaped their clutches on this occasion (Lk. 4.29-30). Now this stands in clear contrast to the role of the crowd in other contexts in which the message is that the crowds that followed and gathered round a prophet protected rather than threatened his person and mission, to the point of people like our travelling magistrates actually fearing what the crowds might do, even though these examining magistrates felt that they had the requisite evidence against the prophet, and therefore contemplated arresting the prophet on the spot and taking him to Jerusalem for trial (see, e.g., the discussion of Lk. 20.1-8 below).

Indeed, as it turns out in the story of Jesus, and as we shall see, the Jerusalem authorities themselves had to wait until Jesus came to Jerusalem to take his challenge to their very doorsteps, a move that he himself knew he had to make at some stage in any case. And even then the high priest had to depend on some informer to reveal in what 'safe house' Jesus slept at night, away from the crowds (Lk. 22.3-6); and even in this event the high priest sought help from the Roman garrison in finally making the arrest (Jn 18.1-14). So perhaps this one instance of the crowd of listeners to the teaching of Jesus shaping up to kill him themselves can be put down to a very local prejudice and might even be overlooked in favour of the way in which the crowds were prepared to behave in defence of the prophet on so many other public occasions. For at least in the case of the most popular of these free-ranging prophets that drew crowds out to the borderlands of the wilderness, it was the utterly transparent power and persuasiveness of the teaching itself, of the 'word' that Jesus, like all the great prophets of Israel received, that brought about a situation in which it was more often the case that it was the examining magistrates, bound by an ancient and literally unalterable version of Torah, that had to fear for their lives, rather than the prophet. This view of the matter is supported by the response of the examining magistracy to Jesus, who, when asked by what authority he persisted with his self-styled prophetic mission, retorted that he would indeed respond to that question, but only after they had answered a similar question from him: 'was the baptism of John from heaven or from men?' At which point 'the chief priests and the scribes' agreed, 'if we say "from men", all the people will stone us; for they are convinced that John was a prophet' (Lk. 20.1-8). The examining magistrates knew what they might well expect on such occasions (namely, stoning), so that no matter how substantial and convincing was the incriminating evidence collected, it could be safely and fully processed only at the highest court in Jerusalem, and even there only with certain assurances that the crowd would not be present at the arrest, and certain other policing and military precautions taken.

Now the foregoing must not be read as if it were an attempt to contrast the one occasion on which the crowd tried to kill the prophet with the many occasions on which the crowd was more likely to kill the prophet's legal accusers, and to assign some moral superiority to the latter; for it is seldom that even a residue of morality can be found in mob rule. And in any event there can be an instance of crowd action, as in fact happened in the case of Jesus, in which any who threatened their chosen prophet could be threatened with lynching, only to have it discovered later that his crowds of followers had wilfully misunderstood our prophet's programme, had mistaken him for a pretender to the throne of David, and would then turn on the prophet from Nazareth, and in lieu of supporting him shout for his hanging instead.

The Gospels are peppered with stories to illustrate the fact that, despite anything Jesus himself could say or do, a significant number, and toward the end a clear majority of his followers from his appointed inner circle of the Twelve to the most occasional of followers who turned up only on festivals and holidays, waved their palms and shouted their Hosannah's for a messianic figure who, in their unquestioning and unquestioned view of the matter, was a legitimate heir to David's throne riding into Jerusalem to bring on the ultimate conflict that would see the holy land restored to Yahweh, its rightful king, and to his plenipotentiary on earth, King Jesus. All three of the so-called Synoptic Gospels record Jesus offering a proof from scripture that the messiah cannot be a son of David (Mk 12.35-37//Mt. 22.41-46// Lk. 20.41-44). But even that made no difference to this crowd. Yes, they knew of his claims to be the prophet of the time of fulfilment, and followed him because they judged him an excellent prophet; but that did nothing to prevent them from following him eventually as the rightful pretender to David's throne.

Messianic speculation at the time was capable of endorsing different permutations and combinations of candidates such as king, priest, prophet—any one of these or whatever mixture thereof. But in the case of Jesus, as he approached Jerusalem in order to bring his God-given mission to its climax, if there were votes for some other option, they were easily shouted down and inaudible over the clamour for a king. 'Because (Jesus) was near to Jerusalem . . . they supposed that the Kingdom of God was to appear immediately' (Lk. 19.11). 'A great crowd who had come to the feast (Passover) heard that Jesus was coming to Jerusalem. So they took branches of palm trees and went out to meet him, crying, "Hosannah! Blessed is he who comes in the name of the Lord, even the king of Israel!"' (Jn 12.12-13). And even after the death of Jesus, during his apparition to his chosen apostles in the upper room, they persist with their question: 'Lord, will you at this time restore the kingdom to Israel?' (Acts 1.6). And who can say how many from among this palm-waving crowd can also be numbered among the crowd that shouted down Pontius Pilate and called for the release of Barabbas—a real Zealot leader in prison for fighting to restore Israel's king—and sent Jesus to his death on the cross instead for failing them at the critical hour (Jn 18.39-40)?

Which brings us at last to the arrest of Jesus by a combination of Judean and Roman soldiery, a feat that could not have been accomplished while Jesus was on the road, regularly attended by a crowd that was hugely supportive, if largely for the wrong reasons; and then to his subsequent trial, first before a Judean and then before a Roman tribunal. Two, not just one, of his inner cabinet of the Twelve, betrayed him to the authorities:

Judas called Iscariot (a nickname taken from the short dagger that Zealot assassins favoured), and Peter, who was once the appointed leader of the Twelve but was fired from that job minutes after his appointment, as Jesus discovered that Peter, like James and John and so many others, expected Jesus to win back David's kingdom rather than get himself killed in trying to do so (Mt. 16.16-23). Judas betrayed Jesus by revealing his secret overnight lodgings as the Sanhedrin in council had requested; Peter did so by actually drawing his sword and trying to initiate the great rebellion in the fervent and widespread hope that if some would start the fight for liberation, God would send the heavenly armies to ensure their victory (Jn 18.10-11). Both Peter and Judas were good Zealots in their different ways, and both equally traitors; for both betrayed Jesus for the same reason, namely, that at the critical hour they were seeing him renege on what they believed to be his God-given mission of restoring the kingdom to Israel. They had to be rid of him as the leader of their now far-from-merry band, if their goal was to remain whole and in any way feasible (Jn 18.1-12; Mk 14:32-50). And, of course, the whole baying crowd betrayed Jesus at the Roman tribunal when they realized that he was about to let himself be hanged on a Roman cross rather than bring down the heavenly armies in order to fulfil his God-given mission to restore the kingdom of God and of David; for that, they had long convinced themselves, was the task God had called Jesus to accomplish—at least that is the interpretation of the matter that the crowd's peremptory choice of Barabbas over Jesus would suggest (Mt. 27.15-23). Matthew in fact has Jesus accomplish something similar to the destruction of the enemies of Jesus and the salvation of his followers much later when Jesus, now established 'in his glory, and all the angels with him', would come back on a second tour of duty—the so-called second coming—to win the last great battle between good and evil, by judging the living and the dead, and decreeing for each their very different awards (Mt. 25.31-45).

Now none of this can be taken to mean that the official Zealot movement itself, led by people like Judas of Galilee, had hijacked the prophetic movement with Jesus at its head; only that a majority of those who followed Jesus, especially on his last journey to Jerusalem, did so in the conviction that he was indeed the legitimate heir to the throne of David. However, only some of these, like Peter and Judas, actually acted on that conviction in their different ways. This then explains why the high priest(s) had to have Jesus brought before Pilate on a different charge from the one on which the Sanhedrin found him guilty; and, incidentally, it explains also the so-called messianic secret, referring to the number of times that Jesus tried to put people off proclaiming him as the messiah, without qualification; for that unadorned title would most likely be taken to mean a claim to be David's heir.

Which brings us to the twin trials themselves. Much exegetical ink has been spilled in trying to make sense of the twin trials that come hard on the heels of the arrest of Jesus. Were the charges the same in each? No. And just what was the charge in the forensic examination conducted by the high priests? Was the Judean trial properly constituted as a trial held before the highest court in the land, the Sanhedrin, or did it consist merely in a relatively informal hearing by the high priests Annas and Caiaphas? And was it not said to be held at times that were odd and not quite in keeping with the law? Anyone who has had the misfortune to feel obliged to pour over all that has been written on this matter might well come away a good deal less enlightened than he or she would have had every right to hope. So here is a suggestion: Jesus was tried before a full and duly constituted meeting of the Sanhedrin; but only John records this trial (Jn 11.47-53). On John's account of the matter, some time before the events of arrest and trial in Jerusalem, 'the chief priests and the Pharisees convened the Council' (Jn 11.47). So here certainly we now have the Sanhedrin legally and validly convened. But no Jesus to charge and sentence in person. Obviously, this is in view of the well-nigh impossibility of arresting him, courtesy of the crowds who protected him, mostly for all the wrong reasons. So Jesus is tried *in absentia*, a perfectly legal process if the judges are put in possession of sufficiently reliable evidence to enable them to hand down a just sentence. This they had been given in abundance in the reports of 'the scribes of the Pharisees' that had been sent as examining magistrates to follow Jesus wherever he went, and to report back his every relevant word and deed. The upshot of the whole messy business is that Jesus was condemned to death *in absentia*, and the plaintive plea was sent out for information, any information, that might help in his arrest—information eventually supplied by Judas. The difficulty of arresting Jesus is stressed again by John's observation that when Jesus apparently heard of this sitting of the Sanhedrin and its verdict, he headed for 'the country near the wilderness once more' (Jn 11.54). Yet the fullness of legal justice would be served when, if at all possible, Jesus could be arrested and have the charges put to him personally, so that he had the opportunity to speak in his own defence. And that is what happened at the Judean trial in Jerusalem, where Jesus was given the opportunity to answer two high priests, one retired and one incumbent, the outcome of which was the re-affirmation of the original sentence of death (Jn 18.12-14).

But what is the charge on which the high priest Caiaphas condemns Jesus to death? That is not altogether clear. It is said to be blasphemy, incurred when Jesus claims to be the messianic son of God. But that still does not bring the required clarity for, as pointed out before, the soubriquet 'son of God' could point to a number of candidates, primarily kings, but prophets also, and many others who faithfully promoted God's will on earth as it is in heaven; in none of these cases need blasphemy be involved. So back once more to the evangelists' accounts of the results of the examining magistrates comprised of chief priests, scribes and Pharisees, which must have formed the substance of the material of their regular reports to Jerusalem. The main thrust of that material amounted to the charge that Jesus claimed to be a prophet; no ordinary prophet indeed, but the prophet of the time of fulfilment, the prophet like Moses that Moses promised God would send (Deut. 18.15). But Jesus, armed with this claim, then took it upon himself in the name of God to preach and practice such breaches of the Mosaic Torah as would raise the suspicion that he regards himself as at least God's equal as lawgiver; that is of the very essence of blasphemy, of the kind that Moses himself decreed worthy of capital punishment (Lev. 24.10-16).

A straw in the wind points to this answer to our question, in the passing remark that the ones who guarded Jesus, once the sentence was passed, mocked him as false pretender to the role of the prophet (Mk 14.65//Mt. 26.67-68//Lk. 22.63-64),[2] just as at the conclusion of the Roman trial, the guards mocked and mistreated Jesus as a false pretender to the throne of David (Mk 15.17-20//Mt. 27.28-31; Jn 19.2-3), the charge on which the Judean authorities wanted Pilate to condemn Jesus to be crucified, though Pilate himself refused to the end to find Jesus guilty on that charge of royal zealotry. In both cases, the liberties taken by the guards mirrored as precisely as they were designed to do the crimes for which their victim in the respective trials was condemned to death. Another straw in the wind, pointing in the same direction, is found in the trial and execution of Stephen, a mirror image of the trial of Jesus, in that it centred on the charges brought by witnesses that Stephen had been 'heard to speak words against Moses and God . . . against this holy place and the law; for we have heard him say that this Jesus of Nazareth will destroy this place, and will change the customs that Moses has delivered to us' (Acts 6.11-14). And again the matter is clinched with clarity by John when he observes, 'This is why the Jews sought all the more to kill him, because he not only broke the Sabbath but also called God his Father, making himself equal to God' (Jn 5.18).

And in any case, in effect, the attentive reader of the Bible will scarcely feel the need to try to follow such straws in the wind, for the nature of the capital charge and the justice of the condemnation of Jesus are already established within Torah as it came from Moses himself when, transmitting God's promise that a prophet like himself would be sent at the time of fulfilment, he decreed in God's name that if a prophet claiming this role would so abuse it as to 'speak a word in my name that I have not commanded him to speak, or who speaks in the name of other gods, that same prophet shall die' (Deut. 18.20).

2. The Lukan version has this mocking taking place just prior to the trial.

The charge of blasphemy on which Jesus is condemned to death by the highest court in his land has nothing whatever to do with the kind of blasphemy that would indeed be incurred if Jesus, or any human being, claimed that he or she was a member of a divine and equal trinity of persons of the same divine substance (*homoousios*) and status as the first person, known as the Father, and as the third person, known as the Holy Spirit. Nor, a fortiori, is such a trinitarian doctrine present or even presaged in the Bible. The blasphemy involved in a human person claiming to be as such a divine person equal in substance and status to two other divine persons is definitely not, then, the kind of blasphemy of which Jesus is accused by his Judean judge. Quite to the contrary, the kind of blasphemy of which Jesus is there accused is that of a human person who knowingly remains fully and only a human person, however in-breathed by the Holy Spirit (i.e. God), yet behaves as if he were the one that could decide what in detail the rule and reign of God in the world should be; so that all who took it to heart might arrive at eternal shalom already in this life and for all eternity. And it is that equality of legislative power and status, and not a matter of an equality of being or substance (*ousia* in Greek is translated by both of these terms), that then constitutes an alleged claim to equality of a human with a divine person that, in the case of the Judean trial of Jesus, draws down the charge of blasphemy on his head. It is a proper charge to level against a mere man who acts as if he could alter or break at his own recognizance a law laid down definitively by the one, true God, through Moses; for such a man acting in such a manner could clearly be accused of acting as, at the very least, the equal of God. John the Evangelist, once again, is the one who expresses this view of the matter with brevity but total historical accuracy when he writes, 'This is why the Jews sought all the more to kill (Jesus), because he not only broke the sabbath but also (in doing so) called God his Father and made himself equal to God' (Jn 5.18).

So Jesus responds to the high priest by insisting that he is indeed a uniquely beloved son of God, not in the sense of some 'oneness in being or substance' with other divine persons nor in the sense of an anointed king of Israel, but rather in accordance with an understanding of the term 'son of God' that denotes a person, whatever his or her profession or persuasion—prophet, priest, king, or commoner—who does God's will on earth as it is revealed from heaven in order to ensure the perfect shalom of paradise restored both here and hereafter: the rule of relentless grace.

Accordingly, Jesus denies that he ever breaks the law of God that Moses brought down from the mountain; for he is the one that Moses promised would come. 'He wrote of me' (Jn 5.46), just as the transfiguration scene in Luke's Gospel confirms, when Moses and Elijah come to meet Jesus on another mountain and appear in glory with him, and a voice out of the clouds proclaims, 'This is my son, the chosen, listen to him' (Lk. 9.28-35).

Jesus fulfils and perfects the law in a manner of which Moses would certainly approve. That is the answer of Jesus to the high priest; for it forms his denial of the charge of blasphemy in the only sense of that word that the high priest could have had in mind—acting as a prophetic 'seer' of the rule of God's kingdom on this earth in a way that contradicted God's known version of that rule as Moses brought it directly from God. It is an answer that Jesus presses home with the threat to the high priest that God will vindicate Jesus, not him, in the fullness of time (Mk 14.61-64).

It is also this understanding of blasphemy that John has in mind in another reported incident when he has Jesus specifically refute the Temple authorities who accuse him of blasphemy, 'because you being a man make yourself God' (Jn 10.22-39). This refutation takes specific account of such accolades as Jesus himself promoted or accepted: 'son of God', or 'the Father is in me as I am in the Father' (Jn 14.10), or 'I and the Father are one' (Jn 10.30). And this refutation is capped by the assertion that who or what they think he is, is of virtually no significance when compared with our readiness to imitate and do on earth, and to obey in all of our lives, a rule of unconditional grace to all others such as is laid down in heaven, and by which God also abides, so that we also may be true sons and daughters of God, here and hereafter.

There is not a scintilla of evidence here, or indeed anywhere else in the Bible, to show that a second, much less a third divine person, all co-equal in divinity, exists; or, a fortiori, that Jesus of Nazareth who was tried and sent to his death by the Sanhedrin on the charge of being a false prophet, could possibly have been the second of some such trinity of personae of the one God. The Irish, as usual, get this right; for their most common way of referring to Jesus our Lord is as 'The Man Above', our kinsman and advocate, now sitting at the throne of grace, having with his last breath on Calvary breathed definitively into a dying world the most powerful inspiration possible of God's unconditional grace to all. This was the breath of the Great Spirit that breathed through Jesus in his life and most of all in his death, the breath of final fidelity to the divine reign of unconditional divine grace. This was the breath that would alone send into remission the originating sin of the race, the sin that consists, as the creation story in Genesis puts the matter in its own mythic language, in homo sapiens wanting to be the equal of God in wisdom and power so as to create a world that would serve the selfish needs and benefits of any particular people, at whatever cost to others.

Which brings us finally to the second trial of Jesus before the Roman governor, Pontius Pilate. Having established that the real, valid and legal trial of Jesus and his condemnation to death was the trial and sentencing before the Sanhedrin that John records, it remains only to establish a credible account of the trial before Pilate, its motive and method. This can be done by a careful reading of John's narrative of the trial before the Sanhedrin, taken together with the accounts that all four evangelists offer of the trials before both priests and Pilate. So here is a suggestion that would seem to make most sense of this material taken as a whole.

Bluntly put, the trial before Pilate is nothing more, nothing less, than a pure show trial forced upon Pilate by the high priest in order to save his own skin and his Temple headquarters. The trial before the Sanhedrin should have been over and done with once the sentence of death on Jesus as a false prophet was handed down. But clearly Caiaphas then noted something about the Jesus affair that could cause further serious problems for them even if the sentence for the alleged blasphemy of playing the law-giver superior to God were carried out and Jesus were executed, like Stephen was later executed on much the same charge, by stoning (Acts 6.14; 7.58). So it had to be something else about the public mission of this pretend prophet of the end-time that would bring down the wrath of Rome, a wrath that would not be mollified in the least by a purely Judean process of having Jesus stoned for some idiosyncratic Judean crime of blasphemy. This something concerning the Jesus-cause the Sanhedrin hinted at broadly enough in declaring that 'if we let him go on, the Romans will come and destroy both our holy place and our nation' (Jn 11:47). It is quite obvious that what is in question here is that feature of the Jesus movement which consists in this: although there is no evidence whatever to show that the official Zealot movement tried to absorb the prophetic movement of which Jesus was founder and leader, nevertheless very large numbers who went to see and hear Jesus and many who only heard of him, took it that he would be the messiah who would liberate Israel from grinding Roman oppression; so anxious and urgent was their long-suffering wish for such liberation. The Roman authorities would hear of this mob clamour; and the distant ones in Rome might take it more seriously than the local authorities such as Pilate, who knew perfectly well that Jesus was no Judas of Galilee, and in the event refused absolutely to convict him as such.

But the Jewish priestly authorities knew only too well that if word of this unorganized mob clamouring for Jesus as king of the Jews reached Rome, the authorities there might come to take away their place and their nation, as they put it; and perhaps take out Pilate in the process. Hence their decision to take Jesus before Pilate and have Pilate condemn and execute Jesus as pretender to the throne of David. The punishment of insurgency was crucifixion, as devotees of the film *Spartacus* will know. The Judean authorities, as they remind Pilate, cannot hand down that sentence; only the Roman tribunal can do so (Jn 18.31). Yet an insurrection is an insurrection, and if the local authorities do not deal with this threatened insurrection, the central power of Rome will do so, as in fact happened some two to three decades later, destroying nation, Temple and puppet government together, as Caiaphas predicted. So, if Pilate is not prepared to move at least against the obvious leader of this brewing insurrection come to boiling point, the priest will complain of him to Rome as 'no friend of Caesar' (Jn 19.12), and Pilate will perish with the rest of them.

It has all the makings of a great Greek tragedy. Pilate knows perfectly well that Jesus is no zealot leader; it would be as odd to suggest that he did not know this, as it would be to suggest that the intelligence unit of the British army of occupation in Northern Ireland did not know the names of every member of the army council of the insurgent Irish Republican Army; but as with Jesus, capturing them was the problem. Yet Pilate also knows that if the priest complains of him to Rome for ignoring a large mob of Jesus-followers who insist that Jesus was the pretender king of Israel, despite anything that Jesus did or could do to dissuade them, Rome would destroy him also. And yet, to his credit, Pilate never did pass a guilty sentence on Jesus. Instead, Pilate insisted to the end that 'I have found no crime deserving death'. It is only when the Judeans, despite this 'not guilty' finding, insisted that Jesus be crucified as befits a zealot, so that neither they nor Pilate (about whom they would duly complain to Rome) can be blamed for allowing him to go free. Thus, 'Pilate gave sentence that their demand should be granted'. But he did not change the not-guilty verdict. He simply washed his hands of what he knew was an injustice, told the priests to take it on their own conscience (which they did), 'but Jesus he delivered up to their will', and put the required facilities for crucifixion at their disposal; satisfied, as he had to be, with the parting gesture of nailing the crime to the cross that suggested they were crucifying their own pretender to the throne, with Pilate's permission, of course (Lk. 23.20-24).

That was the cause of Calvary, and it had nothing to do with the sacrificial killing of a human being—a human sacrifice then—to satisfy God's justice as punishment for the sins of the race. Jesus never was a cultic priest in reality, offering a blood sacrifice to divert God's justice, although that term was used metaphorically of him in the letter to the Hebrews. The only priests present at Calvary on that Friday afternoon were there to confirm the execution, and mock the victim as they did so. It was and is the Spirit that breathed through Jesus in his life, and breathed most powerfully in dying for that for which he had lived, the spirit of unconditional grace breathed by the Great Spirit, breathing through us through him, and not any procedure in a divine court of criminal justice that sends the original sinning of the race into remission.

To conclude, in terms of the opening proposals about him at the beginning of this piece: Jesus of Nazareth was neither a priest nor a king; nor was he, nor is he, a divine person equal in being and substance with the person of the Father God he prayed to and obeyed. He was what he claimed to be, a prophet in Israel, and in his own recognizance the prophet of the time of fulfilment that Moses is said to have predicted. But how can that be verified, until the time of fulfilment comes and it is proven true? Simply because the time of fulfilment is no date already fixed on some cosmic calendar. The time of fulfilment for any and all of us is any time at which we change our hearts and minds so as to let in, in gratitude (eucharist), God's unconditional grace, given daily as life, the supports, healings and enhancements of life offered always unconditionally and equally to all, saints or sinners, together with the eternal shalom that forever comes with it and is ever on offer both here and hereafter. Change your hearts, for the reign of grace is forever at hand. It could not be simpler; but it can be costly. As Dietrich Bonhoeffer once said, grace may be free but it is not cheap. Yet it is always worth it, in the end.

Note

I am acutely conscious of the fact that the portrait of Jesus, and even his self-portrait in the Bible as a man who is not one of three persons in a Divine Trinity of equals, is fleshed out above with a minimum of exegetical evidence to back it up. Context and space are my only excuse for this; and the only remedy I can offer readers consists in a reference to my earlier work, *The Christian Experience of God as Trinity* (London: SCM Press, 1983), in which the fullest exegetical evidence is supplied, and every extant theology of Trinity is analysed, from the early fathers to Moltmann, in order to show that the only holy Trinity that can be detected in our Christian experience of God is that of an economic Trinity, as Tertullian would call it; a Trinity of God our Father, of the Spirit-filled prophet we know as Jesus of Nazareth, the Father's most beloved son, and of the called-out community of saints and sinners insofar as it is in-breathed by the prophet Jesus as he was and is in-breathed by God who is spirit. Nothing more, nothing less.

WERE THERE 'AUTHORS' IN NEW TESTAMENT TIMES?

Bruce J. Malina

I wish to dedicate this essay to Jack Elliott, colleague and friend. His career has been marked by frequent, valuable historical insights, insights meant to eradicate anachronisms and ethnocentrisms. I would like to honor Jack and his work by raising the question whether ascribing the term 'author' to any writer in the first century (or earlier) is anachronistic or ethnocentric. I begin with a range of insights from the literary critic Martha Woodmansee. She has stated, with good reason:

> In my view the 'author' in its modern sense is a relatively recent invention. Specifically, it is the product of the rise in the eighteenth century of a new group of individuals: writers who sought to earn their livelihood from the sale of their writings to the new and rapidly expanding reading public. In Germany this new group of individuals found itself without any of the safeguards for its labors that today are codified in copyright laws. In response to this problem, and in an effort to establish the economic viability of living by the pen, these writers set about redefining the nature of writing. Their reflections on this subject are what, by and large, gave the concept of authorship its modern form (1984: 426).

Woodmansee unpacks the term 'author' in its Renaissance usage as follows:

> In the Renaissance and in the heritage of the Renaissance in the first half of the eighteenth century the 'author' was an unstable marriage of two distinct concepts. He was first and foremost a craftsman; that is, he was master of a body of rules, preserved and handed down to him in rhetoric and poetics, for manipulating traditional materials in order to achieve the effects prescribed by the cultivated audience of the court to which he owed both his livelihood and social status. However, there were those rare moments in literature to which this concept did not seem to do justice. When a writer managed to rise above the requirements of the occasion to achieve something higher, much more than craftsmanship seemed to be involved. To explain such moments a new concept was introduced: the writer was said to be inspired—by some muse, or even by God. These two conceptions of the writer—as craftsman and as inspired—would seem to be incompatible with each other; yet they coexisted, often between the

covers of a single treatise, until well into the eighteenth century (1984: 426-27).

Based on Woodmansee's observations, I offer the following comparative chart distinguishing writer from author:

Writer	**Author**
A writer was first and foremost a craftsman; that is, he was master of a body of rules, preserved and handed down to him in rhetoric and poetics, for manipulating traditional materials in order to achieve the effects prescribed by a particular audience to which he owed both his livelihood and social status.	An author is an individual(ist) who, while using prevailing genre (deriving from the social system) expresses his/her own individual perspective on some subject to achieve the effects prescribed by the author's professional or social ingroup.
When a writer managed to rise above the requirements of the occasion to achieve something higher, much more than craftsmanship seemed to be involved. To explain such moments a new concept was introduced: the writer was said to be inspired—by some muse, or even by God.	When the author rises above the usual requirements of the genre, the author's work is claimed to be creative, insightful and rooted in the author's genius.
The two conceptions of the writer—as craftsman and as inspired—would seem to be incompatible with each other; yet they coexisted, often between the covers of a single treatise, until well into the eighteenth century.	The author, then, may be well schooled in the prevailing genres, producing products of lackluster quality or exceptional products of genius and insight.
It is noteworthy that in neither of these conceptions is the writer regarded as distinctly and personally responsible for his creation. Whether as a craftsman or as inspired, the writer of antiquity is always a vehicle or instrument.	In either case the modern author is distinctly and personally responsible for his creations, unless he/she 'plagiarizes', that is, impinges on the intellectual property of another.
As a craftsman, he is a skilled manipulator of predefined strategies for achieving goals dictated by his audience; understood as inspired, he is equally the subject of independent forces, for the inspired moments of his work—that which is engaging, absorbing and most excellent in it—are not any more the writer's sole doing than are its more routine aspects, but are instead attributable to a higher, external agency—if not to a muse, then to divine dictation.	As a writer, the author has benefited from the training received in the process of education. As an enthralling and engaging writer, he/she has drawn these qualities from within the self where they have been nurtured and developed over time.

Before the eighteenth century, the prevailing theory of writing maximized the element of craftsmanship (in some instances it was the sole purpose of writing) as well as the element of inspiration. At times, when a particular writing was not simply functional but engaging and absorbing, readers sought to identify the source of that inspiration. That is, inspiration was always regarded as emanating from outside or above, never from within the writer himself. 'Inspiration' was explicated in terms of some deity, or good demon/spirit/genius. As a consequence, the inspired work was made peculiarly and distinctively the product—and the property—of the people to whom it was delivered.

Eighteenth-century theorists departed from this compound model of writing in two significant ways. They minimized the element of craftsmanship (in some instances they simply discarded it) in favor of the element of inspiration, and they internalized the source of that inspiration. That is, inspiration came to be regarded as emanating not from outside or above, but from within the writer himself. 'Inspiration' came to be explicated in terms of original genius, with the consequence that the inspired work was made peculiarly and distinctively the product—and the property—of the writer (see Woodmansee 1984).

The connection between inspiration and craft can also be seen in musical composition and performance in the Arab world.

> The traditional musical jargon provides insights into the ṭarab learning-process and sheds light on ṭarab entertainers as a professional group. Reminiscent of, and apparently rooted in, the earlier guild culture, the jargon is craft-based and essentially presents music as a type of manual labor. For example, it embraces such expression as *shughl* which literally means 'work', but denotes performing music especially in professional contexts. *Yimsuk ālah* or to 'carry a tool', may also mean 'to play an instrument', especially in a less formal, or 'make-shift' performance, or when the performer is less skilled on the specific instrument being played, for example when he is asked to play an instrument that is not his main specialty. *Fihā shughl*, or 'it has work' is said of a musical piece with intricate workmanship. *Naḍhīf*, literally, 'clean' describes a flawless rendition of a musical piece. The jargon also identifies the instrumentalists through craft-related expressions that point literally to the mechanical aspect of working or to the working tools themselves, for example: a *raqqāq* for a riqq player, a *qānūnjī* for a *qānūn* player, *nāyātī* for a *nāy* player, and so forth. In these expressions, the suffixes are similarly used in words that refer to the practitioners of manual professions in general (Racy 2003: 31-32).[1]

Similarly, 'Whether as a craftsman or as inspired, the writer of the Renaissance and neoclassical period is always a vehicle or instrument: regarded as

1. *Ṭarab* refers to musically induced alternate states of consciousness; there is an array of music and of instruments that can do this, *if* the musician is 'inspired'.

a craftsman, he is a skilled manipulator of predefined strategies for achieving goals dictated by his audience; understood as inspired, he is equally the subject of independent forces, for the inspired moments of his work—that which is novel and most excellent in it—are not any more the writer's sole doing than are its more routine aspects, but are instead attributable to a higher, external agency—if not to a muse, then to divine dictation' (Woodmansee 1984: 427).

By contrast, writers in the eighteenth century, leading up to the psychological singular subject of the Romantic period, emerged as 'authors'. 'Self-focused' and 'self-generated' writing emerged along with them. And even more significantly, this 'author' had ownership rights to this material as 'intellectual property'. The writings belonged to that singular 'author', and could be bought and sold, inherited or given away like any other property.

Such was not the case in antiquity. As the indefatigable researchers Ede and Lunsford observe:

> What does it mean to be an author? This question has been interrogated from just about every imaginable angle, as the status of the author has been problematized, deconstructed, and challenged to such an extent that discussions of the author problem now seem decidedly old-hat. Scholars now understand—in theory, at least—that the notion of author (like that of the founding or sovereign subject on which it depends) is a peculiarly modern construct, one that can be traced back through multiple and over-determined pathways to the development of modern capitalism and of intellectual property, to Western rationalism, and to patriarchy. Foucault's assertion that '[t]he coming into being of the notion of "author" constitutes the privileged moment of individualization in the history of ideas, knowledge, literature, philosophy, and the sciences' no longer surprises. The author, like the autonomous individual of Descartes's cogito, is, we understand with Raymond Williams, "a characteristic form of bourgeois thought"' (Ede and Lunsford 2001: 354).

New Testament Writers Not Authors

If it is true that there were no authors in antiquity (in any modern sense of the word), it would be inappropriate and anachronistic to introduce that term into New Testament interpretation. The Pauline letters, for example, do have senders but not authors. The senders are co-workers; so it is a short step to consider the Pauline letters as works of collaboration, that is co-working. If one assesses the product, the letters, according to the categories of crafts and/or inspired writings, perhaps such categorization depends on the content and purpose of the letter. A letter to a family member to send one's sandals (like the personal letters found at Oxyrhynchus) are crafted according to rather fixed literary genre. While the Pauline letters do follow the genre of Hellenistic letters (otherwise how could one recognize them as letters), they move several steps beyond the pigeonhole of crafts—even Philemon, which is the most craftlike letter of the corpus.

What might clinch the argument for categorizing the Pauline letters as inspired is the context in which spirit plays a vital and substantive part. First of all, in 1 Corinthians 12 apostles have their role from the spirit; it is a spirit-driven role, an inspired role. All the senders of the Pauline letters were involved in the work of apostles. Then, the context of both the original proclamations and the ongoing interpersonal network was equally suffused with the spirit. The opening of 1 Thessalonians attests:

> For our gospel came to you not only in word, but also in power and in the Holy Spirit and with full conviction. And you became imitators of us and of the Lord, for you received the word in much affliction, with joy inspired by the Holy Spirit (1.5-6).[2]

Thus it would seem that the co-senders of the Pauline letters would have their documents considered both crafted in distinctive ways and falling within the canons of Hellenistic letters. Yet they fall into the realm of the inspired, the work of the Spirit of the God whose gospel these co-senders proclaimed. The letters then might be ascribed to the secretary (writer) of Paul or the Pauline team but ultimately the 'copyright' and owner of the 'intellectual property' known as the Pauline letters is the inspiring agent, the Spirit of the God of Israel.

Further, there is a significant consensus among contemporary writers that the term 'co-author' or 'co-authoring' is rather impossible to define with any precision. Instead, the preferred term is 'collaborator' or 'collaborate'.[3] Of course the Anglo-Saxon 'co-worker' works just as well. And in its Greek garb, this is the term used in the Pauline corpus for that group and its members who worked along with Paul in his task of proclaiming the good news.

2. For 'spirit' in all the co-sent letters: 1 Cor. 1.7; 2.4, 10 (2x), 11 (2x), 12 (2x), 13 (3x), 14 (3x), 15; 3.1, 16; 4.21; 5.3, 4, 5; 6.11, 17, 19; 7.34, 40; 9.11; 12.1, 3 (2x), 4, 7, 8 (2x), 9 (2x), 10, 11, 13 (2x); 14.1, 2, 12, 14, 15 (2x), 16, 32, 37; 15.44 (2x), 45, 46 (2x); 16.18; 2 Cor. 1.22; 3.3, 6 (2x), 8, 17 (2x), 18; 4.13; 5.5; 6.6; 7.1; 11.4; 12.18; 13.14; Phil. 1.19, 27; 2.1; 3.3; 4.23; 1 Thess. 1.5, 6; 4.8; 5.19, 23; Phlm. 25. Of course the presence of the spirit and spirit-effects are common in the letters sent by Paul alone: Rom. 1.4, 9, 11; 2.29; 5.5; 7.6, 14; 8.2, 4, 5 (2x), 6, 9 (3x), 10, 11 (2x), 13, 14, 15 (2x), 16 (2x), 23, 26 (2x), 27 (2x); 9.1; 11.8; 12.1, 11; 14.17; 15.13, 16, 19, 27, 30 (39 instances); Gal. 3.2, 3, 5, 14; 4.3, 6, 9, 29; 5.5, 16, 17 (2x), 18, 20, 22, 25 (2x); 6.1 (2x), 8 (2x), 18 (22 instances).

3. However, Yancey and Spooner 1998: 46, claim: 'we're still without the definitions, critique, and articulation of the range of collaborative engagement that one might wish for'. They offer some in their article.

Collaborative Writing: Hierarchical vs Dialogic

In another, much quoted article, Lunsford and Ede report that many specific forms of collaboration in writing which they have discovered might be covered by two major categories of collaboration: hierarchical and dialogic.

> In our research the hierarchical mode of collaborative writing emerged early on; it is a widespread means of producing texts in all the professions we studied. This form of collaboration is linearally [*sic*] structured, driven by highly specific goals, and carried out by people who play clearly assigned roles. These goals are most often designated by someone outside of and hierarchically superior to the immediate collaborative group or by a senior member or 'leader' of the group. Because productivity and efficiency are of the essence in this mode of collaboration, the realities of multiple voices and shifting authority are seen as problems to be overcome or resolved. Knowledge in this mode is most often viewed as information to be found or a problem to be solved. The activity of finding this information or solving this problem is closely tied to the realization of a particular end product. This mode of collaborative writing is, we would argue, typically conservative. It is also, need we say, a predominantly masculine mode of discourse (Lunsford and Ede 1990: 235).[4]

They note that the hierarchical mode of collaborating was predominant in the professions (i.e. in technological and natural scientific writings). As for the dialogic mode, they note:

> This dialogic mode is loosely structured, and the roles enacted within it are fluid; one 'person' may occupy multiple and shifting roles as the project progresses. In this mode the process of articulating and working together to achieve goals is as important as the goals themselves. Those who participate in dialogic collaboration generally value the creative tension inherent in multi-voiced and multivalent ventures. . . . In dialogic collaboration this group effort is seen as essential to the production—rather than merely the recovery—of knowledge and as a means of individual satisfaction within the group (Lunsford and Ede 1990: 235).[5]

Simply put, the dialogic manner of collaboration has an affective as well as effective dimension. It gets the task of producing a written document done (effective dimensions) while the persons working on the task enjoy themselves (affective dimensions) in the process.

Yancey and Spooner offer an interesting contrast between collaborators and cooperators. 'Collaborators achieve a critical level of congruence in understanding, in purpose and in other intellectual dimensions of a project. Cooperators organize themselves differently: clear structure, division of roles, division of knowledge, efficiency—"hierarchy" in its neutral or posi-

4. See also Dale 1994: 342-43; Yancy and Spooner 1998: 52.
5. See also Stokes and Hartley 1989.

tive dimension.' A sort of middle-range cooperation has 'individuals more or less isolate, but working in concert with others on a joint project. As the degree of integration increases, we move into the range of collaborative models. Here, the individuals contribute more and more to a group solidarity, constituted in the dynamic that Smith calls "collective intelligence"' (1998: 52).

In summary, I offer the following comparative chart of collaborative styles:

Hierarchical Collaboration	**Dialogic Collaboration**
Linear	Collateral
Specific goal driven, with people playing specific roles.	The dialogic mode is loosely structured, with fluid roles; one 'person' may occupy multiple and shifting roles as the project progresses.
Goals designated by persons outside of and hierarchically superior to the immediate collaborative group or by a senior member or 'leader' of the group.	Goals derive from the interactions of collaborative group members.
Because productivity and efficiency are of the essence in this mode of collaboration, the realities of multiple voices and shifting authority are seen as problems to be overcome or resolved.	Those who participate in dialogic collaboration generally value the creative tension inherent in multivoiced and multivalent ventures. In this mode the process of articulating and working together to achieve goals is as important as the goals themselves.
Knowledge in this mode is most often viewed as information to be found or a problem to be solved.	Knowledge in this mode is viewed both as mutually beneficial experiences as well as information to be found and communicated.
The activity of finding this information or solving this problem is closely tied to the realization of a particular end product.	In dialogic collaboration this group effort is seen as essential to the production—rather than merely the recovery—of knowledge and as a means of individual satisfaction within the group.
This mode of collaborative writing is conservative, a predominantly masculine mode of discourse.	The dialogic manner of collaboration has an affective as well as effective dimension. It gets the task of producing a written document done (effective dimensions) while the persons working on the task enjoy themselves in the process.

As for *modes* of collaboration, collectivists stand opposed to individualists, of course.

Individualists	**Collectivists**
In other words, when individualists choose to or are forced to collaborate, they can do so either in a lineal mode or a collateral mode.	When collectivists choose to or are forced to collaborate, they too can do so either in a lineal mode or a collateral mode.
Individualists normally act individualistically, but can also act collectivistically.	Collectivists cannot act individualistically.
Individualists are introspective and psychologically oriented. They can believe in individual responsibility for what they write.	Collectivists are anti-introspective and not psychologically minded. They believe in external, personal influence on what they have written.
Individualists believe in individual property rights, individual authorship and individual intellectual property.	Collectivists believe in group maintenance and group support, with collective (social) property rights, collective 'authorship', i.e. group censorship, approval, engagement.

The descriptions these authors present of the two modes of collaboration fit very well the lineal (hierarchical) and collateral (dialogic) modes of interpersonal relationships (see Pilch and Malina 1998: xxiv-xl). As modes of collaboration, they stand opposed to individualism, of course. In other words, when individualists choose to write, they can do so individualistically or adopt a collaborative mode, and in collaborating, they can choose a lineal mode or a collateral mode. Collectivists can only write in a collaborative mode, either hierarchical or dialogic/collateral.

Returning to the example of Paul, while Paul uses patriarchal language to describe his relation to Timothy, his ingroup language moves along collateral pathways rather than in hierarchical modes. Timothy and other senders are co-workers, collaborators. One main reason for this is that Paul behaves as fictive father to fictive son, a dynamic rooted in mutual attachment rather than legal authority or entitlement (like that of maternal uncle in a patriarchal world).

The Pauline co-working group, furthermore, consisted of collectivistic persons. The cultural norm was group support and group integrity. In the case of Timothy and Paul (and Silvanus and Sosthenes), the group in question was the Jesus groups they founded, to which they belonged and whose welfare was their priority. What is closed to collectivists like Paul and Timothy is the individualist mode of discourse; a collectivist can only write in a collaborative way, either hierarchically or dialogically, that is, either in a lineal or collateral way. Their letters were successful feats of collaboration, given that modern scholars find that aside from the patchwork of 2 Corinthians, their works have no seams. In fact, some find a distinctive Pauline style, even in most of the 2 Corinthian patches. Yet since the collaborators were not individualistic, it was not mutual trust that produced the effect of 'seamlessness'. Rather it was their sense of group identity, their mutual and reciprocal devotedness to the collectivity, the Jesus groups that they founded and of which they were a part. In any event, while modern successful co-authoring produces a single, unified work of two (or more) individualistic persons, ancient collaboration produced a single, unified work of a group realized by two (or more) collectivistic persons. Just as the folk are responsible writers of their folk songs, although one or two individuals in the group actually composed those songs, the same is true of the collaborated letters of Paul. They are not only letters to the Thessalonians or Corinthians or Philippians, but they are the collective work of the Thessalonians, or Corinthians, or Philippians. Paul and Timothy and Silvanus and Sosthenes were the craftsmen who crafted them, duly inspired by the Spirit of the God of Israel, an inspired quality recognized and appreciated by their recipients. The authority of these letters comes from their reception by the Jesus group to whom they were written and by whom they were preserved.

Conclusion

Christians owe their New Testament documents to their ancestors in faith, and these do include Paul and Timothy and Silvanus and Sosthenes, 'Mark', 'Matthew', 'Luke' and 'John' among others. But more importantly they are indebted to the people who made up the Jesus groups of Thessalonians and Corinthians and Philippians along with Romans, Ephesians, Colossians and the rest. They were responsible for the articulation of the faith in the documents addressed to them. For the New Testament writers and their documents, the 'their' in 'their documents' is as ambiguously oscillating as the 'we' who speak in some of them. I think the collectivistic writers would be very happy with this formulation of their activity as 'authors'.

In conclusion, I should like to list the anachronistic words that have no place in any historical or historically based explanation or description of first-century Israel and its Jesus groups: Christian, Jew, Jewish, Greece (as political region), state, nation, Old Testament, pagan, paganism, eschatology, apocalypse, economics, religion, religious sect, counter-cultural and city. To these I would now add 'author'.

References

Dale, Helen

1994 'Collaborative Writing Interactions in One Ninth-Grade Classroom', *Journal of Educational Research* 87.6: 334-44.

Ede, Lisa, and Andrea Lunsford

2001 'Collaboration and Concepts of Authorship', *PMLA* 116: 354-70.

Lunsford, Andrea, and Lisa Ede

1990 'Rhetoric in a New Key: Women and Collaboration', *Rhetoric Review* 8.2: 234-41.

Malina, Bruce J.

2008 *Timothy: Paul's Closest Associate* (Collegeville, MN: Liturgical Press).

Pilch, John J., and Bruce J. Malina

1998 *Handbook of Biblical Social Values* (Peabody, MA: Hendrickson Publishers).

Racy, A.J.

2003 *Making Music in the Arab World: The Culture and Artistry of Tarab* (Cambridge: Cambridge University Press).

Stokes, T.D., and J.A. Hartley

1989 'Coauthorship, Social Structure and Influence within Specialties', *Social Studies of Science* 19.1: 101-25.

Woodmansee, Martha

1984 'The Genius and the Copyright: Economic and Legal Conditions of the Emergence of the "Author"', *Eighteenth Century Studies* 17.4: 425-48.

Yancey, Kathleen Blake, and Michael Spooner

1998 'A Single Good Mind: Collaboration, Cooperation, and the Writing Self', *College Composition and Communication* 49.1: 45-62.

Jesus beyond Nationalism—in Light of Terrorism

Halvor Moxnes

In Norway, July 22, 2011, will become a defining moment—a moment that shook the basis of our society and questioned our values.[1] The immediate response was an affirmation of the democratic values of our society and expressions of solidarity when confronted with the horrors of terrorism.[2] But in the aftermath of the immediate shock, this unthinkable event must lead to a rethinking of what we have taken for granted; we must question our presuppositions about society, about community and the way we see the world. Will July 22 become what the Second World War was for my parents' generation, what the Vietnam War was for my generation and the fall of the Berlin Wall for many of us: an event that provided a new paradigm for how we viewed the world?

Reflecting on the possible effect of a paradigm shift caused by this act of terrorism, I remembered the description that John H. Elliott gave of the effect of the Vietnam War on biblical scholarship. In his essay 'Refugees, Resident Aliens, and the Church as Counter-Culture', Jack describes how he and other church people were involved with individuals and families affected by the war in Vietnam. Since the moral theology and ethics of the church were primarily personal and individualistic, theologians and church activists 'had little training or means to investigate and understand the social dimensions of war, militarism, corporate structures and interests, and national programs' (2011: 204). This experience of lack of personal and

1. A lone terrorist (Anders Behring Breivik) attacked the government headquarters in Oslo with a car bomb that killed eight people and destroyed several of the main buildings. Afterward he carried out a massacre at the youth camp of the ruling Social Democratic party on an island outside of Oslo, killing sixty-nine people, mostly children and youth.

2. The prime minister, Jens Stoltenberg, vowed that the attack would not hurt Norwegian democracy, and said the proper answer to the violence was 'more democracy and more openness'. Three days after the attack, around 200,000 people responded by taking part in a march carrying roses, illustrating the statement by a girl belonging to the youth movement that had been attacked: 'If one man can show so much hate, think how much love we could show, standing together'.

theological resources for the tasks at hand made him realize that 'to get a handle on such comprehensive and interlocking issues, we needed to look at things from the vantage point of the social sciences' (2011: 204).

Jack and his colleagues in the San Francisco area started to study the social sciences in order to be able to address the social, personal and political issues of the Vietnam War. This engagement also made them realize that such interdisciplinary interactions were necessary to understand other conflicts as well, including those conflicts represented in the Bible. For Jack, that led to his lifelong work on the Bible from a social-science perspective, most impressively in his many contributions to the study of 1 Peter. Importantly, he has done this always with the clear intent that the academic study must be closely linked to the social, personal and political, that is, the way faith in God is integrated in the life of human communities.

Based on Jack's insight that a crisis may change the way we do biblical studies, I want to reflect on the terror of July 22 and how that might affect historical Jesus studies, particularly the prevailing paradigm in European scholarship that has interpreted the historical Jesus in light of the central category of 'nationalism'. My hypothesis is that terrorism has exploited an implicit monocultural emphasis within the nationalism paradigm that conflicts with the *aims* of the historical Jesus. The nationalism paradigm leads to a dystopic vision of society that radically conflicts with the utopian vision of society envisioned by Jesus' 'kingdom' sayings and actions.

Terrorism—A Challenge to the Paradigm of Nationalism

What are the issues that we will have to consider? The 'we' in my question are, of course, first my own 'we', theologians and biblical scholars in Norway; but it extends beyond that restricted circle. Since such acts of terrorism are planned, executed and defended by groups or movements of the extreme right in many parts of the world, they represent a challenge to all who are engaged in theological and biblical studies, and who think that they should make a difference outside narrow academic circles. The most important challenge of the horrors of terrorism is that of the worldview presented by these terrorist acts, and how they require us to rethink our views of the world, of society and the paradigms we use to interpret history.

My own context for these reflections in the aftermath of July 22 was that on that very day I was doing the final proofreading of my book *Jesus and the Rise of Nationalism* (Moxnes 2012).[3] In this book I investigated how, from the beginning of historical Jesus studies in the nineteenth century,

3. The present essay, especially the last sections, builds partially on the last chapter of *Jesus and the Rise of Nationalism*, 'Jesus beyond Nationalism: Imagining a Post-National World' (Moxnes 2012: 179-98).

Jesus was interpreted in light of central categories of nationalism that in this period became the dominant ideology in Europe.[4] Terms like 'people', 'country' and 'nation' were reaffirmed in the presentations of Jesus, with his people described as nation, in a certain geographical region ('the land of Israel'). In the following period and up to the present time, these terms have been used in presentations of the historical Jesus. Therefore they have also had a hermeneutical and political function, since Jesus was seen as a model for society understood in terms of the nation-state.

Since nationalism became the dominant ideology and political system, it was used to establish new states when empires were dismantled or when colonial systems were transformed into independent states. It was soon taken for granted that nation-states were the 'natural' way to organize people and regions. However, while nationalism in Germany started out as a democratic movement it was soon coopted by princes and leaders of autocratic governments and used to reach their political goals, for instance, by Bismarck to establish the German Empire in 1871. A recent example of how nationalism can be used as a political weapon in power struggles was the breakup of the former Yugoslavia in the 1990s, where nationalism was a card skillfully played by the Serbian leader Slobodan Milošević in the division of the federal state into different 'ethnic' entities. The result was one of the most horrible examples of how nationalism could be used to legitimate ethnic cleansing (Denitch 1994).

Dystopia—How Terrorism Exploited the Paradigm of Nationalism

This political use of ethno-nationalism for state terrorism in the former Yugoslavia may illuminate also the ideology behind the terrorist attack upon Norway in 2011. Part of the argumentation of ultraright groups and their legitimating of terrorist acts is an ethno-nationalism with very strong boundaries around a narrow concept of the main social group that makes up the nation. The terrorist attack was not a result of a moment of madness; it was a deliberately planned attack to prevent a development of Europe into Eurabia (Breivik 2011). 'Eurabia' is the codeword in this worldview for a Muslim strategy to take over Europe, supported and made successful by socialists and multiculturalists (Ye'or 2005). According to the terrorist, Europe was now at a critical, even apocalyptic moment in the process toward the abyss, and that justified mass murder and terror.

There is an extreme dystopia underlying this terrorism: it is based on the conviction that mass killings are justified, even required, because history is taking a totally wrong direction. The ideas of the Norwegian terrorist Anders

4. My examples were important European scholars like the Germans F. Schleiermacher and D.F. Strauss, the French E. Renan and the British G.A. Smith.

Behring Breivik, although not based on a strong, 'personal' Christian faith, show similarities with those of American violent apocalyptic groups (Stern 2003: xiv-xvi). He introduced himself using crusader imagery, as a Christian Templar Knight, fighting for a Christian Europe. What his manifesto made clear was that this worldview has wide support on the far right of European politics, in ultranationalist groups and even among intellectuals who subscribe to the 'clash of civilizations' view (Huntington 1993). Muslims are the main targets, but state politics of equal rights and integration of immigrants and refugees are responsible for the rapid development toward the catastrophe. The main danger is presented as a multiculturalism that does not lead to equality, but actually, in the words of a prominent advocate of this view, 'promotes the radical deconstruction of the majority culture, the idea of the nation itself and the values of Western democracy' (Phillips 2006: 62).

For Breivik, the only solution is to create a monocultural society: 'Good welfare arrangements', he opines, 'requires a solid cooperation and [this] is only possible in a monoculture where everyone has complete confidence in everyone else' (Breivik 2011). The idea of a monoculture is that of a society consisting of a 'pure' group, with strong boundaries against impure outsiders—in short, an extreme example of a 'we-against-them' mentality of irreconcilable conflicts between religions and cultures. The desire to create a pure group and to exclude those who do not belong to this group are part of the ideology that has led to the Holocaust and many other examples of genocide. In its weaker form it is part of an ethno-nationalism that privileges one ethnic group as the basis for the nation. This was what happened in the breaking up of Yugoslavia; Bogdan Denitch describes it as '[w]hat happens when *ethnos* becomes *demos*', when ethno-nationalism destroyed the previous coexistence of different groups as one people of one state (Denitch 1994: 51-75).

The defense of 'the traditional cultural group' is a common theme in ultraright movements (Phillips 2006). Focus on the threat from Muslims, as in the Eurabia thesis, and on acts of terrorism as a strategy to combat the threat is not necessarily based on a nationalistic ideology. However, in his defense during his trial in 2012 Breivik presented himself as a 'militant nationalist', along with other Nordic and European militant nationalists (Sørensen 2012). This might have been an attempt by the terrorist to create a broader alliance and to point out similarities with more acceptable forms of nationalism.

Terrorism is not accepted in any society outside extremely small groups, but skepticism toward multiculturalism and 'others' is shared by larger segments of the Norwegian population. Until recently, Norway, like the other Nordic countries, was a very homogenous society, so that 'Norwegian' and 'nation' were synonymous. However, over the last two generations a rapid growth in the number of immigrants, foreign workers, refugees and asylum seekers has made Norway into a much more multicultural and multi-religious society. Among many inhabitants, this development has led to changes in their understanding of 'Norwegian' and 'nation', making these identity markers more inclusive. But among many others it has resulted in resistance, for instance in claims that the meaning of 'Norwegian' should remain 'the same', and that 'newcomers' must accept and adapt to traditional values and norms. As a result, Norway is facing issues and questions that are found in many other societies around the world.

Alternatives to Dystopia: Utopian Visions of a World beyond Nationalism

Is there an alternative to this dystopia of a monocultural Europe being destroyed by multiculturalism and a militant Muslim aggression, a dystopia where regions, different ethnic and religious groups are pitted against one another? There is a long, but little known, tradition of the utopian idea of an inclusive 'world people' instead of the existing divisions into nations and nation-states. Political thinkers from the Stoics to Rousseau and Kant to the internationalist Socialists of the early twentieth century have argued for ideas of a single world community (Özkirimli 2005: 195). However, since the nationalist discourse has been so successful, it has suppressed alternative forms of political thinking and continues to present itself as the 'natural' way of doing politics and of understanding the world.

But we should remember that at its beginning nationalism was itself a utopian idea and not a reality. Early German nationalism provides the best illustration (Moxnes 2012: 1-2). The political structure of Europe in the eighteenth century was not based on the idea of nations; it was built on a system of emperors, kings and princes ruling over territories that sometimes were acquired by war, by marriage or by inheritance. The inhabitants of these territories were subjects of the kings, who ruled 'by the grace of God'. By contrast, nationalism was built on the idea of the *people* as the source of the nation. Inhabitants were not subjects of the king; they were citizens of the state with rights to political participation (Moxnes 2012: 29). But nationalism, especially in its German form, was based on the idea of a unitary group, based on a common language, culture and, increasingly, the notion of a common race.

However, there were strong movements of utopian socialism in the nineteenth and early twentieth centuries that had a vision of a universal solidarity based on the working class cutting across nations and state boundaries. But increasingly the strongest movement in nineteenth-century Europe was nationalism, and the nation-states became the dominant political form and model for the establishment of new states. The nation-states dominated also the attempts to build global structures. After the First World War, the attempt to create an international organization to secure peace, the League of Nations, was based on the structure of nation-states. The same was the case with the United Nations after the Second World War. But even if these organizations were built on a vision of a world at peace, they could not do more than the most powerful member states wanted. This has become painfully visible in the role that the United Nations has been able to play, or, especially, *not* been able to play, in many political crises in the world.

The problems for utopias are partly that communism and fascism presented utopias that had catastrophic consequences in terms of destruction of human lives. That created distrust in grand-scale utopias. But utopias are not totally dead. For instance, the Yale historian Jay M. Winter has attempted to revive utopias not as total concepts but on a more modest scale, as 'utopian moments' (Winter 2006). One of these moments is that of global citizenship. Over against the structures built on nations and states, the concept of global citizenship represents a different approach. It starts from below: it is based on women and men who share a vision of a common humanity, of a global 'civil society' or a 'world people'. The building of a global community of human rights and civil rights starts with individuals, groups and movements. It spreads through social contacts, through news channels, through mobile phones and social media. One significant example is the 'Arab spring', which at least at the outset was democratic and inclusive, for instance, in terms of gender and religion.

But what can visions or utopias actually do up against the structures and powers of the world? What are their possibilities to influence these powers? Winter points us toward an answer when he says that 'Utopia . . . is a fantasy about the limits of the possible, a staging of what we take for granted' (Winter 2006: 3). The philosopher Paul Ricoeur said something similar, that 'utopia extends the boundary line between the possible and the impossible' (Ricoeur 1986: 310). Utopias are at a preparatory stage for actions, but they represent a necessary step. Without visions and ideas that question 'the limits of the possible' we will never move forward to what is now regarded as 'impossible'.

Reading Jesus from a Utopian Perspective: Jesus beyond Nationalism

What will be the result if we see Jesus in a utopian perspective, pushing the limits of the possible and pointing toward a new landscape with different configurations of possible and impossible? One of the results of the acts of terrorism on July 22, 2011, was to make me question the way nationalism has been considered as the only possible way to organize the world. And it made me question nationalism as the context for interpretations of the historical Jesus. My studies of nineteenth-century *Lives* of Jesus by scholars who have influenced historical Jesus scholarship, like Schleiermacher, Strauss and Renan, made me aware of how the historical and hermeneutical Jesus are combined. The descriptions of Jesus in Galilee and Jerusalem by these authors reflected the nationalism of their day. I think that this is still the case; consciously or unconsciously modern ideas of 'people' and 'nation' are present in the descriptions of Jesus in Palestine, notwithstanding the protestations of recent Jesus scholars that they write only as historians.

Bearing in mind both the limitations and the dangers of nationalism and the nation-state as paradigms of interpretation, I will ask if it is possible to read the story of Jesus within a different context. I suggest taking a different position on the present global challenges for the world, based not on a wish for monoculture but on an acceptance of 'cultural complexities' (Moxnes, Blanton and Crossley 2009: 1-7). The term 'cultural complexities' 'connotes the coexistence of two or several cultural traditions, their permutations and their anti-traditions. . . . Mixing, reinterpretation and resistance to mixing and reinterpretation are part and parcel of any culturally complex situation and contribute to making it volatile' (Eriksen 2009: 9-10). I think it makes a difference to ask the questions 'what is a people?' and 'who belongs to a people' from the position of cultural complexities instead of from the point of view of a monocultural nation-state. Likewise, the question of solidarity takes a different form in a situation of cultural complexities than within a monoculture (which Breivik saw as necessary for social cooperation). Since so many of the relations between people in our world are expressed in economic terms, it seems relevant to phrase the question as 'what is the economy of a people'?

What does it mean to raise these questions in interpretations of Jesus? The perspective of utopia is a way to take seriously that Jesus was an apocalyptic prophet, something that cannot be only a historical statement about Jesus in the distant past; hermeneutically it must also imply a reflection of the meaning of such a statement today. I suggest that this means we ought see Jesus and his sayings as representing utopia. Jesus had a name for utopia—the 'kingdom of God'. All who have studied Jesus agree that the kingdom of God was the most central part of his message. He spoke of the kingdom of God in parables and images, and he illustrated his sayings with symbolic acts of healings and communal meals. In what follows I will explore this more fully in consideration of cultural complexities by addressing the questions proposed above: What are a people? What is the economy of a people?

What Are a People?

I propose that it is Jesus' sayings about the kingdom of God, as well as his actions, that represent his answers to the question 'what is a people' and 'what is the economy of the people?' Therefore I will take a different starting point than the recent discussion that focuses on Jesus as a Galilean. This is a trend based on the new interest in Galilee, which started in the 1980s.[5] It may be more correct to say that the interest in Galilee has returned, since it was a topic of importance in the *Lives* of Jesus in the nineteenth century (Moxnes 2001). At that time the common view was that the population was mixed, due to people from different areas and backgrounds being moved into Galilee after the deportation of many of the Israelites in 586 BCE. The terminology of the nineteenth century was 'race', and as is well known, some nineteenth-century scholars (primarily German) suggested that Jesus might come from a racial background that was mixed, and maybe was not 'Jewish' (the Aryan hypothesis; see Heschel 2008).

'Ethnicity' is the new term in common use, coined by social anthropologists after World War II had discredited 'race' (Jones 1997: 55-59). Building on different theories of ethnicity developed by social anthropologists, this has been a popular term among biblical scholars in studies of identity. It has been much used in the discussion of the identity of the Galileans at the time of Jesus (Moxnes 2010: 392-98). In contrast to the general agreement of scholars in the nineteenth century, today the viewpoint that is most accepted is that the Galileans, Jesus included, descended from Judeans, that is, people from Judea in the south, who had populated Galilee in the Hasmonean period. But when drawing conclusions about their ethnicity most scholars use the terms 'Jews', 'Jewish' and 'Judaism', with religious practice as the determinative factor in ethnicity (Reed 2000: 53, 216-18). This appears to be an understanding of 'ethnicity' that is found primarily among scholars of religion; among anthropologists religion does not play as significant a role in definitions of ethnicity. Moreover, 'Jew', 'Jewish' and 'Judaism' are categories that carry with them modern presuppositions. An argument for using these terms, rather than 'Judean', to describe the historical situation of the first century is that they convey the continuity of practice and belief between antiquity and the contemporary situation (Levine 2006: 160-66). The problem with this argument has been pointed out by Sian Jones in his *Archaeology of Ethnicity*, where he warns against 'the desire to trace the genealogy of present peoples back to their imagined primordial origins' (Jones 1997: 1). Thus, it may be the modern desire for heritage and not concerns for adequate ways of describing history that determines the choice of categories. In this discussion it appears that 'Jew' and 'Judaism' are understood in terms of 'normative Judaism'. As a result, scholars who have suggested that the situation of Galilee in the first century was culturally more complex, so that Jesus might have been influenced by Hellenistic philoso-

5. It was initiated by Sean Freyne 1980, and followed by archaeological excavations, historical studies and Jesus studies. For an overview see Crossan and Reed 2001.

phy, have been accused of 'de-judaizing Jesus' (Chancey 2002: 182). This sounds like a claim that there was a 'monocultural Judaism' in Galilee in the first century. Much like in the discussions in the nineteenth century, it appears that Jesus has become a symbol for claims to modern identities that go beyond the historical discussion of Galilee. William E. Arnal has proposed that the aggressive arguments for the Jewishness of Jesus reflect a contemporary desire for stable identities and clear boundaries around communities that understand themselves as coherent and homogenous (Arnal 2005; 2009: 100-110).

These identifications with modern categories of nation and religion are avoided if the ancient term *Ioudaioi* is translated 'Judeans', which would correspond to the association between people and land, as both Jack Elliott (2007) and Philip Esler (2003: 62-74) have convincingly argued. This is an ethnic identity that does not have to be understood as monocultural, but can be complex and fluid (Esler 2003: 49-50, 62-68); recent historical studies describe the situation in Galilee as one in which 'multiple and complex identities may have been almost the rule, rather than the exception' (Zangenberg 2007: 2).

Instead of defining Jesus with a monocultural identity, we need to consider a broader context. Ethnicity is not the only factor to describe identities; other components like gender and class must be included (Jones 2007: 85-86). To understand Jesus it is not sufficient to define him on the basis of his ethnic background; it is important also to consider how he interacted with, influenced and even transformed his environment. My suggestion here corresponds to the way modern biographies pay attention to the question of the *aims* of their subjects when they construct their lives. According to one view that appears to be widespread among historians, individuals should be placed in their context and social structures, but they are not limited to this context. They have 'the capacity of going beyond created structures in order to create others' (Nasaw 2009: 577). This approach makes sense also when we write of the historical Jesus. I suggest that we do not limit our interest in 'who Jesus was' to his ethnic context, but describe him in terms of *what he aimed to do*, how he was an active agent in his life (Meyer 1979).

Jesus was a Judean, and he was living in the context and tradition of Judean beliefs, but within this context he had 'the capacity of going beyond created structures in order to create others'. In his engagement with the Judean world around him, Jesus did not seem to be very concerned with boundaries and ethnicity. If we ask about Jesus' specific contribution, it is not best described as creating a new ethnicity. He did not, in the manner of Paul, speak of breaking down ethnic boundaries between Judean and Greek. Jesus seemed to be more concerned with boundaries *within* his ethnic group, boundaries of gender, class, purity. He broke down divisions that were based on social or moral positions, giving priority to the outsiders and the marginalized; he invited all to an inclusive fellowship around meals. Sociology might describe this as an 'alternative community', a beginning of a new sociability that would link people together in new ways, across boundaries and other distinctions.

Rather than using ethnicity as a measure, it makes more sense to say that Jesus saw society from the perspective of *social categories*, for instance, of outsiders versus insiders, and marginal versus centre. Most importantly, these categories were also purity rules, which always have been central to traditional societies. When Jesus placed himself together with the outsiders, with those at the margins, he seemed to suggest, at least in view of his followers, that this was where God was present. He was clearly aware of and concerned about relations between people, between rich and poor, and elites and outcasts, taking the position of those who suffered exclusion. This is also where Jesus starts in his sayings that speak of 'who belongs in the kingdom?' Spoken in a traditional society based on the household, the kingdom sayings did not replicate the household with its 'inside' members. The model of household as a social group was kept, but its composition was different (Moxnes 2003: 104-107). When Jesus spoke of the household it was not as a closed group; it was a community that included outsiders and the marginalized.

Several examples illustrate this point. In one of the most controversial Jesus sayings, about those who made themselves 'eunuchs for the sake of the kingdom of heaven' (Mt. 19.12), Jesus questioned the very idea of male superiority as the basis for traditional society (Moxnes 2003: 72-90). This saying seems so strange that it has been little used in discussions of the historical Jesus; apparently it has been considered as 'out of place' with regard to Jesus' message. But it actually fits well with other sayings of Jesus about who belongs in the kingdom, sayings that likewise question the 'normal' structures of society. The eunuch saying in Mt. 19.12 is immediately followed by a saying about children (19.13-15). In an act of reversal of the social order, the kingdom is ascribed not to adults but to infants. Starting from the inferiority of the children, Jesus' lifting them up becomes a way of presenting a new picture of the community. Sayings about barren women constitute another group associated with the eunuch saying (Lk. 23.29, *Gos. Thom.* 79). The Lukan version with 'blessed are the barren' (Lk. 23.29) emphasizes the motif of status reversal for women who do not have children, a situation of social shame. In these sayings the male world where everybody knows his or her place, with strict lines and ordered authorities, is turned upside down. It is the least valued; the impure and those of little status are lifted up, blessed and accepted into the kingdom. These are sayings of Jesus that break with the idea of a pure, 'monocultural' society.

These sayings should not be understood as a historical description of Judean society at the time of Jesus, or in general as claims about Judaism versus Christianity. They are polemical sayings; some may also reflect conflict situations at the time when the Gospels were written down. But more importantly, this criticism was also directed at the addressees in groups of Christ-believers. *Hermeneutically*, these sayings against temptations and tendencies to make 'pure' societies are directed at us who are the readers and hearers today; these criticisms cannot be passed on to somebody else, modern Jews for instance. Therefore, the hermeneutical function of these sayings is that they should make present readers consider the categories we use when we speak of 'what are a people'. In particular, we should question all forms of monocultural markers like race and ethnicity that lend themselves to ideas of purity in contrast to the impurity of 'others'.

Translating Jesus' sayings and his relations to people into modern categories requires the broader term *intersectionality* in speaking about human communities. The term *intersectionality* has its background in feminist approaches to discrimination and inequality, and looks at the fluid relationship between socio-cultural categories and identities and how they work together (Kartzow 2012). Intersectionality helps to identify important categories for identities on a much broader scale than nation, people and ethnicity; it considers, for example, race, religion, gender, social class, age, disability, bodies, place and the position of the majority or minority (Schüssler Fiorenza 2009). Intersectionality provides a way to see how various forms of discrimination in many areas and all over the world are connected. These practices go across and beyond nation-states and require global solutions. Intersectionality is a way to look at human lives without being limited by national boundaries, and a way to identify a people by starting from those most in need. Instead of the present policy whereby many nation-states exclude the weakest 'others', a global society would start precisely among them. The utopia of a global human society should be based not on race, ethnicity or power but on the needs people have for peace, food, health, community—needs that in modern terms express the fullness of 'the kingdom of God'.

What Is the Economy of a People?

The question of who makes up a people is intimately linked to the economy of a people. This link is not always understood, or rather, it is often disguised. Economy is presented as something that belongs to nations and politics, for instance, the powerful states that make up the groups of G8 or G20. And even more, economy is considered to be the domain of big, often multinational, companies. Some of them control more resources than the national gross product of many states, and they determine much of the world economy. But when they fail, their failure threatens national economics, so that politicians find themselves pressured into bailing them out from bankruptcy.

In this way economy is presented as a separate, powerful sphere in society with rules of its own. But this is a mystification, and only possible when the links between people and the economy are hidden. The social anthropologist M.H. Nash expressed these links in traditional societies in one sentence: 'Economic action is only part of the system of social action' (Nash 1981: 9). This is an insight that is valid also in modern societies and is exemplified by the large gaps between the rich and the poor. This gap is often supported by the politics of a state, for instance by providing great tax breaks for the rich. Another example is the strong resistance in the United States against a shared responsibility for health coverage and pensions for the poor, a position that many Europeans find difficult to understand. A third example is the economic crises in many European states, especially, but not only, in southern Europe (Greece, Spain and Portugal). The downturn in the economy has led to massive unemployment, especially among young people. Another serious effect of the economic crisis is that in many European countries it has led to attempts to effectively close borders against poor refugees and immigrants, and sometimes to totalitarian measures against 'the others' and xenophobia.

This attitude of excluding 'the others' from the economy of the nation is expressed by Breivik when he writes, 'Good welfare arrangements requires a solid cooperation and [this] is only possible in a monoculture where everyone has complete confidence in everyone else'. This statement from the Norwegian terrorist reflects that he comes from a Nordic society. 'Good welfare arrangements' are recognized as a positive goal, but since they are based on solid cooperation, they require a monocultural society. In the case of Norway the solidarity that Breivik envisages is between 'ethnic Norwegians', excluding those who do not belong to this monoculture, presently at least 10 percent of the Norwegian population.

I wonder what a situation with power and profit for multinational financial corporations and an economic crisis for millions and millions of people means for our reading of the historical Jesus. It seems that we need to do the same as Jack Elliott and his colleagues did in the 1960s, applying 'a socially comprehensive view of things' also to social movements in biblical times (Elliott 2011: 204). But I will do it also with a hermeneutical interest: can the experiences of the economic and social crises of today help us see patterns in Jesus' teachings and actions that will make us see our own situation in a different light? First of all, we must realize that with his kingdom proclamation Jesus was engaged in a criticism of the structure of his society. The meaning of the term 'kingdom of God' has been the subject of endless discussions; but at least one of its meanings is to be found in its contrast to contemporary kingdoms and rulers, that of both Rome and the emperor, and the tetrarchy of Herod Antipas. Jesus' parables are stories about individuals, but they represent 'typical' figures, so that they present what we with a social-science mindset think of as 'structures'.

One particularly relevant example is the way in which the household (*oikos*) is at the centre of many of Jesus' parables and kingdom sayings. The term 'householding' (*oikonomia*) is used both for the organization and rule of the small household and for city–state politics. Thus, in this term the economic and the social are combined, as the social anthropologist Nash pointed out. In an earlier study of the Gospel of Luke, I coined the term 'the economy of the kingdom' to express how Jesus used the terminology of exchange to present an alternative to the dominant system of a Hellenized economy of the time (Moxnes 1988). The specific Hellenistic terminology may be attributed to Luke, but the main perspective is found in parables and sayings that belong to the oldest layers of the Jesus material. Jesus' alternative was modeled on ideal behaviour in a household, but it extended beyond its boundaries. In the parables of the kingdom, God is presented not as king but as a father who gives his children what they need; parental giving and care is emphasized as God's role (e.g. Lk. 11.2-4; 12.22-31; Moxnes 2003: 113-21). Trust in that care is encouraged in those who are addressed, who are those in need. Jesus promises a kingdom where the ideals of security and support associated with the home were extended to those who had left or fallen out of their household and village network. Several sayings and parables of Jesus encourage a break with the social customs of a group of insiders or equals who have a strong cohesion and who share resources and hospitality only between themselves. The Parable of the Wedding Feast (Mt. 22.2-10; Lk. 14.15-24) typically includes as guests 'the poor and crippled and blind and lame' (Lk. 14.21). Thus the economy of the kingdom, understood in the classical tradition as householding, now could stand for the total range of human relations. This household represents a solidarity that breaks with social and cultural divisions. Jesus' parables represent a criticism of insiders and privilege outsiders.

Economy of the Kingdom and Solidarity in World Community

The kingdom of God in Jesus' sayings and actions clearly belong in the domain of utopia in that they push the limits of the possible; but they do so with a clear reference to present conditions and customs. In the context of the present world crisis I find that Jesus' message of the kingdom with the ancient understanding of economy as householding takes on a new and sharpened meaning. It introduces the moral solidarity from the household or family as a model for the economy and the politics of culturally and socially complex communities. Therefore I shall conclude with an attempt to establish a dialogue between my reading of Jesus and his economy of the kingdom and the German philosopher Jürgen Habermas and his reflections on how to create solidarity in a world community beyond the boundaries of the nation (Habermas 2001).

Habermas sees the present situation of the world as a 'post national constellation' and is concerned with the future of democracy. He has for many years been engaged with the question 'What is a people?', seeing the development of a citizens' democracy as the lasting result of the nation-state. His present concern is how this democracy can be preserved and developed in a postnational situation. The main problem, as Habermas views it, is that globalization with globalized markets has threatened the autonomy of nation-states and limited their possibility to shape policies of social solidarity. He sees a global scene under the framework of a restructured United Nations as the next stage in a postnational constellation. The goal for such a global community would be a politics that can end a situation where the economics of the world society are out of democratic control, and instead 'make a change of course toward a world domestic policy' (Habermas 2001: 104-12).

The terminology of 'a world domestic policy' is an interesting neologism. It combines two terms that seem to be at different ends of a spectrum: domestic policy and world politics. Domestic policy represents the social solidarity that is the mark of Habermas's idea of national democracy. When he combines the two terms into 'a world domestic policy', he suggests that such domestic solidarity should be extended to the world as a whole in a global society. His suggestions for how this system of world solidarity should be reached are rather vague. But the term 'a world domestic policy' itself is suggestive; it has a utopian character and could potentially transform the way in which we view the world. Bringing it closer to the terminology of Jesus, we might speak of Habermas's idea as one of 'global householding'. There is a structural similarity between Jesus' paradoxical sayings of household as kingdom and Habermas's vision of a 'world domestic policy'. In both instances, the domestic solidarity of home is transferred from the local to a larger scene: in Jesus' parables from household to kingdom, and in Habermas's from the nation to the world. The goal is to create a new identity and sense of belonging based on a different and larger collectivity than the original one, ultimately the global community.

Jesus after July 22

From their beginning, historical Jesus studies have been part of the discussion of the origin and goals of society. In the nineteenth century this was above all the case in European societies, where philosophers, Bible scholars and theologians used their interpretations of Christian origins to envision the future of Europe (Blanton 2007). The renewed interest in the historical Jesus in the second part of the twentieth century was undertaken with claims by scholars that they were doing 'objective' studies; but a closer reading reveals that they obviously were based on cultural and political presuppositions (Crossley 2008, 2012). In this essay I have tried to be open about the presuppositions I bring to the question of the historical Jesus, not as an excuse but as a necessary part of an interpretation process that shall interact with contemporary issues.

The terrorist attack of July 22, 2011, forced me to face the issue of monocultural nationalism behind the interpretations of Jesus. It became important to explore whether the sayings and actions of Jesus about the kingdom of God could point to an understanding of identity, people and solidarity that was not exclusively based on ethnicity and nation, but that could be inclusive, pointing toward a world community. I started with how Jesus created a community from the margins, with people who were in a marginal position in terms of resources, status and acceptance. He thus challenged the distinctions between insiders and outsiders, 'us' and 'them', that are created and upheld by divisions of ethnicity, culture and religion. The other challenge was the way Jesus' 'economy of the kingdom' was based not on the logic of market and profit but on sharing of resources according to need, extending the trust of close family relations to a larger community.

In the aftermath of July 22 I realized that the quest for the historical Jesus must start with a questioning of my own presuppositions and paradigms. And I think I have come to see that the most important question to ask is not 'Who was Jesus?' but 'What were the aims of Jesus?' (Meyer 1979). This is a historical question, but also a hermeneutical one; it points toward Jesus' vision of a future in the form not of a dystopia but of a utopia.

References

William E. Arnal

2005 *The Symbolic Jesus: Historical Scholarship, Judaism and the Construction of Contemporary Identity* (London: Equinox).

2009 'Jesus as Battleground in a Period of Cultural Complexity', in Moxnes, Blanton and Crossley (2009): 99-117.

Blanton, Ward

2007 *Displacing Christian Origins: Philosophy, Secularity, and the New Testament* (Chicago: University of Chicago Press).

Breivik, Anders Behring

2011 'Manifesto', http://info.publicintelligence.net/AndersBehringBreivik.pdf (accessed July 11, 2014).

Chancey, M.

2002 *The Myth of a Gentile Galilee* (Cambridge: Cambridge University Press).

Crossan, John Dominic, and Jonathan L. Reed

2001 *Excavating Jesus: Beneath the Stones, behind the Texts* (San Francisco, CA: Harper).

Crossley, James G.
2008 *Jesus in an Age of Terror: Scholarly Projects for a New American Century* (London: Equinox).
2012 *Jesus in the Age of Neoliberalism: Quests, Scholarship and Ideology* (Sheffield: Equinox).
Denitch, Bogdan
1994 *Ethnic Nationalism: The Tragic Death of Yugoslavia* (Minneapolis, MN: University of Minnesota Press).
Elliott, John H.
2007 'Jesus the Israelite was neither a "Jew" nor a "Christian": On Correcting Misleading Nomenclature', *JSHJ* 5: 119-54.
2011 'Refugees, Resident Aliens, and the Church as Counter-Culture', in *Liberating Biblical Studies* (ed. L. Dykstra and C. Meyers; The Center and Library for the Bible and Social Justice Series, 1; Eugene, OR: Cascade Books): 197-212.
Eriksen, Thomas Hylland
2009 'What Is Cultural Complexity?' in Moxnes, Blanton and Crossley (2009): 9-24.
Esler, Philip F.
2003 *Conflict and Identity in Romans: The Social Setting of Paul's Letter* (Minneapolis, MN: Fortress Press).
Freyne, Sean
1980 *Galilee, from Alexander the Great to Hadrian, 323 B.C.E. to 135 C.E.: A Study of Second Temple Judaism* (Wilmington, DE: Michael Glazier).
Habermas, Jürgen
2001 *The Postnational Constellation* (ed. with intro. by M. Pensky; Cambridge: Polity).
Heschel, Susannah
2008 *The Aryan Jesus: Christian Theologians and the Bible in Nazi Germany* (Princeton, NJ: Princeton University Press).
Huntington, Samuel P.
1993 'The Clash of Civilizations?' *Foreign Affairs* 72.3: 22-49.
Jones, Sian
1997 *The Archaeology of Ethnicity: Constructing Identities in the Past and Present* (London: Routledge).
Kartzow, Marianne Bjelland
2012 *Destabilizing the Margins. An Intersectional Approach to Early Christian Memory* (Eugene, OR: Wipf & Stock).
Levine, Amy-Jill
2006 *The Misunderstood Jew: The Church and the Scandal of the Jewish Jesus* (New York: Harper).
Meyer, Ben F.
1979 *The Aims of Jesus* (London: SCM).
Moxnes, Halvor
1988 *The Economy of the Kingdom: Social Conflicts and Economic Relations in Luke's Gospel* (Philadelphia, PA: Fortress Press).
2001 'The Construction of Galilee as a Place for the Historical Jesus', *BTB* 31: 26-37, 64-77.
2003 *Putting Jesus in his Place: A Radical Vision of Household and Kingdom* (Louisville, KY: Westminster John Knox).

2010 'Identity in Jesus' Galilee—From Ethnicity to Locative Intersectionality', *BibInt* 18: 390-416.

2012 *Jesus and the Rise of Nationalism: A New Quest for the Nineteenth-Century Historical Jesus* (London: I.B. Tauris).

Moxnes, Halvor, Ward Blanton and James G. Crossley (eds.)

2009 *Jesus beyond Nationalism: Constructing the Historical Jesus in a Period of Cultural Complexity* (London: Equinox).

Nasaw, David

2009 'Historians and Biography: Introduction', *American Historical Review* 114: 573-78.

Nash, M.H.

1981 'The Organization of Economic Life', in *Tribal and Peasant Economy* (ed. G. Dalton; Austin, TX: University of Texas Press): 3-12.

Özkirimli, Umut

2005 *Contemporary Debates on Nationalism: A Critical Engagement* (Basingstoke: Palegrave MacMillan).

Phillips, Melanie

2006 *Londonistan: How Britain Is Creating a Terror State Within* (London: Gibson Square).

Reed, Jonathan L.

2000 *Archaeology and the Galilean Jesus* (Harrisburg, PA: Trinity Press).

Ricoeur, Paul

1986. *Lectures on Ideology and Utopia* (ed. G.H. Taylor; New York: Columbia University Press).

Schüssler Fiorenza, E.

2009 'Introduction: Exploring the Intersections of Race, Gender, Status, and Ethnicity in Early Christian Studies', in *Prejudice and Christian Beginnings* (ed. L. Nasrallah and E. Schüssler Fiorenza; Minneapolis, MN: Fortress Press): 1-23.

Sørensen, Øystein

2012 'Ideologi og galskap. Anders Behring Breiviks totalitære mentalitet', in *Høyreekstremisme: Ideer og bevegelser i Europa* (ed. Ø. Sørensen, B. Hagtvet and B.A. Steine; Oslo: Dreyer): 14-44.

Stern, Jessica

2003 *Terror in the Name of God: Why Religious Militants Kill* (New York: HarperCollins).

Winter, Jay M.

2006 *Dreams of Peace and Freedom: Utopian Moments in the 20th Century* (New Haven, CT: Yale University Press).

Ye'or, Bat

2005 *Eurabia: The Euro-Arab Axis* (Madison, NJ: Fairleigh Dickinson University Press).

Zangenberg, J.

2007 'A Region in Transition: Introducing Religion, Ethnicity and Identity in Ancient Galilee', in *Religion, Ethnicity, and Identity in Ancient Galilee* (ed. J. Zangenberg, H.W. Attridge and D.B. Martin; Tübingen: Mohr Siebeck): 1-10.

Cross-Cultural Psychology and the Bible: A Model for Understanding Jesus' Psychological Development*

John J. Pilch

It is with great admiration that I dedicate this article to honor my long-time friend and colleague, Professor John Hall ('Jack') Elliott. We first met at a Catholic Biblical Association of America Meeting, St John Vianney Seminary, East Aurora, NY, in 1969. Since that time we have collaborated at meetings of the Catholic Biblical Association, the Society of Biblical Literature Annual Meetings, and the Context Group Annual and International Meetings. I have profited immensely not only from his exhaustive bibliographies but especially from his insightful and helpful comments on my various research projects on the way to publication. I look forward to many more years of fellowship and collaboration because (with apologies to Robert Frost), 'we have miles to go before we sleep'. *Ad multos annos*.

Introduction

Except for Luke's pronouncement story about Joseph and Mary finding the twelve-year-old Jesus in the Temple with the teachers (Lk. 2.41-52; see Fitzmyer 1981: 436), the Synoptic Gospels provide no information about Jesus' youth. Inspired by Luke's story, authors of the apocryphal Gospels readily remedied that deficiency. The *Infancy Story of Thomas*, for example, reports what Jesus did and/or said at the ages of five (2.1), six (11.1), eight (12.2), and twelve (19.1-5, a paraphrase of Lk. 2.42-52; see Hennecke-Schneemelcher 1991: 439-52). The apocryphal stories of Jesus are of the same genre as similar stories in other cultures and literatures that created boyhood stories for great figures such as the Buddha in India, Cyrus the Great in Persia, and Alexander the Great in Greece. Making use of contemporary social-scientific work in cross-cultural psychology, I attempt in this essay to construct a model of culturally plausible scenarios about the

* A similar though not identical version of this essay appeared in Pilch 2013.

life-stages of ancient historical figures such as Jesus. Especially relevant to this endeavor is the notion of 'indigenous psychology' suggested in Gary Gregg's path-breaking study (2005) on the psychological dimensions of traditional ways of life in Middle East North Africa (MENA).

Part 1 of this essay, therefore, provides a brief history and defines the nature of cross-cultural psychology. Part 2 sets out elements of the MENA social ecology of psychological development. Part 3 describes Gregg's adaptation of Erikson's ages and stages of psychological development and applies it to biblical data. I lean heavily on Gregg's research. The models in each of these parts of my essay strive to achieve what models customarily do: one, they help to retrieve data; and two, they help to interpret the data retrieved.

Cross-Cultural Psychology

The specific social science used in this essay is cross-cultural psychology. Western psychology (and psychiatry) is a monocultural and ethnocentric science and not at all helpful in analyzing subjects from other cultures (Nsamenang 1992: 9; see also Pilch 1997). It has been appropriately and derisively termed WASP ('Western academic scientific psychology'). Biblical scholars who use Western psychology to interpret ancient sources produce culturally implausible readings of ancient texts and persons (see Van Os 2011). 'Cross-cultural psychology is the study: of similarities and differences in individual psychological functioning in various cultural and ethnocultural groups; of the relationships between psychological variables and socio-cultural, ecological and biological variables; and of ongoing changes in these variables' (Berry *et al.* 2002: 3).

Cross-cultural psychology is similar to, yet very different from, psychological anthropology, which is rooted primarily in anthropology and psychoanalytic psychiatry. Psychological anthropology developed in the 1920s. Anthropologists, mainly from the United States, were interested in psychological explanations of cultural phenomena. In their research, population-level concerns predominated. From the perspective of cross-cultural psychologists, psychological anthropology was 'untidy' and 'fuzzy' (Berry *et al.* 2002: 245, quoting Jahoda 1980 and Hsu 1972). It relied too much on Freud and ignored differences within groups or even between persons. Critics of psychological anthropology point to studies of envy as an example. Psychological literature is nearly silent on this topic, but anthropological literature is rich, based on methods and theories criticized by psychologists, notably personal immersion in the culture. Anthropologists call this 'participant observation', that is, living in a culture not one's own and recording careful observations. Biblical scholars who have applied these anthropological insights to their interpretation of envy in the Bible have uncovered hitherto unnoticed cultural aspects generally unknown to or ignored by Western psychologists (see the studies of envy by Hagedorn-Neyrey 1989; and Elliott 2007).

Cross-cultural psychology began to develop in the 1950s, especially with the work of John Whiting (Whiting and Child 1953) and Robert LeVine (LeVine and LeVine 1963). The cross-cultural approach to psychological anthropology emerged when attention shifted from intensive examinations of single cultures and the collective personality of their members to extensive examinations of relationships across cultures between cultural and personality variables. Cross-cultural psychology is rooted in academic psychology. In its methodology, the predominant focus is on individual processes and inter-individual differences.

From the development of cultural psychology it is but a small step to the next level, developing indigenous psychologies. 'At the present time, the highest priority for MENA psychologists has to be the creation of an *indigenous psychology*—or, perhaps more accurately, of *indigenous psychological theories*' (Gregg 2005: 376). What Western psychology (or WASP) imported into the 'majority world' (preferable to the terms 'developing' or 'Third' World) is equivalent to an imposed etic strategy (Pilch 2011: 5-7). Indigenous psychology, the psychology of a particular culture, is an emic reality (Adair and Diaz-Loving 1999). A working definition of indigenous psychology would be 'a psychology of a cultural group based on the day-to-day behavior of its members, for which local points of view provide the paradigms that guide the collection and interpretation of psychological information' (Berry *et al.* 2002: 459-60). This is the task some biblical scholars pursue in their analysis of ancient texts (see Elliott 2007; Hagedorn-Neyrey 1998; Malina 1994; Pilch 2012).

Elements of the Social Ecology of Psychological Development

Social ecology studies the way in which families interrelate, how they govern themselves and how these social structures adapt to society's ecological setting. Scarcity of resources is very significant (e.g. unpredictable rainfall) in MENA ecology. MENA's *traditional* social ecology is a mixture of three ways of life: pastoral nomadism, peasant agriculture, and urban trades and commerce found throughout the ancient Mediterranean and stretching into central Asia (Gregg 2005: 50). This combination occurred around 9,000 to 5,000 BCE with the emergence of grain cultivation and domestication of animals. But perhaps the most important feature of premodern MENA cultures is the elementary 'face-to-face' character of domination (Gregg 2005: 48). Learning how to respond to varying patterns of authority and domination exercises significant impact on psychological development. Seniors dominate juniors, husbands exercise authority over women, men dominate poorer kinsmen and neighbors, etc. Thus in MENA societies, a key developmental task is accommodating to relationships and decisions about one's life that one has not personally chosen.

Malina (1994) has analyzed face-to-face modes of social interaction in the biblical world, an ancient MENA society. In face-to-face societies, people associate mainly by co-presence. Kinship, which means being born into extended lines of blood relationship, is a key social form of face-to-face integration. However, it should be noted that such a mode of integration is not 'natural'. It has to be learned, hence Gregg's emphasis on learning how to accommodate to and negotiate with varying patterns of domination (Gregg 2005: 49). In rearing boys in MENA, the patriarch must be able to impose his will and expect loyalty and obedience (Pilch 1993).

The key figure in MENA societies is the patriarch, the *paterfamilias* (e.g. Jonah, father of Simon Peter and Andrew). Most traditional MENA societies have kinship systems that are simultaneously *patrilineal* (descent and rights are reckoned in the male line), *patrilocal* (newly married couple lives with the husband's father's family; e.g. Simon Peter, his wife and children live in Jonah's compound at Capharnaum) but also *matrifocal* (e.g. Prov. 31.10-31, where the mother is really in charge of things while the father sits outside with his peers, boasting) and *patriarchal* (men have authority over women, and senior males have authority over juniors). The patriarchal family, therefore, is central in biblical society, and generalized reciprocity rules (i.e. giving to others with no expectation of a repayment or return) apply. Contacts are personal, person-to-person. In other words, each person has or can have direct contact with authority. People see one another as fellow kin, fellow village mates. This develops and promotes a sense of collectivistic personality (though individualism is not lacking, as I point out below). People are either nomadic or settled: they either wander or have fixed places of residence. Further, people relate to authority by co-presence. The interactions are reciprocal and continuous with concrete other persons (see Malina 1994: 13-14).

Another aspect of political social interaction has been dubbed 'face-to-space' interaction (Malina 1994: 14). Here we are concerned with one's *patria* (Greek: *patris*), birthplace or locale of one's immediate ancestry and family (see Danker 2000 *a.v.*; for Jesus, this was Nazareth: Mt. 13.54; Mk 6.1; Lk. 4.23-24); space is people inhabiting a place. Polity is coterminous with kin groups and ancestors, since people remain bound by blood and affinity even after death (hence the significance of ancestry in ancient Israel, e.g., Gen. 35.2-29; 48.29-33; 50.22-26). Adherents of the polity are kin, because birth processes define polity. Information is shared by face-to-face memory. Co-presence is central: individuals are engulfed and supported by the close physical presence of others. Moreover, tradition rooted in shared memory engulfs and supports the group. Space is determined by the place of the kin group's origin and location. The sum of these characteristics of face-to-face interaction fleshes out the impact of such domination upon the psychological development of each individual in the group.

Further, while kinship is the basic building block of psychological development, in MENA societies it has three distinctive features: (1) it is endogamous (the ideal marriage partner is father's brother's daughter, or patrilateral parallel cousin; Gregg 2005: 59); (2) social groupings (family, kin, village, etc.) are segmentary in nature, that is, they are split into smaller competing groups but also sometimes into larger cooperating groups; (3) the basic building blocks are *not* families or lineages but rather 'patronymic associations', that is, fluid and flexible family-like groupings that are extended by patron–client relations with non-kin. Sometimes these groupings seem to resemble what anthropologists call 'lineages'. Malina observes that when persons engage in patron–client relationships, the interactions change from face-to-face to face-to-grace relations (Malina 1994: 6-8, 13-14).

In general, MENA societies of antiquity manifest:

- a symbiotic relationship of agricultural and pastoral ways of life (e.g. Gen. 4.1-2, Cain and Abel)
- tensions between honor-based and religion-based ethical systems, which provide the primary etiquettes of interpersonal relationships. (Honor-based system: lying is an acceptable strategy for maintaining honor [Pilch 1992]; religion-based ethical system: 'Thou shalt not lie to one another' [Lev. 19.11]).
- a 'dialectic' of rural and urban ways of life (see the parables of Jesus, e.g., Lk. 16.1-9).
- the 'endogamous' organization of marriage, family and kinship systems (patriarchs, e.g., Genesis 24; 27.46–28.5; etc.).
- the 'segmentary' nature of social groupings (nested groups are both unified and fractured; MENA proverb: 'I against my brother; I and my brother against our cousin; etc.').
- the centrality of 'patronymic associations'—family-like groupings extended by patron–client relationships—to both social life and individual life cycles. Here ties of kinship, friendship and patron–clientship mingle and merge.

Description of Gregg's Model and its Application to Biblical Data

Gregg builds his models on an adaptation of Erik Erikson's *life-stage theory of development* combined with the theory of *three levels of personality organization* presented by G.H. Mead, Robert LeVine and Dan McAdams.

Gregg reduces Erikson's eight developmental stages to six since MENA research is not specific enough to address the eight. The six life stages are:

1. infancy through the second year
2. early childhood, ages three to seven
3. late childhood, ages seven to puberty
4. adolescence from puberty to late teens
5. young adulthood from late teens to mid-twenties
6. adulthood from mid-twenties on (2005: 136).

I discuss Gregg's use of levels of personality organization in the appropriate places below.

A recent lexical semantic study (with no interest in psychological development) offers the following Hebrew words that describe stages of the (male) life cycle in the Bible (Eng 2011: 127):

ילד ('infant'; zero to three years)
נער קטן / נער ('boy'; three to thirteen years)
נער ('young man'; thirteen to twenty-five years)
גבר / איש ('mature, adult'; twenty-five to sixty years)
זקן ('old age'; sixty to seventy years)
טובה שׂיבה / ימים שׂבע / מאד זקן ('extreme old age'; over seventy years)

While not paying explicit attention to psychological development, biblical authors appear to have consistently identified life stages corresponding to those proposed by contemporary social scientists.

Stage1: Infancy through the Second Year

The relevant features of Stage 1 development concern conception and birth, naming, swaddling, nursing and weaning. The basic MENA society notion of how conception and birth take places is that women are considered as the field; males provide the seed (Wis. 7.1-2). The child is presumed to get its bones from the father, and blood (or sometimes flesh) from mother. In traditional contexts, motherhood fulfills a woman's destiny, confirms her adult status and solidifies her marriage—all of which are put in jeopardy by failure to conceive (as with Hannah in 1 Samuel 1). Also in MENA societies, conception by wind/spirit takes place with animals and with humans (see Martin 2010). Thus Mary's conception of Jesus by a 'Holy Wind' (Holy Spirit) is not as culturally puzzling in 'traditional' MENA societies as in modern, Western scientific societies. A pregnant woman also becomes vulnerable to evil spirits and the evil eye, and she may conceal her pregnancy as long as possible.

In MENA societies a child is typically named after seven days. In the biblical world, this is also when boys are circumcised (Lk. 1.59; 2.21; Lev.

12.2). Research indicates that in many societies that circumcise boys, the foreskin is regarded as a bit of feminine tissue that must be removed to masculinize the penis (Gregg 2005: 200). However, being circumcised at this young age, the boy remains in the woman's world. Thus, for the biblical world, circumcision does not mark a transition since there is no transition. Thus, interpreting the rite is tricky and confusing. Scholars think, however, that it may play a role in reproducing the patriarchal orientation. Boys blame the mothers as mutilators (because they allowed it) and direct anger toward them and not toward the fathers. This is because the infant is taken from the women's world and returned there after the procedure. In the life of Jesus, this experience might be one explanation (among others) for his apparently negative exchanges with his mother.

After the birth, the mother and baby usually observe a forty-day period of seclusion, during which her relatives care for her as she cares for her baby (Lk. 1.56, Mary plausibly helps Elizabeth). The loss of blood—said to be 'black' or 'dirty' just like no-longer-productive menstrual blood—and the opening of the body puts the mother in a state of pollution (Leviticus 12; Lk. 2.22-24, 39). The woman is protectively enclosed or 'covered' during the period in which her body is 'open', impure and vulnerable (see the Kypseli video, and compare the old Christian custom of 'churching', that is, allowing a woman to return to public worship after forty days of confinement by conferring a special blessing at the door of the church).

Infants are swaddled (Wis. 7.4; Lk. 2.7, 12). However, in most of MENA societies, women carry infants in slings and gradually move them from the chest to the hip and to the back (see Nemet-Nejat 1998: 130, for ancient Mesopotamia). Swaddling usually extends only for the first five months. This practice contrasts with the 'cradle' or 'crib' in Western or European cultures. Mothers give many different 'health' explanations for the practice: swaddling keeps the baby warm, makes its limbs straight and strong; it is also easier to keep a child clean. A cultural explanation is that swaddling confines the infant and teaches it that s/he is not 'free', cannot wave his/her arms wildly but must lie still. She or he is not in control of life; others are.

Throughout the MENA region, mothers nurse frequently and on demand. In some instances, it may be as much as fifteen to twenty times a day! Nursing is the immediate response to restlessness, because in this MENA world, the ideal child is a quiet child. The child should be 'seen and not heard'. Most women nurse up to the second or third year (or the next pregnancy). 'I enveloped you for nine months and have fed you with my breast' is supposed to be one of the most effective and compelling entreaties in MENA societies (Gregg 2005: 166; Boddy 1989: 51; compare the mother of the Maccabees in 2 Macc. 7.27). Women use this plea when they want obedience or assistance in later years. MENA's 'pediatric model' seems to facilitate the development of 'secure attachment' and of what Erikson terms 'basic trust'. (In general, a pediatric model of raising children promotes subservience; a pedagogic model promotes curiosity.) The pediatric model also soothes distress and modulates emotional excitement. Perhaps most of all, it builds a strong bond of compassion and interdependence between mother and infant. This bond becomes so strong and intense that in the West among adults it is viewed as co-dependency.

This pediatric period ends with weaning. However, this diminishing maternal care is replaced by a wider circle of caretakers, namely, all the women of the household or village. This delays individuation, but group attachment grows. Identification now with the household forms a 'group self' that serves as a psychological 'bridge' from the interdependent mother–son dyad to the larger society beyond the family (collectivism). Nevertheless, weaning is abrupt and often traumatic. Boys are breast-fed longer than girls to promote an interdependence of mother and son that will serve her well in the future, a form of 'social security'. Msefer (1985) believes that prolonged and abruptly terminated indulgence roots the pervasive fear of the evil eye, evil spirits and other malevolent beings, since the mother is not there to protect the child as before. Now extended families become an important 'object' to the weaned child. Mediterranean ethnographies suggest that over and above people's attachments to individual members of their households, they become attached to the 'house' as an idealized, honor-bearing entity that persists through generations as individuals come and go (*beth 'ab*). Family or 'house' serves as a 'self object', an 'other in which one participates and derives a sense of self' (Gregg 2005: 176).

Swaddling and nursing on demand are used to quiet crying, carrying and co-sleeping. These coalesce to establish a protective, soothing, excitation-dampening maternal bond during the first year or so. Mothers talk to children, but these are nothing at all like the stimulating, face-to-face conversations typical of American mothers. As Judy Brink observes, 'These infants do not have toys to play with and do not form attachments to blankets or dolls as do American children. They learn to play with people, not inanimate objects' (Brink 1995). However, these child-rearing practices associated with birth and infant care involve serious development discontinuities. In addition, they establish sharply different trajectories for boys and girls. For further results of these practices see French (1988).

Stage 2. Early Childhood (Ages Three to Seven): Level 1 of Personality Organization

This is the stage at which Level 1 of personality organization begins to develop. This level of personality organization contains three broad classes of dispositional traits:

1. *basic, probably genetically determined*, parameters of individual functioning.
2. the *motivational residues* of early experience. The child's representations of its wishes and fears concerning other persons in its early life provide unconscious prototypes for its *emotional response to others in subsequent environments*.
3. *adaptive organizations* that monitor and regulate responses to stimuli coming from the external environment and internal needs.

This 'core personality' thus encompasses the 'emergent self', 'the core self', 'the subjective self' and 'the verbal self' that emerge in succession in infancy and early childhood, as well as the 'personal disposition' that Dan McAdams theorizes as forming 'Level 1' personality characteristics (McAdams 1995: 365-96).

Toddlers now bereft of breastfeeding (security, all the more significant for boys but still serious for both genders because of food shortages) develop an interactional style of 'assertive dependency' and learn modesty and politeness relative to differing situations and kin relations. These are useful in subsequent kinship and patron–client relationships. In other words, boys and girls learn how to manipulate situations to their advantage. They become masters at it. Particularly between the ages of five and seven there is a shift from a *pediatric model* of infant care (insures survival) to an *apprenticeship-and-obedience model* of child rearing in MENA societies. We view this development of Level 1 personality in two sections (1) attachments and social behavior, and (2) gender development.

Attachments and Social Behavior

Relevant aspects of attachments and social behavior are maternal caretaking, poor health and fears of invisible beings, hunger and food supply, sibling rivalry, and children's social groups. The caretaking role of mothers shifts from weaned children to new infants. Older sisters or female cousins from age five to fifteen often become a toddler's primary caretakers, carrying them in slings on their backs, cleaning and feeding them, and taking them along on errands. Mothers sometimes hit the toddlers, which contributes to an aggressive style of dependency (competition). The child now has to 'fight' with siblings as it were to get its mother's attention. The child is raised in the women's quarters, and fathers have little contact and do little caretaking with infants and toddlers.

The period between age two to four is typically filled with health problems in MENA societies, perhaps due to reduced maternal care. In traditional milieus, many childhood ailments are believed to be caused by evil spirits (possession, e.g., Mt. 17.14-21) and the evil eye. Anxious parents take a great many precautions. Since boys are so prized in MENA cultures, parents sometimes dress young boys like girls, and they affix apotropaic talismans (e.g. blue stones or scarlet ribbons) to their clothing to protect against the evil eye. Some problems thought to be caused by evil eye are illnesses, nightmares, 'hysterical' paralyses, illicit sexual thoughts, accidents, injuries and even death. The Gospels report the near death or death of a twelve-year-old girl whom Jesus restored to life and well-being (Mk 5.22-24, 35-43//Mt. 9.18-19, 23-26//Lk. 9.40-42, 49-53). Given the high rates of infant and child mortality in ancient MENA societies, this girl was fortunate to have survived to the age of twelve. She may well have been the envy of others in the village who lost children at an early age. It is culturally plausible that this girl may have been the victim of the evil eye cast by the other villagers (Pilch 2011: 89-105). In societies that believe in the evil eye, perfectly healthy members can die if they are convinced someone has cast it upon them.

During childhood, food continues to come primarily from the mother and other household women, both because women and children customarily eat separated from the men (Mt. 14.13-21, esp. v. 21), and because women work with food nearly all day long and intermittently give morsels to children (see Kypseli video). However, it is important to remember that the context was endemic hunger, a condition of long-term food deprivation (MacDonald 2008: 58). Eating meat was a rarity, and availability of grains depended on unpredictable and often insufficient rain. Moreover, taxation was so high (perhaps as high as 40 to 60 percent of crop production) that it is more appropriately called exploitation. In such circumstances, endemic hunger led to chronic malnutrition. One can readily appreciate the value of developing assertive dependency by a youngster in the struggle for the limited good, food; yet the mother and other women still might not have had much to share with the youngsters.

Sibling rivalry is openly encouraged by the shaming of a child with the strategy of comparing him with another. The purpose of this strategy is to encourage competitiveness. Paul gives a good example of a similar strategy (Rom. 11.11, 13). According to Paul, since God's firstborn (Israel) did not respond to divine overtures, God was disappointed and therefore welcomed non-Israelites, but not a great number and only on a temporary basis in order to make Israel jealous (Malina and Pilch 2006: 74). With his preaching, Paul intended to do the same (Rom. 11.14). In traditional MENA societies, the mother generally bonds with the firstborn. However, the firstborn does not always respond appropriately. To elicit a favorable response, the mother will give the firstborn a gift, then tear it away and give it to another sibling, hoping to make the firstborn jealous and to win his affection and devotion. Parents do not provoke such competition from girls, whom they rarely tease with sibling comparisons.

In the world of 'limited good', children—especially boys—need to become assertive, competitive, clever and persistent. Gregg (2005: 179) prefers the term 'assertive dependency' (rather than 'aggressive dependency') for it lays an interpersonal foundation for building subsequent client–patron relations with both kin and non-kin patrons.

As MENA societies traditionally follow the patrilineal-extended pattern, they should be expected to facilitate more 'authoritarian-aggressive' social behavior than 'sociable-intimate'. In MENA societies, segregation of men and women, both inside and outside the household, is often more pronounced than in sub-Saharan Africa. MENA ethnographers note relatively high levels of competitive aggression among children. Older siblings and cousins are expected to act as parental authorities with younger ones, often carrying out this role with zest as they grow older and begin to be given responsibility for maintaining the family's honor in the community.

According to John Meier, Jesus probably had brothers and sisters. 'Hence, from a purely philological and historical point of view, the most probable opinion is that the brothers and sisters of Jesus [mentioned in the NT] were his siblings' (Meier 1991: 332). These were plausibly children of Joseph and Mary after the birth of Jesus. Joseph, of course, was not Jesus' father. The siblings named in the New Testament are James, Joseph, Simon and Judas, and unnamed sisters (Mt. 13.55-56//Mk 6.3). Jesus was apparently the oldest. This position entails obligations toward the siblings, not to mention 'social security' for his mother after the death of Joseph. Perhaps this explains why there is no evidence that Jesus was married. How did he relate to his younger siblings, and they to him? What impact did this have on his and their psychological development? In his adult life, we are told 'even his brothers did not believe in him' (Jn 7.5). On another occasion, his family attempted to save his life by declaring him 'crazy' after he had seriously offended powerful authorities who resolved to destroy him (Mk 3.6, 21-22).

Gender Development

Gender differences seem to emerge around five to seven years of age. Gender is constituted of three surprisingly independent components, formed by different processes and different time schedules: *gender role behaviors*, *gender identity*, and *sexual orientation*.

MENA societies' child care and socialization practices described above entail the modeling/reinforcement/punishment-driven learning of *gender role behaviors:* how to act as a boy or girl. About the ages of five to seven they learn this. By five or six years, girls are assigned the responsibility of helping their mothers, thus becoming 'nurturant-responsible'. Boys at this age have fewer tasks that require cooperation or caretaking, are less likely to be closely supervised, and more likely to be prodded or teased into competition, that is, to become more 'assertively dependent' or 'dependent-dominant'.

Biological maleness and femaleness usually solidifies before the age of three. Constructing masculine and feminine *gender identity*, however, is a much more complex process that takes longer.

Sexual orientation appears both more biologically based and culturally determined than it does the outcome of parent–child interactions. Boys and girls start out life 'as if' they were girls, strongly attached to their mothers. They each develop a core sense of self that is fundamentally feminine. Then the developmental tasks of boys and girls diverge. Girls have to shift erotic and love attachment from mothers to men, while retaining their core feminine sense of self and identification with mother. By contrast, boys must shift identification and sense of self from early femininity to an achieved masculinity, while retaining their sensual attachment to women. For boys, this results in 'male gender ambiguity'. The New Testament gives two hints of gender ambiguity. As he laments over the Holy City—'O Jerusalem, Jerusalem, killing the prophets and stoning those who are sent to you'—Jesus continues: 'How often would I have gathered your children together as a hen gathers her brood under her wings, and you would not' (Mt. 23.37-39). The image of rooster would be more appropriate than mother hen. Or Paul writing to the Jesus groups in Galatia: 'My children, I am going through the pain of giving birth to you all over again, until Christ is formed in you' (Gal. 4.19). Even if anachronistically Paul were familiar with and experienced in the Lamaze method, he would have no real empathy for birth pains.

The prevailing cultural model for rearing boys into men entails 'feminizing' or 'emasculating' them by forcing their subjection to harsh authority (usually in the age seven to twelve period), which then motivates them to achieve and prove their manhood via competition with peers, domination of women and juniors, and identification with figures of authority. The Wisdom literature (notably Proverbs) that prescribes severe physical discipline of young boys proposes this as a strategy for making a man out of possibly effeminate young boys who were raised by all the women with little to no male influence (See Pilch 1993; 1995). This results in a kind of machismo masculinity, whereby boys reject their 'feminine' side but idealize and worship the woman as mother or virgin while despising the loose or wanton woman.

Stage 3 Late Childhood (Ages Seven–Twelve to Puberty): Level 2 of Personality Organization

The self-concept developed in Level 1 is now especially shaped by requirements of the honor–modesty system and also religious values and practices characteristic of Level 2 of personality organization. To describe the Level

2 structures shaped by these two predominant value systems, Gregg uses the terms *sentiment* rather than 'emotion', *motive* rather than 'trait', and *social persona* (or *social self*) rather than self (Gregg 2005: 106).

A *sentiment* is longer lasting than an emotion. It entails an active, continuous pursuit or avoidance of a state. The honor–modesty system shapes universal human emotions into culturally distinctive sentiments: 'honor', 'modesty' and 'shame'. These further include sentiments of purity and pollution (see Leviticus), a sense of blessedness and its depletion (blessedness, e.g., Psalm 1; depletion of blessedness, e.g., anxiety over evil eye, Sir. 31.13; 37.11), a sense of receiving divine mercy and compassion (Exod. 33.19; Rom. 9.15); an 'awe' or 'fear' of divine power and judgment (Prov. 1.7; frequent in Proverbs and Sirach), and, closely allied with this awe, sentiments of righteousness and propriety associated with taking Jesus as one's model and staying on 'the straight path' of virtue (1 Cor. 4.16). These may converge into a sense of oneness or union with God, which overcomes a competing sense of estrangement from the divine.

A *motive* influences the long-term course of lives. The honor–modesty system fashions a set of *needs* or *motives* that define important dimensions of individual personality in the MENA culture area. The concepts of *need* or *motive* best describe how honor, modesty and shame become psychological dispositions. Four psychological needs or motives stand out as important dimensions of individual variation in MENA societies: a need for purification (e.g. Leviticus), a need for blessedness (e.g. Temple pilgrimages), propriety (e.g. fear of God fuels the need for propriety), and mercy (understood as refuge and haven from social strife, life disappointments, sinful acts, or the terror of mortality). Mercy is equivalent to paying one's debt of gratitude. Thus, one who seeks mercy equivalently says, 'I need your help right now, and you owe me!' (Malina 2009: 93).

MENA research indicates that a pair of potentially complementary *social personae* (or *social selves*) coalesce during this period, organized around the culture's predominant value orientations: the honor–modesty system and ancient Israel. These value orientations mold culturally distinctive sentiments, motives and social selves that begin to emerge after viewing one's self from the perspective of society's primary roles and values. The *pediatric model* of care now evolves into an *apprenticeship and obedience model*. The submission and obedience fostered by the pediatric model is now further strengthened as respect for parents. This forces children to learn their adult responsibilities. Boys have to learn how to fight for family, village and kin group.

'By the age of six or seven, many children will have been cared for, comforted, ordered about, reprimanded, entertained, and taught by a variety of older siblings, grandparents, and aunts and uncles' (Gregg 2005: 216). A boy is called by relationship ('my grandson'), and only after he has learned his kinship lesson is he called by his given name. The challenge, therefore, is to learn how to deal with patronymic relations. Recall that this is more than the family, even the extended family. Children must learn a core set of values, etiquettes and strategies needed to maneuver within the patronymic association and the larger community. These strategies include deference (a sort of cultural humility calculated to obtain a request from another); hospitality (reciprocity for dyadic relations); assertive dependence (competition with siblings for limited goods); sacrifice (to force a response from others); protection (girls nurture siblings, boys defend them); intimidation (in order to maintain one's status); and mediation (strategies for defusing potential hostility, e.g., Mt. 5.9; Lk. 12.13-21). This family or kin-centered 'we' consolidates in late childhood with mastery of the just-mentioned repertoire of etiquettes, forming an honor-oriented *social self* or *social persona*.

The cultural model of fatherhood in MENA societies requires a shift from warmth, affection and playfulness (even limited as it may have been) in early childhood to distance, formality and discipline during this period (late childhood). In biblical society, it is possible that the father played little to no role in a child's life during early childhood. The majority of emotional care came from the women of the household. What the father must do when a boy enters the men's world at puberty is teach the boy 'how to be a man'. As noted above, that is one purpose of physical discipline of sons recommended in Proverbs (e.g. Prov. 13.24; see Pilch 1993; 1995).

The predominant cultural model prescribes no fundamental change in mothering during late childhood as it does for fathers. Mothers spontaneously continue indulgent nurturing as a natural and necessary counterweight to the father's 'new' responsibility to impose authority, especially for boys. Mothers employ such strategies as nurturing, indulgence and protection to build interdependent loyalties. This is especially true with sons. Since affection and companionship are often lacking in the (arranged) marriage (viz. Fathers' Brother's Daughter, or FBD), mothers turn to sons for emotional ties. Moreover, the son is social security after the death of the husband. 'Mother and son constitute the only heterosexual couple that remains a stable unit in this patrilineal and patriarchal society' (Gregg 2005: 226). She also has to be able to control the daughters-in-law but will be aided in this task by daughters, at least until they marry and move into their husband's patriarch's compound. *Idealization* of the mother by her sons serves as a linchpin of the patriarchal system, constraining women to the role of nurturing mother, and men to the role of her guardian (Stevens 1973). At the heart of the patriarchal order there lies a psychological 'kingdom of Mothers'.

Throughout late childhood, gender differentiation increases still further. This manifests itself mainly in terms of the spaces in which boys and girls move, and the activities in which they take part. Girls experience continuity (learn homemaking skills, but more segregated from boys); boys experience discontinuity (paternal harshness replaces maternal warmth). With both male authorities and peers, boys face tests of strength, courage, endurance, and self-control and may be teasingly or humiliatingly insulted as 'donkeys', 'women', or 'homosexuals', or threatened with castration. Emerging from intense nurturing by the women, the adolescent boy will spend the rest of his life trying to learn how to be a man and to prove it, endlessly.

Traditional parents don't usually play with children of this age (though they do play with younger ones). Neither do they give them toys nor organize their play. Children associate mainly with relatives and neighbors, so most relationships continue to be governed by principles of familial hierarchy. As already noted, they learn the etiquettes of deference and how to relate to various family members and associates in the patronymic association.

Children's groups are as important to their socialization as family interaction at this stage. Children gain vital experience with peers in the interpersonal strategies—assertive dependence, sacrifice, protection, intimidation, mediation and so on as noted above—that they later will use to build networks of personal relations. It is practice or rehearsal that complements what they learn in family interaction.

Girls play separately and differently from the boys. Girls' games imitate women's chores. Many rhyming games that girls play tend to focus on personal possessions, sexual organs and excrements. In the context of play this bawdy language is beyond reprimand.

Boys' peer play and organized games constitute an essential arena for establishing a sense of masculinity. The games include three key elements: (1) the negotiation of hierarchical senior–junior, leader–follower, ruler–commoner dyads, important for adult life; (2) courageous physical competition (and insults) against equals; and (3) domination of girls and 'womanly' boys. Quite likely the children's games to which Jesus referred (Mt. 11.17-18) involved only boys. Games provide youngsters with an opportunity to experience various roles and scenarios that help them learn to see the self from the perspective of the Generalized Other ('who do people say I am?' [Mk 8.27]; on games, see Pilch 2012: 273-78). If MENA's social order, as Eickelman (2002) writes, is woven of 'dyadic relations of domination and subordination', then much of the learning of attitudes, styles and strategies appropriate to both stances appears to be rehearsed in late childhood play.

In addition to sentiments and motives related to states of purity–pollution, children also develop a sense of seeking to please God, an awe and often fear of God (that is, knowing who God is and who one is as a human being; see Ps. 111.10), a sense of receiving divine mercy and compassion when needed. Very likely these sentiments help consolidate a 'social self'—that is, a self as viewed from the perspective of a Generalized Other consisting of God, the prophets, divine and demonic beings, and the community of believers into which the child is maturing. The reaction of fellow townspeople to Jesus' behavior in the synagogue at Nazareth indicates that they did not approve of the 'social self' that Jesus constructed for himself (Mk 6.1-6; Lk. 4.16-20; Mt. 13.53-58).

Gregg observes that traditional Moroccan and probably MENA society did not recognize adolescence as a developmental period (Gregg 2005: 252). It was quite brief for boys, and practically didn't exist for girls. The major psychological task of this period consisted of subordinating burgeoning individualistic strivings to family and community authority (collectivism). Adolescence in MENA societies—as in nearly all traditional societies—ended with marriage. Girls married within two years of puberty in 60 percent of societies examined.

For boys, new developmental themes now come to the fore. Rough games evolve into more serious business of 'performing manhood' (machismo). These may entail deadly games of challenge and riposte, dramatic displays of filial loyalty, or ascetic feats of religious devotion. By late childhood most are familiar with bawdy talk and romantic poetry and song. The play in which boys engage entails a good deal of obscene, sexual and explicitly phallic imagery. It persists into adulthood. This raises a point worth pursuing. 'Then Saul's anger was kindled against Jonathan, and he said to him, "You son of a perverse, rebellious woman, do I not know that you have chosen the son of Jesses to your own *shame*, and to the same of your mother's *nakedness*?"' (1 Sam. 20.30 [NJB translates 'rebellious woman' as 'slut']). 'Shame' and 'nakedness' in Hebrew refer to the genitals. Mayer (1983) says that in the collected sayings of Jesus, he uses seventy adjectives from daily, low-class living. For example, Jesus uses a Greek word for toilet (*aphedron*, Mt. 15.17; Mk 7.19) that is definitely low class. It is best translated as 'shit house', a good Greek proletarian word. The upper classes used the word *ochetos* (Mk 7.19 D). Even today, MENA society adolescents begin telephone conversations with an exchange of friendly obscenities before getting to the business at hand. Is Jesus' use of the insulting word *hypokritēs* in Matthew when referring to the Pharisees a remnant of his adolescence though not as obscene as Saul's statement? (Pilch 2012: 158-62). For boys in traditional milieus, there may still remain some years of 'youth' between sexual maturity and marriage. The challenges at this period are that they can hone, test and perform the components of honorable manhood and assimilate the symbolic associations of masculinity: outside rather than inside, right rather than left, seed rather than soil, bone rather than flesh, pure rather than pollution, etc.

Stage 5. Early Adulthood (Late Teens to Mid-Twenties): Level 3 of Personality Organization

The characteristic feature of Level 3 of personality organization is the social self. The social persona is an identity anchored in a life story. Religious belief and practices constitute a *social persona* that coexists alongside the *social persona* formed by internalizing the honor–modesty system (see above). There is a large literature on identity in MENA societies but little is by psychologists. The internalization of cultural constructions of *social personae* in accord with the imperatives of honor–modesty and religion (as, e.g., in the religion of ancient Israel) does not assign identities, but challenges individuals to fashion them in terms of these two value systems. The development of the third level of personality organization—for which Gregg uses Erikson's term *identity*—begins with the individual taking up the challenge to prove that he or she can live up to the culturally assigned ideals, or to revise or reject those ideals (Pilch 2012: 158-62).

The culture's 'sociocentric' emphasis on familial loyalty coexists with powerful individualistic imperatives, and these readily come into conflict in late adolescence and early adulthood. The majority of young men and women resolve these in favor of family loyalties, making the key psychological 'task' one of renouncing individualistic strivings—rather than that of separating from familiar interdependencies and achieving autonomy, as Western theories assume (Pilch 2012: 116-21).

In traditional milieus, adolescents become full participants in the honor–modesty system and religion (again, e.g., in the religion of ancient Israel). The honor system presented men with a prototype of a truly honorable man along with a complement (idealized, of course): the modest and fecund woman, as well as a number of revolting *opposites,* in particular, the weak, cowardly, or unbalanced man (e.g. Prov. 11.17, 20-21; 12.8) and the dishonorable and/or barren woman (Prov. 2.16; 5.3; 5.20; etc). The image of woman as polluting, lacking reason, subject to desires and therefore a source of chaos and discord provides men with a ready vehicle for projectively denying their own negative qualities as they define their identities in terms of purity, reason and self-control.

Stage 6 Mature Adulthood

Western theories of adult development appear to have limited applicability to MENA societies. Scholars conjecture that women may not have lived longer than thirty, and men longer than forty years (Meyers 1997: 28). Given the harsh demands of peasant life, they had little time for anything else but to struggle for survival. Individualism versus collectivism of MENA societies emerges as an important topic of discussion among contemporary researchers, especially since MENA societies are assumed to be purely and exclusively 'collectivist' (Pilch 2012: 119). Kagitcibasi (1996: 96-97) and Joseph (1999: 13) argue that MENA societies cannot be termed 'collectivist' but that they foster forms of 'connectivity' or 'interrelatedness' in some spheres of life and individualism in others.

Studies of MENA women show that they often acquire a good deal of power and prestige in mid-life and later. Think of Sarah commanding a reluctant Abraham to cast out Hagar and her son (Gen. 21.8-14), or Rebecca forcing her son Jacob to deceive his father and her husband (Genesis 27), or Bathsheba arranging for Solomon to succeed David (1 Kings 1).

Two significant issues that bear on psychological development in adulthood in MENA societies are (1) the 'sociocentrism' versus 'egocentrism' of MENA culture and self as already noted, and (2) culturally patterned shifts in gender orientation in mid- and later-life, that is, becoming more masculinely feminine, and more femininely masculine.

Gregg briefly summarizes research on basic personality traits (introversion–extroversion and neuroticism; and the 'Big Five' traits) and on anxiety (Gregg 2005: 326-34). The Big Five traits are (1) surgency (or extroversion), (2) agreeableness, (3) conscientiousness, (4) emotional stability (or neuroticism) and (5) culture (or intellect or openness to experience; Gregg 2005: 108; Wiggins 1996).

Introversion–extroversion and neuroticism are probably inherited dimensions of personality. In general, the studies of these personality traits provide relatively strong evidence that general anxiety levels tend to be higher in MENA societies than in Western ones, and higher than in at least some other developing societies (e.g. '*ataque de nervios*'; see Guarnaccia and Rogler 1999). As already noted, 'Several non-Western psychologists have argued that individualism and collectivism do not form a continuum on which cultures can be ranked, and proposed that the (1) I and C are specific to *domains* of life, or (2) I and C form independent *dimensions*, so a person can be "high" or "low" on both' (Gregg 2005: 336-37). Kagitcibasi argues that individualism versus collectivism is perhaps the most significant dimension on which cultures differ. However, either one of these does not form a single dimension that characterizes all social domains. She also believes that the psychological orientations of 'separatedness and relatedness' coexist in most individuals, who can experience them either in conflict or confluence (see Gregg 2005: 337).

Suad Joseph uses the term 'connectivity' to describe the strongly interdependent bonds that develop in MENA society families. These differ from Western ideals of nuclear family relations in that they emphasize group ties over individuality and in that they blend bonds of love and nurturing with the 'patriarchal' authority of men over women and seniors over juniors. It is this blending of affection and authority, she believes, that makes the patriarchal system so resilient: 'in patriarchal societies connectivity can become a psychodynamic instrument of domination' (Joseph 1999: 13). Connectivity exists side by side with individualism in the same culture, and perhaps even in the same person. These are not oppositional polarities.

As in many cultures that emphasize more 'machismo' ideals of manhood, in MENA societies gender differentiation appears to peak in early adulthood. Then in mid-life, men and women begin to develop in ways that can be construed as significant modifications, if not reversals, of the 'masculinity' and 'femininity' they fashioned as young adults. Or as noted earlier, one becomes more masculinely feminine or more femininely masculine. While 'gender reversal' is probably not an appropriate term, MENA cultures do appear to foster a shift in gender roles during this time of life that can enlarge men's and women's interaction styles and self-conceptions.

Conclusion

This essay drew heavily upon insights from Gregg (2005) to sketch an outline of periods of psychological development in one MENA society, ancient Israel, fleshing it out with some select examples from the Bible. Cross-cultural psychology is the most appropriate discipline for pursuing this project. The high-context document known as the Bible simply doesn't report as much information as we would like for this project. However, it is legitimate to use cross-cultural psychology to fill in the blanks left by the past. As the medievals noted, *ab esse ad posse valet illatio; a posse ad esse non valet illatio*. From what exists it is legitimate to infer what might have been in the past; but from what is possible now, it is not legitimate to infer that the same thing existed in the past but somehow disappeared. The elements of psychological development in MENA societies that exist at present may well have existed in the past. Following this principle, we have attempted to fill in blanks in the Bible. In the final analysis, however, this is the first stage of a work in progress.

References

Adair, John G., and Rolando Diaz-Loving
1999 'Indigenous Psychologies: The Meaning of the Concept and its Assessment', *Applied Psychology* 48: 397-402.

Berry, John W., Ype H. Poortinga, Marshall H. Segall and Pierre R. Dasen
2002 *Cross-Cultural Psychology: Research and Application* (Cambridge: Cambridge University Press, 2nd edn).

Boddy, Janice
1989 *Wombs and Alien Spirits* (Madison, WI: University of Wisconsin Press).

Brink, Judy
1995 'Changing Child-Rearing Patterns in an Egyptian Village', in *Children in the Muslim Middle East* (ed. Elizabeth Fernea; Austin, TX: University of Texas Press): 84-92.

Danker, Frederick William
2000 *A Greek–English Lexicon of the New Testament and Other Early Christian Literature by Walter Bauer* (Chicago: University Press, 3rd edn).

Eickelman, Dale F.

2002 *The Middle East and Central Asia: An Anthropological Approach* (Upper Saddle River, NJ: Prentice-Hall, 4th edn).

Elliott, John H.

2007 'Envy and the Evil Eye: More on Mark 7:22 and Mark's "Anatomy of Envy"', in *In Other Words: Essays on Social Science Methods and the New Testament in Honor of Jerome H. Neyrey* (ed. Anselm C. Hagedorn, Zeba A. Crook and Eric Stewart; Sheffield: Sheffield Phoenix Press): 87-105.

Eng, Milton

2011 *The Days of our Years: A Lexical Semantic Study of the Life Cycle in Biblical Israel* (New York: T. & T. Clark).

Fitzmyer, Joseph A.

1981 *The Gospel according to Luke I–IX* (AB, 28; New York: Doubleday).

French, Valerie

1988 'Birth Control, Childbirth, and Early Childhood', in *Civilization of the Ancient Mediterranean: Greece and Rome,* vol. 3 (ed. Michael Grant and Rachel Kitzinger; New York: Charles Scribner's Sons): 1355-62.

Gregg, Gary S.

2005 *The Middle East: A Cultural Psychology* (Oxford: Oxford University Press).

Guarnaccia, Peter J., and Lloyd H. Rogler

1999 'Research on Culture-Bound Syndromes: New Directions', *American Journal of Psychiatry* 156: 1322-1327.

Hagedorn, Anselm C., and Jerome H. Neyrey

1998 "It was out of envy that they handed Jesus over' (Mark 15.10): The Anatomy of Envy and the Gospel of Mark', *JSNT* 69: 15-56.

Hennecke, Edgar, and Wilhelm Schneemelcher

1991 *New Testament Apocrypha,* vol. 1 (Louisville, KY: Westminster John Knox).

Hsu, Francis L.K. (ed.)

1972 *Psychological Anthropology* (Cambridge: Schenkman Publishing, 2nd edn).

Jahoda, G.

1980 'Theoretical and Systematic Approaches in Cross-Cultural Psychology', in *Handbook of Cross-Cultural Psychology. Vol. 1: Perspectives* (ed. H.C. Triandis and W.W. Lambert; Boston: Allyn & Bacon): 69-141.

Joseph, Suad (ed.)

1999 *Intimate Selving in Arab Families* (Syracuse, NY: Syracuse University Press).

Kagitcibasi, Cigdem

1996 *Family and Human Development across Cultures* (Mahwah, NJ: Erlbaum).

Kypseli Video

http://www.d.umn.edu/cla/faculty/troufs/anth1604/video/Kypseli.htm.

LeVine, Robert, and Barbara B. LeVine

1963 'Nuyansongo: A Gussi Community in Kenya'. in *Six Cultures: Studies of Child Rearing* (ed. Beatrice B. Whiting; New York: John Wiley): 19-202.

MacDonald, Nathan

2008 *What Did the Ancient Israelites Eat? Diet in Biblical Times* (Grand Rapids, MI: W.B. Eerdmans).

Malina, Bruce J.

1994 'Religion in the Imagined New Testament World: More Social Science Lenses', *Scriptura* 51: 1-26.

2009 'Gratitude (Debt of)', in *Handbook of Biblical Social Values* (ed. John J. Pilch and Bruce J. Malina; Grand Rapids, MI: Baker House; repr. of 1998 *Handbook of Biblical Social Values*, Peabody, MA: Hendrickson Publishers): 92-94.

Malina, Bruce J., and John J. Pilch

2006 *Social Science Commentary on the Letters of Paul* (Minneapolis, MN: Fortress Press).

Martin, Troy W.

2010 'Animals Impregnated by the Wind and Mary's Pregnancy by the Holy Spirit', unpublished research report presented at the Annual Meeting of the Catholic Biblical Association, Loyola-Marymount, Los Angeles, CA.

Mayer, Anton

1983 *Der zensierte Jesu: Soziologie des Neuen Testaments* (Freiburg im Breisgau: Walter Verlag).

McAdams, Dan

1995 'What Do We Know When We Know a Person?' *Journal of Personality and Social Psychology* 63: 365-96.

Meier, John P.

1991 *A Marginal Jew,* vol. 1 (New York: Doubleday).

Meyers, Carol

1997 'The Family in Early Israel', in *Families in Ancient Israel* (ed. Leo G. Perdue, Joseph Blenkinsopp, John J. Collins and Carol Meyers; Louisville, KY: Westminster John Knox): 1-47.

Msefer, Assia

1985 *Sevrages et interdependence* (Casablanca: Editions Maghrebines).

Nemet-Nejat, Karen Rhea

1998 *Daily Life in Ancient Mesopotamia* (Peabody, MA: Hendrickson Publishers).

Nsamenang, A. Bame

1992 *Human Development in Cultural Context: A Third World Perspective* (Cross-Cultural Research and Methodology Series, 16; London: Sage Publications).

Pilch, John J.

1992 'Lying and Deceit in the Letters to the Seven Churches: Perspectives from Cultural Anthropology', *BTB* 22: 126-34.

1993 '"Beat his Ribs While He Is Young" (Sir 30:12): A Window on the Mediterranean World', *BTB* 23: 101-13.

1995 'Death with Honor: The Mediterranean Style of Death of Jesus in Mark', *BTB* 25:65-70.

1997 'BTB Readers' Guide: Psychological and Psychoanalytical Approaches to Interpreting the Bible in Social-Scientific Context', *BTB* 27: 112-16.

2011 'Flute Players, Death, and Music in the Afterlife (Matt. 9:18-19, 23-26)', in John J. Pilch, *Flights of the Soul: Visions, Heavenly Journeys, and Peak Experiences in the Biblical World* (Grand Rapids, MI: Eerdmans): 89-105.

2012 *A Cultural Handbook to the Bible* (Grand Rapids, MI: Eerdmans).

2013 'Exploring Periods of Psychological Development in MENA (Middle East North Africa) Societies: A Tentative Model', *BTB* 43: 196-210.

Stevens, Evelyn P.

1973 'Marianismo: The Other Face of Machismo in Latin America', in *Female and Male in Latin America: Essays* (ed. Ann Pescatello; Pittsburgh, PA: University of Pittsburgh Press): 89-101.

Van Os, Bas
2011 *Psychological Analyses and the Historical Jesus: New Ways to Explore Christian Origins* (London: T. & T. Clark).
Whiting, John W.M., and Irvin L. Child
1953 *Child Training and Personality* (New Haven, CT: Yale University Press).
Wiggins, J.
1996 *The Five-Factor Model of Personality* (New York: Guilford).

The Social Function of Genealogies in the New Testament and its World

Richard L. Rohrbaugh

More than three decades of working with Jack Elliott in the social-scientific criticism of the New Testament has been one of the most richly rewarding experiences of my scholarly life. I count him as the best of colleagues I have known, admiring not only his thorough and groundbreaking scholarship but also his solid commitment to the cause of justice for those our society dumps beside the road. My first experience of collaborative work with Jack was in 1991 in the old 'Social Facets' group of the Jesus Seminar where we each contributed a chapter to a volume on the social world of Luke–Acts (Neyrey 1991). That group eventually split off and re-emerged as a separate group, the 'Context Group', of which Jack and I are both founding members. It is an association we both treasure to this day. Thus dedicating this chapter to him is both a pleasure and an honor.

The discussion that follows—on the social function of genealogies and ancestry in the New Testament—focuses attention on biblical texts that gain little traction in contemporary America; indeed, they are typically ones deemed to have no real-world consequences for anyone. Yet genealogies unmistakably functioned as claims to power and privilege in the ancient world, perhaps the equivalent of educational pedigrees and financial statements in contemporary America. Moreover, they are a form of sociopolitical legitimation that highlights as well as any the fact that even texts we consider obscure and strange once had consequences in the real world.

Genealogy and Descent

It has long been recognized of course that unilineal descent groups are found in all types of preindustrial societies in all regions of the world (Goody 1968: 402). They typically gain importance whenever (1) a certain level of geographical stability and density of settlement is reached and (2) whenever the amounts and types of property transmitted between generations are significant (Forde 1947). Moreover, especially where centralized government is weak, descent group membership and personal lineage are the primary avenues of access to a whole range of social benefits. In such societies, pedigrees matter. The evidence for this fact in the world of the New Testament is actually quite overwhelming. We cannot sample all of it, of course, but Roman funerary practices can provide an important and cogent illustration. That is because the funeral rituals and funerary processions of elite families were far more than an occasion to mourn or celebrate a recent death: they offered 'splendid opportunities for the display of familial, political and personal symbolic capital' (Johanson 2011: 408).

Polybius (*History of the World* 6.53–6.54.3 [Shelton 1998: 95-96]) describes these Roman funeral processions in full detail:

> After the interment and the performance of the customary rites, a wax image of the deceased is placed in a very conspicuous spot in the house, in a little wooden shrine. The image is a mask made strikingly similar to the facial features and expression of the deceased. The family puts these images on display during public sacrifices, arranging them with great care. When any illustrious family member dies, the family takes the images or masks to the funeral, putting them on men who seem to be most similar in height and size to the men represented by the masks. These 'actors' put on the purple-bordered toga, if their 'character' was a consul or praetor, an entirely purple toga if he was a censor, and a gold-embroidered toga if he had celebrated a triumph or done some other such thing. They all ride in chariots, and, according to the respective rank of political office held by each 'character' during his lifetime, the 'actors' are preceded by the fasces, axes, and other such things which usually accompany the magistrates. When they reach the Rostra, they all sit down on curule seats.

In short, funeral processions were a splashy, public way to remind onlookers of the 'clout' and 'claims' of the deceased's family (Shelton 1998: 95; Bodel 1999: 260-65). An especially extravagant example was the funerary procession for Marcellus, the nephew of Augustus, when more than six hundred such masks were paraded along city streets to the forum of Rome (Garnsey 1970: 237). The message was clear to all: ancestry matters.

This was obvious in elite homes as well. In the hall or the atrium of the elite homes the busts of ancestors were prominently displayed to celebrate a family's status (Huskinson 2011: 527). In some homes the *tablinum*, an alcove off the atrium containing family records (*tabulae*), housed the wax *imagines* in wooden cabinets on the walls, connected by lines showing relationships. In other homes the family *stemma* was painted on the walls of entryways for arriving guests to admire. The stemma of the emperor Galba, displayed in his atrium, traced his paternal ancestry to Jupiter and that of his mother to Phasiphae, the wife of Minos (Suetonius, *Galba* 2).

Of course, such ostentatious display did not impress everyone. Seneca (*De beneficiis* 3.28.2 [Basore 1935: 177]), ever the Stoic, took a rather dim view of the practice:

> Those who display ancestral busts in their halls, and place in the entrance of their houses the names of their family, arranged in a long row and entwined in the multiple ramifications of a genealogical tree—are these not notable rather than noble?

That said, Philo reminds us that the 'multitude' took the standard view (*Deus imm.* 150).

Critical Study of Genealogies

The modern critical study of biblical genealogy goes back to the late nineteenth and early twentieth centuries when a number of scholars rejected the historical accuracy of biblical genealogies, understanding them as either mythological constructs or simple reflections of the social and political relationships of their era.[1] More recently a number of scholars have compared the historical and literary character of biblical genealogies with those of the wider ancient Near East. Among New Testament scholars, the genealogies of Jesus in Matthew and Luke continue to attract considerable attention, though most analyses continue the long tradition of mining them exegetically to uncover their relation to the Christology and major themes in each of these Gospels. The women in the genealogy of Matthew continue to draw considerable attention as well. And a few are still trying to reconcile the differences in the Matthean and Lukan versions or square their apparent contradiction with the notion of virgin birth. Yet while much of this work is important and worthwhile, we will leave these and similar issues to others because our interest lies elsewhere. I wish to focus on the *social* function of genealogies, which is often *mentioned* in work on the New Testament but rarely explored in any depth.

First, a word about form. Two types of genealogy are usually recognized. 'Linear' genealogies are those that trace the line of a subject back to a single (usually auspicious) ancestor. They display depth (number of generations) but not breadth (siblings, marriages, branches of the family). They can be short (*x*, the son of . . .) or long (. . . the son of Adam, the son of God) and either oral or written. By contrast, 'segmented' genealogies are those that record the multiple branches of a family, following the lines of siblings to produce the familiar 'family tree'. Segmented genealogies can display both depth and breadth and are more often written than oral.

One of the unquestionable results of the anthropological study of genealogies has been recognition of their fluidity. With oral genealogies, that is obvious because they function primarily in living, face-to face settings

1. Of course substantive discussions of genealogy go all the way back to antiquity. For comment on the historical accuracy of personal genealogies see Josephus, *Apion* 1.7; *Life* 1. For rabbinical comment see *Ed.* 8.7; *b. Qidd.* 69a-71a; and *Gen. Rab.* 82.11.

where they are recited and heard (Levin 2001: 32). They depend on memory and can easily be manipulated according to the needs of the moment. If longer than four generations (grandfather, father, son, grandson), oral genealogies usually retain only significant ancestors rather than all ancestors because persons of minor significance or those from the distant past are quickly forgotten. Of course written genealogies can also be fluid, but written genealogies often survive over long periods of time in virtually fixed form. When they are significantly altered, however, it is more likely the result of deliberate manipulation than simple forgetfulness.

It is also true that genealogies, especially written genealogies, can serve many functions—political, economic, religious, social—and, in fact, can perform several or all of these functions simultaneously (Wilson 1977: 37; Hanson and Oakman 1998: 28; Johnson 1969). That is because long, written genealogies are not primarily concerned with biological facts but with the symbolic value they represent (Plum 1989: 69-70). As such, they can be easily manipulated to serve the agenda of their makers. Plutarch, for example, is critical of writers who produce fictitious genealogies for noble Roman families in order to ingratiate themselves with potential benefactors (*Numa* 21.2). The crucial point, then, is that though retrospective in form, written genealogies are contemporary or future-oriented in practice. They are intended to serve the *contemporary* needs of their users. Thus, the genealogy of Jesus in Matthew likely has more to do with Matthew's agenda and the issues of his own day than it does with the origins of Jesus himself.

The Social Function of Genealogies

As indicated above, the social functions of genealogies are more often *mentioned* by biblical scholars than studied in any depth. A significant exception to that has been the work of Robert R. Wilson (1975; 1977), who compared the genealogies of the Hebrew Bible with those of the wider ancient Near East. He has described the social functions of genealogies in some detail, grouping their functions in three broad spheres of ancient life: domestic, politico-jural and religious (1977: 37-55). Each is important in its own right, though there is considerable overlap among them.

(1) *Domestic*. Domestically, genealogies relate individuals to other individuals and to related lineage groups. In the process they define familial rights and obligations in a way that sanctions the social structure of a family or tribe. They specify and organize roles, status and authority among lineage members. Moreover, in very basic ways genealogies enable persons to participate in daily life. The terms used to address other persons, for example, can be dependent on place in a lineage. Priority in choice or action can be lineage-dependent as well. Some behaviors permitted toward outsiders (lying, cursing, theft) may be forbidden toward anyone regarded

as inside the lineage. In addition, inheritance, control of land and potential marriage partners (Tob. 4.12; Hanson 1989; Hanson and Oakman 1998: 26-31) can all be dependent on one's place in a family lineage.

(2) *Politico-jural.* In the political arena, genealogies can structure relationships of authority, power and legality. They can legitimate a wide range of positions or offices and designate lines of royal succession. In many societies genealogies are used to define community membership and thus allocate community resources or the right to live on certain land. Legal rights can also be legitimated or clarified via genealogy. They can even determine what punishments are applied in criminal proceedings.[2] When the settlement of conflicting claims requires recourse to the courts, genealogies often become a primary form of legal evidence.

(3) *Religious.* Genealogies can also serve a variety of religious functions, and when they do, they are usually long and elaborate (Wilson 1977: 44).[3] They can be used to determine membership in a religious community or legitimate claims to religious office. Ancestors can be invoked in religious rituals to aid the living, heal the sick or protect the dying. Obviously genealogies can also play a central role in an ancestor cult. Long ago, Fustel de Coulanges (1979) argued that proper and regular ancestor worship (both in public and in the home) was essential in legitimating Roman descent claims and actually led to the expansion of the patriarchal family into the ancient *gens*.

Elaborating the Model

Grouping the social functions of genealogies as Wilson does is a helpful start, and we can make good use of it in what follows. But Wilson has missed several of the most important social functions of genealogies. Moreover, detail can be added to most of the functions Wilson cites by (1) using the insights of cultural anthropology that have so benefitted our study of the New Testament (which Wilson's work predated) and (2) providing illustrative and supporting evidence from the wider cultural environment. Such elaboration of the model of social function is what we intend to provide in the comments that follow.

We shall begin by piggybacking on a little-known study by Rodney T. Hood (1961) in which he lists, and very briefly annotates, six purposes of

2. E.g. the Code of Hammurabi provides for different punishments for men, women, citizens and slaves. Roman law likewise had different levels of punishment for citizens and non-citizens.

3. Josephus claims that the Hebrews had scrupulously preserved the accuracy of priestly genealogies back two thousand years (*Apion* 1.8).

genealogies he intends to use in analyzing the genealogies of Jesus.[4] Though the list requires some serious reordering and recharacterization in light of contemporary social-scientific study of the New Testament, nonetheless it can help us add some detail to what we have so far.

(1) *Identification.* Hood understands the simple identification of persons to be the most basic and obvious of genealogical functions. Identifiers such as 'Joshua, son of Nun', or 'Simon, son of Jonah', are brief but familiar personal identifiers. Hood also cites evidence of longer identifying genealogies in legal documents, contracts, wills and other documents from Egypt during the Ptolemaic and Roman periods (1961: 1-2). This is a good start but is problematic in some degree because Hood essentially assumes the individualism of modern societies. Thus he understands 'identification' to mean the act of distinguishing, say, Simon the son of Jonah from Simon of Cyrene.

What is missing here is any recognition that the concept of the 'self' is a cultural construct that differs markedly from one society to the next. At one end of a spectrum there are societies that understand persons individualistically. The United States is the prime example. For them, the individual is seen as a bounded and unique center of consciousness, a more or less integrated cognitive and motivational universe. Their key to understanding persons is thus the psychological makeup of the individual. At the other end of the spectrum are societies viewing the self as fundamentally collective. For them, persons are so embedded in groups that group and individual identity are in large measure coextensive, both psychologically and in every other way. One does not have a self, an identity, apart from the group. Moreover, as F. Sushila Niles has recently argued, there is now a near-consensus among social scientists that such individualist–collectivist differences may be the single most important factor in determining social behavior (1998: 315-16).

Individualist cultures typically base identity on personal experiences, personal achievements, possessions, abilities and personal preferences (Triandis 1995: 71). They attribute motives and actions to internal causes and personal choices in ways that collectivists simply do not. They focus on personal rights, needs and abilities. They give greater priority to attitudes than to norms and treat values as matters of individual choice. Career, lifework or mission, purpose and even religion are all matters to be worked out by individual choice. Above all, individualists assume that ability, effort and responsibility are the basis for personal success.

The fact is, however, that this sort of individualism has been rather rare in human history. It is nearly absent in the Middle East today, and almost certainly was in antiquity as well. In fact there is virtually nothing in the

4. Hood does not use the term 'social' when describing the functions of ancient genealogies. He simply calls his list a set of 'basically representative functions'.

New Testament or the Jesus tradition that suggests anything like what we have been describing (Malina 1993: 67).

By contrast, persons in collectivist cultures are literally defined by the groups to which they belong. They do not understand themselves as having a separate identity. They are motivated by group norms rather than individual needs or aspirations and strenuously avoid articulating personal goals or giving them priority over the goals of the group. And most significantly, for nearly all collectivists the primary identity-group is the family (though belonging to additional in-groups is common).

What this means is that the genealogical or descent identifiers in the New Testament do more than distinguish one individual from another. Instead, they identify the groups (families) from which the actors take their identity. Moreover, since the individual's values are deemed irrelevant, and all group members are assumed to have the same outlook, values, attitudes and loyalties, an identifier like 'Simon son of Jonah' is really saying that Simon views the world exactly the way his father Jonah does. Likewise, a written genealogy or set of *imagines* paraded in public implies that the current members of the family share, or are expected to share, all the attributes of their illustrious ancestors.

(2) *Characterization.* The collectivist understanding of human identity allows us to be far more specific in describing another of Hood's 'representative' functions for New Testament genealogies (1961: 5-6). In antiquity it was assumed that a son inherited not only a father's property but also his character. The ancients articulate it clearly: 'For the first Adam, burdened with an evil heart, transgressed and was overcome, as were also all who were descended from him' (2 Esd. 3.21). Or as Jesus says, 'If you knew me, you would know my Father also' (Jn 8.19). In other words, like begets like.

Stereotyping is thus the principal way in which collectivist persons know one another. And while stereotyped character can be constructed from more than biological ancestry (geographical location, food types, city or region, water source, gender, age), ancestry is its primary source. As Tit. 1.12 claims, 'Cretans are always liars, vicious brutes, lazy gluttons'. Cicero claimed that Carthaginians were a fraudulent and lying nation, that Campanians were proud and puffed up, with a fondness for deceiving, that Ligurians were wild and tough (*De lege agraria* 2.95). Philo thought Egyptians were by nature envious people infected with the evil eye (*Flacc.* 29).

This kind of stereotyping was nearly universal at all social levels in the ancient world and Plutarch (*De sera* 16 [De Lacy and Einarson 1959: 247-49 (559D)]) explains why it is legitimate:

> If a city is a single and continuous whole, surely a family is so too, attached as it is to a single origin which reproduces in the members a certain force and common quality pervading them all; and what has been begotten is not severed from the begetter, as if it were some product of his art; it has

> been created out of him, and thus not only contains within itself a portion of what is his, but receives a portion of his due when rightly punished or honored.

Genealogies or descent indicators thus convey far more than biological information. They tell you about values, attitudes, aspirations and agendas. Very simply, they tell you what kind of persons you are encountering, what behavior you can expect from them and where their loyalties lie. It would be hard to overestimate the importance of this for ancient societies. In agrarian, largely non-literate societies, plagued by unstable and insecure life chances, preoccupation with the character of people was a matter of survival. It was necessary to know all one could about competitors, supporters, rivals, insiders, outsiders, friends and enemies. Loyalties and alliances mattered. Close attention to character indicators was therefore much more than 'mere pastime' (Goitein 1988: 189-90).

(3) *Honor* (*Magnification*). 'Magnification' is Hood's term (1961: 3-5). By this he means that genealogies provide support for individual or family pride and are 'the fundamental ground of reputation or discredit for human beings' (Aristotle, *Rhet. Alex.* 35.1440b.24-25 [Hett and Rackham 1937: 405). While this is clearly correct, it is necessary to acknowledge that the term 'magnification' does not say nearly enough. Today we would highlight the function of genealogy in establishing family and individual *honor*, the term that is ubiquitous in the ancient sources themselves (Malina 2001: 27-57; Rohrbaugh 2009). However because so much has been written in recent years about the centrality of honor in the biblical world there is no need for a long explanation here. We need only acknowledge the important distinction between 'ascribed' and 'acquired' honor, noting that genealogies articulate the former.

'Acquired' honor is the honor gained from laudatory public behavior. Aristotle calls it the 'reward of virtue' (*Eth. nic.* 8.14.1163b.3-4). It is to be distinguished from the more fundamental 'ascribed' honor that comes from position, office, or, above all, from birth family. As Sirach (3.11) puts it, 'the glory of one's father is one's own glory'. This is what makes it relevant to our topic. In fact we can say almost categorically that before they are anything else, *all* genealogies are honor claims because honor is automatically ascribed to those who come from honorific families. That is why families decorated hallways with ancestral busts. That is why *imagines* were paraded in funeral processions and why the family *stemma* appeared on entryway walls. It was all about family honor.

Sampling some of the ancient evidence for the centrality of ascribed honor is instructive. Plutarch lays it out on the first page of his *Moralia* (1.1.2 [Babbitt 1927: 5]):

> For those who are not well-born, whether on the father's or on the mother's side, have an indelible disgrace in their low birth, which accompanies them throughout their lives, and offers anyone desiring to use it a ready subject of reproach and insult. Wise was the poet who declares:
>
> The home's foundation being wrongly laid,
> The offspring needs must be unfortunate.
>
> A goodly treasure, then, is honorable birth, and such a man may speak his mind freely, a thing which should be held of the highest account by those who wish to have issue lawfully begotten. In the nature of things, the spirits of those whose blood is base or counterfeit are constantly brought down and humbled, and quite rightly does the poet declare:
>
> A man, though bold, is made a slave whene'er
> He learns his mother's or his sire's disgrace.

Aristotle (*Rhet.* 2.15.2 [Freese 1939: 257]) agrees: 'Noble birth is a heritage of honor from one's ancestors'. Philo (*Deus imm.* 150 [Colson and Whitaker 1930: 85]) is no less definitive:

> Will you take no heed of the honors of high ancestry on either side, or the pride of noble birth, which the multitude so extol? Will you leave glory behind you, glory, for which men barter their all, and treat it as though it were a worthless trifle?

In his *Moral Essays* Seneca makes two comments that would startle most Americans:

> . . . in the competition for public office some of the most disreputable men are preferred to others who are industrious, but of no family, by reason of their noble birth (*De beneficiis* 4.30.1 [Basore 1935: 267]).

And again:

> So-and-so was the father of great men: whatever he may be, he is worthy of our benefits; he has given us worthy sons. So-and-so is descended from glorious ancestors: whatever he may be, let him find refuge under the shadow of his ancestry. As filthy places become bright from the radiance of the sun, so let the degenerate shine in the light of their forefathers (*De beneficiis* 4.30.4 [Basore 1935: 267]).

In other words, birth-status trumps bad behavior, even in the matter of holding public office. Obviously genealogy mattered.

Yet one other kind of evidence is worth describing. Honorific statues set up in public places were an important means of celebrating 'ancestral pride'. They were prominent earlier in Greece (*koroi*) and first became so in Rome during the late republic. During the imperial period they proliferated, with some families placing statues of the emperor next to those of family members in an obvious attempt to draw associations. Though the statues were of individuals, 'they brought "reflected glory" on the whole family, particularly through the emphasis on ancestors' (Huskinson 2011: 525).

The ultimate honorific genealogy of course would relate a mortal to a god. So Cyrus Gordon (1977: 1) has pointed out that paternity at two levels—human and divine—was common in the ancient world. The Egyptian pharaoh had a human father from whom he inherited the throne and was also considered the son of the solar deity Ra. Odysseus was the 'Zeus-born son of Laërtes'. Suetonius (*Julius* 6) tells us that in his eulogy for his aunt Julia, Caesar claimed her descent from kings on her mother's side and from the 'immortal gods' on her father's side. 'We therefore unite in our descent the sacred majesty of kings, the chiefest among men, and the divine majesty of gods, to whom kings themselves are subject'. That would be as exalted an honor claim as one could possibly make.

(4) *Qualification*. Genealogies could be used to legitimate office, claim rights and privileges, or establish authority. In fact this is probably the most commonly cited function of genealogies in the ancient world, and examples of it are plentiful. According to the *Lex Julia* (18 BCE), the descendants of Roman senators held that rank to at least the third generation of agnatic descent (Garnsey 1970: 237). Descent from Aaron in order to hold priestly office is an oft-cited example from ancient Israel (Josephus, *Apion* 1.30-31). In addition to office or position, those with the right ancestors qualified for a variety of special privileges. *Curule* seats (ivory) in the theaters and stadiums, regalia and distinctive clothing, residence in certain areas, access to contracts, lesser punishments in the legal system and a host of other privileges came to those of noble birth.

One item that has been overlooked in all this, however, is the fact that an honorific genealogy also qualified a person to write and speak in public. Note the comment of Plutarch above: 'A goodly treasure, then, is honorable birth, and *such a man may speak his mind freely*'. Two examples may be cited. First, there is Josephus, who states that Judean priestly descent was the gold standard of honorific birth (*Life* 1). He then starts off his own biography by making a genealogical claim that is clearly designed to display his credentials and disarm critics or detractors: he claims to be a priest in the first of the twenty-four priestly courses and justifies it by tracing his lineage back five generations. In his book *De bello judaico*, he begins by asserting he is the 'son of Matthias, by birth a Hebrew, and a priest' (*War*, 1). In *Apion* (1.8), he repeats the claim that he was a 'priest by birth'. [5] In other words, lest his readers doubt him or imagine him an unworthy author, he cites his birth status to underscore his credibility and establish his authority to write.

A second example comes from the Gospel of Luke. In the ancient Mediterranean world honor status determined who talked and who listened.

5. He asserts that the Hebrews kept accurate genealogical records of their priesthood back two thousand years, taking extraordinary pains to insure the accuracy of the records even in times of war (*Apion* 1.7-8).

Inferiors did not initiate conversations, nor were they accorded a public audience. They had no 'authority' to speak or act as public figures. Thus Jesus' opponents offered him a challenge: 'Tell us, by what authority are you doing these things?' (Lk. 20.2). His interrogators assumed that Jesus had no *ascribed* honor justifying the public initiative he was taking, so they pressed the proper question: 'Who is it who *gave* you this authority?' In other words, because the birth status of Jesus warranted nothing like the behavior he exhibited, his challengers naturally assumed the honor must have been *acquired*, that is, given to him by someone with the right to confer it. By contrast, a person of publicly recognized honorific birth might have been challenged about *what* he did or said but never about *his right to do so*.

(5) *Organization*. According to Hood, social organization demands continuity, stability and definition. Thus the relationships of both groups and individuals are often systematized and legitimated by the use of genealogies (1961: 2-3). Genealogies can specify roles and organize responsibilities. They can incorporate outsiders brought into a group or articulate the merger of families via marriage. They can even become a vehicle for carrying family or tribal myths, legends and traditions down the generations.

All that is true enough, but there is much more to say. Genealogies defined the primary natural grouping (common blood) in a society where group membership was everything (Malina 1991; Malina and Neyrey 1991). In ancient agrarian societies group membership (and the consequent collectivist sense of identity) was critical because, for all but a few of the elite, group membership was the primary defense against the exigencies and insecurities of ancient life. This meant that while competition was sharply constrained or regulated within groups it was virtually unlimited between groups. As a result, collectivist societies demanded group loyalty above all else.

The implications of this are far reaching. It meant that group boundaries had to be carefully defined, constantly guarded and uncompromisingly tested. Purity laws clarified who was in, out or marginal. Group norms needed constant public reaffirmation, and transgressions against family honor were considered deeply sacrilegious (Malina 2001: 45). Personal opinion was irrelevant or dangerous. One's public self and in-group self had to match, that is, family members were expected to display public behavior in perfect consonance with internal family values (Rohrbaugh 2007: 70). Moreover, the all-pervasive gossip network kept everyone accountable and their lives transparent (Rohrbaugh 2007: 125-46). In other words, genealogies were the credentials for membership in the most significant survival mechanism in ancient life.

(6) *Motivation and inspiration*. Once again we must be careful not to assume the individualism of contemporary American culture. Today we

assume that motives and aspirations originate in the desires of an individual. Examining them is a study in psychology. But ancient collectivists considered individual desires to have no place; only group aspirations really mattered. Thus Sirach (48.22) can say with considerable satisfaction, 'Hezekiah . . . kept firmly to the ways of his ancestor David'.

This meant that living up to the reputation of one's ancestors was an expectation and ambition on the part of sons throughout the ancient Mediterranean world, and illustrations of it are not hard to find. The 'lives' of Plutarch perform exactly this function. So also do the histories of the great generals of various nations by Cornelius Nepos. He makes clear that each subject is to be judged not by some universal criteria or rule, but by the standards and merits of their respective forefathers (*De excellentibus ducibus exterarum gentium* Pref. 4-7).

Polybius lays all this out quite precisely. After describing the splendid funeral processions of illustrious families he writes:

> It would not be easy to find a more splendid sight for a young man who loves honor and virtue to behold. For who would not be moved by the sight of the images of men renowned for their excellence, all together in one place, portrayed as if still alive and breathing? And therefore . . . the fame of men who have done great deeds is made immortal, and the glory of those who have faithfully served the fatherland becomes well known to the people and is handed down as a model to future generations (*History of the World* 6.53–6.54.3 [Shelton 1998: 96]).

Of course the fact that successors did not always live up to the standards of their predecessors was frequent and obvious to everyone, but the social ideal remained intact.

(7) *Additional functions*. Several additional social functions of genealogies are worth mentioning. If they could be used to justify writing or speaking, they could also be used to obtain an audience. That is no doubt part of Josephus's intent in citing his own genealogy so frequently. We could add that they were likewise used to tell a reader why a story was worth reading. This is almost certainly part of the purpose of Matthew and Luke in providing their genealogies for Jesus. If some in the audiences of Matthew and Luke were outside Palestine and non-Israelite, they might have wondered why anyone should bother with the story of an obscure, low-born peasant/artisan from a strange land about which they knew nothing. The long, honorific genealogies are thus 'attention-grabbers' that justify the effort and interest of the reader.

Yet another function of genealogies, one related to their broader political function, is their use as weapons in conflict situations (Acts 23.6). Richard Kalmin, for example, describes the Babylonian rabbis of late antiquity using genealogies against non-rabbinic opponents in local power struggles to 'cast aspersions' on their lineage (1996: 79). They likewise used genealogies as weapons against the distant Palestinian rabbis over whom they claimed religious superiority. Similarly, Geoffrey Dunn (2001) explores Tertullian's discussion of the genealogy of Jesus in which he argues, *contra* Gnosticism, for Jesus' Davidic descent through Mary—thereby rescuing the notion of a genuinely human incarnation.

New Testament Examples

We turn now to the New Testament. But before looking at specific examples of what we have been describing three qualifications are necessary. First, there are far too many genealogical and other descent indicators in the New Testament to examine all of them closely, so we must be satisfied with representative examples. Second, we must acknowledge that much of the information embedded in ancient descent indicators is forever lost to us. Those who knew Jonah and his family knew immediately what was encoded in the term 'Simon, son of Jonah'. Knowing Jonah, they knew all about Simon. But that local knowledge is not available to us and never will be. Third, because any genealogy performs a number of social functions simultaneously, we cannot neatly pigeonhole the descent indicators in the New Testament into the list of functions described above. Matters are always more complex than pigeonholing would imply.

Nowhere is that clearer than when dealing with the genealogies of Jesus. Many scholars have described the literary, historical and theological functions these genealogies perform. We have also suggested that they are attention-grabbers designed to convince readers the story of Jesus is worth reading. But it is not hard to see how the genealogies of Jesus simultaneously perform other social functions as well. They qualify him for the office of king (Mt. 21.5; Mk 15.17-18//Mt. 27.29; Jn 1.49; 18.37; 19.2-3) and high priest (Heb. 5.5). They tell the reader what the opponents of Jesus (in the story world of Luke) do not know when they challenge his authority. As 'son of Adam, son of God', Jesus also gains a legitimate place at the right hand of the father (Mt. 26.64). Finally, perhaps drawing an analogy with the *imagines* of Roman funerary processions, the author of Col. 1.15 can say, 'He is the *image* of the invisible God, the firstborn of all creation'.

But we can say more. Earlier I argued that above all else genealogies are honor claims. Moreover, the ultimate honor claim is one declaring dual paternity from both a mortal and a god. Significantly, in the cases of Galba, Julius Caesar, Augustus, Alexander, Scipio Africanus and, according to Luke, Jesus, the mortal claim is on the mother's side and the divine one on the father's side. Would any literate or even status-conscious Roman miss the point? Luke has just moved Jesus from village artisan, a status below that of landed peasant (Rohrbaugh 2007: 19-30), to the pinnacle of ascribed honor in the Roman world. Moreover, placing the genealogy immediately following the baptism scene in which Jesus is proclaimed God's 'beloved son', as Luke does, makes the author's intention in this staggering honor claim crystal clear.

To get a sense of what this genealogy is really claiming for Jesus, contrast it with the challenge that erupted in Nazareth (Lk. 4.16-30; Mt. 13.55): 'Where did this man get this wisdom and these deeds of power? Is this not the carpenter's son? Is his mother not called Mary? And are not his brothers James and Joseph and Simon and Judas?' In other words, whatever else Luke's genealogy might be theologically or in any other way, it is before all else an astonishing honor claim for the central figure in the story.

Beyond the genealogies of Jesus other descent indicators are exceedingly common in the New Testament. In fact there are well over a hundred brief descent markers we could list. They function as simple identifiers, as honor claims, as expressions of character, as weapons in the heat of conflict and as claims to office or position. What follows are representative examples.

Some are simple identifiers such as the 'sons of Zebedee' (Mk 1.19// Mt. 20.20) or the blind beggar known only as 'the son of Timaeus' (Mk 10.6). Encoded in those identifiers are character and loyalty statements that are now lost to us. But there are also simple identifiers where we do have some clues. Philip tells Nathaniel that he has found the one written about by Moses and the prophets, 'Jesus, son of Joseph, from Nazareth' (Jn 1.45). The part about Joseph and Nazareth suggests an artisan low-life from a village that is stereotyped as producing nothing good (1.46). But that is sharply counteracted by the comment about Jesus' acknowledgment in the writings of Moses and the prophets. Stereotype is being countered with honorific information.

There are other identifiers that function to signal ascribed honor. Typical would be the notice in Lk. 1.5 that Zechariah belonged to the priestly order of Abijah and that his wife was a descendant of Aaron. Or again, Jesus is repeatedly called 'son of David' by those seeking help or seeking to praise him (Mt. 9.27; 12.23; 15.22; 20.30, 31; 21.9, 15; Mk 10.47, 48; Lk. 1.32; 18.38, 39). His own claims raise questions of comparison with Israel's most honorific forebears. In Jn 4.12 Jesus is asked if he is greater than the ancestor Jacob. In 8.53 he is asked if he is greater than Abraham. Honorific genealogy is also offered as the basis for royal inheritance. In Lk. 1.32 we are told that he will receive the throne of his ancestor David.

Family and lineage are invoked in a variety of other ways. In the synagogue of Antioch in Pisidia (Acts 13.23), Paul addresses those present as 'brothers, descendants of Abraham's family', clearly evoking family solidarity in an attempt to ingratiate himself with his hearers. By contrast, Jesus makes the shocking statement that in the time of judgment, loyalty to biological family members will break apart (Lk. 12.53). Given the fact that family solidarity was the basis of survival in the ancient world, this was no minor threat.

In Lk. 14.26 Jesus goes even further, declaring that those who wish to be his disciples must 'hate' their own family members. Of course we must understand this carefully. 'Hate' does not refer here to the emotion we so describe in English. 'Love' in the New Testament refers to group 'attachment' or group 'loyalty', while 'hate' is simply the opposite: group 'disloyalty' (Malina and Rohrbaugh 2003: 380-81). To say one 'hates' one thing and 'loves' another is simply a colloquialism describing priorities between the two. In other words, what Jesus demands is not negative emotions toward family but something deeply radical nonetheless: greater loyalty to him than to one's biological descent group. To the family-centered society in which he lived that is perhaps the most radical thing Jesus ever said. In John's Gospel Jesus even adds (15.23), 'Whoever hates (is disloyal to) me hates (is disloyal to) my father also'.

Quite common in the New Testament are descent identifiers where the issue is character—often in settings of conflict. Perhaps the best example is the charges and countercharges in John 8 between Jesus and the Judeans: 'Abraham is our father' . . . 'If you were Abraham's children you would be doing what Abraham did'. Character is also the focus of Jesus' comment in Jn 14.9: 'Whoever has seen me has seen the Father'. In Mt. 3.7 John the Baptist uses as nasty a character insult as one could possibly imagine in a society where birth-status was a matter of pride: he calls the Pharisees and Sadducees the offspring of snakes (literally, 'snake bastards'!). He then warns them not to claim Abraham as an ancestor as if that guaranteed character.[6] Jesus uses the same insult in Mt. 23.31-33. After claiming they were better than some of their ancestors who had killed the prophets, Jesus angrily tells the scribes and Pharisees, 'You testify against yourselves that you are descendants of those who murdered the prophets'. He then punctuates the charge by calling them 'snakes, and the offspring of snakes'. Not only are they evil themselves, they come from a line of ancestors with similar character.

In a similar fashion during a heated confrontation at Paphos (Acts 13.10), Paul hurls a character-focused genealogical charge at Elymas the magician: 'You son of the devil, you enemy of all righteousness, full of all deceit and villainy, will you not stop making crooked the straight paths of the Lord?' On a more positive note Paul can state (Rom. 8.29) that those whom God foreknew he also predestined to be 'conformed to the image of his Son, in order that he might be the firstborn (in character and honor, not simply chronology) in a large family'.

6. In Lk. 3.7, John the Baptist says this to the whole crowd.

Finally, ancestors are frequently cited as positive or negative examples to follow. Jesus claims that he does what his Father asks so the world will know that he 'loves' (is loyal to) him (Jn 14.31). In Acts 28.17 Paul claims he has done nothing against the customs of the ancestors. He repeats the claim in Gal. 1.14, saying he has always been zealous for the ancestral tradition. Furthermore, Paul specifies Abraham as the ancestor to be imitated by both the circumcised and uncircumcised (Rom. 4.12). The elder of 2 John (1.4) is delighted to find the children of the elect lady walking in the Father's truth. A negative example can be found in Acts 7.35-53, where Stephen recounts the ancestral history and the failure of his opponents to follow Moses, the greatest ancestor of them all.

Conclusion

In conclusion, then, we can say that it is precisely because such descent indicators are loaded with *social* information and significance that they are worthy of more attention than contemporary readers customarily give them. While space does not permit a look at all the ones in the New Testament, the examples above should make this clear. And while we can acknowledge that many other factors besides family origin contributed to ancient allocations of status, power and privilege, pedigree really did matter. Low-born types were supposed to beget their own kind, and the great were expected to produce the next generation of stars. When that did not happen, when a low-born person attained unexpected rank or position (Moses, Jesus), social compasses went awry. Stability and order were threatened. Such anomalies required out-of-the-ordinary explanation because birth-status was not sufficient to justify or explain the position or privilege being held. That is why ancient cultures had a stock of stories to explain how such things could possibly happen: a divine birth, a virgin birth, or even the divine rescue of a low-born infant, destined for greatness, who was threatened by a king intent on killing infant rivals. Stories of portents in the heavens or honorific gifts from foreign dignitaries could help as well. But ultimately divine intervention of some sort *had* to be involved because biologically 'like begets like'. No other explanation sufficed in a world where pedigree was everything.

In sum, genealogies and other descent indicators had real-world consequences for the first readers of the New Testament. For Americans, however, learning to 'read' and catch the implications the indicators contain requires the hard work of cross-cultural communication. That is because these references come in a language Americans do not speak. Yet if we can never know completely what is encoded in the descent indicators that ancient persons understood as part of their daily experience, nonetheless theirs is not a language that is totally beyond our reach. In fact, it is yet another example of what can be gained if we are willing to move beyond our Western ethnocentric and anachronistic reading of the Bible and learn the culture from which it came.

References

Babbitt, Frank Cole (trans.)
1927 *Plutarch's Moralia,* vol. 1 (LCL; New York: Putnam's Sons).

Basore, John W. (trans.)
1935 *Seneca: Moral Essays,* vol. 3 (LCL; Cambridge, MA: Harvard University Press).

Bodel, J.
1999 'Death on Display: Looking at Roman Funerals', in *The Art of Ancient Spectacle* (ed. B.A Bergmann and C. Kondoleon; New Haven, CT: Yale University Press): 259-81.

Colson, F.H., and G.H. Whitaker (trans.)
1930 *Philo,* vol. 3 (LCL; New York: Putnam's Sons).

De Lacy, Phillip H., and Benedict Einarson (trans.)
1959 *Plutarch's Moralia,* vol. 7 (LCL; Cambridge, MA: Harvard University Press).

Dunn, Geoffrey D.
2001 'The Ancestry of Jesus according to Tertullian: *ex David per Miriam*', *Studia patristica* 36: 349-55.

Forde, Daryll
1947 'The Anthropological Approach in Social Science', *Advancement in Science* 4: 213-24.

Freese, John H. (trans.)
1926 *Aristotle: The Art of Rhetoric* (LCL; Cambridge MA: Harvard University Press).

Fustel de Coulanges, N.D.
1979 *The Ancient City: A Study on the Religion, Laws, and Institutions of Greece and Rome* (Gloucester, MA: Peter Smith).

Garnsey, Peter
1970 *Social Status and Legal Privilege in the Roman Empire* (London: Oxford University Press).

Goitein, S.D.
1988 *A Mediterranean Society: The Jewish Communities of the Arab World as Portrayed in the Documents of the Cairo Geniza. Vol. V: The Individual* (Berkeley, CA: University of California Press).

Goody, Jack
1968 'Kinship: Descent Groups', in *International Encyclopedia of the Social Sciences* (ed. David Sills; New York: Macmillan): 401-13.

Gordon, Cyrus Herzl
1977 'Paternity at Two Levels', *JBL* 96: 101 [Critical Note].

Hanson, K.C.
1989 'The Herodians and Mediterranean Kinship. Part I: Genealogy and Descent', *BTB* 19: 75-84.

Hanson, K.C., and Douglas E. Oakman
1998 *Palestine in the Time of Jesus: Social Structures and Social Conflicts* (Minneapolis, MN: Fortress Press).
Hett, W.S., and H. Rackham (trans.)
1937 *Aristotle: Problems Books 22–38; Rhetorica ad Alexandrum* (LCL; Cambridge, MA: Harvard University Press).
Hood, Rodney T.
1961 'The Genealogies of Jesus', in *Early Christian Origins: Studies in Honor of Harold R. Willoughby* (ed. Allen Wikgren; Chicago: Quadrangle): 1-15.
Huskinson, Jane
2011 'Picturing the Roman Family', in Rawson (2011): 521-41.
Johanson, Christopher
2011 'A Walk with the Dead: A Funerary Cityscape of Ancient Rome', in Rawson (2011): 408-29.
Johnson, Marshall D.
1969 *The Purpose of Biblical Genealogies: With Special Reference to the Setting of the Genealogies of Jesus* (SNTSMS, 8; London: Cambridge University Press).
Kalmin, Richard
1996 'Genealogy and Polemics in the Rabbinic Literature of Late Antiquity', *Hebrew Union College Annual* 67: 77-94.
Levin, Yigal
2001 'Understanding Biblical Genealogies', *Currents in Research: Biblical Studies* 9: 11-46.
Malina, Bruce J.
1991 'Is There a Circum-Mediterranean Person? Looking for "Stereotypes"', *BTB* 22: 66-87.
1993 'Let a Man Deny Himself (Mark 8:34//): A Social Psychological Model of Self Denial', *BTB* 24: 106-19.
2001 *The New Testament World: Insights from Cultural Anthropology* (Louisville, KY: Westminster John Knox, 3rd edn).
Malina, Bruce J., and Jerome H. Neyrey
1991 'First Century Personality: Dyadic, Not Individualistic', in Neyrey 1991: 67-96.
Malina, Bruce J., and Richard Rohrbaugh
2003 *Social Science Commentary on the Synoptic Gospels* (Minneapolis, MN: Fortress Press).
Neyrey, Jerome H. (ed.)
1991 *The Social World of Luke–Acts* (Peabody, MA: Hendrickson Publishers).
Niles, F.S.
1998 'Individualism–Collectivism Revisited', *Journal of Cross Cultural Research* 32: 315-41.
Plum, Karin F.
1989 'Genealogy as Theology', *Scandinavian Journal of the Old Testament* 1: 66-92.
Rawson, Beryl (ed.)
2011 *A Companion to Families in the Greek and Roman Worlds* (Malden, MA: Wiley-Blackwell).

Rohrbaugh, Richard L.

2007 *The New Testament in Cross-Cultural Perspective* (Matrix: The Bible in Mediterranean Context; Eugene, OR: Cascade Books/Wipf & Stock).

2009 'Honor: Core Value of the Biblical World', in *The Social Context of the New Testament* (ed. Richard DeMaris and Dietmar Neufeld; New York: Routledge): 27-43.

Shelton, Jo-Ann

1998 *As the Romans Did: A Sourcebook in Roman Social History* (New York: Oxford University Press, 2nd edn).

Triandis, Harry C.

1995 *Individualism and Collectivism* (San Francisco, CA: Westview).

Wilson, Robert R.

1975 'Old Testament Genealogies in Recent Research', *JBL* 94: 169-89.

1977 *Genealogy and History in the Biblical World* (New Haven, CT: Yale University Press).

Intimation of the Year of Jubilee in the Parable of the Wicked Tenants

Herman C. Waetjen

The honoree, Dr John H. Elliott, and I have enjoyed a warm collegial friendship for fifty-five years. It was initiated in the academic environment of a course in contemporary philosophy that I had been invited to teach at Concordia Theological Seminary in St Louis in 1957, and it has continued to grow into a maturity that we share in the biblical mandate to 'do justice, to love kindness and to walk humbly with God'. Jack was oriented to New Testament scholarship at Concordia, and, with encouragement from me, he entered the University of Münster in Westfallen to pursue a doctorate in biblical studies and complete a dissertation on 1 Peter. While there, he met and married Linde, and she has worked alongside him in translating German New Testament writings into English. We reconnected after they left Concordia Seminary, where Jack taught briefly, to take up residence in northern California in order to enable Jack to teach New Testament at the Jesuit University of San Francisco. As war-protesting academics, we were drawn together with colleagues in biblical studies to form 'the Bay Area Seminar for Theology and Related Disciplines' (or 'BASTARD'), which pioneered the introduction of social-scientific criticism into biblical scholarship, a historical-critical discipline with which Jack has gained world-wide recognition. His work on 1 Peter has culminated in two magisterial publications: *A Home for the Homeless,* the finest social-scientific interpretation of 1 Peter that has been published, and his commentary on 1 Peter in the Anchor Bible series. While he has continued his biblical scholarship, he has also been involved in circles and communities working for social, economic and political change. It is to him that I dedicate this essay on the Parable of the Wicked Tenants, which culminates in the liberation of the poor and the dispossessed from the subjugation of the ruling elite.

The institution of the Year of Jubilee and its economic regulations, detailed in Leviticus 25, may never have been put into practice in the history of Israel. But the ideals of redemption and restoration, which it envisioned for the nation's covenantal relationship with God and its intended actualization of justice, were appropriated and applied by Israel's prophets to the social, economic and political conditions of their times.

> And you shall hallow the fiftieth year and you shall proclaim liberty throughout the land to all its inhabitants. It shall be a jubilee for you: you shall return, every one of you, to your property, and everyone of you to your family. When you make a sale to your neighbor or buy from your neighbor, you shall not cheat one another. When you buy from your neighbor, you shall pay only for the number of years since the jubilee; the seller shall charge you only for the remaining crop years (Lev. 25.10, 14-15, NRSV).

The anonymous prophet of Isa. 61.1-11 simulates the essence of the Year of Jubilee in his summation of 'the year of Yahweh's favor', and Yahweh's 'love of justice'. Jesus' ministry appears to have been directed toward the fulfillment of these jubilary ideals. Indeed, his actualization of the eschatological reality of 'the kingdom of God' expresses vital aspects of the redemption of the jubilee year, 'the year of the Lord's favor', as he announces it in the synagogue of Nazareth at the commencement of his ministry (Lk. 4.18-21). The Parable of the Wicked Tenants functions as a mirror confronting the ruling elite with their eviction from God's vineyard and their replacement by the very people they oppressed and dispossessed, the poor and the destitute.[1]

The Parable of the Wicked Tenants[2] *(Mark 12.1-11; Matthew 21.33-42; Luke 20.9-17; Gospel of Thomas 65-66)*

There are four versions of this parable: one in each of the Synoptic Gospels of Mark, Matthew and Luke and one in the *Gospel of Thomas*.[3] Of the four, the Marcan version is the earliest, and, although it includes some allegorical elements, it is, nevertheless, a parable attributable to Jesus. Both Matthew and Luke appropriated the parable from Mark, but edited it, either adding or deleting features derived from Isa. 5.1-2, according to

1. On parable functioning as mirror, see Antoinette Clark Wire 1983.

2. The interpretation of this parable is determined by John Dominic Crossan's definition of parable as figurative language: 'Figurative language has two quite different functions. One is to illustrate information so that information precedes participation. The other is to create participation so that participation precedes information.' Also, 'A parable tells a story which, on its surface level, is absolutely possible or even factual within the normalcy of life' (Crossan 1973: 15).

3. See Robert W. Funk, Roy W. Hoover and the Jesus Seminar (1993: 100-101), where the parable has been printed in gray, indicating the inclination of the Jesus Seminar to attribute the parable to the creativity of the early church. But note: 'A version of this parable without allegorical overtones, could be traced to Jesus' (1993: 101). *Gospel of Thomas*'s simpler edition is considered to be closer to the original parable.

the character and conditions of their socio-economic context.[4] The *Thomas* version has no narrative setting, the initial allusions to Isa. 5.1-2 have been eliminated, and its original parabolic character has been forfeited by the reduction of its structure and content. Its abbreviated form, however, has elicited the opposite conjectures about the earliest dating and the lateness of its distinctive version, representing either a more primitive edition of the parable or the continuation of a process of abridgment already begun by Luke.[5] Its appearance in the *Gospel of Thomas* intimates that, in its historical transmission, it is the final rendering of the story, deliberately abbreviated in order to present the gnostic perspective of the son, namely Jesus, who, by being sent 'by the good man who owned the vineyard', enters the material world of the vineyard in order to bring light to its tenants but suffers their rejection.[6]

Jesus is the narrator in all three Synoptic versions of the parable. But it is only in the contexts of its Marcan (11.27 and 12.1) and Matthean (21.23) redactions that the story is explicitly addressed to chief priests (ἀρχιερεῖς), lawyers (γραμματεῖς) and elders (πρεσβύτεροι), the three groups who constitute the Sanhedrin.[7] Of the three Synoptic renderings of the parable, the Marcan version, minus its allegorical features, is the original. Its immediate context is the challenge directed at Jesus by these three groups of religious leaders to disclose the source of the authority by which he has shut

4. Which of the four versions should be prioritized as the original parable has continued to evoke extensive discussion. Klyne R. Snodgrass (1983: 45-71) compares the various accounts and then proceeds to determine the development of the tradition. His analysis shows that the *Thomas* version, which has two linguistic features in common with Luke (δώσουσιν αὐτῷ and ἴσως), may be dependent on Lk. 20.10 and 20.13, or at least a similar tradition. Snodgrass prioritizes the Matthean version of the parable. William R. Herzog II (1994: 98-101) and Arland J. Hultgren (2000: 355-67) also review the judgments regarding the relationships of the four versions of the story to one another to determine priority of origin.

5. Crossan (1973: 86-96) considers the *Thomas* version to be the authentic parable of Jesus. Bernard Brandon Scott (1989: 245-46) is unable to make sense of the story and struggles to recover an 'originating structure' of the parable, cleansed of all its allegorical details. His judgment: 'The story frustrates metaphorical referencing and consistency building, thus creating an alienating and defamiliarizing experience that blocks closure and resolution, forcing upon the hearer the one item that stands out: the tenants' recognition of the son as *heir* and their proposal to gain the *inheritance*. This makes no sense at the level of narrative structure, because it is impossible' (the italics are Scott's). Charles Harold Dodd (1935: 124-32) offers a hypothetical reconstruction of the original parable, which, after the *Gospel of Thomas* was found in 1945, proved to resemble the *Thomas* version of the parable.

6. Hultgren (2000: 366) offers the same verdict of the *Thomas* parable.

7. The allusion to Isa. 5.1-2 in both the Marcan and Matthean versions, and most likely also the Lucan, is drawn from the Septuagint.

down the Temple institution (11.15-17). After declining to reveal the origin of his authority in response to their refusal to acknowledge the heavenly origin of John's baptism, he proceeds to address them with a parable that is introduced by imagery drawn from the opening two verses of Isaiah's 'Song of the Vineyard' (5.1-2) and constructed to serve as the entrance to the story.[8]

> And he began to speak to them in parables: 'A vineyard a human being planted, and he set a hedge around it and dug a wine trough and built a tower, and he leased it to tenant farmers, and he departed' (Mk 12.1).[9]

Matthew's redaction of Jesus' introductory use of Isa. 5.1-2 is virtually identical to his Marcan source. The human being who plants the vineyard, however, is specifically identified as a housemaster (οἰκοδεσπότης), a term that the evangelist employs seven times, primarily in his rendition of Jesus' parables. Its deliberate use in Matthew's narrative world is determined by the presence of upper-class landowners and businessmen among the addressees of his Gospel.

> Hear another parable: 'A human being was a housemaster who planted a vineyard, and he built a wall around it and dug a wine press and built a tower, and he leased it to tenant farmers, and he departed' (Mt. 21.33).

In the Lucan edition Jesus addresses the people (ὁ λαός), the term by which the evangelist generally acknowledges the people of Israel as God's elect people.

> Now he began to speak to the people (τὸν λαὸν) this parable: 'A human being planted a vineyard and he leased it to tenant farmers, and he departed for a long time' (Lk. 20.9).

In contrast to the Marcan and Matthean versions of Jesus' introduction of the story, the reference to Isa. 5.1-2 in Lk. 20.9 is limited to the words 'he planted a vineyard'. To what extent they would enable the Gospel's addressees to identify the metaphorical referents of the tenants can only be determined after the objective of the parable is disclosed. Noteworthy is the Lucan redaction of 20.16. The people, the λαός, disavow the story's concluding destruction of the tenants and the transfer of the vineyard to others by exclaiming *μὴ γένοιτο* ('may it not happen').

8. Although the narrator states in Mk 12.1 that Jesus spoke to them in parables (παραβολαῖς), only one parable follows. The use of the plural is typical of Mark, as 3.23; 4.2, 11 indicate. 'It is Jesus' manner of speaking parabolically' (Hultgren 2000: 367).

9. Jesus' use of Isa. 5.1-2 in Mk 12.1 is based on the LXX translation of the Hebrew text of Isa. 5.1-2. I have indicated by underlining in the introduction of this parable in the four versions of Matthew, Mark, Luke and *Thomas* where the wording corresponds to the wording of Isa. 5.1-2 in the LXX.

In all three versions the owner and planter of the vineyard is an ἄνθρωπος, a human being who departs after leasing the vineyard to tenant farmers, and therefore is identifiable as an absentee landlord. Jesus' introductory use of Isa. 5.1-2 readily lends itself to an immediate identification of this vineyard owner, for the 'Beloved' of Isaiah's 'love-song', who planted a vineyard, hewed out a vat and built a watchtower is identified in 5.7 as '[the] Lord of hosts'. But who, on the basis of Isa. 5.1-2 and its context, would be inclined to identify '[the] Lord of hosts', the planter and owner of the vineyard as an absentee landlord? Particularly if the vineyard metaphorically represents 'the house of Israel'?

The final features of the parable's introduction, specifically leasing the vineyard to peasant farmers and departing as an absentee landlord, move the story Jesus will tell into the contemporaneous realities of Galilean agriculture. Historical records indicate that for many generations Galilee had been royal territory subject to the control of prebendal domains, that is, 'stipend' property or grants for income. The land was awarded to officials of the state who derived their income from it by leasing it to the peasantry for a stipulated rent to be paid in the form of agricultural produce, money or labor. The Zenon papyri of the third century BCE disclose that the Hellenistic monarch of Egypt, Ptolemy Philadelphus (283–246 BCE), had granted property in Bet Anat in Galilee to his finance minister, Apollonius (Freyne 1980: 156-62). The estate, which he owned as an absentee landlord, appears to have been a large holding of grain fields and a vineyard of 80,000 grapevines. It is estimated that a workforce of at least twenty-five people was required to carry out the work that was involved in such a large operation, but this seems to be a minimal figure. Herod the Great advanced this kind of latifundialization during his reign in the first century BCE by expropriating large tracts of farmland and selling them to wealthy landowners (Oakman 1986: 141-49; Fiensy 1991: 24-43, 49-60). Consequently the best agricultural lands of Galilee fell into the hands of a few land barons who preferred to live in another part of Palestine or even abroad while their estates were managed by estate managers (οἰκονόμοι) and worked by tenant farmers (γεωργοί). Michael Rostovtzeff offers a comprehensive view of land tenure in Palestine:

> Judaea, Samaria, and still more Galilee are studded with hundreds of villages inhabited by peasants, above whom stands a native aristocracy of large landowners, who are patrons of the villages. . . . Still more opulent are the officials of the kings and tetrarchs, and the kings and tetrarchs themselves and their families. Lastly, we find estates of the Roman emperor himself and the imperial family, and even a military colony established by Vespasian at Emmaus after the Jewish War. Such were the conditions of life in Palestine, and in later times there was clearly no change, except that

> landed proprietors of other than Jewish origin, like Libanius, increased in number (Rostovtzeff 1957: 1.270).[10]

Rostovtzeff's and Willy Schottroff's socio-economic analysis of the realities of latifundialization and the concomitant dispossession of the peasantry during the Hellenistic and Roman domination of Palestine establish the real-life plausibility of Jesus' Parable of the Wicked Tenants (Rostovtzeff 1957: 1.270; 2.663-64 n. 32; Schottroff 1996: 26-32).

The story recounts a local peasant revolt and its activation of a spiral of violence, but it does not 'open with a description of a familiar process, the takeover of peasant land and its subsequent conversion into a vineyard' (Herzog 1994: 104).[11] That is a projection into the introduction of the parable. Nothing more can be presupposed by the opening of the story than a large holding of land, a latifundium, owned by a member of the political or religious elite who, by planting a vineyard and leasing it to tenant farmers, is engaged in the production of a cash crop. The purpose of Jesus' allusion to Isa. 5.1-2 should not be limited to the building of a vineyard (Herzog 1994: 101-104). As reality oriented as the story is, the failure of the peasant revolt, which Herzog interprets as a codification of 'the futility of armed rebellion' (1994: 113), eradicates the parabolic character of the story.[12] For if Mk 12.9 is assumed to be its conclusion, and 'the parable ends as abruptly as most peasant revolts', the story has been reduced to an action narrative that investigates world.[13] As such, the story merely illustrates what is already known. Consequently, there is no need to subvert the credibility of 'the themes of ownership, inheritance, and heir' by calling into question the accepted version of those generative themes (Herzog 1994: 113). They are already comprehended by the addressees.

10. On land tenure, see Rostovtzeff 1957: 1.270; 2.663-64 n. 32, and Rostovtzeff 1967: 2.1181-82; more recently, Schottroff 1996: 20-26. Also Horsley and Hanson 1985: 58-63.

11. Herzog, who, adopting Paulo Freire's 'codification' as the most incisive way to interpret Jesus' parables, maintains that 12.1-2 presupposes that peasant land has been expropriated and converted into a vineyard. Mark the evangelist chose to utilize Isa. 5.1-2 'to describe the building of the vineyard' (1994: 102). On Herzog's use of 'codification', see 1994: 20-24.

12. On Herzog's employment of Freire's 'codification', see 1994: 20-24. Herzog applies this codification to Jesus' stories as generative images 'designed to stimulate social analysis and to expose the contradictions between the actual situation of its hearer and the Torah of God's justice' (1994: 28). If Jesus' stories are interpreted as codifications, they disclose only the contradictions, and the subversion of world is lost.

13. This is the result of Herzog's codification of the story of the parable (1994: 110, 113). See Crossan 1988: 40-45 (p. 42: 'Action narratives investigate world').

This parable should also not be interpreted as a 'transparent, fictive narrative about real life that teach[es] the listeners to "see" in the full sense of the word: to recognize the God of Israel and God's action in this distorted world' (Schottroff 2006: 21). Who are these listeners who are to see? And what is there about 'real life' that the parable would teach them to see? If they are absentee landlords, they are consciously extracting 'the last penny' from the tenants. If they are peasants, they already are experiencing the conflict between the landowner and themselves as tenants, and therefore there is no need to make that reality transparent to them.[14] Where or how 'God's action in this distorted world' may be discerned in or through the events of the story is not explicated.[15] And the realities of 'economic exploitation at the hands of foreign property owners, the counter-violence of their victims, and Roman dominance' that are supposedly transparent in the parable are neither overt nor implied.[16] Concomitantly, nothing in the parable intimates that the religious leaders of Judea, the stipulated addressees in the Marcan and Matthean contexts of the story, are being accused of political failure (Schottroff 2006: 24). They may be representative of the human being who planted the vineyard and who, by dispossessing the tenants of the economic surplus they produce, exacerbates their revolt and in retaliation slaughters them and gives the vineyard to others. But much more is being communicated by Jesus' parable. What that may be depends entirely on the function of Jesus' introductory use of Isa. 5.1-2. To maintain, however, that its reference to a vineyard simply applies to 'the life of the people of Israel' and that any allegorization of Jesus' appropriation of Isa. 5.1-2 contributes to the anti-Judaism that has been promoted in the history of Christian interpretation ignores the mirror-oriented objective of his story (Schottroff 2006: 24). If the history of God's people is concentrated within this narrative, the parable has been reduced to an illustration. The parabolic character of the story, the comparison it insinuates and the metaphorical character of the language have been lost.

14. Schottroff 2006: 24 recognizes that 'the parable in Mark and Matthew addresses Jewish leadership groups', but earlier in her exposition she claims that the parable is intended to teach the listeners to see. What are the listeners to see?

15. But Willy Schottroff, the late husband of Luise Schottroff, concludes that the anger of the vineyard owner portrays the anger of God (1996: 41).

16. See Schottroff 2006: 103, who maintains that parable narratives are intended to describe 'the structure of political rule or the structure of the world of work and social relationships' and offers the following examples: 'the injustice of wealth and the suffering of poverty; the role of the patriarchal father in relation to sons'. Her interpretations treat the parables simply as transparent, fictive narratives about real life, but she ignores their subversive character as well as their function to create participation so that participation precedes information, as Crossan shows (1973: 15).

The addressees of Jesus' parable can easily be identified in the Marcan and Matthean contexts of the story. As already noted, they are chief priests, lawyers and elders, and the impact that the story has on them is noted pointedly by both evangelists in Mk 12.12 and Mt. 21.45. But what specifically elicits that impact is not indicated; it is a matter of the reader's construction. The question, therefore, is critically decisive: with whom do these religious leaders identify themselves as they listen to the parable? The owner and planter of the vineyard who is an absentee landlord or the revolting tenants? If the story evokes within their consciousness a self-identification with the absentee landlord, particularly if they are owners and planters of vineyards, they would be confronted with the contemporaneous realities of peasant revolts against landlords, particularly absentee landlords. That would simply transform Jesus' parable into an action story that ends with the destruction of the tenants who have continued to pay the required rent fund.[17] If, however, the story's introductory allusion to Isa. 5.1-2 arouses within them a recognition that the owner of the vineyard is identifiable as the God of Israel and the vineyard as the house of Israel, they, in terms of their professional identity as the ruling elite, would be compelled to identify themselves with the caretakers of the vineyard, the tenants.

Many of the chief priests, lawyers and elders in Jerusalem undoubtedly were both vineyard owners and absentee landlords, and, as such, they would easily be drawn into Jesus' story. But at the same time, the context of Isa. 5.1-2, would compel them to identify the planter of the vineyard and absentee landlord as God. Consequentially, they are confronted with multiple self-identifications. Jesus' use of Isa. 5.1-2 in the opening verse of the parable in Mark 12 is overpowering in its mirror-like function. It reflects that the ruling elite see themselves in a presumptuous God-like self-understanding, that they and the God who has entrusted to them the vineyard of Israel are alike in their relationship to the vineyard as absentee landlords. A self-understanding, however, that is entirely foreign to the scriptures of the Old Testament! Yet simultaneously they are also compelled to view themselves as the tenants to whom God has committed the care of the vineyard, the house of Israel.[18] Consequently, they would be 'seeing' themselves in mirror-like fashion from an ironic perspective, a perspective that they had never viewed before. In their self-understanding as absentee landlords, they are induced to identify themselves with the revolting tenants to whom God, presupposed to be like them as absentee landlords, has leased his vineyard.

The explicit preparatory activities of the owner of the vineyard—planting vines, building a wall, digging a vat for a wine-press and constructing a watchtower—intimate an anticipation of good harvests. Although no

17. On rent funds, see Lenski 1966: 266-70.

18. Also Dodd 1935: 126; Jeremias 1963: 70; Hultgren 2000: 359.

time period is specified in the story, Jesus' original audience, as well as the readers of the Gospels, would infer a rather considerable period of tenancy before the first payment was required. Even though the vineyard would not be profitable for four or five years, peasant labor would be necessary to tend the vines and to carry on the continuous process of cultivation and weeding (Snodgrass 1983: 32-33). The expenses that would be incurred during this period of time would be defrayed by growing grain and vegetables between the rows of vines. Rent might also be paid on this produce, but at least four years would elapse before a rent fund would be due on the fruit of the vines.

A single slave is stipulated in the Marcan version of the parable as the first to be sent by the owner to collect the rent fund, 'the fruits of the vineyard'. One individual might be all that would be needed to supervise the transfer of the grapes to their predetermined destination.[19] But he is beaten by the tenants and sent away empty. No motive is specified, but a conflict between the landowner and the peasants would be implied, and the hearers of the story would fill this gap accordingly. The unjust rent fund, generally extracted by landowners in an agrarian society, would naturally motivate their refusal to pay 'the fruits of the vineyard'. A second slave is sent to oversee the transfer of the owner's share of the harvest, and he is wounded in the head and dishonored. Obviously the tenants are resolved to resist the payment of the rent fund. Their violence in striking this second slave in the head has elicited the possibility of an allusion to the beheading of John the Baptizer (Crossan 1973: 87). The verbs are almost identical: the tenants struck the slave in the head (ἐκεφαλίωσαν); an executioner decapitated (ἀπεκεφάλισεν) John.[20] In the light of the similarity between the two verbs and the correspondence between this feature of the parable and Mark's earlier narration of John's death, the treatment of the second slave in 12.4 may have been intended to convey a simulation of John's fate. The treatment of the second slave, particularly if it reflects the killing of John the Baptist, would continue the gradual escalation of the violence within the narrative world of Mark's Gospel. It is the murder of the third slave that climaxes the crimes of the tenants against the slaves of the owner of the vineyard and precipitates his decision to send his own son.

However, between the triple sending of the slaves and the murder of the owner's son, Mark has edited into the story a summary account of multiple slaves in 12.5b: 'and many other slaves, some they beat and some they killed'. Its intrusiveness, in all probability, suggests that it is a Marcan

19. How many slaves are necessary to carry out the transaction is disputed. One of the features that convinces Snodgrass (1983: 56-61) of the originality of Matthew's version of the parable is the landowner's sending of a number of slaves to collect the rent.

20. The verb used to denote John's decapitation is simply a compound form of the verb that denotes the slave's being struck on the head.

redaction. It appears to interrupt the movement of the parable, yet it serves to multiply the escalating violence into the culminating event of the murder of the son.

Most likely Jesus originally continued his story from the killing of the third slave into the episode of the sending of the son: 'One he had, a beloved son; he sent him last (ἔσχατον) to them, saying, "They will have respect for my son"'. Frustrated by his slaves' unsuccessful efforts to collect the rent fund, he sends his son last. The adjective ἔσχατος intimates this sending as an eschatological reality; that is, the 'beloved son' is the owner of the vineyard's final representative.[21] There will be none to follow! He is sent as his legal representative, to coerce the tenants to fulfill the contract that they had underwritten. The verb ἐντραπήσονται ('to show deference to') implies the recognition of his high status. Only someone who was involved in the ownership of the land could represent the landlord and serve as a legal claimant. To support the son's legal status, Snodgrass conjectures that the owner of the vineyard had 'transferred a small portion of ownership to the son for this purpose' (1983: 37). But this is an unnecessary projection into the text.

The adjective 'beloved', which characterizes the son in his relation to the landlord, namely, υἱὸς ἀγαπητός ('beloved son'), must also be regarded as a Marcan redaction. It is inconceivable that Jesus would project himself into the narrative world of his own story and identify himself with the son of this absentee landlord. Only the original addressees of the parable, the landowning ruling elite, would naturally be inclined to identify the planter of the vineyard as God on the basis of the parable's introductory allusion to Isa. 5.1-2 and its added observation, 'he leased it (the vineyard) to tenant farmers and went away'. For the evangelist, however, the insertion of the word 'beloved' would be natural because the parable belongs to the narrative world of Mark's Gospel in which the heavenly voice at Jesus' baptism and transfiguration identified him as 'my son the beloved' (Mk 1.11 and 9.7). Mark's redaction of the son as 'beloved', in order to intimate an identification with Jesus, would, of course, be directed to the addressees of his Gospel. But such an implied identification of Jesus with the son of the landowner in the original version of the parable, that is, the story as Jesus may have told it during his ministry, is incongruous because it supports the religious leaders' identification of the absentee landlord as God and therefore the identification of the 'beloved son' as God's son. Yet because of its location in the narrative world of Mark's Gospel, the Marcan redaction would convey to its addressees that the very God, with whom the religious leaders identify themselves as absentee landlords, is nevertheless the God of Israel who has a 'beloved son'. Both the preceding baptism and transfigu-

21. Also Hultgren 2000: 368.

ration stories and the so-called suffering Son of Man sayings in 8.31, 9.31 and 10.33-34 would facilitate the identification of Jesus with the 'beloved son' of the parable who, in the story of the parable, was killed by the revolting tenants who personify the ruling elite. In turn that would anticipate the fulfillment of that part of the story when the chief priests, the lawyers and the elders, to whom the parable is addressed, deliver Jesus to the Romans for crucifixion. Consequently, Mark's version of the parable is disposed toward an allegorization of Jesus' story; however, the parable as Jesus probably told it during his ministry is neither an allegory nor an illustration. In its remarkable mirror-like metaphorical character it is a parable that creates participation so that participation precedes information.[22]

Noteworthy in this context is the intertextual relation between Mk 12.7 and LXX Gen. 37.20. The mutual inducement of the tenants to kill the son, 'Come, let us kill him' (δεῦτε ἀποκτείνωμεν αὐτόν), replicates the incentive of Jacob's sons to kill their brother Joseph.[23] Both texts, the Parable of the Wicked Tenants and the story of Jacob's sons planning to kill their brother Joseph, are oriented to the critical issue of inheritance. That coincidence between Mk 12.7 and LXX Gen. 37.20 in the matter of inheritance is repeated in the correspondence between the parable's spiral of violence culminating in the murder of the 'beloved son' and Mark's account of the death of Jesus. The inheritance of 'the kingdom of God' that Jesus is inaugurating for the poor and the dispossessed is directly opposed to the efforts of the ruling elite to establish themselves as the true heirs of the house of Israel at the expense of those whom they subjugate and whom they simultaneously disinherit.

The motive for killing the son that is attributed to the tenants is their expectation of taking over the possession of the vineyard, 'Come, let us kill him, and the inheritance (ἡ κληρονομία) will be ours'. But how they would be able to claim it for themselves is not indicated. What projection at this point in the story is Jesus' original audience or Mark's addressees expected to make in order to fill this gap? Does the sending of the son, the heir of the vineyard, imply that usucaption, the acquisition of title to the vineyard by the tenants, has become a possibility because of their long-undisturbed settlement on the property? Concomitantly, must the landowner reassert his authority of ownership after a period of four years in order to continue to possess the land (Derrett 1970: 296-306)? According to the Mishnaic tractate *B. Bat.* 3.1, usucaption, the acquisition of property, is legally possible after a period of three years. To this *B. Bat.* 3.2ab adds, 'There are three regions as securing title through usucaption: Judah, Transjordan, and Galilee. If one was located in Judea, and [someone else] took possession

22. Again, Crossan 1973: 15.

23. Scott (1989: 252) connects this moment of intertextuality with the theme of inheritance that is prominent in the Hebrew scriptures.

of his property in Galilee', securing title by usucaption would be legal.[24] However, *B. Bat.* 33i forbids 'tenants' as well as 'joint-holders and guardians to secure title by usucaption'. Consequently, none of these projections can fill this gap in the parable.[25] Laws, such as those of *B. Bat.* 3, would very likely be enacted after the fact of such attempts at land seizure. In all probability, peasant sharecroppers would have enjoyed few, if any, options to claim property during the time of Jesus' ministry. During the rule of the Herodians, absentee landlords would protect their stipend property from any and every possibility of usucaption. The closure of Jesus' parable, Mk 12.9, in fact, supports this conclusion.[26] The outcome of the story proves the senselessness and foolhardiness of the tenants to seize the vineyard.

Matthew has heightened the allegorical character of the story. While Mark's version has three different sendings of a single slave each time during the initial harvest, Matthew has only two sendings, but of multiple slaves.

> Now when the season of fruits drew near, he sent his slaves to the tenant farmers to receive his fruits. And the tenants taking his slaves, one they beat, one they killed and one they stoned. Again he sent other slaves, more than the first, and they did the same to them (Mt. 21:34-36).

The multiple slaves of both of these two sendings probably represent the differentiation between the earlier and the later prophets and the persecution and martyrdom of the judges, prophets and priests in the course of Israel's history (Jeremais 1963: 72; Hultgren 2000: 371). The use of the adverb ὕστερον ('finally') at the beginning of v. 37, which introduces the sending of the son, sustains the implied history of Israel represented by the two missions of the multiple slaves. The son is killed, but only after he has been thrown out of the vineyard. Undoubtedly, this signifies the rejection of Jesus by crucifixion that condemns him to the curse of Deut. 21.23 and therefore his separation from Israel as the people of God. Analogously, therefore, the correspondence between Matthew's allegorized version of the parable and Matthew's distinctive narrative world parallels the congruity between Mark's allegorized version of the parable and Mark's narrative world. This is evident in the coincidence between the murder of one slave and the stoning of another in Mt. 21.35 and Jesus' bitter polemic against 'the scribes and the Pharisees' in Matthew 23, specifically his denunciation of 'all the righteous blood shed on earth from the blood of righteous Abel to

24. *Baba Batra* 3.1ac and 3.2ab (Neusner 1988: 563).

25. Herzog (1994: 107) considers it unlikely that the tenants could stake a legal claim to the vineyard.

26. Mark 12.9, rather than Mt. 21.41 and Lk. 20.16b, probably is the original conclusion of Jesus' parable.

the blood of Zechariah son of Barachiah' in v. 35.[27] The parallels between the allegorization of this parable and the allegorization of the Parable of the Wedding Feast of 22.2-10 offer additional evidence of their correspondence to the structure and character of the Gospel's narrative world. Jesus' question at the end of Matthew's version of the parable (21.41) is answered by the addressees, the chief priests, the lawyers and the elders. Ironically, they pronounce judgment upon themselves.

The Lucan version of the parable (20.9-19) is addressed to the λαός, a term that is used thirty-eight times in the Gospel to designate God's elect *people* Israel. They have been present throughout Jesus' ministry. They were baptized by John, heard Jesus' Sermon on the Plain, witnessed his healing, ate of the bread and fish that he provided in the desert, and were spellbound by his teaching (19.48). They are present in the Temple when the chief priests, lawyers and elders challenge Jesus to legitimate the authority he exercised in cleansing the Temple and in teaching *the people* (ὁ λαός). At their refusal to reply to his critically defining question, 'Did the baptism of John come from heaven or was it of human origin?' he turns to the people (ὁ λαός), and tells them this parable. Only a fragment of Isa. 5.1 is used in Jesus' introduction to the story, 'he planted a vineyard' (ἐφύτευσεν ἀμπελῶνα).[28] Correspondingly, the allegorical character of the Marcan story has also been mitigated, and consequently the narrative recounts events that appear to reflect more realistically the contractual relationship between the landlord and the tenants.[29] The vineyard, however, remains representative of God's people Israel. As in Mk 12.1, the landlord leases the vineyard to tenant farmers and departs. Luke has added the note 'for a considerable length of time'.[30] When the rent fund is due, a single slave is sent to receive the 'fruit of the vineyard', and the tenants, 'beating him, sent him away empty' (20.10). Another slave is sent, and this one is beaten and dishonored and, like the first slave, sent away empty. When the third slave is wounded and thrown out, the owner initially appears to be equivocal about the response he must make, 'What shall I do?' Equally his decision seems

27. 2 Chronicles 24.21 recounts the stoning to death of Zechariah, the son of the priest Jehoiada. See also the litany of the sufferings and killings of Israel's prophets in Heb. 11.36-37.

28. Snodgrass (1983: 47-48) rightly contends that the Lucan omission of Isaiah 5 is unfounded.

29. Also Crossan 1973: 91. On the basis of 20.10 ('At the season he sent a slave to the tenants so that they might give him from the fruit of the vineyard'), Hultgren (2000: 376) states that 'the owner appears less aggressive; the tenants are expected to respond freely of their own accord and without pressure from the slave of the owner'.

30. Hultgren (2000: 375) has correctly observed that this time reference, 'a considerable length of time', cannot refer to the *parousia* because the owner of the vineyard is representative of God, not Jesus.

to reflect a degree of reluctance, 'I shall send my son the beloved; it may be that they will have respect for him'.[31] In spite of his redaction of the allegorical character of his Marcan source, Luke appears to be deliberate in his adoption of the substantive adjective 'the beloved' (ὁ ἀγαπητός) to characterize the owner's son. In Luke's Gospel, as in the Gospel of Mark, its appropriation intimates an echo of the heavenly voice's identification of Jesus at his baptism in 3.22, 'You are my son *the beloved* (ὁ ἀγαπητός)'. When he appears at the vineyard, the tenants debate with one another as to what they should do. Recognizing that he is the heir, they decide to kill him 'so that the inheritance becomes ours'. As in Mt. 21.39, they throw the son out of the vineyard and then kill him, and that sequence of actions appears to reinforce the correspondence between these acts within the parable and the events of the forthcoming crucifixion of Jesus outside of the city. In Lk. 20.15b-16a, Jesus ends the parable, as he did in Mk 12.9 and Mt. 21.40, with a question and an answer, 'What, then, will the lord of the vineyard do to them? He will come and destroy these tenants?' The people, the λαός, who have heard the story, reject his conclusion by exclaiming, 'By no means!' They are the house of Israel, and the judgment that will fall upon the revolting tenants, their religious leaders, will include them. And Luke, as 20.19 indicates, observes that the lawyers and the chief priests realize that Jesus spoke this parable against them.

In contrast to Isa. 5.5-6, the vineyard is not destroyed. Jesus' concluding question and answer convey the unexpected reversal of the episode. Those who killed the heir of the vineyard are dispossessed by the owner, and the vineyard is leased to others. Without this ironic conclusion the story is incomplete and therefore cannot function parabolically. Without this ironic conclusion there would be no surprise twist; there would be no subversion of world, no mirror of disclosure. The story would simply be 'a deliberately shocking story of successful murder' (Crossan 1973: 96).[32] The ending of Mk 12.9, Mt. 21.40-41 and Lk. 20.15b-16a is essential for the integrity of the story to function as a parable, in terms of both its mirror-like and subversive functions. To object on the basis that Jesus did not end his parables with a question and answer imposes a limit on the creativity of Jesus in his story-telling and overlooks similar instances in Mt. 20.15 and Lk. 12.20.[33]

But who are the 'others' to whom the vineyard will be leased? Jesus does not identify them. The addressees of each Gospel would fill this gap by their own projection, but it would be a projection that would be deter-

31. Hultgren (2000: 378-79) perceives this sense of uncertainty in the decision of the vineyard owner to send his 'beloved son'.

32. This is Crossan's conclusion on the basis of his judgment that the *Thomas* parable is its original version.

33. Against Scott 1989: 248.

mined by their own socio-political self-understanding in their Roman-dominated society and concomitantly by the effects of their interaction with the Gospel that has been addressed to them. Jesus' ministry in Mark's Gospel is directed toward drawing the disenfranchised lower classes into 'the kingdom of God', and most likely, therefore, the identity of the 'others' that would be projected would be the actual tenants of Palestinian latifundial agriculture. In Mark's version of Jesus' parable they are implied to be the ruling elite, but in the socio-economic world of Palestine these 'others' would be those subjugated to poverty and dispossession by the ruling elite.[34] The same identification would apply to 'the stone which the builders rejected' in Jesus' quotation of Ps. 118.22 in Mk 12.10-11.

> Did you not read this scripture, 'A stone which the builders rejected, this became *unto* (εἰς) the cornerstone; this is from [the] Lord, and it is marvelous in our eyes'.

In place of a vineyard, a building is implied, and instead of tenant farmers, builders. Although this image of the rejected keystone is generally interpreted christologically by being identified with Jesus, by analogy, and in view of the change in metaphor, it more appropriately refers to the 'others' who receive the vineyard at the conclusion of the parable. The stone that becomes the cornerstone in the house of Israel should be identified as the disenfranchised lower classes.

Matthew has also appropriated the tradition of the rejected keystone of Ps. 118.22 and placed it immediately after the religious leaders have replied to Jesus' question with the answer, 'He will give forth the vineyard to other tenants'. Jesus, according to Matthew's redaction in 21.43, enunciates the identification of the 'other tenants' himself: 'On account of this I say to you, "the reign of God will be taken from you and will be given to a *nation* (ἔθνει) producing its fruit"'. The word ἔθνος usually refers to the gentiles, but, on the basis of the conclusion that Matthew's Gospel intimates, it will be a new Israel of God that unites both Jews and gentiles. Accordingly, the rejected cornerstone of Ps. 118.22 should also be identified as this New Israel.

Jesus, in the Lucan conclusion of this episode, does not identify the 'others'. He responds to the people's rejection of the ending of his parable by asking them, 'What then is that which has been written?' and proceeds to quote an abbreviated version of Ps. 118.22, 'A stone which the builders rejected, this became *unto* (εἰς) its cornerstone'. As in Mk 12.10-11 and Mt. 21.42, a building has been substituted for the vineyard, and builders in place of tenants. The implication is that the reality that the rejected stone

34. Eduard Schweizer (1970: 241) identifies the 'others' as the gentiles. But in Mark's Gospel they must necessarily be the poor. See Waetjen 1989: 188.

represents has already begun to take its place as the keystone in the building that is being constructed through the ministry of Jesus. But, as in the other Gospels, the readers must determine the identity of this stone. Throughout Luke–Acts, it is implied to be 'the Son of the Human Being' (ὁ υἱὸς τοῦ ἀνθρώπου), the corporate reality of Jesus and the community of disciples that he is constituting.

This parable, as originally composed by Jesus, draws the ruling elite, identified in the context of the Synoptic Gospels as chief priests, lawyers and elders, into an identification with sharecroppers, and, in a mirror-like fashion, they, as absentee landlords, ironically find themselves in an unaccustomed role. Jesus has lured them into a self-representation of the peasantry, which they exploit for the maintenance of their wealth and power by appropriating a grossly unjust proportion of their agricultural produce through exorbitant rent funds. For a brief moment, perhaps, they may perceive the injustice of the socio-economic system that they themselves, as guardians of God's elect people, maintain. Simultaneously, they would also be constrained to see themselves as the tenants of God's vineyard who, in their rebellion against God, are refusing to fulfill the covenant by rejecting their divinely appointed role as the caretakers of the house of Israel. They are guilty of forfeiting their ministry of nurturing God's people into a greater self-understanding of their privileged membership in their inheritance as the household of God. This double disclosure, which is conveyed to them through their participation in the story, shrewdly draws them into a circular continuity of cause and effect. As absentee landlords who exploit the peasantry, they would naturally be inclined to condemn the revolting peasants of the story for illegally withholding the rent fund, beating and humiliating the landlord's slaves and murdering the landlord's son and heir. Accordingly, they would have no difficulty in justifying the revenge of the vineyard owner. Ironically, at the same time they would be pronouncing judgment on themselves for their failed guardianship of God's people and the injustices and violence they continue to perpetrate as the tenants of God's vineyard.

Inheritance (κληρονομία), that is, the inheritance of the vineyard, is the unusual term that the tenants expect to attain according to Mk 12.7, Mt. 21.38 and Lk. 20.14. By killing the son, they evidently hope to take possession of the vineyard as their inheritance. In Mediterranean antiquity, 'the State was the "house" (οἶκος) of the king, and its territory his estate (χώρα). So the king managed his State as a plain Macedonian or Greek would manage his own household' (Rostovtzeff 1967 [1941]: 1.269). Analogously, the religious leaders of Second Temple Judaism would be inclined, quite naturally, to regard the house of Israel as their domain, their house. By confronting the religious leaders through the mirror-like experience of viewing themselves as the tenants in his parable, who kill the son in order to acquire the inheritance of the vineyard, Jesus is also confronting them with their determination to manage the house of Israel as though it were their own possession. But it could never be theirs as an inheritance! They are not the offspring of the landlord. The initial allusions to Isa. 5.1-2 at the very beginning of the parable govern the story: God is the owner and planter of the vineyard, the vineyard represents the house of Israel, and the tenants are its caretakers. The house of Israel is God's inheritance, and this is explicitly certified by Isaiah and Jeremiah.[35] The religious leaders, therefore, have no legitimate claim to it. They are only its caretakers. By attempting to make it their inheritance, they are in fact dispossessing God of his sovereign lordship of the vineyard.[36] In effect, they are guilty of committing deicide.

References

Crossan, John Dominic

1973 *In Parables: The Challenge of the Historical Jesus* (New York: Harper & Row).

1988 *The Dark Interval: Towards a Theology of Story* (Sonoma, CA: Polebridge Press).

Derrett, J.N.D.

1970 *Law in the New Testament* (London: Darton, Longman & Todd).

Dodd, Charles Harold

1935 *The Parables of the Kingdom* (London: Nesbet).

Fiensy, David A.

1991 *The Social History of Palestine in the Herodian Period: The Land Is Mine* (Studies in the Bible and Early Christianity, 20; Lewiston, NY: Edwin Mellen Press).

Freyne, Sean

1980 *Galilee from Alexander the Great to Hadrian: 323 B.C.E. to 135 C.E. A Study of Second Temple Judaism* (Wilmington, DE: Michael Glazier).

Funk, Robert W., Roy W. Hoover and the Jesus Seminar

1993 *The Five Gospels: The Search for the Authentic Words of Jesus, New Translation and Commentary* (New York: Macmillan).

35. According to LXX Isa. 19.25, God blesses Egypt as 'my people', Assyria as 'the work of my hands', and 'Israel as my *inheritance* (κληρονομία)'; also Isa. 63.17; Jer. 10.16; and also 12.7-8.

36. Snodgrass (1983: 109), after examining the development of the tradition behind the parable and analyzing its origin and meaning, has concluded that it is a genuine parable of Jesus. As valuable as his study is, he has not determined the distinctive character of the genre 'parable', and, consequently, he has not ascertained the function of the story. His renaming the story 'the Parable of the Rejected Son' discloses a one-sided christological emphasis in his interpretation of the parable: 'The parable is an accusation and a threat against the Jewish leaders, but at the same time it is a veiled claim of Jesus to be the authoritative and decisive representative from God'. But this is more applicable to the allegorized version of the story in Mark's Gospel than to the original parable of Jesus.

Herzog, William R., II

1994 *Parables as Subversive Speech: Jesus as Pedagogue of the Oppressed* (Louisville, KY: Westminster/John Knox Press).

Horsley, Richard A., and John S. Hanson

1985 *Bandits, Prophets, and Messiahs: Popular Movements at the Time of Jesus* (Minneapolis, MN: Winston Press).

Hultgren, Arland J.

2000 *The Parables of Jesus: A Commentary* (Grand Rapids, MI: Eerdmans).

Jeremias, Joachim

1963 *The Parables of Jesus* (London: SCM Press, rev. edn).

Lenski, Gerhard

1966 *Power and Privilege: A Theory of Social Stratification* (New York: McGraw-Hill).

Neusner, Jacob (trans.)

1988 *The Mishnah: A New Translation* (New Haven, CT: Yale University Press).

Oakman, Douglas E.

1986 *Jesus and the Economic Questions of his Day* (Studies in the Bible and Early Christianity, 8; Lewiston, NY: Edwin Mellen Press).

Rostovtzeff, Michael

1957 *Social and Economic History of the Roman Empire* (2 vols.; Oxford: Clarendon Press, 2nd edn).

1967 *The Social and Economic History of the Hellenistic World* (3 vols.; Oxford: Clarendon Press, from corrected sheets of the original 1941 edition).

Schottroff, Luise

2006 *The Parables of Jesus* (Minneapolis, MN: Fortress Press).

Schottroff, Willy

1996 'Das Gleichnis von den bösen Weingärtnern (Mk 12,1-9 parr.): Ein Beitrag zur Geschichte der Bodenpacht in Palästina', *Zeitschrift des deutschen Palästina-Vereins* 112: 18-48.

Schweizer, Eduard

1970 *The Good News according to Mark* (Atlanta, GA: John Knox Press).

Scott, Bernard Brandon

1989 *Hear Then the Parable: A Commentary on the Parables of Jesus* (Minneapolis, MN: Fortress Press).

Snodgrass, Klyne R.

1983 *The Parable of the Wicked Tenants: An Inquiry into Parable Interpretation* (WUNT, 27; Tübingen: J.C.B. Mohr).

Waetjen, Herman C.

1989 *A Reordering of Power: A Socio-Political Reading of Mark's Gospel* (Minneapolis, MN: Fortress Press).

Wire, Antoinette Clark

1983 *The Parable as Mirror* (General Assembly Mission Board; Atlanta, GA: Presbyterian Church, U.S.A.).

1 Peter 2.13-17 and Martyrdom

Robert Louis Wilken

In 1960 when Jack Elliott and I graduated from Concordia Seminary in St Louis, he sailed to Germany to study New Testament at the Westfälische Wilhelms-Universität Münster, and I enrolled at the University of Chicago to study patristics. Over the years our friendship has been nourished by the intersection of our two fields. One summer, when I was teaching at the University of San Francisco, we met together in the morning to read the letters of Ignatius of Antioch in Greek. Ignatius died at the beginning of the second century and is usually considered one of the earliest church fathers, but he is also a bridge to the writings of the New Testament.

In thinking about an essay to honor my good friend I got to wondering when 1 Peter began to be cited by early Christians, and I discovered that the letter was well known by second-century writers. According to Eusebius, Papias, who was born (c. 60 CE) while Paul and Peter were alive and died in 130, drew on material from 1 Peter in his teaching (*Hist. eccl.* 3.39.17). Papias's contemporary Polycarp, who was born c. 70 CE and died a martyr c. 155, makes extensive use of 1 Peter in his letter to the Philippians, written in the thirties of the second century. There are more than a dozen citations or allusions to 1 Peter in the letter. No other writer before Origen draws so deeply on the epistle.

In reading through these second-century writings anew, what caught my attention was an allusion to 1 Peter in the *Martyrdom of Polycarp*. According to this, the earliest account of the martyrdom of a Christian, the Roman proconsul pressed Polycarp to swear 'by the fortune of Caesar' and to 'curse Christ' (*Mart. Pol.* 9.2-3 [Shepherd 1953: 152]). To which Polycarp responded: 'Eighty-six years I have served him, and never did he do me any wrong. How can I blaspheme my King who saved me?' (9.3 [Shepherd 1953: 152]). I cannot do that, he added: 'I am a Christian'. Then he urges the proconsul to 'give me a hearing' (10.1 [Shepherd 1953: 152-3]). And in the few moments allowed him Polycarp explains to the governor that 'we have been taught to render honor, as is befitting, to rulers and authorities appointed by God, so far as it does us no harm; but as for these, I do not consider them worthy that I should make defense to them' (10.2 [Shepherd 1953: 153]).

Polycarp had in mind either Rom. 13.7 or 1 Pet. 2.17, both of which use the word 'honor'. Here is the passage in Romans: 'Pay all of them [the ruling authorities] their dues; taxes to whom taxes are due, revenue to whom revenue is due, respect to whom respect is due, honor to whom honor is due'. And in 1 Peter: 'Honor all men. Love the brotherhood. Fear God. Honor the emperor.'[1] Either is possible, but I am inclined to think Polycarp had 1 Peter in mind. For only 1 Peter draws a distinction between the kind of reverence shown to the emperor and that which is appropriate for God. The emperor is 'honored', but God is to be 'feared'.

Support for this interpretation of Polycarp's words can be found in an account of Christians executed later in the second century. Scillium was a city not too far from Carthage in Africa Proconsularis and the *Acts of the Scillitan Martyrs* is a concise, even austere, account of the martyrdom on July 17, 180 CE of seven men and five women for refusing to renounce worship of the one God. It is a precious document, the first Christian writing in Latin and the first to give evidence of a Latin Bible, or at least of the translation of some letters of the New Testament. One of the martyrs, Speratus, says to the Roman governor: 'I do not recognize the empire of this world. Rather, I serve that God whom no man has seen, nor can see, with these eyes' (6). A few lines later another Christian, Cittinus, said: 'We have no one else to *fear* but our Lord God who is in heaven' (8 [emphasis added]). And one of the women, Donata, chimes in: 'Pay *honor* to Caesar as Caesar; but it is God we *fear* (*Honorem Caesari quasi Caesari; timorem autem Deo*)' (9 [emphasis added]).[2]

It is noteworthy that in these two early Christian writings, one from a Greek-speaking community in Asia Minor, the other by a Latin author from Scillium, the language of 1 Pet. 2.17 surfaces in the context of martyrdom. When early Christians spoke about giving honor to the emperor, they often had in mind the words of St Paul in Romans 13. But when they are faced with martyrdom 1 Peter served far better, for Peter made a clean distinction between the respect owed to Roman authorities and the worship or fear of God.

How significant martyrdom was in shaping the interpretation of 1 Pet. 2.17 can be seen in another Latin writer, Tertullian of Carthage. He was in his early twenties when the Scillitans were martyred and surely knew of them. Some thirty years later, most likely after a persecution of Christians in Carthage in 212 initiated by the Roman governor Scapula, Tertullian wrote a little essay entitled *Scorpiace*, usually rendered in English as 'antidote to

1. Biblical citations are from the RSV.
2. The text and translation are taken from Musurillo 1972: 87-89.

the scorpion's sting'. Its aim was to rebut the gnostics—the scorpions—who held that it was unnecessary to suffer martyrdom. Christ died for us, they said, so that we might not be slain. If Christ died for us, why is it necessary to 'hope for salvation from my violent death (*de mea nece*)?' (*Scorp.* 1.8).

Toward the end of the treatise Tertullian brings forth Paul as a witness. Though he had been a persecutor, when he became a Christian Paul 'exchanged the sword for the pen' and in his letters 'speaks in favor of martyrdom' (*Scorp.* 13.1). Tertullian further notes that Paul urged Christians to be patient in the midst of persecution and tribulation that they may be 'worthy of the kingdom for which they suffer' (*Scorp.* 13.2, citing 2 Thess. 1.4). In writing to the Corinthians, Paul said, 'sufferings (*passiones*) must be endured' for we 'bear in our body the dying of Christ' (*Scorp.* 13.5-6, citing 2 Cor. 11.23 and 4.8). Tertullian also cites 2 Timothy: 'The saying is sure. If we have died with him, we shall also live with him. If we suffer with him, we shall also reign with him; if we deny him, he also will deny us; if we are faithless, he is faithful. He cannot deny himself' (*Scorp.* 13.11, citing 2 Tim. 2.11-13).

After citing these and other passages from the letters of Paul, Tertullian turns to Romans 13, where Paul admonishes the Romans 'to be subject to all power because there is no power but God' (*Scorp.* 14.1, citing Rom. 13.1). He notes that Paul said the ruler 'does not carry the sword without reason' and 'rulers are not a terror to good conduct, but to bad' (*Scorp.* 14.1, citing Rom. 13.3). In persecuting Christians, however, rulers use the sword against those who do good. Nevertheless, Tertullian takes Paul at face value that Christians should be subject to the ruling authorities even when it leads to martyrdom. He is, however, uneasy about leaving things at that point and notes that in the same passage Paul said that one should pay 'taxes to whom taxes are due, and revenue to whom revenue' is due (*Scorp.* 14.2, citing Rom. 13.7). For Christ had taught that one should 'render to Caesar the things that are Caesar's and to God the things that are God's' (*Scorp.* 14.2, citing Mt. 22.21). From these passages he draws the conclusion that 'man is the property of God alone' (*solius autem dei homo*) (*Scorp.* 14.2).

To support his citation of the words of Jesus, Tertullian turns to 1 Peter. For Peter had written that 'the king must certainly be honored', yet he says that the 'king is to be honored only when he deals with those things that belong to his sphere (*suis rebis*), and does take to himself the honor due God'. For just as one loves one's parents along with God, but does not make them equal to God, so with the emperor. 'For not even life can be loved more than God' (*Ceterum super deum diligere nec animam licebit*) (*Scorp.* 14.3).

Tertullian draws on 1 Pet. 2.17 to give a more precise and nuanced understanding of what Paul meant when he spoke of being subject to the ruling authorities. Peter's language, complemented by the words of Jesus, gave Tertullian a scriptural basis to emphasize that there was an honor due God incommensurate with the honor due human beings, even someone as exalted as the emperor. Peter's way of putting this is to distinguish the reverence due the emperor and the worship due God. 'Honor all men. Love the brotherhood. *Fear* God. Honor the emperor' (*Omnes honorate. Fraternitatem diligite. Deum timete. Regem honorificate*) (1 Pet. 2.17). Jack Elliott recognized the significance of this feature of the text in his commentary on 1 Peter. 'The Petrine author, however, pointedly distinguishes the reverence appropriate for God from the honor due the emperor, as to all persons' (2000: 500). Tertullian's treatise *Scorpiace* was written when the church in Carthage was being persecuted, most likely by the Roman governor Scapula in 212. In that setting it was necessary to explain the admonition of Paul and Peter, 'be subject to the ruling authorities', in light of the social reality Christians were facing. Hence he reminded his readers that there was a higher obligation, to give honor and worship to God alone. In the fifth century, Christians made up the majority in the empire, the emperor was Christian, and many magistrates, judges, generals and provincial governors were Christian. Yet the passage from 1 Peter 2 still resonated in the Christian communities of North Africa.

In 397 Augustine preached a sermon celebrating the 'birthday' (i.e. the day of martyrdom) of the Scillitan martyrs.[3] At the outset he cites two lines from the Psalms: 'The Lord is my strength (Ps. 118:14)' and 'I will love you Lord, my might (Ps. 18:1)' (Hill 1994: 263). Then he cites Paul's words in Philippians, 'to live will be Christ, and to die will be gain (Phil. 1:21)' (Hill 1994: 263). Do not fear the 'bitter cup of death', for 'precious in the sight of the Lord is the death of his saints (Ps. 116:15)' (Hill 1994: 264). When Jesus stood before Pilate he said, 'You have no authority over me unless it had been given to you from above (Jn 19:10-11)' (Hill 1994: 265).

In saying that we should 'be submissive not to men but to God', Jesus 'was teaching martyrs when they suffer anything from men, to fear, not men, but the one . . . who gives men authority' (Hill 1994: 265). In support, Augustine cites the words of the woman among the Scilittan martyrs who spoke out: 'Give honor to Caesar as to Caesar, but fear to God' (*Honorem Caesari quasi Caesari; timorem autem Deo*). '[T]hat most valiant woman', says Augustine, made the right and proper distinction because she 'paid attention to what the apostle [Peter] said'. However cruel the emperor may be, he should be honored and treated with proper respect, but he is not the pinnacle of authority. 'Supreme authority' belongs to God alone 'in whose

3. This sermon is listed as Sermon 30.2 in *Miscellanea agostiniana* (Morin 1930: 1.550-57). In the new translation of Augustine's works by Edmund Hill (used here), the sermon is numbered 299E (Hill 1994: 263-70).

hands we are, both we ourselves and our words (Wis. 7:16)' (Hill 1994: 265).

In the *Confessions*, Augustine says that in 'my needy life, Lord, my heart is much exercised by the pummeling of the words of your holy scripture' (*pulsatum verbis sanctae scripturae tuae*) (*Conf.* 12.1.1). What Augustine says of his own life is an apt description of the way the *words* of the Scripture penetrated the minds and hearts of Christians in the early centuries. This was surely the case with the epistle of 1 Peter. Two little words, first spoken to a Roman governor by the martyrs, became part of the vocabulary of Christian speech and carried the weight of a profound biblical truth: honor and respect the ruling authorities, but give worship and adoration to God alone.

References

Elliott, John Hall
2000 *1 Peter: A New Translation with Introduction and Commentary* (AB, 37B; New York: Doubleday).

Hill, Edmund (trans.)
1994 *The Works of Saint Augustine, A Translation for the 21st Century*: *Sermons*, vol. 3.8 (Hyde Park, NY: New City Press).

Morin, D.G. (ed.)
1930 *Miscellanea agostiniana*, vol. 1 (Rome: Tipografia Poliglotta Vaticana).

Musurillo, Herbert (ed. and trans.)
1972 *The Acts of the Christian Martyrs*: *Introduction, Texts and Translations* (Oxford: Clarendon Press).

Shepherd, Massey Hamilton (ed. and trans.)
1953 *The Martyrdom of Polycarp*, in *Early Christian Fathers* (ed. Cyril Richardson; New York: Macmillan): 141-58.

The Interests of the Shrewd Steward and his Interpreters

Ritva H. Williams

Introduction

Among Jack Elliott's many contributions to the field of New Testament interpretation is his 1993 volume defining the parameters of the subdiscipline of social-scientific criticism: *What Is Social Scientific Criticism?* He describes the aim of social-scientific criticism as analyzing, synthesizing and interpreting the social, linguistic, literary, and ideological dimensions of the text as both a reflection of and a response to a special social and cultural context (1993: 7). He asserts that ideology emerges from the articulation of ideas that explain and justify self-interests. The result is 'an integrated system of beliefs, perspectives, assumptions and values, not necessarily true or false' (1993: 52).

Elliott advocates for an 'ideology critique' that investigates both interpreters and the texts they interpret (1993: 52). With respect to the latter, he encourages the exegete to ask questions about the self-interests and/or group interests of the author, to consider how they are expressed or inferred in the document and how they compare and contrast with other social groups of the time (1993: 74). Elliott cautions that self-interests and group interests are difficult to ascertain because they are generally concealed from view. He writes, 'In many cases they can only be inferred from the content and strategy of a text and from what is known about its producers' (1993: 84).

The focus of this essay is the Parable of the Shrewd Steward, more commonly known as the Parable of the Dishonest Manager, in Lk. 16.1-8a.[1] The goal is to engage in an ideologically conscious reading of this text. It begins

1. A majority of scholars regard Lk. 16.8a as the conclusion of the original parable, with the applications that follow in 16.8b-13 as Lukan interpretations or misinterpretations. See discussions in Scott 1983: 175-77; Herzog 1994: 233-37; Landry and May 2000: 288-89. Hultgren 2000: 147-48 argues to include 16.8b as Jesus' interpretation of the parable. Mathewson 1995: 30-34 argues that vv. 8b-13 are part of the original parable.

by recognizing that texts convey their ideologies indirectly through literary features such as irony, plot, characterization and point of view, through 'who speaks, who sees, and who acts in a text—and especially in who does not' (Yee 1999: 536). Therefore, the initial focus of this essay will be on the characters in the parable, asking questions about their self-interests. Insights from the cultural anthropology of the ancient Mediterranean will reveal that these are quite different from the self-interests of twenty-first century first-world, especially American, readers. This analysis will demonstrate that the common assessment of the rich man as the good guy and the allegedly 'dishonest manager' as the bad guy is rooted in an anachronistic and ethnocentric reading that is not ideologically conscious at all. Following an examination of the characters, this essay will ask questions about the self-interests of Jesus in telling the parable, Luke in incorporating it into his Gospel narrative, the resurrected Christ groups he was addressing and subsequent early interpreters.[2]

Ideology in the Text—Resolving Conflicting Interests

The first character that we meet in this parable is described as a 'rich man' (ἄνθρωπός τις ἦν πλούσιος [16.1]). In the societies of the ancient Mediterranean where all goods were regarded as permanently limited, the acquisition of wealth was considered the result of theft, fraud or extortion. As Malina and Rohrbaugh remind us,

> To be labeled 'rich' was therefore a social and moral statement as much as an economic one. It meant the power or capacity to take from someone weaker what was rightfully not yours. Being rich was synonymous with being greedy (2003: 400).

The label 'rich', thus, points to the social location of the storyteller (Jesus and/or Luke) and his audience as non-elites. They immediately learn that the primary interest of this man is the acquisition of wealth at the expense of those who are socially, economically and politically weaker.

The rich man has a steward (16.1), indicating that he is the owner of a large estate, which he desires not only to maintain for his posterity but also to increase in ways that the audience regards as greedy, that is, as morally reprehensible. The man himself operates from a different social location from the storyteller and his audience. He is a relatively high-status person who may simply consider his riches as one expression of his power over others in a world where male honor depended on a man's ability to socially

2. Thank you to John Kloppenborg and the members of the Context Group for their constructive responses and suggestions to an earlier version of this paper, presented at the 2006 annual meeting of the Context Group.

dominate others and where wealth was one means of acquiring honor (Kloppenborg 1989: 489). In other words, his greed may not be so much for material wealth as for social capital in the form of honor, an important aspect of which would be his perceived ability to control the members of his *oikos*. Failure to do so would not only result in making him look like a fool in front of his peers but would also reduce his capacity to exercise power over his subordinates, thus negatively impacting his ability to demand both material and social goods from them (Kloppenborg 1989: 489).

The second person we meet in the parable is the steward (οἰκονόμος [16.1-2]). He is probably a slave, perhaps born in the household itself, who has the authority to act on behalf of his master in arranging for the rental of his property, making loans, reducing and liquidating debts, and keeping the accounts of such transactions. He may have received wages, a *peculium*, and/or some form of commissions or fees for his services (Kloppenborg 2006; Malina and Rohrbaugh 2003: 292; Ukpong 1996: 201). Like other slaves and low-status persons, the steward would have been socialized to believe that his 'well-being was completely wrapped up in the well-being and benevolence of the patron. Slaves and freedman who had been put in charge of their patron's wealth were proud when they were able to increase it, as their tombstones show' (Martin 1995: 28). A slave or freedman coveted such a position since it was one of the almost nonexistent avenues available for upward social mobility within an elite household, social club, or even a municipality (Martin 1995: 48). The steward's interests, initially, are to do whatever is necessary to ensure the well-being and benevolence of his master and thereby secure his own welfare. It is imperative that we recognize that the 'steward represents the master, negotiates the master's interests, and takes his own cut and lives with the hostility that results from doing his job' (Herzog 1994: 253).

The third set of characters that we hear about are the anonymous informants who never actually appear in the scene but about whom it is reported that they διεβλήθη, 'bring charges', against the steward (16.1). The root of this verb, διαβάλλω, means to 'make a complaint about a person to a third party, bring charges, inform either justly or unjustly' (Danker 2000: 226). The range of meanings includes to 'bring into discredit', 'attack a man's character', 'speak or state slanderously' and 'deceive by false accounts, impose upon, mislead' (Liddell and Scott 1996: 389-90). The fact that accusations are made against the steward does not mean that he is actually guilty of any wrongdoing. We cannot rule out the possibility that the steward is being unjustly accused by these unidentified persons (Lygre 2002: 23; Landry and May 2000: 297; Bryan 1999: 123-24; Beavis 1992: 48). Not knowing who they are makes it difficult to ascertain their specific interests. But at least two scenarios might be envisioned.

Scenario one: If the accusers are tenants or other dependents of the master such as merchants responsible for marketing his goods, they may be motivated by envy. They either covet the steward's position or are motivated by a desire for revenge because of what they perceive as excessive rigor and greed in administering their contracts. It is important to note that should the tenants complain of the steward's severity, the master is likely to see that as testimony to the steward's thoroughness (Herzog 1994: 244, quoting Gachter 1950: 126-29). Their false accusations could be seen as 'tactics in the endless resistance that is part of everyday life in agrarian societies', and are intended to 'place the villagers or merchants in a stronger bargaining position' with the landowner (Herzog 1994: 252).

Scenario two: If the accusers are other landowners, they may regard the steward as an uppity slave who needs to be put in his place, especially if he was engaging in status displays and conspicuous consumption that they felt were inappropriate to his social status as a slave-manager (Herzog 1994: 252). High-status persons in the ancient world particularly resented having to deal with οἰκονόμοι in soliciting access to potential 'friends', and saw the upward social mobility of managerial slaves as a threat (Martin 1995: 44; Saller 1982: 64-66). If the accusers are other landowners, we might also interpret their accusations as a challenge to the steward's master. In other words, the slave-manager may be the relatively innocent victim caught in a challenge–riposte situation between his master and his master's elite rivals.[3]

Whoever the accusers are they are hostile to the steward, and allege that he is 'squandering' his master's property (16.1). The participle used here, διασκορπίζων, is based on the same verb that is used to describe the activity of the prodigal son, who fritters away his inheritance in dissolute living (15.13). It means to 'scatter, disperse', or 'squander, waste' (Danker 2000: 236). The steward is thus anonymously and perhaps falsely charged with engaging in activities that are inappropriately dissipating his master's resources (Landry and May 2000: 298; Lygre 2002: 23-24). Their accusations set the story in motion.

The rich man summons the steward and demands from him an accounting of his stewardship, not in order to determine whether the charges are true but because he has already decided to remove the slave from his managerial position (16.2). Surprisingly, the master does not demand repayment of the squandered resources. This may signal that he is a merciful man willing to acknowledge an interpersonal obligation to a slave whom he has entrusted to represent him (Malina and Rohrbaugh 2003: 292). It is more likely, however, that he is not particularly concerned about the loss of the

3. The story of the steward Arion recounted by Josephus in *Ant.* 12.4.1-9 provides an analogous situation of a steward caught in the midst of competing demands.

money or other material goods. Rather he is more intent on repairing any damage to his honor that may result from the steward's activities.

Public reputation is at least equal to, if not more important than, wealth in establishing social status and prestige in ancient Mediterranean societies. The rich man will be judged on the basis of his ability to control the behavior of his subordinates. If his steward carelessly wastes his master's resources by engaging in inappropriate behavior then it is the master who will lose prestige and status among his peers. To prevent such a disaster the master unilaterally dismisses the steward without giving him an opportunity to defend himself (Landry and May 2000: 298-300; Kloppenborg 1989: 487-89). In doing so, however, he lives up to the storyteller's labeling of him as 'rich'—he is a man motivated by greedy self-interest.

Like the prodigal son, who scatters and wastes the resources entrusted to him, the steward devises a plan. Unlike his counterpart in the former story who admits that he 'sinned' and is 'no longer worthy', the manager acknowledges no wrongdoing (compare 16.3-4 with 15.17-19). The tone of his soliloquy, rather, suggests a lack of control over his situation (Lygre 2002: 25). Particularly if he is a slave, or even a freedman to a somewhat lesser degree, he is quite dependent on his master's goodwill and favor. So he contemplates his prospects: removed from his position as manager he will be reduced either to 'digging', that is, working in the fields, or running away and becoming a beggar (16.3). He acknowledges that he is not physically strong enough to do the former and is ashamed to do the latter (16.3). Unable to countenance these socially degrading options (Herzog 1994: 242), he concludes that 'he must do something that will allow him to keep his position as a steward' (Landry and May 2000: 300). He understands that he is being dismissed because of allegations that his actions dishonor his master. He therefore comes up with a plan that he hopes will enable him to retain his managerial position and/or to gain a new circle of patrons (Malina and Rohrbaugh 2003: 293).[4] An additional aspect of his plan may include getting even with his master for threatening to dismiss him, without, of course, actually suffering the penalty of losing his position (Scott 1983: 183; Beavis 1992: 51).

The steward's plan involves granting favors to his master's debtors in anticipation of their future hospitality and goodwill once word gets out that he has been removed from his position. He summons them individually and has them rewrite their contracts. The debtors do not speak in the parable. They silently do what the steward tells them to do seemingly without question or protest, no doubt because it is in their best interests to do so. The first owes the rich man 'a hundred jugs of olive oil' (16.6), the equivalent

4. Martin 1995: 25 provides inscriptional evidence to demonstrate that slaves could have patrons who were not their owners.

of eight or nine hundred gallons of oil, the yield of approximately 150 olive trees (Herzog 1994: 240; Malina and Rohrbaugh 2003: 293). The steward reduces the amount owed by 50 percent. The second debtor owes his master 'a hundred containers of wheat' (16.7), about a thousand bushels, the yield of one hundred acres of land (Herzog 1994: 240; Hultgren 2003: 151).[5] In other words, these are large-scale debtors, perhaps renters near the social status of the landlord or village elders negotiating on behalf of an entire village (Kloppenborg 2006; Malina and Rohrbaugh 2003: 293).

The debtors do not appear to have been informed of the rich man's decision to remove the steward from his position and so believe that he is acting legitimately in his capacity as the rich man's agent. They do not know what motivates him to rewrite their contracts in this favorable way. Yet having accepted these favors the debtors are now morally obligated to him if they are honorable men. Not only are they obligated to receive him into their homes, they will publicly praise him *and* his master for relieving their burden of debt. The steward has acquired important social capital for himself (and by extension for his master also) by reducing the debts owed to his master (Herzog 1994: 255).

The steward has thus placed his master in a serious predicament. The rich man knows that the steward acted after being informed of his dismissal; therefore, the redrawn contracts are not legally binding on his master (Malina and Rohrbaugh 2003: 292). It is up to the rich man to decide if he will honor them or not. On the one hand, if he nullifies them he risks alienating his clients and tenants. Not only will his reputation suffer, but the situation could easily deteriorate into the sort of relations illustrated in the Parable of the 'Dispossessed Peasants', better known as the 'wicked tenants' (Mk 12.1-12 and parallels). On the other hand, if he 'allows the reductions to stand, he will be praised far and wide as a "noble and generous man", as will the manager for having made the "arrangement"' (Malina and Rohrbaugh 2003: 293). The master's enhanced honor includes an increase in the obligations that are now owed to him by his clients. By honoring the rewritten debt contracts the rich man indicates that he stands behind the steward despite the allegations—perhaps unfounded—of his wastefulness. Indeed the steward is counting on his master to see in his actions proof that he knows quite well how to use his master's material resources in the most appropriate way.

The parable concludes with the master commending the steward for acting φρονίμως—sensibly, thoughtfully, prudently (Danker 2000: 1066). This adverb refers to the practical, streetwise wisdom of people 'of less repute' in Plato's *Apology* 22, hence, 'shrewdly' may be a more apt translation (Harrill

5. Malina and Rohrbaugh 2003: 293 suggest 150 bushels of wheat.

2006: 76). The master thus praises his manager's street-smarts. The master recognizes that while the steward made him take a short-term financial loss, he has placed new cards in his hands (Herzog 1994: 257).

Yet the master's praise appears to look like a left-handed compliment; the steward is shrewd but remains unjust. He is in his master's words, *τὸν οἰκονόμον τῆς ἀδικίας*, which can mean either 'the unjust or unrighteous steward' or 'the steward of unrighteousness or injustice'. If translated as the 'unjust steward' then it seems to refer to some quality or action of the slave himself. In this scenario, the master's judgment of his steward reflects 'the exploitative economic system's concept of justice, which is giving to everyone their dues' (Ukpong 1996: 203). From the master's perspective his wealth is due to him and should be given to him regardless of the extent of exploitation involved. In this instance, the injustice consists in the fact the steward has deprived his master of rents contractually and legally due to him (Ukpong 1996: 204).

If, on the other hand, we translate *τὸν οἰκονόμον τῆς ἀδικίας* as 'the steward of unrighteousness or injustice' then it is possible to see the steward as an agent responsibly handling the fruits of his master's unjust economic pursuits (Brown 1992: 141; Lygre 2002: 24). Remember that the man was 'rich', that is, by definition a greedy man who accumulates wealth at the expense of his tenants and clients. The steward has participated willingly in his master's exploitative economics until he himself becomes a victim of this man's so-called justice. Confronted by immediate dismissal based on anonymous, perhaps even spurious allegations, the steward suddenly finds himself in a position where standing in solidarity with his master's debtors is the best way to secure some sort of future for himself. He turns a no-win situation into a win-win situation for all involved. The master is forced to take an immediate short-term loss that has the potential to produce long-term gains in both social and material resources. The tenants have their debts reduced. Instead of being dismissed, the steward is commended by his master for his clever financial management (Lygre 2002: 27; Herzog 1994: 257-58).

The steward bests his master in a way that could be understood as an implied critique of his 'master as an exploiter, and of his former self as an agent of the oppressive system' (Ukpong 1996: 205-206). The master acknowledges this critique by labeling his manager a steward of injustice in the very act of praising his cleverness and ingenuity (Ukpong: 1996: 207).

The Parable of the Shrewd Steward raises important questions about strategies for survival in the real world of ancient Mediterranean societies. What is the appropriate behavior of a person who finds him or herself in a position of responsibility within a household, a business, an association or a city? Is it really in one's best interests to collaborate slavishly in the rapacious schemes of the rich who are one's earthly masters, employers or supervisors? Is one's welfare dependent solely on courting the benevolence of the rich? The parable highlights alternative strategies that might be used by non-elites to produce results that are favorable to their interests (Herzog 1994: 258).

The steward's best interests are served by shrewdly and subversively playing on his master's conflicting goals and desires. By using his master's material wealth to acquire social capital, the steward reminds his master that wealth exists for the sake of honor, that generosity is more desirable than greed, that networks of human relations are more valuable than oil and wheat. The master's commendation of his 'unjust' steward for his shrewdness points to a validation of the steward's values rather than those of the master.

The Shrewd Steward and the Interests of Jesus

The story of the shrewd steward is presented by Luke as a parable of Jesus, and is regarded by many as an authentic parable of Jesus.[6] The way that this parable highlights the ability of a non-elite character to subvert his master's agenda is analogous to the way that Jesus deals with household relations.

The group bound together by kinship bonds, common residence and shared livelihood was 'everything' in the world of the first-century followers of Jesus. Without a place in a household acquired either at birth or adoption or some other social arrangement, a person quite literally had no social identity (Moxnes 1997: 23; van Aarde 1999: 102). To leave this family—willingly or unwillingly—was to become radically marginalized in a culture where the household was the primary source of social identity. Jesus' promise to Peter that he and others who leave everything for the sake of the gospel will receive 'houses, brothers and sisters, mothers and children, and fields' (Mk 10.28-30) is a response to that reality. Those who leave their homes and families to follow Jesus will be compensated with a new family based not on biological, kinship relations, but on 'personally chosen, intentionally embraced and shared commitment to the will of God' (Bartchy 1978: 69). Like the households that the disciples left, this new family will consist of brothers, sisters, mothers and children. It will even include houses and fields. It will not, however, have any human fathers. This exclusion of human fathers is affirmed in Jesus' statement that those who do the will of God are his brother and sister and mother (Mk 3.31-35//Mt. 12.45-50//Lk. 8.19-21), and even more forcefully in his instruction to call no man father (Mt. 23.9). As disciples they are all ἀδελφοί—brothers and sisters—recog-

6. See Funk *et al.* 1988: 32.

nizing only the Father in heaven (Mt. 23.8-9). In this way Jesus used one aspect of what we might call 'traditional family values', specifically sibling solidarity, to subvert another element of those very same family values, patriarchal domination (Bartchy 1978: 73).

Similarly, in this parable Jesus does not endorse the normative social scripts of ancient Mediterranean agrarian life, specifically that 'masters distrust stewards; peasants hate stewards; stewards cheat both tenants and masters' (Herzog 1994: 257). Rather Jesus' parable asserts that shrewd action within such a world can bring about a reversal of these very same scripts so that stewards can relieve the debt of tenants and clients while enhancing the honor of their masters so that clients and tenants praise both steward and master, and master commends steward. In this parable Jesus provides, as Herzog writes, 'a glimpse . . . of another order, one in which forgiveness of debt would be more than a petition in a prayer' (1994: 258). Such a new order is to be brought about not by violent resistance, as in the Parable of the Dispossessed Peasants (Mk 12.1-12), but by shrewdly evoking the value of honor and general reciprocity.

The Shrewd Steward and the Interests of Luke

A quick survey of Luke's use of the term 'rich man' (ἄνθρωπός τις ἦν πλούσιος) indicates that it always has a pejorative sense, consistently occurring in passages that critique material wealth. We see this for example in Jesus' curse on the rich (6.24), the Parable of the Rich Fool (12.16), his discouragement of invitations to rich people (14.12-13), the story of the rich man and Lazarus (16.19, 21, 22), the story of the rich noble man saddened by the prospect of selling all his property (18.23, 25) and the story of the rich but repentant tax-collector Zacchaeus (19.1-10). Based on this evidence it is quite unlikely that Luke would have regarded the rich man as a positive role model, even less as a God-figure.

Comparing Lk. 16.1-8 with the parables that precede and follow it further confirms our assessment that Luke was not presenting the rich man as a God figure. In ch. 15 Jesus introduces three characters—a shepherd (15.1-7), a woman (15.8-10) and a father (15.11-32)—who are 'anxious about and search for what is lost' (Ukpong 1996: 198). The father welcomes back the son who has squandered his property in dissolute living (15.11-32), in sharp contrast to the rich man who acts to immediately dismiss the steward for allegedly squandering his property (16.1-8). The steward's master is more similar to the rich man who ignores the plight of the beggar Lazarus lying before the rich man's gate (16.19-31). These contrasts and comparisons mean 'that while it is reasonable to understand the main figures in chapter 15 as they are generally understood to stand for God, it is not reasonable to understand those in chapter 16 the same way' (Ukpong 1996: 198). It should be clear therefore that Luke is not interested in promoting the rich man as a model or exemplar of discipleship.

We demonstrated above that the steward's shrewdness consisted in his ability to broker a deal with his master's clients and tenants that brought debt relief to them, secured his own future and resulted in greater honor for the master. That Luke is holding up the steward as a model for discipleship is affirmed in the verses that he adds to the original parable. The first moral that he draws from the parable is that 'the children of this age are more shrewd in dealing with their own generation than are the children of light' (16.8b). 'Children of light' refers to the disciples of Jesus in Jn 12.36 and to Christ-followers in 1 Thess. 5.5 and in Eph. 5.8. Here in Luke's immediate literary context it must refer to the disciples, but in the social circumstances of the performance of Luke's Gospel it is intended for his audience of resurrected Christ followers living in the urban centers of the Greek east. They are criticized for lacking the shrewdness of the 'children of this age', and are exhorted to 'make friends . . . by means of dishonest wealth' (16.8b-9). The disciples and Christ-followers are here encouraged to act like the steward, a child of this age, who shrewdly translated material wealth into relational debt (deSilva 1993: 261). In other words, the only appropriate purpose and use of wealth are mutually beneficial benefactions that serve to build up networks of reciprocity. For Luke this is what constitutes being 'faithful with the dishonest wealth' that really belongs to others (16.11-12). The disciple and the Christ-follower must commit his or her love, devotion and service either to God or to wealth (16.13). The Parable of the Rich Man and Lazarus dramatizes the eternal consequences of failing to make the right decision (Lk. 16.19-31).

Another shrewd steward appears in Lk. 12.41-48. That parable is set within the context of a discourse on the need for alert vigilance in anticipation of the establishment of God's rule. Here the absent master is intended to be read as a God-figure. Jesus urges his listeners to behave like slaves awaiting the return of their master from a wedding banquet. They are to be 'dressed for action' (12.35) and 'alert' (12.37). In a radical reversal of roles, the slave who is thus prepared will not only be 'blessed' but will also be served a banquet by the master himself when he returns (12.37-38). A warning not to be caught unawares like the owner whose house was broken into (12.39-40) is followed by Peter's question about the intended audience of this parable: 'Lord, are you telling this parable for us or for everyone?' (12.41).

Jesus' responds with another question, 'Who then is the faithful and prudent manager (ὁ πιστὸς οἰκονόμος ὁ φρόνιμος) whom his master will put in charge of his slaves, to give them their allowance of food at the proper time?' (12.42).[7] The use of the title οἰκονόμος emphasizes the managerial role that sets this slave apart from the others. During his master's absence this slave-manager has two choices. He may concern himself with the welfare of those over whom he exercises authority by ensuring that they receive their food allotments in due time. This is the path of upward mobility that will culminate in the steward being put in charge of all of his master's possessions (12.43-44; Martin 1995: 53). Alternatively the steward may use his owner's absence as an excuse for abusing the other slaves, self-indulgence and drunkenness (12.45). The steward who chooses this path can expect his master to 'cut him in pieces and put him with the unfaithful when he returns' (12.46).

In this parable the absent master's interest is in ensuring the well-being of the household slaves entrusted to the care of the steward—not in acquiring wealth. In this instance a shrewd steward's self-interests, understood as achieving upward mobility, greater authority and power are most easily served by aligning his behavior with his master's expectations. What connects these two parables in addition to the presence of a shrewd steward in each is their concern for the right use of wealth (Lk. 16.1-13) and authority (Lk. 12.41-46). In both cases faithful stewardship involves looking out for the interests of those over whom one exercises authority.

Luke uses these parables to address the situation of Christ-followers living in and near urban centers in the eastern Mediterranean at the end of the first century. He seeks to answer a number of questions. What are the responsibilities of Christ-followers embedded within the hierarchically organized households, businesses and associations located in the cities of the Greek east? Whose interests should he or she serve? How does one seek to enact as well as one can an alternative order in which material resources are seen as gifts from God to be shared equitably so that no one does without, in which it is a crime to exploit another human being, and in which the rich use their wealth to benefit others (Ukpong 1996: 206)?

The Shrewd Steward in Subsequent Interpretations

Since it is beyond the scope of this paper to provide a comprehensive analysis of how the Parable of the Shrewd Steward has been used by subsequent interpreters, I will focus on two bishops of the early church, Asterius of Amasea and Cyril of Alexandria, and Martin Luther. What these three

7. This parable calls into question the contention that shrewdness (φρόνιμος) does not ordinarily indicate a Christian virtue in Luke (Harrill 2006: 78).

have in common is a conviction that the Parable of the Shrewd Steward is intended to promote benefactions and good works toward one's neighbors.[8]

Asterius, bishop of Amasea in the Roman province of Pontus c. 375–405 CE, was a contemporary of the Cappadocian fathers. Little is known about his life except that he was a lawyer before becoming bishop and had been educated by a Scythian or Goth slave who had himself been trained in Antioch in Syria. Five of his sermons are available in English translation.[9] Asterius regards the Lukan text as a 'fiction of a parable, which by obscure sayings inculcates moral virtue' (Anderson and Goodspeed 1904: 49). He focuses on the steward as a person analogous to all believers in that just as he is 'the steward of other men's goods' so every one of us is 'an administrator of what belongs to another' (1904: 49). Asterius understands the 'remission of debts that the unjust steward contrived' as an 'allegory' (1904: 69), which he explains as follows:

> All of us who busy ourselves about the rest to which we are destined, by giving what is another's, work to our own advantage; now by what is another's I mean what belongs to the Lord. For nothing is our own, but all things belong to him. When, therefore, any one anticipating his end and his removal to the next world, lightens the burden of his sins by good deeds, either by canceling the obligations of debtors, or by supplying the poor with abundance, by giving what belongs to the Lord, he gains many friends, who will attest his goodness before the Judge, and secure him by their testimony a place of happiness. Now they are called witnesses, who have secured for their benefactors favor from the Judge, not because they inform him of anything, as though he were ignorant, or did not know, but in the sense that what has been done for them relieves those who have helped them from the punishment of their sins (1904: 69-70).

Asterius, like Luke, interprets the parable as having a lesson to teach about the appropriate attitude toward and use of possessions. His logic does not appear to be all that different from Luke's: benefactions granted in this life that bring relief to debtors and to the poor have an ultimate payoff for the benefactor in the afterlife.

Cyril was enthroned patriarch of Alexandria from 412 to 444 CE, following in the footsteps of his maternal uncle, Theophilus. He was well educated in grammar, rhetoric, the humanities, theology and scripture. He was a major player in the Christological controversies of the fourth and fifth

8. These ancient writers answer positively the question, 'Is almsgiving the point of the "unjust steward"?' (Williams 1964: 293-97).

9. Galusha Anderson and Edgar Johnson Goodspeed 1904. Apparently physical copies of the book are very rare, limited to the British Library in the United Kingdom and Harvard University in the United States. An on-line version is available at http://www.tertullian.org/fathers/asterius and at http://www.ccel.org/p/pearse/morefathers/home.html.

centuries, especially at the Council of Ephesus, which condemned Nestorius. Cyril wrote extensively, not only on matters related to Christology, but also commentaries on the Gospels of John and Luke. Commenting on Luke 16, Cyril expresses the common ancient Mediterranean view that wealth is gathered often by extortion and covetousness (1983: 443). It leads men to be careless about their piety to God, contemptuous of others and hedonistic (1983: 440). He asks,

> Is there, then, no way of salvation for the rich, and no means of making them partakers in the hope of the saints? Have they fallen completely from God's grace? Is hell and the fire necessarily prepared for them, such as is the fitting lot of the devil and his angels? Not so, for lo! The Savior has shown them a means of salvation in the present parable. They have been entrusted with worldly wealth by the merciful permission of Almighty God; according nevertheless to his intention they have been appointed stewards for the poor (1983: 440).

Cyril urges the wealthy, if they are unwilling to divide all their wealth among the poor, at least to use part of it to gain friends, who will serve as witnesses to their charity at the final judgment. The distribution of all of one's wealth to the poor is in Cyril's words 'worthy of perfect praise'. He sees as a slightly lesser act of piety 'the employment of a sort of artifice', namely to obtain as friends those who are especially near to God by giving them some portion of one's wealth (1983: 441). Cyril reiterates his contention that in this parable Christ 'was teaching the rich to feel especial delight in showing kindness to the poor, and in opening their hand to whoever are in need' (1983: 442).

Remnants of these perspectives are still present in Martin Luther's sermon on Lk. 16.1-9. He defines 'mammon' as

> that which we have above our needs and we will not use in helping our neighbor; for this we possess unrighteously, and before God it is stolen goods. . . . Therefore, as the saying runs, the greatest owners of property are the greatest thieves; because they possess far more than they need, and give the least possible to others.

Although Luther regards the steward as a rogue, he nevertheless sees him an example of what Christians ought to do, albeit the steward does it for all the wrong reasons. Luther urges his medieval audience to use their wealth to care for the poor, not to earn salvation but to demonstrate their faith. In Luther's reading, as in that of Asterius, the poor will serve as witnesses for their benefactors before the judgment seat of God.[10]

10. The text of Luther's 'Sermon for the Ninth Sunday after Trinty; Luke 16:1-9' may be found in *The Sermons of Martin Luther* (Grand Rapids, MI: Baker Book House, 1983): 4.292-301, and on-line at http://www.orlutheran.com/html/mlselk161.html.

What is noteworthy about these ancient interpretations is that they hold up the steward as a character to be emulated, in stark contrast to so many modern readings that consistently condemn the steward as being a cheat, a sloth or some other despised character.

Conclusions

Contemporary readers of the Parable of the Shrewd Steward in Lk. 16.1-8a are frequently baffled by the story, unable to comprehend how the master can commend such a seemingly shady character. Thoroughly embedded in a culture rooted in capitalist ideology, they immediately side with the master and blame the steward (Herzog 1984: 245; Ukpong 1996: 189-90). An ideologically conscious reading of the text that highlights the interests of the various first-century Mediterranean characters in their own preindustrial agrarian context reveals an entirely different scenario. The steward is caught in the middle between his rapacious master and exploited tenants and clients. The steward's shrewdness is demonstrated in the way that he cleverly resolves their conflicting interests in such a way that everyone emerges as a winner. His strategy is subversive; its success rests on the premise that his master will value the social capital of honor and benefaction over and above material goods.

The outcome of the steward's actions is consistent with the interests of Jesus. The parable demonstrates how a non-elite person can transform a no-win situation into a win-win situation. Just as Jesus promotes sibling solidarity to subvert patriarchal family and household arrangements, he endorses reciprocal relations rooted in benefaction in order to undermine the greed of the wealthy elite. The parable works well with Luke's agenda to disparage commitment to material wealth, as is evident by the applications he adds (16.8b-13) and his strategic placement of the parable in his text. The shrewd steward exemplifies the correct use and attitude toward material wealth unlike the rich man in the parable that follows in 16.19-31. Luke's position might be summed up as follows: faithful stewardship of material resources consists in benefactions that enact the relief of debt and suffering. These result in the establishment of reciprocal relations that will pay off both now and in eternity. This reading is reflected in the early history of interpretation, as we have seen from the sermons of Asterius of Amasia, Cyril of Alexandria and Martin Luther.

The pay-off of an ideologically conscious reading of the text, informed by the cultural anthropology of the ancient Mediterranean, is not only a deeper and richer understanding of the story in the text but also a heightened awareness of how much our own ideological environment can obscure our understanding of our ancient scriptures.

References

Aarde, Andries G. van
1999 'Fatherless in First-Century Mediterranean Culture: The Historical Jesus Seen from the Perspective of Cross-Cultural Anthropology and Cultural Psychology', *HTS* 55.1: 97-119.

Anderson, Galusha, and Edgar Johnson Goodspeed
1904 *Ancient Sermons for Modern Times by Asterius, Bishop of Amasia Circa 375–404 AD* (Cleveland, OH: Pilgrim Press). On-line versions available at http://www.tertullian.org/fathers/asterius and http://www.ccel.org/p/pearse/morefathers/home.html.

Bartchy, S. Scott
1978 'Power, Submission, and Sexual Identity among the Early Christians', in *Essays on New Testament Christianity: A Festschrift in Honor of Dean E. Walker* (Cincinnati, OH: Standard): 50-80.

Beavis, Mary Ann
1992 'Ancient Slavery as an Interpretive Context for the New Testament Servant Parables with Special Reference to the Unjust Steward (Luke 16.1-8)', *JBL* 111: 37-54.

Brown, Colin
1992 'The Unjust Steward: A New Twist?', in *Worship, Theology and Ministry in the Early Church: Essays in Honor of Ralph P. Martin* (ed. Michael J. Wilkins and Terence Paige; JSNTSup, 87. Sheffield: Sheffield Academic Press): 121-45.

Bryan, Christopher
1999 'Editorial: The Slandered Steward', *Sewanee Theological Review* 42.2: 123-26.

Cyril (St), Patriarch of Alexandria
1983 *Commentary on the Gospel of Saint Luke* (trans. by R. Payne Smith; Astoria, NY: Studion Publishers).

Danker, Frederick William
2000 *A Greek–English Lexicon of the New Testament and Other Early Christian Literature* (Chicago: University of Chicago Press, 3rd edn).

deSilva, David A.
1993 'The Parable of the Prudent Steward and its Lucan Context', *Criswell Theological Review* 6.2: 255-68.

Elliott, John H.
1993 *What Is Social-Scientific Criticism?* (Minneapolis, MN: Fortress Press).

Funk, Robert, James R. Butts, Bernard B. Scott and the Jesus Seminar
1988 *The Parables of Jesus: Red Letter Edition* (Sonoma, CA: Polebridge Press).

Gachter, Paul
1950 'The Parable of the Dishonest Steward after Oriental Conceptions', *CBQ* 12: 121-31.

Harrill, J. Albert
2006 'The Dishonest Manager (Luke 16:1-8)', in *Slaves in the New Testament: Literary, Social, and Moral Dimensions* (ed. J. Albert Harrill; Minneapolis, MN: Fortress Press): 66-83.

Herzog, William R., II.
1994 *Parables as Subversive Speech: Jesus as Pedagogue of the Oppressed* (Louisville, KY: Westminster/John Knox Press).

Hultgren, Arland J.

2000 *The Parables of Jesus: A Commentary* (Grand Rapids, MI: William B. Eerdmans).

Kloppenborg, John S.

1989 'The Dishonored Master (Luke 16:1-8a)', *Biblica* 70: 474-95.

2006 'Response to Ritva Williams' Interests of the Shrewd Steward', presented at the annual meeting of the Context Group, Menucha Retreat Center, Corbett, OR.

Landry, David, and Ben May

2000 'Honor Restored: New Light on the Parable of the Prudent Steward (Luke 16:1-8a)', *JBL* 119: 287-309.

Liddell, Henry George, and Robert Scott

1996 *A Greek–English Lexicon with a Revised Supplement* (Oxford: Clarendon Press).

Luther, Martin

1983 'Sermon for the Ninth Sunday after Trinity; Luke 16:1-9', *The Sermons of Martin Luther* (Grand Rapids, MI: Baker Book House); 4.292-301. Reprint of John Nicholas Lenker's *The Precious and Sacred Writings of Martin Luther* (1905). Available on-line at http://www.orlutheran.com/html/mlselk161.html.

Lygre, John G.

2002 'Of What Charges? (Luke 16:1-2)', *BTB* 32: 21-28.

Malina, Bruce J., and Richard L. Rohrbaugh

2003 *Social-Science Commentary on the Synoptic Gospels* (Minneapolis, MN: Fortress Press).

Mathewson, Dave L.

1995 'The Parable of the Unjust Steward (Luke 16:1-13): A Reexamination of the Traditional View in Light of Recent Challenges', *JETS* 38.1: 29-39.

Martin, Dale B.

1995 *Slavery as Salvation: The Metaphor of Slavery in Pauline Christianity* (New Haven, CT: Yale University Press).

Moxnes, Halvor

1997 'What Is Family? Problems in Constructing Early Christian Families', in *Constructing Early Christian Families: Family as Social Reality and Metaphor* (ed. Halvor Moxnes; London: Routledge): 13-41.

Saller, Richard P.

1982 *Personal Patronage under the Early Empire* (Cambridge: Cambridge University Press).

Scott, Bernard Brandon.

1983 'A Master's Praise', *Biblica* 64.2: 173-88.

Ukpong, Justin S.

1996 'The Parable of the Shrewd Manager (Luke 16:1-13): An Essay in Inculturation Biblical Hermeneutic', *Semeia* 73: 189-210.

Williams, Francis E.

1964 'Is Almsgiving the Point of the "Unjust Steward"?', *JBL* 83: 293-97.

Yee, Gale A.

1999 'Ideological Criticism', *Dictionary of Biblical Interpretation* (ed. John Haralson Hayes; Nashville, TN: Abingdon Press): 534-37.

A Bibliography of Works by John H. Elliott

Books

1966

The Elect and The Holy: An Exegetical Examination of 1 Peter 2:4-10 and the Phrase Basileion Hierateuma (NovTSup, 12; Leiden: E.J. Brill; repr., Eugene, OR: Wipf & Stock, 2006).

Doxology: God's People Called to Celebrate his Glory: A Biblical Study of 1 Peter in 10 Parts (St. Louis, MO: Lutheran Laymen's League).

The Christ-Life: Jesus Christ the Sacrament and Sacramental Living (Chicago: Walther League).

1975

Proclamation: Aids for Interpreting the Lessons of the Church Year. Series A. Pentecost 3 (co-authored with Bruce Vawter; Philadelphia, PA: Fortress Press).

1979

1 Peter: Estrangement and Community (Herald Biblical Booklets; Chicago: Franciscan Herald Press).

1981

A Home for the Homeless: A Sociological Exegesis of 1 Peter, its Situation and Strategy (Philadelphia, PA: Fortess Press; British edn, London: SCM Press, 1982; 2nd edn with a new Introduction, 1990; 3rd edn, Eugene, OR: Wipf & Stock, 2005; Portuguese trans. J. Rezende Costa of 1981 edn as *Um lar para quem não tem casa: Interpretação sociológica da primeira carta de Pedro* [Coleção Bíblia e sociologia; São Paulo: Edições Paulinas, 1985; republished, Sao Paulo: Editora Academia Cristã e Editora Paulus, 2011]; Spanish trans., Constantino Ruiz-Garrido of 1990 edn as *Un hogar para los que no tienen patria ni hogar: Estudio crítico social de la carta primera de Pedro y de su situación y estrategia* [Estella (Navarra): Verbo Divino, 1995]).

1982

Elliott, John H., and R.A. Martin. *James* (R.A. Martin), *I–II Peter/Jude* (John H. Elliott) (Augsburg Commentary on the New Testament; Minneapolis, MN: Augsburg Publishing House; Chinese trans., Barbara Luk [*James*] and Amy Chow [*I–II Peter/Jude*] [Hong Kong: Taosheng Publishing House, 1988]).

1986

Social-Scientific Criticism of the New Testament and its Social World (ed. John H. Elliott; Semeia, 35; Decatur, GA: Scholars Press).

1993

What Is Social-Scientific Criticism? (Guides to Biblical Scholarship; Minneapolis, MN: Fortress Press).

1995

Social-Scientific Criticism of the New Testament: An Introduction (London: SPCK, British edn of *What Is Social-Scientific Criticism?*).

2000

1 Peter: A New Translation with Introduction and Commentary (AB, 37B; New York: Doubleday/Random House).

2007

Conflict, Community, and Honor: 1 Peter in Social-Scientific Perspective (Eugene, OR: Wipf & Stock).

2013

La primera carta de Pedro: Edición bilingüe y comentario (trans. Francisco Javier Molina de la Torre; Biblioteca de estudios bíblicos, 141; Salamanca: Ediciones Sígueme, 2013).

Forthcoming

Beware the Evil Eye: The Evil Eye in the Bible and the Ancient World (Eugene, OR: Wipf & Stock).
Jesus and the Family of God: A Core Symbol of Community (Grand Rapids, MI: Eerdmans).
Jesus the Gesturer: Gestural Communication in the Gospel of Mark (Grand Rapids, MI: Eerdmans).
Jesus the Israelite and Wooing Crocodiles (Eugene, OR: Wipf & Stock).
Rehabilitating First Peter: Fresh Perspectives on an Exegetical Stepchild (Eugene, OR: Wipf & Stock).

Articles, Essays and Chapters in Books

1958

'With An Outstretched Arm', *The Seminarian* 49.2: 16-20.
'Exegesis: The Royal Priesthood', *The Seminarian* 49.3: 53-56.

1959

'Stir Up . . .', *The Seminarian* 51.1: 2.

1960

'Faith, Works, and the Paradox', *The Seminarian* 51.2: 28-30.
'Wanted: A Liberal Theology', *The Seminarian* 51.4: 4-5.
'Not So Beatific Vision', *The Seminarian* 51.4: 43-48.

1961

'Rudolf Bultmann and the Sacrament of Holy Baptism', *Concordia Theological Monthly* 32.6: 348-55.

1962

'Shirer, the Third Reich, and Modern Germany', *American Lutheran* 45.7: 23-24.

'Correspondence from Germany', *The Seminarian* 54.1: 23-27.

Rengstorf, Karl Heinrich, 'Old and New Testament Traces of a Formula of the Judean Royal Ritual', *NovT* 5.4: 229-44 (trans. from the German orig. by John H. Elliott).

1963

Wendland, Heinz-Dietrich, 'Brotherhoods in Church and World', *Una Sancta* 20.4: 40-50 (trans. from the German orig. by Richard Knudsen and John H. Elliott).

1964

'Homiletics: Outlines on the Standard Epistle Series (Misericordias Domini: 1 P 2:21-25; Jubilate: 1 P 2:11-20)', *Concordia Theological Monthly* 35.4: 228-34.

'Infant Baptism: A Review of a Controversy'. *Una Sancta* 21.3-4: 70-73.

1965

'Love Is a Many Splendored Thing. Sermonic Resource Material. The Epistle for Quinquagesima, The Second Sunday in Lent. 1 Cor. 13', St. Louis, MO: Published by the Lutheran Laymen's League for Lutheran Hour Sunday.

'Two St Louis Clergymen Tell Why They Demonstrated', *The St. Louis Lutheran* 20.3: 1-2.

'The Ten Best', *Arena* 74/4 (1965): 23.

1966

'The Chosen People', *American Lutheran* 41.2 (1966): 14-16, 22-25. A paper originally delivered in Fourth Lutheran–Jewish Seminar in St Louis, November 4, 1965. Separate reprint of essays by Rabbi Polish and John H. Elliott published in *American Lutheran* also published by the Anti-Defamation League of B'nai B'rith: 'The Chosen People', by Rabbi David Polish (pp. 4-8) and 'The Chosen People', by John H. Elliott (pp. 8-12).

'The New Testament Is Catholic: A Reevaluation of Sola Scriptura', *Una Sancta* 23.1: 3-18.

'Living Life with a Capital S', *Youth Programs* 16: 36.

'The Gospel and Social Change', *Una Sancta* 23.2: 9-20.

'Teaching Christian Doctrine from the Viewpoint of an Exegete', in *Religion for the Restless: Teaching Bible Doctrine to Youth* (ed. John F. Choiz; Twenty-Third Lutheran Education Association Yearbook): 40-55.

'The Preacher and the Proclamation: Some Architectural Reflections on Gaps and Bridges', in *The Lively Function of the Gospel: Essays in Honor of Richard R. Caemmerer on Completion of 25 Years as Professor of Practical Theology at Concordia Seminary, St Louis* (ed. Robert W. Bertram; St. Louis, MO: Concordia Publishing House): 99-130.

'The Historical Jesus, the Kergymatic Christ, and the Eschatological Community', *Concordia Theological Monthly* 37.8: 470-91.

'The Chosen People', *The Lutheran Scholar* 23.4: 3-16.

1967

'Lutheraner und Juden: Ein Meinungsaustausch. Dialog in USA', *Friede über Israel. Zeitschrift für Kirche und Judentum* 50.2: 34-38.

Comment on 'What Synod Needs', *Lutheran Witness* 86.6: 15.

'The Theology and Practice of Worship', *Una Sancta* 24.3 (1967): 59-61. Review article on *Worship: Its Theology and Practice,* by J.J. von Allmen (trans. from the French orig.; New York: Oxford University Press, 1965).

'Kittel Says' (a review article on *Theological Dictionary of the New Testament,* vols. I–IV [ed. G. Kittel; trans. and ed. G.W. Bromiley; Grand Rapids, MI: W.B. Eerdmans, 1964-1967]), *Una Sancta* 24.4: 85-89.

1968

'Law and Eschatology: The Antithesis of the "Sermon on the Mount"', *Lutheran World* 51.1: 16-24.

'Die Antithesen der Bergpredigt: Gesetz und Eschatologie', *Lutherische Rundschau* 18.1: 19-29.

'Symposium: Lutheran Reactions to the Arab–Israel War', *Lutheran Quarterly* 20.3: 276-89.

John H. Elliott *et al.*, 'Lutherans on Roman Catholic Campuses: Teachers Are Not Missionaries', *Lutheran Forum* 2.9: 8-10.

'Death of a Slogan: From Royal Priests to Celebrating Community', *Una Sancta* 25.3: 18-31.

1969

'A Catholic Gospel: Reflections on "Early Catholicism" in the New Testament', *CBQ* 31: 213-23.

'The Particularity of the Gospel: Good News for Changing Times', *Concordia Theological Monthly* 40.6-7: 369-78.

Review article by David Noel Freedman and J.H. Elliott of *The Jerome Biblical Commentary* (ed. R.E. Brown, J.A. Fitzmyer and R.E. Murphy; 2 vols.; Englewood Cliffs, NJ: Prentice Hall, 1968), *CBQ* 31: 405-15.

'Thanksgiving Apocalypse', *The Cresset: A Review of Literature, the Arts, and Public Affairs* 33.1: 18.

1970

Review article of Peter Stuhlmacher, *Das paulinische Evangelium: I. Vorgeschichte* (FRLANT, 95; Göttingen: Vandenhoeck & Ruprecht, 1968), in *Lutheran World* 17.1: 78-81, and *Lutherische Rundschau* 17.1: 102-106.

'Ministry and Church Order in the New Testament: A Traditio-Historical Analysis (1 P 5:1-5 plls.)', *CBQ* 32: 367-91.

'Man and the Son of Man in the Gospel according to Mark', in *Humane Gesellschaft: Beiträge zu ihrer sozialen Gestaltung. Festschrift für Heinz-Dietrich Wendland* (ed. T. Rendtorff and A. Rich; Zurich: Zwingli): 47-59.

'Dualism or Integrity? The Quest for an Eschatological Ethos', *Seminar* (Concordia Seminary, St Louis) 3.1: 3-13.

1971

'We Have Met the Enemy and They Are Us—A Parable', *The University of San Francisco Foghorn* (December 3, 1971): 4.
'Adam's Atoms: Gehenna or Garden?'; 'Eve's Peeves: St Paul and the Women's Liberation Movement', A Tape of Two Lectures, distributed by Camelot Publications, Minneapolis, MN.

1972

'The Gospel: Riddle or Irrelevancy?', *Event* 12.6: 3-6.

1973

With William G. Thompson, S.J., 'Peter in the New Testament: Old Theme, New Views', *America* 130.3: 53-54.

1974

'On Being Catholic and Jesuit: A View from the Bridge', *University of San Francisco Foghorn* 69.1: 4, 12.

1975

'Everyone a Priest? No!', *Lutheran Forum* 9.4 (1975): 40-42. A review article of Oscar E. Feucht, *Everyone a Minister: A Guide to Churchmanship for Laity and Clergy* (St. Louis, MO: Concordia Publishing House, 1974).
Elliott, John H. *et al.,* 'A Group Discussion: Implications of a Class Approach to the Bible', *Radical Religion* 2 (1975): 7-18.

1976

'The Rehabilition of an Exegetical Step-Child: 1 Peter in Recent Research', *JBL* 95: 243-54.
'The Second Sunday in Advent', Preaching Helps. *Supplements to CTM* 3: 85-86.
Elliott, John H. *et al.,* 'A Group Discussion: Implications of a Class Approach to the Bible', in *The Bible and Liberation: Political and Social Hermeneutics. A Radical Religion Reader* (Berkeley, CA: Community for Religious Research and Education): 7-18.

1979

'Christian Unity: What Surprises Are in Store for Us?' *CTM* 6.5: 300-302.

1980

'Peter, Silvanus, and Mark in 1 Peter and Acts. Sociological-Exegetical Perspectives on a Petrine Group in Rome', in *Wort in der Zeit: Neuetestamentliche Studien* (Festgabe für Karl Heinrich Rengstorf; ed. Wilfred Haubeck and Michael Bachmann; Leiden: E.J. Brill): 250-67.

1982

'Salutation and Exhortation to Christain Behavior (1 Peter 1:1–2:10)', *Review and Expositor. A Baptist Theological Journal* 79.3: 415-25.

'The Image of Mary in the Lutheran–Catholic Dialogue: The Image of Mary, a Lutheran View', *America* 146.2: 226-29.

'Mary, the Mother of our Lord—a Lutheran View', *Lutheran Forum* 17.4: 16-20.

1983

'The Roman Provenance of 1 Peter and the Gospel of Mark: A Response to David Dungan', in *A Time for Reappraisal and Fresh Approaches: Colloquy on New Testament Studies* (ed. Bruce Corley; Macon, GA: Mercer University Press): 181-94.

'Seminar Dialogue with David Dungan', in *A Time for Reappraisal and Fresh Approaches: Colloquy on New Testament Studies* (ed. Bruce Corley; Macon, GA: Mercer University Press): 157-79.

'Introduction' to Jerome Murphy-O'Connor, *St Paul's Corinth: Texts and Archeology* (Good News Studies, 6; Wilmington, DE: Michael Glazier): xiii-xvii.

1984

'Philemon and House Churches', *The Bible Today* 22.3: 145-50.

1985

'Backward and Forward "In his Steps": Following Jesus from Rome to Raymond and Beyond. The Tradition, Redaction, and Reception of 1 Peter 2:18-25', in *Discipleship in the New Testament* (ed. Fernando Segovia; Philadelphia, PA: Fortress Press): 184-209.

'The Bible from the Perspective of the Refugee', in *Sanctuary: A Resource Guide for Understanding and Participating in the Central American Refugees' Struggle* (ed. Gary MacEoin; San Francisco: Harper & Row): 49-54.

A review essay of Wayne A. Meeks, *The First Urban Christians: The Social World of the Apostle Paul* (New Haven, CT: Yale University Press, 1983), in *Religious Studies Review* 11.4: 329-35.

1986

'Social-Scientific Criticism of the New Testament and its Social World: More on Method and Models', in *Social-Scientific Criticism of the New Testament and its Social World* (ed. John H. Elliott; Semeia, 35; Decatur, GA: Scholars Press): 1-33.

'1 Peter, its Situation and Strategy: A Discussion with David Balch', in *Perspectives on First Peter* (ed. Charles H. Talbert; National Association of Baptist Professors of Religion Special Studies Series, 9; Macon, GA: Mercer University Press): 61-78.

'The Rehabilitation of an Exegetical Step-Child: 1 Peter in Recent Research', in *Perspectives on First Peter* (ed. Charles H. Talbert; National Association of Baptist Professors of Religion Special Studies Series, 9; Macon, GA: Mercer University Press): 3-16. Reprinted from *JBL* 95 (1976): 243-54.

1987

'Patronage and Clientism in Early Christian Society: A Short Reading Guide', *Forum* 3.4: 39-48.

1988

'The Fear of the Leer: The Evil Eye from the Bible to Li'l Abner', *Forum* 4.4: 42-71.

1989

Review article of *Theologische Realenzyklopaedie*, vols. 1–10 (ed. Gerhard Krause and Gerhard Mueller *et al.*; Berlin: Walter de Gruyter, 1977-82), *Religious Studies Review* 15.2: 117-19.

1990

'Introduction' to Jerome Murphy-O'Connor, *St Paul's Corinth: Texts and Archaeology* (Good News Studies, 6; Collegeville, MN: Liturgical Press, 2nd expanded edn): xii-xvii.

'Paul, Galatians, and the Evil Eye', *CTM* (F.W. Danker Festschrift) 17.4: 62-73.

'With the Bible toward the Year 2000: Scriptural Engagement as Barometer, Beacon and Bellwether', *In die skriflig. tydskrif van die Gereformeerde Teologiese Vereniging* 24.3: 213-26.

1991

'Temple versus Household in Luke–Acts: A Contrast in Social Institutions', in *The Social World of Luke–Acts* (ed. Jerome H. Neyrey; Peabody, MA: Hendrickson Publishers): 211-40. Published also in *HTS* 47.1 (1991): 88-120.

'Household & Meals vs. Temple Purity: Replication Patterns in Luke–Acts', *BTB* 21.3 (1991): 102-108. Published also in *HTS* 47.2: 386-99 as 'Household and Meals versus the Temple Purity System: Patterns of Replication in Luke–Acts'.

'With the Bible toward the Year 2000. Scriptural Engagement as Barometer, Beacon and Bellwether', in *Theology toward the Third Millennium: Theological Issues for the Twenty-First Century* (ed. David G. Schultenover; Toronto Studies in Theology, 56; A Joint Publication of the Center for the Study of Religion and Society, Creighton University, and the Edwin Mellen Press; Lewiston, NY: Mellen): 23-40.

'The Evil Eye in the First Testament: The Ecology and Culture of a Pervasive Belief', in *The Bible and the Politics of Exegesis: Essays in Honor of Norman K. Gottwald on his Sixty-Fifth Birthday* (ed. David Jobling *et al.*;Cleveland, OH: Pilgrim Press): 147-59.

Foreword to Piet van Staden, *Compassion—The Essence of Life: A Social-Scientific Study of the Religious Symbolic Universe Reflected in the Ideology/Theology of Luke* (Hervormde theologiese studies Supplement, 4; Pretoria: University of Pretoria): iv-vi.

1992

'Matthew 20:1-15: A Parable of Invidious Comparison and Evil Eye Accusation', *BTB* 22.2: 52-65.

'Peter, First Epistle of', in *ABD* (ed. David Noel Freedman *et al.*; New York: Doubleday): 5.269-78.

'Peter, Second Epistle of', in *ABD* (ed. David Noel Freedman *et al.*; New York: Doubleday): 5.282-87.

1993

'The Epistle of James in Rhetorical and Social Scientific Perspective: Holiness-Wholeness and Patterns of Replication', *BTB* 23.2: 71-81.

'Sorcery and Magic in the Revelation of John', *Listening: Journal of Religion and Culture* 28.3: 261-76.

1994

'The Evil Eye and the Sermon on the Mount: Contours of a Pervasive Belief in Social Scientific Perspective', *BibInt* 2.1: 51-84.

1995

'Disgraced yet Graced: The Gospel according to 1 Peter in the Key of Honor and Shame', *BTB* 25.4: 166-78.

'The Jewish Messianic Movement: From Faction to Sect', in *Modelling Early Christianity: Social-Scientific Studies of the New Testament in its Context* (ed. Philip F. Esler; London: Routledge): 75-95.

1996

1 Timothy, 2 Timothy, Titus by Jouette M. Bassler (ed. John H. Elliott; Abingdon New Testament Commentaries; Nashville, TN: Abingdon).

1998

'The Church as Counter-Culture: A Home for the Homeless and a Sanctuary for Refugees', *Currents in Theology and Mission. Essays in Honor of Edgar Krentz* 25.3: 176-85.

'The Anthropology of Christian Origins. An Extended Book Review of Destro, Adriana and Pesce, Mauro, *Antropologia delle origini cristiane* (Quadrante, 78; Rome: Laterza, 1997, 2nd edn), *BTB* 28.3: 120-22.

1999

'Phases in the Social Formation of Early Christianity: From Faction to Sect—A Social Scientific Perspective', in *Recruitment, Conquest, and Conflict: Strategies in Judaism, Early Christianity, and the Greco-Roman World* (ed. Peder Borgen, Vernon K. Robbins and David B. Gowler; Atlanta, GA: Scholars Press): 273-313.

'Social-Scientific Criticism of a Biblical Text: 1 Peter as an Example', in *The Social Sciences and New Testament Interpretation: Contemporary Approaches* (ed. David Horrell; Edinburgh: T. & T. Clark): 339-58. (Excerpted from *What Is Social-Scientific Criticism?* [Minneapolis, MN: Fortress Press, 1993: 70-86]).

2001

'On Wooing Crocodiles for Fun and Profit: Confessions of an Intact Admirer', in *Social Scientific Models for Interpreting the Bible: Essays by the Context Group in Honor of Bruce J. Malina* (ed. John J. Pilch; Biblical Interpretation Series, 53; Leiden: Brill): 5-20.

'Elders as Leaders in 1 Peter and the Early Church', *CTM* (Everett Kalin Festschrift) 28.6: 549-59.

2002

'Jesus Was Not an Egalitarian: A Critique of an Anachronistic and Idealist Theory', *BTB* 32.2: 75-91.

2003

'Elders as Honored Household Heads and Not Holders of "Office" in Earliest Christianity. A Review Article' *BTB* 33.2: 77-82. Review of R.A. Campbell, *The Elders: Seniority within Earliest Christianity* (Edinburgh: T. & T. Clark, 1994).

'The Jesus Movement Was Not Egalitarian but Family-Oriented', *BibInt* 11.2: 1-38.

'Household/Family in the Gospel of Mark as a Core Symbol of Community', in *Fabrics of Discourse: Essays in Honor of Vernon K. Robbins* (ed. David B. Gowler, L. Gregory Bloomquist and Duane F. Watson; Harrisburg, PA: Trinity Press International): 36-63.

'"Worthy Is Christ": A Modern Hymn and its Apocalyptic Pedigree', *CTM* (Robert H. Smith FS) 30.6: 406-22.

2004

'Look It Up. It's in BDAG', in *Biblical Greek Language and Lexicography: Essays in Honor of Frederick W. Danker* (ed. John A.L. Lee, Peter Burton, Bernard Taylor and Richard Whitaker; Grand Rapids, MI: Eerdmans): 48-52.

'No Kingdom of God for Softies? Or, What Was Paul Really Saying?', *BTB* 34.1: 17-40.

2005

'Deuteronomy—Shameful Encroachment on Shameful Parts: Deuteronomy 25:11-12 and Biblical Euphemism', in *Ancient Israel: The Old Testament in its Social Context* (ed. Philip F. Esler; Minneapolis, MN: Fortress Press): 161-76, 330-32.

'Deuteronomy 25:11-12 LXX: No Tweaking the Twins. More on a Biblical Euphemism and its Translation', in *Kontexte der Schrift.* Band 2. *Kultur, Politik, Religion, Sprache—Text. Für Wolfgang Stegemann zum 60. Geburtstag* (ed. Christian Strecker; Stuttgart: Kohlhammer): 323-42.

'Lecture socioscientifique. Illustration par l'accusation du mauvais oeil en Galatie', in *Guide des nouvelles lectures de la Bible* (ed. André Lacocque; trans. Jean-Pierre Prévost; Paris: Bayard Éditions): 141-67 [collection of fourteen essays in French on various new methods of biblical interpretation]. Eng. trans., 'Social-Scientific Criticism within the Historical Critical Method: Perspective, Process, and Payoff. Evil Eye Accusation at Galatia as Illustration'.

'Jesus, Mark, and the Evil Eye', *LTJ* (Festschrift in Honour of Victor C. Pfitzner) 39.2-3: 157-68.

2006

'Hunting for Homosexuals at Corinth: Exegetical Tracking Rules and Hermeneutical Caveats', in *From Biblical Interpretation to Human Transformation: Reopening the Past to Actualize New Possibilities for the Future. A Festschrift Honoring Herman C. Waetjen* (ed. Douglas McGaughey and Cornelia Cyss-Wittenstein; Salem, OR: Chora Strangers): 3-43.

2007

'Envy and the Evil Eye. More on Mark 7:22 and Mark's "Anatomy of Envy"', in *In Other Words: Essays on Social Science Methods and the New Testament in Honor of Jerome H. Neyrey* (ed. Anselm C. Hagedorn, Zeba A. Crook and Eric Stewart; Sheffield: Sheffield Phoenix Press): 87-105.

'Jesus the Israelite Was neither a Jew nor a Christian. On Correcting the Nomenclature', *JSHJ* 5.2: 119-55.

'Envy, Jealousy and Zeal in the Bible. Sorting Out the Social Differences and Theological Implications—No Envy for YHWH', in *To Break Every Yoke: Essays in Honor of Marvin C. Chaney* (ed. Robert Coote and Norman K. Gottwald; Sheffield: Sheffield Phoenix Press): 344-63.

2008

'Critical Background for Lectionary Reading: Easter Five 1 Peter 2:2-10', in *Bible Workbench: Living our Story through God's Story* 15.3 (Easter 2–Trinity Sunday, March 30, 2008 through May 18, 2008; St Louis, MO: The Educational Center): 67-70 (excerpted from *A Home for the Homeless* [Minneapolis, MN: Augsburg Fortress Press, 1990]: 132-36).

'La crítica socio-cientifica: La configuración colectiva y cooperativa de un método' ['Social-Scientific Criticism. The Collective and Collaborative Shaping of a Method'], in *Reimaginando los orígenes del cristianismo: Relevancia social y ecclesial de lose studios sobre Orígenes del cristianismo. Libro homenaje a Rafael Aguirre en su 65 compleaños* (ed. Carmen Bernabé and Carlos Gil; Agora, 23; Estrella (Navarra): Editorial Verbo Divino): 101-15.

'Elders as Leaders in 1 Peter and the Early Church', *HTS* 64: 681-95 (reprinted from *CTM* 28.6 [2001]: 549-59).

'The Epistle of James in Rhetorical and Social Scientific Perspective: Holiness-Wholeness and Patterns of Replication', in *The Social World of the New Testament: Insights and Models* (ed. Jerome H Neyrey, and Eric C. Stewart; Peabody, MA: Hendrickson Publishers): 105-22 (reprinted from *BTB* 23.2 [1993]: 71-81).

'From Social Description to Social-Scientific Criticism. The History of a Society of Biblical Literature Section 1973–2005', *BTB* 38.1 (2008): 26-36.

'God—Zealous or Jealous but Never Envious: The Theological Consequences of Linguistic and Social Distinctions', in *The Social Sciences and Biblical Translation* (ed. Dietmar Neufeld; Symposium Series, 41; Atlanta, GA: Society of Biblical Literature): 79-96.

'Meals and Food in the Jesus Movement: Decoding Social Meanings', in *Nuovo Testamento: Teologia in dialogo culturale. Scritti in onore di Romano Penna nel suo 70° compleanno* (ed. Nicola Ciola and Giuseppe Pulcinelli: Bologna: Edizioni Dehoniane): 421-31.

'Paul, Galatians, and the Evil Eye', in *The Social World of the New Testament: Insights and Models* (ed. Jerome H. Neyrey and Eric C. Stewart; Peabody, MA: Hendrickson Publishers): 223-34 (reprinted from *CTM* 17.4 [1990]: 262-73).

2009

'1 Enoch, 1 Peter, and Social-Scientific Criticism. A Review Article on a Major 1 Enoch Commentary', *BTB* 39: 39-43.

2010

'A Biblical Creation Faith and Jesus as Embodiment of the Creator Spirit. A Review Article', *BTB* 40.2: 93-99. A review of James P. Mackey, *Christianity and Creation: The Essence of the Christian Faith and its Future among Religions. A Systematic Theology* (New York: Continuum, 2006), and James P. Mackey, *Jesus of Nazareth: The Life, the Faith and the Future of the Prophet (A Brief History)* (Blackrock, Co Dublin: Columba Press, 2008).

2011

'Social-Scientific Criticism: Perspective, Process, Payoff. Evil Eye Accusation at Galatia as Illustration of the Method', *HTS* 67.1 (A.G. van Aarde Festschrift):114-23.

'Refugees, Resident Aliens, and the Church as Counter-Culture', in *Liberating Bible Study: Scholarship, Art, and Action in Honor of the Center and Library for Bible and Justice* (ed. Laurel Dykstra and Ched Myers; Center and Library for the Bible and Social Justices Series, 1; Eugene, OR: Wipf & Stock/Cascade): 197-212.

Forthcoming

'Jesus, Paulus und der Böse Blick: Was die modernen Bibelversionen und Kommentare uns nicht sagen', in *Alte Texte in neuen Kontexten: Wo steht die sozialwissenschaftliche Bibelexegese?* (ed. Wolfgang Stegemann and Richard E. DeMaris; Proceedings of the International Context Group Meeting, Tutzing, Germany, June 2009; Stuttgart: Kohlhammer).

'Fresh Screwtape Revelations: How to Bash Gays with the Bible' (FS S. Scott Bartchy) Volume not yet titled (Eugene, OR: Wipf & Stock).

'Social-Scientific Criticism of the Bible—Emergence, Features and Contributions', in *Reading a Tendentious Bible: Essays in Honor of Robert B. Coote* (ed. Marvin L. Chaney, Uriah Y. Kim and Annette Schellenberg; Sheffield: Sheffield Phoenix Press).

Index of Ancient References

Index of Modern Authors

CPSIA information can be obtained
at www.ICGtesting.com
Printed in the USA
LVOW04*1008201215
467280LV00004B/6/P

9 781907 534928